JOSEPH JEFFERSON
DEAN OF THE AMERICAN THEATRE

John White Alexander painting of
Joseph Jefferson as Bob Acres
in *The Rivals*

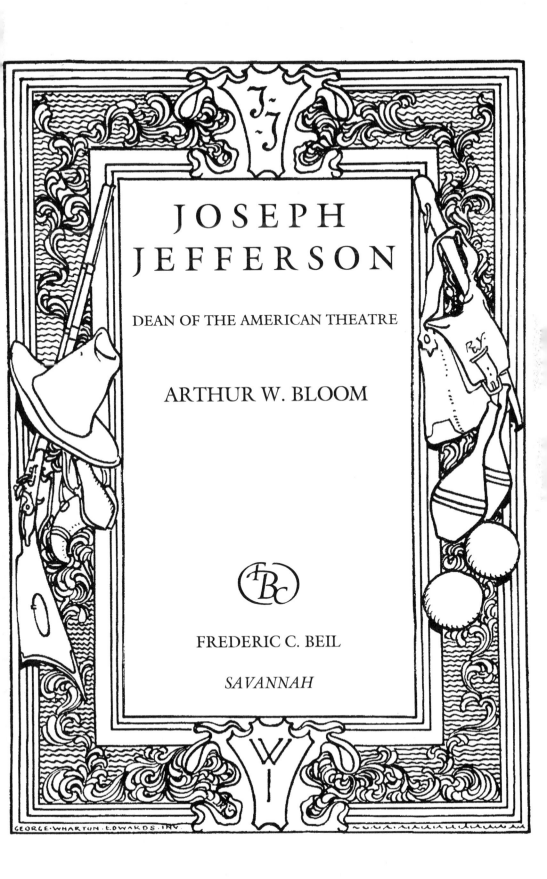

JOSEPH JEFFERSON

DEAN OF THE AMERICAN THEATRE

ARTHUR W. BLOOM

FREDERIC C. BEIL

SAVANNAH

GEORGE·WHARTON·EDWARDS·INV

Copyright © 2000 by Arthur W. Bloom

Published by
Frederic C. Beil, Publisher, Inc.
609 Whitaker Street
Savannah, Ga. 31401
http://www.beil.com

LIBRARY OF CONGRESS CATALOGING-IN-PUBLICATION DATA
Bloom, Arthur W., 1939–
Joseph Jefferson: dean of the American theatre /
by Arthur W. Bloom.
p.   cm.
Includes bibliographical references and index.
ISBN 0-913720-55-0 (alk. paper)
1. Jefferson, Joseph, 1829–1905.
2. Actors–United States Biography.
I. Title
PN2287.J4B66   1999
792'.028'092–dc21
[B]   99-21148
                                                                  CIP

First edition

All rights reserved

This book was typeset by SkidType, Savannah, Georgia;
printed on acid-free paper; and sewn in signatures.

Printed in the United States of America

The frontispiece is a painting by John White Alexander
of Joseph Jefferson as Bob Acres in *The Rivals*.
Courtesy of the Hampden-Booth Theatre Library at
The Players.

The title-page design is revived from the title page of
Rip Van Winkle as Played by Joseph Jefferson (1896).

For

Rena Fraboni Bloom

Sarah Evelyn Bloom

and

Jessica Elizabeth Bloom

CONTENTS

ILLUSTRATIONS

Figures

ACKNOWLEDGMENTS

Research on the Jefferson family in Chicago in 1838 was made possible through grants from the American Philosophical Society and Loyola University of Chicago.

I am grateful to Rena Fraboni Bloom, John Callahan, James F. Coakley, Ben McArthur, Timothy Running, Robert Smith, and above all to Julius Novick for editorial assistance; to Michael Burgess for his assistance in obtaining information about the Jefferson home in Buzzards Bay, Massachusetts; to John Callahan and Patricia Flynn for accesss to their collections; to the staff of the Jefferson Home in New Iberia, Louisiana, for access to their collection; to Mr. Robert Hewitt for his assistance in locating the Jefferson home in Hohokus, New Jersey; to Mr. Raymond Wemmlinger, librarian at the Hampden-Booth Theatre Library at The Players; to Ms. Geraldine A. Duclow, librarian, Theatre Collection, the Free Library of Philadelphia; to the library staffs of Loyola University of Chicago, Trinity University, Loyola Marymount University, and Kutztown University for their assistance in obtaining newspaper microfilm; and to Hulya Sowerwine, Colleen Whitefield, and above all to Matthew Small for their secretarial assistance. Finally I would like to express my deep appreciation for the lifetime of inspiration provided by the late professors Henry B. Williams of Dartmouth College and Rollin G. Osterweis and Alois B. Nagler of Yale University.

INTRODUCTION

There is a moment when any biographer, overwhelmed by the details of a particular life—in this case, by a succession of performances over seventy-nine years—asks: What is the story? What links the endless travels, the opulent homes, the carefully constructed image of rusticity, the landscape painting, the fishing, the concealed domestic life, and the scrawled handwriting? That is the moment when any biography acquires a plot and that plot, a series of themes that produce the significance—in this case, of the life and work of Joseph Jefferson III.

What then is the Jefferson story? It is often a story of endless travel, an itinerary maintained long after the traveler ceased needing further fame or money, long after he had played every reasonably sized American city several times, long after he was bored with his major role and physically exhausted. It is a story of the theatrical rootlessness that has always typified American actors. By the age of fifteen, Joseph Jefferson had lived in Pennsylvania, Washington D. C., Maryland, New York, Ohio, Illinois, Iowa, Missouri, Indiana, Mississippi, Tennessee, and Louisiana, and this at a time when travel was a combination of stage-coaches, wagons, and riverboats. With the explosion of railroad transportation after the Civil War, Jefferson crisscrossed the continent, bringing his art to the furthest reaches of America. Eventually, he lived for months at a time on a train.

It is simultaneously the story of an endless search for home by a man who spent his life in rented rooms and railway cars. Jefferson never lived in a house he owned until he was forty, but by the time he died, he owned homes in Hohokus, New Jersey, Buzzards Bay, Massachusetts, New Iberia, Louisiana, and Palm Beach, Florida. These homes indicate a continual tension in both his personal life and in his times, a tension between the call of rustic country living, with its nostalgic appeal to a simpler age, and the cultural and commercial predominance of urban life that emerged after the Civil War. Jefferson spent most of his career in cities, because that was where the theatres were, but he preferred to live in the country. The exteriors of his homes were rustic, but their interiors were stuffed with the upholstered comforts of urban upper-class Victorian life.

Jefferson never resolved this dichotomy. There is, in fact, no evidence that he was aware of it. He loved rusticity. He fished; he painted romantic Corot-like landscapes devoid of human beings; he built furniture with his own hands; he puttered around his estates in battered clothing, raising livestock and growing oranges. But there were photographers around to catch him in picturesque poses; the iced catch from his fly fishing was sent hundreds of miles from Cape Cod to Princeton, New Jersey, to delight the family of former president Grover Cleveland; and the gilt-framed paintings wound up in gallery shows.

Rusticity was Jefferson's delight, but it was also his image, because he presented it to the public for almost fifty years in the guise of his most famous role, Rip Van Winkle. His audiences came to expect that Jefferson was Rip, and he always gave them exactly what they wanted. Late in life he attended a costume party in Henry Flagler's Floridian palazzo, at which the captains of American industry appeared decked out in the rouge, headdresses, and hoopskirted finery of Versailles ladies. Jefferson stood among them perfectly at home in the chamois rags of Rip Van Winkle. They would have been disappointed at anything else.

Jefferson learned the way all actors learn that he had no other choice but to please. And because he learned it well, his story is a Horatio Alger rags-to-riches saga of a young boy from a financially and socially impoverished family who rises to opulence and honor through hard work and his own abilities. It is the American story. Industry and talent bring wealth and success. In the end, the hero lives happily ever after, in opulent style, while still humbly attached to his rustic origins.

Like his country's, Jefferson's life began in the East, moved West, suffered a period of physical and emotional darkness during the Civil War, and was reconstructed to achieve material wealth and international recognition. After 1865, Jefferson became a national power, an icon of the Gilded Age, the dean, as he was called, of the American stage, the most important comic actor in America—and the most financially successful.

His is also the story of the American theatre, developing from small itinerant touring companies, performing everything and everywhere, to specialized urban stock companies, to combination companies— the nineteenth-century equivalent of the modern road show. Yet what Jefferson brought to the opulence of late nineteenth-century theatres was nostalgia about a bygone era, the rude vigor of an eighteenth-century Dutchman who wakes up to find a strange new world.

Any version of Jefferson's story has to investigate the version he wrote, an immensely popular 1888 biography, first serialized in magazine form and later published by Century Press. The *Autobiography* is a collection of amusing personal and theatrical anecdotes brimming over with nostalgia. It is exactly the sort of book audiences would have expected from Rip Van Winkle, and Jefferson—who could, in private, refer to the role as "the theatrical swindle"—never disappointed an audience.

He wrote little else. Late in life there were numerous interviews and public addresses at distinguished universities, but his correspondence is of more interest to the autograph-seeker than the biographer: a collection of hastily written thank-you notes and business letters scrawled in an unschooled hand. But then again that was exactly the hand his correspondents expected from Rip.

And like Rip, he was beloved, as beloved as Bob Hope or Jack Benny. His death, in 1905, made front-page national headlines. The clearest modern equivalents would be a handful of television or film actors whose characters became so indelibly linked to them that audiences were disturbed to see them "out of character"—whether in real life or performing another role.

This identification generally occurs to comic actors. Audiences seem willing to allow "serious" actors the right to transmute from character to character, but they insist on Groucho's mustache or Benny's stinginess or Lucy's red hair. Jefferson knew this, and constructed and maintained a personal image so consonant with the role that it actually enhanced the popular myth that the only part he played was Rip. He certainly played other roles, but the most important role he performed was indistinguishable to an outsider from the image he created about the rest of his life. An anecdote told by the American producer Daniel Frohman illustrates how Jefferson was typically perceived.

> Jefferson [was] in a town where he was playing Rip. He went to the bank to draw some money. The cashier, not knowing him, asked if there was anybody who could identify him. Jefferson replied with the words of Rip, "If my dog Schneider were here, he would know me." The cashier instantly recognized him.[1]

Jefferson told one of his biographers, the actor Francis Wilson, that the story was not true, "but it ought to be." No one expected that Edwin Booth was really Hamlet—but no one would have accepted that Jefferson was not Rip. Francis Wilson contended that "He was Rip and Rip was he . . . the play . . . was Jefferson's whole existence." But if his Rip image was not completely false, it also could not have been completely true. While he lavished money on his family, he often withheld it stingily from the dilapidated productions in which he toured. Expectations that he would make some prodigal contribution to the theatrical profession on the order of Booth's gift of The Players went unfulfilled. Performers who threatened to detract from Rip's centrality by deepening their characterizations were brought into line. And other actors found him not only defensive of his own stage territory but invasive of theirs.

Jefferson was a hard-working, tough, professional, nineteenth-century actor. At the height of his career, long after he had become accustomed to the most luxurious of existences, he could still perform with the scenery literally falling down around him. Jefferson was a survivor. He had been brought up hard, and he was never soft. If this biography seems to seize upon the negative aspects of his life, I must plead the necessity of humanizing a figure lavishly praised, devoutly admired, and publicly adored throughout most of his life. If I seem to insist that he could not have been that charming or lovable, it is probably because the overwhelming evidence tells me that he was.

JOSEPH JEFFERSON

DEAN OF THE AMERICAN THEATRE

1

A PROPERTY CHILD
1829–1837

Joseph Jefferson III (who was called Joe all his life) was born on February 20, 1829, in a four-story brick house that still stands on the southwest corner of Spruce and Sixth streets in Philadelphia. When the building was constructed in 1805, it was located in the center of the city's most prestigious neighborhood. The house had a central mahogany staircase, Georgian mantels, and marble fireplaces. Joe's parents could never have afforded such a place; they had rented the house when its owners moved to a more elegant setting because the neighborhood was going downhill. The Jeffersons were middle-class actors, always bordering on genteel poverty, always beset by the vicissitudes of theatrical economics.[2]

Three blocks north of his birthplace was the Chestnut Street Theatre, where the Jefferson family worked. Joe's father, twenty-five-year-old Joseph Jefferson II, was a scenic artist, a painter of coral fairy grottoes and rear scenes "showing a ship rolling in the tossing storm billows." Joe's mother, Cornelia Francis Burke Jefferson, was of French descent and eight years older than her husband. At the time of their marriage, on July 27, 1826, she was a widow with a four-year-old son, Charles Burke, by her first marriage. A contemporary described her as "the first vocalist of American birth who traveled as a star" as well as "a lively actress, much better than the generality of the singers who were her contemporaries." Like her husband, she worked at the Chestnut, performing through her fifth month of pregnancy, and gave birth to Joe while the rest of the company was on tour in Baltimore. A month and a half after her baby's birth, Cornelia was back on stage.[3] The Jeffersons had little time for family life outside the theatre, but then they did not need much, because the theatre was their life, an occupation and a place that involved their entire family.

Figure 1. Joseph Jefferson's birthplace at the southwest corner of Sixth and Spruce streets, Philadelphia, Pennsylvania. Courtesy of the Van Pelt Library, University of Pennsylvania.

In the early nineteenth century, acting was a family business, as it had been since the Renaissance and continues to be for various theatrical and film families. Today, however, the wealth earned by successful actors, together with compulsory education, enables their children to make career choices closed to the Jeffersons, whose limited income and itinerant life denied their children formal schooling. The only thing Joe was educated to do was work in the theatre; the sons and daughters of theatre people normally followed their parents' profession. Actors married actors and produced actors. Even their theatrical roles were inherited, like the inventory of a family business. Today, the last thing a young actor would consider doing is repeating his father's most famous role, but it was the first thing a nineteenth-century actor was trained to do, and the very thing nineteenth-century audiences wanted to see. Acting was passed down as a craft, from generation to generation; Jefferson learned comic roles from his stepbrother, Charles Burke, and from his father

Figure 2. Jefferson's birthplace as it appears today

that they in turn had seen Jefferson's grandfather perform. It would have been as unlikely for Jefferson to become a tragic actor as it would have been for his friend Edwin Booth to become a comedian.

By the time Jefferson was born, American actors were working primarily in stock companies. Along with scene painters, musicians, and box-office personnel, they were hired for a September–May season by a manager who was, in turn, leasing the theatre from local businessmen who had invested in building it. If popular enough, the same actors might return to a city year after year, becoming known and respected members of the community. Others, in search of better wages or roles, might move from company to company.

Financially and artistically above the stock-company actors were touring stars who traveled from city to city, performing pieces for which they were famous and using stock actors as supporting cast. These might be individuals, like Junius Brutus Booth; husband and wife teams like Mr. and Mrs. Barney Williams; or small companies, such as the Seguin Opera Company or the acrobatic Ravels. Below stock-company actors were itinerant groups playing the hinterlands,

Figure 3. Joseph Jefferson (1774–1832),
grandfather of Joseph Jefferson

going from place to place, performing in each for a short period of time, the way English companies had performed in eighteenth-century America. These three levels were, however, not theatrical castes, and actors moved up and down the scale artistically and financially. In the summer, for instance, when many metropolitan theatres closed, stock-company actors and even stars barnstormed through rural America.

At the time of Joe's birth, the dominant Jefferson family member was his grandfather, Joseph Jefferson I (1774–1832), for over twenty years the foremost comedian of the Chestnut Street Theatre company, the premier troupe of eighteenth- and early nineteenth-century

America. Jefferson had worked at the top of the American theatrical profession, but by the time Joe was born, his popularity was waning. In December 1829, when Joe was ten months old, the eldest Jefferson, stung by the success of a rival comedian as well as the financial failure of two benefit nights, declared: "I am not wanted here any longer." He left the Chestnut Street company, never to return to the Philadelphia stage, and moved the Jeffersons to Baltimore.[4] This began his grandson's life as an itinerant actor. Joe spent most of the next seventy-five years on the road, giving his last performance in 1904, a year before his death.

In Baltimore, Joe's grandfather appeared at the New Theatre and Circus—a combination theatrical company and equestrian troupe—first as a traveling star and then as a company member. The progression was typical. Nineteenth-century troupes played six nights a week and were in constant need of new plays and new performers. Novelty was used up in the theatre as regularly as it is consumed in modern television. Indeed a new actor in town had star potential, only insofar as he or she was "new." In the elder Jefferson's case, this potential was real; he was one of the established stars of the American theatre. But even a star's potential, like any nineteenth-century actor's, was soon exhausted, and if the star remained, he became a salaried employee of the troupe. This was the position Jefferson had occupied at the Chestnut Street Theatre, but the Baltimore company was far less prestigious, and he was probably paid less money.

Accompanying the elder Jefferson were his wife, Euphemia; his eldest daughter, Euphemia Anderson; his son and daughter-in-law, Joseph and Cornelia Jefferson; Charles Burke; and young Joe. Through the spring of 1830, the Jefferson family shuttled between Baltimore and Washington, where their Baltimore manager ran another theater. In Washington two more family members began to make stage appearances. The first was Joe's half-brother, "Charley," age eight; the second was Joe's aunt Mary-Anne Jefferson, his grandfather's third daughter.[5]

Joe's immediate family grew during the summer of 1830. After his eldest aunt, Euphemia Anderson, died on June 13, her orphaned daughters, Elizabeth and Jane, ages twelve and eight, came to live with Joseph and Cornelia. Young Joe grew up with these older cousins as members of the family. They all became actors, and Jane Anderson's professional life was to intersect with her cousin's throughout the nineteenth century. By December 1, 1830, Joe's grandfather had formed his own eighteen-member company, featuring Joe's uncle, John; Joe's parents; Charles Burke; and Joe's aunts Mary-Anne Jefferson and Elizabeth Jefferson Chapman. Joe spent his childhood sur-

Figure 4. Joseph Jefferson (1804–1842), father of Joseph Jefferson

rounded by relatives who worked together, and he would spend much of his adult life replicating the family company in which he grew up.[6]

His grandfather leased the Washington Theatre, a 700-seat house, too small to be profitable or imposing by nineteenth-century standards. The Jeffersons enlarged its capacity from seven hundred to a thousand, but in the eyes of the touring English star, Fanny Kemble, it still looked "absolutely like a doll's playhouse . . . the tiniest little box that was ever seen, not much bigger . . . than the baby's playhouse at Versailles."[7]

For young Joe Jefferson it was a playhouse, a toy-shop filled with stock scenery and props where he produced amateur theatricals with other children and fell in love with acting. He was, like the child of any nineteenth-century theatrical family, "taken on 'in arms' as a property child in groups of happy peasantry." In 1881 he recalled: "As to when I first appeared on the stage, I am not quite clear. I know that when I was an infant 'muling [sic] and puking in its nurse's arms,' our family hired me out to the theatre, and the chances are that whenever a baby was wanted on the stage, either for the purpose of being murdered or saved, I did duty on those occasions."[8]

Figure 5. Cornelia Jefferson (1796–1850),
mother of Joseph Jefferson

Like all theatrical families of the period, the Jeffersons worked incessantly. Between their opening in Washington on December 1, 1830, and the season's close on March 26, 1831, the company offered a full-length play and a one-act farce every night of the week except Sunday. Occasionally they performed three plays or parts of plays on a given bill. They had a repertory of ninety plays, and thirty-four of them were given only once during the season. Few were ever performed more than twice.[9] Long runs were unknown, because plays went out of fashion quickly. The Jeffersons, consequently, could never earn enough money to rest. Joe grew up working under these conditions, and they molded his character; long after he could have retired he continued to perform, working until he was seventy-five years old, as if driven by a need for money.

When the season closed, the company began to tour, reverting to the theatrical life that had characterized American actors in the eighteenth century, when companies moved from town to town without a home base. It was exhausting work, because it meant not only performing but also setting up scenery for the production, constructing stage spaces for the actors, and arranging seats for the audience.

Joe's grandfather, then fifty-seven, could no longer function as the family's artistic head. His wife, Euphemia Fortune Jefferson, had died on January 11, 1831, during the Washington season, and he was ill. A letter written to a friendly physician who was treating him free of charge reveals the old actor's charm and his predilection for puns even amidst the pain of gout.

> Allow me to trouble you with my thanks for your kind attention and liberal present—You are a most humane physician to not only prescribe, but furnish the medicine without fee. My first glass was to your health, in which glass I joined most *cordially*—(there's no making wry faces at such physic).
>
> I hope to meet you on a better footing—when the gout has left me in *toe toe*. Till then I am and ever shall be your grateful
> & humble Servant
> J. Jefferson.[10]

With the eldest Jefferson indisposed, the company's leadership fell to Joe's uncle, John Jefferson, a handsome, athletic twenty-seven-year-old who specialized in low comedy. Under his leadership, the company played Alexandria, Virginia, and then moved to rural Pennsylvania, where between April 29, 1831, and October 25, 1831, they worked a circuit from York to Lancaster to Reading to Pottsville to Harrisburg and then back to Lancaster. They were particularly successful in Harrisburg, where the elder Jefferson had always been a favorite among the governor, his cabinet, the state's legislators, and its supreme court, many of whom attended the theatre and financially underwrote the season. Joe grew up dependent on the good opinion and friendship of wealthy influential people. Long after he had become one of these people, he continued to court them. He learned to charm them as a child, and he continued to do so for the rest of his life. As a star, his life would be an endless succession of performances alternating with social events arranged by people who attended those performances. He was a charming child; he became a charming adult who could use his personality to his advantage both offstage and on.[11]

The Jeffersons played in what the modern theatre refers to as found spaces—Mr. Cooper's Ball Room in the Red Lion Tavern in Lancaster, Mr. Boyer's Ball Room in a tavern in Reading, and the Masonic Hall in Harrisburg. Even Lancaster's Chestnut Street Theatre, named for its famous Philadelphia counterpart, was actually a converted "large brick barn" fitted up with a pit, gallery, and proscenium arch.[12] These were the spaces available in any American town, and Joe grew up in the tradition of American actors who moved easily between sophisticated urban venues and the type of primitive rural performance sites found in Pennsylvania towns. It was an ability he maintained throughout the rest of his life. Long after he was a star, accustomed to the most opulent theatres in America, Jefferson could still perform in a second-rate house with the scenery falling down around him. In April 1903, when the lights in a theatre in Savannah failed, he performed part of *Rip Van Winkle* in total darkness. Critics who damned the production could never fault the performance.

On October 25, 1831, in Lancaster, John Jefferson fell down a flight of stairs at his hotel and died of a fractured skull. Had he lived, the family's fortunes might have improved, but John's death insured that his nephew's childhood would remain impoverished and itinerant. The company's leadership now devolved upon two men of lesser ability: Joe's father and his uncle, a Scots newspaper agent, publisher and bookseller named Alexander MacKenzie, who had recently married Joe's aunt Hester.[13]

Jefferson's father was a poor businessman, the sort of person whose personal optimism allowed him to avoid responsibility and deal cheerfully with adversity. As a result of his father's lack of financial sense, Joe grew up attuned to the value of money. In later life, when he became wealthy, he had a reputation for being tight with a dollar as the head of a theatrical company, although he was extravagant in support of his family. His father had been able to support neither the acting troupe he headed nor the family dependent on it.[14]

On December 5, 1831, Jefferson and MacKenzie reopened in Washington with an eighteen-member company. Like most urban American companies of the period, they existed to back up touring stars who provided the quality and variety that audiences craved.

These ranged in importance from Charles Kean and Edwin Forrest down to Mr. Frimbley, the delineator of "living statues." These performers provided young Joe's theatrical education. His aunt Bess (Elizabeth Chapman) remembered:

> When little more than two years old, he gave an imitation of [Frimbley] the Statueman, and it was . . . an astonishing feat. My mother chanced to notice the child . . . trying this experiment, and she . . . found that he had got all the 'business' of the statues, though he could not have pronounced the name of one. . . . She made him a dress, similar to that worn by [Frimbley], and he . . . gave these imitations upon the stage when only three years old.[15]

According to Jefferson, his earliest performance was on December 28, 1831, in Richard Brinsley Sheridan's *Pizarro*, a standard piece in the nineteenth-century repertoire. Jefferson, not quite two, played the role of the child of the Peruvian heroine Cora and the noble Spaniard Alonzo.[16] Although mute, the child is vital to the play's plot and appears in seven scenes. During his first appearance in Act II, Cora comments on the child's rapid growth: "I am sure he will speak soon." "As she said this on the occasion of the infant 'Joe' Jefferson's first appearance, he . . . walked toward the foot-lights and addressing the leader of the orchestra . . . said: 'Green, why don't you play the fiddle?'"

In the play's last act, Cora leaves the stage to seek Alonzo and momentarily abandons her baby, who is kidnapped by Spanish soldiers and then recaptured by the Peruvian hero Rolla. Rolla is later shot holding the baby while crossing a wooden bridge over a chasm. Jefferson, retelling the family legend in his *Autobiography*, pictured himself

> as a startled child in a white tunic beautifully striped with gold bands, and in the grasp and on the shoulders of a . . . tragedian crossing a shaky bridge amid the deafening report of guns . . . and in a blaze of fire and smoke. . . . The situation seemed perilous, and . . . I seized *Rolla* by the hair of his head. "Let go," he cried; but . . . I tightened my grasp upon his tragic top-knot. The battle was short but decisive, for in the next moment, I had pulled off his feather-duster head-dress, wig and all, . . . and as he was past the prime of life, the noble Peruvian stood bald-headed in the middle of the bridge. . . . This story has the flavor of an old anecdote, but I am credibly informed that I was the original scalper.[17]

At an early age, Joe also demonstrated an interest in drawing and painting, an interest derived from his father and grandfather, that would grow into a substantial hobby. His aunt, Elizabeth Jefferson Chapman, told the American critic William Winter:

> My father could not keep his drawing-box away from the boy. . . . I remember his . . . daily salutation would be, "Joe, where's my paint?" "It's gone," said the child. "Yes sir, I know it's gone; but where? where?" "Him lost," was Joe's reply. "Yes sir, I know it's lost and gone; but how and where?" The boy would look up roguishly and say, "Him hook um"; and then his grandfather would prophesy what a great artist that child would . . . become . . . and let him destroy . . . anything he chose. The inheritance of talent was never more clearly shown than in the case of the present Joseph Jefferson: his habits, his tastes, his acting . . . seems just a reiteration of his grandfather.

Mrs. Chapman's statement, as well as the *Pizarro* anecdotes, were published when Jefferson was a major star. Both were part of the mythology that grew up around his life. The image is that of a lovable rogue; it is both the stage image and the life image that Jefferson fostered. As both child and adult, Jefferson really was lovable, but he also learned to be lovable, how to play lovable, and how being and playing lovable produced substantial rewards. It was his grandfather who began this education.

It is significant that his aunt looked not to her brother, Jefferson's father, as the progenitor of his talent, but to his far more successful grandfather, yet another indication that Joe's family was emotionally and financially dependent on Jefferson I. Unfortunately the elderly comedian, weighed down by the emotional burden of the deaths of his wife and three children, continued to decline. Depressed by the loss of his son John, he refused to work in plays they had performed together. Thus the company lost its primary comedian, and the comedies that had dominated the troupe's earlier repertory disappeared; an editorial late in the season complained of "an undue proportion of tragedy," expressing the desire "to see our old favorite Jefferson out again."[18]

When the company left on a summer tour to Lancaster and Harrisburg, the elder Jefferson went with them, but by June 29 he was too ill to perform. He died at the age of sixty-two in Harrisburg on August 4, 1832. His funeral the next day was attended by "a large concourse" of the town's citizens. Unfortunately his family could not afford a headstone, and Jefferson lay in an unmarked grave in St. Stephen's Episcopal graveyard until 1843, when a justice of the Supreme Court provided a marble slab monument.[19]

The Jeffersons never had time to mourn. Despite the death of Joe's grandfather, they toured for three and a half months, performing works from their Washington repertory. The troupe's leading man had become David Ingersoll, a circus performer turned actor who had joined the company during its Washington season to play juvenile leads. Ingersoll, a "silver-tongued" young man possessed of "extraordinary talent" and a "tall and symmetrical figure," eventually married Joe's youngest aunt, Mary-Anne.[20]

In mid-September 1832 the Jeffersons returned to Washington, forming a twenty-one-member troupe that opened on October 3 for 122 nights. Joe's cousins and childhood companions, Elizabeth and Jane Anderson, began to perform, and even his father played roles in the line of old men. Joe's earliest appearance documented by an extant theatre program occurred on November 23, 1832, when, at the age of three, he appeared as Theodore in J. R. Planche's *Legion of Honor*. On January 10, 1833, he was Julio in W. Dimond's *Hunter of the Alps*. Julio is one step above a prop baby. He and his brother Florio are the poor but deserving children of Rosalvi, a destitute peasant, wrongfully accused of stealing his master's purse. Julio exists to increase the play's pathos with lines like: "Have you brought us some breakfast? I am very hungry."[21]

On February 2, 1833, Jefferson's cousin Elizabeth Jefferson made him up in blackface for an appearance with T. D. Rice, the progenitor of the American minstrel show. Jefferson later remembered this performance in his *Autobiography*.

> The comedian saw my imitation of him and insisted that I . . . appear for his benefit; . . . I was . . . blacked up and dressed as a . . . miniature . . . of the original. He put me in a bag . . . and carried me upon the stage on his shoulders. No word of this proceeding had been mentioned in the bills. . . . After dancing and singing the first stanza, he began the second, the following being the two lines which introduced me:
>
> > Oh Ladies and Gentlemen, I'd have you for to know
> > That I've got a little darky here that jumps Jim Crow;

and turning the bag upside down, he emptied me out head first.
. . . The picture . . . is as vivid . . . as any recollection of my . . . life.[22]

It was an ambitious year for all the Jeffersons. Joe's uncle Alexander
MacKenzie established a small company at the Holliday Street Theatre in Baltimore that ran from January 2 through March 26, 1833.
Thus, in mid-year, the Jeffersons were operating two theatres in cities
several hours apart. Elizabeth Chapman, Mary-Anne Jefferson, and
David Ingersoll spent the winter shuttling between Washington and
Baltimore, and the results were disastrous.[23] Fanny Kemble, a niece of
the great English actors, John Philip Kemble and Sarah Siddons,
undertook an American tour in 1832–33 and recorded what she
called "my immediate impressions of what I saw and heard." Her on-
the-spot account of playing Juliet with the Jeffersons in Washington
is devastating.[24]

> My Romeo had gotten on . . . trunk breeches that looked as
> if he had borrowed them from some . . . Dutchman of a hun-
> dred years ago. . . . They were of a . . . dull, heavy looking blue
> cloth, and . . . crimson satin, all be-puckered and be-plaited and
> be-puffed, till the young man looked like a . . . figure growing
> out of a . . . strange-coloured melon, beneath which descended
> his unfortunate legs, thrust into a pair of red slippers. . . . The
> play went off . . . smoothly, except that they broke one man's
> collar-bone and nearly dislocated a woman's shoulder by fling-
> ing the scenery about. My bed was not made in time, and when
> the scene drew, half a dozen carpenters in patched trousers and
> tattered shirt sleeves were discovered smoothing down my
> pillows and adjusting my draperies. The last scene is too good
> not be given verbatim:

> *Romeo.* Rise my Juliet, and from this cave of
>   death, this house of horror
>   Quick let me snatch thee to thy Romeo's arms.

> Here he pounced upon me, plucked me up in his arms . . .
> and staggered down the stage with me.

> *Juliet.* (*aside*), Oh, you've got me up horridly!—that'll never
>   do; let me down, pray let me down.
> *Romeo.* There breathe a vital spirit on thy lips.
>   And call thee back, my soul, to life and love!

> *Juliet.* (*aside*), Pray put me down; you'll certainly throw
> me down if you don't set me on the
> ground directly.

In the midst of "cruel cursed fate," his dagger fell out of his dress; I embracing him tenderly, crammed it back again, because I knew I should want it at the end.

> *Romeo.* Tear not our hearth string thus!
>   They creak! they break! Juliet! Juliet! (*dies*),
> *Juliet.* (*to corpse*), Am I smothering you?
> *Corpse.* (*to Juliet*), Not at all; could you be so kind, do you
>   think, as to put my wig on again for me?
>   It has fallen off.
> *Juliet.* (*to corpse*), I'm afraid I can't, but I'll throw my
>   Muslin veil over it. You've broken the
>   phial, haven't you?
> (*Corpse nodded*),
> *Juliet.* (*to corpse*), Where's your dagger?
> *Corpse.* (*to Juliet*), 'pon my soul, I don't know.[25]

Fanny concluded: "I wonder if any body on earth can form the slightest idea of the interior of this wretched little theatre; it is the smallest I ever was in. The proprietors are poor, the actors poorer, and the grotesque mixture of misery, vulgarity, stage finery and . . . raggedness is . . . revolting."[26]

This is the theatrical world in which Joseph Jefferson grew up as his family operated theatres in Baltimore and Washington through the spring of 1834. On October 12, 1833, Joe, then four years old, may have acted the Duke of York to Junius Brutus Booth's Richard III in Washington. Certainly on March 12, 1834, shortly after his fifth birthday, he performed Robert in *Rob Roy or Auld Lang Syne* at the Front Street Amphitheatre in Baltimore.[27]

In Washington the Jeffersons' troubles increased. The 1833–34 season was marked by newspaper complaints about smoking in the theatre, nails protruding from the box and pit benches, rowdiness, waits of half an hour between the main play and the afterpiece, a lack of music, and insufficient heat. The Jeffersons made improvements. Additional stoves were installed; music was added between the acts and between the play and the farce, and police officers were engaged to keep order. Jefferson and MacKenzie published reassurances of respectability and comfort aimed at Washington's ladies, who were reluctant to attend. Nothing worked. The company was in financial trouble by the end of the season and forced to raise prices to cover its expenses.[28] It rarely mounted new productions, and its stars, Elizabeth Chapman and David Ingersoll, left for other cities. Even Charles Burke, age eleven, went off to perform at New York's Park Theatre. By May 1834 female members of the company were running a concert and ball to make ends meet. Finally the Jefferson troupe went bankrupt. The next day, a friend called on Joe's father to offer sympathy and was told he had gone fishing. Fearful that the senior Jefferson might attempt suicide, he rushed to the river, only to find the ex-manager lying in the grass, a book open at his side and his fishing rod stretched over the water.

> "Why, Jefferson," asked the friend, . . . "how can you devote yourself to . . . pleasure . . . when your . . . misfortunes ought to be driving you to . . . despair?"
>
> "Confound it, old boy!" was the answer: "I have lost everything and am so poor . . . that I can't . . . afford to let anything trouble me."[29]

The three seasons in Washington were the most theatrically ambitious of Joe's father's career. He may not have been a financially astute manager, but he failed in part for reasons beyond his control. First was the public's insupportable demand for novelty. By 1834 the Jeffersons had a repertory of at least 271 plays, but they performed 100 to 125 evenings every season and eventually ran out of new material. Audiences became bored and stayed away.

Second, the physical condition of the Washington Theatre was difficult for both actors and spectators. Audience members in the boxes and pit were too close to the stage. The seating capacity was not large enough to compensate stars sufficiently on their benefit nights. The stage was too small for elaborate scenery. Heavy columns obstructed sight-lines, and the auditorium ceiling was only painted canvas. The boxes had no aisles, forcing audience members to climb over uncushioned backless benches to get to their seats. The *Daily National Intelligencer* condemned the house as cold, dirty, and small, "insufferable in winter from the cold and in summer from the heat." Tyrone Power, the Irish comedian, wrote that it "was a most miserable-looking place, the worst I met with in the country, ill-situated and difficult of access."[30]

A third problem involved complimentary tickets. Each of the theatre's sixty stockholders, to whom the Jeffersons paid rent, was entitled to free admission except on benefit nights. They could also assign their seats to others. Because the theatre only sat a thousand, sixty complimentary tickets a night was a severe drain on its income. A fourth problem, the lack of street lights in Washington, made it inconvenient for patrons to attend evening performances.[31]

The American character of the period, still bound by the Puritan work ethic, may also have mitigated against theatregoing. The English traveller Francis J. Grund, writing in 1836, noted: "Of all the theatres in the United States, there is but one (in New York), which is . . . a profitable business. . . . Americans are not fond . . . of public amusement and are best pleased with . . . business. Their pleasure consists in being . . . occupied, and their evenings are either spent at home or with a few of their friends, in a manner as private as possible."[32]

The failure of MacKenzie and Jefferson's Washington Theatre led to a dispersal of the family between the summer of 1834 and the fall of 1835. The range of Joe's travels increased. In the next three years, the Jefferson family broke apart and reunited in Philadelphia, New York, Wilmington, and Baltimore.

In October 1834 Joe's parents moved back to Philadelphia, where his father, still determined to be a manager, opened the Northern Exchange Theatre. But by December 10 the elder Jefferson was writing: "I am not able with all my exertions to support my family," and by the end of the month the Northern Exchange closed. By January 5, 1835, Joseph and Cornelia had reverted to their status as occasional actors, and Cornelia was pregnant again.[33]

Between January and August 1835 Joe's immediate family shuttled between the Walnut Street Theatre in Philadelphia and the company's summer theatre in Wilmington, Delaware. Cornelia, although six months pregnant, was still performing, as were Joe (now six), Charles Burke, and Jane Anderson. Of particular note is a July 22 Wilmington performance by "Master Jefferson" in the role of Alexis in William Barrymore's *The Snow Storm*, the earliest newspaper reference to Joseph Jefferson III.[34]

Alexis is the child of Lowina of Tobolskow, the melodrama's virtuous heroine who attempts to reach her exiled husband in Siberia and escape the clutches of the powerful Baron Ostroff. For most of the play, Alexis is a wordless role, mainly requiring pantomimic action. Act II, however, gave the six-year-old Jefferson a moment of glory. Lowina, missing her trusted servant Michael, exits to find him,

> . . . and in her anxiety leaves ALEXIS on the stage, who follows her to the wing crying "Mother, mother." Finding his cries not heeded, he returns . . . to the front of the stage and begins to show the effects of the cold; he writhes with pain and staggering towards the cloak which his mother had left upon the stage, gets possession of it. Offering up a prayer for the protection of heaven, he folds himself in the cloak and sinks upon the earth.[35]

When the Wilmington Theatre closed on August 21, 1835, the Jeffersons returned to Philadelphia. There, on August 28, the seven-months-pregnant Cornelia played Ophelia at the Walnut Street Theatre, a performance presumably made possible by the hoop-skirted dresses of the period. Opening at Baltimore's Holliday Street Theatre on September 26, Cornelia was still performing three days before her third child and only surviving daughter, Cornelia, was born on October 1, 1835. The younger Cornelia was known as Connie, or later Auntie Con, and grew to be a small delicate woman. Like all Jeffersons, she was destined to be an actress. After her birth, her mother took five days off from work and was back on the stage by October 6.[36]

In 1836 the Jeffersons migrated to New York to work at the Franklin Theatre on Chatham Street. Joe's father knew the neighborhood, having performed and met Joe's mother there in 1824. David Ingersoll joined the Franklin company during the summer of 1836, and Joseph Jefferson II, Cornelia Burke Jefferson, Charles Burke, Elizabeth Richardson, Mary-Anne Jefferson Ingersoll, Jane Anderson, and Elizabeth Anderson, followed him to New York.[37] The Jeffersons no longer had their own company; they were now salaried actors, but they were still together, and Joe attempted to recapture this family solidarity forty-three years later when he came to form his own company.

They lived nearby on the Lower East Side, on the third story of a tenement at 26 James Street. The ground floor was occupied by the landlord, Mr. Titus, and the second floor by another company member, John Sefton. Next door was a Catholic church and in the rear the old Pearl Street Jewish cemetery, where Joe played among the tombstones. It was a poor neighborhood, beginning to house the immigrant populations pouring into New York.[38]

The Jeffersons had doubts about staying. On December 30, 1836, Joe's father wrote to the St. Louis theatre manager, Noah Ludlow, inquiring about work. On January 11, 1837, Ludlow replied offering him a position as acting manager and scene painter. Cornelia was to sing, play old women, and fill in as a chorus member, and Charles Burke was to work as an artist in the paint room, function as a call boy (someone who notified actors in their dressing rooms that their cue was coming up), act, sing, and dance. Ludlow wanted them in St. Louis immediately and set February 20, 1837, as a deadline for their arrival. The Jeffersons made a bad mistake by turning him down.[39] They would eventually wind up in the West, destitute, separated from one another, and working for Ludlow.

During the 1836 and 1837 seasons, they remained in New York, where Joe's father was employed at the Franklin Theatre as a scene painter and occasional actor. Jane and Elizabeth Anderson became members of the theatre's stock company, the former specializing in chambermaids and walking ladies, the latter in old women. Within a year, both women had married actors in the troupe. Cornelia Jefferson worked occasionally at the Franklin, primarily at her husband's benefits. She had not appeared in New York in ten years, and "her voice and person . . . in the interim suffered sadly from the ravages of time." Even Joe was pressed into service on September 20, 1837, when, at the age of eight, he engaged in a mock battle with a juvenile performer named Master Edwin Titus (possibly his neighbor's son), for the latter's benefit night.

> Young Titus was attired as an American sailor, I being dressed to represent a Greek pirate. I was much smaller than my antagonist, but as the fight was for his benefit, good taste suggested that he should . . . slay me—which he did—and as the curtain came down, I was flat on my back, and the American sailor, waving a star-spangled banner over me, placed his foot . . . on the chest of the vanquished Greek. The fight was encored; so I had to come to life . . .—quite a common thing for stage pirates— and die twice.[40]

Most New York theatres closed in the summer. Consequently from July 18 to September 23, 1837, the Jeffersons became part of an attempt by their neighbor, John Sefton, to turn Niblo's Garden into a "legitimate" house. Sefton's company produced English one-act farces disguised as French "vaudvilles," alternating with the concerts that comprised the garden's usual fare. As both the Franklin and the Park theatres were closed for the summer, he had his pick of unemployed actors, and the company included Joseph Jefferson II, Jane Anderson, Charles Burke, and Elizabeth Richardson. In 1903 Jane Anderson Germon remembered that

> Mr. Sefton took charge of a pavilion in Niblo's Garden, and . . . we appeared three times a week with salary paid by the night. We closed minus our salaries and with the alternative of getting the whole amount by note or two-thirds in cash. Uncle Joe was angry with me, because I took $40 instead of the $60 due; he never got a cent.[41]

In 1837 New York suffered a financial panic and a run on the banks caused by President Martin Van Buren's fight against the Bank of the United States. Social activities, including theatregoing, ground to a halt.[42] Seeking financial advantage, the Jeffersons left New York for Albany, and from Albany began their journey west.

2

THE JEFFERSONS
IN THE WEST

1836–1847

The Jeffersons had begun to migrate west in 1836. Joe and his immediate family joined them when he was nine years old; he would not
return east until shortly before his eighteenth birthday. His childhood
had been spent primarily in New York and Washington; his adolescence was to be a series of brief stands in Illinois, Wisconsin, Iowa,
Missouri, Indiana, Mississippi, Tennessee, Louisiana and Texas.
Although his *Autobiography* treated this period as an adventure in
theatrical pioneering, there is ample evidence of its financial, physical,
and emotional hardship. The Jeffersons had never been wealthy, but
the adolescent Joe saw the dissolution of the family company and his
parents' descent into desperate poverty. In 1836 Joe was living in a
New York tenement while his family made a living in the theatre, but
by 1846 he was working in a bar in a Mexican border town. He was to
spend his life amassing money and buying houses, making sure that
no one in his family experienced the poverty and homelessness of his
adolescent years.

Joe's uncle and aunt, Alexander and Hester Jefferson MacKenzie,
were the first family members to move west. By fall 1836 MacKenzie
was stage-managing the Italian Hall in Cleveland for the theatrical
firm of Edwin Dean and David D. McKinney. In the late spring of
1837 the Dean and McKinney troupe moved to Detroit, and another
aunt and uncle, Mary-Anne and David Ingersoll, came west to join
them.[43]

When the Detroit season ended, MacKenzie formed a partnership with Harry Isherwood, the actor whose wig the two-year-old Joseph Jefferson had scalped on stage. Isherwood had become a scenic artist, and he and MacKenzie broke off from the parent troupe and returned to Cleveland with a small company. At that point Ingersoll left his wife, Mary-Anne, with the troupe and moved south where he died in August 1838.[44]

The troupe he left behind, under the leadership of Isherwood and MacKenzie, took the steam packet *Pennsylvania* through the Great Lakes to Chicago. There they fitted up a theatre in an existing space and opened in October, becoming the town's first theatrical company. The following January they left for a tour of southern Illinois, promising the citizens of Chicago they would return in a few months with an enlarged troupe and establish a theatrical circuit in the region. The expanded company would include Joe Jefferson.[45]

While MacKenzie was opening up Chicago as a theatrical territory in the fall and winter of 1837, Joe's father was working at the Pearl Street Theatre in Albany. There, on December 11, the eight-year-old Jefferson played a fop in a production of *Gulliver in Lilliput* in which the title role was performed by Mr. Porter, the "Kentucky Giant," and the Lilliputians by an assortment of children and a stage dwarf.

In early 1838 the Jeffersons toured with the Albany company to the western part of New York, traveling "in a fast-sailing packet-boat" on the Erie Canal and performing along the way to pay their passage. With them were Joe's cousin Jane Anderson, her husband Greenbury C. Germon, Charles Burke, and William Warren. Warren, then twenty-six, was Joe's father's first cousin and would become Boston's most famous comic actor.[46]

After a brief run, beginning May 31, at the Eagle Street Theatre in Buffalo, the Jeffersons took a steamboat through the Great Lakes to Chicago, a place that Jane Anderson Germon recalled as primitive: "We played in a big drafty hall. . . . The streets of the town were not paved, . . . and the ways were so dark that we had to use lanterns strung on big sticks to light us to and from the playhouse."[47]

The playhouse was a small theatre located on the second floor of a three-story wooden building in one of the most congested streets of the young city. The building, called the Rialto, was a glorified tavern. It rented rooms to lodgers, provided a bar, and had enough space for a 2,400-square-foot theatre. The theatre, which had just been built by Isherwood and MacKenzie, had a pit of planed board benches, a tier of individual boxes with straw-stuffed seats, and a gallery of benches. The stage was hidden by a ludicrously painted drop curtain and lit by oil that smoked in tin lamps and sconces.[48]

In 1888 Joseph Jefferson III later remembered this period as "a short season in Chicago, with the varying success which in those days always attended the drama," but this recollection was part of his charming deprecation of his barnstorming days. The 1838 season lasted a month and a half longer than the 1837 season, and the Jeffersons were able to save money by bartering theatre tickets for printing costs and the tin lanterns and oil they needed for lighting. Moreover, the company's return for another season in 1839 implies that the previous year had been at least reasonably profitable. Actors were unlikely to return to cities where they had not made money.[49]

By October 27, 1838, the Jeffersons were on their way to Galena, Illinois, traveling westward across the prairie in open wagons with their wardrobe trunks for seats. In Galena the foundations of a theatre had already been laid, but the building was not yet complete. The twelve-member company was forced to perform in a large hall on the second floor of a store. By this time nine-year-old Joe was serving his theatrical apprenticeship, singing and acting "occasionally when a role suitable for a girl or a boy happened to be on the bill." Audiences were receptive. Jane Germon later wrote that "nearly every gambling house in the place was broken up. We simply drove them out of business."[50]

The Jeffersons closed their season on February 6 and traveled on sleighs along the frozen Mississippi to Dubuque to perform in a theatre on the second floor of the Shakespeare Coffee House and Free Admission News Room.[51] Jane Germon remembered that "we left [Dubuque] just when the ice was breaking, and every little stream was swollen to twice its normal size. It took us three days' driving, . . . and we had to forge the streams on horseback."

They toured to southern Wisconsin at the end of February and returned to Galena when the spring thaw of 1839 opened navigation on the Mississippi. In April the company proceeded to Burlington, Iowa, by steamboat. From there they traveled south along the Mississippi playing small towns, often under crude conditions. Cornelia Jefferson wound up singing "Home, Sweet Home" to the accompaniment of squealing pigs in Pekin, Illinois.[52]

The company opened in Springfield on July 4, 1839, the day the town officially became the state capital. Remembering their Springfield adventure in his 1888 autobiography, Joseph Jefferson launched into a story about how his father and MacKenzie built a new theatre there; how the town, in the throes of a religious revival, attempted to impose a heavy license fee on the company; and how Abraham Lincoln came to their rescue. Unfortunately, none of it was true. Jefferson and MacKenzie never built a theatre in Springfield. They performed in a "commodious building" that had recently been completed by a wood "stapler" or supplier named James P. Langford. The town council did impose an unusually high tax of $3 a day on the company, but Lincoln, although a member of the board of trustees, was absent.

Why did Jefferson make up such a story? In part it reflects his lifelong aversion to organized religion, an aversion he had to express carefully, but which the readers of his autobiography in the late nineteenth century would have known, because Jefferson had publicly exposed a minister who refused to bury a professional actor. But the anecdote also reflects his desire, in 1888, to associate himself, in a positive way, with Lincoln. A nostalgic link with the martyred president, who had led nineteenth-century America through its premier event, was what Jefferson needed to deflect attention from the facts—that he had been a good friend of the Booth family (he had certainly known John Wilkes Booth) and that he had actually declined to participate in the Civil War, choosing to sit it out in Australia, New Zealand, and England.[53]

The Illinois Theatrical Company, as the Jefferson family troupe now called itself, remained in Springfield until August 9, 1839, and then returned to Chicago for their third and most artistically ambitious season.[54] Their ranks were augmented by two touring stars, Mary Ann Meek McClure and Charles Kemble Mason (a nephew of the English stars Sarah Siddons and John Philip Kemble and a cousin of Fanny Kemble, with whom the Jeffersons had performed in Washington). They produced new scenery and costumes for both a spectacular musical and a melodrama as well as a production of *Oliver Twist*.

The short duration of the 1839 season—only two months—and the fact that the Jeffersons never returned to Chicago signal financial failure. Chicago had been hurt by the financial panic of 1837 and did not recover until the late 1840's. People did not have enough money to buy tickets. Moreover, by end of their third season the Jeffersons' Chicago repertory was wearing thin, and they were forced to move on.[55]

When the Chicago season closed on November 2, 1839, William Warren returned to Buffalo, and Greenbury Germon left for Georgia. The rest of the troupe embarked on a tour along the Fox River and by mid-month were again in Springfield. There they announced their intention of remaining "during the ensuing session of the legislature."[56] By this time Joe was earning his living singing and dancing. The *Sangamo Journal* reported: "Joe is . . . a chip off the old block" and the shower of bits [fourpence] which fell around him . . . proved how those present appreciated his efforts to please."[57]

The company remained in Springfield until February 7, 1840, a few days after the legislative session ended, and then proceeded south to St. Louis. When Sol Smith and Noah Ludlow, the city's reigning theatrical managers, refused to rent their new St. Louis theatre, the Jeffersons fitted up what they advertised as a "splendid Ball Room" in a concert hall on Market Street with a "parquette" or seated pit and a gallery for "persons of colour." The *Daily Missouri Republican* thought that the space was unsuitable for "pieces requiring much scenic effect," and the Jeffersons, opening on March 9, closed on March 28. Announcing their intention of touring the principal towns of the Missouri and Mississippi Rivers, they left, probably to avoid competition, just as Ludlow and Smith returned from Mobile to begin their spring season.[58]

Through the spring and summer of 1840, the Jeffersons toured with Augustus A. Addams, a once-promising American star, by then degenerating from alcoholism and forced to play the provinces. Shortly thereafter the company began to disintegrate, splitting into two smaller operations, one playing Illinois, the other touring rural Missouri. The two groups were reunited by mid-May in Palmyra, Missouri, and spent the summer and winter of 1840 in Missouri and Illinois.[59]

In May 1841 the company performed in Vincennes, Indiana, where an elderly settler remembered them as a group of nine or ten people in dire financial straits. They set up an "impromptu stage, seats etc." with a curtain at the rear of the stage, behind which the actors dressed, but no front curtain. An audience of fifty to sixty people, on plank seats, saw a performance in which Joe served as prompter and played a minor role as a comic servant. After the performance the Jeffersons moved south to join a troupe managed by John S. Potter in Nashville, Tennessee in the fall of 1841. There Hester MacKenzie and Cornelia Jefferson played mature character roles; Joseph Jefferson II painted scenery and occasionally played elderly men; and Charles Burke danced and specialized in comic afterpieces.[60]

At the age of nineteen, Charley had become a tall, thin, angular young man with a "small round head set on square broad shoulders" and "arms of unusual length." A contemporary, John A. Ellsler, who would later be one of Joe's managerial partners, remembered Charley as having "combined the qualities of both pathos and comedy, an excellent singer and dancer and an expert with the foils." In Nashville, Burke and Mrs. Margaret Mervine Maynard (called Mary), another member of Potter's acting company, were married on October 24, 1841. When the troupe broke up, the Burkes left the family, accompanying Potter to Mississippi.[61]

After the Nashville season closed, Joseph and Cornelia Jefferson moved their family to Vicksburg. Cornelia acted; Joseph acted and painted scenery; and in Vicksburg, Joseph Jefferson III, age thirteen, and his sister, Cornelia age seven, began to contribute substantially to the family's income. Advertisements in the *Vicksburg Daily Whig* highlighted the comic duets, Tyrinnian Waltzes, and Highland Flings performed by the Jefferson children as prominently as the titles of the plays being performed.[62]

The Vicksburg company disbanded in late April 1842, and by May 2 the Jeffersons were in financial trouble. Cornelia Jefferson wrote to Noah Ludlow in St. Louis asking him to employ her husband as an "actor, artist or both" and saying that their financial position was poor. Ludlow, who had offered them jobs five years before, now did nothing for them. The Jeffersons then joined a small troupe led by Alexander MacKenzie, opening in Hart's Saloon in Memphis on May 4.

MacKenzie's company gave short dramatic performances, followed by a dance. By June 17 they joined forces with John S. Potter again to open Memphis' New Theatre. The company was not successful. The theatre was a converted livery stable and warehouse, and D. S. Lathan, editor of the *Memphis Eagle*, noted that during the summer the odor of the place led him to believe that "livery stables and Theatres make a very bad co-partnership." Joseph Jefferson III remembered that "bad business . . . closed the theatre, and my father turned from scene painter to sign painter." Potter failed to pay their salaries, and the Jeffersons were broke again.[63]

They were temporarily saved by Joe's aunt, the now-widowed Elizabeth Richardson, who was touring the South. In Alabama she had attracted the attention of Charles J. B. Fisher, secretary of the Mobile Gas Company, who was to marry her four years later. Fisher had been delegated to employ actors for the Royal Street Theatre and, wanting to befriend the Jeffersons, hired Mrs. Richardson, Alexander and Hester MacKenzie, Mary-Anne Jefferson and her new husband, John S. Wright, Joseph and Cornelia Jefferson, and Greenbury and Jane Germon as members of the company. Although working as salaried actors, the Jefferson family troupe was back in business.[64]

They were scheduled to open at the Royal Street Theatre on November 14, 1842, but Joseph and Cornelia Jefferson, their children, and their housekeeper, Mary, came early. They traveled steerage on the steamboat *Creole* from New Orleans and arrived in Mobile on October 10 so that Jefferson, the company's scenic artist and chief comedian, would have time to repaint the theatre's stock scenery. The Jeffersons settled in a house on the west side of Conception Street, and the two children began one of their rare periods in school.[65]

Yellow fever had been raging in Mobile. In mid-October a local newspaper claimed that the sickness had subsided, but by November 23 Joseph Jefferson II had contracted the disease and was replaced on the nightly bill. He died at midnight the following day, at the age of thirty-eight, and was buried on November 25 in the Magnolia Cemetery in Mobile beneath a wooden grave marker. T. Allston Brown, the theatrical agent who became one of America's earliest theatre historians, spoke of him as "an actor of great talent and an artist of unquestioned excellence. . . . Guileless as a child, he passed through life in perfect charity to all mankind, and never, by his nearest and dearest, was he ever known to utter an unkind word or entertain an illiberal opinion."[66]

Years later his son removed the wooden marker, buried it on his estate in Hohokus, New Jersey, and replaced it with a marble stone. Jefferson is said to have visited his father's grave whenever he played Mobile and to have planted the red camellia that blossoms on the site today.[67]

The Jeffersons had little time to mourn. Four days later they were back at work. The now-widowed Cornelia Jefferson retired from the stage to support herself by running a boarding house for actors. Joe, then almost fourteen, later recalled:

> My sister and myself were . . . engaged . . . to act such children's parts as our size and talent warranted . . . appearing in . . . dances and comic duets, added to which I was to grind colors in the paint-room—assistant artist, I was called in the playbill—. . . for which services we were to receive six dollars a week. . . . This employment was . . . a charity; . . . One of the programmes . . . announced that after the play, Master and Miss Jefferson were to "execute a fancy dance." Now as our terpsichorean education had been rather limited, it is quite likely that the execution was complete.[68]

Jefferson's denigration of his dancing is an example of the self-mockery typical of his public persona by 1888. He was a great star being charmingly modest. Joe was a modest person, but he knew that his public loved his modesty, and he always played to that public. Although he came to joke about it, his dancing ability served him well as a child performer, and he continued to dance as a mature actor, even in *Rip Van Winkle* and *The Cricket on the Hearth*. In 1843 his stage work was actually central to the company rather than a charitable employment. From December 31, 1842, when "the interesting child, Miss Jefferson performed a hornpipe," the two children appeared regularly in the Mobile company's advertisements. Except for Elizabeth Richardson, the resident leading lady, they received more advertising space than any other family members. In the program, Joe, at the age of thirteen, was listed as Master Jefferson.[69]

It was in Mobile that Jefferson first met George Holland, a comic actor whose death in 1870 would make him nationally famous. It was also here that he first fell in love—with Julia Dean, the daughter of Edwin Dean, the Buffalo theatre manager. Born on July 21, 1830, she was a year and a half younger than he was. In the late nineteenth century, after Dean's death, Jefferson told his fellow actor Francis Wilson: "This sweet girl and I fought our early professional battles side by side. We were in the ballet, front row together. Happy peasants and gypsies—alternately Catholics and Protestants, Whigs and Tories—ready to change our religious or political opinion for six dollars a week."[70]

The Mobile company formed by Charles Fisher was not successful. Two days after the season closed, Elizabeth Richardson assumed its management, making her one of the few women to work as a theatre manager before the Civil War. The troupe was described as "half a company, only half paid, consisting of those with small salaries who could afford one-third or one-half of nothing." Richardson also failed, and on May 27, 1843, she announced the close of "her managerial career." She remained in Mobile, while the Wrights, MacKenzies, Germons, and Jeffersons returned to Nashville by August 28.[71]

The Nashville troupe broke up in November 1843, and the Jeffersons dispersed. Joseph Jefferson III later recalled: "Business was bad, and on one occasion, the gentlemen of the company, myself included, walked from Gallatin to Lebanon—not however for the exercise." The family company was finished. They constructed a barge, using scenery as a sail, and floated down the Cumberland River to Clarksville, from there to the Ohio, and from there to the Mississippi. Accompanied by their mother, Joseph and his sister Cornelia joined Ludlow and Smith's troupe in their first season in the theatre on Royal Street in Mobile. Here, for the first time, young Joe was called Mr. Jefferson in advertisements. He was fourteen years old.[72]

Along with his sister and mother, Joe remained with Ludlow and Smith for the next two years. After Mobile they played New Orleans, where Joe was fined for "boisterous and noisy" behavior in his dressing room in November 1844. The Ludlow-Smith company returned to Mobile and finally traveled north to St. Louis. When the fall 1845 season began, Joe sang comic songs and duets with his sister and occasionally performed a wooden shoe dance.[73] It was during this season that Jefferson, appearing in a theatrical celebration of the Fourth of July, suffered what he described as one of his great adolescent humiliations. He had been selected to sing the national anthem.

> I was in a . . . state of excitement . . . having been selected to give the first stanza. I had studied it . . . so often that I knew it backwards, and that is . . . the way I sang it. . . . We were arranged in the . . . conventional half-circle with the "Goddess of Liberty" in the center. The "Mother of her Country" had a Roman helmet —pasteboard . . . —on her head and was . . . draped with the American flag. My heart was in my mouth as the music started

..., but I stepped ... forward. ... I got as far as "Oh, say, can you
see—" and here the world left me. My mind was blank. I tried it
again: "Oh say, can you see—" ... I was blind with fright; ... The
audience began to hiss. ... I heard the ... voice of the Goddess of
Liberty say, "Poor fellow!" ... The hissing increased. Old Mul-
ler, the German [orchestra] leader, called out ... , "Go on, Yo!"
but "Yo" couldn't go on, so "Yo" thought he had better go off.
I bowed ... and made a ... retreat. My ... mother stood at the
wings in tears; I threw myself into her arms.[74]

It made a terrific story, and, of course, it may have happened. Any
actor can blank on stage. Certainly newspapers attest to the company's production of a Fourth of July pageant in 1845. But Jefferson
was sixteen at the time. He had been performing steadily since the age
of three under the most adverse theatrical conditions imaginable. At
sixteen, he would not have had difficulty memorizing "The Star-
spangled Banner." Whether the anecdote was true or not, it served to
remind Jefferson's 1888 readers that he had not always been a star—
which consequently let them realize how great a star he had become.
It is an example of the real but simultaneously self-serving deprecation
that he practiced publicly all his life. When he had become "the dean
of the American theatre," he could afford to be humble.

By November 21, 1845, Master and Miss Jefferson were performing "La Polka" with the Ludlow and Smith company at the St. Charles
Theatre in New Orleans. They remained there through the spring of
1846, when Jefferson, now seventeen, played Zeke, the black servant
in *Fashion*, opposite the play's author, Anna Cora Mowatt.[75]

The season at the St. Charles closed on April 14, and according to
the local newspaper, the following day "there was a general breaking
up and departure of the comedians." Joseph, his mother, and his
sister Cornelia set sail on the *Galveston* for the three-day, eight-
hundred-mile journey to Texas. They did what was typical of nineteenth-century actors in the summer—they broke off from a parent
company to barnstorm the provinces. The Jeffersons played Galveston and then "embarked on board a small stern-wheel steamer" for
Houston, where, beginning July 4, 1846, they acted at the Market
Square Theatre "for several weeks . . . but with a feeble kind of
patronage."[76]

By midsummer they had joined an even smaller theatrical corps that followed Zachary Taylor's army into Mexico. In his *Autobiography* Jefferson contended that in "May 1846, we embarked on board a condemned Mississippi steamer for Point Isabel," a westward port on the Gulf of Mexico near the Rio Grande and the present site of Brownsville. Thus he placed himself near the decisive battles of Palo Alto and Resaca de la Palma. Taylor's forces entered the captured city of Matamoras, Mexico, on May 8, and Jefferson's autobiography has "our gallant band of comedians bringing up the rear."[77] Like his earlier evoking of Lincoln's intervention on behalf of the family troupe, Jefferson was determined to assert his patriotic credentials, here through a connection with the Mexican War.

More likely he was part of a troupe that reached Matamoras after the fighting was over in mid-July 1846 and was seen by a Maryland volunteer named John R. Kenly at the mouth of the Rio Grande. Kenly's remarks illustrate the ragtag condition to which the Jeffersons had fallen.

> [A] company of strolling players, bound for Matamoras and hailing from New Orleans, stopped at the landing. I must confess to looking upon them with . . . interest and . . . pity. The *ladies* of the troupe gratified the men of our troop by casting bottles of wine from the steamer's deck into their midst, whilst to add to the *hilarity of the occasion*, they . . . sang . . . a few of their favorite airs. Ah, me! poor women! Though full of apparent gaiety, my heart bled for them.[78]

Matamoras was a quiet Mexican town suddenly transformed into a rough military camp, filled with drunken soldiers. Audience members carried their weapons and made so much noise that John Kenly reported: " I do not believe that anybody ever did know what was . . . played that night."[79] The plight of the professional actors was exacerbated by the necessity of using amateurs during performances, a standard nineteenth-century theatrical ploy to attract business and a necessity on the frontier. Mexican War soldiers were accustomed to seeing their officers and fellow men on stage. (Lieutenant Ulysses S. Grant had been scheduled to play Desdemona until an actress arrived from New Orleans to replace him.) A letter to the New Orleans *Daily Picayune* in August 1846 provides a first-hand description of the Jeffersons in Matamoras. The writer is apparently a soldier accustomed to more sophisticated fare.

I visited the theatre . . . to see *Richard III.* I expected to see *Richmond kill Richard*, but what a tragedy! It was a wholesale *murder* out and out. Not only were the . . . children in the Tower and "good King Henry" slaughtered, but one indiscriminate hacking . . . and slaying . . . took place. If the field of Bosworth drank as much blood as was spilt on the stage . . . it must have been an awful field. . . . The tragedy was *carried off.* On came the pretty little Miss Jefferson who gave us the *cracovienne* [a dance she had performed in New Orleans].[80]

The Jeffersons were still performing on September 5, 1846, but General Zachary Taylor set September 1 as the beginning of his campaign to capture the Mexican city of Monterrey. By mid-September American troops had left Matamoras, and the theatre was closed. Abandoned by their manager, without money in a country at war with their own, the Jeffersons and a fellow actor named Edward Badger opened what Joe later described as "a coffee and cake stand in a barroom of an adobe building facing the main plaza of Matamoras."[81] What they actually ran was a tobacco shop in Foyle's Lunch House, where they sold "Good chewing tobacco always on hand, ready for use."

In his *Autobiography* Jefferson describes this period of his life as an idyllic adventurous existence that included a romance with "a simple child of nature" named Metta. Following a murder in the saloon and a touching farewell scene, Jefferson deserted Metta with promises to return "to claim her as my bride and bear her off with the whole family—there were sixteen of them—to my own country." He claimed to have forgotten her within a month, a breach of promise apparently acceptable both to him and to nineteenth-century readers, because "she had that rich olive complexion that one sees in a pale Key West cigar." On the other hand, Metta was given far more attention in Jefferson's autobiography than either of his two wives.

Although the mature Jefferson portrayed Matamoras in his memoirs as the site of a youthful adventure, life there could not have been pleasant. The town was filthy; the upper-class Mexican population had fled; and both the local population and invading Americans were infested with lice. Within two months, in early November 1846, the Jeffersons received a permit to leave Matamoras in a government boat taking wounded soldiers to Brazos Santiago and sailing from there to Louisiana.[82]

Jefferson arrived in New Orleans on Saturday, November 28, 1846, to find the Ludlow and Smith company at the St. Charles Theatre. The afterpiece was John Baldwin Buckstone's *A Kiss in the Dark* with John E. Owens. Jefferson went to the performance and later reported in his autobiography that his desire to rival Owens' ability had determined his life as comic actor. It is probable, however, that the careers of his grandfather and his half-brother Charles Burke were equally influential. The Jeffersons, after all, were comedians.[83]

It was Charles Burke who provided Jefferson's next career opportunity. Burke and his wife were working in Philadelphia and gradually ascending into the mainstream of American theatre. Joe left his mother and sister in New Orleans he set off by steamer for Wheeling, West Virginia. Although the Baltimore and Ohio Railroad already ran from Wheeling to Cumberland, Maryland, he apparently could not afford the train. Instead he took an arduous twenty-four-hour stage coach ride to Cumberland, and thence to Philadelphia. Immediately upon arrival, he was cast as the lead in two farces and opened on New Year's Eve of 1847 at the Arch Street Theatre. Joe was not quite eighteen, and this was the beginning of his apprenticeship as a mature professional actor.[84]

3

APPRENTICESHIP
IN THE EAST
1847–1850

Jefferson began his eastern apprenticeship in a second-string urban stock company at the Arch Street Theatre in Philadelphia under the management of the comic actor William E. Burton. The company employed dozens of actors, but unlike Philadelphia's more prestigious theatres, it did not at first feature touring stars. Although this policy may have been an economic limitation for Burton, it was fortunate for rising young actors like the Burkes and Jefferson. Middle-level urban companies, like western touring troupes, provided inexperienced performers with roles usually reserved for seasoned actors and traveling stars.

In 1847 Jefferson was a "utility" actor working his way up the theatrical ladder. Being a "super" or a "utility" actor were the first steps in a theatrical apprenticeship in "lines of business" that led to being a "second walking gentleman" or a "second old man and character," and from there to lines designated as "juvenile," "character," "light comedy," "first old man," and finally "leading business." It took between seven to twelve years to complete this apprenticeship, and many actors stopped along the way, having found a line of business that suited them in the lower ranks of a company. Jefferson's cousin Jane Germon, for instance, performed old women most of her life.

Performing a "line of business" meant knowing every legitimate part in the line, a considerable proportion of the best-known and most frequently played pieces on Lacy's (now French's) list of plays.

Consequently, before actors could move from one line to the next they spent hours memorizing the text and traditional stage business for every role they might perform. The first season when an artist took such a step meant performing six new parts a week and staying one or two hours after each performance to memorize lines. An actor named Frank C. Bangs, who performed with Jefferson in 1890, remembered his stock company origins: "I often acted three and four parts a week and sometimes five and six. Many and many a time have I had to study a part all night . . . to memorize my lines for rehearsal on the day following."[85] John L. Saphore, a contemporary of Jefferson's, writing in 1901, explained the system.

> In the "palmy days," . . . a player was trained [by a] system of study and could act acceptably any role in his particular line in four hours' notice, whether he had ever seen the part before or not. One of the rules posted up in the greenroom was . . . that every actor was expected to be ready to play any part in his line within that length of time. The method that made this possible was this: The grade of role above first walking gentleman was that of juvenile. The walking gentleman was understudying all the juvenile roles, and the juvenile was understudying the grade of role above his, and so on; throughout the entire company, each member was preparing himself . . . to take a better line of parts, should opportunity offer. By this system, we were continually raising a new force of thoroughly equipped actors, to most of whom the now arduous committing of lines was . . . child's play and but the . . . beginning of their work. Incidentally, we were able to change the bill nightly without the . . . strain that would . . . attend . . . such an undertaking now.[86]

The actress Eliza Young, three years younger than Jefferson, recalled in 1902 that "I have absolutely no idea how many parts I have played. . . . The number must be in the thousands. In the old days, I often went home on Monday night with five new roles to learn for the next week. We had to be quick at learning them. I remember once playing Helen in *The Hunchback* at one day's notice. During the latter days of my career, the work seemed easy, despite my age, because I often played one part for weeks at a time."[87]

Not everyone was successful. According to a local newspaper review, an actor named Allen, appearing with Jefferson, in Wilmington, North Carolina, could not keep up. "He has been cast in a . . . new round of characters and has had too many parts to study to admit . . . doing justice to them. . . . The chief drawback . . . has been an imperfect committing of the words of his parts, which may readily be excused and accounted for by the shortness of the notice."[88]

Jefferson made the transition from utility actor to "leading business" in only ten years, but the roles he performed were roles that had served his father and his half-brother, Charles Burke. They were staples of the Jefferson family troupe, and Joe had seen and heard them since boyhood. In 1847, however, at the beginning of his adult career, he was a minor company member whose name seldom reached the daily newspapers' abbreviated cast lists. His most notable part that season was The Artful Dodger in a stage version of *Oliver Twist* with Burke as Fagin and Mrs. Burke as Nancy Sykes. Jefferson, in his autobiography, remembered that Burke "would often persuade Mr. Burton to cast me for parts far beyond my reach." If so, newspaper cast lists provide no corroboration, and it is possible that Jefferson, in 1888, was being sentimental about his long-dead brother.[89]

On February 15, 1847, the Burton company went on vacation. Faced with unemployment, the Burkes and Jefferson moved to a less prestigious house, Peale's Philadelphia Museum and Gallery of Fine Arts. It was the urban equivalent of barnstorming in the summer. At Peale's, Charley and his wife were the leading attraction. Jefferson was relegated to minor parts such as David in *The Rivals* and the villainous schoolmaster Squeers in a version of *Nicholas Nickleby* entitled *Poor Smike and His Friend Nicholas.* His name, however, appeared more often in Peale's advertisements than in Burton's, because in a less prestigious theatre, a less prestigious actor could attract attention.[90]

The Burkes and Jefferson remained at Peale's until April 22 and then returned to Burton's Arch Street Theatre, where Jefferson performed comic songs and minor roles. In June 1847 they were joined by eleven-year-old Connie, who had come east with her mother. For a while at least four of the Jeffersons were acting together again. Burke, however, moved on to an engagement at New York's Bowery Theatre in mid-July, leaving his wife and the rest of the family behind. He was always one step ahead of Jefferson, always higher on the bill. Consequently, his move proved a break for Joe, who took over some of Charley's roles. Unfortunately the Arch Street soon turned to visiting star performers as attractions, and his name disappeared from newspaper cast lists.[91]

He had, however, attracted Burton's attention, and the seasoned manager featured the young comedian that summer in a thirteen-member company that performed at Baltimore's Front Street Theatre for eight days beginning July 2, 1847. Jefferson was billed as the "son of the celebrated comedian; his first appearance." He was, of course, the grandson of the comedian cited, and this was not his first appearance. It also may not have been successful, because Jefferson's name disappeared from cast lists at the end of three days. Apparently Burton had tried him out as a first comedian, and the results were not good.[92]

By mid-July 1848 Jefferson returned to Philadelphia to appear again at Peale's Museum, this time as the theatre's lead comedian. Although Peale's was a step down in theatrical prestige from Burton's, it provided Jefferson with a step up in his "line of business." He appeared in a series of farces culminating in his first benefit as a mature actor on July 28. A benefit was a performance featuring or honoring a member of the company who received the proceeds after expenses were deducted.[93]

That fall, on October 22, 1848, Joe's mother, Cornelia Jefferson, died at her home on 207 South Ninth Street in Philadelphia and was buried two days later. She left her eldest son Charles Burke, then twenty-six; Joe, not quite twenty; and Cornelia, who had just turned thirteen.[94] Both Jefferson and Burke were out of town. The story of their mother's funeral became a family legend, eventually written down by Jefferson's granddaughter, Eleanor Farjeon:

> Cornelia's children are summoned by telegram to Philadelphia and arrive only in time to bury their mother. That day Charles and Joe walk the streets in misery, and in the evening, not knowing where to go or what to do, they turn into their natural home, the theater. I heard this tale when I was . . . small. . . . My grandfather must have told this . . . to his daughter, who made *her* daughter see so vividly—the two unhappy brothers, sitting . . . through a theatrical performance on the day of their mother's funeral.[95]

On December 23 Charles reopened at Philadelphia's Arch Street Theatre, and simultaneously Jefferson began appearing as the lead comedian at the Athenaeum and National Museum, two blocks away.

The two brothers competed on friendly terms for three weeks—Joe, of course, performing in the less-prestigious house. But Charley always took care of his brother. He took a benefit on January 12, but stayed on to perform at Joe's benefit three days later in order to insure a good house.[96] On that occasion Jefferson performed the role of Nicholas, a part he interpolated into John Maddison Morton's *The Midnight Watch,* and received his first notice as an adult actor. "Mr. Jefferson . . . was very well; yet he failed, in many good points, to produce the desired effect. He is a young actor of . . . ability, and with care and study, he is destined to rise in the profession."[97]

To fail "in many good points" meant that Jefferson was not yet receiving the audience reaction expected in nineteenth-century theatres, namely applause that literally stopped the show. Actors were expected to "score points"—to deliver a line or gesture that produced a spontaneous response. Nineteenth-century actors actually counted their points and judged their performances by their ability to get the same number of reactions performance after performance. In 1869 Jefferson, by then a star, instructed the fledgling actor James O'Neill: "My boy, you got six rounds of applause tonight, and that is good. Very good. But there are eight rounds in the part and we must get them."[98] In 1849 he was learning how.

By January 17, 1849, the *Pennsylvanian* reported that Jefferson was "to leave this place." Although his name disappeared from cast lists, he spent the winter of 1849 at the Circus and National Theatre on Chestnut Street. As he remembered, "at this establishment . . . the circus used to amalgamate with a dramatic company and make a joint appearance in equestrian spectacles." Jefferson received $20 a week and a third-clear benefit, and he worked hard for his money. While carpenters hammered behind the drop, he sang comic songs in "frontscenes," scenes performed in front of a curtain while the scenery was changed.[99]

Jefferson moved to a more prestigious position on April 18, 1849, when he and a fellow actor named John Ellsler became the artistic managers of the Philadelphia Museum, a new name for the Masonic Hall on Chestnut Street. They performed with a company of nineteen until June 4, 1849, when the theatre turned to minstrel entertainment, and Joe was out of a job.[100] Once again Charley came to his rescue.

By May 23, 1849, Burke had contracted to appear at Chanfrau's

National Theatre on Chatham Street in New York. Just as his presence had eased Joe into a career in the Philadelphia theatre, so too Charley's success in New York brought Jefferson into the center of the American stage, a city of half a million people. The National was to be the scene of his New York debut.[101]

It was close to the bottom of the New York theatrical ladder. Chatham Square and the streets radiating from it were a rough neighborhood teeming with "adroit adolescent lamp smashers, ball-throwers, marble-shovers, kite flyers and their ungenital [*sic*] spirits." Frank S. Chanfrau, the National's manager and chief comedian, came from this neighborhood and catered to the audiences he knew—the local newsboys who carved their initials in the pit benches to secure a place, the Jewish merchants and their "gaily-dressed" wives and daughters seated in the dress circle, and the area's prostitutes in the gallery.[102]

Charles Burke opened at Chanfrau's four months before Joe. New York was hot and rainy, but the theatre was "nightly crowded to overflowing." By June 8 the *New York Herald* was writing: "Such unprecedented success of the performances at this theater . . . caused a repetition of the . . . programme, and it is no marvel, for Burke is there . . . to the delight of all its patrons."[103]

That summer Chanfrau also hired a sixteen-year-old actress named Margaret Lockyer, who became Joseph Jefferson's first wife. Margaret Clements Lockyer had been born in Burnham in Somersetshire, England, on September 11, 1832, the eldest daughter of Thomas and Elizabeth Stuart Lockyer. Shortly after her birth, the family had emigrated to New York, where Thomas had become a "forwarding merchant." Margaret, known as Maggie, grew up in the city and appeared as a dancer at New York's Bowery Theatre as early as November 6, 1847, when she was fifteen years old. By the summer of 1849, in addition to dancing, she was performing in the comedies and one-act farces that were the staples of Chanfrau's National, playing opposite stars such as T. D. Rice, the minstrel progenitor who had given Jefferson his start.[104]

Chanfrau hired Burke as stage manager for the 1849–50 season, a position equivalent to an artistic director or production manager today. The company that gathered together in the greenroom on September 6 included Margaret Lockyer, Joe, and John Ellsler, Joe's Philadelphia partner. Burke hired Margaret before he hired Joe; he knew her before Joe did, and he may have introduced them. He was certainly responsible for bringing them together, because he hired them to work together.[105]

The company opened on September 10, 1849, and Jefferson made his New York debut that night as Jack Rackbottle in *Jonathan Bradford*. The next morning the *New York Herald* reported that "Mr. Jefferson, as Jack Rackbottle, was . . . much applauded. We believe this gentleman is a very near relation of Mr. Burke; the likeness between them in figure, face, gait &c. is surprising."[106]

By mid-October, Jefferson's name began to appear frequently in the theatre's advertisements. He worked every night, sometimes in two or even three separate plays, but he received little critical attention. He was simply a stock company actor doing his job. By December 1849, however, he was occasionally performing leads, and his name began to be mentioned in the *Herald*'s reviews. The citations were brief but favorable.[107]

Jefferson remained in New York until November 28, 1850, performing a total of fifty-eight roles at the National Theatre and later at the Brooklyn Museum. Most of his parts typified the daily drudgery that formed the learning experience of mid-nineteenth-century actors. With the exception of the first witch in *Macbeth* (traditionally a male role) and a minor part in Bulwer-Lytton's *Richelieu*, Jefferson stuck to comedy. He seldom played a piece more than once, and only two of the roles, Bailie Nicol Jarvie in *Rob Roy* and Diggory in *The Spectre Bridegroom*, were to become longstanding parts of his repertoire.

Isaac Pocock's *Rob Roy or Auld Lang Syne*, described by its author as an operatic play in three acts, is a nineteenth-century melodrama with a plot of inexplicable complexity occasionally punctuated by songs set to traditional melodies in the mode of eighteenth-century ballad operas. Bailie Nicol Jarvie, a subordinate comic role, is a Scots salt merchant and magistrate with a warm heart, a noble conscience, and colorful dialect speech punctuated with homey aphorisms and constant references to "my worthy father the deacon." He was one of the first of Jefferson's rough-hewn characters with a heart of gold —a type he would return to in *Our American Cousin*, *The Octoroon*, and *Rip Van Winkle*.[108]

On January 7, 1850, Jefferson performed Knickerbocker, the schoolmaster engaged to Rip's sister Alice in "a new version" of *Rip Van Winkle* that Charles Burke had written to provide himself a starring role.[109] Burke's was one of the texts that Jefferson used, ten years later, when he began to work on what would become the definitive role of his career. From Burke's version, Jefferson took Rip's story to his wife about trying to shoot a rabbit and a duck and hitting the family bull, the attempt to defraud Rip of his property, the conversation between Rip and Seth Slough when the aged Dutchman returns to his village and the play's most famous line— the moment for which Jefferson became celebrated—"Are we so soon forgot when we are gone?"

Jefferson, remembering how his brother spoke that line, purpose-fully avoided Charley's intonations. "It is possible" he said, "that I might speak it as he did, but . . ." Reminiscing about his brother in 1879, Jefferson said: "Charles Burke was to acting what Mendelssohn was to music. He did not have to work for his effects, as I do: he was not analytical, as I am. Whatever he did came to him naturally as grass grows or water runs; it was not talent that informed his art, but ge-nius." He intended the remark as a compliment, but it also inferred a criticism of Charley's lack of discipline. Jefferson came to believe that acting was the meticulous reproduction of what appeared to be spontaneous behavior. Charley was apparently far less technical.[110]

On March 1, 1850, Burke took a farewell benefit before embark-ing upon a tour of the South. Just as in Philadelphia, his departure boosted Jefferson's career. Joe began to play Charley's roles, appear-ing opposite Frank S. Chanfrau, who was one of the leading comedi-ans of the period. When Chanfrau went back to touring and sold his share of the company, Jefferson was left as the National's principal comedian.[111] On April 29 he appeared with the Irish comedian Barney Williams. The next day the *New York Herald* commented that "Two such comedians would make any piece succeed. Jefferson, as usual, commanded the risible muscles of the audience at will."[112]

By May 10, 1850, Burke was back in New York, but instead of working at what was now called the National Theatre, Chatham Street, he appeared at the Astor Place Theatre. It is tempting to think that he chose not to interfere with Joe's ascendancy into the first line of comic business at the Chatham, but in all likelihood the fact that Chanfrau had sold his interest in the establishment, and the presence of Barney Williams, who was as eminent a comedian as Burke, proba-bly dictated the change. As soon as Williams was gone, Burke re-turned to the Chatham. A "large and crowded audience" greeted Charley's return, and next day the *New York Herald* noted: "he and

Jefferson now constitute a constellation of comic genius at this popular theatre."[113]

Between the fall of 1849 and the spring of 1850, Jefferson and Margaret Lockyer decided to marry. The wedding was performed "in the old church in Oliver Street" on May 19, 1850, when he was twenty and she was seventeen. According to Jefferson's granddaughter, Eleanor Farjeon (whose dating of their ages is somewhat incorrect), it took place against Charles Burke's wishes.

> Charles hastens to delay the imprudent match. He reminds Joe how short a time he has known his bride; warns him that he is barely twenty-one . . . Margaret, but eighteen; [Charles] is just a little jealous. There are almost "words" about it. But Joe is obstinate, or rather, is in love. He spends two months' salary on a lavender suit, issues a batch of expected invitations—and, on the appointed Sunday morning, sneaks with shy Margaret to another church.[114]

Charley's opposition to the wedding is best evidenced by the fact that, although the obvious choice, he was not Joe's best man. He was certainly in New York at the time. Cornelia, Joe's fourteen-year-old sister, was the maid of honor, yet Jefferson chose the Irish comic actor Barney Williams to be his groomsman. When Barney asked Joe why there were so few people present, he supposedly said: "They would have been here, Barney, but I sent them to the wrong church."[115] Whom was he hiding from? The family legend points to Charley, whose displeasure is also reflected in L. Clarke Davis' description of Burke's relationship to Margaret:

> We . . . remember Charles Burke standing in the wings, nervously absorbed in the acting of Mrs. Jefferson, a lady of . . . culture . . . and loveliness but, in those . . . days, lacking force in her art. His love for Joe extended to all that belonged to Joe, and sometimes, when the little lady was speaking her lines too quietly . . . , Burke, in his eagerness for her success, would hiss out to her, as to be heard beyond the footlights, "More fire, more fire, Margaret!"[116]

Although Charley's love for Joe may have extended to "all that belonged to Joe," it is doubtful that Margaret appreciated being coached so loudly from backstage that the audience could hear. Nor is it clear that Burke's opinion of her acting was shared by those around him. For instance, on February 22, 1850, the *New York Herald* commended Margaret for her "neatness, elegance and simplicity." On March 27 the same newspaper commented that "Jefferson and Miss Lockyer filled remarkably well their respective parts." "Neatness, elegance and simplicity" might be a polite manner of describing a lack of fire, and the *New York Herald* was hardly rigorous in its standards. But there were many actors to commend in any company. The newspaper chose Margaret.[117]

Margaret and Joe lived together for the next eleven years until her death in 1861. She became pregnant a little more than a month after their marriage, and they were to have six children, two of whom died in infancy.[118] Yet in his autobiography, Jefferson never mentions her name. Was it grief? His sudden departure from America after her death raises that possibility, and his friend and chronicler William Winter suggests as much. Was it reticence? This is also possible. Jefferson's second wife, Sarah, who was alive in 1888 when the *Autobiography* was published, is mentioned only once. By 1888 Margaret had been dead for twenty-seven years. Jefferson could not remember the date of her death with precision and believed, or at least contended, that his reading public was not interested in his private life.

On May 17, two days before the wedding, Cornelia Jefferson joined the Chatham company, playing opposite her brother Joe. On May 22, Margaret Lockyer appeared as "Mrs. Jefferson" in cast lists. With five members of the Jefferson family in the company, the Chatham was, like Burton's Philadelphia theatre, beginning to resemble the Jefferson family troupe of Joe's boyhood, the troupe he would perpetuate in his starring years. But family companies did not last if the family did not control the business, and the season was drawing to a close. By July 8 the management of the Chatham had engaged "a new and very talented company of comedians," and Jefferson's name disappeared from its cast lists.[119]

The regular theatrical season ended in the summer. Company members dispersed, and the Jeffersons, facing unemployment, descended a rung in the theatrical evolutionary ladder. On July 4, 1850, Burke joined forces with his old boss, Chanfrau, and opened the Brooklyn Museum; Charley was the "Director of Amusements." The establishment was part natural history museum, part wax museum, and part theatre. The Chatham was hardly a high-class establishment, but at least it was a theatre. The Jeffersons had reverted to a venue like Peale's Museum in Philadelphia. Their Brooklyn venture was the equivalent of Joe's grandfather's summer tours to rural Pennsylvania.[120] By August 5 the Brooklyn venture had closed, and Jefferson, Margaret, and Connie returned to the National on Chatham Street for a short summer season.

The National Theatre reopened on September 23, 1850, with the British-born American star Junius Brutus Booth as its first attraction, and Jefferson and his wife as company members. Jefferson, who had performed opposite Booth as a boy in 1833, now had the opportunity of observing him from the point of view of a mature actor. He was also able to strike up a friendship with the seventeen-year-old Edwin Booth, who accompanied his father on tour. Jefferson was to remember him as "a handsome youth. . . . A lithe and graceful figure, buoyant in spirits, and with the loveliest eyes I ever looked upon. We were friends from the first."[121] This friendship would sustain both men for the rest of their lives.

By the fall of 1850 Jefferson was a reasonably successful member of a third-rate theatre in New York; he was married; his wife was pregnant; he could have stayed in New York, continued to make a living, and settled down. Instead he consciously chose to revert to the pattern of eighteenth-century American actors and become a strolling player, and eventually the head of a theatrical troupe that went from town to town. Joe could not have been motivated by money. He had spent his childhood watching his uncle, his father, his aunt, and many others fail as managers. Why then did he want to become one? The reason was a desire for control. He wanted roles unobtainable at the Chatham. He wanted more artistic authority than being a member of a minor New York theatre could afford. In modern parlance, by the spring of 1851 Jefferson had decided to direct.

4

A PROVINCIAL MANAGER: A PROVINCIAL ACTOR

1850–1857

Between 1850 and 1857 Jefferson became, in his own words, "a small tyrant manager in the country." He ran theatres in Richmond, Baltimore, Washington and Philadelphia and even led a touring company through the rural South just as his father had led the family troupe through the Midwest twenty years before. In his autobiography he remembered these managerial stints as summer jaunts on which he squandered money earned as a stock actor the rest of the year, but his memory was inaccurate. From 1850 to 1852 he actually spent each fall and spring as a manager and then earned extra money in the summer as a stock actor when the theatres he managed closed. Moreover, managerial duties never prevented Jefferson from performing. In reality, they gave him access to roles denied him as a minor member of a New York company. The 1850–1857 period saw his development of Mr. Golightly in *Lend Me Five Shillings*, Dr. Ollapod in *The Poor Gentleman*, Bob Acres in *The Rivals*, and Dr. Pangloss in *The Heir-at-Law*—a series of characters from the standard repertoire that he used for the next fifty-four years. His decision to leave New York enabled Jefferson to spend seven years as a provincial manager and actor, honing his craft and preparing for the stardom that would be his when he returned.

Jefferson's managerial work may have been unexpected. He left New York to be an actor, not a manager. He left for the opportunity to be a star, albeit a star in a provincial touring company. On January 6,

1851, he and Margaret, who was seven months pregnant, opened in Savannah, Georgia, as part of a twenty-to-thirty-member company managed by Charles Kemble Mason. For opening night at the Savannah Athenaeum, Jefferson performed Dr. Ollapod in George Colman's *The Poor Gentleman*. It became one of his standard roles.[122]

Figure 6. Joseph Jefferson, *ca.* 1850's.
Courtesy of the Performing Arts Research
Center, New York Public Library.

Leaving Savannah on January 14, the Kemble company took the steamer *Metamora* to Charleston, opening on January 20, 1851, again with Jefferson as Ollapod. Charleston, with its population of almost forty-three-thousand people, was able to support such a company far better than Savannah. In the course of a run that lasted until March 5, Jefferson performed twenty-five roles, including Grumio in *The Taming of the Shrew*, Tony Lumpkin in Goldsmith's *She Stoops to Conquer*, and Bob Acres in *The Rivals*.[123] This is the earliest documented performance of Jefferson's Acres, eventually the second most important character of his career.

By March 5, 1851, internal dissension had split the Mason company. The management claimed the actors were attempting to control the theatre. The actors were aware that Mason intended to replace them with an opera company. Consequently they did what any group of nineteenth-century actors caught in the provinces would do: they formed their own company. Jefferson entered into partnership with two fellow members of the troupe, John Ellsler (his comanager from the Philadelphia Museum) and William Dearing, to run a theatre circuit south of Richmond. Joe painted the scenery; the male members of the company built the sets, and the women sewed costumes. Everyone performed. Margaret Jefferson, then eight months pregnant, played ingenue roles, just as Jefferson's mother had done when she was pregnant with Connie. Jefferson had instantly reverted to barnstorming and was managing the kind of company his father had run.[124] He could not have been unaware of the financial risks, but his entire career manifests a desire for artistic control that made managing attractive.

The breakaway actors, styling themselves the New York Dramatic Company, left Charleston and by March 19 were playing Macon, Georgia. The company was small, and their space was only a flat-floored concert hall renovated so that its seats were raised. But they produced *Othello, Macbeth,* and *Richard III* as well as traditional afterpieces like *The Spectre Bridegroom,* in which Jefferson "kept the house in a perfect uproar." L. Clarke Davis, writing in 1879, says that Joe began making money in the early 1850's as a manager, and Jefferson remembered the Macon season as financially profitable. But the constant movement of the New York Dramatic Company suggests an impoverished group of actors going from one rural theatre to another, like the Jefferson troupe when Joe was a teenager.[125]

On March 20, 1851, the day after the company opened in Macon, Margaret gave birth to a boy. They named him Charles Burke, which was, for Jefferson, comparable to naming their firstborn after his father. Professionally and personally, Charley Burke was the most important influence in Jefferson's life. Jefferson's father had died when Joe was thirteen; Charley was twenty at the time and lived another twelve years. Between the ages of thirteen and twenty-five, Joe looked to his half-brother for personal and professional guidance.

He admired Burke's skill as a comic actor all his life, saying that if "my brother Charley had only lived, the world would never have heard of me." In one of his autobiography's rare personal moments, he admitted that "only a half brother, he seemed like a father to me." Jefferson was to have ten children, seven of whom survived, but the bond that

Figure 7. Joseph Jefferson's half-brother,
Charles Burke (1822–1854)

he shared with Charley Burke transferred to this particular son, twenty-two years his junior and named for the man Jefferson loved most. Charles Burke Jefferson would accompany him to Australia and England, manage his father's business affairs, see him to his grave, and be the last family member to leave the cemetery.[126]

In 1906, a year after Jefferson's death, Charles Burke Jefferson wrote:

> My father was just twenty-one . . . when I was born in Macon. . . . He was . . . playing a week's engagement in that town and

went from there to Savannah, leaving my mother behind with me until we were able to travel. It was in Savannah we joined my father, and I was sent on as a property babe. I made a failure. I spoiled the play by wailing at the wrong time. In Augusta, I repeated that failure. But, notwithstanding that fact, I was with my father constantly up to the time of his death. I was with him in Australia, Van Daimen's Land, South America and in England. In fact, there is not an English-speaking country in which he did not appear, and there was hardly a day, I was not with him.[127]

Charles Burke Jefferson was slightly incorrect. Following his birth, Margaret became ill, and Jefferson, detained in Macon, actually considered running a theatre there. Eventually, however, the company went on to Savannah, opening on April 9, 1851. Margaret joined her husband within a week and played Lucy, the maid in *The Rivals*.[128] The fact that she was not playing Lydia Languish, the play's heroine, indicates that even in the provinces she was a minor actress. Jefferson was the star and support of the family.

In August 1851, after six months as a provincial manager, Jefferson reverted to being an actor at Philadelphia's Arch Street Theatre, where his brother was the stage manager and leading actor. Jefferson performed through September 13, 1851, playing eight roles in a two-week period, and then returned to his own work as a manager, assembling a fourteen-member company in New York for a Southern tour.[129]

They left on a dilapidated schooner for Wilmington, North Carolina, opened on October 20, 1851, and played until November 15. Joe and Margaret performed regularly in full-length plays and one-act afterpieces and sang comic duets. By the end of the month, houses were "very respectable." The local critic thought the company's production of *Othello* "too heavy business to attempt, although they succeed in it beyond expectation." The expectation could not have been much; the Jeffersons were comedians. Jefferson also played Peter, the Nurse's servant in *Romeo and Juliet*, in a manner that, according to the local newspaper, "made more out of Peter than we have ever seen before"—a trait for which Jefferson would be both commended and criticized for the rest of his life.[130]

The company opened in Charleston on January 1, 1852, and ran through the end of March. Jefferson's first love, Julia Dean, came in

February for a starring engagement, and Jefferson bought a watch from the engagement's profits. Charles Burke played Charleston for two weeks beginning March 10, and Joe had another chance to watch Charley perform his version of *Rip Van Winkle*. When Junius Brutus Booth began a two-week engagement on March 22, 1852, Jefferson renewed his friendship with Booth's son Edwin.[131]

Figure 8. Julia Dean (1830–1868)

The Charleston season ended on March 30, 1852, with Jefferson having performed twenty-three roles. Jefferson, Ellsler, and Junius Brutus Booth left the next morning by train, arrived in Augusta that afternoon, and opened that night in the concert hall. Booth left after four nights, and Jefferson and Ellsler immediately reduced ticket prices from one dollar to fifty cents. During their final week of performance, Ellsler played Richmond to Jefferson's Richard III, a casting decision designed "to induce the many warm friends and admirers of these gentlemen to be present, in order to satisfy themselves as to whether their favorite actors in the temple of mirth also possess the faculty of tearing a passion to tatters in the stormy seas of high tragedy." As it turned out, Jefferson and Ellsler did a burlesque version of the play, with Jefferson as "the hump-back tyrant" alias Mose—the hero of Chanfrau's *A Glance at New York*.[132]

At best, the Jefferson-Ellsler company remained in one place for a week or two. The Southern cities in which they played lacked the population to support a resident company longer, and the brevity of the company's seasons indicates financial failure, as does Jefferson's decision to return to work as a resident stock actor.[133]

By the summer of 1852, he was back in New York earning money. In July he played one performance at Niblo's Garden in a troupe that illustrates the interrelationships of nineteenth-century acting careers. Included in the company were members of the Front Street Theatre, with whom Jefferson had appeared in 1847, including his old boss, William E. Burton; John Sefton, the comedian who had shared a New York tenement with the Jeffersons in 1836; and Mrs. John Drew, who was to perform Mrs. Malaprop with Jefferson from 1881 until 1892. The careers of nineteenth-century actors continually intersected as companies formed, dissolved, and reformed. Because "lines of business" as well as repertory were constant, at any moment Jefferson was likely to perform opposite people he had already worked with in plays they had all worked on either separately or together. Like any nineteenth-century actor, he could easily step into a performance for a night.[134]

In the fall of 1852, after a year and a half in provincial companies, Jefferson gave up managing his own company completely and accepted an engagement, in the line of first comedy, at Philadelphia's Chestnut Street Theatre. He brought Margaret with him, and during the fall she became pregnant with their second child. Although back as a stock-company actor, Jefferson was now in the position his grandfather had filled thirty years before, first comedian of the Chestnut. There he played Dr. Ollapod in *The Poor Gentleman*, Bob Acres in *The Rivals*, and Dr. Pangloss in *The Heir-at-Law*.

The Philadelphia engagement is the earliest record of Jefferson's having performed Pangloss who, like Ollapod, is a comic descendent of the learned *dottore* of the *commedia dell'arte*. As written, Pangloss is a pedant inflated by his learning and motivated by sheer avarice, but Jefferson refined the character, giving him a sentimental underpinning that lent the doctor sympathy, particularly at the end of the play when his pretensions are exploded. Joe's godson, Jefferson Winter, remembered Jefferson's Doctor Pangloss pocketing a gratuity with the remark that "honesty is the best policy" or plaintively expostulating: "Don't damn Plato! the bees buzzed round his mellifluous mouth." While there is no evidence about his early work as Pangloss, descriptions of his performance late in life are typical of Jefferson's approach to characterization. In 1890 the *New York Times* noted that

> he employed all of his . . . humor in bringing out the . . . comedy element of the pedantic tutor, who quotes Latin and Shakespeare on the slightest provocation. His make up was . . . ludicrous, principally on account of a conspicuous wig of bushy gray hair that made the doctor's head seem unduly developed.
>
> Colman intended . . . to satirize a type of scholar . . . who paraded his shallow learning for mercenary gain and social preferment. . . . Jefferson . . . however, placed the . . . pompous tutor in . . . sympathy with the audience. Everyone was glad to see him treble his income and felt sorry for him when his pupil Dick Dowlas, compelled him to dance in a public thoroughfare. Mr. Jefferson was deliciously droll without ever resorting to exaggeration or overstepping the bounds of high class comedy.
>
> Jefferson actually puts a soul into the preposterous tutor whose scraps of Latin . . . and . . . learned appellations of LL. D. and A. S. S. help to gain for him a . . . respite from the . . . poverty of Milk Alley. The Pangloss of Colman's play is a shallow, selfish humbug, whose imposture is finally rewarded, just before the rhyming tag, by a high-sounding rebuke from priggish Mr. Henry Moreland; but Jefferson, without adding a line to the text, except a few of those accretions that have adhered to it during long years of service in the theatre, . . . makes us . . . sympathize with the quaint . . . humbug and feel that there is a man's heart under his shabby black coat in spite of his mendacity.
>
> This is partly owing to the . . . personality of the actor but more to his . . . art, which is employed here . . . not to repeat the old Pangloss' traditions but to . . . recreate the man; to make his utterances seem to be the spontaneous expression of thoughts emanating from a not very ponderous brain. [M]ost of the audience last evening felt sorry after the play . . . that a fellow-creature, . . . so genial and so helpless, should be left . . . with so dubious a prospect before him—nothing indeed but a return to

Milk Alley and starvation. Not that any of the fun of the part was lacking. On the contrary, people laughed till they cried whenever the learned doctor was in sight.[135]

Jefferson's characters were always costumed with painstaking detail consonant with his realistic approach to farce. Like all nineteenth-century actors, he performed roles from the standard repertoire, but Jefferson reinterpreted them so that audiences re-experienced them as real, albeit farcical, human beings. And once he gained any degree of artistic control, he either played sympathetic characters or re-created the characters he played sympathetically. He portrayed their faults—Pangloss' avarice, Bob Acres' cowardice, Rip's drunkenness —as the external foibles of someone with a good heart. Audiences and even critics came to believe that he did so out of his own natural goodness. It is at least as likely that he understood what would warm the hearts of his audience and that the complexity of a wayward disposition in an essentially good person produced a character that was compelling on stage and good at the box office. Jefferson knew that his audiences came to the theatre to laugh and cry. He enabled them to do both in the same play.

By December 1852 Jefferson had left Philadelphia to perform at Niblo's Theatre in New York, just as his father had done in the summer of 1837. He was a stock-company actor, playing in a theatre that alternated "legitimate" plays with variety nights. Margaret followed him to New York and stayed there for the rest of her pregnancy. On January 10, 1853, when his wife was three months pregnant, Jefferson opened in a stock company at the Albany Theatre under the direction of Madame Julie de Marguerittes, one of the few female theatrical managers of the period. By January 31, Margaret had joined him to perform in the one-act farces that ended each performance.[136]

In early February the Albany Theatre ran into financial trouble and was sold. Joe simply moved to another stock company. It was what he had been trained to do all his life, and in typical Jefferson fashion he moved to a company with relatives in it. On February 12, 1853, he joined his cousins Elizabeth Thoman and William Warren at the Boston Museum. By March 17 he was at the Howard Athenaeum starring in the farces that opened the evening or followed the main piece. His name occasionally headed the playbills distributed as advertisements, appearing in larger type than the rest of the company.[137] And he earned one of his first extended newspaper reviews.

> I have had . . . little opportunity . . . of witnessing the efforts of [Mr. J. Jefferson]; but, from what I have seen, have concluded that he partakes . . . of the comic humor as well as versatility of his . . . grandfather. I can detect a . . . streak of dry and quaint humor in the . . . expression of Mr. Jefferson's face; his acting seems legitimate and free from buffoonery, while it evinces care and study.[138]

Jefferson remained at the Athenaeum through April 19, when he appeared in the benefit of a fellow company member named Henry Willard. Four days later he and his sister Cornelia opened in a company Willard formed at the diminutive Eagle Theatre. Again what Jefferson had done was what any unemployed nineteenth-century actor did: he joined a less prestigious venue and began to perform.[139]

Shortly after his Boston engagement, on July 4, 1853, Jefferson's second child, Margaret Jane, was born in New York City. She was called Tid as a child, later Tiddie, and finally Maggie, and was named, of course, for her mother, who within a few months of Tid's birth was back at work. Jefferson's relationship to this daughter was never the same as his relationship to his son Charles Burke, although he was always financially generous to her. Her life must have been strange. She was born to lower-middle-class itinerant actors. When she was seven years old her mother died, and her father left her for five years. Until she was twelve she lived with her grandparents, and then was brought up by the family "housekeeper," Nell Symons—for whom she named her eldest daughter. When Jefferson returned, he was a major star touring America and away from home for nine to ten months at a time. By the time she was a teenager, Margaret was living in an upper-class home with a stepmother only a few years her senior. When she was twenty-four she married an Englishman who was almost her father's age, settled in London, and saw her father only once again. Maggie spent her entire adult life abroad, but the major barrier between her and her father was occupation, not distance. She never went on the stage. Theatre was the bond that tied Jefferson to his sons, and although Margaret was brought up as a wealthy young woman, given music lessons and ponies to ride, she was denied access to the heart of what made the Jeffersons a family.[140]

The Jeffersons continued working in stock for the 1853–54 theatrical season, returning to Philadelphia's Chestnut Street Theatre, where Jefferson was billed as "the star comedian of America." Between August 23, 1853, and May 19, 1854, Joe and Margaret performed afterpieces and acted in a lengthy run of George L. Aiken's *Uncle Tom's Cabin*, "portraying the happiness of the Negroes of the South —introducing the Harmony that prevails upon Plantations, their Holiday Festivals, Marriages, Congo Dances &C." Joe played Grumpton Cute, the type of Yankee role that would make him one of America's most popular actors within a few years. At first his name appeared frequently in Philadelphia newspapers, and a theatrical correspondent referred to him as one of the male members of the cast worth mentioning in a poorly run theatre. After the first month, however, his popularity diminished, and he became just another member of the company, performing thirty-seven roles in one season.

When Charley Burke appeared as a touring star, Jefferson played Knickerbocker opposite his half-brother's Rip Van Winkle. At Charley's benefit he and Joe alternated in the role of Diggory in *The Spectre Bridegroom*, two actors playing the same character at different parts of the same performance. Nineteenth-century audiences knew these plays so well that comparative nuances in performance provided the novelty that the plot lacked.[141]

Beginning in the fall 1854 season, Jefferson began a two-year professional relationship with the Baltimore-Washington theatre manager Henry C. Jarrett, opening on August 28, 1854, as stage manager and lead comic actor at Jarrett's Baltimore Museum. He headed a company of fourteen actors, eleven actresses, an orchestra, and fifteen support staff, including a machinist, a costumer, two property masters, a furniture maker, an upholsterer, two purveyors of carpeting, a painter, and a paperhanger. While the New York Theatrical Company's tours through the South in 1851 had been a risky financial investment, here Jefferson was a paid employee with the artistic, but none of the financial, responsibilities. He had control without risk.[142]

By the second week of performance, the theatre had been pretentiously renamed the Baltimore Museum and Gallery of the Fine Arts. Its troupe supported traveling stars in their specialty pieces and performed the one-act farces that followed. The English actress Agnes

Robertson appeared in early October 1854. The relationship Jefferson began with Robertson and her husband, the actor-playwright Dion Boucicault, proved the most important contact of his professional life. It resulted in his later work in *Dot, Nicholas Nickleby, The Octoroon,* and *Rip Van Winkle.*[143]

On November 10, 1854, while Joe was stage-managing in Baltimore, Charley Burke died of pulmonary tuberculosis in New York's Florence Hotel, where he was a resident. He was thirty-two years old, and as he died in Joe's arms he said: "I am going to our Mother." Jefferson arrived just in time. He was performing in Baltimore on the evening of November 9, and it was a sixteen-and-one-half-hour train trip to New York. On October 11 he accompanied his brother's body to Philadelphia, where Charley was buried next to Cornelia Jefferson in Ronaldson's Cemetery, not far from the home where Joe was born. Charley died from what was then called consumption. His mother had died of the same disease, and Joe was probably afflicted with it. He told friends that by the time he married, he had only one lung, and he spent much of his adult life in warm climates.[144]

Five days after Charley's death, Joe was performing again in Baltimore; it was the longest period of mourning he had ever taken, which reflected both his stature in the Baltimore company as well as his love for Charley. Margaret, who had become pregnant in October, continued to act with him. On December 4, 1854, they opened in Jefferson's production of a spectacle opera entitled *The Naiad Queen.* It was an enormous success, playing seventy-three performances. Within two days of its opening, the local newspaper was cautioning the public: "Those who wish to see it would do well to procure their seats before night as it will then be impossible to obtain one in the parquette or dress circle." A month later the newspaper noted that "the Saloon is thronged every evening to see [the performance] and numbers are unable to gain admittance. The gorgeousness of the scenery and dresses and the admirable drill of the female soldiers [led by the three-month-pregnant Margaret Jefferson] are unsurpassed."[145]

It was in Baltimore, during the 1854–55 season, that Jefferson first performed the role of Mr. Golightly in *Lend Me Five Shillings,* a brilliantly paced one-act farce by John Maddison Morton.[146] As in the case of Pangloss, he infused what had traditionally been a farcical role, played in the broadest manner, with a sense of realism. In 1877 the *London Times* critic wrote of his work:

It would seem . . . that there can be no . . . acting of farce without noise . . . and . . . pantomimic behavior. . . . To be . . . everywhere on the stage at once; to gabble out one's words so that they tumble over one another's heels, as the actor is applauded for tumbling over . . . chairs and tables; to be forever slapping somebody on the back or digging somebody in the ribs, such are the . . . actions which . . appear . . . to constitute that . . . quality known as "go." It is possible to hear every word [Jefferson] says. . . . He is . . . quiet and natural. . . . His voice, his face, every gesture, every movement is brimful of fun. . . . When Mr. Golightly discovers in the pocket of that "shocking bad" coat, which has been substituted by some dishonest guest for his own brand new "Raglan," those five shillings for which he has been begging, . . . that face is the . . . essence of comicality, and the jaunty air with which he turns on his heels with a "Jack's alive again" is inimitable.

In 1900 the *New York Times* wrote:

As Golightly in Morton's old farce of *Lend Me Five Shillings*, Mr. Jefferson lifts . . . the character and the piece out of the domain of . . . farce by the . . . naturalness of his manner. Time was when it was . . . quite the thing to "mug" through . . . a farce. Mr. Jefferson acts Golightly as if he were a human being. . . . He omits many of the old catchphrases in the text and has . . . recreated the character. It would not be becoming . . . to inquire if the . . . old piece, even in these circumstances, is . . . worth while.[147]

Instead of interpolating comic business in his roles, Jefferson developed a style of acting that allowed the play's comedy to arise naturally out of the situations on stage. Having established a character as sympathetic and real, he allowed the character's predicament to push him to logical and simultaneously farcical extremes.

Toward the end of May 1855, members of the company began taking their benefits, and Jefferson was often performing two roles a night, including parts he had not played that season. When his second benefit occurred on May 29, he performed four roles, ending with the last act of *Richard III*, presumably in the burlesque version he had used before. By the time the theatre closed on June 2, 1855, he had played fifty-seven parts in one season. To the modern actor it

seems an overwhelming amount of work, but Jefferson had performed ninety roles at Chanfrau's Theatre in New York in 1849–50.
As his theatrical career advanced, he was able to control what he
performed and how much he performed. This was the goal of every
nineteenth-century actor. The season over, the Jeffersons stayed in
Baltimore, where Margaret Jefferson gave birth to her second
daughter, Frances Florence, on July 9, 1855, almost exactly two
years after her previous child had been born. For the first time in his
life, Jefferson was able to spend the summer with his family.[148]

On September 1, 1855, he resumed work as stage manager at the
Baltimore Museum. Margaret appeared opposite him in one-act
farces that ended each evening's performance, and the company also
included a fifteen-year-old girl named Mary Devlin, who was to
become the first wife of Jefferson's lifelong friend, Edwin Booth.[149]
As Jefferson remembered it, his employer, Henry Jarrett, had

> one day brought a . . . girl who had been given to his care and
> placed her in mine—a beautiful child, but fifteen years of age.
> Her family, a most estimable one, had met with some reverse,
> and she had decided to go upon the stage to relieve them from
> the burden of her support and . . . to contribute to the comfort
> of her father. . . . She lived in my family as the companion of my
> wife for three years and during that time became one of the
> leading actresses of the stage.[150]

Attendance at the Baltimore Museum, in Jefferson's words, "was
so poor that even the wax figures seemed to hold up their hands in
protest at being put upon two-thirds salaries." Consequently, on
October 3, 1855, Jarrett began to produce a series of performances
at the "handsomely refitted" National Theatre in Washington with
Jefferson as stage manager and lead comedian. But Joe was back in
Baltimore performing at the Museum the following Saturday, and he
began to split his time between the two cities just as his grandfather
and father had done. Jefferson and Jarrett brought a small number of
actors down from Baltimore once or twice a week and filled out their
Washington company with local amateurs billed, in one instance, as
"a large corps of Supernumeraries, Choctaw Indians, Attaches &c."
The limited number of Washington engagements whetted the appetite of a theatrically starved audience. Performances were advertised
locally two days in advance, an unusually lengthy newspaper notice

in a period in which performances were generally advertised in the press only on the day they occurred.[151]

In Baltimore, business was not good; Henry Jarrett engaged a troupe of juvenile comedians at the Baltimore Museum, and "our Jeff," as the local newspaper called him, was out of work. He returned to the stage on October 29, opening at Baltimore's Charles St. Theatre. There he and his boyhood idol, John E. Owens, performed the Dromio roles in Shakespeare's *A Comedy of Errors*. When the museum reopened on November 12, the Charles St. Theatre closed, and Jefferson continued to commute between Baltimore and Washington, focusing most of his activity on the capital. There, on November 19, he was the first witch in a production of *Macbeth* starring James William Wallack and featuring "the whole force of the Baltimore Museum Company." By late November, Jarrett and Jefferson were capitalizing on the fact that they were running companies in both cities by having the Irish comedienne, Mrs. Barney Williams, perform in the first piece in Baltimore and then hop on a train for a fifty-five minute ride to Washington, where Jefferson announced her arrival to a cheering audience assembled to see her perform the last piece of the evening.[152]

Margaret Jefferson stayed on in Baltimore, where their five-month-old child, Frances, died on December 12, 1855. Jefferson performed Dr. Pangloss in *The Heir-at-Law* the night his child died, took one day off to bury Frances, was back at work in Baltimore by December 14, and commuted to appear in Washington by December 17. Margaret, who appeared next on December 31, became pregnant again almost immediately after the child's death.[153]

On New Year's Eve, January 31, 1855, Jefferson stage-managed and played the moneylender Moses in an all-star Washington production of Sheridan's *The School for Scandal*. In a puff for the production, the Baltimore newspaper lauded him as "one of the best low and eccentric comedians of the day." Washington's *Daily National Intelligencer* wrote: "Mr. JEFFERSON, though a young actor, makes good his title to the inheritance of the family name and fame." The following day he opened in the same role at the Holliday Street Theatre in Baltimore. In the company were his cousin Jane Anderson Germon as Lady Sneerwell and Mary Devlin as Maria. Simultaneously he performed Jacques Strop in *Robert Macaire* at Jarrett's Baltimore Museum. *The School for Scandal* began at 7:30

P.M., and Moses appears only in Act I; the evening of three plays at the Baltimore Museum also began at 7:30, but *Robert Macaire* was the second play performed. Jefferson performed Moses at the Holliday Street, got out of costume and makeup, rushed to the museum, got into costume and makeup, and thus performed in two theatres on one evening. He must have been desperate for money.[154]

Joe continued as leading comedian and stage manager in Baltimore and Washington, and Margaret appeared periodically, although she was clearly a minor company member in comparison to Mary Devlin.[155] Jefferson acted virtually every day, doing as many as three parts in an evening, but he seldom performed a role more than twice. Only one role that season, Schnapps in Jefferson's revival of *The Naiad Queen*, was given a significant number of performances, including a then-rare matinee, probably because of its scenic spectacle featuring a grand march of female warriors.

Jefferson continued to stage-manage and act simultaneously in Washington and Baltimore through the spring of 1856. The Washington company ended its season on March 1 with a benefit for his employer, Henry C. Jarrett. Two days later Joe began stage-managing the National Theatre under Thomas Kunkel and John T. Ford.[156]

Washington was Jefferson's first venture with Ford, the theatrical producer with whom he would work for the next two years. Under Jefferson's artistic direction, the Washington company performed every night of the week except Sunday until June 16, 1856. Its nineteen actors, "comprising the prominent members of Jarrett's company, together with . . . members of the Holliday-street Theatre, Baltimore" included Mary Devlin and Jefferson's cousin, Jane Germon. Almost every night it presented a visiting star's chosen vehicle, followed by a farce featuring Jefferson, who performed twenty-seven different roles that season, only six of which he had done the preceding season in Washington. Joe also got a chance to sing and to perform two Shakespearean parts: the frantic Francis in *Henry IV, Part I* and, for his benefit on May 31, 1856, the role of Macbeth, his only attempt at a tragic part. It is possible he burlesqued the role, and if it was a serious performance, there is no reason to believe he was successful.[157]

When the Washington season ended, Jefferson and his friend John Sleeper Clarke went off to star in country towns. Clarke was four years younger than Jefferson; he had been a boyhood friend of

Edwin Booth and would marry Booth's sister, Asia, in 1859. He also specialized in the same comic characters that Jefferson performed. L. Clarke Davis' retelling of the story provides the earliest reference to Jefferson's passion for fly-fishing, a lifetime hobby.

> He and Clarke agreed to star in the country towns, and their first appearance was made at Oakland, Maryland, a summer resort on the summit of the Blue Ridge. [R]eceipts were just twelve dollars. Dividing that sum, . . . they ended their starring-tour in the . . . highlands. Mr. Clarke, in relating this experience, . . . adds that Jefferson beguiled him to Oakland, not because he thought there was an audience there but because he knew there were trout-streams . . . , for Jefferson loves fishing better than playing or making money.[158]

Davis' view of Jefferson the man was the audience's view of Rip Van Winkle, a carefree loafer unmindful of practical affairs. The fact is that Joe devoted time to fishing and painting, but never loved anything better than acting or making money. And by the time of his Washington benefit, he had made enough to announce his intentions to visit Europe "on professional business." In June 1856 he sailed for London in the clipper *Neptune*, leaving Margaret, who was six months pregnant, in the sweltering heat of a Washington July.[159] By his own admission, he squandered "two years salary" on a trip when his wife, who had suffered the death of a child six months before, was at home with a five-year-old boy, a three-year-old girl, and a baby on the way.

Jefferson's "professional business" trip was a vacation that took him to London and Paris. He did not perform in England, but his friends, Mr. and Mrs. Barney Williams, were playing the Adelphi Theatre. Jefferson visited them and met the theatre's manager, Benjamin Webster, who would produce *Rip Van Winkle* nine years later. Although wealthy enough to undertake a European trip, Jefferson was still in a financial pinch; he sailed to Europe in steerage, traveled from London to Paris in a second-class coach, and spent most of his time window shopping. He particularly admired works by Rousseau, Corot, Diaz, and D'Aubigny, paintings he would later see in American museums and lament that he had been too poor to buy.[160]

Joe spent three weeks in Paris and then sailed for home. Pausing in

Washington to perform on September 2 and 3 at the National Theatre, he headed for Richmond, where Margaret joined him. Their new daughter, again named Frances Florence, was born in September 1856, in Richmond, just as Joe reopened there as stage manager of John T. Ford's theatre. Within a few months, the child died from scarlet fever in the old Swan Tavern at the corner of Ninth and Broad streets, where the Jeffersons boarded. Margaret was pregnant again by December.[161]

Jefferson opened in Richmond on September 5, 1856, and remained with the company until November 14. He then returned to Washington, where at a cost of $1,500 he "altered, adapted and produced" *The Naiad Queen* with a cast of forty people and "rich and gorgeous scenery, gold and gem-studded dresses, silver and steel armors, Fairies, Nymphs, Danscuses, and the Female Army of Sixteen Lovely Girls." Anticipating "out-of-town" business from patrons in Alexandria and Georgetown, the National Theatre ran an unusual Saturday matinee performance "for the special accommodation of ladies, families and children."[162]

Jefferson then returned to Richmond, where the season lasted through June 5, 1857. Richmond audiences braved the "impassable condition" of the city's streets to witness a company of approximately seventeen men and seven women, large by provincial American standards, perform 105 plays in the course of nine months. Only twenty plays were performed more than once, and only two were given more than three performances during the season. Jefferson is listed in newspaper advertisements for only twenty-two roles, although he undoubtedly performed more often.

Joe's progress as an actor was clear He played ninety roles at Chanfrau's in New York during the 1849–50 season, thirty-seven roles in Philadelphia in 1853–54, fifty-seven roles in Richmond in 1854–55, and twenty-seven roles in Washington in 1856. He was begining to specialize. Among his parts was Grumio in David Garrick's version of *The Taming of the Shrew* (entitled *Katherine and Petruchio*), opposite Edwin Booth as Petruchio and Mary Devlin as Katherine.[163]

It was in Richmond on November 25, 1856, that Booth and Mary first met, when she played Juliet to his Romeo. Jefferson later recalled: "One morning I said to her: 'To-morrow you are to rehearse Juliet to the Romeo of our new and rising young tragedian. . . . I knew at the conclusion of that rehearsal that Edwin Booth and Mary Devlin would soon be man and wife."[164]

Jefferson was speaking in 1894, with Booth recently and Devlin long dead. He was actually in Washington when they performed Romeo and Juliet, but he returned to Richmond in time to see their romance develop. Joe disapproved of Mary's attraction to Edwin and demanded that she return a turquoise bracelet that Booth had given her; but "at the end of the week," as he recalled, "he came to me in the green-room, with his affianced bride by the hand, and with a . . . smile, they fell upon their knees. . . and said: 'Father your blessing,' to which I replied in the same mock-heroic vein, extending my hands like the old Friar: 'Bless you, my children!'" The scene was probably less romantic than Jefferson remembered because Edwin and Mary were not engaged and did not marry for another four years, but Jefferson told the story to the members of The Players on the first-year anniversary of Edwin's death, and it has become part of the Booth legend. At the time Booth, like any touring player, moved on; Mary stayed behind with the company to which she was contracted, and Jefferson replaced the rising young American actor with the money-making production of *The Naiad Queen* that he had developed in Washington.[165]

The spring 1857 season in Richmond ended Jefferson's managerial career until 1878, and he reverted to being the leading comic actor and "stage manager" of a stock company. Management provided artistic control, but in the provinces it produced no money. The combination of stage management and first comic business allowed for artistic control and the security of a contractual salary. On May 16, 1857, Jefferson and Mary Devlin opened in Philadelphia at the National Theatre in a company under the management of John Drew, whose wife would later become Joe's Mrs. Malaprop in *The Rivals*. Jefferson functioned as the "stage manager," and the opening performance featured W. J. Florence, who would later play Sir Lucius O'Trigger opposite Mrs. Drew and Joe. During Florence's two-week stay, Jefferson did not perform. With Florence still the more famous of the two, there was no need for Jefferson. Immediately after Florence left, however, his name began to appear in the company's newspaper advertisements.[166]

On August 18, 1857, the *New-York Daily Times* announced that Jefferson would join Laura Keene's company in New York for the fall season. Other than his choice of Rip Van Winkle, it was the most important professional decision of his life. He stayed with Keene in the line of "first low comedian" for the next two years and established himself as a star in the American theatre. Joe's days of playing fifty to ninety roles in a season were finally done.[167]

5

THE YEARS WITH LAURA KEENE

1857–1859

The English actress Laura Keene began managing American theatres by taking a five-year lease on New York's Metropolitan Theatre, which she renamed Laura Keene's Varieties and opened on December 27, 1855. She specialized in genteel drawing-room comedies mounted with close attention to realistic detail. When, at the close of her first season, the Metropolitan was sold to Jefferson's former boss, William E. Burton, Keene negotiated the building of a new theatre a block away. It opened on November 18, 1856, during a boom period in New York when fifteen hundred people could spend as much as $15,000 a night at the city's theatres and concerts.[168] This was the economic atmosphere in which Jefferson became a star.

When she employed him a year later, Laura Keene had never met Jefferson, seen him act, or auditioned him. Presumably she knew him by reputation. She employed him because, despite her theatre's promising opening, business had fallen off by the end of the first season. In late May the *Spirit of the Times* attributed poor attendance to "the wretched weather of the past few days," but by the end of the month the newspaper admitted that there were problems in the quality of the plays.[169] Jefferson's *Autobiography* confirms the newspaper's opinion: "Laura Keene's judgment in selecting plays was . . . bad; she . . . allowed herself to be . . . influenced by their literary merit. . . . I do not say that polished dialogue or delicate . . . characters are detrimental, . . . but if these qualities are not coupled with a sympathetic story, . . . told in action rather than in words, they seldom reach beyond the footlights."

Unlike Keene, Jefferson never hesitated to alter text or subordinate words to action. In his first performance at Keene's Theatre on August 31, 1857, he appeared as Dr. Pangloss and was praised for his "mobile face, lithe active figure, good distinct delivery and emphasis and evident familiarity with stage effects."[170] "He is a low comedian of . . . originality. . . . Such a . . . twitchey, nervous . . . little man was never seen. MR. JEFFERSON was . . . funny as *Dr. Pangloss* and gave several new readings to the character, occasionally using the text prepared by MR. COLMAN but frequently deviating from that authority. . . . He may . . . reckon on a brilliant career in this city."[171]

In his *Autobiography*, written thirty-one years later, Jefferson, stung at that point by criticism of his interpolations in *The Rivals*, regarded this early review as negative and defended the substitution of new stage business, which he called "introductions," for traditional stage business. "Old plays and particularly old comedies, are filled with traditional introductions, good and bad. If an actor . . . presumes to leave out any of these respectable antiquities, he is . . . considered sacrilegious. . . . And . . . if in amplifying the traditional business, he introduces new material, he is thought to be . . . impertinent; whereas the question as to the introduction should be whether it is good or bad, not whether it is old or new."[172]

For Jefferson, ever the practical theatre practitioner, the question was whether or not interpolations worked in front of an audience. By the time he wrote this defense, such "introductions" had become the basis of his career, but earlier on they ran contrary to the genteel atmosphere Keene was creating. The *Spirit of the Times* noted: "This . . . little theatre reminds us . . . of a Club-room, or . . . of a . . . reunion of friends, . . . so pleasant . . . is everybody and everything about the establishment. Nothing is ever said or done upon the stage to offend the . . . 'straight-laced,' and still enough is said and done . . . to instruct and amuse the numerous patrons."

Jefferson's willingness to subordinate text and character to a good laugh produced problems within the genteel clubroom of Keene's Theatre. When a comedy entitled *Victims*, by the English playwright Tom Taylor, was produced on September 7, 1857, Joe was cast as Butterby, a weak-minded man who puts up with his fiancée's bad temper in order to enjoy her financial support. When his character presented the lady with a gift, Jefferson opened the parcel to reveal a pair of male trousers, creating an absurd and risqué situation in a period when women hid their legs under elaborate dresses designed to disguise their shape. The *Spirit of the Times* found him "cast for a part entirely out of his line. Genteel comedy, or anything approximating to it, is not his vocation." In time Jefferson would prove the newspaper wrong, but in 1857 he was being typecast as a broad extravagant comedian. On September 14 Keene produced what the *New-York Daily Times* described as a "romantic drama of the atrocious school" entitled *Judith of Geneva*. The newspaper's critic wrote: "Mr. Jefferson has an opportunity to get drunk, and this is his specialty."[173]

Jefferson was a success, but the theatre was soon caught up in the financial panic of 1857 caused by the failure of the Ohio Life Insurance and Trust Company, which set off a chain of financial disasters resulting in the closure of almost every bank in the country. Laura Keene responded by reducing prices and seeking a wider audience by successfully producing a melodrama entitled *The Sea of Ice, or A Mother's Prayer*, which had been a great success when Jefferson produced it in Baltimore.[174] It was the hit of Keene's season, and the *Spirit of the Times'* reviewer wrote of Jefferson's performance: "Joe Jefferson, a second edition of the lamented Charley Burke, . . . personates Barnabas, a sailor, to perfection. . . . I have seen . . . the best comedians of the age but . . . no one who equals Jefferson in his *role*."[175]

In the course of the season Margaret Jefferson gave birth to their second son, Thomas, on September 10, 1857. Charles Burke was seven years old; Margaret was four. Thomas would become an actor and vainly attempt to take over his father's most famous role when Jefferson's health declined in the early twentieth century.[176]

Jefferson's first New York benefit took place on February 13, 1858. He performed three roles, two of them in plays not yet seen that season at Laura Keene's. After the first piece, Jefferson was "called out and . . . presented . . . with a . . . purse containing a considerable amount of specie." On February 27 the *Spirit of the Times* described him as displaying "a degree of comic talent seldom witnessed in any theater, which . . . stamps him as one of the first low comedians of the country."[177]

He performed at Laura Keene's throughout the spring of 1858. A letter from his friend Edwin Booth, writing on April 26 from Louisville, Kentucky, must have been a reminder of the barnstorming days behind him. Its initial comic complaints attest to Jefferson's lifelong aversion to writing letters, an aversion that may have resulted from his lack of schooling and consequent poor handwriting. Even his beloved half-brother chided him with "A letter from you I look on as a *friend*; think of that, Joe, and don't let me have to remind you again."[178] Booth's letter, the longest piece of correspondence to Jefferson extant, reveals the close friendship between the two men as well as the vicissitudes of touring and the concerns of actors in the period. Booth is sitting in his dressing room, after a performance as Sir Giles Overreach in *A New Way to Pay Old Debts*. He is waiting for Ben Baker, his manager, to knock at the door, the signal for him to go on in a one-act farce that will end the evening's performance.

Louisville, April 26th 1858
Friend & Brother Joe-ferson
We will *suppose* the letter written, sent and received—I mean the one you've promised me, . . . and I will . . . answer . . . the . . . questions which we will *suppose* you to have asked . . . , but knowing . . . how you arrange those questions . . . , I will give a bunch of answers, and you may dispose of them accordingly. *Yes. No. Umpse. Guess so. Don't know. First rate. Shy. Spec so.* There they are—now fix 'em to your fancy. We left Baltimore on Friday last . . . arrived here—after a delightful gut-shaking—last evening, right side up with care—neuralgia and sore throat abroad. . . . Opened tonight with "Sir Giles" to a slim house—my share amounting to somewhere between ought and eighty-ought—"who steals my purse steals . . . ."

I must give you . . . details of my journey hither, . . . because it led me to that delightful retreat where you and [John Sleeper] Clarke—in days gone by—pourtrayed [*sic*] in mimic guise the muse's thought sublime etc. (high falutin').

"Brevity is the soul of wit"—I guess it is of pleasure too, for "work that's sweet is quickly done," and I spare you the brevity of my visit to that sweet-scented hole. [It would have been] a source of greater pleasure to me had we staid long enough to get . . . dinner—which we didn't at any point on the route. I say *sweet-scented* on your authority, not from my personal experience—for I smelt nothing but coal-smoke . . . which, Heaven knows is not "balmy," though the "sense does ache at it." I could see nothing but a house and a blacksmith shop, the latter consisting of a pair of bellows and a coal of fire, superintended by "a handy maintainer" who looked as if he didn't know more than to chew tobacco and not swallow the juice; I wondered if he was one of your patrons.

The car took a jerk . . . , and we travelled . . . within its empty stomach and on our own, 'till six at night, when we arrived at *Morrow* and grubbed—I thought we'd never reach there, and I mentally ejaculated . . . "To Morrow and to Morrow and to Morrow," [we] creep in this petty pace" hungered and athirst and mad'er'n hell. However, "it's a long lane that has no turning," and that one had turns enough—it's the most *serpentine* road I ever travelled . . .—and found the end of it (guess you wish I'd do the same by this letter).

I see by the Cin[cinnati] papers that a John Clarke of Phil. was found in the river with his throat cut—is it *ourn*? I wouldn't write to him, for he wouldn't answer—dead or alive—but knowing you to be so punctual . . . in your correspondence, I thought it the speediest mode of arriving at the truth—I'd like to know in time—before he stinks—for I'm in a poetic mood just now and would like to set about his epitaph.

I hope to do a smashing business here, and if tonight is any criterion, I undoubtedly will, but where the smash be, I leave you to imagine.

I'm told by Chanfrau (He's here courting Henrietta Baker) that Willard will probably have Laura [Keene]'s place next season, for a star theatre.—why don't you try it on?—I think it would be a good hit— put the sharing terms down to the lowest match, and play the stars—t'would knock the others—for stars are sick of acting in N.Y. for *nix*—I speak feelingly, and "am zealous in the cause."

Joe—I've got a pipe that knocks hell out of the blues—a perfect "bougee," will let you smoke it next summer in the *Kontry.*

Give my kindest *how d'ye do's* to Mrs. Joe and "ye smaller Jeffs." "How are ye's" to the boys, and answer this—d—m you! if you don't I'll wish the curse of Rome into a load of sand, and drop it at your door.

Knock, Joe, *Knock*; Baker sleepeth, but he giveth voice.

I remain here two weeks; and shoot for St. Lou's—don't stop
in Cincin.
No news. Write soon. Health ditto toujours le meme
Thine
EDWIN[179]

Booth's letter assumes Jefferson's knowledge of the vicissitudes of
rural acting—the difficulties of train travel, the health dangers, the
small illiterate audiences, the limited earnings, the inedible food, the
dirty conditions of rural America, the constant sense of being under-
paid and overworked. The letter presumes the continual importance
and uncertainty of earning money as an itinerant actor. It also assumes a line-by-line knowledge of Shakespearean plays (*Hamlet*,
Othello, and *Macbeth*) as well as the typical star vehicles of the period
such as Bulwer-Lytton's *Richelieu*, with its renowned "Curse of
Rome" speech. Thus while Joe's education may have been informal,
his theatrical background provided him with easy references to major
dramatic texts. It is also interesting that Jefferson was a smoker in
this period, a habit that may have served him poorly in later life. He
had already lost the use of one lung and would spend most of his life
working in theatres whose sizes necessitated considerable vocal
power. Finally the letter points out the difference between the two
men. Booth, a minor traveling star in 1858, was still subject to the
disasters of a poor house and the discomforts of nineteenth-century
travel. Jefferson had chosen financial comfort as a salaried employee
in the most prestigious theatrical center in the country.

Booth's letter caught Jefferson in professional turmoil. The *New
York Times* contended that "MISS LAURA KEENE'S successes are few in
number" and that she had sustained "heavy losses . . . in the earlier
and less prosperous portions of the season." As a means of avoiding
bankruptcy, Jefferson dramatized George Lepard's revolutionary war
story, *Blanche of Brandywine*, a spectacular melodrama filled with
"battles, marches and counter-marches, murders, abductions, hair-
breadth escapes, militia trainings and extravagant Yankee comicali-
ties." Keene's opening night advertisement promised audiences the
Battle of Bunker Hill, a sinking ship, Washington Crossing the Delaware, the battle of Trenton, and a grand military tableau. The level of
scenic difficulty forced Keene to close the theatre the night before
opening, something done for no other production that season.[180]

In his *Autobiography* Jefferson claimed that the "soul-stirring drama" that he and the stage manager James G. Burnett "concocted" from Lepard's novel was "a shocking innovation in a legitimate Broadway theater" and quite beyond Miss Keene's abilities, trained as she was in light comedy and serious drama. The production opened on April 22, 1858, and the review indicates that Jefferson had produced a series of spectacular scenes and a juicy role for himself.

> There is no . . . plot in the piece, but there are . . . a succession of scenes which keep the audience in a . . . state of anxiety or good humor. . . . The first scene is an American farmer's kitchen, in which the lads and lasses of the village are assembled for . . . merry-making. . . . A . . . dance by the company closes the scene. . . . The first scene in the second act, an old church and graveyard by moonlight . . . was . . . beautiful and elicited . . . applause. But the most beautiful of all . . . was the grand tableau, illustrating Trumbull's . . . picture of the Battle of Bunker Hill. . . . The storm on the Delaware was one of the best scenes of the kind we have ever witnessed, and the new drop curtain which fell at the close of the third act elicited . . . praise. . . . Mr. Jefferson is . . . continually before the audience, whom he keeps in excellent humor. . . . It should have a long run. . . . Do not neglect to take your wives, daughters, sisters and sweethearts.[181]

Blanche of Brandywine and his later revision of *The Rivals* represent Jefferson's only attempt at playwrighting outside of his contribution to *Rip Van Winkle*. Although his name is listed in the printed edition, he was given no credit in advertisements at the time. The text is a melodramatic excuse for scenic spectacle, requiring twenty-three characters and twenty-two supernumeraries. There is, in fact, no dramatic reason whatsoever for the Battle of Bunker Hill. The action stops. The curtain opens, and the audience sees the tableau. The title character, Blanche, is endangered by the play's nemesis, Gilbert Gates, described as "half villain, half Quaker" and by a Tory lord named George Percy of Monthermser. Both perish in a spectacular shipwreck that provides yet another opportunity for scenic display. Blanche is saved by her sweetheart, the Yankee rebel Randolph, who also enables George Washington to win the battle of Trenton Falls. Jefferson appeared as a "live Yankee" named Seth Hope who spends his time cavorting with a Pennsylvania Dutchman named Kraut and a Negro servant called Sampson. The three eventually form a local militia battalion for General Washington, and Seth drills his compatriots, urging them on with: "The inemy's [*sic*] in front of you, and glory's behind you; let each man feel as strong as Julius Caesar, when he cuts off the head of Goliah [*sic*], with the jawbone of an ass."[182]

Blanche of Brandywine, of course, is not about the Revolutionary War, but about the Civil War. The descriptions of warfare put into the mouths of both Washington and the English general Howe presage the carnage that would overtake the play's audience within the next two years. The English, who should be the natural villains of the piece, are seen as courteous, loyal, and noble adversaries. The villains of the piece are the Tories, described as rebels turning against their country.

On May 12, 1858, Jefferson took his second and "farewell" benefit and "the house was filled by his friends and admirers." In the course of his first New York season with Laura Keene, Jefferson had appeared in thirty-six different plays. Of these, twenty-nine were performed fewer than ten times, and only seven were performed between eleven and twenty times. *Blanche of Brandywine* had not been the success that Jefferson hoped, and Keene's only hit that season was *The Sea of Ice.* Nevertheless, Jefferson had established himself as the most important performer in the company and was the only person, aside from Keene, to be given two benefits. Moreover, he was moving away from the drudgery of life as a minor stock company actor. In 1849–50, at the Chatham Street Theatre, he had performed ninety roles. In Baltimore, in 1854, he had played fifty-seven parts. A season with only thirty-six roles must have seemed leisurely. The more important a nineteenth-century actor became, the fewer parts he or she played. In Laura Keene's theatre, Jefferson had time to rehearse, time to develop new roles. At the end of his first season with Keene, however, he had not found a part on which to base his career. He was a famous stock company actor now, but he was not yet a star.[183]

That summer the Jeffersons and Mary Devlin began to vacation at Paradise Valley in eastern Pennsylvania. Joe had already been refused an insurance policy on the basis of a family history of consumption and a poor upper part of one lung. According to his granddaughter, Paradise Valley was part of his lifelong pursuit of a suitable climate. The Jefferson family boarded at what Jefferson described as "a queer old Dutch farm-house at the foot of the Pocono Mountains." His father-in-law, Thomas Lockyer, had just purchased an inn there, and the Jeffersons lived in a small adjacent cottage, which is still standing. Jefferson began to sketch, a hobby that, along with fishing, came to dominate his leisure hours.[184]

Figure 9. Modern appearance of the house where Jefferson and his family lived in Paradise Valley, Pennsylvania, when he made the decision to do Rip

The family's life was simpler at Paradise Valley than in New York. There were no stores and the menu, prepared by the Jeffersons' "housekeeper," Aunt Nell Symons, was limited. (Thursday, for instance, was always boiled beef-and-dumplings.) But although the setting was rustic, the Jeffersons now enjoyed the trappings of upper-class Victorian life. A music master arrived weekly to instruct the children. Tiddie Jefferson played the guitar. A sewing woman was employed to do the family mending. Joe drove a team of Australian ponies, and above all, he did not have to work in the summer. He now had enough money to enjoy his leisure surrounded by rural nature. It became the style typical of all his homes.[185]

Jefferson returned to New York by August 18, 1858, when Laura Keene called her company together to prepare for the opening of the 1858–59 season. On September 6 she embarked upon a series of standard English comedies, with Jefferson performing Bob Acres in *The Rivals* and the dandyish Crabtree in *The School for Scandal*. And

Figure 10. Joseph Jefferson as Asa Trenchard in *Our American Cousin*

then on October 18, 1858, Jefferson opened as Asa Trenchard in Tom Taylor's *Our American Cousin*, a performance that established him as a major star of the American theatre.[186]

The play, now associated only with the death of Abraham Lincoln, was one of the great theatrical successes of mid-nineteenth-century America. It had everything audiences of the period wanted:

sentimentality, Yankee humor, a wonderful English nobleman named Lord Dundreary (for whom E. A. Sothern created elaborate sneezes), a villain, a damsel in distress, a happy ending, and verbal duels between the American and English cousins played by Jefferson and Laura Keene. The plot revolves around an uncouth American Yankee, played by Jefferson, who visits the English branch of his family, where he comes up against the barbed wit of his cousin Florence Trenchard, played by Laura Keene. Florence's prejudices against Yankees are well established before Asa's first entrance as she speaks to Augusta (played in the original production by Jefferson's cousin Effie Germon):

> *Augusta*: I can imagine the wild young hunter   an Apollo of the Prairie.
>
> *Florence*: With a . . . nasal twang, and a taste for smoking Cigars and drinking Coblers. . . . He's seven feet high . . . and has long hair and a red skin, and shoots with a bow and arrows and scalps people who offend him.[187]

Asa is Florence's worst nightmare. In the original text he introduces himself as "Asa Trenchard raised in Saginaw, suckled in the Bloody Creek, about the tallest gunner and the slickest dancer, and loudest critter in all pints [*sic*], by snakes in all Michigan. . . ." But Jefferson suggested making him an easterner from Brattleboro, Vermont, rather than a westerner, possibly because he knew that a New York audience would have no concept of Saginaw's location. In creating Asa, Jefferson also abandoned the traditional long hair, short trousers, and nasal twang characteristic of stage Yankees in favor of a finely textured light grey cloth suit with long trousers and matching hat, a wig the length of his own hair and a . . . normal speech pattern.[188]

Asa may not have European manners, but, like all of Jefferson's most successful characters, he has a good heart. He meets Mary Meredith, an impoverished dairymaid of noble blood due to inherit the property that Asa has been left, if no will is presented.

> A shrewd, keen Yankee boy of twenty-five falls in love . . . with a simple, loving, English dairymaid of eighteen. She innocently sits on the bench, close beside him; he . . . draws closer to her; she raises her eyes in innocent wonder at this, and he glides gently to the farthest end of the bench. He never tells her of his love, nor does she . . . suggest her affection for him; and though they . . .

talk of other things, you see plainly how deeply they are in love. He relates the story of his uncle's death in America, and during this recital asks her permission to smoke a cigar. With apparent carelessness, he takes out a paper, a will made in his favor by the old man, which document disinherits the girl; with this, he lights his cigar, thereby destroying his rights and resigning them to her.

Asa's true-blue nature wins out in the end. When his English cousins are threatened by an unscrupulous villain, he drinks the man under the table, blackmails him into paying the family debts, and wins the pretty milkmaid. What Jefferson did with Asa was to take a stage stereotype and humanize it, a characteristic trait of his later performances. Jefferson made stereotypes work by making them human.

The *New York Times* gave Jefferson most of the credit for the success of *Our American Cousin*, and Jefferson agreed. In a lawsuit in which he testified against Keene in 1865, he remembered: "A comedy this loosely . . . put together is apt to be varied from night to night. There were alterations made in the business, until it was quite a different play from Mr. Taylor's manuscript. I introduced many alterations in the play." This, of course, was typical of his work. Whether or not Jefferson's view of his own contributions was justified, the money rolled in, and Laura Keene began to sport diamonds around the theatre. Keene had been planning a production of *A Midsummer Night's Dream*, but the success of *Our American Cousin* kept delaying it. On December 11 the *Spirit of the Times* reported that "this pretty house is crammed in all kinds of weather and the audience frequently uproarious in applause." By December 18, ninety-thousand people had seen *Our American Cousin*, many of them content to find standing room. In all, the production initially had 139 consecutive performances and was then revived nine more times during the season for a total of 148 performances, netting $46,000 for the management.[189]

By the end of the run of *Our American Cousin*, Jefferson had decided to become a star performing the play without Keene. Margaret was pregnant again. With three children and a fourth on the way, he was becoming more ambitious. He had visions of his name in large type on theatrical advertisements, of foreign tours, and more money.[190] His decision to perform the play by himself also reflects the growing deterioration of his relations with Laura Keene. Keene viewed criticism or even a lack of sympathy as a personal attack. When the *Daily Express* failed to sympathize with her problems as a manager, she published what, to a modern perception, is essentially a feminist rebuttal.

> Why my endeavors to use my share (however humble) of professional talent and experience, as the Directress of a Theatre, should be converted into grounds for wanton attacks, . . . unjust allusions, malicious insinuations and undeserved outrage, I have yet to learn; or why, because there happen to be other establishments with which . . . the one I am about to conduct may . . . interfere, I am to refrain from doing precisely what was done by the gentlemen directing those Theatres,—viz: try my powers of catering for the public,—appears to me a still greater riddle. I seek no newspaper warfare. I am a woman, and at your mercy. If you think you add to the value of your columns, the pleasure and instruction of your readers, or the character for manliness and generosity of yourselves or reporters, by . . . wounding the feelings and . . . endeavoring to injure the prospects of one who, as an antagonist, is . . . helpless, and who is unconscious of . . . having merited such treatment, do so. I must submit to you as an individual but to the public as a manageress. Let them judge between us.
>   I am gentlemen, your obedient servant
>   LAURA KEENE[191]

Laura Keene was no one's obedient servant, and she could play the injured victim to the hilt. And, for his part, Jefferson was feeling his new-found power as a celebrated actor. "I think she found that I was becoming too strong to manage. . . . I have no doubt that I perhaps unconsciously exhibited a confidence in my growing strength that made her . . . apprehensive lest I should try to manage her."[192]

Keene favored E. A. Sothern at Jefferson's expense, and when Joe interrupted a piece of new stage business that she and Sothern had interpolated into the performance, the tensions became public.

> The Duchess—as she was . . . called by the actors, on the sly —had arranged some new business with Mr. Sothern, neglecting to inform me of it. I got the . . . cue . . . , and I came upon the stage. I . . . unintentionally interrupted their preconceived arrangements. . . . Miss Keene, speaking out so loudly . . . that

. . . the audience could hear her, said: "Go off the stage sir, till you get your cue for entering." I was thunderstruck. There was a dead silence, . . . and . . . I replied: "It has been given, and I will not retire."

When the curtain fell, she was furious and . . . discharged me. . . . I might leave now if I liked, and she would dismiss the audience rather than submit to such a public insult. . . . I informed her that I could not take a discharge given in the heat of temper, and would remain.The play proceeded, but she was singularly adroit, and by her manner in turning her back on me . . . made the audience believe that I was a cruel wretch to insult her in so public a way.[193]

By the end of the season, on June 4, 1859, Jefferson had performed in fifteen different plays, a significant reduction from the preceding season because of the popularity of his Asa Trenchard. He had also had his first taste of a long-running success, of what it was like to perform the same part night after night in a play of limited literary value that served as a star vehicle for his talents. *Our American Cousin* set the pattern that he followed with *Rip Van Winkle,* and by the end of the run he determined to leave the company and pursue a career as a touring star. When he asked Keene for permission to perform *Our American Cousin,* she refused, saying: "The play is my property, and you shall not act it outside of this theater." She then requested that Jefferson resign the role of Bottom in her upcoming production of *A Midsummer Night's Dream,* a role to which he was entitled as the company's chief comedian. "This I positively refused to do. I told [her business manager] plainly that Miss Keene had taken an antagonistic stand towards me and that . . . she would not appreciate a favor . . . and would treat any concession . . . as weakness."[194]

Keene stopped talking to Jefferson, but she had the right to order him to undertake any role in his line of business. He began rehearsing for Bottom, found himself unsuited for the role, and resigned the character on the condition that he might take *Our American Cousin* out on a starring tour and give Keene half of the profits as a royalty.

When William Winter's *Life and Art of Joseph Jefferson* was published, John Creahan, who became Keene's biographer, denounced its characterization of her in a letter written to Jefferson in December 1894. Jefferson replied that "If you will refer to my autobiography, you will find that I have treated Miss Keene with every respect."[195] After the Civil War Keene and Jefferson made up their differences, and Jefferson remembered with pride in 1888 that "the last letter she wrote was penned upon her death-bed, and was addressed to me." Certainly she willed him pictures of the English actor-managers Edmund Kean and Madame Vestris that he had admired, but the animosity between the two actors was well known, and in his autobiography Jefferson reserves for her a level of nastiness directed at no one else. They met at a period when his self-assertiveness made Jefferson difficult.

This same quality led to a another quarrel within the company. When Jefferson began what the critic William Winter describes as an "excellent custom of expunging the indelicate lines from the old comedies," a fellow company member named W. Rufus Blake referred to him as "the Sunday school comedian." When Blake made the accusation in the theatre's greenroom, Winter reports that Jefferson turned on him with: "You take an unfair and unmanly advantage of people . . . when you force them to listen to your coarseness. They are for the time imprisoned and have no choice but to hear and see your ill-breeding. You have no better right to be offensive on the stage than you have in the drawing room."[196]

Even Jefferson, whose recollection of the quarrel is far more gentle than Winter's, notes that "Mr. Blake was a much older man than I, and more than my peer as an actor. . . . I was angered, and doubtless my manner was more offensive than what I had said. I apologized, . . . and we were friends.[197]

Jefferson wrote about the quarrel thirty-one years after the event. Blake had been dead since 1863. Jefferson was a major star, and there was no need to rehash the quarrel, because who would have remembered it? Yet Joe felt the need to justify himself and to show his good will by an apology. In demonstrating his rashness as a young man, he reminded his 1888 readers of how great a star and how good a person he had become. Yet who but Jefferson could have provided the exact quotation used by William Winter? In the period of his ascent, he was clearly driven to impose his taste on others and to grab and hold center stage both onstage and off, and his autobiography's treatment of Keene and Blake indicate that, even as a star, he was not above settling old scores.

6

BOUCICAULT
AND STARDOM

1859–1861

By the spring of 1859 Jefferson's name was widely associated with *Our American Cousin*, and he was determined to capitalize on the play's and his own popularity. Given the fact that he had never performed Asa Trenchard outside New York City, his popularity in the "provinces" indicates an audience that read about and remained aware of what was playing in the country's theatrical capital. Jefferson embarked on a tour of the Northeast on April 18 and even contemplated taking *Our Amerian Cousin* to London. Once again he was planning to leave his pregnant wife for a trip abroad. Mary Devlin wrote to Edwin Booth: "Joe thinks of going to England—has had very fine offers."[198]

Porter's *Spirit of the Times* encouraged Jefferson to go to London, where Tom Taylor had arranged for him to perform at the Haymarket Theatre, but the *New York Clipper* warned that the London theatre could be inhospitable to Americans. Jefferson was still planning the trip in late June 1859, but it never materialized. After what he described as a "qualified success" in the provinces, he was back in New York by mid-June planning a nine-day engagement at the Howard Athenaeum in Boston. On June 27 he opened there with *Our American Cousin*, but his cousin William Warren had performed the role for two months at the Boston Museum that season, and the play's popularity had been exhausted. Porter's *Spirit of the Times* again reported that Jefferson planned to "rusticate in the interior of Pennsylvania for a few weeks, preparatory to making arrangements for his contem-plated visit to our English cousins." But by July 23, 1859, he was back in New York, appearing at Niblo's Gardens, opposite Margaret, now five-months pregnant, who was making her first appearance on the New York stage in nine years. The performance was advertised as a benefit for Jefferson before his departure for England in order to attract audiences with the possibility of not seeing him for a while, but Jefferson announced from the stage that he had "not fully deter-mined" to go. The *New York Clipper* found this deliberate attempt at money-grubbing "refrigerating."[199]

By early August, Jefferson had decided to stay in America, and on September 3 he began rehearsals for *Dot*, a version of Dickens' *The Cricket on the Hearth*, adapted and directed by Dion Boucicault.[200] Here Jefferson was to find his second starring role, the impoverished toymaker Caleb Plummer, who laments the loss of his son in the "golden South Americas" and pretends to his blind daughter, Ber-tha, that their impoverished surroundings are luxurious. Boucicault later wrote that at first Jefferson was reluctant to play the part.

> [W]hen I opened the Winter Garden, in 1859, having en-gaged Joe Jefferson as leading comedian, it struck me that *Caleb Plummer* was a character he could grasp. He was called to re-hearsal, and the part was placed in his hand. I shall never forget the expression on his face. Approaching him, I said: "What's the matter, Joe?" "Oh," he replied, "don't ask me to play this. I have tried it in the old edition and failed in it conspicuously. . . . Is this to be my opening part?" I tried vainly to persuade him that he would make a hit in it. He would not see it. However, I was obliged to insist, and he went to his duty.[201]

Jefferson was a paid employee; his "duty" was his only choice, but he was so concerned about undertaking the pathos-ridden role that he insisted on performing in the concluding farce to maintain his reputa-tion as a low comedian, a stipulation he dropped once *Dot* was a hit. In rehearsal Jefferson emphasized the pathetic nature of the toymaker, but Boucicault saw that he had approached the role incorrectly.

> During my rehearsal of the first scene, which I went through just as I intended acting it at night, I saw by [Boucicault's] man-ner that he was disappointed with my rendering of the part, and

I asked him what was the matter. He replied . . . "Why, you have acted your last scene first; if you begin in that solemn strain, you have nothing left for the end of the play."

Figure 11. Joseph Jefferson as Caleb Plummer in *Dot*. Courtesy of the Hampden-Booth Theatre Library at The Players.

In his own version of what happened Boucicault is far more intrusive:

I saw at once he had struck the wrong key. He mistook the character. He made it a weary, dreary, sentimental old bore. Rising from my managerial chair, I stopped the rehearsal. "Sit there, Joe," I said, placing him in my seat. I took his place on the stage, . . . giving an imitation of himself, playing the character as

I knew he could play it, in a comic, simple, genial vein. I had not spoken three speeches before he began to wriggle in his chair and then, leaping up, he cried, "Stop! I see! I know! That is enough."

Under Boucicault's direction, Jefferson lightened Caleb's opening scenes, emphasizing his deceit of Bertha as a result of the character's whimsy rather than as a pathetic attempt by a poor old man to make life pleasant for his stricken child. The critic Laurence Hutton described the first scene.

> How plainly we can recall that scene in the toymaker's cottage; the dolls and Noah's arks and small fiddles and barking dogs; *Bertha* making the dolls' dresses; and *Caleb*, in his sackcloth coat, which she, in her blindness and her fondness, believed to be a garment that the Lord Mayor might have been proud of, finishing up a . . . toy horse. How plainly we . . . see the . . . goodness of the old man, as he described to *Bertha* the beautiful things by which they were surrounded and which existed only in his loving . . . heart; that . . . humorous look on *Caleb's* face as he painted the numerous circles and dots and stripes, which gave to his . . . horse a likeness to nothing known in natural history, and held it up with the satisfied remark that he did not see how he could outlay any more talent on the animal, at the price.[202]

Jefferson had always been a comedian, and Caleb Plummer was his first venture, as a celebrated New York actor, into the mixture of pathos and comedy that would become his specialty. In 1862 a critic in Melbourne, Australia, provided a detailed description of his performance.

> His make-up is a study in itself. . . . The scanty grey hair which fringes his furrowed temples, the worn face, the thin voice, "that pipes and whistles in its sound," the bowed figure of the man, the occasional dreaminess of his manner are all true to nature. . . . The part is not an easy one to play. The cheerfulness which he imposes upon his daughter has to be assumed when Caleb's heart is heavy with sorrow and his accents tremulous with emotion so that it gives rise to a quaint turn of expression, odd inflections of the voice and abrupt transitions of manner. And while he dissembles . . . , Bertha's blindness ab-

solves him from the necessity of any falsification of his features so that, in the play of these, the spectator is enabled to detect the double part which the old man is assuming and to perceive the struggle which it costs him. As Mr. Jefferson is describing the fictitious appearance of the place he is in, the imaginary freshness of his own attire and the youthful vigour of his person, the glance he casts at the dismal realities is full of dolour, not untinctured with remorse. . . . It was not enough that his head was frosted with age and that his coat of packing-canvas bore "Glaze with care" on . . . his back, but every item of his costume, gesture of his body and inflection of his voice were carefully designed . . . to bring out . . . the character [rather] than to immediately affect his audience.[203]

Whereas other actors had emphasized Caleb's senility, Jefferson's Caleb was younger and even frisky in movement. Taking Boucicault's advice, he saved his pathos for the last scene of the play, when Caleb confesses his pathetic deceit and discovers that the mysterious stranger in his house is his long-lost son from South America. His godson, Jefferson Winter, remembered Caleb "momentarily in his agony of joy shrinking from the son whom he has long thought dead as he utters his heartrending cry: "My boy! My son—that was drowned—don't tell me—don't tell me—that he is alive!" Winter saw Jefferson perform the role approximately fifty times—each time in an identical way. "I knew exactly what he was going to say and do and when and where and how he was going to say and do it."[204] By the time Winter saw it, Jefferson had been performing Caleb for forty years and prided himself on the precision with which he repeated effects night after night. Eventually, as Jefferson revived the part over the span of his career, some critics complained that Caleb's mannerisms were reminiscent of Rip's. In a letter to the editor of *The Century*, J. Rankin Towse defended Jefferson by saying that a certain similarity of manner in characterization is natural to any actor.[205]

Dot opened on September 14, 1859, to successful notices, ran for twenty-nine consecutive performances, and was revived for eight more later in the season. By September 27 Boucicault and his co-manager, William Stuart began a string of advertisements for the production citing only the names of characters and actors. One such advertisement read, "MR. JEFFERSON AS THE TOY MAKER EVERY

EVENING." There was no mention of the name of the play or the theatre; none was necessary. The *New York Times* referred to Jefferson as "the greatest comedian of the age."[206] It continued its praise of him in mid-October, by which time the rest of the cast was becoming sloppy.

> The dialogue . . . is now . . . clogged with cheap and worthless . . . interpolations. . . . After a certain period, this . . . evil is . . . inevitable. . . . Something of the discretion that Mr. JEFFERSON brings to bear . . . would not be unacceptable if displayed by other members of the company. The truest test of this gentleman's . . . powers is . . . the fact that he excites emotions of a totally different character to those which he is expected to create by the audience. He is one of the few . . . low comedians who can command pathos and the only one . . . who perceives the true Dickensonian balance—which topples you over into an agony of emotion before you know where you are. The scene with Bertha and the recognition of his boy "from the golden South Americas" are . . . beautifully true to . . . human nature.[207]

The "Dickensonian balance"—that mixture of comedy and pathos ensured by Boucicault's direction—would become Jefferson's specialty, but over the next forty years his "discretion" in the role disappeared as he added more and more "interpolations." Eventually even J. Rankin Towse, certainly a Jefferson fan, decried Joe's decision to kiss the slow-witted comic servant, Tilly Slowboy, during the dance that ended the play as an "extravagance," one probably motivated by the fact that Tilly had become a specialty role for Jefferson's sister Cornelia. Cornelia was a member of the original company, and she must have had ample opportunity to study the part as originally performed.

Jefferson had taken a minor character and made it into a starring role, a path he would follow throughout his career. The production was such a hit that speculators bought up tickets during the afternoon to sell at increased prices that evening. Despite *Dot*'s success, however, all was not well at the Winter Garden: Boucicault was having financial difficulties with the management. On October 22, as part of a new contractual agreement, he decided to adapt *Nicholas Nickleby,* and his version, entitled *Smike,* opened ten days later with the title role performed, as a "britches part," by Agnes Robertson.

On the night his second surviving daughter was born, Jefferson went to work as usual performing Ralph Nickleby's drunken clerk, Newman Noggs.[208]

Josephine Duff Jefferson, called Josie and sometimes Dode, was born on November 10, 1859, at the family's home at 97 East Twelfth Street. Like her sister, Margaret, she never went on the stage, although all of her brothers eventually followed their father's profession. This may have been a result of some sense on Jefferson's part that it would be inappropriate for female members of the family to work as actresses. Certainly Margaret was an actress when he married her, but the continuation of her career was a financial necessity. Once Joe was a success, she all but abandoned the stage. And although Joe's second wife, Sarah, came from a theatrical family, she never appeared on the stage. In any event, a stage career for Josephine would have been impossible. A careless nurse dropped her in infancy, which resulted in a twisted spine, a limp, and intermittent spasms. Josie remained in pain all of her life and was financially dependent on her family. Eleanor Farjeon, the daughter of Josie's older sister Maggie, recalled that as a girl her mother, "kept a spoon in her pocket . . . ready to slip between the child's teeth at the first alarm." According to his granddaughter, Joe Jefferson spent his life "trying to spare [Josie] pain, to compensate her for the pain she couldn't be spared." Jefferson now had three children, one of whom would require constant care. He needed to make money.[209]

Smike received rave reviews. The *New York Times* praised Jefferson's ability to adapt his persona from role to role, an ironic comment in hindsight, because six years later he eventually became so identified with a role that he came to feel that audiences would not believe him in any other character.[210] Washington's *Daily National Intelligencer,* in 1866, gives a rare picture of Jefferson's Newman Noggs.

Who . . . will ever forget the scene in which, resting on his stool, with his goosequill behind his ear, he stands over his old desk, gives his employer the old rascal *Ralph Nickleby,* "a raking down," and then, when *Ralph* breaks from the room in a rage, settles hard upon his stool, pulls out his bottle from the desk, and draws courage from it? And then there is the scene of the drunkard's last drink in the last act.[211]

Smike ran for nineteen nights and was revived later in the season. It is an odd version of Dickens' novel, featuring its minor characters and relegating its hero, Nicholas, to such a subordinate role that the name of the actor playing the part never appeared in newspaper advertisements. Indeed the version is subtitled *Scenes from Nicholas Nickleby*. The fact that Newman Noggs survives in Dickens' novel would never have fazed either Boucicault or Jefferson, who would immediately have seen Noggs' death as simultaneously pathetic and morally righteous. Nineteenth-century audiences expected a drunkard to have a tragic end, a notion that Jefferson would later challenge in *Rip Van Winkle*.[212]

The season's second major hit, Boucicault's antislavery drama *The Octoroon*, opened on December 5, 1859, three days after the execution of the abolitionist John Brown. Jefferson appeared in the character role of Salem Scudder. In a conversation with Francis Wilson, he recalled:

> [Boucicault] remembered that I had had some success in playing Yankee roles. . . . He remembered also that a certain actor made a most effective Indian, and when he, Boucicault, adapted Mayne Reid's novel of *The Quadroon* under the title of *The Octoroon*, he worked these two characters into the piece and engaged the other actor and me to play them.[213]

Boucicault was writing for a company of actors employed for the season. If they lacked roles, they were paid without performing. It was in Boucicault's financial interest to provide Jefferson with a role, but it was not easy. *The Octoroon* dramatizes the pathetic fate of Zoe, the illegitimate daughter of a kindly white plantation family. Salem Scudder, a comic Yankee overseer, provided Jefferson with only a small part overshadowed by the play's abolitionist melodrama. When announcements first appeared in the local newspapers, his name was not even mentioned, and Jefferson, accustomed to turning small parts into major roles, reacted with vigor.

> I sent my part . . . to the theater, with a note to Mr. Stuart [the lessee and producer], saying that I considered my engagement canceled by my name being publicly ignored in the announcement of the play, and I concluded my resignation by saying that

. . . if Mr. Stuart or Mr. Boucicault would call on me, I would be pleased to enter into a new engagement with them . . . ; otherwise I must decline to act again in the theatre. As the play was ready and to be acted on the following Monday night, this being Saturday, I felt pretty sure that my note of resignation would . . . explode with considerable force in the office.

Jefferson "had been for some time suffering with an attack of dyspepsia," and when Boucicault and William Stuart arrived at his home, they found him boxing with "an old retired champion of light-weights" whom he had engaged as a personal trainer in the hope that exercise would alleviate his condition. The contractual agreement was settled, and Jefferson opened in the play at a salary of $150 a week, with his name second only to Agnes Robertson's.[214]

The script was controversial. The *Spirit of the Times* called it "a disgrace to the North, a libel on the South" and claimed that Boucicault, in order to make money, had "taken advantage of the existing anti-Southern excitement . . . to bring out a play which . . . is more pernicious than anything which has heretofore . . . conceived in the spirit of sectional hate." The *Herald* assailed the play "as an Abolition drama . . . intended to excite the public mind against the South, and . . . part of the gigantic conspiracy . . . against the integrity of the Union." Jefferson had a more tolerant view on the play, which simultaneously condemns slavery and romanticizes the old South.[215]

On December 13 the external conflict over *The Octoroon* led to Boucicault and Robertson's withdrawal from the Winter Garden. With Robertson gone, Jefferson got top billing, despite his small role, and the play, enhanced by newspaper reports of litigation, soared in popularity. In the subsequent lawsuit Jefferson sided with Stuart and his partner Thomas C. Fields who were, after all, paying his salary, and contended that "Bourcicault's [*sic*] conduct as stage manager has been offensive to the artists of the theatre" and that he had himself on "two occasions actually resigned his place in said theatre by reason of . . . unfair dealing."[216]

Jefferson's backing of Stuart and Fields against Boucicault, as well as his ability and reputation, led the managers to appoint him as stage manager by January 6, 1860. Although Joe did not appear in his first production. advertisements even cite him as the play's "director," an unusual practice for the period, when play direction was in its infancy. Jefferson was now the artistic head of the Winter Garden company.[217]

There is no evidence that he was successful. On February 2, 1860, his adaptation of *Oliver Twist* opened with Charles Burke's step-daughter, Ione Sutherland, in the title role. The *Spirit of the Times* noted that the "scenes are made . . . effective, and the audience is hurried to the denouement," but the production lasted less than two weeks. By mid-February, Jefferson was serving the company primar-ily as its lead comedian in a series of spectacle pieces.[218] On April 11 the Winter Garden was given over to operatic spectacle, and Jeffer-son began a tour to Baltimore and Washington. This was the kind of provincial engagement he no longer needed to do, a throwback to his life ten or fifteen years before. He simply could never resist the opportunity to earn money performing.[219]

On May 16 Jefferson opened the Winter Garden for a three-month summer season with "a company selected with especial regard to burlesque and extravaganzas," including his former boss F. S. Chanfrau, James Simmonds, with whom he would tour Australia, his sister Cornelia, his cousin Hetty Warren, and Ione Sutherland. It was a version of the Jefferson family troupe in which Joe had grown up. They produced a series of hit comedies that appealed to the city's summer tourists as well as a burlesque celebrating the opening of diplomatic relations with Japan. Jefferson not only acted, but also danced "his original Grape Vine Twist and Burlesque Breakdown." Actors were continually "called out" during performances, forced to come before the curtain to acknowledge the audience's applause and often make a short speech; bouquets tossed on stage became such a nuisance that an actress, having been the object of one, simply reached down and tossed it unceremoniously offstage. The season netted $20,000.[220]

On July 23 Jefferson, responded to a request in the *Spirit of the Times* for more legitimate drama by reviving *Our American Cousin* with members of the original cast. The company were showing signs of boredom and introducing "gags" into the production, much to the annoyance of a local critic: "Putting a tin pan on Lord Dundreary's head, is a liberty which no Yankee, however impudent, would . . . take. . . . We are . . . sorry to see such things . . . from gentlemen who know better and . . . have . . . shown . . . more legitimate taste."[221]

Jefferson's management of the Winter Garden ended on August

31, 1860. That fall he took his family to Paradise Valley, and there, on a rainy day, he went out to a barn loft to read *The Life and Letters of Washington Irving*. Joe was amazed to find a reference to himself. Irving had been to Laura Keene's Theatre on September 30, 1858, and had seen him act.[222] Flattered by the attention, Jefferson went back into the house and returned with Irving's *The Sketch Book*, in which the tale of Rip Van Winkle appears. He was, of course, aware of versions performed by his father and stepbrother, and he determined to create a version for himself. But the material was not inherently stageworthy.

> I was disappointed with it . . . . the tale was purely a narra-
> tive. . . . The character of *Rip* does not speak ten lines. What
> could be done dramatically with so simple a sketch? How could it
> be turned into an effective play? . . . Still I was so bent upon acting
> the part that I started for the city and in less than a week, by
> industriously ransacking the theatrical wardrobe establishments
> for old leather and mildewed cloth, and by personally superin-
> tending the making of the wigs, each article of my costume was
> completed; and all this before I had written a line of the play or
> studied a word of the part.

Rip Van Winkle began not with a revision of the play, but with a costume including Charles Burke's leggings, which Jefferson used as late as 1883. The script that developed was first and always an actor's piece. Jefferson was less concerned with the originality and quality of the script than with the originality and quality of his performance. He had been brought up in stock, and with the exception of his work on Asa Trenchard, Salem Scudder, and roles in some of the minor plays produced by Laura Keene, he never performed characters he had not already seen. He was, like most nineteenth-century actors, a refiner and reinventor rather than a creator. That summer, Jefferson rehearsed *Rip*, developing his own characterization. In his *Autobiog-raphy* he speaks of writing the play. It would be truer to say that he pieced together three old printed versions of the drama and the Irving story, expanded the action from two acts to three, and made the scene of Rip's encounter with the spirits of Hendrik Hudson and his crew the centerpiece of the drama. It was here that his most effective "writing" occurred.

[B]y far the most important alteration was in the interview with the spirits. In the old versions, they spoke and sang. I remembered that the effect of this ghostly dialogue was dreadfully human; so I arranged that no voice but *Rip's* should be heard. This is the only act on the stage in which but one person speaks while all the others merely gesticulate. . . . It required . . . thought to hit upon just the best questions that could be answered by a nod and shake of the head and to arrange that at times even *Rip* should propound a query to himself . . . , but I had availed myself of so much of the old material that in a few days after I had begun my work, it was finished.[223]

There is no extant copy of Jefferson's first version of *Rip Van Winkle*, but a full description of one moment was provided by a Philadelphia reviewer in 1871. It occurs in the scene in which the old Rip finds out that his shrewish wife Gretchen has died, a moment omitted from the version that made Jefferson famous and in which Gretchen lives. The 1871 reviewer preferred the earlier *Rip*.

How much better it would be were Mr. Jefferson to modify the version he plays so as . . . to do away with the second marriage of "Rip's" wife. In that which he used to play, . . . Gretchen was made to die during Rip's long sleep, and her death gave him an opportunity for a bit of acting which we have never seen equaled. When in conversation with the friendly inn-keeper, Rip learns of her death, his first feeling is one of intense joy and relief, finding expression in the words, "Vot! te old woman's clapper stappit at last?" but, as his satisfaction reaches its climax, a consciousness of what she really was to him, how much she had done for him and how little he had done for her, begins to come over him; his laugh gradually dies away; his face softens and saddens; his eyes become yearning and suffused, and in a voice almost broken with feeling, he sadly and lovingly prefaces a tribute to her worth with "But she vos mine own frau."[224]

As he did with Caleb Plummer, Dr. Ollapod, and Dr. Pangloss, Jefferson took what had been an essentially comic role and found pathos in the part. Although the more famous version of the play that Boucicault would write for him in 1865 substitutes Gretchen's repentance for her death, Jefferson consistently emphasized the ambiguity of their marriage. Gretchen is a shrew, but she is a shrew who loved Rip. Rip is constantly tricking Gretchen, but he is crushed when she drives him out of the house.

Laura Keene resumed her managership of the theatre in the fall of 1860, and despite their differences she offered Jefferson a *carte blanche* engagement with the company. Whatever personal or professional animosity she may have felt for him, Keene knew that hiring him was good business, but Jefferson decided to play a series of short starring engagements in "principal cities" with a repertoire that included *Rip Van Winkle*. He was now, and would be for the rest of his life, a touring star, first alone and later with his own company.

His ability to tour was dependent on the burgeoning development of the American railroad. The cheapness of land (particularly in the West, where Congress made significant land grants to railway companies), the desire of Americans to occupy the vast territories available to them, and the need to transport goods rapidly had, by 1857, led to the construction of twenty-six-thousand miles of railway in the United States. Jefferson's career, indeed the entire nineteenth-century American theatre, could never have occurred without them.[225]

On November 5, 1860, with only a few days rehearsal, Jefferson opened the fall season of the Washington Theatre with a twelve-night engagement that included *Rip*.[226] By the end of the run he was satisfied with his own character, but not with the play's construction. He would resume work on it five years later in England, where Dion Boucicault would make the final "alterations and additions" that turned it into one of the great starring vehicles of the nineteenth century. In 1860 Rip was only one of a series of roles Jefferson performed. Following engagements in Baltimore and Richmond, he returned to New York's Winter Garden Theatre on December 24 in what local papers deemed "his first appearance as a 'star.'" Reviews were hostile.

> A new version of . . . "Rip Van Winkle" . . . introduced Mr. JEFFERSON in the . . . character of "a star." It seems but the other day that we gave welcome to this gentleman as a desirable addition to Miss LAURA KEENE'S Theatre, and now we find him . . . going through the egotisms of a star engagement . . . hence the necessity for a piece like *Rip Van Winkle* which . . . demands but

a single actor and a variety of supernumeraries. Of its kind it is good enough, but we object to its kind and regret the occasion which has brought Mr. JEFFERSON from the . . . position of the first stock actor of the Metropolis to . . . a mere comic star. His performance . . . was as good as any man could make it but the applause . . . will not . . . contribute to the fortunes of the engagement.[227]

Rip played for only a week; The *New York Clipper* said that it "put people to sleep, and it will take something extraordinarily good to wake them again."[228] Jefferson went on to other roles, and he closed at the Winter Garden on January 19, 1861. His run was a financial failure. The *New York Times* reported:

Mr. JEFFERSON closed, . . . playing to the only unprofitable week this theatre had seen. . . . It is one of the misfortunes of our drama, that the moment a good stock actor contributes to the success of a piece, he . . . sets up at once for "a star." . . . We have only to hope that . . . Mr. JEFFERSON . . . may be . . . disenchanted . . . of the . . . delusion that because an actor shows himself a good stock actor and plays two or three parts . . . well, he is able to carry alone the weight of attraction of a first-class metropolitan theatre.[229]

Following one of the few critical setbacks in his career, Jefferson went out on the road, as any nineteenth-century actor in need of work would do. The tour did not last long.[230] On February 18, 1861, Margaret Clements Lockyer Jefferson died in their home at 97 East Twelfth Street in New York, leaving Joe with four children—the eldest, Charles Burke, not quite ten years old, the youngest Josephine, a fifteen-month-old infant. Margaret was only twenty-eight. Her death was apparently unexpected, the result of a brief illness.[231] The official cause was asthenia, defined as a lack of strength, a diminuation of vital powers, or general debility. The funeral took place at the Jefferson home on February 21. Friends of the family were invited, and presumably Edwin Booth, who was playing in New York at the time, attended. Margaret was buried in Calvary Hills Cemetery on Long Island. In his autobiography Jefferson is characteristically taciturn: "At the death of my wife, which occurred in March, 1861, I broke up my household in New York, and leaving three of my children at school, left home with my eldest son for California. Through the act of an overzealous agent, my engagement in San Francisco was an unmistakable failure."

Margaret gets half a line, and he is back to his career. His reticence about personal matters throughout the autobiography was based on his stated assumption that his reading public was not interested in such details. In addition his memory had apparently become blurred; he got the month wrong, but then Margaret had been dead for twenty-seven years when he was writing. The drama of his statement, however, is unmistakable. Margaret dies, and he leaves. His friend, the critic William Winter, echoed the theme: "Early in 1861, being oppressed by a domestic bereavement and by failing health, Jefferson was persuaded to seek relief in travel and new scenes."

Jefferson's health was the reason presented to the public. The *Baltimore American and Commercial Advertiser* noted that Margaret's death "has had a more unfavorable effect on the . . . delicate health of her husband." Readers of the *Spirit of the Times* were told that Jefferson was leaving New York to "act for some time in San Francisco, where he trusts to recover his health which has been somewhat shaken." Dr. G. A. Kane, who seems to have known Jefferson both in the 1840's and the 1880's, believed that Joe "thought he had consumption or that he was predisposed to that disease." The *New York Clipper* in 1866 said that "the cause of Mr. Jefferson leaving his native country was ill health, as he was rapidly going into consumption," and reiterated in 1872 that Jefferson was "in poor health, being seriously threatened with pulmonary consumption." According to E. H. Sothern, Jefferson had told him "that his doctors declared that his only hope was to be out in the fresh air as much as possible" and that "his life depended on it." Shortly before his death, Jefferson said that "as a boy I was very delicate. Nobody thought I could last. I always had to be careful of myself. Fifty years ago I was refused an insurance policy. My family history was bad—Consumption in the family, and the top of this lung affected."[232]

The truth, however, is more ambiguous. Jefferson may have heard of theatrical opportunities in California from Edwin Booth, who had performed there from 1852 to 1856. Moreover, the Civil War was about to begin. South Carolina had already withdrawn from the Union on December 20, 1860, and by February 1, 1861, six other states had followed. On April 12 Confederate troops fired on Fort Sumter. At the time of Jefferson's death, a friend, Henry Watterson, wrote:

Early in 1861 Jefferson came to me and said: "There is going to be a great war of sections. I am not a warrior. I am neither a Northerner nor a Southerner. I cannot bring myself to engage in bloodshed or to take sides. I have near and dear ones North and South. I am going away and I shall stay away until the storm blows over. It may seem to you unpatriotic and it is, I know, unheroic; I am not a hero; I am, I hope, an artist. My world is the world of art, and I must be true to that; it is my patriotism, my religion. I can do no manner of good here, and I am going away.[233]

L. Clarke Davis, writing in 1879, remembered:

When the Southern troubles began he was prophetic, telling his lifelong friend, John T. Ford, that Mr. Seward's prediction of a three-months' struggle was folly; that war once begun between men of such courage and determination as his countrymen would last for years; and that, for himself, he would have no part or share in it: he would not fight with brother against brother. He was in Baltimore in 1861, when the Massachusetts troops were fired upon by the mob, and he then resolved to go abroad and remain there as long as the fratricidal conflict lasted. Speaking of it afterward, he said: "I felt myself growing very old in those dreadful years."[234]

In 1906 Charles Burke Jefferson, who was ten years old when the events in question occurred, wrote of his father:

His sympathies were with the south but his judgment was against the war. It was not the war that made him leave. My mother had just died. God rest her soul, and my father was in poor health. It wasn't generally known at the time, but the truth is one of his lungs was in mighty bad shape. In fact, it wasn't a whole lung. He started to California, hoping that climate would benefit him.[235]

And Jefferson's daughter-in-law, Eugenie Paul Jefferson, quoted him as saying that "I loved my country so much, I could not bear to see her suffer—some were kind enough to say that I ran away."[236]

Jefferson's decision to leave America as the Civil War began haunted him for the rest of his life. It was certainly not the result of a sole cause. Margaret's death, his own health, a desire to avoid being called upon to take sides, and quite possibly an eye to financial profit all contributed. Nor did he leave New York immediately upon Margaret's death, as the *Autobiography* implies. He reappeared on the New York stage at the Winter Garden Theatre on April 29 and continued there through May 25, 1860. The season was not over, and there was still a chance to make money. Emille Marguerite Cowell reported that the "House looked very good but . . . full of orders [complimentary tickets]." The war had just begun, but the *New York Times* reported that Jefferson was playing "to magnificent houses" despite the fact that interest in the war had become New York's most popular form of entertainment.[237]

When the season was ended, Jefferson left his three younger children, Margaret, Tommy, and Josie, in the care of his dead wife's parents. Six days after he closed at the Winter Garden, on June 1, 1861, he and his eldest son sailed for San Francisco and arrived on the 26th.[238]

Jefferson and Charles Burke each paid about $600 for their passage, and could each bring fifty pounds of luggage with them on the trip to California, more if they were willing to pay ten cents a pound for overage. All passenger baggage was stored together, and passengers lived out of carpet bags they brought with them. On the first night aboard ship, passengers presented themselves to the ship's purser and exchanged their boarding passes for tickets that designated their table places. First-class passengers—and Jefferson was certainly wealthy enough to be one—dined last to allow them time to eat their meal leisurely rather than being rushed out of the dining area to make room for others. The ship sailed out of New York harbor around Sandy Hook and then south past the Bahamas, the eastern end of Cuba, and the western point of Haiti.

Seven and a half days out of New York, the boat stopped at Aspinwall on the east side of the Isthmus of Panama. The baggage was unloaded and weighed, and then it disappeared until the party reached the western side. Black porters hired for twenty-five cents transported the carpet bags to the railroad station. Aboard a wood-burning train, steerage and first-class passengers mixed during the three-hour journey across the Isthmus. The train stopped to replenish its wood supply, and local inhabitants rushed to sell fruit, claret, lime juice, and ice water to the travelers.

Passengers went by barge out to their boat on the Pacific side. The boat steamed out of the Bay of Panama, going southwest before it turned northward. At 6 A.M. the gong rang for breakfast. Mornings were spent reading or card-playing. Lunch was at noon, dinner at 4:30. In the evening there was a light supper, card-playing, dancing, and singing. It took three weeks to get to Acapulco, where the weather was scorching hot. Passengers were rowed ashore to buy fresh bananas, oranges, sugar, and cakes and watch Mexican boys dive for dimes. A week later the boat reached San Francisco; baggage was loaded into a cab and transported to a hotel.[239]

Jefferson made his San Francisco debut at Maguire's Opera House on July 8, 1861, and played in California until November 4. As early as July 3, ads for his engagement began to appear in San Francisco's *Daily Alta California*. Anticipating an enormous demand for tickets, Tom Maguire, the Opera House's manager, put seats on sale for each performance three days in advance. The *New York Clipper*'s correspondent reported that "Joe . . . opened to a 'crusher'" and that "there has been no abatement of people to witness the performances of the noted J. J."[240] The local reviewer, however, felt that Jefferson's choices of *A Conjugal Lesson* and *Mazeppa* were unfortunate. Jefferson had, in his own words, been "overbilled" as "the celebrated American comedian" with a "national reputation," and the reality did not live up to hype.

> It is pity that this actor selected two . . . insignificant characters in which to start. . . . Some misgivings have been felt that Mr. Jefferson does not merit all that has been . . . said and puffed about him. There is a delicious bit of pantomime in *Mazeppa* where Cassimir parodies the circus-rider, that is almost worth sitting out a couple of hours to see.[241]

Business immediately fell off, and the local critic demanded that Jefferson offer "something better." He countered with a performance as Bob Acres that was described in the newspaper as "gloriously triumphant": "It is wonderful how limber Jefferson becomes in the duel scene in this piece, literally wilting into his boots."[242]

Despite his success in *The Rivals*, however, Jefferson had still not found favor with the local critics:

This gentleman labors under some natural disadvantages on the stage. His features are so sharp-cut and his face so thin, that he is always recognizable as the same man in all his chracters. That Punch-like nose and that chin cannot be transmogrified. His natural dapper figure is likewise ever present. . . . His voice too—not of the strongest or finest quality at best—is at once recognized in every part.

He cannot disguise his voice and features. His broad stares and grins are always before us.

[Of *Our American Cousin*] It is to be hoped that there is at least one other character left in the piece besides Asa Trenchard, as the plays heretofore presented by Mr. Jefferson have been so cut up as to be barely recognizable.

Between the author and the actor, Asa Trenchard is made a disagreeably prying, evesdroping, fliching [*sic*] fellow. Mr. Jefferson is not responsible for the part as written, but his interpretation . . . is very coarse. . . . His Yankee is offensively vulgar and a buffoon. He continually plays to the spectators in his conceited . . . looks and his chuckling grimaces.

Rip could hardly be deemed a good conception of the character. The Yankee showed too clearly through the small disguise of Dutch dialect, and Rip was converted into low comedy.[243]

It was the worst set of reviews of Jefferson's career, and when he returned to San Francisco after an early August tour to Macguire's Theatre in Sacramento, he reopened at another theatre, San Francisco's Opera House, on September 16 with *The Naiad Queen*, a spectacle drama he had produced in his managerial days prior to 1857. The production was expensive, but most of the performers were, in the opinion of the *New York Clipper's* correspondent, "incompetent." At least two of the actors were drunk on stage, and *The Naiad Queen* played to poor houses. In addition, Jefferson became severely ill. He was reduced to playing burlesques and pieces he had not performed since becoming a New York star.

When he reappeared at Maguire's Opera House in a series of English comedies, business improved, but in 1888 Jefferson remembered the entire California engagement as "an unmistakable failure." At the time, the *New York Clipper* admitted that "Jefferson's expectations of

success in California . . . were not realized." A five-month engagement, however, could hardly have been said to be totally unsuccessful.[244] One of the problems may have been that the general financial
status of the population was poor. A correspondent for the *New York
Times* reported: "We have had no balls and parties yet, the universal
cry being: 'Can't afford it'—and that's so; there are not half a dozen
families in the place that can afford to give parties. It's no joke where
ice cream is a dollar and fifty cents to two dollars per quart, chickens
in proportion. To give a plain party to fifty couples costs about $600.
It don't pay."[245]

Charles Burke Jefferson remembered that his father "was then
comparatively unknown, and while we made money, it was not a
grand successful trip. He did not improve much, and hearing of the
delightful climate of Australia, he decided to try it."[246]

Jefferson's decision to tour Australia was not made until he
reached San Francisco. New York newspapers mentioned only a
California trip. Moreover, while in San Francisco he had miniatures
painted of the children, presumably from photographs, because he
did not expect to see them again for some time. Had he intended to
go to Australia when he left New York, he almost certainly would
have had the miniatures painted then. Joe closed at Maguire's Opera
House on November 4, 1861, and sailed the next day; and although
the *New York Clipper* believed he was leaving for "a short season" in
Australia and would soon return to San Francisco, he would spend
the entire Civil War period abroad.[247]

7

YEARS ABROAD—
AUSTRALIA, NEW ZEALAND
1861–1865

Jefferson sailed from San Francisco on the *Nimrod*, bound for Port Phillip and Sydney, with his son Charles Burke, his agent, James Symons, and his agent's mother, "Aunt Nell" (Mrs. H.) Symons, who served as Jefferson's "housekeeper" for the next fifty years. The ship carried seven first-class passengers and another fourteen in steerage. Included was a Catholic priest whom Jefferson, never one for traditional piety, teased about celibacy and theology. The ship left San Francisco on November 6, 1861, met "with very light winds and calms throughout the [seventy-two-day] passage," and landed in Sydney on January 7, 1862.[248]

James Symons, who had managed theatres in Australia, introduced Jefferson to the Cockney ex-convict who ran Sydney's Royal Victoria Theatre, but the manager, who had never heard of Jefferson, had no interest in hiring him. Jefferson was forced to rent the house and company for $2,000 for two weeks.[249] The deal was struck quickly. Four days after he landed, the Royal Victoria announced Jefferson's engagement "for a limited number of nights." He did not open, however, until February 3, 1862. The long period between announcement and opening was due to a lack of scenery, particularly for *Rip Van Winkle,* which was not part of the standard repertoire. Jefferson supervised and worked on the painting of new sets and opened as Rip and Cassimir in the burlesque *Mazeppa.* The audience called him before the curtain at the end of *Rip,* and the reviews, next morning, hailed him as "not merely a good comedian; he is an *artiste* of . . . excellence, quite as . . . able to draw tears as to excite laughter. His acting is . . . *natural*—nothing ever appearing to be . . . forced or overstrained."[250]

Charles Burke Jefferson remembered that "at the end of two weeks, that opera-house owner wouldn't rent the house any more." Instead he insisted on managing the theatre while Jefferson appeared as a touring star. Managing a theatre in which Jefferson appeared had become more profitable than renting out the space. As Charles Burke put it, "We had a hog-killing time of it. Cash was abundant. . . . My father had more money at the end of those two weeks than all the Jeffersons put together ever had before."[251]

In his first Sydney engagement Jefferson played Rip, Dr. Pangloss, Newman Noggs, Asa Trenchard, Caleb Plummer, Bob Acres, Mr. Golightly, and Salem Scudder. By mid-February the Sydney newspaper was calling his success "the chief—indeed . . . the only—event . . . in the Australian world of Music and Drama." Jefferson took a farewell benefit on March 13 and closed two days later. He had performed twenty characters in six weeks. After his years in New York with Laura Keene and Dion Boucicault, he was back in the world of the touring actor.[252]

On March 19, 1862, Jefferson and his manager took the steamer *Wonga Wonga* to Melbourne, arriving on March 21. By March 27 Symons had rented the Royal Princess Theatre for three months, and Jefferson opened four days later with *Rip Van Winkle* and *Mazeppa*, the same combination he had used in Sydney. Once more he was forced to rent the theatre himself rather than be a touring star. And as in Sidney, there was a wait—in this case, ten days between his arrival and his performance because of problems in negotiating for the space. Jefferson was not known in Australia, and there was no rush to engage him.[253]

Jefferson performed in Melbourne for 164 nights, and in the words of his son: "We just simply coined it. It was like a mint." But the limited size of Australian cities, in comparison to New York and Boston, challenged him to find new material, and he turned to another English farce, opening on April 7 as Hugh de Brass in *A Regular Fix*. It was his first new role since Rip and would become one of Jefferson's staples for the next sixteen years.[254]

Hugh de Brass gave him an opportunity to play the same type of character he had created in Mr. Golightly—a harassed gentleman in an uncomfortable social situation. And as in all of his work, Jefferson emphasized the humanity of the character, so that the audience, absorbed in realistic detail, was gradually drawn into the farcical situation.

> Not a smile flickers on his . . . face while the spectators are convulsed with merriment; there is no straining after points and no grimacing at . . . people in the pit. . . . Mr. Jefferson exhibits an . . . unconsciousness of . . . anybody beyond the footlights. . . . Of course Mr. Jefferson's American accent jars . . . upon English ears. [His] characteristic as an actor . . . consists in . . . being natural and in avoiding clap-trap and caricature, even in farce. As a minor illustration of this, we . . . refer to his costume. Most actors . . . dress the hero of a farce in suits of such a pre-posterous cut, material and pattern, as are never seen off the stage; and the make-up is frequently more diverting than the dialogue and the by-play. Mr. Jefferson presents Hugh de Brass in the evening dress of a gentleman, nor is there anything in his deportment . . . at variance with that character.[255]

On April 21, 1862, the day after Easter, observed in Australia as a national holiday known as Easter Monday, Jefferson opened *Our American Cousin* in Melbourne. It was the hit of the season; some people came half a dozen times, and it ran continuously for twenty-eight days. In contrast, the appeal of the next show, *The Octoroon*, was as much in its scenery as in Jefferson's performance. His Salem Scudder had become "the central figure of the drama," reflecting both his reputation and a significant enlargement of the role. In like manner, *Nicholas Nickleby* was retitled *Newman Noggs* when Jeffer-son performed the role, and he was castigated by a local critic for subordinating the novel's well-known characters to his own.

> Mr. Dickens has no reason whatever to be grateful to Mr. Boucicault for mangling *Nicholas Nickleby* in the way he has done in the melodrama . . . which was played last night at the Princess's Theatre. Great liberties have been taken with the story; fresh incidents introduced, and the fate of one important character . . . altered. . . . Many of the well known characters

appear upon the scene. . . . They are merely . . . imperfect copies of the originals and seem to be thrown in as foils to Newman Noggs, who becomes the central figure of the motley group.[256]

By August 1862 Jefferson had embarked on an ambitious foray into Shakespeare. He opened as Bottom in *A Midsummer Night's Dream*, the role he had rejected at Laura Keene's Theatre only three years before. The results were imperfect. The *Argus* reviewer felt that Jefferson's Bottom lacked the careful detail that his other characters had shown, and this is not surprising. By 1862 Jefferson had been performing Rip Van Winkle, Caleb Plummer, and Salem Scudder for three years; Asa Trenchard for four; Dr. Golightly for six; Bob Acres for eleven; and Mr. Ollapod for thirteen. In comparison, any new role would have seemed under-rehearsed. It was a problem that Jefferson, like all nineteenth-century actors, faced. In order to tour, they needed to perform stock pieces that stock companies knew. Putting on a new play was difficult as long as a "star" was on tour. Consequently, touring actors were seldom able to undertake new characters, and their new characters were less developed than the ones they normally played. Moreover, mid-nineteenth-century actors looked as much to the perfection of standard roles as to the creation of new parts to build their careers.[257]

By September 8 Symons leased the recently built Royal Haymarket Theatre in Melbourne, and Jefferson opened there on September 15 in *Our American Cousin*. Both men were counting on the excitement of a new house to draw an audience, but the results were disappointing. Jefferson closed on September 27 and, leaving Symons behind to manage the new house, embarked on what he described as a tour into "the small mining and provincial towns" of Ballarat, Bendigo, and Castlemaine. The Australian mining towns lay west and north of Melbourne in the state of Victoria, where some of the world's richest deposits of gold had been discovered in the 1850's, producing a boomtown economy like that of California during the same period. A passenger train had just begun running from Melbourne seventy-one miles west to Ballarat, which had a population of forty thousand. Jefferson performed there at the Theatre Royal. Bendigo, somewhat north of Ballarat, was Victoria's richest gold-mining town. Castlemaine, which had about thirty thousand miners, was the central market place for central Victoria's gold fields.[258]

Jefferson reappeared twice in Melbourne between December 1862 and June 1863. In Melbourne, perhaps because it was so distant from any theatrical center, Joe experimented with expanding his repertoire. He wanted to find a new play or at least a part he had not performed in a number of years; he tried five different roles, one after another, but none of them attracted an audience sufficiently to warrant development. While he worked on new or seldom-revived roles, Jefferson periodically reverted to Newman Noggs and Asa Trenchard, particularly on Saturday nights when audiences filled the theatre. By June 15 another comedian was headlining at the Royal Haymarket, and Jefferson's Asa Trenchard, Solon Shingle, Tobias Shortcut, and Rip Van Winkle were getting second billing. His repertoire was wearing thin, and consequently his popularity in Melbourne was waning. He received a complimentary benefit, on June 25, closed on June 26, and left for Adelaide.[259]

At Adelaide's Victoria Theatre, Jefferson performed all his major roles, receiving particular notice for Salem Scudder in *The Octoroon*. He then returned to Sydney, opening at the Prince of Wales Opera House on September 12, playing his repertoire to audiences that ranged from the governor to "swarms of bedouins of the streets" who "tramped and raced about all over the seats" and "planted themselves . . . in front of the footlights, . . . shutting out the view of the stage from at least half of the rest of the pit."[260]

In the fall of 1863 Jefferson and Charley took a month's vacation. On October 28, 1863, they left for Melbourne, arriving there three days later, and then went north to Daylesford in the mining area; after a performance Jefferson visited a Chinese theatre. He continued into the interior of Australia and stayed for three weeks at a 3,500-square-mile ranch. Sending his son back to Melbourne to study at the Scotch college, he began a trek toward the Murray River, which runs north of Bendigo and Melbourne from the Great Dividing Range in northeast Victoria to Encounter Bay in South Australia. He camped at the river for a fortnight and witnessed an aboriginal dance. It is at this point in his autobiography that Jefferson embarks upon a ten-page story—the longest in the entire book. It involves meeting a former alcoholic living as a recluse in the blue-gum forest and how Jefferson, in accidentally putting temptation in the man's way, actually enables him to confirm his commitment to abstinence and thus return to human society. By 1888, when he was writing,

Joe was celebrated and simultaneously criticized for playing an unreformed drunkard. In this elaborate tale he reminded his audience that liquor is part of life and that alcoholism is not caused by drinking but rather by the abuse of it. He was justifying the performance that made him one of the richest actors in America.[261]

Jefferson was engaged to perform at the Princess Theatre in Dunedin, New Zealand, by mid-November 1863, and "daily expected to arrive," but the trip was postponed. Instead he played eleven roles during a ten-day engagement at the Lyceum Theatre in Bendigo. It must have seemed like touring the Midwest as a teenager. Returning to Melbourne, he immediately gave a few performances under James Symons' management starting November 23, 1863. Then, possibly ill from the weak lungs that had plagued him since adolescence, he settled down in a home called Warren Cottage, from which Charley wrote to his sister Tiddie.[262] Charley's spelling, capitalization, and punctuation at the age of thirteen imply a level of education much closer to his father's than to the kind of training the younger children in the family received.

> Warren Cottage
> Decb. 23rd 1863
> *My dear Sister*
>   I just wright you a few lines to tell you how Papa and I where pleased with your letter Dear maggie you don't know how we want to get back to see the family I suppose Tommy is as wiled as ever we haver a grait many curious things to show you when we get back papa is liked by every body in the colonys. We want your lines as quick as possible.
> I remain you
> aff brother
> *C. Jefferson*[263]

In January 1864 Jefferson took a steamer from Melbourne to New Zealand and performed *Our American Cousin* in Dunedin late that month. While there, he met an Englishman named Benjamin Farjeon. Farjeon, a member of a London Jewish family, had emigrated to Australia in 1854 and worked as manager, sub-editor, contributor, and compositor for the *Otago Daily Times*, the first daily newspaper in New Zealand. The two men were contemporaries, Jefferson thirty-five and Farjeon twenty-six. Jefferson opened an oval green-velvet case, showed Farjeon a miniature painting of the golden-haired eleven-year-old daughter whom he had arranged to have educated at the Convent of the Sacred Heart in America, and said: "And this is Tid." The event is recorded by his granddaughter, because thirteen years later Farjeon married Margaret Jefferson.[264]

After a successful engagement in New Zealand, Jefferson returned to Australia via Melbourne and left with Charley for Hobart Town, the capital of Tasmania, on February 6, 1864. He arrived on February 15, but Hobart Town lacked a professional company, and it took time to paint the scenery for *Rip* and construct the special effects for Boucicault's *Octoroon*. Consequently, on February 17 Jefferson began giving performances at the Theatre Royal in nearby Launceston, probably much the way his grandfather had toured rural Pennsylvania in the 1830's. His first night in Hobart Town itself was not advertised until February 20, and he did not open there until February 29.[265]

In his autobiography Jefferson contends that he gave Tom Taylor's *The Ticket-of-Leave Man* its first performance in Hobart Town to an audience that included at least one hundred ticket-of-leave men (ex-convicts) in the pit. As he remembered it, the crowd was furious opening night, believing that an American was going to make fun of them, but *The Ticket-of-Leave Man* is a melodrama in which an innocent man, Bob Brierly, has his reputation restored. When Jefferson's character won the day, the crowd, according to Charles Burke, "went wild. Instead of throwing chairs and benches . . . , it was hats and coins that fell upon the stage with the flowers. That play went on . . . until father was worn out, and it was the greatest money-maker we had. Instead of mobbing the yankee mountebank, as he was called before the play . . . , the entire town was ready to dance attendance upon father.[266]

The wild-west story the Jeffersons remembered was, in reality, far less adventurous. They arrived in Hobart Town as part of a troupe organized in Melbourne, and Jefferson's popularity resulted as much from the novelty of professional actors in a town accustomed to amateurs and one-person shows as it was to his ability. He performed *The Ticket-of-Leave Man* only twice in Hobart Town, and its premiere was his benefit and next-to-last performance, attended by the governor of the state and his wife. Jefferson would never have risked the profits of a benefit night on a controversial play.

The big hit of what was termed "a short summer season" was not

The Ticket-of-Leave Man but *The Octoroon*, admired as much for its spectacular scenic effects as for Boucicault's writing or Jefferson's Salem Scudder. In all Jefferson performed fifteen roles in Hobart Town in a season that lasted until April 5. The longer he stayed, the more his reputation grew. On opening night the pit and boxes of the Theatre Royal were crowded, but the dress circle was only moderately filled. The performance, however, was deeply appreciated by a theatre-starved audience that called him out before the curtain after the first and last acts of *Rip*. But Hobart Town's limited population made it difficult to sustain any production for a long time. The local critic, for instance, thought it amazing that *Rip* could be performed for three nights running, and the theatre was never packed until the last night of *The Octoroon*. Scheduled to close on March 23, the company stayed on to catch the business generated by the local horse races on Easter Monday.[267]

Jefferson returned to Adelaide and reopened *Rip* at the Victoria Theatre on July 11, 1864. He stayed until August 11 and went on to Melbourne and finally Sydney, where on September 2, he headed a "Grand Dramatic Festival" at the Prince of Wales Theatre. On October 10 he took a farewell benefit "prior to his departure for London" and sailed back to Melbourne for a thirty-seven-night "farewell engagement."[268]

Jefferson lingered in Australia and finally left in April 1865, bound for South America on his way to England. The fifty-seven-day voyage ended at Callao, six miles from Lima, Peru. Upon landing, Jefferson learned that the Civil War was over. The moment is recreated in his son's reminiscence in 1906:

> When we left Australia, the war was still going on, and we were anxious to hear the news. A row boat with caulkers came out to meet our sailing ship, and upon it was a man who recognized my father. The instant he saw father, he yelled out:
>
> "Well I'm damned that aint Joe Jefferson. Why Joe, where in the h—— did you come from?"
>
> Father asked him for the war news, but the man wanted to know where father had been, and it was some time before he condescended to talk. Then he said:
>
> "The war's over. Richmond has fallen, and Lee has surrendered."

I was standing close beside my father, and I heard him heave a heavy sigh as though he were disappointed.

"And Lincoln has been assassinated," added the man in the boat.

"That's a great pity," said father.

"Wilkes Booth shot him in the Ford theater, in Washington," yelled the man.

Father tottered, and I believe he would have fallen had not the captain and I caught him. He was as white as a sheet, and for a minute trembled like an aspen. He and Wilkes Booth had been friends. They had played together, and the bond of friendship was a strong one. Presently father recovered and, turning to me, remarked:

"My God, that's awful. What could Booth have meant? He must have been crazy. Son, take me to my room."

I can't recall the time I ever saw father so moved as that information moved him. He was depressed for days, and for days he was as taciturn as I ever saw him. He appeared unable to drive that feeling of depression away. In fact, he never succeeded until after we reached London.[269]

Jefferson's version of the above story in his *Autobiography* is interesting in its departure from his son's recollection:

We had several passengers, two of whom enlivened the trip with their political arguments. One was from South Carolina, the other from Massachusetts, and their disputes were . . . violent. I was a . . . mediator between these hostile parties and helped to settle . . . their quarrels. At times they were the best of friends and really liked each other very much. . . . On the fifty-seventh day, we dropped anchor in the bay of Callao, six miles from the beautiful city of Lima. . . . The two belligerents were . . . restless, . . . desiring some bulletins of the war. Presently . . . a boat darted . . . out of the mist. . . . In the stern there sat . . . a man . . . [who] caught sign of my face, "Joe Jefferson, by thunder!"

"My friend," said I, "as you seem to recognize me, perhaps you will . . . give us some news of the war." He answered this question by asking me how long it was since he saw me act in New York with Laura Keene. I told him about six years but that

I would be . . . obliged if he would give me the . . . news concerning Richmond."

"Where's old Ned Sothern now?" said he to me. I was between the two belligerents, who were both writhing . . . at the . . . delay of my new-found acquaintance. I told him that Mr. Sothern was in England but that I . . . could not answer . . . more questions until he told me . . . about the war.

"Is he actin' old *Dundreary* now before the Britishers?" said he. Finding I could get no satisfaction from him, I turned to the captain and said: "You had better interrogate this man yourself. . . . "

Here the captain broke in, hailing him with, "My friend, I am the captain of this ship and would like to get a paper from you concerning the war, as you don't seem . . . communicative yourself."

"Will your ship want calkin', Captain, before she loads?" said the impenetrable calker—for that . . . was his profession.

"You don't calk my ship . . . until you answer my question," said the captain.

The man . . . became thoughtful, and, . . . turning over in his mind that he might lose a job . . . , said, "Oh, the war—that's all over; the South caved in, and Richmond is took."

The crestfallen gentleman from South Carolina sank upon a stool . . . , and the lively gentleman from Massachusetts danced a hornpipe over him, whistling "The Star-Spangled Banner."[270]

Charles Burke Jefferson's account of his father's reception of the news of the war's end and Lincoln's assassination is tragic. It was published a year after Jefferson's death, and his son was remembering an event that occurred when he was fourteen—one of the most important events of American history. He was not likely to have forgotten what happened, and his account implied that his father was a Southern sympathizer.

It also connects him with John Wilkes Booth, a connection Jefferson did not want made. Although there is no evidence that the two men ever performed together, Jefferson knew John Wilkes Booth well. At one point he even volunteered to help him find a position in a stock company. He told his son Charles that the "art of Wilkes Booth was like a divine flash, an inspiration. . . ." Charles, who was still a boy when he knew Wilkes Booth, remembered him as "a charming fellow off the stage. A man of wit and magnetic manner, he could hold a group by the very force of his eloquence and personal charm." The Booths and Jeffersons were family friends. Jefferson's granddaughter, Eleanor Farjeon, wrote that her mother would show her a picture in a family album of "an Edgar-Allan-Poe-like man in a cape— That's John Wilkes Booth, Edwin's brother. He was fascinating."

Margaret and her husband, B. L. Farjeon, eventually became close friends of John Wilkes's and Edwin's sister, Asia Booth Clarke, and of her husband, John Sleeper Clarke, whom she had married in 1861. When Asia lay dying in Bournemouth, England, she told Farjeon about a manuscript she had written concerning John Wilkes Booth. The manuscript was apparently based on the text of a "squat black book with JWB stamped on its leather cover. "After her death on May 23, 1888, Asia's daughter and son-in-law, Dollie and Rhys Morgan, sent Farjeon Asia's handwritten memoir. He in turn had the manuscript typed, and in mid-July 1901 sent it to William Winter Jefferson, Joe's youngest son, who presented it to his father. Farjeon's typescript manuscript was an abridged version of what Asia had written, omitting many of her negative comments about her husband, who was one of Jefferson's and Edwin Booth's best friends. Farjeon wanted to publish this version and asked Jefferson for his assistance. But even in 1901, thirty-six years after the assassination, Jefferson "suggested" that he would prefer not to be involved; he wanted no public connection between himself and John Wilkes Booth.[271]

When he was writing his autobiography, thirteen years earlier, Jefferson knew he had to say something about the Civil War. But he omitted all mention of Booth's assassination of the president, and he converted the Callao incident into a comic routine in which he is completely neutral and, in fact, a mediator between North and South. Once again, he was covering his tracks. In 1888, twenty-three years after the war's end, Jefferson was not going to allow himself to be associated with the man who had shot Lincoln. It was bad for business. The neutrality that his *Autobiography* demonstrates toward the Civil War was part of Jefferson's public "neutrality," his avoidance of all controversial issues. When he returned to America in 1866, Jefferson became an instant favorite in both parts of the country without any taint of partisanship. Audiences could love *Rip Van Winkle* without worrying about which side its creator had favored. Jefferson never allowed his name to become associated with political causes that might hurt his box-office receipts.

From Peru, Jefferson went to England. In his *Autobiography* he claimed that he wound up there as an accidental result of missing a boat in South America. His son Charles Burke echoed this story, adding the possibility of death had not Jefferson been lucky.

> Father was getting homesick [in 1865]. His health had mended, and he was practically a well man again. The oceans weren't then dotted with steamers. . . . From South America, we came to Jamaica to catch the Evening Star, a vessel for New York but arrived in port after that vessel had left. We were booked for passage on it. Two days out, the Evening Star went down with every soul on board. That was a narrow escape for us. Missing the Evening Star gave the American people the greatest Rip Van Winkle on earth. . . . We found a vessel going to Southampton, and rather than wait for a vessel to . . . America, father decided to go to England, pass a few days in London and then cross the Atlantic for home.[272]

Charles Burke's recollection was incorrect. Australian newspapers show that Jefferson had no intention of returning immediately to the United States. The contention that he did, in his autobiography, served two purposes. First, it gave Jefferson yet one more excuse for missing the Civil War. In this section of the autobiography he was again at great lengths to disguise the evasion. For a public figure to have avoided the primary event of nineteenth-century America would have set poorly with an audience Jefferson was always careful not to offend. Second, it made his new version of *Rip* accidental and thus more charming and dramatic to his reading public. If he had not missed the boat, if he had not gone to England, if he had not met Dion Boucicault, *Rip* would not have flowered into the artistic triumph and moneymaker of his life. As it were, by accident, Jefferson went to meet his destiny.

8

JEFFERSON AS RIP
1865–1867

In early August, Jefferson sailed for Panama, crossed the Isthmus with his son, and took an English mail steamer from Colon to Liverpool. In mid-September 1865 he arrived in London where his boyhood idol John E. Owens was in the middle of an unsuccessful engagement. Feeling "disgusted," Owens asked Jefferson to fill out his time, but Jefferson needed and wanted a new role for his English debut. He approached Dion Boucicault, who had written *The Octoroon* and *Dot,* with a proposal to rewrite *Rip Van Winkle,* which Jefferson considered "a great part in an indifferent play."[273]

Boucicault saw little hope in the material and told Jefferson: "Joe . . . this old sot is not a pleasant figure. He lacks romance. I dare say you made a fine sketch of the old beast, but there is no interest in him. He may be picturesque, but he is not dramatic. I would prefer to start him . . . as a young scamp—thoughtless, gay, just such a curly-headed, good-humored fellow as all the village girls would love and the children and dogs would run after. Jefferson threw up his hands in despair. It was totally opposed to his artistic preconception." Boucicault insisted, and Jefferson gave in. Boucicault had the upper hand; he was far more important in London than Jefferson, and Joe may have remembered the sound advice he had given about Caleb Plummer. Three or four weeks after the London production opened, Jefferson conceded to Boucicault: "You were right about making Rip a young man. Now I could not conceive and play him in any other shape."[274]

Boucicault rewrote *Rip* for what Jefferson terms "a consideration agreed upon between us." In a lawsuit against the managers of Chicago's Crosby's Opera House in 1870, Jefferson contended that the "consideration" was $15,000, but the amount was probably exaggerated for legal purposes. In 1865, $15,000 would have been an enormous speculation. And Boucicault did not, at the time he was writing, think that the play would be a hit. It is unlikely that he would have asked, or that Jefferson would have given, that much. Boucicault was not proud of the finished work. He told Jefferson: "It is a poor thing, Joe," to which Jefferson responded: "Well, it is good enough for me. Will you accept a royalty or cash?" Boucicault replied: "Cash for me, for it will not go. They'll never stand for a man sleeping twenty years!"[275]

How great was Boucicault's contribution? When published for the first time in 1895, *Rip*'s title page bore the inscription "as played by Joseph Jefferson." In his introduction to the edition, Jefferson repeated the story told in his *Autobiography* and also referred to earlier versions by Yates, Hackett, and Charles Burke. Boucicault's name was not mentioned. But, according to Francis Wilson, Jefferson gave Boucicault substantial credit for the play's success in private conversation.

> "Much the best of the play," I [Wilson] advanced,—"weird, unspeaking gnomes, the recognition scene between Rip and Meenie—had all been added by Jefferson."
>
> "And Boucicault," he [Jefferson] added. "Don't forget Boucicault. The children at the end of the first act" (as it was then, but it has since been made into two acts) "and the Rip and Meenie scene are his, and mighty fine they are."
>
> "As developed and played by Jefferson," I ventured.
>
> "Yes I must be frank," he answered. "I added to it, enlarged upon it," he acknowledged modestly. "I am not a fool about such things. Ideas come, and I seize and apply them, but that idea and that outline were Boucicault's."
>
> "And keeping the spirit crew of Hendrick Hudson silent and giving them an act to themselves, in which Rip so cleverly supplies them with words—that was not Boucicault, was it?" I asked.
>
> "No, no, no, no, no, no, no," he said sweetly; "that was Jefferson, and he is very, very proud of it."

Figure 12. Jefferson as the young Rip Van Winkle.
Courtesy of the Performing Arts Research Center,
New York Public Library.

"When he [Boucicault] had finished writing the recognition scene between Rip and Meenie," Jefferson said, "he read it to me, and pausing, asked me if I liked it. I assured him of my delight."

"Do you recognize it?" he said.

"Why no—what do you mean?" I asked.

"Why, it is the Lear and Cordelia scene reversed. In *King Lear* it is Cordelia who longs for recognition; here it is Rip—the man—who seeks to be known."[276]

While Boucicault worked, Jefferson "made an engagement" with Benjamin Webster to act the part at the New Theatre Royal, Adelphi, not for a salary but for a share of the nightly gross receipts after seventy pounds had been deducted for expenses. It was a risky proposition. Jefferson was staking his own cut of the profits against the possibility that the play might flop. But he must have anticipated success, because he sent for his three children to join him in London and set up housekeeping at 5 Hanover Street, Hanover Square. He also had the play copyrighted in the Southern District of New York on August 26, 1865. Jefferson knew he had a hit.[277]

The production was almost canceled when Boucicault and Webster got into a dispute, but *Rip Van Winkle or The Sleep of Twenty Years* opened on September 4, 1865. Jefferson's name was not printed in large letters on advertisements or the program. It was Boucicault's reputation that drew the crowd. On the first night, he arrived in Jefferson's dressing room and said: "I'm sorry for you, Joe. . . . The piece won't go here; but I hope you'll get through." The first-night house proved him wrong. The cast was given five or six curtain calls after the first act. Mrs. Billington, who played Gretchen, told Jefferson: "It will run a hundred nights," to which Jefferson replied: "I'll wager you a new silk dress to a new silk hat that it doesn't." Mrs. Billington won.[278] Charles Burke Jefferson remembered: "Father melted . . . into that character, and before the play was half through, people . . . were asking: 'Who is this man? Where's he from? How does it happen he has been hidden out so long?' After that it was Joe Jefferson's Rip Van Winkle, not Boucicault's."

Opening night reviews were ecstatic. The London *Times* referred to Jefferson as "one of the most original and . . . finished actors ever seen upon any stage." The review, however, also pointed out the play's and Jefferson's inconsistencies.

In Mr. Jefferson's hands, the character of Rip van Winkle becomes the vehicle for a . . . refined psychological exhibition. In the first act, he appears as a . . . hearty man, aged about thirty years [Jefferson was actually thirty-six at the time], with a . . . countenance rendered . . . picturesque . . . by . . . dishevelled hair and tattered garments. . . . In the short second act, which is occupied by the meeting of Rip Van Winkle with . . . Hudson and his spectral crew, there is no further development of character;

but when the Dutchman wakes in the third act, after a sleep of twenty years, the portraiture progresses. He is now an aged man, with white flowing hair and beard, who might be seventy or eighty years of age, and although the change from the Rip of the first act is greater than could possibly have been effected by the mere lapse of four lustra; we would rather attribute . . . the transformation to the effect of Hudson's infernal beverage than suggest a correction of the . . . exaggeration. A man of fifty would not be old enough to present that contrast of senility with vigour. . . . On the other hand, a lapse of more than twenty years would render the other personages too old for the purposes of the story. Let us accept, then an age-bestowing power in the Hudsonian still, just as we tolerate the . . . dialect which Rip talks among persons supposed to be of the same country and habits with himself. Common sense teaches us that all should talk alike, but if Mr. Jefferson talked mere English, he would drop one of the . . . peculiarities of his part, and if all the other personages indulged in . . . dialect, the infliction would be awful.

Jefferson, of course, used the accent to establish Rip as an eccentric comic-dialect role and to set himself up as the star of the production. He also knew that the heart-rending pathos of an old man who awakes in a strange world would never work if Rip had merely slept into middle age. The *Observer* praised Boucicault's version for "retaining . . . the leading characteristics of the legend, with so much . . . added as makes it an interesting, if not an altogether well-constructed drama. [Boucicault has taken] great pains with those scenes in which the hero appeared and . . . little trouble with the others."

The *Pall Mall Gazette* critic called Jefferson "an actor whose range may possibly be limited, but whose execution within that range surpasses anything to be seen on our stage." The *Standard*'s critic wrote: "The drunken sot—good natured at heart, and fond of everything but his wife, whose ill-temper . . . makes him a vagabond —was sustained with skill throughout the first act, . . . while the semblance of old age, in the last act, was even more striking and had only one fault—that it was too real."

The only negative comments came from Henry Morley in the *Examiner* who disparaged the play for its melodramatic scenes, its comic set-pieces, and its third act, in which Rip's repentant wife is returned to him along with all of his land. At the same time, Morley had nothing but praise for Jefferson as an actor, particularly in the third act when "retaining his old Dutch-English with a somewhat shriller pipe of age, . . . he quietly makes the most of every opportunity of representing the old man's bewilderment." Morley's review reads:

> Mr. Jefferson's Rip Van Winkle is . . . a play that seeks dramatic effect by tasteless variations from the tale . . . Irving told. . . . The harmless school master, Derrick Van Bummel, is selected for the villain's part. The first act is brought to a melodramatic close by Rip's wife driving her husband from her hearth into a thunderstorm. He goes out snivelling. She, of course, cries in vain to him to return, and as the curtain descends, plumps on the ground in [a]. . . melodramatic swoon.

> In the second act . . . the story is closely followed, except in the melodramatic change that substitutes for Rip's attendance on the company, . . . a formal attendance of the company upon him . . . and the conventional "Ha! ha! ha! ha!" when he drinks. The original story made them . . . mute. . . .

> In the third act . . . surely there can be no actor . . . who would not rather have his Rip left on a bench astonishing the gossips by the door of Doolittle's hotel, than presented with the claptrap effects of a wife who has been borrowed and improved during his absence, and a . . . collection of town lots to make him happy ever after.

> In the scene with his wife in the cottage . . . it is impossible to cover the defect of bad invention by the dramatist. A long story about shooting at a rabbit and not hitting it is . . . tedious fun, and it is but a coarse stage-effect to make Rip drink out of a spirit-flask over his wife's back, while she is embracing him, because he has again "swored off" his evil habit.[279]

What made *Rip Van Winkle* hold the stage for the next forty years was not Boucicault's plot and dialogue or even Washington Irving's story. It was Jefferson's performance, particularly what audiences of the day perceived as his realism on stage. Of the opening production, The *Standard*'s critic wrote: "There is no. . . exaggeration in anything he does or says, and it was . . . astonishing to observe the effect he produced on an audience who are accustomed to . . . caricature."

Realism on stage is a convention in which the audience participates, by a willing suspension of disbelief, induced by specific stage techniques. Although the text of *Rip Van Winkle* is not realistic, Jefferson brought to the script acting abilities that made the plot plausible, because his character was believable. The first of these techniques was the level of physical detail he developed in the role over a forty-year period. A silent film of the play's second act, made in 1896, demonstrates this in Jefferson's treatment of the barrel of magic brew given to Rip by the dwarf he encounters in the mountains. The dwarf indicates, in pantomime, that he wants Rip to help him carry the heavy barrel. Rip picks it up, staggers under the weight, and then later shifts the barrel on his shoulder to retain his balance as he moves uphill and down. It was Jefferson's moment-by-moment examination of the barrel's weight under different physical conditions that conveyed the realism of the character's behavior and consequently made a supernatural situation seem believable. A Chicago reviewer wrote that "Mr. Jefferson charms the audience by his quiet and conversational style of acting. . . . Every motion, every gesture, the nervous twitching of the hand, the weakness of the knees, the almost tottering walk [portrays the] feeling of old age."[280]

A second technique to produce the illusion of realism was Jefferson's use of alterations in movement patterns. In the first act Rip talks to Derrick Von Beekman musing about what he might do if Gretchen, his shrewish wife, were in a capsized boat:

"But surely, Rip," says Derrick, "you would not see your wife drown? You would rescue her."

Rip rocks back and forth on the table, his hands clasped over one of his knees, and a smile half reflective and half amused on his face.

"You mean I would yump in and pull Gretch out? Would I? Humpf!" (still rocking. After a moment's pause and with a sudden thought:) "Oh, den? (Stops rocking.) "Yes I believe I would den. And it would be more my duty now."[281]

The audience understood Rip's thinking through Jefferson's body language. When Rip comforts Gretchen in the second scene, her head is down on the table. Putting his arms around her shoulders, he

rocks back and forth as he sits on the table, gently patting her on the shoulder and keeping time to his motion.

"Oh if you would only treat me kindly!" sobs Gretchen.

Figure 13. Jefferson as the elderly Rip Van Winkle.
Courtesy of the Performing Arts Research Center,
New York Public Library.

"Well I'm going to treat you kindly," returns Rip, still patting Gretchen at regular intervals as he rocks.

"It would add ten years to my life," says Gretchen. Rip's
hand is up, about to descend in its regular stroke on her back,
but it stops short. It is the announcement of Gretchen that
kindness will add ten years to her life that stops it . . . no need of
a word from Rip to indicate that he considers the inducement
questionable.[282]

Jefferson's ability to make his audience understand what Rip was
thinking even when he did not speak produced the illusion of psychological depth, although the actual moment may have been only a
comic "hit." In addition, his attention to external physical realism led
him to what was one of the most daring decisions any nineteenth-
century actor could make—turning his back to the audience, allowing
them to understand his emotion through body movement as opposed
to facial expression—a device that would not come into popular use
until the modern innovations of Konstantin Stanislavski and Anton
Chekov. Jefferson found the move accidentally by moving his chair
downstage one day at rehearsal to look at the action. When warned by
an older member of the cast never to do so "dangerous" a thing on
stage, he became determined to introduce it into the action.[283] He
used it in the second scene when Gretchen orders Rip out of the
house, and he combined it with an alteration in physical movement in
the play's opening act, when the villain, Derrick Von Beekman, leaves
Rip with a purse of money. Jefferson sat with his back to the audience
tossing the purse uneasily in his hands.

> [He] looks . . . at the purse and then at the retreating form of
> the man who has pretended to befriend him. His back is to us,
> but we know that he is perplexed and is . . . considering the
> reasons for this unexpected kindness on the part of Derrick.
> Then come the words, "I don't know about dot," the uneasy
> tossing of the purse again, and the exclamation, "It don't chink
> like good money, any way."

Jefferson also used costume props to delineate internal states.
Suspicious of the document that Derrick has read to him only in part,
Rip, who is illiterate, cons the young boy, Hendrick, into reading the
paper to him:

He has placed his hands over his head, leaning back in the attitude of listening, and as he tells Hendrick to read on, lifts his limp hat from his head, and holds it in his fingers. Hendrick proceeds:

"Do bargain, sell, and convey all my houses, lands, and property whereof I hold possession."

Then the hat drops—a perfect expression of sudden surprise.[284]

Jefferson's use of Rip's hat is also apparent in the silent film version of Act II. Collapsing elaborately after he drinks the magic brew, Jefferson tilts his head back and puts his hand to his brow. Instantly his hat falls off, dramatizing Rip's mental collapse. A frame-by-frame examination of the moment reveals that surreptitiously Jefferson tips the hat backward off his head when his hand goes to his brow. When the film is run at normal speed, the sleight of hand is imperceptible— a technique perfected over forty years of performing the role.[285]

Above all, Jefferson's realism was produced by not playing directly to the audience and by avoiding the obvious choices through which actors of the period made "points." The concept of "scoring a point" or "scoring a hit" referred to the nineteenth-century actor's habit of punctuating his or her performance with emotionally charged dramatic moments or comic effects so that the overall reality of a performance was sacrificed to a series of individual line readings or bits of stage business for which the audience could then applaud. Jefferson subordinated individual moments to a consistent level of truthfulness that struck contemporary audiences as realistic. Of course such realism is always relative to the standard performances with which it is implicitly being contrasted, and Jefferson's acting must be seen in light of the prevailing practices, particularly among comedians of his day. A reviewer for the *Chicago Tribune* wrote:

The stereotyped stage-walk—a sort of comico-heroic strut which has been pressed into service for all sorts of characters . . . the stage gestures . . . the rolling of the eyes . . . the mouthing of phrases in a set manner . . . the hackneyed entrances and exits; the rant and the making of points are . . . foreign to Mr. Jefferson. . . . He completely identifies himself with the character. . . . Mr. Jefferson never talks above the ordinary conversational tone of voice, uses only a few gestures and those of the simplest description . . . attempts no tricks of facial expression.[286]

The audio recording of Jefferson's performance supports his reputation for quiet realism.[287] Although the rising inflections of his "Dutch" accent are monotonous, the tone seems, to the modern listener, so casual, so conversational as to be emotionally inadequate, particularly in the recognition scene with Meenie. The lifelike quality of this delivery amazed his contemporaries. Individual lines, individual dramatic and comic moments certainly became his trademarks, but at his best Jefferson was able to subsume these moments into an artistic whole so that they did not jump out at an audience, but seemed to proceed naturally from the dramatic situation of the play. L. Clarke Davis noted:

> He leans lightly against a table, his disengaged hand holding his gun. The kindly, simple, *insouciant* face, ruddy, smiling, lighted by the tender, humorous blue eyes, which look down upon his dress, elaborately copied bit by bit from the etchings of Darley. . . . The impersonation is full of what are technically known as *points*, but the genius of Mr. Jefferson divests them of all "staginess." . . . From the rising of the curtain . . . until its fall . . . , nothing is forced, sensational or unseemly.

As Derrick Von Beekman prepares to get Rip to sign a paper that will swindle Rip out of his remaining property, he reflects on the future:

> "Ah where will we be then?" [twenty years from now] . . .
> "I don't know about myself," responds Rip, as if speaking to himself,—never to the audience; "but I can guess pretty well where you'll be about dot time."

The obvious way to play such a punch line was to look at the spectators as if letting them in on the joke, but Jefferson never played it that way. By delivering the line as an internal aside or verbalized subtext, he allowed his audience to get the joke themselves.

Throughout Jefferson's career, critics particularly cited the realism of Rip's banishment by his wife:

> He is sitting upon a chair partially turned from the audience. . . . His wife orders him to leave her house. . . . He pays little heed to it. She repeats the order in a louder tone of voice, but still he pays no heed to it. He has stretched out his arm and

raised his head as if to speak, when she again issues her order. . . .
He sits as if that instant petrified. . . . He rises quietly . . . stoops
and kisses the little one and . . . passes from the doorstep to the
outer darkness.[288]

Despite his seeming avoidance of points, Jefferson was well aware
of what did and did not work on stage and of the ways in which
actors could milk applause from audiences at important moments in
the show—in other words, the way in which they could score "hits."
During the 1869 Washington run the part of the young sailor,
Heinrich, was performed by the twenty-three-year-old actor James
O'Neill, who would later find his own perpetual starring vehicle in
The Count of Monte Cristo and father Eugene O'Neill. On opening
night, O'Neill stopped the show six times. At the close, Jefferson
sent for him. O'Neill arrived, panic-stricken, thinking he was about
to be criticized. Jefferson then proceeded to instruct the young actor
in methods of getting audiences to interrupt the play with applause,
a custom so standard in the period that actors expected and even
worked for it. The next night O'Neill got seven rounds, and Jefferson's comment was "Better, my boy, better." Finally O'Neill got
eight rounds, and Jefferson ended the engagement by praising the
young man's acting.[289]

Jefferson spent the rest of his life performing and perfecting his
characterization and Boucicault's version of the play. Over the next
forty years he cut about twenty minutes from the performance and
inserted new bits of business. In 1896, for instance, after thirty-one
years in the role, he discovered a new way of performing a specific
piece of business in the second scene through an accident recorded
by Mary Shaw, his Gretchen that season.

> In the third [scene], *Rip* is attempting to excuse himself for
> being drunk, and makes a promise to *Gretchen* that he will never
> drink again. . . . In her joy at his . . . reformation . . . , [she] goes
> from the scene to bring on the children. Returning, she finds
> *Rip* drinking out of the bottle and chuckling at his success in
> being able . . . to fool her. Berating him, she snatches the bottle
> away and thrusts it into a pocket which she wears on the outside
> of her dress. . . . When, a short time after, he is . . . cajoling her,
> *Rip* . . . feel[s] about for the bottle and tak[es] it out of its
> hiding-place without her knowledge. To my horror . . . I found

I had forgotten to put on the pocket. What in the name of heaven should I do with the flask! As I had been washing, the costume I wore had the outer skirt turned up and pinned behind; but as it was not pinned in front, to put the bottle in there meant to run the risk of its slipping out.

My blood . . . ran cold; but I dropped the bottle into the turned-up skirt and depended upon being able to warn Mr. Jefferson that it was there. But, alas! he was deaf and occupied with his part. . . . All the time Rip, while holding *Gretchen's* attention with his story, is feeling about with his hand for the bottle, and Gretchen is getting angrier and angrier at his not coming to the point. That evening it was *real* business. The pocket was not there. As Mr. Jefferson hunted for it, there was a touch of realism that . . . was never in his performance afterward. Meanwhile I was reiterating . . . loudly . . . : "it is in my dress."

"Where in your dress?" he asked presently.

"In the turned up part" I answered. He dived into the turned up part, produced the bottle and the scene went on. . . . At last the scene was over, and . . . Mr. Jefferson looked at me a moment and said: "What a splendid idea! You know, I have always had a feeling that it was a mistake to have that pocket hanging on there. A woman washing wouldn't have it, you know. Yet there didn't seem to be anything to do with the bottle but that. You have accidentally hit upon a ripping scheme. That would be the natural thing to do with a bottle, wouldn't it? Just sew up your dress so that the bottle can't fall out. You have added a piece of splendid business to the scene. I am very much obliged to you."[290]

Innovations, however, that detracted from the audience's sympathy for Rip were not tolerated. When Shaw, who was a proponent of the newer naturalistic school of acting, made Gretchen a sympathetic believable character, Jefferson insisted on a more caricatured approach so that all sympathy would go to him. Shaw later wrote:

[It] came to the place where *Gretchen* turns *Rip* out of the house. . . . I launched into this scene with all the . . . feeling . . . of what that outraged woman would feel and do in those circumstances. I was wholly in sympathy with *Gretchen*. When I cried: "Out you drunkard! Out, you sot! You are a disgrace to your wife and child. Out! I hope I shall never see your face again as long as I live," there was . . . continued applause. . . . It was the first time this had . . . happened in the play.

Mr. Jefferson said nothing to me that evening, but the next day he sent for me, and we had a long talk about the part. . . . "The little details of *Gretchen's* sufferings and all the things which grow out of *Rip's* wrong relationship with society are unimportant compared with the great human study of a lovable ne'er-do-well who has become a living personality to the majority of American readers. . . . Therefore, in playing *Gretchen* you must . . . make her . . . a shrew. What lines have been put in her mouth that would indicate an . . . ability to suffer, you must toss over lightly. Take my word for it, two thirds of the power and charm of this . . . play would be destroyed [by] truthfulness. You must not once . . . , except in the last act, call the attention of the audience to any ordinary rule of conduct. . . . You must play everything with the idea of putting forth this central figure, *Rip Van Winkle*, as more and more lovable, the more and more he outrages the sensibilities, that being the ethical meaning of the play.[291]

In the forty years that Jefferson performed Rip, there grew to be two constant complaints about him and about the play. The first was that he had limited his range as an actor by sticking so constantly to one part. Jefferson would often reply wittily: "It is certainly better to play one part and make it various than to play a hundred parts and make them all alike." The criticism was perhaps unfair. While Jefferson played Rip for the rest of his life, he also continued to work on Mr. Golightly, Dr. Ollapod, Caleb Plummer, Bob Acres, and Dr. Pangloss. As time went on, however, he began to distrust his memory; he was afraid of forgetting his lines onstage and unable to memorize a new role. As his reputation increased to national proportions, he also came to fear the possibility of public failure and to depend on the financial success that *Rip* produced. When he finally turned to Bob Acres in *The Rivals* as a substitute, he returned to a role which he knew as well and had actually been performing longer.

The second criticism was that *Rip* encouraged intemperance, particularly since its hero, having suffered for his drinking, winds up toasting his fellow villagers at the end. An 1869 review in the *Nation* mixes admiration for Jefferson's acting with grave doubts about the play:

Jefferson . . . never rants; he never gives utterance to a stage laugh; his asides are not stage asides. From the moment when he first appears on the stage, with . . . Dutch children rolling and playing and tumbling about him, to the . . . recognition of his child in the last scene, all is as natural as if there were no footlights, no audience, no orchestra, no scenery and no prompter. He seems unaware of the audience's presence. . . .

Considering the excellence of Jefferson's talent, it is . . . surprising to find him acting on such a low level. . . . The play is bad enough, but the corruption of the character is worse. Those who remember . . . the old story cannot be . . . pleased at seeing their Rip Van Winkle transformed into a drunken loafer. . . . The [play's] moral is the advisability of drinking to excess inasmuch as the hero, after a life of . . . dissipation, . . . triumphs over his enemies, retrieves the ruin [his] intemperate habits had . . . induced and, finally, is presented . . . with a glass of clear liquor by his wife, who . . . attributes to his old ways his final success. . . . Can they find nothing better for a man to do who has gone through the tragedy of Rip Van Winkle's life than to call for something to drink? . . . However . . . nothing seems to tickle the audience so much as the drunken part of the play, and nothing so much excites their approbation as the *denouement*.[292]

In 1874 the local critic in Wheeling, West Virginia, wrote:

Whether . . . there is any . . . moral in *Rip Van Winkle*, we have never been able to discover. The sympathy of the audience is . . . with Rip, who would be turned from every respectable door in the city and compelled to seek a lodging in the lock-up, if he were . . . to visit Wheeling to-day.[293]

In the fall of 1878 the *New York Times* wrote:

Rip Van Winkle represents not only beauty, love and sympathy, but also drunkenness, moral degradation and heartlessness. Suffering virtue and wifely devotion are held up . . . to contempt while he, the arrant knave and . . . faithless husband and father, pleads successfully to the dishonest sentiments of a tearful audience. . . . People who love *Rip Van Winkle* unconsciously approve what is . . . detestable in human nature and contrary to good morals.[294]

The criticism of Rip accepting a cup from Gretchen at the end of the play haunted Jefferson throughout the play's history. He answered it in his *Autobiography*:

> Should *Rip* refuse the cup, the drama would become at once a temperance play. . . . The action would have . . . a modern flavor. I should as soon expect to hear Cinderella striking for high wages or a speech on woman's rights from old Mother Hubbard as to listen to a temperance lecture from *Rip Van Winkle*; it would take . . . the poetry and fairy-tale element . . . out of it.[295]

Critical doubts about the play's value never marred Jefferson's financial success. The initial London production ran for 170 nights. The Prince and Princess of Wales came the second week. By late October 1865 the theatre's free list (shareholders entitled to complimentary tickets) was suspended. At Christmas, Jefferson was drawing "still increasing houses," and the management decided to cancel its annual pantomime. So many people wanted to take Jefferson to dinner after the show that he took to having a hansom cab waiting at the stage door. He later told his daughter-in-law Eugenie Paul: "I . . . got in and put up the window and went home, no matter who was out after me." By late February 1866, newspaper advertisements were numbering each performance as if compiling batting statistics. The production closed on March 24, 1866, with Jefferson's benefit followed by a supper on stage attended by William Makepeace Thackeray, Charles Dickens, and Wilkie Collins. After the London engagement, Jefferson performed the play in Manchester and Liverpool. On July 30 he embarked on the clipper *Sunrise* for New York, arriving on August 13, 1866.[296]

Jefferson opened Boucicault's version of *Rip Van Winkle* at New York's Olympic Theatre on September 3, 1866. It was his first New York performance in five years, and his London success had preceded him. The house was packed, particularly with theatre people. Jefferson's old employers, John T. Ford, Frank Chanfrau, Henry Jarrett, and John Brougham, were there, as well as his future theatrical partner, Billy Florence. When Jefferson made his first entrance, the applause that filled the hall was, in the words of the *New York Clipper*, like "an electric shock." During the evening he was given several curtain calls, and at the end he made a speech thanking the audience.

Local reviewers had almost nothing but praise for the play, the production, and the actor.[297]

Jefferson's acting and the realism of the production's "new and elaborate scenery," costumes, and props made American audiences believe in a period of nostalgic rusticity.

> With Mr. Jefferson's acting . . . , we are transported into the past, and made to see . . . the old-fashioned Dutch civilization as it crept up the borders of the Hudson—the quaint and quiet village; the stout Hollanders, with their pipes and schnapps; the loves and troubles of an elder generation. It is a calmer life than ours; yet the same elements compose it.

In 1874 the *New York Times* wrote of the play: "It has the flavor of a remote period, and, in truth, is a product of a time when in this new land, . . . the world may be said to have been fresh and golden." The appeal to nostalgia, to America in its most innocent period, remained part of *Rip*'s appeal through the forty-year period Jefferson performed it. As late as 1896, a reviewer, in an apostrophe to the leading character, wrote:

> Come with your shiftless . . . ways and teach the work-ridden citizens of a working city to sympathize . . . with your . . . exemption from the . . . curse which bears . . . heavily in these later days . . . the avarice that drains men's blood of . . . kindliness and the ambition that tramples down . . . affections.[298]

Jefferson's Rip linked post–Civil War America to

> a rural world, a land of farms, hamlets and vast wilderness areas, of handscraftsmen, homesteaders, small merchants, country lawyers, clergymen and landed gentry. Its pace was set by the jog trot of a horse, the lurch of a two-wheeled ox car, the draft of a canal boat; its work tempo set by a man plowing, a woman at a spinning wheel. It was not Golden Age, but life was linked to the . . . seasons rather than to a clock, a factory machine or railroad timetable.[299]

Ironically, although Jefferson's life would eventually be tied to a railroad timetable, his character Rip reminded Americans about the changes that occurred between the 1830's, when average Americans felt they were in control, democraticizing American political, economic and cultural institutions—shaping the nation and its destiny in their own image—[and] the late nineteenth century, when unmanageable incomprehensible forces seemed to be running their lives, when common people seemed more like puppets dancing on strings than free men determining their own fate.[300]

Such an approach to *Rip* was hardly the one in either Boucicault or Jefferson's minds. Jefferson took the traditional Yankee character, gave it a Dutch accent, and softened it, "substituting jocularity for acidic wit, sentimentality for social criticism." He established that Rip's foibles disguise his innate goodness so that when he is punished by sleeping through twenty years of his life, the audience sympathizes with an old man in a new world, his sense of bewilderment and nostalgia matching their own discomfort in the rapid industrialization of post–Civil War America.

Jefferson was originally scheduled to appear at the Olympic for two months. Within a week of *Rip*'s opening, the theatre was "densely crowded every night," despite the triumphant opening of *The Black Crook,* a musical spectacle now regarded as a milestone in the development of the American musical and, at the time, an enormous crowd-pleaser. But no nineteenth-century play could sustain the long runs enjoyed by modern musicals, and *The Black Crook* eventually began hurting business at the Olympic. Theatres were larger; city populations were smaller; theatregoing was a ubiquitous diversion open financially to a wide variety of people. Nineteenth-century theatre audiences demanded change; the decision by nineteenth-century managers to pull a production was financially based. When the management announced that after September 30 *Rip* would be replaced by *Our American Cousin*, it was admitting that Jefferson's big hit had been less financially successful than anticipated.[301]

Our American Cousin was even less successful. The text had been cut, and some of the best scenes eliminated, presumably to make it more a vehicle for Jefferson. Business was poor, and on October 17 Joe began to appear as Caleb Plummer. He performed two other roles during the season, and by the end of the New York engagement on October 27, 1866, Jefferson had four plays running in repertory.[302]

Joe was a star, but *Rip*, at this point, was not his only starring vehicle. His scope was admittedly narrow. In comparison, Edwin Booth's range as an actor continued to be wider than Jefferson's after the Civil War. Booth performed Hamlet, Iago, King Lear, John Howard Payne's Brutus, Macbeth, Benedick, Ruy Blas, Richelieu, Othello, Shylock, Bertuccio in *The Fool's Revenge*, Richard III, Brutus in Shakespeare's *Julius Caesar,* and Sir Giles Overreach in *A New Way to Pay Old Debts.* Jefferson never ventured out of comedy, or at least out of a kind of comedy mixed with pathos. Caleb Plummer and Rip were the most serious roles he ever attempted, and both are actually characters in sentimental melodrama.

But Booth and Jefferson, like all American stars, continued to limit their repertoires. It was the hallmark of success for a nineteenth cen tury actor. The more important you were, the fewer parts you performed. Jefferson had been a stock-company actor, and by 1866 he had performed in at least three hundred plays. In limiting his roles, he was adhering to the standard procedure of his time. The fact that he is now remembered for only one role, if at all, is a trick of time. No nineteenth-century actor could have made a living from only one role. Nineteenth-century audiences depended on theatre the way twentieth-century audiences depend on television, films, or videos. There was a continual need for variety. Productions could last almost indefinitely but not continuously. Rip and later Bob Acres were Jefferson's staples, but he always maintained a cupboard of other works. In a financial pinch, Jefferson could always go back on the road, traveling from town to town. If business was bad on Wednesday, he could switch plays on Thursday, throw together some scenery, and put on another show. In a pinch, Jefferson became his father.

9

"MY LATEST NOVELTY"
1867–1870

Rip was not an immediate success, and Jefferson's return to America was not the triumph he had envisioned. Audiences in New York were "pretty good" for three weeks, but attendance at subsequent performances was only "fair," and his revivals of *Our American Cousin* and *Dot* were both financial failures. The Olympic took in $23,380 in September, but only $17,761 in October. In comparison, Niblo's Garden, home to *The Black Crook,* took in $43,008 in September and $70,525 in October. Then, as now, the musical prevailed.[303]

If New York had been disappointing, Jefferson knew where to make money; he began to tour and spent the rest of his life amassing a fortune as a touring actor during the economic boom that followed the Civil War. His prosperity, like that of America, was the result of the emergence of the railroad. His youth was characterized by the laboriously slow progress of itinerant actors, traveling by foot, by wagon, and by steamboat across the country. In 1857 it took two days to travel from New York to Philadelphia. But by the late nineteenth century, he could move quickly, able to perform a matinee in one city and an evening performance in another.

Eventually he traveled in comfort in a private railway car, but at first, train travel was difficult. Between September 1864 and September 1865 there were between sixty-seven and 128 railway accidents in America. More than three hundred people were killed and six hundred injured. One report listed 1,500 casualties. A British newspaper correspondent wrote in 1865:

Travelling is not expensive, but is impossible to conceive anything more disagreeable. . . . In the course of the line from Rochester to Niagara, and Niagara to Buffalo, I noticed that the rails looked patchy and broken, the iron had worn off in flakes, and the edges were chipped and broken like a piece of rock. The joints of the rails were far apart, and the cars jumped over them in a way which threatened an accident every moment. . . . The cars are so . . . dirty that it would be hopeless . . . to convey a fair idea of their condition to anyone who has not travelled in America. No wonder that Americans always travel by the steamboats . . . , notwithstanding that the chances of accident or robbery . . . are by no means contemptible.

The cars oscillate wildly from side to side, and jump at a rate which proves that it is not so easy a thing as it looks to cause a railway accident, but that great pains are necessary. The country roads across the line are not fenced in, and the level crossings have no gates . . . , but merely a notice . . . , "Railway crossing; look out for the cars." Hundreds of such roads run across every line. The railway is rarely properly fenced in . . . so that cattle stray upon the line constantly. . . . All classes being huddled together in one long car—[the] tobacco-chewer, the shoeblack and the . . . fastidious Englishman or American alike—the atmosphere is loathsome . . . , and there is almost sure to be a woman who claims the traveller's seat and turns him out of it. . . . Behind each seat is often a stuffed pad, on a projecting piece of iron, for the traveller's head to rest against—a foul, greasy offensive pad— which could not fail to be an object of interest to the diligent student of insect life. . . . Every now and then, the guard walks through the cars and does not ask the tourist for his ticket but knocks him in the side if his head happens to be turned the other way or pinches his arm. . . . The man never speaks, but always uses his fist. . . . There are sleeping cars to travel in by night, but they are simply storehouses of vermin.[304]

No matter how disagreeable, touring was a necessity for nineteenth-century actors. Stars traveled by railroad from city to city where they performed the roles for which they were famous, supported by resident troupes whose actors had dozens and dozens of parts in their memories. As the tragedian Edmon S. Conner remembered: "Stock

companies were always very complete, and . . . I could start on a starring tour from New York or Philadelphia to Mobile, playing en route
at all the important cities and find, in each one, a full company from
the leading man and woman down to the smallest utility person, all
"up" in the legitimate parts and ready to go on . . . at a moment's
notice."[305]

In 1867 Jefferson encountered difficulty touring, because the
Boucicault version of *Rip Van Winkle* was not part of the standard
American repertory, not yet a "legitimate part," although at least three
other versions had long been standard theatrical fare. Jefferson could
not count on finding companies who knew his version of the play.
Actors in the period memorized quickly, but audiences did not know
the script and at first did not know Jefferson's version of it. Jefferson
needed to establish the play in people's minds. Moreover, although it
was written to conform to the stock sets found in any nineteenth-
century theatre, companies could not mount *Rip* scenically in the
elaborate style the New York production had set. Yet touring was the
only way to position the play within the theatrical repertoire.[306]

Jefferson had decided, even before opening in New York, to
perform *Rip* in his birthplace, in the theatre in which his grandfather
had been a star: the Chestnut Street in Philadelphia. He opened on
October 30, 1866, for his first appearance there in thirteen years,
and by that Saturday night "it was difficult to obtain even decent
standing room by the time the curtain rose." Yet although critically
successful, Jefferson again failed to take in the amount of money
anticipated. *Rip* was new, and the Philadelphia management, having
spent a lot of money on its scenery, withdrew the play after eight
nights when audiences did not come. *Our American Cousin* also
failed, and by closing, when he was guaranteed a benefit, Jefferson
was performing, like a stock actor, in three one-act farces. A benefit
night was simply too important financially to risk using a play audiences had already seen. Before the engagement ended on November
24, Jefferson had appeared in eight different roles. Rip was intended
as the major draw, but there was no sign, at this point, that Jefferson
thought of it as his only role. Again its financial failure may have
resulted from competition with a Philadelphia production of *The
Black Crook*.[307]

Jefferson had failed to draw significantly in both New York and
Philadelphia. In need of a new strategy, he turned to his old boss,

John T. Ford, who was managing both the Holliday Theatre in Baltimore and the National in Washington. Ford had arranged a joint engagement in both cities, a longstanding practice that Jefferson's father had used in the 1830's.

On November 26, two days after he closed in Philadelphia, Jefferson inaugurated the "Winter Season" at the National Theatre in Washington, where he was welcomed after "years of absence, [by] a community which witnessed and encouraged the efforts of his earliest professional struggles." But he did not open in *Rip*; in fact, he did not perform *Rip* at all. Realizing that his reputation in the part had not spread sufficiently, he decided to reestablish himself with his audience before dazzling them with his newest role. *Rip*'s absence in Washington was a ploy to build anticipation; Jefferson opened in Washington knowing that he was coming back, and when he closed on December 1 to go to Baltimore, he was immediately advertised for a reengagement to include *Rip Van Winkle*.

Back in Washington, however, Jefferson chose to postpone the play's appearance again and instead performed seven other characters during the first week of his reengagement. The strategy worked. Houses were now "running over." Finally that Saturday, the local newspaper announced *Rip* for Monday, and Jefferson went on to play the role for thirteen performances to rave reviews and sold-out houses. But even then he took no chances. Anticipating a "bumper" on New Year's Eve, he switched to *The Octoroon*.

After a tour of the Midwest and South, Jefferson returned East at the end of spring 1867, and on June 3 he opened another engagement at the Walnut Street Theatre in Philadelphia. By this time he had generated a taste for his newest role. Starting with *Rip*, he continued to play nothing but Rip for sixteen consecutive performances, taking a benefit every Friday night to packed houses despite rain and heat. At the beginning of the tour he had used his better-known roles to entice audiences for *Rip*. Now he used *Rip* to bring them back for his other parts. Jefferson closed his Philadelphia engagement and his first American tour on June 29, 1867, having acted continuously since September 3, 1866. He had performed for almost ten months, almost exclusively in major cities, in runs lasting from one to four weeks. He could command benefit performances every Friday night; he had established his reputation as Rip, at least outside New York, and the show was popular enough for Jefferson to perform it twice in one season in cities the size of Baltimore and Philadelphia. By the end of the 1866–67 tour, however, he was still playing nineteen other parts. This range would rapidly narrow the following year.

Jefferson played Rip for the rest of his life, but his national reputation for the role was built in the period from 1867 through 1874. Although it was never the only role in his repertoire, it soon acquired and still retains that reputation. For forty years *Rip*'s popularity allowed Jefferson to perform it without an afterpiece, whereas his other major roles, Bob Acres and Caleb Plummer, were often followed by one act farces.

Jefferson was always of two minds about the play. He was well aware of how important *Rip* was to him financially. Nat Goodwin, who specialized in impersonations of fellow actors, imitated Jefferson waking up as Rip and commenting: "Gallery is a little off tonight! House about fifteen hundred, I should think." Jefferson's response was: "He knows how much I like to play to a good house." He spoke of *Rip*'s financial and artistic success as "the greatest pleasure I have ever known." At the same time he was casual and unsentimental about the play itself. Late in his career, he wrote to Francis Wilson: "I will be in New York early in May, where I hope to see you. In the meantime on the road producing my latest novelty, *Rip Van Winkle*, as I find the public still blind to my dramatic defects. . . . Think of it! What a triumph it is for artistic duplicity to have deceived the public for fifty years—and in view of my present health, I am good, as King Henry says, for much more slaughter."[308]

With *Rip*'s success came repetition, and with repetition came boredom. A year after his return to America, Jefferson was already looking for variety. He spent part of the summer of 1867 in Paradise Valley with his sister Cornelia, and part of that time directing or working as a production supervisor, the nineteenth-century equivalent of an artistic director. In Baltimore he produced an extravaganza entitled *The Woodcutter of Baghdad, and the Lovely Forty Thieves*, eventually destined for a Washington production. In Philadelphia he produced a spectacle version of *A Midsummer Night's Dream*. He had planned to open in New York in *Forty Thieves*, but the plan fell through when the Olympic's manager went bankrupt, and the new management needed a hit. Jefferson reopened *Rip Van Winkle* on September 9, 1867. The *New York Times* damned the supporting cast, but the production was a financial success. Reserved seats sold out each day, and "at night the line of eager applicants for admission extended across the entire lobby and from the box-office to the outer edge of the pavement."[309]

At the beginning of the 1867–68 season Jefferson was forced to give into the demand for what became known as the "the Rip matinee." In New York this meant performing seven times a week, including a 1:30 P.M. show on Saturdays that ended two and a half hours later so that suburban patrons, particularly those with children, could get home early. Matinees had been slow in coming to America, and Jefferson, like all actors, hated them. They were the result of a Boston prejudice against Saturday evening performances, based on a religious belief that the Sabbath began at sundown. For years Boston managers had substituted a Saturday matinee for an evening performance. When, in 1855–56, the religious ban was lifted, managers retained the custom without increasing salaries, claiming that the extra performance was really a rehearsal to which actors were contractually obligated.[310]

The custom spread to New York during the Civil War, but the results were disappointing. Daylight crept through open doors into lobbies and auditoriums. Unpaid actors gave sloppy performances. Musicians were few in number, and respectable women were forced to share the theatre with painted prostitutes, their hair *à la chinoise*, dressed in brightly colored shawls and bonnets, accompanied by men with diamond breast pins, patent leather shoes, and dyed black moustaches. The *New York Times* reported: "Scenes are carelessly set; actors are carelessly dressed; parts are carelessly remembered. . . . In tragedy whole scenes are slurred over; in comedy the silliest balderdash replaces the author's language. Levity is the rule of such assemblages, and the very atmosphere of the place seems tainted with Bohemianism."[311]

After the Civil War, public attitudes changed. New York had a larger wealthy leisure class, and Jefferson's "*Rip* matinees" were part of the vogue that swept the city for matinee performances. The results were financially dazzling. During his two-month engagement in 1867, the Olympic took in $52,714, and although Jefferson may have hated the extra matinees, he earned $15,000 during the run, in part because he had enough power to insist on being paid to perform them. He also had an opportunity to direct. Encouraged by the

Olympic's new manager, he staged the theatre's next show, a spectacle version of *A Midsummer Night's Dream*. Using models he had brought from London for the Philadelphia production, he refurbished that production's properties and transferred it to New York, complete with a moving panorama scene.[312]

Rip Van Winkle was scheduled to close on October 12, and *A Midsummer Night's Dream* to open on October 14, but *Rip* was doing good business, and no manager pulled a financially successful show. *Midsummer* was first put off until October 21, and then, when the management announced that the scenery was not ready, it was delayed until October 28. Meanwhile Jefferson began to tour.[313]

He had intended to return to Washington that fall, and his name appeared as one of a series of stars slated for the National Theatre. But the *Daily National Intelligencer* pointed out a number of factors that influenced whether a particular star would appear in a particular city. "A series of stars arranged in and for New Orleans may be completely broken and disarranged by an accident in Montreal or a fire in Rochester, and it is not till the autumn has fairly set in, that certainty can be approximated. New York, as the great theatric and advertising centre, determines, in some degree, the season's plans of every other city."[314]

That November, instead of Washington, Jefferson performed for three weeks in Chicago, where he met his second cousin, Sarah Isabel Warren. She was not only the daughter of Henry Warren, the treasurer of McVicker's Theatre, but also the niece of the famous Boston comedian, William Warren; and she was related by marriage both to John Blake Rice, a Chicago theatrical entrepreneur who had become the mayor of the city, and to the celebrated Yankee comedian Danforth Marble. When Jefferson met her, Sarah was living with her father, in whose home Joe and Sarah were married in December. Jefferson mentions the wedding in his *Autobiography*, but immediately assures the reader that he has no intention of committing an "impertinent intrusion" by discussing his personal life. Sarah's name never appears again. They lived together until his death in 1905 and had four children.[315]

Toney, as she was known in the family, had been born on November 26, 1850, and consequently was not quite seventeen when she met Joe. He was thirty-eight, more than twice her age. She had just turned eighteen when they married. Her oldest stepdaughter, Margaret, was fourteen; her oldest stepson, Charles Burke, was slightly older than she was. Given the closeness of the two men, Charles must have seemed more like Jefferson's brother than his son to her. Writing about the Jeffersons two years later, in 1869, James B. Runnion, Jefferson's first biographer, noted that "Mrs. Jefferson . . . married to Mr. Jefferson something more than a year ago in Chicago—is an amiable lady, never has been, and probably never will appear, on the stage."[316]

Sarah never went on the stage, although she spent her honeymoon on the road and traveled with Jefferson as he got older. On their wedding night she and Joe left for Cincinnati, where he opened a two-week stint in *Rip* on December 23.

Sarah was the perfect wife for Jefferson. She was a middle-class "lady" from a theatrical family, but she was not an actress. She was a respectable woman who understood the stage, but did not work on the stage. Indeed there was no need for her ever to work, because she had married into immense wealth. How great that wealth was had become a matter of public speculation. In the course of Jefferson's engagement that year in Mobile, the local newspaper published an article stating that "Mr. Joseph Jefferson has the reputation of being one of the most financially successful members of the theatrical profession. . . . His profits at the present average two thousand dollars a week. The 'season' is about thirty weeks." The newspaper's contention was supported in 1869 by James B. Runnion: "Mr. Jefferson has acquired a considerable fortune during his successful career and now acts less than the greater number of our hard-working American actors."

Jefferson's personal income was, of course, based on his ability to produce astounding box-office receipts. When he performed on April 14, 1868, in Washington, with generals Ulysses S. Grant and William Tecumseh Sherman in the audience, the management took in almost $1,200. For extended runs, managers reaped enormous financial profits from his appearances. In 1869 James McVicker took in $23,562.00 during the month of Jefferson's engagement, far more than any other theatre in Chicago made that season.

Jefferson's percentage of this take varied, but it was always lucrative. In Boston a twenty-four-performance run over a four-week period beginning May 3, 1869, netted him $15,000, and the proprietors of the theatre an equal amount. In Brooklyn, after expenses were cleared, four performances of *Rip* in the fall of 1869 netted

$8,000, which Jefferson and his manager split in half. In two weeks in Memphis, in December 1869, Jefferson's share of the house was $7,000. That fall, at Booth's theatre in New York, he received $500 a night and half of the gross receipts of his matinee performances. Receipts averaged $1,600 a night, and Jefferson was paid almost one-third of the gross. In seven weeks at Booth's, he earned at least $25,000. But during the month of August alone, Booth's theatre grossed $41,834, almost twice the take of its nearest competitor, and during the month of September it grossed $49,144. Jefferson closed on September 21, and the gross for October went down by $15,000. When a theatre manager earned $90,000 and paid the star actor $25,000, the star was a good financial investment. Jefferson made money for himself because he made money for others. In 1869 the *New York Star* contended that he was worth half a million dollars, second only to his boyhood idol John E. Owens, said to be worth $800,000.[317]

On the other hand, Jefferson demanded a high salary, and theatre managers often raised prices in order to meet his demands and still show a profit. Faced with higher prices, audiences were sometimes reluctant to attend. Consequently, in Memphis in 1868, the theatre lost money on Jefferson's engagement. Ten years later, in July 1878, Jefferson was touring through the West, playing Central City (Colorado), Denver, and Salt Lake City. By then he was the highest priced star in America. Tickets ($1.50 for the parquette in Salt Lake City, $2 for all seats in Denver) were incredibly expensive for that region. The managers took in $750 a night, but they were forced to guarantee Jefferson $500; and after the rest of their expenses were cleared, they wound up losing money.[318] A local correspondent for the *New York Clipper* wrote:

> I know Mr. Jefferson is independent and not obliged to act, but he ought to remember that the public gave him his money, and the five-hundred-a-night business was well enough during the flush times of 1862 and 1863, and as long thereafter as good times lasted; but now money is close, and theatres have been obliged to reduce their scale of prices, while good stars won't reduce their terms. Someone may reply by saying "Don't play stars," but that don't mend the evil, for managers must play what the public demands.

The tricky part of hiring Jefferson was to figure out what the audience would pay higher prices to see. The answer was increasingly *Rip*. The 1867–68 tour ended on June 17; Jefferson had been performing since September 9, 1867. It was again a ten-month season, one of the longest he ever performed. Jefferson was still playing ten roles, but his repertoire was narrowing. By the end of 1868–69 he would be down to eight parts; Rip was coming to dominate his performances. In 1869 the Memphis *Sunday Morning Appeal* wrote that "Mr. Jefferson, or *Rip Van Winkle*,—for the names have become identical—commences his engagement next Monday."[319]

Jefferson, however, was not content to be a star actor. On August 31, 1868, he opened his 1868–69 season with *Rip* at McVicker's Theatre in Chicago and immediately began to revive the production of *A Midsummer Night's Dream* which he had already staged in Philadelphia and New York. By Jefferson's second week in Chicago, the theatre was advertising for "fifty young ladies for *A Midsummer Night's Dream*." By September 9, an advertisement asked that "a number of good female singing voices apply at the stage door between ten and twelve A.M." On October 5 McVicker's opened the production, "given in gorgeous style, under Mr. Jefferson's careful and critical eye." The performance offered transformation scenes in the mode of the English producer, Charles Kean, as well as nineteenth-century musical spectacle. The production was favorably reviewed, and Jefferson was praised for producing the play in an artistic rather than a sensational manner, although the level of scenic spectacle involved hardly seems to justify such a claim. Initially the *Chicago Tribune* heralded the play's financial success: "Jefferson and McVicker have made so much with it already that money is becoming a drug, and they are utterly indifferent about laying up any more greenbacks."[320]

Jefferson was never "utterly indifferent" about money, and there is evidence that the production of *A Midsummer Night's Dream* was not the financial success the *Tribune* claimed. The assertions of undiminished attendance and the images of wealth pouring in were "puffs," designed to attract an audience. By October 29 the *Tribune* was admitting that receipts had not been equal to expenses. Faced with an artistic success and a financial failure, Jefferson supposedly told McVicker: "It is all right. We have done our duty and have made an artistic success of the piece. If the people will not come to see it, it is more their misfortune than ours." The statement, if true, is uncharacteristic of

Jefferson. Any positive feelings he had about the production probably reflect the fact that it took in $17,974.00 at the box office during the month of October. This put McVicker $6,000 ahead of his nearest competitor. What is most important about Jefferson's venture into Shakespeare, however, is that as early as two years after his great success with *Rip*, he was already looking for new artistic ground.[321]

Unfortunately he did not find it, and by October 26 Jefferson had gotten together a group of Chicago actors to form a company to troupe *Rip* for six nights to the Milwaukee Music Hall where his cousin, William Warren, was the manager. He was still following the same pattern his father and uncle had followed in the Midwest thirty years before—a band of actors in an urban company broke off to form a smaller troupe and play the hinterlands. According to the *Chicago Tribune*, the results in Milwaukee were disastrous.

> Now Jefferson might better have given a hundred dollars to the Trinity Mission than to have gone to Milwaukee and lost no one knows how many, playing Rip Van Winkle to dismal houses. A circus is the only show that stands any chance in Milwaukee. . . . No legitimate amusement can depend upon over seventeen men, a woman and a child, and the woman and a child belong in Kenosha. One of the men has got an opera glass, quite worn from lending round. One habit in Milwaukee militates against amusement, and that is the fact that nine-tenths of the inhabitants go to bed just after sundown. The other tenth comprise the seventeen men, woman and a child of whom I have spoken, and they like amusements so well that the janitors always have a hard time explaining to them when the curtain is down for the last time. They have a place set apart for amusements in Milwaukee, which is a music hall and when it isn't a music hall, is an opera house, when not an opera house, a theatre, when not a concert saloon, a circus pavilion, when not a circus pavilion, a temple of the muses and when not a temple of the muses a rink, and so on. As a German cheap boarding-house, it would be a success.[322]

Jefferson had intended to perform for six nights in Milwaukee; he left after five and began to tour the Midwest and then Washington, Baltimore, and Boston. His success in *Rip* was so great that he could stay in a particular city as long as he wanted and make up his itinerary as he went along. Joe could, as the saying went, "open with the privilege," meaning the privilege of staying as long as he chose. He could also be uncertain as to where he would play next, but whatever city he chose would still want him. Edwin Booth wrote to William Winter that "Joe is really uncertain about his movements—I see he has suddenly determined to lengthen his engagement in Boston & his Cincinnati trip must be again deferred."[323]

On the road, however, Jefferson could not do what he did in New York, namely play *Rip* to inexhaustible audiences. He always needed a wider repertoire. By 1870 at least two-thirds of any run was devoted to *Rip*, the rest to a combination of seven other roles. The work was still exhausting. Although the rumor mill had him performing as little as thirty weeks a year, in 1869–70 he actually worked ten months straight before returning home.

Jefferson had failed as a producer-director; he certainly could not have seriously contemplated a life as a manager of a provincial touring company in the Milwaukee mode. He had a hit play; he was very wealthy; but by 1869 he was recognizing the possibility that he might spend the rest of his life touring *Rip Van Winkle*. It appears to have been a mixed blessing. By February 1870 Jefferson was thinking of leaving America again for England.

10

HOME
1868–1870

With *Rip* came money. The Jeffersons were a wealthy family by the summer of 1868. When they vacationed at Paradise Valley, Joe's daughter Maggie, then fifteen, was given a young black mare for her birthday. She called her Topsy, after the famous comic character in *Uncle Tom's Cabin*. The horse proved difficult to ride, and Joe bribed his daughter with $100 if she would "sell him" the pony. She insisted on receiving the money in installments. The story told by Maggie's daughter, Eleanor Farjeon, may be meant to counteract the widely held image of Jefferson as stingy.

> Joe reckons that Topsy cost him Five Hundred in the end, but he laughs and forks out—as he would, if no Topsy at all stood as security. Any child . . . could demand five or ten dollars . . . and no questions asked, but let them go to him for a quarter or fifty cents, and it was. . . : "What *do* you want a quarter for? Don't grow up mean, whatever you do!"[324]

Jefferson was handing out $5 and $10 bills to his children at a time when expensive theatre tickets cost a dollar. He had been born poor and was determined that his children and ultimately his grandchildren would never know such want.

In the fall of 1868 Sarah accompanied him to Chicago to visit her family and became pregnant during the Chicago run. On July 6, 1869, in New York City, she gave birth to their first son, Joseph

Warren Jefferson. Jefferson was forty; Sarah was not quite nineteen. Joe Jr. was almost ten years younger than his next older sibling, his half-sister, Josephine. He was nineteen years younger than his oldest half-brother, Charles Burke. The Jeffersons were starting a second family, and three weeks later, on July 27, spurred on by the birth of his new son, Jefferson purchased two lots in Hohokus, New Jersey for $30,000, the equivalent of approximately sixty performances of *Rip*. It became the first Jefferson family home. The site in the Saddle River valley, a forty-nine-acre estate complete with trout streams, was "a charming spot, lying on both sides of the river, with a fine brook for trout in the rear, a capital old brown stone house and spacious outbuildings, the whole surrounded with innumerable fruit and shade trees." It eventually became the rural retreat of a wealthy man living in an elaborate garden setting.[325]

Jefferson lived at least part of the year in Hohokus until 1887. In November 1874 he purchased more land near the original site. By then his property contained a spring-fed pond that remained a steady fifty-five degrees all year round. He built two rustic bridges, divided the pond with dams, and stocked one side with trout and the other with black bass. Joe fished under the shade of a giant elm and hired a gardener who lived in a nearby cottage to ward off poachers.[326]

He built greenhouses, one entirely devoted to the camellias he eventually brought from Louisiana, and cultivated a vineyard; he planted long avenues of fir trees that led to the lawns and gardens surrounding the house. He expanded the half-stone, half-timber house in a series of irregular additions and surrounded them with vines, firs, pines, climbing rosebushes, wisteria, honeysuckle, evergreens, oaks, and birches.

Great front doors led into a wide hall that ran from the front to the rear of the house and in which a broad staircase led to the second floor. To the right were the "dining room, opening out into the conservatory, the sitting room, a boudoir and . . . a guest's room." Beyond the guest room was Jefferson's painting studio, "with its fifteenth-century mantel of carved black oak, its fireplace of old Dutch tiles and its brass grate and fender." To the left of the entrance hall was a large low-ceilinged drawing room with windows jutting out on three sides. This became Jefferson's museum, filled with "carved teak-wood furniture from India, upholstered in rare silk and gold fabric; embroideries from Turkey, China and Japan; Oriental rugs; skins of

tigers and lions from India and of bears and wolves from the Rocky
Mountains; pottery; bronzes from Italy and France; old cabinets of
carved oak; inlaid chairs and tables from Holland and France and
pictures everywhere."[327]

Jefferson had become a collector, gathering mementoes from
exotic civilizations to produce the interior decoration suitable to an
age of imperialism. The poor boy who had spent his youth in boarding houses and tenements now surrounded himself with the trappings of wealth, including an art collection devoted to theatrical
portraits, contemporary European artists, and his own landscapes.[328]
His tastes were in part motivated by private and professional interests. But the bulk of the collection indicates his attraction to the
work of the Barbizon school, a group of artists painting from the
natural landscape they found in the forest of Fontainbleu. The critic
James Henry Moser, wrote:

> Those poetic truths which Constable, Corot, Daubigney,
> Rousseau and Mauve saw clearly are open secrets to Jeffer-
> son. . . . There is . . . a . . . picturesque quality . . . which betrays
> long familiarity with theatrical scenery. . . . There are . . . typical
> old water mills, cascades and shady dells. The pervading color is
> rich gray greens and the shadowy tones of wet, mossy rocks and
> tree trunks with somewhere on the canvas a note of silvery grey
> and Delft blue. . . . This sort of art is distressing to the apostle of
> impressionism, who revels in violets and pale yellows; but let
> that pass.[329]

Unfortunately for his heirs, Jefferson let Impressionism pass,
preferring its *plein air* antecedents. He had been in no financial
position to collect paintings before 1857, and probably bought most
of the works he owned after 1865. He might have purchased Millet
or John Singer Sargent, who painted him twice, so why did he buy
Barbizon art?[330] To begin with, it is not clear how much he determined his artistic purchases. Later in life, he worked through an art
dealer. Moreover, Jefferson purchased conservatively. By 1865,
works of the Barbizon school were considered masterpieces, winning
gold medals year after year at the official Paris salon. But in acquiring
paintings by an artist like Jean-Baptiste Camille Corot, Jefferson was
not merely a wealthy man purchasing what he had been told was
good. He shared a vision with the Barbizon school. Corot, like other

Barbizon painters, was reacting against the changes in nineteenth-century life created by the Industrial Revolution. And what motivated Corot's audience also motivated Jefferson's—the desire to return to a period of unspoiled nature, to a pastoral world, to a vision of life being systematically destroyed by nineteenth-century transportation and industrialization.

By 1870 Corot was the most revered artist in France. When he exhibited that year in the Paris salon, one critic wrote: "I salute that . . . master, that virgilian poet—-no, even better, that peasant's soul, Corot. Before . . . his work one forgets what one has seen in art and what one knows about criticism. It is no longer a canvas, and he no longer a painter . . . . I open a window and I am at home in a poet's nature." Another critic wrote: "Always the same thing· a master-piece. But what do you expect? Corot does not know how to do anything else." Jefferson's reviews read like Corot's. "Of course nobody wastes ink in criticism of Mr. Jefferson's acting; the time for that is passed. What he does is accepted as perfection, and in its way, it is perfect." William M. Reedy, editor of St. Louis' *Sunday Mirror,* wrote: "What can one say of Jefferson, save that he is Jefferson. . . . He is an appeal to pleasant memories no less than a delight to the artistic sense."[331] Theatrical reviewers almost immediately gave up criticizing or describing Jefferson's art. *Rip* was an acknowledged masterpiece, and there was nothing else to say.

Like Corot, Jefferson worked without stopping. The demand for both men's art was inexhaustible. Both were aware of the commercial mass appeal of their work, and both replicated an artistic product for an audience hungry for more of the same. Real and phoney Corots flooded America. Jefferson remarked to Francis Wilson that upon Corot's death it was found he had painted some eight hundred canvases and "that there were over nine hundred in America alone!"[332] Because Corot was a visual artist, "more of the same" meant variations on a theme—the trees, the stream, the occasional peasant, the off-center construction, could change from painting to painting. But, Jefferson, as an actor, felt bound to replicate exactly his portrait of Rip Van Winkle, performance after performance, for almost fifty years.

This caused him no serious anguish, although he felt the artistic pressure of critics pushing him to expand his repertoire. To see Jefferson as the comic equivalent of James Tyrone, Eugene O'Neill's guilt-ridden fictional father in *Long Day's Journey into Night*, would be incorrect. He was brought up in a theatrical tradition in which the ability to make a role one's own, one's specialty, was the hallmark of success. Jefferson had no illusions about the artistic merits of Rip Van Winkle; he experienced boredom, perhaps a sense of bitterness, but he suffered no agony. He was brought up working hard and continued to do so all of his life, enjoying his rural leisure as the well-earned reward of an urban profession.

Jefferson shared his public's desire for a return to a simpler rural existence. The location of his homes, his interest in agriculture and gardening, the casual clothes in which he slopped around, his love of fishing, all of these mirror the setting for *Rip* as well as Jefferson's paintings and those of his Barbizon masters. His choice of New Jersey as a home may have resulted from his recognition that he would be performing frequently in New York, but the relationship between the actor's surroundings and his most famous character's setting was not lost on others.

> He chose his home . . . among the hills of the Passaic, surrounded by . . . forest trees, which he loves as Rip loved them. . . . "Is Mr. Jefferson ever quite sure, as he walks about, that Schneider is not at his heels?" When he is at home, Schneider *is* always at his heels in the shape of a . . . setter of purest blood, presented to him by a son of Horace Howard Furness, Esq., the eminent Shakespearian scholar, or a beautiful Scotch collie of unsullied strain, bought by him of a Highland shepherd . . . on the shores of Loch Lomond or of a . . . dun mastiff called Schneider, sent him by an enthusiastic admirer.

Jefferson's lifestyle displayed the ambivalence of late nineteenth-century America. He lived in the midst of romantic rusticity, but he lived in baronial splendor. Rip's Schneider was probably a mutt; Jefferson's dogs were blue bloods. His external environment may have suggested Rip, but the oriental carpets and the art work were the upper-class trappings typical of a nineteenth-century country home. Jefferson could afford to ship collies from the highlands of Scotland and drink fresh milk from an imported she-ass.

Although the subject matter of both Jefferson and Corot's art eschewed the technological advances of their period, the careers of both men were deeply affected by the Industrial Revolution. The

American railroad brought Jefferson to his audience; the French railroad system carried Corot into the countryside to find his subjects. The village of Barbizon and the forest of Fontainbleu were an easy train ride from Paris, and by 1860 over a hundred thousand Parisians a year traveled out from the capital for a day in the country. They thought they were going to see nature; they were actually watching a stage set. "The 42,000 acres of dense woods intercut with rocky gorges, marshes and shady clearings may have looked like a wilderness to city folk, but it was actually tamed and tractable; guideboooks steered artists and tourists alike along one hundred miles of footpaths."[333]

The artifice of *Rip Van Winkle* was far more obvious. Audiences always knew they were watching a play. But the combined realism of scenic detail and acting made the fairy tale seem believable, and only Jefferson and those who watched closely and continuously realized that the naturalness of his acting was the result of a technique as studied as the landscaped forest of Fontainbleu. Nineteenth-century audiences in the theatre, like nineteenth-century audiences in the forest, wanted an idealized, improved version of nature.

For twenty years Jefferson improved on nature at what he called "My Farm in Jersey" and regaled audiences with anecdotes about his unsuccessful attempts. His listeners knew him as Rip, and Jefferson knew they expected him to be Rip-like in everything he did.

> I was attracted by a townsman, and I bought a farm in New Jersey. I went out . . . to examine the soil. I told the honest farmer who was about to sell me this place that . . . the soil looked . . . thin; there was a good deal of gravel. He told me that . . . gravel was the finest thing for drainage. . . . I told him I had heard that, but I had always presumed that if the gravel was underneath, it would answer the purpose better. He said: "Not at all; this soil . . . will drain both ways." . . . I bought the farm and set . . . to work to increase the breadth of my shoulders. . . . I even . . . split the wood. I did not succeed. . . . But as I only lived at my farm during the summer . . . , it became . . . unnecessary in New Jersey to split wood in July, and my farming operations were not successful.
>
> We bought . . . chickens and they . . . turned out to be roosters, . . . but I resolved . . . I would carry on that farm as long as

my wife's money lasted. . . . My Alderney bull got into the
greenhouse. There was nothing to stop him but the cactus. He
tossed the flower-pots right and left. . . . I never saw such a
wreck, and I am . . . convinced that there is nothing that will
stop a . . . well-bred bull but a full-bred South American cactus. . . . I found him there; everything was smashed, and he was
quietly eating the Hamburg grapes. . . . The bugs got into the
potatoes; we put paris green upon them to such an extent that
we were afraid to eat them.[334]

Jefferson's remarks, part of a dinner speech given in 1893, are
typical of his self-deprecating public image. That he had ever lived on
his wife's money is unlikely. Sarah Jefferson did not have any money;
she came from a middle-class theatrical family, and by the time they
married, Joe was making enough to support her in luxury. This
money was made through touring, and Jefferson's schedule made it
unlikely that he spent enough time in New Jersey to undertake
serious farming himself. Moreover the presence of a greenhouse with
South American cactus and a growing art collection makes it more
likely that he was playing gentleman-farmer in New Jersey.

The image of rustic simplicity that Jefferson projected was not just
a public relations device. It was also part of his personal taste. The art
he collected and the art he created mirrored the tamed nature
around him rather than the upholstered interiors of his home. The
landscapes that surrounded his homes, first in Hohokus and later in
New Iberia, Louisiana, and Buzzards Bay, Massachusetts, became
the imaginary landscape of his painting.

Like Corot, Jefferson always painted when he traveled. The young
actor Otis Skinner, later one of the stars of the early twentieth century,
toured with him in 1899 and remembered: "When the scenery was
hauled out of the baggage car, he would go down to the railroad yards,
set up his easel in the empty car, paint landscapes and be happy."[335]

Touring with his own company late in the century decreased the
need for rehearsals, and there was little else to do except attend the
fund-raisers and lunches in which he served as a trophy star. Painting
filled the void. Like Corot, Jefferson made sketches that could then be
reworked into formal canvases in his home studio. Both men worked
en plein air—outdoors—but neither always painted exactly what he
saw. Jefferson used painting in the heat of Louisiana or the briskness

of Cape Cod as a healthy restorative for a professional life spent in railway cars, hotels, and theatres. The scenery around him inspired his work, but the paintings themselves, like Corot's *souvenirs*, were invented landscapes composed of details he had observed and remembered. The primary difference between the two is that Corot painted for a living. Although far more talented than the average gentleman painter, Jefferson was not a professional visual artist. He created his roles to please audiences, but he created his paintings to please himself. Although they were occasionally exhibited, there is no indication that he ever created them to sell.[336]

In spite of the urban interior trappings of his home, Jefferson did not want to live in the city. His health may have mitigated against metropolitan life, and it eventually drove him south to warmer climates. But his visual art betrays a love of splendid solitude, both in the paintings he bought and in the paintings he made. Painting afforded Jefferson the solitude he sought and which the theatre, by its nature, denied him. "If I like to be alone when I paint," he said, "I have no objection to a great many people when I act."[337]

He modeled his own works on Corot's dark landscapes illuminated by bursts of light; but unlike Corot, Jefferson painted few architectural details, nor even the most indistinct human figure. Barbizon paintings, as well as the photographs of the Barbizon photographer Eugene Cuvalier, focus on nature rather than people. Jefferson's landscapes go further and depict a virgin wilderness generally untouched by civilization. In July 1879 L. Clarke Davis published a drawing of the actor in his studio. Jefferson, dressed in a suit, sits in an ornate chair next to an ornate fireplace and mirror with a completed picture on the easel before him. The picture, which features a harbored boat at midnight in a craggy landscape, is one of the few Jefferson paintings with any indication of human life.

It is tempting to attribute the moodiness of Jefferson's tastes in visual art to some dark night of his soul. The truth is much simpler. Jefferson's painting was an inheritance from his father; like his father, he became a painter of scenery. On stage, there was no need to paint people on backdrops. The people presented were live actors. The all-purpose scenes of the nineteenth-century theatre were idealized landscapes. It is these same landscapes that Jefferson reproduced in his visual art.

Yet even his father's scenery had "Ships tossing in a billowy sea."

Figure 14. Jefferson in his studio in New Iberia, Louisiana.
Courtesy of the Performing Arts Research Center,
New York Public Library.

Most Jefferson paintings betray virtually no human presence at all.
Part of this has to be a predilection for privacy, for solitude. He lived
and even worked surrounded by his family for most of his life. As an
actor, he was constantly sought after for private after-the-show

dinner parties, but he was a public man who loved solitude. He spent his life working in cities, but he lived in the country as soon as he was wealthy enough. Yet although he played and painted the rustic, he made sure that the conditions under which he lived never replicated the poverty of real rustic life. His *Autobiography* is a charming recollection of an impoverished childhood, which he made sure his children never experienced.

Rip allowed Jefferson to overcome forever the poverty of his youth. Joe and Margaret had lived in New York and only vacationed in the country. Joe and Sarah could afford several country estates and never bought property in a city. If the decision to live in the country reflected Jefferson's taste, the heavy Victorian furniture of his homes, must, in part, reflect Sarah's. Joe's theatrical background, as well as the poverty and constant travel of his youth, would have mitigated against any significant exposure to Victorian finery on his part, but Sarah had been brought up in a middle-class urban home. Her uncle was the mayor of Chicago. It is likely, therefore, that the plethora of possessions in the Jefferson household reflected both her aspirations for upper-class elegance and his desire for the respectability and comfort denied him as a boy.

Eight months after he purchased his Hohokus estate, Jefferson bought land for yet another home, this time in Louisiana. On March 4, 1870, he purchased Orange Island near the present town of New Iberia for $28,000. Money was rolling in, and Jefferson was determined to have both a winter and a summer residence. Given his lung condition, the winter residence had to be in a warm climate. Jefferson chose Louisiana in part for the healthy influence of its heat. Francis Wilson describes him as "a sun hunter . . . thin and quickly chilled."[338]

He found the site with a friend named James A. Lee, a druggist in New Iberia, whose home he had visited. The elliptically shaped island, really part of the bayou system of Louisiana, was a seventy-foot-high salt dome bordering Lake Peigneur on the north, five or six miles from the Gulf, approximately 1.8 miles in diameter and containing 1,200 acres. Jefferson continued to purchase land in the area and eventually had a 9,000-acre estate. On the dome's summit, the highest point of the orchard overlooking an arm of the Gulf of Mexico called Vermillion Bay, he had a local architect named George Francis build a summer home. Materials for the home were brought up the Teche, as the bayou was called, in boats from New Orleans to

New Iberia, and from there were transported by ox cart over twelve miles of difficult roads to the island.[339]

Eventually visitors to Orange Island crossed by ferry from New Orleans to Algiers and boarded a Southern Pacific Railroad train for the four-hour, 125-mile trip that took them to a station named Bob Acres. They then drove in a wagon over twelve miles of flat prairie. The road was full of soft places, and guests were often obliged to abandon the wagon or carriage so that the Cajun driver could pull it out of the mud. They crossed the prairie to a little settlement called "The Bridge," named for the fact that the road took a sharp curve there and crossed a stream. The traveler was then confronted with a succession of barbed-wire fences and thick hedgerows of blossoming rosebushes seven miles around and ten feet tall. The outer enclosure was given over to hundreds of cattle. Two miles further on, visitors passed through locked gates and approached the house still two miles away "through a broad lane, hedged for three miles on either side with Cherokee or McCartney roses" that formed an "impenetrable thickness . . . of white blossoms." They then rode on "a narrow levee" that formed a "wagon way or carriage drive across the marshy ground," leading to the foot of the hill on which the house was sited.

There the traveler went through a large gate in a high dense osage hedge designed to protect the house from grazing cattle, and began to climb a mile-long hill to the house. Halfway up, yet another low hedgerow protected the lawn. Although the orange trees were eventually killed by a sudden freeze, the house remained surrounded by large oaks hung with Spanish moss, Cherokee or Chickasaw rose hedges, magnolias, and green shrubbery. It could take as much as five hours for the twelve-mile trip from the station to the Jefferson home. Jefferson built his house so that it was nearly inaccessible and then invited guests; he eventually filled it with children and grandchildren. He had been brought up in a family troupe crowded with relatives, so he constantly needed the society of others even as he sought a place to be alone.

The house on Jefferson's Island was a white frame octagonal two-story building with verandas on three sides, surrounded by evergreen hedges and oak trees covered with moss. Its front door faced south. The square columns were connected by a balustrade of wooden filigree on top, and in the center of its roof a square cupola or belvedere was flanked on all four sides by dormer windows. The cellar stored boats and eventually a device for maufacturing gas. Jefferson maintained a painting studio on the second floor on the rear or north side of the house. The kitchen and servants' quarters were separate from the main house in the rear.

Figure 15. Joseph Jefferson's home in New Iberia Parish, Louisiana, as it appeared in Jefferson's time. Courtesy of Joseph Jefferson House, Jefferson Island, New Iberia, Louisiana.

Inside, a twelve-foot-wide hallway ran through the length of the building and terminated in a dining room, in which visitors found a large fireplace containing a five-foot log in full blaze as well as a table with a white cloth, in the center of which might stand a huge steaming pot of Boston baked beans and, at each plate, a broiled quail and a glass of wine or a bottle of beer. To the left were large and commodious bedrooms; to the right were parlors and drawing rooms. Oranges, tangerines, and pecans were always available in an open crib. Outside, Jefferson eventually built a series of cottages for his sons; on the right were the servants' quarters and barns. Behind the house, an arched corridor of trees, mistletoe gourds, and hanging vines led to Lake Peigneur, which provided Jefferson with the fishing grounds he craved. Toward the east was a jungle of cypress trees in which alligators bayed at night.

Eventually Jefferson raised cattle, which netted him $10,000 annually, as well as sugar cane, oats, and rice. A windmill on the property provided water to its extensive herds of cattle and horses.

The Brazilian and Mandarin orange trees set out in groves were killed by the severe winter of 1881 and replaced by new orange as well as pecan trees overseen by Jefferson's land agent, Joseph Landry. Each winter Jefferson would repair to Orange Island to paint, fish, rest his lungs, and play country squire with "the finest imported pointers and setters."[340]

The region was populated with Cajuns and Negroes. Both groups were illiterate or semiliterate, and both had speech patterns that seemed comic to Jefferson. At a breakfast held in his honor in the 1890's he read the following letter "for the amusement of his host and his guests":

IBERIA PARISH, LA.

MY DEAR MR. JEFSON:

I spose you don't like to hear from myself, but sir, I am in a bad way sure. Your overseer don't like me mity well and that the reason that I write to you. Sometime the wether is bad, and I can't get cross the prary for to do my work on that plantation that you hone yourself, then he cuss me awful bad befo all those black nigger hands on the place. I think he been writing you bout me, thats why I go writing bout himself. Now look for yourself, no christian cant cross a prary in bad wether. You think that overseer is putty good man yes. I don't think him a fust rate man, no. I wish you could come down here wen that overser ant round. I wil show you some things that you never can't see. So please sir don't let him send me away for sure because then what will I do for myself. Please write that overseer to make me stay if I wil and I don't never forget your kindness caus some day that overseer he is a good kind man and next day he is just like a son of a Gun.

I am your good fren

Saturday morning

I am

JAN LARUE

P. S. You see I am in a bad way sir cause my old mudder is dead for a long time. My fader she cant see out of both his eyes and what will I do? My wife is going to have a leetle baby, and you wouldn't like to be that way yourself.[341]

The humor of the piece, particularly as it might have been performed by a skilled mimic of the local dialect, is obvious. Rip was a Dutch dialect role, and there is no reason why Jefferson might not have been as skillful in Cajun. And the postscript is clever enough to have been invented. But the idea of Jefferson's reading it in public in an elegant setting of leisure and wealth sets him aside from the modern period and places him squarely within the calloused class-conscious society of the nineteenth century. The sadness of the letter seeps through its humor. Indeed that may have been why he chose it. This is what Rip and Caleb are all about; this is even what he made of Dr. Pangloss. The letter's mixture of pathos and humor was Jefferson's specialty.

11

THE LITTLE CHURCH
AROUND THE CORNER—
BLINDNESS
1870–1875

In 1870 Jefferson, although in complete control of his touring schedule, was restless with a career dominated by one play and was contemplating a return to Europe. Edwin Booth, who wanted Joe to perform in his New York Theatre, wrote to their mutual friend, the American critic William Winter:

> I'm trying to hook that queer fish Joe & if he don't take my bait now he's a "Jack" [John Dory—a common fish]. . . . Drop Joe a line at Balto. & urge him to play a long engagement here before he goes abroad & advise him to begin early in the fall. I don't know whether he listens much to advice in such matters —but it's for his good.[342]

Baltimore audiences were warned that they might not have the opportunity of seeing Jefferson for several years, but in reality he had no immediate plans for Europe. By February 1870 he was already booked for a four-month run at Booth's Theatre. Jefferson loved the place and was often quoted as saying that "Booth's theatre is conducted as a theatre should be—like a church behind the curtain and like a counting-house in front of it." Opening on August 15, he played Rip and nothing but Rip for a hundred and forty-nine consecutive performances until January 7, 1871. On opening night the receipts were over $2,000, and the grosses for September were $41,830,

$15,000 more than Booth's nearest competitor. By mid-December Rip had been seen by a hundred and fifty thousand persons, and Jefferson's identification with the role was complete.[343] The *New York Times*, in an article on theatrical "bills," satirically characterized the play's posters.

> [T]he general street reader is . . . well acquainted with the *Rip Van Winkle* poster. How its big blue letters straddle over the paper, . . . seeming to say, "Oh we don't want to stop you. If you can afford to wait awhile before coming to see us, pray do so. This is our five thousandth representation; it is by no means impossible we may run on to the ten thousandth."[344]

The numbers are greatly exaggerated for comic effect. Had he performed Rip every night for five years, Jefferson would not have reached his two-thousandth performance by the end of the 1870 season. Given a ten-month season, with seven performances a week, and assuming that Rip was performed seventy-five percent of the time, Jefferson had probably given one thousand performances in the role by 1870. But his identification with the part was such that he could stand near the fruit stand on the southwest corner of Twenty-third Street and Sixth Avenue, eating Malaga grapes out of a paper bag and watching crowds file into Booth's, and still not be recognized. People only knew him as Rip.

The role had become an American icon. The editor of *Harper's New Monthly Magazine* likened Jefferson's Rip "to shrines at which worship is imperative like the Pieta in St. Peter's." Yet he was also aware of the play's moral detractors.

> "Yes, but look at it," says Conscience, . . . "here is a . . . rascal, who wastes his substance in riotous living, who breaks his wife's heart and enslaves her to the hardest labor; and when the catastrophe comes, what happens? He goes quietly to sleep for twenty years, and she, for her daughter's sake, marries a man who abuses her, and she is wretched beyond words, as if she had been guilty; and at last my lazy lord opens his eyes and rubs them and descends after his sound nap to have his wife fall upon her knees before him, as if she were the sinner, and to beg him to drink at his pleasure. . . . What do you think the Rev. Dr. Sabine would think of it?"[345]

The Reverend William T. Sabine was part of what became the most famous legend of Jefferson's life. On December 20, 1870, the actor George Holland died in New York at the age of seventy-nine, leaving a widow and five children. Jefferson was godfather to Holland's son, Joseph, who turned ten on the day his father died. Upon the wishes of the widow, Joe and one of Holland's three sons approached the Reverend Mr. Sabine, the Episcopal minister of the Church of the Atonement at Madison Avenue and Twenty-eighth Street, where Holland had rented a pew and made regular donations. Jefferson asked Sabine to officiate at the service. Sabine recorded his own refusal: "I said I had a distaste for officiating at such a funeral and that I did not care to be mixed up in it. I said . . . that I was willing to bury the deceased from his house but that I objected to having the funeral solemnized at church." Sabine would not allow the funeral of an actor in his church.

Jefferson retold the rest in his *Autobiography.*

> I was hurt for my young friend and indignant with the man—too much so to reply, and I rose to leave the room with . . . mortification. . . . I paused at the door and said:
>
> "Well, sir, . . . is there no other church to which you can direct me, from which my friend can be buried?"
>
> He replied that "there was a little church around the corner" where I might get it done, to which I answered:
>
> "Then, if this be so, God bless 'the little church around the corner';" and so I left the house.[346]

Jefferson proceeded to the Church of the Transfiguration on Twenty-ninth Street near Madison Avenue. He met with its pastor, the Reverend Dr. George H. Houghton, and told him that Holland had been an actor. Houghton said: "This did not concern him. I only know that your friend is dead, and my services are asked." By early 1871 the church was known and has since been known as "the little church around the corner."[347]

It took time for the story to get around. On January 7, 1871, *Frank Leslie's Weekly* published an obituary for Holland without mentioning the incident, but that same day *The Clipper*, a New York newspaper devoted to theatre and sports, carried the story and a later edition continued to publicize it. By the following week the *New*

York Daily Times suggested that Sabine contemplate a paraphrase of Laertes' lines over Ophelia's grave:

> I tell thee, churlish priest,
> A minist'ring angel shall my *"father"* be
> When thou liest howling.

On February 11, 1871, *Leslie's Weekly* praised Dr. Houghton, noting with unintentional irony that his willingness to bury Holland derived from "his custom to labor with suffering humanity in all forms of wretchedness in this city." While, to a modern reader, the newspaper betrayed its prejudices by linking actors with "the poor, the unfortunate and the lowly," its intentions were good, and the incident marked a moment of recognition of theatrical respectability. Sabine was pilloried as having done "a deed unworthy the humanity of the nineteenth century, in conformity with the spirit of the Dark Ages." His name appeared in verse lampoons, while a minstrel show song, "The Little Church Around the Corner," became beloved.[348]

How much of this did Jefferson engineer? Certainly he had little respect for organized religion and enough professional prestige to make any newspaper editor listen. Jefferson was not a religious person, in the churchgoing sense. In fact, what he was reported as having said was: "All honor to that little church," a far more appropriate remark for a man who apparently had no belief in God. Holland's death, however, gave him the opportunity to publicly condemn religious hypocrisy while simultaneously making himself the virtual creator of a religious institution. While his name is forever connected with "the little church around the corner" and is now memorialized in one of its stained-glass windows, his family passed up the opportunity to have Jefferson's funeral service there, and he was eventually buried out of his own home with brief services in its parlor and at graveside.

By January 5, 1871, plans were underway for a Holland benefit organized by William Winter. On January 19 benefit matinee performances were presented at twelve theatres in New York. Special tickets were available that admitted the holder to any participating theatre, and groups of New Yorkers got up parties to go from one performance to another, a plan made difficult by the inclement weather and almost impassable street conditions. Although he did not appear on the nineteenth, Jefferson played Mr. Golightly in two special performances at the Academy of Music in benefit of Holland's widow and children on January 21. There were simultaneous Holland benefits in Boston, Philadelphia, St. Louis, Baltimore, Washington, San Francisco, and Vicksburg. Managers in New York sent their receipts without deducting any expenses. The benefits netted $13,608.41. But they were far more valuable for Jefferson, because his involvement in the Holland incident gave him a beloved public image that matched his stage persona. When, on April 17, he opened for a week of *Rip* at Holliday Street Theatre in Baltimore, the local critic noted: "His conduct in this matter, outside of his merits as an actor, should endear him to the heart of every liberal-minded man and woman. But, to know the man, go and see Rip Van Winkle."[349]

Given the publicity he had reaped from "The Little Church Around the Corner" incident, it would have been natural for anyone as commercially minded as Jefferson to follow up with a substantial tour. Instead he went south to New Iberia and did not reemerge for three months. He may have used the time to plan and supervise the construction of the plantation house that eventually occupied the Louisiana property, but he may also have been experiencing the effects of glaucoma, which would interfere with his career the following season. Joe began a spring tour in Washington in mid-April, performing Rip primarily in Baltimore, Boston, and Philadelphia. It was the kind of season he would adopt in old age, a performance schedule geared to someone who needed to take it easy.

Jefferson spent the summer painting in Hohokus, opened in Brooklyn on September 4, 1871, and then toured the West. The New Orleans *Daily Picayune* reported that he was earning $10,000 per year and playing only six months. In actuality, he was still performing nine months every season, but problems began to appear. Audiences and critics were annoyed at the inflated prices being charged for a Jefferson performance, particularly when they sensed that the performance did not live up to their expectations. In Albany "attendance at the Trimble Opera House" was "only . . . fair . . . owing to the double rates of admission, being charged without previous notice." In St. Louis "a slight cold" interfered with Jefferson's enunciation. On January 14, 1872, after a week of the engagement, the New Orleans newspaper noted that Jefferson "was more animated than at any time during the present engagement, and his interpretation was more like what it used to be." The note is ominous. By that Wednesday, the same newspaper commented that "an admiring crowd . . . appeared to enjoy [Rip] heartily, notwithstanding the fact that Mr. Jefferson does not . . . play . . . with the . . . vigor that he formerly did." He was still turning away customers at matinees.[350] But as soon as he closed, the newspaper let Jefferson have it full blast:

> Never before has Mr. Jefferson appeared to such small houses in New Orleans. . . . On the first night . . . there was such a house as formerly greeted him, but that house made a painful discovery. . . . The favorite of the stage . . . had fallen from his high estate, and had lost . . . the power to make people weep, although he could yet make them laugh. . . .
>
> We saw a natural manner . . . dwindle into carelessness and indifference. The thrilling tone in which *Rip's* mournful question, "My God! are we so soon forgotten when we are dead?" was once spoken, had shrunk into a mechanical utterance. . . . The farewell to the wife, after expulsion from her house, once so . . . tender . . . was . . . a hard, expressionless dramatic formality. Of the "recognition scene," in the third act, we cannot speak from personal observation. We did not stay to witness it.
>
> We learn that Mr. Jefferson will take a vacation. It would be well for him to improve . . . by studying some other "specialty," since he has . . . ceased to feel any interest in *Rip Van Winkle*, save as an equivalent for $500 per night.[351]

After New Orleans, Jefferson retreated to New Iberia for a couple of weeks of rest. On February 6, after five days rehearsal with an inexperienced company, he opened *Rip* in Galveston, the city in which he had landed as an impoverished young actor in 1846. It could have been a moment of triumph, but Jefferson was in no condition to relish it. He had contracted glaucoma in his left eye and was going blind. But he continued on, performing in rural Kentucky, Ohio, Indiana, New Jersey, Delaware, and Pennsylvania during the spring of 1872. In general the cities in which he performed were far smaller than the ones he had previously visited, and the stays were shorter—three days in Syracuse, three days in Rochester, two days in Peoria, one day in Newark. At the end of the season Jefferson played a three-week engagement in Boston and a one-week engagement in Baltimore, but was forced to cancel his performances in Philadelphia. The glaucoma was getting worse. He wrote to a friend:

My left eye has been overcast by a mist, for some time; the pain became so intense that I was alarmed and called upon Dr. Chisolm, of the celebrated oculists of Baltimore, who told me that I was threatened with the loss of sight in one eye and possibly in both. Today I had another examination under the ophthalmoscope, by the eminent oculist Dr. Reuling, and . . . he give me the same . . . intelligence. Nothing can save my sight unless at once I give up my profession and submit to an operation, which will not only keep me in bed for two days, but [also] confine me in darkness for a longer time. Dr. Reuling, who will at once perform this operation, gives me every hope of recovery, by attending to my case in this its early stage but cannot take the responsibility if I expose my eye to the continual glare of the light or delay in . . . submitting to an operation.[352]

The operation was performed by a young German occulist, Dr. George Reuling, at Jefferson's home at Hohokus, New Jersey on June 13 or 14. Following the surgery, Jefferson had to remain in a darkened room for several days, but after a visit to the occulist on August 16 he reported:

I have just returned from a visit to Dr. Reuling at Baltimore. He made a final examination of my eye and gives me the pleasing intelligence that all traces of the disease have entirely disappeared. I no longer wear glasses and . . . am as good as new. The doctor says I could act tonight, without the slightest risk.

Apparently the only scar left was what Francis Wilson describes as "an unusual white mark" in Jefferson's eyes.[353]

By early August 1872 Jefferson was already accepting engagements for the following season, but he could no longer count on a long opening run in New York as he had the year before. Instead he began performing on September 2 in Augusta, Maine, moving south into Massachusetts. But Dr. Reuling's reassurances were premature. By September 14 Jefferson's eyes forced him to cancel further performances. He returned to Baltimore for more treatment. Sight in one eye was fine, he reported to a friend, but the other eye was sore and became painful when he attempted to act, presumably from the lights on stage. Jefferson was able to recognize an acquaintance in daylight six to seven hundred feet away, but he was unable to read, and he decided to retire from the stage until the spring of 1873. When he reappeared on January 1, 1873, in Baltimore, his performance was billed as "the first appearance of Mr. Jefferson since his late affliction."

By late June the tour was over, and Jefferson was enjoying the rustic life at Frontenac in Lake Pepin, Minnesota. He vacationed abroad, setting sail on July 9, 1873, for England accompanied by Sarah and by his first cousin William Warren, and returning on August 27. By the time he opened his 1873–74 season with a five-week engagement at Booth's, he was back to his old form. Edwin Booth had retired from the management of the theatre at the end of the 1872–73 season, and it was now run by his brother, Junius Brutus. Jefferson was making his first New York appearance in three years. He performed *Rip* each week for five nights and a 1:30 Saturday matinee. He could still pull in audiences and had enough clout to force the new manager to schedule another play for Saturday night, because Jefferson did not "care to perform twice daily." The *New York Times* wrote of *Rip* that

> its impressiveness upon an audience that filled the theatre . . . was, of course, as clear . . . as ever. . . . The weird scene, . . . with its . . . orchestral accompaniment, could not easily be improved upon. . . . The assemblage [audience] was not only large, but . . . enthusiastic, for it summoned Mr. Jefferson before the curtain twice at the close of the drama. If Mr. Jefferson has really suffered from illness for many months, his work, last night, bore no evidence of past ill health.[354]

He may have looked fine, but Jefferson no longer toured for nine or ten months without stopping. During the 1873–74 season, he established what was to be the primary touring pattern of the rest of his career—a fall tour beginning in late August and ending after Christmas; a mid-winter break in New Iberia; and a spring tour beginning in January and ending in May. Jefferson closed his New York engagement on October 4 and began to play major cities along the Eastern seaboard, first in the middle-Atlantic states and then south through the Carolinas and into Georgia and Alabama. After he performed in Montgomery on December 27, he went to rest in New Iberia while the rest of the company left for Baltimore. Joe resumed playing in New Orleans on January 12, 1874, and went from there through the Midwest.

By the 1874–75 season Jefferson sensed that audiences were growing tired of *Rip* as a play. In Philadelphia he played a one-week engagement with six evening performances, a Saturday matinee, and no
benefit. Four years before, he had been able to play Philadelphia for
three weeks, taking a benefit every Friday. By 1875, a review published in *Every Saturday* indicates that *Rip,* long recognized as only
as a vehicle for Jefferson's talents, had lost any validity in the eyes of
a sophisticated spectator, although its lead performance was still
riveting audiences.

> The play in itself is the slightest of sketches, without a
> dramatic situation in it, and with not even probability or possi-
> bility in its plot. . . . Its opportunities for scenic display are . . .
> slight. . . . Its minor personages are tedious. . . . The leading
> character . . . does not make one point such as we are accus-
> tomed to in our experience of the stage—he has not one pas-
> sionate line, not one situation . . . laughable in itself. . . . The
> trait which is . . . the peculiarity . . . of this . . . piece of acting is
> its fidelity to nature. . . . The dialect is as close to the actual
> speech of a certain class of American-Dutch man as the utter-
> ance of one Dutchman is like that of another. . . .
>
> We cannot follow Mr. Jefferson through the play in detail,
> through the broader humor of the scene in the kitchen, where
> the tales of the rabbit and the bull always seemed to us the least
> worthy of . . . the actor . . . and the tragic close of the act, where
> Rip is turned out of his wife's house into the storm, and where
> . . . the spectator is moved without knowing why [by] the bear-
> ing of the man who sits with his back to the audience, and at last
> goes off with hardly a word or a gesture to emphasize his exit. . . .
> And then the last act—that amazing piece of acting at which we
> have seen one half an audience rapt in silence, with glistening
> eyes . . . while the other half . . . were convulsed with laughter.

The *Chicago Tribune* reported that Jefferson was making more than
$12,000 a month, primarily playing Rip, but, according to L. Clarke
Davis, he had grown "weary of the part" and "thought to put it and
the stage away for ever."[355]

> We wished him to have a new play, with a part fitted to him,
> written. "No," he said, "that would not do. I have put myself so
> wholly into Rip that in any entirely new character my personality

would shine through, coloring and warming it, and my audience would still see only Rip in another costume, in other scenes, speaking other words.[356]

Jefferson's estimation of his audience eventually proved correct; they came to see Rip in all of his characters, but then that is what they wanted to see. Even more than Rip, they would eventually come to see Jefferson himself, so that his curtain speeches became an integral part of his performance.

By February 27, 1875, Jefferson, feeling trapped in the part and faced with the prospect of endless touring, decided to visit England. In late March he announced his intention to leave in July. He played Rip in Boston for two weeks beginning May 3, 1875, and by May 24 was in New York, publicly announcing his imminent departure on June 30, for a two-year stay in Europe.

12

ENGLAND AND AMERICA
1875–1877

Jefferson left for England on June 30, 1875, on the steamship *Russia*. With him went Sarah; his twenty-two-year-old daughter Margaret; his son Tom, aged seventeen; his daughter Josephine or Josie, aged fourteen; his and Sarah's oldest son Joe Jr., now six; and his youngest son Henry, nicknamed Harry, who had been born in Chicago at the home of his maternal grandfather, for whom he was named. Aunt Nell Symons accompanied them to take care of the children. According to Eleanor Farjeon, Jefferson's granddaughter, Charles Burke, by then twenty-five, stayed behind in Louisiana with his wife, Lauretta Vultee, whom he had married in 1871.[357]

Immediately upon arrival, Jefferson entered into a contract with F. B. Chatterton, Esq., the manager of the Princess Theatre, and took up residence at 29 Hyde Park Place near Tavistock Square. There he invited his old acquaintance from New Zealand, Benjamin Farjeon, to a 3 P.M. Sunday dinner. Farjeon, now a successful novelist, arrived, played with the younger boys, and met Margaret Jefferson. Two years later, she would become his wife.[358]

The Jefferson family went off for a summer holiday in France. After a short stay at the Hotel Mirabeau in Paris, they took a furnished flat in the Avenue d'Eylau near the Arc de Triomphe. Sarah became pregnant again; they engaged a tutor to teach the family French, and Jefferson spent most of the summer painting in the villages near Paris, replicating the subject matter of the Barbizon school he admired. He had sketched and worked in watercolors since boyhood, but now, with lessons, he began painting in oils. In later life he would say, somewhat disingenuously: "I . . . regret that I did not . . . devote myself to art instead of drama and believe my career would have been more successful." It was the kind of modesty for which he was famous, and it was designed simultaneously to impress listeners with his humility and to remind them of his fame, to score, in other words—an offstage "point."[359]

The family returned to London in the late fall, and Jefferson opened as Rip at the Princess Theatre on November 1, 1875, playing there through April 29, 1876. His return was enthusiastically received. The *Times* wrote of *Rip*:

> The version adopted by Mr. Jefferson is [by] . . . Mr. Boucicault and is . . . satisfactory. The incidents are arranged with . . . skill, and the delineation of the principal character bears evidence of great care. The last act, unlike the first, has a . . . melodramatic aspect, but the defect is . . . redeemed by the humour of the dialogue. The drunkenness of Rip Van Winkle is not such as to exclude him . . . from sympathy. He is . . . good natured, and the more he drinks, the more these qualities become apparent. He rarely allows his super-equanimity to be disturbed, thinking . . . that life is . . . but a farce. There is nothing like malignity in his composition, and even when his . . . wife turns him out . . . on a stormy night, he is only surprised and hurt. It must not be supposed, however, that he is a fool. He is sharp sighted enough to penetrate motives, and it is to no purpose that a . . . rascally settler makes him drunk . . . to induce him to put his cross to a document in which, unknown to himself, he is made to renounce important rights. He is also courageous, as may be seen when he is confronted by the spectres of Heinrich Hudson and his crew. His long sleep on the top of the mountain has no . . . effect upon his good humour, although it produces a great change in his appearance. Indeed, it is certain that, notwithstanding his many faults, Rip will always be liked better, except . . . by the advocates of total abstinence, than his . . . sober and industrious but sharp-tongued wife. . . . Rip's amiable qualities are further set off by the villany [*sic*] of Derrick, in the absence of which the third act would be . . . uninteresting.

Mr. Jefferson has not, for many years, played in any piece except *Rip Van Winkle*, and . . . he will not again play in any other. This decision will occasion some regret, but the performance is so attractive that he may well ask himself why he should put himself to the trouble of undertaking new parts or resuming old ones. The experience of Monday night will not lead him . . . to alter his mind, since, although he represented the character . . . in London ten years ago, the house was crowded and the applause tumultuous. In truth, Rip Van Winkle is one of the most remarkable exhibitions of the modern stage. His humour, though . . . quiet, is so effective that one laugh has scarcely subsided when another is raised. . . . The almost inaudible chuckle which accompanies the expression of any emotions is a well-chosen illustration of the philosophical contentment and mild cynicism of the Dutchman. Mr. Jefferson is successful in depicting the contrast between vigour and senility; his tone in the first act is not the same as it is in the third, and the change is made without apparent difficulty. In the expression of pathos, too, he has lost none of his former power. It remains to be added that the effect of Mr. Jefferson's acting was . . . increased by the excellence of the company and of the decorations.[360]

Jefferson was unable to enjoy the triumph, because Harry was ill. On November 4 the King and Queen of Denmark, along with the Princess of Wales, were present at the theatre. Jefferson, of course, went on, but Harry died the next day. His death was never announced in the *Times*. Jefferson's audiences never knew it occurred. Joe did not miss a performance. It was the family tradition. But his valet and stage-manager, Sam Phillips, recalled the poignancy that night of Rip's line: "My little child, look in my face and don't know who I am!" Harry's body was brought back to America to be buried at Cypress Hills, Long Island. Edwin Booth wrote of the incident to William Winter:

I am delighted to know that Joe J. has grasped the Lion firmly by the jaw with ungloved hands & hope he will shake lots of "shekels" from old Bull's money-bags, but poor fellow! he has his sorrow heavy on him while he struggles to lighten the cares of others; in a letter today from my sister, Mrs. Clarke, the death of his youngest child is mentioned—after a brief illness & about the fourth or fifth day of his engagement.[361]

By March 5, 1876, Booth wrote to Winter: "J. J. is *on deck* in London & is about to have his lost baby replaced by a younger one (Mum!)." Booth's "Mum" may have been a comment on the fact that Jefferson was forty-seven. In April 1876 Sarah Jefferson gave birth to a boy christened William Winter Jefferson at the font of the Stratford-upon-Avon church, in which Shakespeare is buried. Coming so late in life and so close upon Harry's death, Willie, as he was known, became the pampered darling of the family. A visitor to New Iberia, when the boy was eleven, reported that

> the youngest member of the family seemed to think the interest centered in himself. This was Willie, then so delicate a boy that often the only thing he consumed at the table was the brain of a snipe. On this evening Willie was particularly voluble, and his father, at last, suppressed him by a single remark: "Willie, a little of you goes a long distance this evening."[362]

In London, Jefferson's oldest daughter, Margaret, lived the life of a Victorian socialite, going to balls, having dresses made, attending riding school, and entertaining B. L. Farjeon, who became a "constant visitor in Tavistock Square." They went to boat races together. He sent her a box at the theatre and wrote: "If you go, I dare say I should manage to pop in for an hour." In the summer of 1876 Jefferson and his family followed their usual pattern and retreated to the country, spending six months at "Morningside," a mile from Edinburgh in "a fine furnished old mansion" called Canaan Lodge, built 150 years earlier and surrounded by "seven acres of walled ground [and] oak-tree-shaded lawns." Farjeon came up to Edinburgh upon Jefferson's invitation, and he and Maggie fell in love. When Jefferson and Sarah proceeded to Ireland, the rest of the family returned to London, where they lived in Mayo Lodge on Belsize Avenue. There Farjeon and Margaret were chaperoned by Asia Booth Clarke, Edwin Booth's sister, whose daughters had become Maggie's closest friends. In January 1877 Farjeon asked Jefferson for Maggie's hand in marriage. Joe gave his consent and even agreed to speak to Maggie to prepare her. Farjeon arrived the next day, bearing a teapot as a gift for Aunt Nell, and proposed. He and Maggie were married on June 6, 1877. He was thirty-nine and she was twenty-four. Asia Booth Clarke signed the marriage certificate, and Joe gave the couple $100,000 as a wedding gift. In 1877 this was an enormous amount of money. No matter how stingy Jefferson might later become in his stock-company presentations, his generosity toward his family knew no bounds. The Farjeons went on a honeymoon to Paris and Switzerland with the idea of eventually returning to America and living with Joe, Toney, and the younger family members.[363]

On March 1, 1877, Jefferson performed Mr. Golightly in *Lend Me Five Shillings* at Drury Lane in a benefit matinee (called a morning) performance under the patronage of the Prince of Wales. The *Times* was so pleased with his performance that its critic expressed the hope that in his next London engagement, Jefferson would perform works other than *Rip*. As early as March 22, the *Times* announced that Jefferson would reappear at the Royal Princess's Theatre in London on Easter Monday, April 2. No play was announced until March 30, when an advertisement for *Rip* appeared. Performances began at 7 P.M. with a one-act farce, then *Rip*, then another one-act farce. Jefferson appeared only in the main piece. By May 22 the *Times* was announcing the last seventeen performances prior to his departure for America.[364]

The day after closing, Jefferson accompanied William Winter on a tour of Warwickshire. They traveled by train from London through the gentle rain of the English countryside to Warwick and then walked on foot to a local inn. After exploring the castle of Kenilworth, they took a carriage to Stratford-upon-Avon and stayed at the Red Horse Inn, where Washington Irving had stopped. That night they stood in the dark before the house in which Shakespeare was supposedly born; Jefferson put his hand on Winter's arm and said: "This is the place." The next day they saw Shakespeare's tomb and lunched at an old inn, where they got drunk enough on Warwickshire wine to wind up in a graveyard with Jefferson weeping over a tombstone of someone he did not know. A year later Winter published a book describing his travels, and Jefferson provided sketches of the places described. It was typical of the symbiotic relationship that had developed over many years between the two men. Winter adored and promoted American actors. He courted them. In Jefferson's case, the admiration was returned. The correspondence between the two men implies a genuine friendship. Jefferson referred to Winter as "My dear Willie" and had just named a child after him.

Winter had already christened a son Joseph Jefferson. At the same time, Jefferson was well aware of the importance of critics, particularly when so many of them had become hostile to his dependence on Rip, and Winter was virtually sychophantic toward famous actors about whom he wrote glowing biographies. Their personal friendship served the professional needs of both men.[365]

Back in London, Jefferson appeared on June 11 at the Theatre Royal, Haymarket, playing a double bill of Mr. Golightly in *Lend Me Five Shillings* and Sir Hugh de Brass in *A Regular Fix*. Ticket brokers offered seats to spectators on the front page of the *Times*. The newspaper's critic wrote:

> We think Mr. Jefferson's acting of farce . . . very admirable. . . . Objections have been taken to it as being "too quiet," deficient in "point," in "life," or "go." . . . In such a quality, . . . Mr. Jefferson is altogether deficient. . . . Jefferson abstains from that "pestilent heresy" known . . . as "making his points." Mr. Jefferson does not go to his "points;" they come to him. They are not forced into prominence but arise . . . from the . . . sequence of words and actions.[366]

On July 16 the *Times* again began a countdown of Jefferson's remaining performances, and the productions closed on August 11. On August 20, 1877, Jefferson opened for a six-night run of *Rip* in Edinburgh, in what was billed as "his only appearance in Scotland previous to his return to America." In the *Scotsman*, a local critic wrote:

> The celebrity of this performance was . . . attested by the . . . house that assembled in spite of weather . . . calculated to keep people within doors. . . . The drama in which the romantic story has been embodied by Mr. Boucicault is slight . . . in structure and, apart from the central figure, has little in the way either of character or incident. . . . All hinges upon Rip; but to Rip, the actor has succeeded in imparting intense, yet unobtrusive, reality. . . . The style of acting is . . . quiet . . . . Nothing is forced; every look and word seems as . . . natural as the soiled and tattered dress . . . of the good-for-nothing drunkard.[367]

The two-and-a-half-year stint in the British Isles had been an enormous success. In America, *Scribner's Monthly* reported: "Press and audiences were alike enthusiastic. . . . As for the managers, they went to the courts to fight for the possession of him."[368]

This would be Jefferson's last trip to England. The family, including B. L. and Margaret Farjeon, returned to America on the steamship *Abyssinia* from Liverpool on October 17, 1877. By the time they arrived and settled in Hohokus, Margaret was noticeably pregnant. That Sunday's newspapers announced Jefferson's first appearance in New York in three years. He opened as Rip a week later on October 29, 1877, at Booth's Theatre, then under the management of Augustin Daly. He commuted each night from the theatre to his home in Hohokus, crossing the Hudson River at the Twenty-third Street ferry and often not getting to bed before 2 A.M. Sarah stayed up, waiting for him, making sure he had a hot meal when he got home. Joe played five nights a week and a Saturday matinee, but had enough clout to force Daly to allow him to have Saturday night free so he could spend it with his family.[369]

In spite of a severe rainstorm, opening night was a great success. The "free list" was suspended, and only the press was admitted without paying. Jefferson was called before the curtain after every act, and the *New York Clipper* noted that "the sojourn abroad had evidently improved his health." Daly, whose productions were noted for their scenic realism, had given special attention to the setting of the last scene of Act II, in which Rip drinks the fatal schnapps that sends him to sleep for twenty years. The curtain opened on "the rocky summit of one of the peaks of the Catskill Mountains." Stage left were "huge rocks forming a portion of a higher mountain." There seemed to be a chasm between the rocks and the vista upstage center. In previous productions, six or seven dwarfs had been spread around the stage. Now as Rip, bearing the keg of schnapps, climbed up the rocks and came into view over the upstage ground row, he was surrounded by a much larger number of ghostly figures, all alike in appearance, spread picturesquely on the rocky terrain. The dwarf who first gives Rip the keg of schnapps to carry was played by Samuel Phillips, who had served as Jefferson's valet and stage manager in London, and who performed the role without the mask that had customarily been used. At the end of the scene, after Rip's collapse, the demons disappeared gradually, as if melting into the rocks, some of which were probably painted on scrims. Their fading figures were the last thing the audience saw as the curtain descended. The *New York Times* review read: "The . . . theatre was filled . . . , and the applause with which the distinguished actor was received was of no uncertain temper. . . . It was . . . enthusiastic when Mr. Jefferson first came upon the stage; it rang . . . heartily between the acts; it made itself felt at all the well-known passages, and . . . it came in with crowning effect when the play was over."[370]

The combination of Jefferson and Daly's realism was electrifying; the lavish production added to the fact that American audiences had not seen *Rip* for two years. Within a week, newspapers were announcing that Jefferson "would appear every evening until further notice." Box seats were sold two weeks in advance, and audiences were lured by assurances that evening performances, which began at 8:00, would be over by 10:40 and that matinees, which began at 2:00, would be over by 4:30, allowing suburban patrons ample time to reach their trains.[371]

Toward the end of the eight-week run, Jefferson announced that his New York performances would be his only engagement that fall and that he planned to spend Christmas with friends in Baltimore and then to winter in Louisiana. It was completely untrue. Two days after closing in New York, he embarked upon a tour of Pennsylvania, upstate New York, southern New England, Brooklyn, Washington, and Baltimore.

After the Baltimore engagement, Jefferson, in ill health, stopped performing and announced he was going on vacation. He, Toney and the younger members of the family went South to visit Charles Burke and Lauretta Vultee Jefferson in New Iberia. Charlie had decided to retire from the stage temporarily to see if he could make the Orange Island plantation pay as an orange orchard. Margaret and Ben (as Farjeon was known) remained at Hohokus with Josie and Grandpa Lockyer, the father of Jefferson's first wife. By March 20, 1878, Charlie wrote to Maggie that their father's health had improved.[372]

Jefferson's first grandchild, Harry Farjeon, was born in Hohokus on May 6, 1878, with Aunt Nell serving as a midwife. He was named for Maggie's dead brother. Unfortunately B. L. Farjeon was uncomfortable in America, and in late July 1878 Maggie, Ben, and their baby sailed for England. She did not return to America until 1903. The long absence may indicate some cooling of relations between Jefferson and his son-in-law.

Farjeon's American sojourn had not been a happy one. He attempted several public readings in New York from his best-known work,

Blade of Grass, but the public was more interested in whether Joseph Jefferson's son-in-law was a Jew. Farjeon, who had converted to Christianity as a young man, was noncommittal and attempted to amuse his audiences by saying that at least he was not an Irish Jew. The press took the comment unfavorably and warned against possible lawsuits, and Jefferson could not have been pleased. Twenty years later, Francis Wilson told Joe that Farjeon had stopped writing, and Jefferson replied: "His style has gone out of fashion, I suppose. I am ashamed to say I have never read but one or two of his books."

In the late nineteenth century, successful American actors, like Billy Florence and his wife, vacationed in Europe every summer. Jefferson never returned, and Margaret never saw her father again until he was dying.[373]

13

THE JEFFERSON
COMPANY

In the spring of 1878 Jefferson headed west, performing in California for the first time since 1861. He opened in San Francisco on June 3, but refused to play the state's interior cities when local managers could not produce the financial guarantees he demanded. He used the distance from major Eastern theatres to try out a new role—the tutor Tracy Coach in *Baby*, a play translated from the French. Like Dr. Pangloss and Mr. Ollapod, Tracy Coach was one of Jefferson's conniving tutor roles. Coach winks at the antics of his pupil, thought angelic by his parents, but actually prone to mischief. It was Jefferson's first new part in thirteen years, and it was not successful. The fact that Jefferson tried it, however, again signals his understanding that audiences were growing tired of *Rip* as well as his own boredom with the role. As the *New York Times* charged:

> Year after year he returns to this city, . . . appearing in the same character, never making the slightest attempt to win public and critical applause in the variety of his work. This actor, for whom is claimed the position of the most illustrious American comedian, is, in a large measure, responsible for one of the most vicious customs which has ever threatened . . . the drama. He is . . . endowed with . . . talent, [but he] is content to strut the stage . . . as a model one-part actor. . . . It is natural to suppose that an actor who is content to appear in one part, so long as that one is successful, thinks more of his purse than of his profession.[374]

Published in the fall of 1878, the review may have had an effect at the box office. Business was slow at first during Jefferson's three-week run at New York's Fifth Avenue Theatre; but it was Christmas, and the *New York Clipper* attributed the slump to the $1.50 ticket price and the fact that potential audiences were shopping at stores open late for the holiday. After Christmas, ticket sales improved. On the last Saturday matinee and evening, audiences crowded in to see *Rip*, and the receipts for two performances came to $2,200.[375] The *New York Mirror* pointed out:

It now looks as if this engagement, begun amid surroundings, not altogether auspicious, [will] prove . . . successful. There is in New York . . . latent interest in an impersonation so famous as Mr. Jefferson's Rip Van Winkle, but it takes . . . time to arouse it. . . . There are so many people who have heard so much about Jefferson's "Rip" or have been so often "just on the point" of seeing it, that the . . . announcement that he is playing it . . . is sufficient to attract them.

In spite of the engagement's eventual success, not all was well financially at the Fifth Avenue. The theatre's two partners, D. H. Harkins and Stephen Fiske, were engaged in a lawsuit. Harkins, according to Fiske, refused to pay a company to support Jefferson. On January 4, 1879, a fair-sized audience gathered in the theatre and noticed there were no musicians in the pit. A member of the production staff announced that *Rip* would not be performed, because the company and the orchestra refused to play. Patrons were given their money back, and Jefferson cut his engagement short.[376] The Fifth Avenue Theatre incident merely illustrated what Jefferson, like any nineteenth-century actor, knew—namely, that he was at the mercy of managers to supply supporting companies and scenery. But this situation was about to change, because by 1878 the public was demanding combination companies.

Since 1859 Jefferson had been a traveling star, going from city to city, performing plays with resident stock companies across America. By the mid-1870's, however, the stock company was giving way to the touring combination company, what the twentieth century calls a road show. Instead of assembling actors in a given place and having them each perform forty or fifty roles a season, as Jefferson had done in the 1850's, managers now preferred to assemble actors in New

York, have them perfect one or more plays, and send them out across America. This process was again facilitated by the development of the American railroad. In 1849 there were fewer than six thousand miles of railroad track in America. It made sense for actors to stay in one place. By the end of 1860 there were almost thirty-one thousand miles of track. The combination company was a response to the ease of travel and the national demand for the higher artistic quality that came with specialization. In 1871–72 there were fifty stock companies left. By 1877–78 there were only twenty; and by 1880 there were only seven or eight. In contrast, there were one hundred combinations on the road by 1876–77; ten years later, that number had almost tripled. In 1879, the *New York Mirror* predicted:

> It seems [to be] a question of time when all the theatres in the country . . . will conform to the system now in vogue in England—organizing [a company] with a view . . . to the . . . fitness of its members to appear in certain plays. . . . One of the . . . effects of this will be to compel stars to furnish their own support. Players who . . . traveled from city to city, receiving, at each place, the support of the resident companies, must now . . . take combinations with them or organize a new company at each stopping-place.[377]

The combination company meant that the age of specialization had come to the American theatre. Jefferson, of course, had been a specialist since 1865. His specialty was Rip. Now, however, he assumed managerial control over the quality of his productions and casts. Over the next twenty-six years he attracted some of the leading stars of the nineteenth-century theatre into his company, although he usually preferred employing them on their way up. Young actors were cheaper than seasoned professionals. As a touring star, Jefferson was paid his price and walked away; if the weather was bad and no one came, it was the manager's problem. Suddenly Jefferson was the manager, at least the manager of a company; he had a payroll, and he made sure that payroll was as low as possible.[378]

Young actors were also more pliable. Jefferson's productions were vehicles for his own comic talents, and he did not share the stage easily. This was particularly true of *Rip*, in which subordinate characters exist solely as foils for the leading character and had to be performed so as to direct the audience's sympathy toward a drunkard whose dissipation impoverishes his family. Jefferson needed actors who would do the show *his* way.

Mary Shaw, who played Gretchen in 1896, discovered this when she made changes in the character. Jefferson approached her to play the part by mail, writing that "he had had, at some time or other, for *Gretchen* every actress who had attained to any prominence." He charmed her at a personal interview, and she took the job. But Shaw had little preparation with Jefferson himself, who came only to the last two rehearsals before opening. His sons rehearsed the play, filling in for their father, and Shaw later recalled that "they were . . . easy-going young men, and . . . tired of the play. . . . These were the funniest rehearsals. . . . It was wonderful to me, who had been used to very exact training, to hear the young Jeffersons talking down in front on all sorts of matters . . . and permitting the actors to go on in 'any old way they pleased.'"

Referring to the comic impresario of *Nicholas Nickleby*, Shaw described the Jefferson troupe as "a sort of *Vincent Crummles'* company," composed of family members and actors long associated with Jefferson and with the particular plays he performed. She was the only member of the group who did not know the stage business traditionally associated with *Rip*; Jefferson's sons told her nothing, and when the master himself finally appeared he gave her only "a few general directions." Shaw remembered:

> At the end of *Gretchen's* first scene, where *Derrick* prophesies to her that if she continues to live with *Rip*, . . . she will lose everything . . . , she shoulders her wash-board . . . and as she leaves the stage says, "Well, not while *Rip* lives, bad as he is." The audience responded with a round of applause. I was too . . . excited . . . to notice the surprise of the actors, but it appears that it was . . . unprecedented. . . . As I went to my dressing-room, one of Mr. Jefferson's sons tiptoed up to me and said: "the governor won't do a thing to you. There is to be no sympathy for *Gretchen* in this play. You are all off." "Well," I retorted, "if I am all off, it is the fault of you boys, for I did not know how he wanted it played."

Shaw found Gretchen an unrewarding and difficult part. When she had to pull Jefferson by the hair, she could hardly touch him, because by this time he was wearing a wig even to play the young Rip.

Shaw had to "make a vicious lunge, as if she were grabbing his hair, and when she had done so, rest her hand lightly on his head while he wriggled about, . . . never pressing too hard, yet giving the impression of pulling his hair furiously." But she was able to satisfy Jefferson and played two seasons with him—six weeks in the autumn and five in the spring. Eventually she lived with the Jefferson family in their private railroad car, which was put up on a siding in towns to which the company toured. And each evening Jefferson would share a cab with her to and from the theatre. He seldom spoke about the theatre and would get up each morning, call for a cup of coffee, and spend the rest of the day painting. He was not generous with money, but he had a real concern that the poor people in the second balcony who paid only a quarter could see and hear as well as the people in the orchestra and first balcony. And he complained heavily about the carelessness of speech shown by younger actors as well as their lack of clarity in "pose and gesture."

> As he depended . . . , even when sitting in a box, on what he could see rather than on what he could hear, he used . . . to turn to me, when a round of applause occurred, and say: "I suppose it is all . . . fine, but I really don't catch anything, and don't . . . know what it is all about. I see these young gentlemen's cuffs, and they are walking about . . . in a . . . pleasant . . . manner, but what are they doing?"[379]

Between 1879 and 1904 Jefferson employed at least two hundred different actors as company members. Some of them were the leading figures of the nineteenth-century American theatre—Mrs. John Drew, her son-in-law Maurice Barrymore, Julia Marlowe, William J. Florence, James O'Neill, and Otis Skinner. But whenever possible, they were members of his own family—his sons, Thomas, Joseph, Jr., William Warren, and Charles Burke; his daughters-in-law, Blanche Bender and Eugenie Paul; his cousin, Jane Germon; and his godson, Jefferson Winter. When his sister, Connie Jefferson Jackson, joined the troupe in the fall of 1883, she was making her stage comeback after a fourteen-year retirement to play Tilly Slowboy, the dim-witted servant in *The Cricket on the Hearth*. Connie had been rendered deaf in an accident that also disfigured her. She was nearly forty-eight years old and so hard of hearing that her cues had to be given to her by gestures and signs.[380] Connie was not easily employable, but she was family, and Jefferson always employed family. In fact he used his sister's deformity as characterization. His daughter-in-law, Eugenie Paul Jefferson, recounts the following story:

> Mr. Jefferson was seated beside a young woman who was . . . enthusiastic over the performance of *The Cricket on the Hearth.* . . . After telling the actor . . . how she had laughed and cried, she spoke of Tilly Slowboy and the lady playing the part.
>
> "I think she was the funniest thing I ever saw! and *so* ugly! And oh, such a funny turn-up little nose! Tell me, Mr. Jefferson, how do you get people of that kind? Where *do* you pick them up?"
>
> Mr. Jefferson's eyes twinkled . . . as he replied:
>
> "Oh that is not such a difficult matter! We do not have to go so far. Sometimes we find them right in our own family. Tilly Slowboy is my sister."

Many of Jefferson's actors stayed for only a season, although most were employed for both his fall and spring tours. Some of them remained longer, and a few made careers out of being Jefferson actors, locked within a caste system dictated by "lines of business" as if they were in a traditional stock company. Robert L. Downing played young leading men for two years; Viola Allen did ingenue roles for three; Frederick Robinson played Sir Anthony Absolute for four seasons; Emma Vaders played Lydia Languish for five years, until she went insane after a performance in New Haven; Thomas Jefferson played Fag in *The Rivals* for eight years; John Jack did three parts for nine years; George Frederick Nash played secondary young men for eleven years; Edwin Varrey played older men in the company for twelve years; Harry W. Odlin played two minor roles in *Rip* for thirteen years; George W. Denham played the servant David for seventeen years (from 1887 until 1904); and Dudley McCann played nothing but the dwarf in the second act of *Rip Van Winkle* from 1882 until 1904—a total of twenty-two years in a wordless role.

Jefferson's stock company did not always work successfully. Rosa Rand played both the youthful, flighty, romantic Lydia Languish and the down-to-earth middle-aged peasant woman Gretchen Van Winkle in 1881. It is unlikely that she was well suited to both parts. Mrs. John Drew, then a member of the company, would have been far more appropriate, but she was there to play Mrs. Malaprop and would never have consented to undertake as minor a part as Dame Van Winkle. There were years when the Jefferson company fell far below critical expectations. In 1882 the *New York Mirror* praised Rip, but damned the rest.

The support was generally bad—very bad. Rose Wood, though a charming actress, is totally unsuited to the part of the shrewish

Figure 16. Mrs. John Drew as Mrs. Malaprop in *The Rivals*

Gretchen; Sam Hemple was a poor Nick Vedder and Harry Taylor a wretched Cockles. The children were acted by a pair of parroty youngsters. B. T. Ringgold made a stiff Hendrick. The exceptions to the unsatisfactory portions of the cast were Charles Waverly as Derrick, Lillian Lee, a sweet and sympathetic adult

Meenie, and Dudley McCann as the Dwarf. The scenery was fair but hitched and worked unevenly. Manager Abbey's stage-carpenters need a stirring up.[381]

In 1884, in Charleston, the prop baby used in *The Cricket on the Hearth* was handled "awkwardly by everyone," and the cue for the cricket chirp so vital to the third act was missed. In 1887 the *New York Mirror* felt that "with the exception of the mountain scene, which had some points of excellence, the scenery was poor."[382] And even Jefferson himself occasionally received bad notices. In 1882 a Chicago review indicated that both Rip and Bob Acres were showing their age.

> Joseph Jefferson . . . has ceased to be an actor in his presentations. . . . Nowadays Mr. Jefferson permits the situations to . . . drag him along, whilst he rests . . . on a . . . reputation . . . won in the past. Possibly, for . . . business purposes, this is just as well as any . . . artistic effort on Mr. Jefferson's part. What matters . . . if people are made to laugh and applaud over the frame which once held the fine old picture and are not conscious their imaginations are filling in from memory the cherished canvas. The effects, dollars and entertainment are accomplished.[383]

If there were critical doubts now and then, there was always financial success, at least for Jefferson. If houses were occasionally less than full, theatre managers, not company managers, took the loss. The company had already been guaranteed its fee. In 1879 the Cincinnati theatre took in only $500 on Jefferson's opening night. Five hundred dollars in this large city was bad business. One night in Erie, Pennsylvania, a far smaller place, brought in $400. But instances of failure were far outnumbered by financial triumphs. Ten years later Jefferson's advance man, Abraham L. Erlanger, declared:

> The spring tour of Mr. Jefferson . . . was opened at Cincinnati . . . and marked the largest house . . . ever in that theatre. All along the line, . . . the comedian has played to houses phenomenal in their size at increased prices. There were only two points played during the entire season when the receipts fell below the sum of $1,100 per night, and from this sum, they ranged upward to $2,500. There never has been a better opportunity to test the drawing qualities of Mr. Jefferson than was presented in Des Moines and Sioux City, Iowa.

At the latter point Mr. Jefferson's advanced rate [advanced ticket sales] opened on the same day that Booth and Barrett were to play there. With $3,000 and $4,000 tied up at each of these points for Booth and Barrett, the advance sale in Des Moines for Mr. Jefferson was over $600 the first hour, and in Sioux City, enough orders had been taken to more than sell the entire house.[384]

The company's financial success allowed Jefferson to continue to tour until his retirement in 1904, and continual touring allowed him to develop the equivalent of an early nineteenth-century stock company in which certain actors remained fixed in their roles while others advanced through lines of business. Connie's son, Charles Jackson, played a dwarf in Washington in 1881, but graduated the following year to the role of Hendrick Hudson. Charles Duval started as the mute Hendrick Hudson in 1887, but had moved to a speaking part as Jacob Stine by 1904. George W. Denham began with the minor role of Cockles in *Rip Van Winkle*, but gradually advanced to play Nick Vedder, a more significant part. Joseph Jefferson, Jr., began by playing Fag in *The Rivals* and eventually attained the role of Sir Lucius O'Trigger, the play's second comic lead. It was an unusually large jump for a Jefferson actor, but then Joe Jr. was a member of the family.

One of the children who performed with Jefferson in *Rip* grew up to become a leading actress in the company and eventually married Jefferson's godson, Jefferson Winter. Elsie Leslie Lyde, who played Lydia Languish in *The Rivals* and Dot in *The Cricket on the Hearth* from 1898 to 1901, began her career as a Jefferson actor at the age of five. She appeared in *Rip Van Winkle* in 1888, and wrote a memoir of the experience at the age of ten.

> I was Meenie, in a little blue skirt with a red petticoat and a black Gretchen waist, buttoned in front with one button and all the other buttons off, because I was supposed to be very poor, and my dress was torn in the skirt, with a great big black patch on it.
>
> I played for two seasons with him. We had one-night stands then. When we were traveling, Mr. Jefferson would read me funny things he found in the papers, and I would take a sleep in his arms. We would take those corner seats in the cars. Aunt Connie was in the company. She was Mr. Jefferson's sister, and

we . . . called her Aunt Connie, because she was such a little
lady. Her son, a great big boy, could pick her up in his arms and
carry her, she was so little. She wore the same size shoes I wear
now, No. eleven. . . .

The next season, Mr. Charley Jefferson . . . asked me to play
Hendrick, and I didn't feel . . . I could play it, because it was a
boy's part and I liked girls' parts best; but Mr. Jefferson said he
could not find a . . . boy to play Hendrick, and he could get a
little girl to play Meenie. I wore a little Dutch suit with tags on
the knees.[385]

Jefferson's use of actors over lengthy periods meant that the
company could adjust easily to changes in audience. Jefferson told
Otis Skinner that "certain cities need a little more force. 'This is
Pittsburgh,' I always say to my company when we are there, 'and you
must pull things open a little wider.'" Joe had forty years of touring
in which to find out how to play different cities. He played Pittsburgh eighteen times, St. Louis twenty-one times, Cincinnati
twenty-four times, and Baltimore twenty-six times; he played both
Macon and Savannah, Georgia, seven times and Sandusky, Ohio,
twice. There was no American city and few large towns that Jefferson
did not know.

A group of actors that worked together for this length of time
could pick up slight changes in performance. Charles Waverly
began playing Cockles in *Rip Van Winkle* in the spring of 1878,
and went on to larger roles—Derrick von Beekman, Sir Lucius
O'Trigger, and Humphrey Dobbins in *The Poor Gentleman* during
the next five years. When Waverly died in August 1884, Jefferson
wrote to William Winter:

Returned . . . on Saturday to find the sad news of . . . Charles
Waverly's death. . . . I liked him . . . he knew [the play] so well;
if I made an alteration of technical business . . . , he had an
intuition that seemed to complement me.

Now I am rehearsing another actor who tho [*sic*] careful . . .
I fear [will] fall . . . short of poor Charley. . . . If Monday is hot
and you are tired, don't come. [Apparently this is an invitation
to a rehearsal, as Jefferson was not performing.] Rip is such an
old story that there is nothing to say of it.[386]

Jefferson's letter assumes that alterations in the "technical business"—the blocking, the "bits," the way in which props were handled
—were a normal part of a play in performance as long as *Rip*. The
alterations, however, were minor. The drudgery of the early
nineteenth-century stock company, with its demand that actors have
forty or fifty roles at their command, had been replaced by the tedium
of endless road companies in which actors performed the same set of
three, two, or even one part for years at a time. The sloppiness of the
early nineteenth-century theatre was the result of overwork and
under-rehearsing; the sloppiness of the late nineteenth-century theatre was the result of boredom, the boredom of actors trudging from
town to town, night after night. In 1893 Jefferson, standing in The
Players, Edwin Booth's legacy to the acting profession, reminisced
about his recently dead friend: "The walls within which we stand, the
art, the comforts that surround us, represent a life of toil and travel,
sleepless nights, tedious journeys and weary work."[387]

Jefferson knew what he was talking about. The fate of any
nineteenth-century actor was an endless train ride, crisscrossing the
country, city after city, town after town, year after year. In Connecticut in 1889 Jefferson's acting partner, Billy Florence, ran into trouble during a curtain speech.

> He began by saying he never felt more at home than in that
> city. He knew the faces before him, and he was glad they all
> knew him, knew him as a boy, and he felt like one of them.
> Most of his success was due to the training he had received in
> that town, and he wound up by saying that his good old town
> of Hartford was the best place in the world.
>
> Just then a man in the front row said: "That's all right, Mr.
> Florence; but this ain't Hartford. This is New Haven."

The same story was told of John Barrymore, mistaking Cincinnati
for Detroit. Whether it was true is not as important as the fact that the
joke made sense. The tours of nineteenth- and even early twentieth-
century combination companies were a mind-numbing experience.[388]

As combination companies replaced stock companies, booking
became an essential element in theatrical success. As early as 1880,
when resident companies still existed, there were 250 companies
traveling. Touring had become so complex, with combination companies crisscrossing the country, that agents who worked on the

intricate booking schedules became a necessity. Theatre had become a national business moving toward monopoly control. Actors were becoming "talent," disposable commodities. The traffic on the road meant that performers were bound by contracts negotiated by theatrical booking agents with the owners of theatrical chains. Eventually these agents came to control not only the combination companies, but also the theatres in which they played.

In the beginning Jefferson had enough theatrical clout to avoid having an agent. He was a brand name, and as a brand name he had more control than many of his contemporaries; but he was still enmeshed in a system that dominated his life. The forerunner of the theatrical monopolist was A. H. S. Taylor, who scored a coup in the summer of 1880 by becoming Jefferson's agent, and eventually Charles Burke's partner. Taylor was one of the first theatrical agents in America representing actors, companies, and a group of seventy out-of-town managers simultaneously.[389]

It took time, however, before Jefferson completely relinquished control over his own touring arrangements. On February 14, 1883, he wrote from New Iberia to A. H. (Dan) Palmer, manager of the Union Square Theatre in New York, negotiating an engagement there starting October 8, 1883.[390] Joe was working on his fall schedule.

> I take it for granted that it is settled we open at the square on Oct. 8th for a season of six weeks?
>
> Please telegraph me at my expense if this is clearly understood as there are some dates up to this time filled up and I am anxious to know if we are all clear—have contracts made out as before and let them be sent here to C. B. Jefferson.[391]

This is Jefferson the businessman writing, still arranging his own schedule, using his son, Charles Burke, to deal with the paperwork, but clearly in control, making sure that every date is filled, able to take for granted certain terms of the contract, but dependent enough on Palmer to pay for the cost of a telegram. Every day on the schedule had to be filled. The members of the touring company were paid by the season whether they performed on a given day or not. The more tightly Jefferson could fill the schedule, the more money he could make. He would eventually perform matinees in one town and evening performances in another.

One of Jefferson's most influential agents was Abraham L. Erlanger who, with his partner, Marc Klaw, would form the controversial "theatrical syndicate" in 1896. Charles Burke hired Erlanger at the munificent sum of $300 a week to manage Jefferson's tours in the spring of 1888. One of Erlanger's first decisions was to raise the price of orchestra seats to $2 everywhere Jefferson played. Opening night was in Lexington, Kentucky. Jefferson wrote telling Erlanger he had made a mistake, because *Rip* was no longer a novelty. Erlanger replied: "Your letter came too late. Every seat in the house sold at $2!"[392]

With the agent came the publicist, whose job it was to keep the star's name before the public, particularly the New York public. One of the methods Jefferson's agents consistently used was rumors that he intended to quit the stage. They were never true and were probably circulated to encourage business for yet one more "final" performance. Thus Jefferson, in the winter of 1878–79, returned to Orange Island and announced that he did "not intend to resume playing for some time." But by March 24, 1879, he had opened *Rip* and *The Rivals* at the National Theatre in Washington, D.C., for a spring tour. In midsummer 1879 he announced again that he would play only "semi-occasionally" during the upcoming theatrical season. He was, however, already booked at Ford's South Broad Street Theatre in Philadelphia, and by August, 2, 1879, as small a place as Easton, Pennsylvania, was advertising his appearance. If Jefferson was booked into one-night stands in rural Pennsylvania, his intention to play "semi-occasionally" must have been a publicity stunt.

With the coming of the combination company, Jefferson began to re-form the family troupe he had known as a boy. On August 21, 1879, his son Thomas, then almost twenty-two, married the actress Eugenie Paul at Hohokus. She was immediately pressed into service to play the role of Meenie in *Rip* and Lydia Languish's servant, Nancy, in *The Rivals* during the fall 1879 tour. As always, Charles Burke was his father's manager; Thomas joined the company to play Fag; Jefferson's cousin Jane Germon performed Mrs. Malaprop; and William Winter's son, William Jefferson, also joined the company.[393] The family company allowed Jefferson to solve the personal-versus-professional conflict produced by the coming of the combination company, and to keep his family together even on the road. Home, in this system, became a vacation spot—a place to spend summer and winter holidays.

Those holidays were raucous; both the Hohokus and the New Iberia homes overflowed with people. Jefferson spent the summer of

1880 in New Jersey, in a house he described as "partial to full," with his father-in-law and mother-in-law; his son Tom's wife, Eugenie, and her infant baby; his sister, Con; and her son, Charles Jackson. As he wrote to William Winter, "you can imagine that our reserved seats are all taken. Standing room only!"[394] Jefferson reproduced, in a private railroad train going across America, the same crowded family he had experienced at home and the troupe he had known in boyhood. Josephine was ill, and Margaret was gone, but all the other members of the family eventually performed with him.

The one exception, of course, was Sarah. Although brought up in a theatrical family, she was not an actress, and she may have had chronic health problems. On August 3, 1880, Jefferson wrote to Winter: "I am going to take Mrs. J. away for a change as she is not feeling well. Our house has been so full all summer that I fear the activity has told on her. I expect to return in about a week."[395]

Jefferson's mention of Sarah's poor health is one of a long series of nonspecific references in letters to her medical problems. Sarah was ill most of their married life, but unlike Margaret, she was to benefit from the constant care that Joe, as a wealthy man, could lavish on her. His first wife had died as a young woman, and his concern for his second wife reflects a difference not only in his financial situation but in his professional life. Joe and Margaret had lived and worked together for most of the eleven years of their married life. By contrast, he spent as much as ten months of the year away from Sarah when they first married, and at least five months of the year away until he retired. By 1880, they had a family of young children, whom Sarah brought up while Joe traveled. Joe worked to support his first wife's parents, his second wife, his children, and eventually his grandchildren. He was a touring star and the leader of a combination company—but he was also the head of a family who could not stay home. The combination company allowed Jefferson to reestablish a family troupe, but simultaneously took him away from the family waiting at home. This tension would never be resolved in Sarah's case. In the case of his children, it would only be resolved when they grew up and joined the company to become Jefferson actors.

14

JEFFERSON:
THE PUBLIC MAN

Jefferson had been a public man all his life, but his public life had been largely confined to stage performances. There had been forays into offstage philanthropy as early as January 12, 1849, when he participated in the founding of the Actor's Order of Friendship in Philadelphia. Begun as a benevolent association to aid the sick and indigent, the organization eventually became a theatrical union. At its founding Jefferson was not yet twenty years old, but he already regarded himself as a member of a profession. Throughout his career he regularly participated in benefits, but even during "The Little Church Around the Corner" incident he remained essentially hidden from view and did not speak publicly about the event for eighteen years.[396]

Jefferson participated in the popular theatrical traditions of his time—the tribute, the professional matinee, and the benefit. Tributes were recognitions of a theatrical anniversary ("fifty years upon the stage") or of a significant career moment. On June 15, 1880, for instance, a group of eminent New Yorkers held a public breakfast in the large hall at Delmonico's to honor Edwin Booth, five days before his departure for England.

The "breakfast" was a nineteenth-century male ritual in which wealthy men participated in an elaborate, boisterous banquet to mark an occasion—in this case, to display their patriotic support of an American cultural symbol who was embarking upon an English tour. Although called a "breakfast," the tribute began at noon with the 150 guests, all male, assembling in Delmonico's first-floor parlors to await Booth's arrival. Letters from prominent individuals unable to attend were displayed on a table. Booth, as the guest of honor, arrived after the other attendees, and at about 1 P.M. Judge John R. Brady took the actor's right arm under his left and announced in stentorian tones: "Gentlemen, come to breakfast." The doors of the dining hall were thrown open, and the crowd entered while a string band on the south gallery played them in with a march.

The hall was decorated with theatrical pictures, portraits, and busts, including the famous portrait of Edwin Booth as Iago, but few theatre people were there.[397] Jefferson sat on the dais, second from the left of Booth, along with Lawrence Barrett, Lester Wallack, and William Warren, all of whom, like Jefferson, were members of the testimonial committee. Each guest found a *boutonnière* in the folds of his napkin and a watercolor-decorated French menu set on broad ribbons. Grace was said, and the guests tucked into:

Clams

Consommé

Hors d'Oeuvres

Boudine à la Polonnaise [polish sausage]

Cold Salmon, vert pré

Beef Filet à l'Aquitaine

Ailes de volaille à la Béarnaise [poultry wings]

Lamb Cutlets à la Parisienne

Sorbet à la Régence

Bécassines [snipe] and Pigeons

Salad

Terrine de Foie Gras

Galantine de Chapon [capon]

Petits Pois [peas], Haricots verts [green beans], asperges [asparagus]

Gelee aux Ananas [pineapple jelly], Gaufres [waffles] à la Creme

Napolitaine, Soufflé aux Macarons, Strawberries, Petit Fours

Fruits and Desserts

Coffee

The lavishness of the courses symbolically celebrated the importance of the occasion and the honoree; guests were not expected to eat everything on their plates. Once cigars were lighted, Judge Brady began the proceedings, and upon the first mention of Booth's name the guests rose to their feet, cheering and waving their napkins while the band played "Hail to the Chief." It was an appropriate theme song. Booth was the symbolic president of the American theatre, taking the American flag into cultural battle. This was followed by a long line of toasts and formal speeches in response to the toasts. The clergy turned out to bless the event, although the main clerical speaker admitted to hardly knowing the honoree. The relationship between the bar and the stage was toasted, because so many members of the audience were wealthy lawyers. Mrs. Booth was saluted, although the event was thought too raucous to permit female attendance.

And then the actors seated on the dais, in full view of the audience, were called upon one by one to perform by saying a few words to entertain the wealthy and powerful who were, in turn, there to honor an actor. The brevity of their responses implies a reluctance to comply, but they were accustomed to compliance. No matter how famous, actors could never refuse. The people honoring them were not only their audience: They were the icons of a respectability to which they aspired and to which Edwin Booth's personal prestige and generosity had led them.

Jefferson, called upon to respond to a toast to "The Home Life of Edwin Booth," a subject on which he could have said a fair amount, acknowledged that "he had known Mr. Booth since boyhood. Together they had watched the playful kitten and the ball of yarn. His home life was equal to his public life; it was so successful and brilliant that it needed no further comment."

His brevity was matched only by that of his cousin, William Warren, who, when asked to make a few remarks, replied: "I came to breakfast Booth and not to praise him. I wish him God-speed." Booth himself said nothing. The breakfast concluded with the singing of "Auld Lang Syne," and the reporter of the *New York Times*, his attention drawn to the band, noted that "a number of ladies found seats in the balcony with the musicians and seemed to derive as much benefit from the wit and wisdom of the speakers as the boisterous breakfasters on the floor below them." There is no indication that the wealthy men attending the breakfast were disappointed by the remarks made by the professional actors before them. There is, however, a sense of the actors suffering themselves to be displayed offstage.[398]

Sometimes they worked for their meal. On April 4, 1896, the three hundred members of New York's Lotos Club honored Jefferson at a dinner. The nine-course menu was printed on cards decorated with pictures of his most famous characters, and he spent the night autographing them in a signature he described as "getting more and more like the weather report." The dinner was highlighted by bluepoint oysters, striped bass, filet of beef, and roast squab. Ices reached the tables at the end of the meal in the shape of miniature busts of Jefferson, and the old actor rose to, as he put it, "talk shop" because "it is the only thing I know." He regaled the group with a series of career anecdotes whose language so closely paralleled that of his *Autobiography* that they clearly had become set pieces for him. After dinner a clergyman "dwelt upon the manner in which [Jefferson] amid the temptations of a stage life . . . succeeded in keeping his name clean and unsullied." Jefferson rose and said that "he objected to being singled out for a characterization of exclusive respectability. He could not permit a speaker, even a clergyman, to pay him a tribute which implied a reproach to the profession among which he numbered scores of friends." The *New York Dramatic Mirror* noted that "the time has passed when actors need patting on the back by clergymen."[399]

Like the breakfast, the dinner was intended for and attended primarily by people outside the theatre. The actors had "let themselves out . . . to attract curiosity seekers." On the other hand, the professional matinee was closed to the public and open only to theatre people. It occurred on a weekday afternoon other than Wednesday or Saturday, when performances were normally scheduled, and allowed actors to see and honor each other's work. Jefferson took such a matinee on October 26, 1882. It had been announced as early as October 8. The *New York Mirror* reported: "Jefferson's professional matinee today . . . will be a notable event. Nearly every actor and actress in town . . . secured seats. No tickets will be sold to outsiders, as is generally the rule, and the performance will be enjoyed all the more for that reason."

At times the tribute and the theatrical matinee were combined. On March 20, 1890, William H. Crane and Joseph Brooks, managers of the Star Theatre, gave a professional matinee of their hit play, *The Senator*, which only members of the theatrical profession could attend. But the performance was also a testimonial to Jefferson, who was performing in New York at the time. Crane and Brooks were providing an opportunity for him to see the play and to be seen seeing it. The financial beneficiaries were the producers. The demand for tickets was enormous. Everyone wanted front-row seats in the orchestra or balcony. Offended members of the profession returned their tickets with caustic notes. When the management decided against standing room, the crowds in front of the theatre protested against the policy.[400]

Traditionally there were two types of theatrical benefits: those given to augment the income of theatrical personnel, and those given for charitable purposes. In stock companies, virtually every member of the troupe, down to the box office staff, was guaranteed at least one night per season when he or she received the evening's receipts minus expenses. This worked only when stock companies were the primary organizational structure of the theatre, and actors lived and worked in specific places, sometimes for years at a time. They became members of their communities and could count on their neighbors to "give them a bumper" on benefit nights. Stars, on the other hand, negotiated for benefits as part of their contracts. While they might occasionally perform for charity, their primary interest in benefits was personal gain. In the decade between 1865 and 1875, Jefferson commanded a benefit virtually every Friday night (the second most lucrative evening of the theatrical week). This was purely a financial arrangement, a way for star actors to obtain more money from management. But in the last quarter of the nineteenth century, benefits became, as they are now, solely charitable events. Actors in a "combination" company were no longer members of a community, and individual stars traveled with their supporting casts. Local managers paid for a company, and if, like Jefferson, the star was the head of the company, he or she paid the rest of the personnel. Benefits became unusual occurrences.

Like the breakfast or dinner, a benefit depended on the willingness of wealthy people to pay for seats; however, it used actors not as celebrities but as what they really were—performers in a play. Actors had been participating in charitable benefits since the eighteenth century, particularly as a way of gaining public approbation for their work. Joe's father, for example, had arranged a benefit for the Galena Fire Department on February 4, 1839, when the family was touring Illinois.

The success of any benefit depended not only on the charity supported, but also on the reputation of the actors performing. Consequently, as Jefferson became a national icon, getting him to do a benefit meant guaranteeing a lot of money. On December 4, 1884, he went from Philadelphia, where his company was performing, to

New York to play for the Actors' Fund benefit at the Academy of Music at 2:15 P.M. His fare was donated by Samuel Carpenter of the Pennsylvania Railroad. His picture appeared on the front page of the *New York Mirror*, which lauded his generosity. The president-elect of the United States, Grover Cleveland, and the mayor-elect of New York, W. R. Grace, were scheduled to attend. Tickets, ranging in price from $1.50 for the rear balcony to $25 for a proscenium box, went on sale at 9 A.M. the preceding Monday. By 1 P.M. over $2,000 had been taken in at the box office, and the only seats available were in the family circle and one or two boxes. Scalpers were already at work. By 6 P.M. on Wednesday night approximately $3,300 had been collected. The fund estimated that it would net $3,700 on the proceedings. It actually netted $4,036.50. Certainly Jefferson's appearance must have been a factor, because the fund had done very poorly at its benefit the year before.[401]

Benefits allowed theatrical professionals to assist their own— namely, aged and indigent actors and their families as in the famous series of benefits held for George Holland's family after "The Little Church Around the Corner" incident. On May 10, 1887, Jefferson appeared, along with Edwin Booth, Lawrence Barrett, James O'Neill, and Mrs. Drew, in a performance in honor of the semicentennial of C. W. Couldock, who had performed with Jefferson in *Our American Cousin* and was a longtime friend. Jefferson, O'Neill (as Sir Lucius O'Trigger), and Mrs. Drew performed the third act of *The Rivals*. The benefit cleared $4,200 for Couldock, who had just turned seventy-two and announced vehemently from the stage that he had no intention of retiring.[402]

When given on behalf of an individual actor, benefits, as opposed to testimonials, generally signaled the termination of a career, the onset of retirement, the presence of illness, or the imminence of death. Couldock proved to be an exception. Eight years later, on May 17, 1895, Jefferson presided at the Fifth Avenue Theatre at an auction sale of seats for yet another Couldock benefit, this one commemorating the old actor's retirement at the age of eighty. The sale began at 1 P.M., and Jefferson began with a speech praising Couldock. He switched into auctioneer lingo and sold a box for $325. Then he introduced the playwright James A. Herne, who wielded the gavel and in turn sold Jefferson a box for the same amount. The benefit itself occurred at 2 P.M. on May 31, 1895, at the Fifth Avenue Theatre in New York. Jefferson performed in an all-star production of *The Rivals* with Henry Miller, Nat Goodwin, W. H. Crane, DeWolf Hopper, and Mrs. Drew. Sarah Jefferson was in a box in the audience; Charles Burke was in the orchestra. A report was circulating that Couldock was about to enter the Edwin Forrest home for indigent actors, but the old actor appeared on stage, again vehemently declaring: "I am still open to an engagement."[403]

The most famous testimonial or benefit in which Jefferson performed was on May 21, 1888, when he played the First Gravedigger in an all-star production of *Hamlet*. Edwin Booth played Hamlet, Lawrence Barrett was the ghost, Helena Modjeska played Ophelia, and W. J. Florence was the Second Gravedigger. Given as a testimonial to the producer Lester Wallack at the Metropolitan Opera house, the production played to 3,950 people, and the evening's profits came to $21,560.17.[404]

Throughout the 1880's, Jefferson began to assume more and more of a public role, and like any celebrity he was an object of admiration, curiosity, and suspicion. He performed not only onstage but off and simultaneously enjoyed and hated the role. He was gradually encouraged to assume a public lifestyle by Richard Watson Gilder, a poet, man of letters, and editor of the *Century Magazine*, with whom Jefferson became friends in 1874–1876. Years before, when Gilder was working as senior editor of a small newspaper in his hometown of Newark, New Jersey, he had been seized with a desire to act with Jefferson.

> I went to my friend Mr. Taylor who owned the Opera House and told him . . . I wanted to act that night with Jefferson. My friend . . . responded with . . . promptness . . . : "All right; come . . . to the Opera House to-night, and I will arrange the matter." I came, was introduced to Jefferson, who presented me to his stage-manager, who dressed and rehearsed me, . . . first as a speechless ghost of one of Hendrik Hudson's crew, second as an inhabitant of the village of Falling Water. In a single speech . . . I demanded to know of the white-bearded and long-haired Rip, "Who's your barber?" I was standing in the wings when Rip was . . . driven . . . into the storm by . . . Gretchen, and I heard him heave, all unconsciously, a deep sigh as he passed from the door into the darkness. Yet in a moment the actor

went on with the conversation with me . . . where it had been left off a little while before.[405]

For a modern theatre professional, the idea of taking an amateur into a production is unimaginable. But the twentieth century has focused on what were called "combination companies"—groups of actors and technicians united to produce one production night after night. When he first met Gilder, Jefferson was still working with the resident companies found in each city he played. He certainly did not know the young newspaperman, but for that matter he may not have known most people in the company. An amateur with one line meant nothing. Moreover, the senior editor of even a small-town newspaper had potential power, and Jefferson courted the powerful. When they met later in life, "Jefferson spoke of the time [Gilder] played the ghost and villager with him in Newark." Gilder was, of course, impressed that Jefferson remembered him, but it is far more likely that Joe was being polite—and was aware of Gilder's significance, in 1874, as an influential critic and editor. On November 20, 1874, Gilder wrote:

> Joe Jefferson was in the office today. He came in answer to my note and made an appointment to come home with us after the play, Tuesday night. He was much interested in the pictures and was extremely intelligent on the subject of art. . . . Jefferson always speaks modestly. He said, when I nagged him about playing something else, that the play of Rip was greater than he —that is, its reputation was. He said that when he played other things, his friends came to see him, but the crowd stayed away. And yet they say he is delicious in other characters.[406]

Jefferson was a major American actor and had been since 1865. *Rip Van Winkle* was one of the greatest hits of the American theatre. But its star still listened to criticism; he was in the office of an influential editor, and when he contradicted Gilder, he did it by charming the man. The following week they continued their acquaintance.

> The day after Thanksgiving, I went around after the play to Booth's and brought Jefferson to the Studio (Gilder's home]. We thought we were more impressed with his playing that night than ever; he seemed greater. But this Friday Night we had him to ourselves for two hours and a half.

He stayed till half-past one! He brought some new photographs of the ancient Rip and asked us about coming out and spending three or four days with him in the summer.[407]

There is every reason to believe that Jefferson and Gilder were genuine friends. They continued to see each other for the rest of Jefferson's life, and Gilder was a pallbearer at his funeral. But the two men also fed off each other professionally. Gilder published Jefferson's autobiography. He arranged for Jefferson's first speaking engagement, and he introduced Jefferson to his stable of literary people. On September 25, 1882, the Southern poet, novelist, and essayist, George W. Cable, met Jefferson in Gilder's New York home.

They made me a delicious cup of tea. Just as I was dropping sugar in, in walks Mr. Joe Jefferson, the comedian. We had a three hours' talk. I like him extremely. He seems good and *sweet*. He said: "I have done things in my life I am ashamed of; we all do that; but I have no secret. I can't lie, or cheat or steal; yet I am the fifth generation of an unbroken line of comedians." I have promised to go and visit him on his island if I possibly can next Spring.

The conversation is odd and possibly disingenuous. Cable came from a religious puritanical background and harbored a distrust of actors on moral grounds. He was amazed to find Jefferson "good and *sweet*," and Jefferson, who may have picked up on his new-found acquaintance's naïveté, began playing Rip, a man with weaknesses but essentially good at heart. And then comes the astonishing statement: "I can't lie, or cheat or steal; yet I am the fifth generation of an unbroken line of comedians." Is Cable's memory colored by his prejudices or is Jefferson admitting and possibly sharing the prejudice of the age? Why does he invite a man he has just met to Orange Island? Is it because he knows how unlikely it is that Cable will come? Why does he spend three hours talking to someone who is ambiguous about the morality of the theatre? Does he see himself as an apostle to the Gentiles, a theatrical ambassador impressing the nontheatrical world with the respectability of actors? Was he emotionally bound to please everyone he met?[408]

Initially Cable refused to see Jefferson act, but he finally relented and completely changed his mind. A year later, on October 28, 1883, Cable wrote to his daughter Lucy:

I was invited . . . to go and hear Joseph Jefferson play *The Cricket on the Hearth*. I did so, and if there is anything wrong in that—no, I'll not put it that way. [If] it isn't pure and sweet and refreshing and [as] proper a diversion as spending the same length of time over a pretty, sweet and good story book, then I'm a dunce. . . .

Well, I've neither time nor paper left to tell you how lovely—how lovely—Jefferson is in the play. I feel this morning as if I had a bath in pure cool water. I thank God for the pleasure I have had—now let me see if I cannot make some feeble return for it before the rising sun goes down.

Cable's need to atone for his pleasure was part of his Puritan distrust of theatrical entertainment, a distrust Jefferson encountered as a boy in Illinois, as a man trying to bury a friend, and as a public figure chiding an insensitive clergyman at his own testimonial. He fought it all his life. On October 30, 1883, Cable met Jefferson again at the Gilders, this time in the company of the English poet Matthew Arnold. Jefferson arrived late, at 1:30 A.M. after a performance, and Cable recorded: "Oh! then we had a good time. We sat down together at once & had it good. We talked about the principle of the subordination of details in art. Every art except music was represented by some one . . . of noted ability. It was a night to remember all one's days."

It was 1:30 in the morning; Jefferson had just given a performance, changed out of costume and makeup, and gone out for an evening of intellectual entertainment. Is this the perennial need of actors to unwind, or does he feel the necessity of making a public appearance, of continuing to entertain the wealthy and powerful? A week later Cable wrote of a personal encounter with him at a society breakfast:

It was a delightful affair. All nice people. Had some delightful chats with Jefferson, who can talk about . . . many things and always with taste and . . . modesty. . . . He invariably refuses all kinds of alcoholic drink with gentle firmness. . . . Coffee seems to be the . . . limit of indulgence. He delights to talk about painting which he . . . works hard on whenever he is not in the theatrical season.

A very funny . . . thing happened. I noted that the two waitresses were . . . pretty; but in passing dishes, scraping crumbs off the cloth, & c., they were . . . raw and slow. After dinner, as

Mr. Jefferson & myself were sitting . . . talking, Mrs. [William Herbert] Morse [the breakfast's hostess] approached & said they had all had such . . . enjoyment in seeing Mr. Jefferson's plays that they thought it but right to reciprocate & act a little farce for his amusement. I saw him try to hold back the dismay that began to gather in his face. (For his time was limited—he had a matinee at two.) Mrs. Morse, however, opened the door into the hall & called for the "actors to enter." The two waitresses came in, & she proceeded to introduce them . . . to the ancient Joseph. . . . They were two society girls, & the farce had already been played in the dining-room. It was a hit. The laugh was long and hearty.[409]

Cable's pleasure at Jefferson's alcoholic abstinence is a reflection of his expectations. He expected Jefferson to be a drinking man, because he thought of him as Rip. Jefferson, who certainly took a drink in private, avoided public drinking once he had established himself as a drunkard on stage. Rip's alcoholism was still an issue with which critics had to wrestle. Jefferson was acting a role offstage for Cable and others that excused his most famous part in the theatre.

To the modern reader, the "society girls" playing waitresses are distasteful in their implied social condescension, but this is not what bothered Jefferson. His dismay at the possibility of being subject to an amateur theatrical performance underscores the fragility of his position. Jefferson was a public figure, and there is a sense of his being trapped in the role, subjected to the possibility of having to sit through amateur theatricals while simultaneously manipulating his public image so as to strengthen his audience's approbation of his stage performances. Why did he go to society breakfasts? He had been brought up all his life to please the public, to cater to the rich and powerful, and although he was now one of the rich and powerful himself, he retained the notion of being their servant. While the "society girls" are serving food, Jefferson is, in actuality, the main dish being served—the star attraction at breakfast.

His public esteem, however, enabled Jefferson to act in a capacity he enjoyed—namely, that of an expert consulted on his opinion. Letters came soliciting his advice on scripts.[410] In December 1882 the *North American Review* published an article entitled "Success on the Stage," in which it asked six leading actors, Jefferson among them, to discuss how to be successful in the theatre. Jefferson's answer to the *North American Review* reflected his life situation.

> The art must be commenced at the foundation, or the superstructure can scarcely stand. The student should . . . enter upon the lower walks of the profession, and this is his first stumbling-block, because the lower positions are erroneously considered to be degrading. But, to "carry a banner" is necessary and is certainly not degrading to a beginner in the art of acting. All professions require that the student shall master the drudgery of his calling.
>
> . . . The study of gesture and elocution, if taken in homeopathic doses and with . . . care, may be of service; but great effects can only be produced by great feeling, and if the feeling be true and intense, the gesture and the elocution must obey it.

He also gave advice freely to other members of his company. When Mrs. Drew was playing Mrs. Malaprop, she said one night: "Mr. Jefferson, I'm not getting the laughs I used to get. What is the matter?" I replied: "Mrs. Drew, it's because you read the lines as though *you* thought them funny; try reading them seriously." He told the young actor Otis Skinner:

> Work at your part like the dickens when you're studying effects, but don't carry your tools into the theater and let the audience see them. Leave them in the workshop. When I die, I suppose people will say . . . that I was one of the most mechanical actors in America, and they will be . . . right. I am. . . . Real comedy is the most difficult and serious business in the world. [No] two audiences [are] ever alike, and that was why [I] never tire of playing . . . [my] old parts. One must not be caught napping in a performance, for it is from the . . . varying audiences that the tone and tempo of a performance is set. . . . I always . . . tell myself I am playing the part for the first time.

In semipublic occasions, such as tea with the Gilders, he held forth on contemporary actors.

> He said he thought Salvini the greatest tragic actor he had ever seen. He did not like the death-scene in *Othello,* however, where Salvini curls up like a beast. "Art is not imitation of nature but built upon nature. There should be nothing offensive as is that

part of Othello; he could teach any ignorant fellow to do that, but the great artist should know better."

He believed that you actually got some real substance from your audience when you were acting—and gave a real substance back to it. It would exhaust him beyond measure to play his part without an audience. But with an audience, he is not at all tired. The secret of acting is to keep the heart warm and the head cool.[411]

The Gilder correspondence is the earliest record of Jefferson's theories of acting. From a modern standpoint, he was a technician, dropping out of character the instant he was offstage, never so immersed in a role that he behaved indecorously during a performance. But he experienced his work on stage as a combination of intellectual detachment and emotional involvement. He understood that emotional involvement produced appropriate external behavior, but he concentrated on the behavior not on the internal psychological reality. For psychological involvement, Jefferson substituted external detail and commitment to precision in replicating physical gestures on a moment-to-moment basis.

It was a short step from "performing" at tea or in print to lecturing in public. Jefferson began to develop a career as a platform speaker in 1883, when Gilder arranged for a lecture to benefit the Kindergarten Association, of which he was president. Eventually he developed a sub-career as a public speaker with set pieces that could be interchanged so that when he spoke, he could use material over and over just as he did as an actor. He even developed a costume for his role as a speaker.[412]

This disguise consisted of a long black Prince Albert coat, black waistcoat, which, after the Southern fashion, was fastened by one or two buttons at the bottom only or, . . . one at the top and one at the bottom, disclosing peeps of a rather loosely starched white shirt. Gray trousers, patent leather shoes, and a turndown collar with a red and black Windsor tie, completed his costume. The tie gave him an artistic jauntiness but scarcely corresponded with the rest of his dress.[413]

As an actor, Jefferson must have been aware that the formality of a black Prince Albert coat did not match a Southern waistcoat and a Windsor tie. He was simultaneously assuring his audience of his dignity and reminding them of his profession as a comedian. Typically his lectures began with verbal gestures of self-deprecation, an assumed shyness or reluctance that actually prompted his audience to remember how famous he was. On June 7, 1892, as he came forward at the annual business meeting of the Actor's Fund at Palmer's Theatre in New York, the crowd greeted his "droll expression of countenance" with "a tumultuous welcome."[414]

> My Comrades (applause), you seem to be well acquainted with me. I don't mean personally so much as with my nature, for there is nothing I enjoy more than a good round of applause. (Applause). I did not mean that to trick you out of another . . . but simply to say that a round of applause . . . answers two purposes. In the first place, it assures me that I am welcome, and in the second, it gives me time to think of what I am going to say. . . . (Laughter) Possibly if that lovely lady who just sang would pursue that interruption until the close of the entertainment, I might have time to collect my thoughts. . . .
>
> Let me see, where was I? I think I left off where I stuck. Oh! I naturally approach you with some timidity.

The idea that Jefferson, who had been performing since childhood, would approach an audience with timidity at the age of sixty-two was a ploy to charm spectators through a protestation of inexperience on the part of someone they knew to be a thorough professional. From this point Jefferson launched into a series of remotely related issues. Some of them were suggested by questions he had received from audience members, a practice he eventually stopped because of his growing deafness.[415] Eventually working with note-cards, Jefferson turned these questions into part of his act.

> "Did I consider that the stage had improved in its condition during the last, well say, from one hundred to two hundred years?" (Laughter). . . . Of course, you are going a . . . ways back, and though I may claim some . . . experience in the theatrical profession, the date you mention is a little before my time. But I can tell you it has improved. . . . I [could] . . . explain how it had improved. But that would take too long. . . .
>
> "Mr. Jefferson, what is your opinion of the starring system? Don't you think it is . . . pernicious and that it has stood in the way of dramatic advancement and that it has . . . dwarfed the

talents of others?" [It is a] delicate question . . .; there was a time, when I was in the stock, when I thought the starring system was the most pernicious thing I knew of, but since that time, I have somewhat altered my opinion. (Applause). In fact, in the early days, when I was in the stock, I looked upon every manager as a tyrant, but when I became a manager myself, I considered every actor a conspirator. (Loud laughter).

When faced with a "delicate question," Jefferson was usually elusive, preferring to charm his audience with the answer rather than tackle the issue head on. His approach to politics was typical. "I wish you to bear . . . in mind . . . [that] within three days, . . . the Republican party will nominate either Blaine or Harrison, or somebody else. (Laughter). I merely desire that to go upon the record, . . . and . . . I will stand by what I have said."

Jefferson could have very strong political opinions. Richard Watson Gilder records that in 1896 Jefferson thought the state of the nation was "extremely dangerous," remarking that "the hatred of the West for the East is something much deeper than we have any idea of." He saw the West as an over-advertised region with a treacherous climate that was producing an overabundance of wheat and was heavily subject to foreign competition. This is hardly the idyllic prairie he pictured in the boyhood section of his *Autobiography,* and it was the kind of opinion that he never expressed in public.[416]

Jefferson clung to neutrality, as if a public slip might end his career. By mid-December 1897, for instance, he indicated his opposition to the Theatrical Syndicate, the artistic and business monopoly led by Marc Klaw and Abraham Erlanger, which was attempting to control not only theatres but the attractions that could be shown in them. Although he expressed opposition, Jefferson also said he preferred to remain neutral, having friends on both sides. He was unable to come out strongly against the trust because Charles Burke was working with Klaw and Erlanger, but he continued to "insist on his right to determine his own prices based on the exigencies of the season."[417] To some degree, Jefferson's avoidance of controversy was well founded. Actors could not afford to make enemies. But his neutrality toward the trust earned him a good deal of enmity.

His enemies rejoiced. They took occasion to accuse Mr. Jefferson of . . . selfishness. They said that he had not produced a new play in . . . years; that he carried about the country a company of inferior actors; that his scenery had become a byword; in short, that he was non-progressive and mercenary, without . . . love for his art or . . . his profession, and that so long as he was not "squeezed" himself by the Trust, he cared nothing as to what might befall the rest.[418]

Jefferson depended on the goodwill of audiences who came to see him season after season, and when he addressed them as a speaker, he knew he was there to provide charm, not controversy. When asked to compare theatregoers in New York, Boston, Philadelphia, and Chicago, he answered: "That's an odd question to ask a man in my profession. I must be diplomatic. New York, as I am here, but I tell you frankly I should say Boston in Boston."

Again when asked, "What is your favorite role?" [he responded:] "Well I don't know. It is generally the one I don't happen to be acting. When I have been doing Bob Acres . . . , I feel a fondness for Caleb Plummer, and when I grow tired of . . . Caleb, I fancy Rip Van Winkle. On the whole, however, I think I prefer Rip."[419]

Even when faced with a topic on which there could be no real controversy, Jefferson approached the issue with charm. On March 29 the Aldine Club and the Up-town Association gave a complimentary dinner in his honor. Faced with an audience painfully aware of the recent blowing up of the battleship *Maine* and the impending Spanish-American War, Jefferson recalled his 1837 combat with Master Edwin Titus, a battle in which he portrayed the vanquished Spanish pirate, and concluded: "I have often thought lately that I was . . . the . . . cause of the present strained relations between this country and Spain." In his *Autobiography*, ten years before, the pirate had been Greek. Jefferson was simply giving his audience what it wanted.[420]

Jefferson stuck to charming set pieces, including his farm in New Jersey, a rebuttal of the theory espoused by Ignatius Donnelly that Shakespeare's plays were written by Francis Bacon, a description of Shakespeare's burial place in Stratford-upon-Avon, a comparison of the orator and the actor, a discussion of tragedy versus comedy, stories of the English tragedians David Garrick and William Charles Macready, a reading of the Gravedigger scene from *Hamlet*, and the difference between "genius" and "art."

The topic on which he could of course be expected to speak and write with considerable expertise was acting. On April 28, 1897, Jefferson addressed the graduates of the American Academy of Dramatic Art at the Carnegie Lyceum in New York. Referring to the graduates as "fellow students," he emphasized the importance of "craft," or what would be called "technique" in modern acting, as an adjunct to what Jefferson called "genius," or spontaneous inspiration. Jefferson understood the importance of spontaneity on stage, but playing the same roles for forty years had taught him how difficult it was to produce night after night.

> The greatest things . . . on . . . stage are not those that are thought out but those that happen. But suppose they don't happen. Just imagine actually waiting for an hour and keeping an audience waiting until it happens. We must prepare . . . in case it don't happen. . . . Speak each line for the audience as though spoken for the first time. The play is supposed to be performed for the first time, and if the audience sees you rattle if off and keep answering the questions of the next person before they are finished, . . . your work lacking verity, will not be satisfying. That is the greatest error of my profession, the anticipation until the audience don't know where to catch you. They are willing if you will give them time. Of course, you must understand you must not give them too much time. Many of them get the joke at once. Some of them don't for a second or two, so that you simply wait sufficiently long to let one portion of the audience become thoroughly saturated with your effect, keeping the other portion interested in your pantomime. . . . It is almost mechanical and to say that these things cannot be learned or cannot be taught is absurd. . . . You have to play the same part very often—night after night, and yet play as if you never had played it before.

When asked how much an actor should immerse himself in a role, the burning artistic question of the late nineteenth-century theatre, Jefferson, as always, reverted to neutrality.

> That . . . depends upon an actor. Some actors like to entirely forget themselves in a character. Another actor would be confused if he tried to do so. If you can produce a better effect by immersing yourself into the character, it is better to produce it. . . . In nature nobody is looking at us; in art we have an

audience. . . . I always feel best when the emotion is strong but does not run away with the intelligence, that is to speak plainer, with the head cool and the heart warmer.[421]

It was a natural step from lectures and interviews to full-length prose. By October 7, 1886, while performing in Chicago, Jefferson was working on his autobiography. He later told Francis Wilson that he had begun the book as a private memoir for his children, but that he had been encouraged to publish by the American novelist William Dean Howells.[422] He had never published anything and began to write hesitantly, eventually getting up during the night to jot down thoughts that had come to him.

> I have never kept a diary. . . . I am fortunate in having a good memory; I wrote the entire book from that. . . . I would awake in the middle of the night . . . and would think of . . . my past experiences. If I went to sleep again, I would find, in the morning, that . . . I could not think what that something was. After this, I had a pencil and notebook by my bedside, and . . . as I awoke, . . . I would rise and write out the material.[423]

Edwin Booth was in Chicago, and Jefferson wrote to him:

My Dear Ned:

I was on the point of writing you when I read your card.

I am scratching down my memories . . . connected with the Players of the Past. Your father is assured an important position.

I have . . . one or two interesting incidents hitherto unrevealed, and I thought . . . that you would like to review them—it won't take over five minutes—so if I don't hear from you . . . , I'll drop around at your Hotel on Saturday about 11 A.M., and we'll crack some old chestnuts together.

Ever thine

Joe[424]

What is so strange is that Booth, Jefferson's best friend and the person to whom he brought the manuscript for approval, is never mentioned in the autobiography. Francis Wilson attributes this to the fact that Jefferson "did not feel justified in naming and estimating contemporary players," and consequently concentrated on past performers.[425] Again neutrality was his mode of operation.

In spite of the honors that were heaped upon him in later life,

Jefferson never attained the public prestige that Booth enjoyed. In part this was because of a difference in the level of esteem accorded tragedians over comic actors, but Booth also had been highly influential as a manager, theatre builder, and founder of a club for male actors. He set himself up as an artistic icon, whereas Jefferson set himself up as a businessman. But the two were great friends, and Jefferson was always there to support Booth financially when his New York theatre needed a star attraction and personally by lending his presence to Booth's greatest social accomplishment—his establishment of The Players.[426] It was a moment when the theatrical establishment of nineteenth-century America asserted its right to respectability.

As Booth's health declined, Jefferson's stature increased. He began to move into his role as "dean of the American theatre." On April 30, 1892, the producer A. M. Palmer announced that Jefferson had agreed to open the Actor's Fund Fair in Madison Square Garden and had sent a $500 contribution. For the occasion the Garden was converted into a city street filled with theatrical reminiscences—The Globe Theatre, Dickens's Old Curiosity Shop, and even the Chatham Street Theatre in which Jefferson had made his New York debut in 1849. Within each façade there was a boutique stocked with donated merchandise and staffed by society matrons. The fair began at 8 P.M. with its officers mounting a set of stairs into a overhanging box on the south side of the building. Jefferson entered moving "lightly up the stairs" with Palmer and the much-enfeebled Edwin Booth, who was unable to speak publicly. Both actors were warmly applauded, and Jefferson made a brief speech. Then Booth and Jefferson bowed, hand in hand, to an applauding audience, while the band played "The Star-Spangled Banner," and Mrs. A. M. Palmer waved the American flag above them. It was a formal public acknowledgement of their equality in tragedy and comedy.[427]

That fall Booth visited Jefferson at Buzzards Bay, and the two men walked on the beach together. Booth knew he was dying, and Jefferson later recalled that "we walked on the sea beach together, and with a strange and prophetic kind of poetry, he likened the scene to his own failing health—the falling leaves, the withered seaweed, the dying grass upon the shore and the ebbing tide that was fast receding from us. He told me that he felt prepared to go, for he had forgiven his enemies and could even rejoice in their happiness."[428]

On December 30, 1892, the two men celebrated at the annual

banquet held at The Players in honor of the organization's founding. The membership toasted their founder, who took Jefferson aside and said: "They drink to my health to-night, Joe. When they meet again, it will be to my memory."[429]

On April 25, 1893, Edwin Booth retired to his rooms at The Players. At 10:30 the next morning, his brother-in-law, the club's superintendent, John Henry Magonicle, alarmed that Booth had not risen, entered the room and found the actor unconscious in bed. Initially diagnosed with a case of vertigo, Booth had actually suffered a cerebral brain hemorrhage, resulting in a loss of speech and complete paralysis of the right side. By April 28 he was bordering on a coma. His daughter, Edwina Grossman, was at his side, and by midnight on April 29 he was not expected to live. By May 6, however, he had rallied, and his doctor was anticipating that he would recover within a fortnight. That day Jefferson ended his spring tour in Cincinnati, and instead of going to Buzzards Bay, he returned to New York. Booth may have been the reason.

On June 6 Booth's doctor announced publicly that his patient was dying, and Jefferson and his son Charles Burke visited the feeble man in his apartment in The Players overlooking Gramercy Park. At 1:17 A.M., on June 7, 1893, Edwin Booth died. Upon learning of Booth's death, Jefferson, according to the *New York Times*, was deeply affected and sent Charles Burke to convey his condolences and a private letter to Edwina. That Friday morning, Jefferson and Charles arrived early at The Players where Edwina was waiting. At 9:20 A.M. Jefferson appeared with the other pallbearers, wearing a broad sash and rosettes of royal purple ribbon. They formed two lines on the walk in front of The Players and stood there as Booth's coffin was borne to its hearse by six assistant undertakers. The *New York Times* reported that Jefferson looked "quite thin and pale, the result of his recent illness, but his eyes lacked none of their old-time fire and lustre." Jefferson sat in a carriage immediately following the hearse. They processed to The Little Church Around the Corner. Following the service, Jefferson "appeared visibly affected when he left the church and . . . seemed much weakened by the ordeal through which he had passed."[430]

Booth's death left The Players without a president, but the choice was obvious. Jefferson was now the most famous actor in America, and on October 9, 1893, he was elected president of the club by unanimous ballot. Under his leadership, The Players immediately decided to preserve Booth's rooms exactly as he left them and to hold a public meeting celebrating the dead actor. On November 18, 1893, Jefferson presided at a memorial in the Madison Square Garden Concert Hall commemorating Booth's sixtieth birthday. He delivered an address from which the famous story of Booth's introduction to Mary Devlin is derived, and was followed by the main speakers—the great Italian actor, Tommaso Salvini, and his English counterpart, Sir Henry Irving. Ironically, the greatest American actor of the nineteenth century was honored by two Europeans.[431]

Jefferson's ascendancy to the presidency of The Players must certainly have been tangible proof to him that he was now the most famous actor in America, but he wore the honor lightly.

> [At] monthly meetings, . . . his appearance . . . was always an event. The rest of the Trustees were serious business men, carrying on the work of the club, but the details of business, were . . . dry to Mr. Jefferson, for he would begin telling funny stories, holding up the business of the Trustees and then apologize for his aberration, and the business would go on, and again he would tell some more funny stories. The rest of the Trustees . . . waited respectably for him to finish and then would suggest that the business be gone on with.

Jefferson had little interest in The Players. He was generally performing elsewhere during its New Year's Eve celebrations and seldom attended meetings. His business was touring as a star, but he accepted the club's presidency the way he accepted all honors, with a sense that not he, but Rip, was being celebrated. Jefferson was as much a businessman as the other members of the board, but his business was entertaining, so even at meetings he played Rip, the carefree lackadaisical scamp who never gave a thought to practical matters.[432]

The same lack of reverence revealed itself on November 8, 1895, when a silver loving cup, inset with precious stones, was presented to Jefferson at the Garden Theatre. The proceedings were set for 1:30 P.M., and the auditorium was filled. The theatre was decorated with palms and ferns, and a pedestal bearing a laurel wreath stood at the front of the stage. The band played "Auld Lang Syne," and a procession of the older members of the theatrical profession entered, culminating in Jefferson's appearance with Mrs. John Drew leaning on his arm. He sat in the center of a semicircle on stage surrounded by the leading lights of the American theatre—John Drew, Nat Goodwin, Daniel Frohman, Tony Pastor, E. H. Sothern—as well as Sir Henry Irving and Ellen Terry. Among those present were Jefferson's family, including many of his grandchildren, as well as six children who had appeared in *Rip Van Winkle* with him over the years. In the audience were Bram Stoker, Henry Irving's stage manager and the author of *Dracula*, and Mrs. Drew's granddaughter, Ethel Barrymore.[433] After a series of speeches, the audience gave three cheers for Jefferson, whose reaction the moment before rising is recorded by an on-the-spot observer.

> I chanced to sit immediately behind Jefferson, on the stage of the Garden Theatre in 1895, when the loving-cup was presented to him. . . . Just before he was about to rise and speak, . . . I discovered, sticking to his coat, a long . . . fragment of whisk-broom, left there by some careless brusher. I attempted to remove it; when he felt the action, he . . . turned around with an inquiring expression. I held up the object and said, "It is nothing, Mr. Jefferson; only a straw on your shoulder." Immediately with a half-merry, half frightened smile, he replied, "I feel as I had a load of hay on my back."[434]

Whether he wanted to be there, Jefferson, with a lifetime of testimonials, breakfasts, benefits, and luncheons behind him, knew what was expected. His schedule had become an endless round of performances, lectures, and social occasions. On April 12, 1895, while playing Rip in Harlem, he wrote, accepting yet another address, this time to a group of kindergarten children.

> I have to give eight performances next week—a lecture at the Berkeley School of Art and attend two receptions.
> Under ordinary circumstances, I should for the sake of needed rest have to decline your request—But you have put the matter in such an urgent way—and as it is—for the Grand Kindergarten I will comply—please tell at what time you desire me to be at the Amphian on Thursday evening.[435]

The tone is one of wearied compliance—"Just tell me where to go and I'll show up." Jefferson's life as a public figure had become a theatrical tour—one stop after another.

15

"FOR HEAVEN'S SAKE,
GET A NEW PLAY"

1880–1889

When the critic Laurence Hutton went to England in the summer of 1903, Jefferson sent his regards to Sir Henry Irving:

> You are quite sure to see Sir Henry. Tell him . . . that he is remembered here with much affection—and give him my love and respect—I hope that he and I will act together in the other world if not in this.

> > "And on the last day when we leave those we love
> > And move in a mournful procession
> > I hope we'll both play Star Engagements above
> > For I'm sure they 'admit the profession'
> > For myself when I knock at the gate with some fear
> > I know that St. Peter will say
> > Walk in young comedian and act with us here
> > But for heaven's sake get a New Play"[436]

At least twenty-five years before he wrote the poem and fifteen years after he first appeared in Boucicault's version of *Rip*, Jefferson's fame in the role was already anecdotal. A typical joke was: "Do you not admire the principles of Jefferson?" asked an enthusiastic politician of a society friend. "I really don't know much about his principles," was the reply, "but he plays *Rip Van Winkle* superbly."

Jefferson was such a national institution that adulation for him produced doggerel poetry:

JOE JEFFERSON! my Jo, JOE!
  When first we were acquaint,
Your locks were like the raven, Joe,
  Your cheeks were Nature's paint;
Tho' noo we baith are older grown,
  (Time's aye upon the go!)
Ye're still the same braev chiel we've known,
  JOE JEFFERSON, my JOE!
JOE JEFFERSON! my Jo, JOE!
  First time Old "Rip" ye played—
How long, my JOE, that was ago
  To state it, I'm afraid—
We thought it great: Night after night,
  (How many do you know?)
You've played it since, to our delight,
  JOE JEFFERSON, my JOE!
Full five and twenty years ago,
  Fame spread your praise abroad,
As "Doctor Pangloss, L.L.D,"
  "Tony" and "Allapod:"
Now, with the "Cricket on the Hearth"
  Un-"*Rival*"-ed on you go,
To give us new delight and mirth,
  JOE JEFFERSON, my JOE!
JOE JEFFERSON! my Jo, JOE!
  Will ye ne'er be growin' old,
Or still remain "that same old Joe,"
  Till ye're laid beneath the mold?
May all your steps down life's decline
  "*Go-lightly*," as they go!
All earthly joy and weal be thine,
  JOE JEFFERSON, my JOE!
So, here's a health, JOE JEFFERSON!
  A health to thee and thine;
Lang-lang, when frae us ye'll be gone,
  May flourish still your line!
Three JEFFERSONS have graced the name,
  And long may fresh ones show
The GENIUS and acquire the FAME,
  Of JEFFERSON, my JOE![437]

Apparently the writer was better acquainted with the range of Jefferson's work than most of his contemporaries. In August 1886 William Winter felt called upon to defend Jefferson, contending that he

> has . . . played more than a hundred parts and ascribes the fashion of calling him a "one-part actor" to ignorance. . . . But . . . he has obtained his fame and influence mainly by acting one part. . . . [Winter quotes] a remark made by Charles Mathews [the English comic actor] and Jefferson's retort.
>
> "I am glad to see you making your fortune, Jefferson," said Mathews, "but I don't like to see you doing it with a carpet bag" —referring to the limited compass in which our comedian's wardrobe for Rip could be stowed and to his one part reputation.
>
> "It is perhaps better," replied Jefferson, "to play one part in different ways than to play many parts all in one way."[438]

Although this might be considered a barbed retort, Jefferson was unlikely to take on another actor in public. The Mathews anecdote is characteristic of the way in which Joe always sidestepped controversial topics. But he was fully aware that he had done *Rip* far too long. Moreover, aside from the boredom it produced for him, *Rip* was no longer the box-office guarantee it once had been.

By 1880 Jefferson was convinced that he needed to find a "new" part. He had been performing Bob Acres since 1851, but during the 1880 season he began to turn it into a signature role that would rival *Rip*. It was a part that would allow him to escape the charges of being a one-role actor and bring audiences, sated with his portrayal of the mythic Dutchman, back to see him as a character he conceived of as a charming English lord. After Rip, Acres became Jefferson's most famous character; and, as in the case of Rip, Joe began not with the play but with the costume. William Winter remembered:

> Once, in his cottage at Hohokus . . . , I was with him in the garret . . . , and we were inspecting costumes for the comedy of *The Rivals*, which he had determined to alter and revive, resuming the part of *Acres*. . . . His particular quest was for a suitable hat. My attention chanced to be attracted to some play-books . . . , and for a little while, I did not observe him, but presently . . . I saw him . . . put on a . . . hat, and instantly . . . he assumed the

Figure 17. Joseph Jefferson as Bob Acres in *The Rivals*.
Courtesy of the Performing Arts Research Center,
New York Public Library.

face and manner of *Acres*. He had forgotten that any person was present. . . . He never "looked the part" more effectively in the best public performance that he ever afterward gave of it.[439]

The Rivals, however, presented problems that Jefferson had not faced with *Rip*. *Rip* was essentially a one-person show, a starring role surrounded by subordinate characters. *The Rivals* required a series of *bravura* performances. It needed actors who matched Jefferson in reputation and skill. Bob Acres was a minor character, and Jefferson's audiences expected him in the leading role. Moreover, Acres had traditionally been played as a country lout who, although comic, was not necessarily sympathetic. As written, he functions as a rival to the romantic hero, and is a coward. Finally, the play suffered, in Jefferson's view, from an eighteenth-century sentimental subplot involving Faulkland and Julia, whose love affair serves as a serious foil for the comic main plot involving Lydia Languish and Jack Absolute.

Jefferson's solution to the need for star actors was to hire them. The 1879–80 tour had been a family affair, but the following year he began working with a star combination. By mid-July 1880 he had engaged Mrs. John Drew and her son-in-law, Maurice Barrymore, for the company. Louisa Lane Drew was the leading female comic star of the American nineteenth-century theatre, and Mrs. Malaprop was her most famous role. Maurice Barrymore was a handsome athletic young leading man—a matinee idol who had played Laertes to Edwin Booth's Hamlet.

Jefferson's solution to the play's internal problems was to perform the service that Dion Boucicault had rendered for *Rip* fifteen years earlier: he decided to rewrite. It was a daring move. Although *Rip* had a stage history before Jefferson began to perform it, it had never been a distinguished play. *The Rivals* was an acknowledged masterpiece— one of the great comic centerpieces of the eighteenth-century English stage. Audiences and critics had expectations of what the play would be. Jefferson's expectation was that they wanted to see him.

He cut the play from five acts to three, totally eliminated the role of Julia, and confined the part of Faulkland to scenes with Acres. For Christmas 1895 Maurice Barrymore gave him a copy of *The Rivals* with every part cut out except Bob Acres. It was also Barrymore who originated what became the most famous quip about Jefferson's *Rivals*. When asked by William Winter, "And what must you think of the new *Rivals*, Mr. Barrymore?" Barrymore replied: "Well sir, it reminded me of that line in Buchanan Read's Civil War poem, 'And Sheridan twenty miles away.'" The saying went that Jefferson did *The Rivals* "with Sheridan twenty miles away."[440]

Anyone who worked with Jefferson knew that in his version Acres became the central figure of the play, a charming silly English gentleman rather than a lout; the duel between him and Beverly became the central action; and the Acres scene with Sir Lucius O'Trigger became the production's chief set piece. The Philadelphia correspondent for New York's *Daily Mirror* wrote:

> [Jefferson] excelled . . . in the duel scene, where his nervousness and cowardice were inimitably displayed; the look of comic horror his face assumed when Sir Lucius tells him that "a ball or two may pass clean through your body and never do you any harm at all," was marvelous; and the wondering, doubtful way in which he replies, "clean through me! a ball or two clean through me!" was . . . not easily forgotten. His . . . dejection . . . on being told of the approach of his foe . . . , the smile of delight that lighted up his face on his recognition of "Jack! my dear Jack! my dear friend!" and the hearty manner in which he greets his "dear Jack," showed a perception of the requirements of character acting such as is seldom witnessed.

Jefferson had long believed that clarifying and even bowdlerizing old English comedies was the prerogative of the modern actor. He simplified the play's language and emphasized Acres' charm rather than his boorishness.[441] He told a group of theatre students:

> I had been playing from the traditional standpoint. I did not believe I could represent the character so well in that way as I could in another, and I acted it in all sorts of ways. I had played the part of Acres two hundred times before I knew how to end the second act.[442]

Unlike *Rip*, which was a sentimental melodrama with a comic hero, *The Rivals*, in Jefferson's version, became a farce. He resorted to the practice he had been so famous for avoiding—"gags," comic bits of business that scored points with the audience. "At the thought of his improvement in urban ways," Jefferson's Acres "lifted his hat and exposed his hair done up in curl papers." At the moment Sir Lucius paces off the dueling distance, he turned to find Acres right behind him instead of at the other end of the firing line. Jefferson also added tag lines like: "He who fights and runs away, May live to fight another day" to give himself exits that would signal applause. He costumed himself elaborately, entering first in a caped coat with a whip and conical hat and changing later to a $500 hand-embroidered coat with duchess lace at the neck and sleeves.[443]

At the same time, however, the mannerisms so long famous in *Rip Van Winkle* showed through in Bob Acres.

> The charm . . . was not in the evolution of a Bob Acres, but in the exhibition of a Joe Jefferson. Whatever . . . embellishments Bob Acres wore had been worn by Rip Van Winkle. There was the same beamy, irresolute smile; the same doubting repetition of . . . phrases ("You-don't-say so"); the same break in . . . speech; the same endeavor of a weak mind . . . to comprehend an idea by repeating . . . words; the same dreamy pauses; the same sly play upon words; the same weakness of spirit and really . . . the same cadences and inflections.
>
> This persistence of personality despite the change of character is . . . indicative of the fact that Mr. Jefferson has followed the popular weakness which prefers his personality to the assumed characterization and mainly because he has found it easier to do. . . .
>
> To my mind this persistent and amiable personality which . . . colors . . . everything that Mr. Jefferson does, is a badge of artistic weakness, whatever . . . it may be as a personal trait. I hold it . . . a fault in Bob Acres that he . . . suggests Rip Van Winkle. I hold it . . . an artistic vice in Mr. Jefferson that he should cling to the mannerisms of Rip when Rip is not in question, simply because those mannerisms got a laugh in Rip.
>
> In Mr. Jefferson's hands the play of *The Rivals* suffers a pleasant but . . . inexcusable inversion. . . . Bob Acres is embroidered out of all relation to the group.[444]

The following year A. C. Wheeler, writing in the *New York Mirror* under the pseudonym of Nym Crinkle, concurred. He may, in fact, have been the author of the previous year's review.

Mr. Jefferson does not know it, but he has come, with years and the repetition of one or two roles, to a point of . . . delightful Joe Jefferson mannerisms. That little chuckle has become habitual. That repetition of the sentence with a reflective inquiry interludes all his work. One feels . . . that this is not Bob Acres, because it has already been Rip Van Winkle.[445]

The *New York Times*, however, asserted that Jefferson was above criticism.

Bob is a countryman and a simpleton . . . , but he is something more, he is a gentleman . . . , he has refined sensibilities, there is just a touch of pathos in his . . . mishaps; While we are laughing, we cannot help feeling sorry for him. . . . What a world of meaning there is in his . . . soliloquy after poor David has, with a few uncouth words, struck beneath his . . . veneer of polish. It is a little play in itself . . . with Bob trying to remember his bow and his slide, but worried all the while by the memory of David's bluntness. His head does not look exactly like a pickled cabbage, of course, but the jeer struck home. There is a touch of . . . pathos in his expostulation with that same David later on. What is the use, says Bob, when a fellow is writing a challenge to ask him what his mother will think! In the last scene, Bob's . . . admission that when he stands up, to be shot at, he expects to take a little risk, and he don't care how little the risk is, seems to be . . . rational. . . . There is not a trace of artificiality in the whole performance.[446]

In 1898 the *New York Times* wrote:

An Acres for whom one feels the kindliest regard, even when he exhibits his preposterous hair done up in curl papers . . . is one of Mr. Jefferson's great contributions to the stage. . . . This is the only Acres . . . who ever . . . brought a tear of sympathy to the spectator's eye when he protests to David against references to what his mother might think while he is writing a challenge to mortal combat. He is the only Acres associated . . . with the . . . gentle individuality, the lovable disposition, the innocence and the pathos of . . . Rip Van Winkle. . . . To say . . . that the public cares much more for Jefferson than it does for Bob Acres . . . and that the personality of the actor exerts a greater charm upon his audiences than his art . . . cannot be doubted by any person who carefully watches the crowds which . . . assemble . . . at the Fifth Avenue theatre. The public fondness for this . . . actor grows as the years advance. No one on the stage . . . equals him in the affection of his audiences. It has become a . . . tradition to admire Jefferson, and the tradition will not languish while the actor performs so well.[447]

What Jefferson had done again is to take a farcical character and underpin his comic extravagences with sentimental, sympathetic realism. In like manner, Acres' external "gags" were made more realistic by the care that Jefferson bestowed on his costumes and wigs as well as by his internalization of the character—his emphasis on Acres's humanity. Unfortunately this level of care was often missing from the physical production as a whole.

A little more might have been done for the play in the way of scenery and furniture. Some of the scenes were old—two of them being poor. . . . The last scene . . . was very stiff and ugly, although . . . it is painted from [Jefferson's] sketches of King's Mead Fields . . . in England. The furniture displayed in the room at Bob Acres' was execrably bad. Let us suggest . . . a neat chintz set instead of the odd pieces which reminded one of a broker's shop.[448]

Whatever the production's limitations, the 1880–81 tour, a succession of one- and two-night stands with stays up to three weeks in major cities, was a great success. From Harrisburg, Pennsylvania, on October 7, 1880, Jefferson wrote to William Winter: "The comedy draws out good audiences for the country, and our business is very fine, considering the Political Crises [the national election in which Winfield S. Hancock of Pennsylvania was pitted against Ulysses S. Grant]."

Beginning on September 13, 1880, Jefferson played six days a week for six months, ending the tour in early March 1881. He primarily performed *The Rivals*, although he added *Rip* at the end of longer runs, for novelty and in order to pack houses, for Saturday matinees and evening performances. The fifty-one-city tour, however, took its toll. The fall 1880 tour lasted six months; the fall 1881 tour lasted only three.

When the season ended on March 12, 1881, most of the company returned east, but Jefferson, along with Charles Burke and Tom went off to Louisiana to "rusticate," taking Frederick Robinson, a company member, along as a guest. Tom, then twenty-three, did not rusticate long. By March 28, 1881, he was engaged at Wallack's Theatre in New York in Victorien Sardou's *A Scrap of Paper*. But Jefferson's sons were never successful on their own as actors, and by the fall, Tom was back performing with his father. He may never have intended to leave permanently. Jefferson simply did not need him in *Rip*, and when he resumed touring in mid-April, he played nothing but *Rip*. *Rip* was far less expensive than *The Rivals*, because it required no star actors, only Jefferson and a supporting company. Thus while Jefferson played Acres in New York, Philadelphia, Chicago, and St. Louis in the fall, he turned to places like Ottumwa and Keokuk, Iowa, in the spring. A month of one-night stands playing Rip in towns that felt blessed to have a star of Jefferson's stature cost little and brought in the money.

After a summer of fishing in Hohokus, Jefferson opened his fall season with *The Rivals* in Albany, New York, on September 5, 1881. The *New York Times* again lauded his decision to try a new role and looked forward to further innovations. Mrs. John Drew was particularly praised for her Malaprop, and by the end of the New York engagement people were besieging the doors. Although he never gave up Rip, Jefferson now had proof that audiences would come to see him in another character. In Cincinnati on October 7, 1881, he wrote to a fan that he had, by then, played Rip about twenty-five hundred times—for which, as he put it, "may I be forgiven in another and a better world where there will be no matinees and no managers."

The fact that he now had two hit roles was financially beneficial. On November 14, 1881, Jefferson reopened for the second time that year in New York. The fact that his earlier run had consisted solely of performances of *The Rivals* allowed him to return later in the season as Rip. In like manner, he played *The Rivals* for six weeks in September–October 1882 at the Union Square, and then came back to the Grand Opera House on November 20 with *Rip Van Winkle*.

With two starring roles, Jefferson now also had the option of starting a week's engagement with one play and finishing with the other. On December 12, 1881, he opened at the Arch Street Theatre in Philadelphia with three performances of *The Rivals*. On Thursday, Friday, and Saturday (both matinee and evening) he did *Rip*. He

Figure 18. Portrait of Joseph Jefferson (*ca.* 1888),
from a photograph by Pach

could also play both pieces in a single day, attracting audiences to either, or even to both a matinee and an evening performance. In Pittsburgh, on the day after Christmas 1881, he performed *Rip Van Winkle* in the afternoon and *The Rivals* in the evening. The theatre was crowded despite bad weather and muddy streets; chairs were illegally placed in the aisles to accommodate the overflow; camp stools were placed in the rear of the orchestra and dress circle, as well as in front of the doors through which audience members entered and exited; the audience was "disorderly in the extreme"; but the daily take was $2,700.[449]

Jefferson was far more interested in box office receipts than in critical judgments, and by the late 1880's he even hardly needed advertisements. The 1888 New York engagement produced little attention from the press. In fact Jefferson shared a tiny advertisement in the *New York Times* with his friend Edwin Booth, who appeared the following week. But every seat was filled by Friday morning for the final Saturday matinee, and when drenching rains left many New York theatres empty, "men and women were standing six deep behind the orchestra seats" to see Jefferson. On December 29, 1888, Jefferson wrote to John Rogers, Jr., who was producing a sculpture of Joe as Bob Acres: "The fellow seems to be growing in popularity; as I act him all through next season, he will soon become better known."[450]

In addition to *The Rivals*, Jefferson brought *The Poor Gentleman* back into the repertoire during the fall 1882 tour and, in the spring of 1883, added *The Heir-at-Law*, *The Cricket on the Hearth*, and *Lend Me Five Shillings*. He now had six plays he would perform for the rest of his life. *Rip Van Winkle* was, of course, still part of the repertoire, but Jefferson could no longer count on the sellout crowds that attended past performances. Mixing the six plays in various combinations, he continued to tour with his company.[451]

The fall 1885 tour brought public hints of retirement. The public was growing tired. Jefferson, nearing fifty-seven, drew only a "fair house" in Fort Wayne, and the local reviewer noted that "age is beginning to tell upon him." On October 12, 1885, he opened a week-long run in St. Louis with Caleb Plummer, and despite cold weather and a streetcar strike, had a large audience. But the *Missouri Republican* felt that "the grand old man" was nearing "the verge of his retirement." His Washington performances "did not draw as large houses as usual," and the *New York Mirror* referred to them as "the lightest engagement he has ever known in Washington." Although he was still making enormous amounts of money, by the end of the 1888–89 season Jefferson knew that he needed a new way of attracting audiences. He needed a partner, and he chose Billy Florence.

16

THE JEFFERSON-
FLORENCE COMPANY
1889–1892

William Jermyn Florence was born in Albany, New York, on July 26, 1831. After coming to New York and working on a newspaper (and as a clerk) he became involved in amateur theatricals, finally making his professional debut at the age of eighteen. After his marriage on January 1, 1853, Florence wrote plays, in which he and his wife starred in Irish-American roles. He also performed Robertson's *The Ticket-of-Leave Man* and *Caste*. When his wife retired, Florence decided to team up with Jefferson.[452] They had known each other at least since 1857, and by the summer of 1888, inspired by the financial success of the Edwin Booth–Lawrence Barrett theatrical tour, they decided to form a "combine." Both were already booked for the following season, but were discussing the possibility and alerting the public. Florence already knew his roles. "I would quite willingly play Lucius O'Trigger in *The Rivals*, Zekiel Homespun in *The Heir-at-Law*, and John Perrybingle in *The Cricket on the Hearth*. Then again we might play double bills. Yes, indeed, I should be quite content to wind up my career with such an association."[453]

Florence may have been holding out for more money, because one week later, the *New York Mirror* reported that "the two gentlemen cannot see the matter in the same financial light" and that Jefferson was already reemploying some of his old company members for the 1888–89 fall season.[454] If discussions had just begun in the summer of 1888, there was no hope of a combination company for the fall. Star actors were booked long before that. By early February 1889, however, the Theatrical Syndicate operators Klaw and Erlanger had engaged Jefferson for F. F. Proctor's New England and Middle States circuit; by March the troupe going out was referred to as the Jefferson-Florence company. The vision of the two old-time actors was coming true.

On July 6, 1889, the Florences left for Europe, where Mrs. Florence spent the year, while her husband came back to America to begin rehearsals for Sir Lucius O'Trigger in *The Rivals* and Zekiel Homespun in *The Heir-at-Law*. In an interview that summer Florence noted: "Although I shall be an associate partner, I shall have no hand in the management, and Joe and I expect a great time, [as] the young men [Jefferson's sons], will look after business affairs. We shall have our own private car, and . . . we're going to enjoy ourselves."[455]

Accustomed to touring in public transportation, Florence looked forward to the luxury of a private railway car in which he and Jefferson, ensconced in their own compartments, would be serviced by waiters and maids. He was well aware, however, that working with Jefferson meant doing *The Rivals* the way Jefferson played it. Francis Wilson reports a conversation between the two old actors.

> "By the way, Billy, there's a line in *The Rivals* I never speak."
>
> "There's a lot in that piece Joe, if you'd only study it!". . . retorted Florence.
>
> "But I always give you the cues!" comically whined Jefferson.
>
> "Yes," said Florence, "and the cues are about all you do give me!"[456]

Jefferson, however, saw himself as deferring to Florence on stage, adapting his Bob Acres to Florence's Sir Lucius. He told the young Otis Skinner that

> when Billy Florence and I joined forces as a two-star team in *The Rivals* I felt I mustn't take all the situations as *Bob Acres* but must give Billy a show as *Sir Lucius O'Trigger*. In the duel scene, I had been used to working all the tricks of terror, shaking knees, trembling voice, ghastly face, etc., as *Bob* sneaks off the scene with his courage oozing out of the tips of his fingers. They used to laugh tremendously at it; so I piled it up. It rather took the attention from *Sir Lucius*. Of course, I liked the laugh-

ter, but I must be fair to Florence. So I didn't work at all. I gave
Sir Lucius a look, turned and walked quietly into the wings
and, by George! they shouted louder than ever.[457]

Figure 19. W. J. Florence (1831–1891) and Joseph Jefferson
in *The Rivals*. Courtesy of the Performing Arts
Research Center, New York Public Library.

Rehearsals were casual. On August 24 Florence returned from
Europe but continued to vacation well into September, finally meeting Jefferson at Buzzards Bay to "talk over the details of the tour and
fish." As he put it, "I never neglect pleasure for business."[458]

The Jefferson-Florence company opened in *The Rivals* at the Star

Theatre in New York City on October 14, 1889. New York's first-night audience turned out to see their old favorites in full force, the men in evening clothes, the women in huge hats and wraps. It was pouring rain, and the theatre smelled of the India rubber that coated the mackintoshes worn in bad weather. The management, wary of gate-crashers, forced anyone who went out the side entrance for a breath of air to get drenched, walking around the corner in order to be readmitted. But the audience was filled with well-wishers, particularly of the gregarious Florence. These were "the men that he fishes with, dines with, wines with and jests with."[459] The retired Civil War hero, William Tecumseh Sherman, spent the evening in the first row, "flirting with the pretty actresses on stage, leaning forward and pushing his applause on to the stage. When his hands [were] idle, his tongue [wagged] gleefully with a running commentary of criticism. No one ever [said] 'hush' to the general. His voice [was] . . . incidental music to the play."[460]

In addition to Florence, Jefferson had surrounded himself with star actors—C. W. Couldock as Sir Anthony and Mrs. Drew as Mrs. Malaprop. The *New York Dramatic Mirror*, in March 1889, noted that "The tour will probably be Jefferson's farewell. He is rich; he doesn't care of the money side of this enterprise, but he means to make it historical."[461]

The idea that Jefferson had no concern for money was a press agent's fantasy, an attempt to merge the actor's personality with Rip's. Moreover, Jefferson continued to perform for another fifteen years. But press agents marketed the tour to a gullible public as the last grand gesture of his career. Unfortunately the scenery was far from "historical." When the production opened in New York in October 1889, the *New York Herald* critic wrote: "The costuming was excellent. So was the staging. But why did two inevitable little tables turn up right and left in every interior?" By the time it returned in March 1890, the *New York Dramatic Mirror* said flatly: "The piece was poorly mounted."[462]

At sixty Jefferson was far too old to play Bob Acres, a potential rival for the heroine's hand, and both he and Florence had trouble with the brogues they adopted. Jefferson's Acres was an Irish gentleman, although Sheridan's was not. Newspapers accused Jefferson of sounding like a "jaunting car driver," Florence of hardly using any brogue at all. Generally, however, Joe was described as "light, dainty and exquisite." A New York reviewer reported that although he was "rather too old to dissemble the youthful character, his wrinkles were eclipsed by youthfulness and sprightliness." Florence, on the other hand, took a beating in the New York press: "While no improvement could be recommended to the delightful Jefferson, it is difficult to indict Florence of any sin save that of natural unfitness for his part. Perhaps he was apathetic. Maybe he will unbend, relax. We hope he may limber his legs and thaw out the frigidity of his mobile countenance."[463]

Florence continued to run into bad reviews in Scranton, Albany, and Philadelphia, and Jefferson's age was apparent even to the critic of as remote a town as Wilkes-Barre.[464] "Mr. Jefferson. . . [is] not as young as he used to be; yet he is as active as ever. In the opening half of the play, he would not be suspected of being an old man, but in the latter part, divested of some of his facial finish, he was no longer a youth."[465]

It is doubtful that either man cared personally about these criticisms. Florence was paid $1,000 a week, and Jefferson's guarantee was large enough to force local managers to double ticket prices in as small a city as Albany. But the company made money for managers hand over fist. In Dayton they took in $1,400 in one night. Chicago houses were "overflowing" in spite of pouring rain and seats selling for $1.50 and $2.00. In Chattanooga, even standing-room tickets were sold out before the doors opened. Receipts for the first week in Philadelphia were $12,570. Seats in Memphis went on sale on February 11 for a February 14 opening, but the line formed a week in advance. Tents were pitched on the ground, and scalpers tried to buy out the entire house.

Jefferson was due to reopen at the Star Theatre in New York, but its manager, Joseph Brooks, had a hit already playing and persuaded Charles Burke to move his father to the Fifth Avenue Theatre. The reviews acknowledged Jefferson's popularity, but were not positive.

> Mr. Jefferson's acting is always fine and . . . interesting, but it is oftener the revelation of his own personality than . . . the author's character. That personality is . . . winsome . . . and beneath its . . . spell, the spectator is apt to forget the play and the violation of its . . . demands upon the actor. This is true of his Bob Acres, who is . . . a different personage than Sheridan conceived and a long line of . . . comedians interpreted. Mr.

Jefferson, however, does not fail to please his admirers, and his . . . conception of the role finds adequate treatment.[466]

The *New York Times* agreed.

The Sir Lucius of Mr. Florence . . . is indeed much closer to Sheridan and eighteenth century manners than Mr. Jefferson's Acres. . . . Mr. Jefferson has adapted Sheridan's Bob to his own manner of acting, and Mr. Florence adapts his manner to Sheridan's Sir Lucius.[467]

Jefferson had opened with the possibility of substituting *The Heir-at-Law* for *The Rivals* some time during the second New York run. Stung perhaps by box office receipts resulting from the negative reviews, he decided to substitute the Colman piece on March 24, 1890, the beginning of the third and last week of the New York season.[468] It was the first time Jefferson had acted Pangloss in New York since he had left Laura Keene's company in 1859.

During the second New York run, a report circulated that some "differences" had arisen among Jefferson, Florence, and Mrs. Drew and that they would not perform together the following season. These rumors were emphatically denied, and may have been spread to produce more business.[469]

The Brooklyn performances ended the longest touring season of Jefferson's career—a season whose length implies enormous financial success. In early June, Florence left for Europe to join his wife, but announced that he would return to begin the 1890–91 season with Jefferson in late September. The rumors that had circulated about dissension among the stars resurfaced, however, during the summer of 1890. Jefferson and Florence had decided to tour again, but Mrs. Drew declined. She would be replaced by Madame Ponisi from the Wallack stock company. According to the *New York Mirror*,

the reason for Mrs. Drew's retirement is her objection to traveling another season in the Jefferson-Florence private car, which is not . . . a luxurious institution. . . . On the contrary, it is source of discomfort and ill-health.

The stars [Jefferson and Florence] . . . occupy the best part of the car. They enjoy the possession of separate staterooms. . . . The company . . . sleep in the ordinary berths, huddled in like so many sheep.

Eating, sleeping and . . . living in this crowded migratory residence, either subject to draughts or choked by bad ventilation, means . . . a season of noise, cinders, vitiated air and unrest.

The unpleasant part of the private car arrangement is that, although it is supposed to lend . . . dignity . . . to the attraction, a part of the . . . expense has to be borne by the members of the company, who . . . are expected to pay a . . . weekly board for inferior accommodations and pass their nights in narrow bunks on railway sidings, their dreams invaded by the rumble and the shrieks of passing trains.[470]

Jefferson's decision to use a private car was financial. He could get from city to city quickly without depending on commercial train schedules. There was no checking in or out of hotels, no packing or unpacking. The company simply got off the train, took hired carriages to the theatre, and returned to their bunks after the show. Jefferson would not have paid for their room or food had they stayed in a hotel; consequently he charged room and board payments on the train, which subsidized the use of a private railway car. Years of touring in second-rate productions of *Rip* had given him a reputation for stinginess, and this may have been well deserved. In mid-July 1890 the *New York Dramatic Mirror* wrote:

A Boston paper says that Mr. Jefferson is the richest actor in the world. He spends little, saves much and grows liberal only when the purchase of a work of art is concerned.

Mr. Jefferson *is* a very rich man. His engagements are always profitable, and his investments have been made judiciously and remuneratively. . . .

In return for the fortune that he has earned by his artistic gifts and the . . . recognition that they have received . . . , has Mr Jefferson . . . done his duty?

From a representative actor—one on whom prosperity has smiled—people . . . expect something which shall be a tribute to . . . his art when he has passed from the scene.

It might be said that the recollection of Mr. Jefferson's impersonations will be legacy sufficient. That would apply equally to Forrest, Booth and Irving. Yet these men have manifested a . . . moral sense of the duties of their exalted station—Forrest after death bequeathing a noble home to the members of the profession, Booth giving birth to The Players, and Irving beautifying his career by . . . private and public benefactions.

If Mr. Jefferson is one of the richest as well as one of the finest actors in the world, he can attest his love for his art and his desire to benefit the players of posterity in many a fitting way.

The question is, does that love and does that desire exist?[471]

This was one of the nastiest public indictments of Jefferson's career, yet it was thoroughly deserved as far as Joe's contribution to the theatrical profession was concerned. Although generous to his family and to personal friends, he had been born poor and struggled for money for the first twenty-eight years of his life. He was not about to endow institutions. His determination to tour, long after it was a financial necessity, bespeaks a personality obsessed with money and ever fearful that it would run out, that he would one day become his father, and that his children and grandchildren would face the life he had faced as a young man.

On September 6, 1890, Florence returned home from Europe and announced that his wife, weary of one-night stands, was remaining in England.[472] On October 3, in an interview, he addressed the rumor that he was breaking up with Jefferson.

This is the first intimation I have had of anything of the kind, and you may deny the rumor for me . . . emphatically. . . . I have made no arrangements beyond the present season. It may be, that sooner or later, Mr. Jefferson will want to rest. As for myself, I hope to create some new roles and to make another tour of the country with Mrs. Florence before I leave the stage. But I do not think that the . . . companionship of Mr. Jefferson will be lost . . . for some time yet. We are both *en rapport* with our repertoire, and . . . I enjoy acting with Mr. Jefferson very much—he is such a delightful comrade.[473]

It was most likely that Florence was the "delighted comrade," because Jefferson had raised his salary from $1,000 a week to $1,000 plus a percentage of the house if receipts went above a certain amount. Jefferson arrived in New York from Buzzards Bay on October 6 to rehearse the company at Palmer's Theatre, where the second Jefferson-Florence season opened with *The Heir-at-Law* on October 13, 1890. By October 17, ticket sales extended into the following

Figure 20. Joseph Jefferson as Dr. Pangloss in
The Heir-at-Law. Courtesy of the Performing
Arts Research Center, New York Public Library.

week, despite "advanced prices," and Jefferson was considering performing nothing but Pangloss in New York.[474] The *New York Times*
reviewer wrote:

> Mr. Jefferson's Pangloss is the same pedantic, hypocritical,
> avaricious, but . . . humorous pedagogue, whom New York
> laughed at . . . last season. . . .
> A special effort has been made to have the scenery and

properties as . . . perfect as possible, and the result was . . . praiseworthy. The interior of Lord Duberly's mansion . . . was adorned with paintings from the brush of Mr. Jefferson himself, while the old London street scene was massive in its buildings and imposing in its perspective.[475]

The two old troupers had found another hit, and in larger cities they typically played *The Rivals* on Monday, Tuesday, and Wednesday nights as well as Saturday matinees and switched to *The Heir-at-Law* for Thursday, Friday, and Saturday evenings. The schedule implies that *The Heir-at-Law* was the more popular of the two productions, possibly because it was the newer. The schedule was grueling; they toured from October 13, 1890, through May 19, 1891, without the winter break that Jefferson customarily took. On April 10, 1891, Jefferson wrote a letter accepting an invitation to a local club meeting on April 16 at 3 P.M., but indicated that he and Florence would need to leave between 5 and 6 P.M. in order to prepare for that evening's eight o'clock performance. Both men typically arrived at the theatre early each night. An hour before show time, a barber came and shaved Jefferson, including the hair on his temples, so that he could fit into the wigs he wore. Although their makeup and costumes were complex, their arrival two to three hours before curtain time implies that the two men also had to rest.[476]

Again the tour was very successful. In late February the *New York Dramatic Mirror* reported that Jefferson and Florence "are doing a tremendous business in the West and Southwest, playing everywhere to packed houses and at advanced prices." In Nashville the house was "filled out" at $2.00 a seat, and the advanced sale was almost $2,500. In Atlanta "speculators bought up most of the desirable sets and placed them in price beyond the reach of the theatre-going public, engendering a very hostile feeling among the regular theatregoers." When the company played Nashville, Jefferson visited Ward's School for Young Ladies by invitation of one of the teachers, Miss MacKenzie, the daughter of his aunt and uncle, Hester and Alexander MacKenzie, who had led the Jefferson company in the late 1830's and 1840's. The visit, however, was not simply a matter of family nostalgia. Miss Mackenzie brought two hundred young women from the school to the theatre that evening. Jefferson was, as always, utilizing family members to make money.[477]

By late January 1891 Florence and Jefferson had already signed a contract for next season. By September 29 they were rehearsing the company at the Star Theatre in New York for what was heralded as their last tour together. Florence and his wife had announced that

Figure 21. Oil painting (1891) by John Singer Sargent of Jefferson as Dr. Pangloss in *The Heir-at Law*. Courtesy of the Hampden-Booth Theatre Library at The Players.

they planned to resume touring next season and, by late October 1891, had signed contracts for a thirty-week season during 1892–93. The Jefferson-Florence company began performing on October 5, 1891, in Richmond, Virginia, and the company opened a two-week New York engagement on October 12, 1891, at the Garden Theatre. The *New York Times* praised the production and noted sadly that "hereafter Mr. Jefferson will take life very easily, acting only a few weeks in the winter, and then only the character that made his fame—Rip Van Winkle."

After playing Brooklyn and Boston, the tour opened November 9 in Philadelphia. Billy Florence became ill. His health had been poor for some time, and he told friends he expected to live only a short while, although he was still entering into professional contracts. A severe cold he had contracted two weeks earlier in Boston had developed into pneumonia in both lungs. In spite of his physician's advice, he insisted on playing Zekiel Homespun on Saturday, November 14. Billy could hardly stand on his feet during the performance, and yet, in typical Florence style, he hosted a dinner party for the actress Mrs. Kendal and her husband afterward. His condition worsened during dinner, and he was forced to leave the party for his room at the Continental Hotel. By Sunday, he was in critical condition, and a wire was sent to his wife in England. When J. H. Barnes, the company's young leading man, visited him along with Jefferson, Barnes was shocked at Florence's appearance. Jefferson, however, was optimistic. The *New York Times* reported that Joe "could scarcely be reconciled to leaving . . . Florence behind," but that Florence had urged him to go, saying: "Good bye old boy, I'll soon catch up with you." Jefferson and the company left for Buffalo on the following Monday morning. On Tuesday, Florence was still breathing heavily. On Wednesday a priest administered extreme unction. Later that night Florence regained consciousness and began to speak to those around him, but he died in his sleep at 8:20 on Thursday evening. Billy Florence was sixty years old.

The news reached the public by means of a bulletin board in the hotel lobby. Jefferson had just entered his dressing room in Grand Rapids, Michigan, and was seated on one of the huge property trunks when a reporter informed him. "My God, you don't tell me?" was the only thing he was able to say at first. He then asked: "Are you sure it is true?" He left the theatre and went to the newspaper offices, where he spent most of the night reading dispatches about Florence. He later told the reporter that "his death is a great shock to us. You may say that our engagement at Detroit to-morrow night will certainly be deferred out of regard to his memory."

On Friday evening Florence's body was brought to New York from Philadelphia on a special railway car and lay in state at the Fifth Avenue Hotel on Saturday and Sunday. Mrs. Florence cabled directions for the funeral service, and services were held on Monday morning, November 23, at 10:30 A.M. at the Church of St. Agnes. Virtually every major figure in the American theatre attended except

Jefferson, who sent a floral wreath in the shape of a seven-foot-high cross, anchor, and scythe made of white flowers and covered with hearts of roses. On one of the hearts, purple flowers spelled out the word "brother." Jefferson was lucky to have missed the funeral. The Reverend Dr. Brann preached the kind of condescending sermon that Joe had hated all his life. "I know," said Dr. Brann, "that actors constantly stray away from the right path. But their lives are exposed to many temptations." Fortunately Jefferson had commitments to managers and audiences—and money to make.[478]

He had been scheduled to open in Detroit with Florence on November 20, but when his private car arrived at the Michigan Central depot at 12:40 that afternoon, Joe was in no condition to perform. A reporter described the scene.

> As he left the car, his appearance was that of a man who had passed the night in sorrowful reflection. His figure seemed less erect than usual; his face was pale and his eyes heavy. He carried in his hand his huge grip, pushing aside the porter who attempted to relieve him, and followed by Mrs. John Drew and other members of the company, entered a carriage and was driven to the Cadillac [Hotel].[479]

Jefferson canceled the opening performance in Detroit despite a sold-out house on the basis of a "disinclination to appear so soon after the death of his late friend and associate." He told the local reporter: "No, we shall certainly not play tonight. . . . Of course not. I do not know whether we shall play tomorrow or not. My inclinations would be not to do so, but one cannot always do as he would like. . . . It is like a death in my own family. There has never been the slightest friction in our professional relations."

Jefferson, however, knew better than to cancel two performances in a row. This was indeed like a death in his own family, but the Jeffersons never had time to mourn. Joe was shocked by Florence's death, but he also needed time to break in Louis James, who had been hired in New York on November 18, the day before Florence died, and had just arrived that morning to join the troupe. With one day's rehearsal, he opened on the afternoon of November 21 as Sir Lucius O'Trigger and proceeded to play Zekiel Homespun that evening. It was what any competent actor in the nineteenth century was trained to do. The tour had gone on.[480]

17

PRIVATE LIFE AT
BUZZARDS BAY

Jefferson had time for private life only between engagements—summers in Hohokus, and later in Buzzards Bay, Massachusetts; and winters, first in New Iberia, and later in Palm Beach, Florida. He visited friends. He spent time with his family. He painted. But above all he fished.[481] By the 1880's, fishing had been his delight for at least thirty years. Like his father, he used it as a refuge from the world in which he worked. The elder Jefferson had needed a respite from failure; his son needed a respite from success. He also occasionally hunted, but hunting was secondary. A reporter from *The Outlook* visited him in New Iberia.

> The morning after the arrival of his guest, Mr. Jefferson asked him what he would like to do best.
> "Do you shoot?"
> No, the Spectator didn't shoot.
> "You don't shoot! Why not?"
> To which the Spectator hesitatingly replied that he guessed it was because he didn't like to kill things.
> "Well that's queer. Do you fish?"
> Yes, the Spectator confessed that he sometimes slew fish. But very little fishing was done. . . . A year or more after the visit to the Louisiana plantation the Spectator met Mr. Jefferson in New York.

"Do you remember what you said when you were down at Orange Island?" he asked.

The Spectator could not recall anything . . . that he had said. . . .

"You said you didn't like to kill things! It made such an impression on me that I've never been shooting since; but I let Willie kill the jays, because they are such a nuisance. You don't mind our killing jays?"[482]

Jefferson's ambivalence about hunting was also noticed by E. W. Kemble, an artist who visited him in New Iberia:

Suitably dressed in hunting costume, we had gone out in a patent air-boat . . . in hopes of finding . . . sport on the wing. Presently some birds came in view. I took . . . aim and missed. Mr. Jefferson caught up the gun, took . . . aim and also missed. The attendant rowed us on in . . . silence. Presently Mr. Jefferson said dryly:

"I think I've had enough hunting for to-day."[483]

Jefferson did not always miss. In later years he would say: "I don't shoot any more. I can't bear to see the birds die." But any image of reluctance on his part to kill animals must be coupled with the decor of his New Iberia home, which was hung with skins, guns, heads, birds, fishing tackle, etc.[484] Hunting and above all fishing allowed Jefferson to escape the public eye, but it also allowed him to maintain his public image as a rustic, a child of nature reveling in the unsophisticated natural wilderness—in other words, Rip. Jefferson's private life mirrored his stage persona. As he wrote to Edwin Booth: "I've had a glorious month. The boys and I—far 'from the haunts of men.' Endless camp fires, pine boughs for a bed, a noble forest for a front parlor and a crystal river for a washstand." His interest in fishing, like the oils he painted, reflected Rip's life, but it was also the life Jefferson enjoyed.

Gradually he began to spend more time in New England and even Canada.[485] In May 1887 Joe ended his spring tour in Bangor and took off on a trout-fishing excursion "in the 'Down East' wilds of Maine" with his sons and the seventy-two-year-old theatrical veteran C. W. Couldock. Couldock and Jefferson went to relax, to escape life in the theatre. In the days before *paparazzi*, there were no reporters hounding Joe, but his press agent still made sure this idyll reached the *New York Mirror*, the city's leading theatrical newspaper: "On account of mosquitos they are compelled to make up—that is, they smear their faces with something that unnerves the 'insex' and then cast their lines. . . . Both are expert anglers. . . . At present, they are flowers of the Maine forest. . . . The solitude of the rod agrees with these old chums. They are 'far from the madding' etc. and enjoy themselves to the full."[486]

On his way home from Maine, Jefferson spent a day fishing in Buzzards Bay, where Cape Cod joins the mainland. There he sailed around Buttermilk Bay, so named for its foamy white ripples whipped up by the wind. He went ashore, climbed a tall tree (at the age of fifty-eight), and saw the possibilities for a Jefferson family summer compound. He wrote to his sons, who were thinking about purchasing home-sites in the Thousand Islands, and they began buying land in Massachusetts.[487]

Jefferson's summer 1885 fishing trip coincided with the last stages of Sarah Jefferson's last pregnancy, a pattern typical of Jefferson's life, and on September 12, Frank Jefferson was born in New York City. Joe was already fifty-six; his oldest son was thirty-six. Jefferson was inundated with congratulatory telegrams. Frank would be nineteen when his father died, and would live until 1963.

Sarah and Joe needed space. When they played host to a family reunion at Thanksgiving in 1887, they were surrounded by eighteen children and grandchildren. Joe wrote to Lester Wallack that he would be unable to attend a reception, because "if the assembled group—eighteen kids and grandkids—was deserted by their progenitor there would be a 'Mutiny on the Bounty.'" Buzzards Bay was the answer. There the Jeffersons eventually owned virtually all the land around the bay, and an extended family of twenty-six lived in six houses amid pines and oaks that went all the way to the water. By June 1890 Buzzards Bay had replaced New Iberia, and the Louisiana plantation was up for sale. Moss was strangling the giant live oaks, weeds were growing among the roses, the grounds were untrimmed, and the home's furnishings had been placed under sheets. The Jeffersons had moved north in the summer.

During the late winter of 1888, Jefferson began negotiating for land on Cape Cod, specifically in Sandwich. Local legend had it that he "encountered prejudice in the form of inflated prices."[488] But by

March 27, 1888, he had purchased the Allen Bourne farm located on the main road between the village of Bourne and Bournedale close to the juncture of Cape Cod and the mainland. The estate contained a fine trout brook. The house he built sat on a sixty-acre plot to which Jefferson added over the years so that by the time of his death, he owned approximately 156 acres of land valued at over $52,000. Eventually, during the summer, Jefferson's sons lived in cottages some distance from his house, and in the evening the families would gather at Jefferson's home to give concert versions of popular operas and burlesque versions of *Rip Van Winkle*—in which Jefferson played Meenie as a squalling child.

Crow's Nest, as the Jefferson home was called, sat on a hill overlooking Buttermilk Bay and was approachable only by boat or by a two-mile carriage drive from the hamlet of Buzzards Bay. Jefferson had opted again to live isolated from the urban life in which he earned a living, and the approach to the house, although not as formidable as it had been in Louisiana, was still a journey.[489]

The first house Jefferson built on the site was "a large solid substantial structure" surrounded by "a broad veranda" and surmounted by "two great colored clay chimneys" that serviced its fireplaces and basement furnace. Its facade was broken by stained-glass panels with life-sized representations of Edwin Booth as Hamlet and Jefferson's cousin William Warren as Falstaff. In the rear of the front hall was a $2,000 stained-glass window depicting a flamingo with drooping neck standing under rich tropical foliage with clusters of bananas. Rising from the front hall was a stairway whose balustrade contained four carved antique bedposts that Jefferson instructed the architect to use. Off the front hall was a dining room of oak and cherry with a coffered ceiling in which each square had a tile hand-painted by Jefferson. In the corners of the room and about the fireplace were Dutch tiles he had selected abroad. The mantel was cherry carved in the shape of huge dragons. The library, whose walls and ceiling were covered in English oak panels, contained marble busts of Jefferson and other actors and a bronze of Rip Van Winkle. Like his Hohokus home, the interior of Crow's Nest had a palatial, heavy, imported look that belied the rusticity of its surroundings. Jefferson, having retreated from the stage, surrounded himself with mementos of his profession. The decor was meant to remind visitors that they were entering the home of a great actor whose most famous role was a Dutchman.[490]

By mid-July 1888 the Jeffersons were entertaining guests in a house called "Crow's Nest" built on the property, but it was apparently the original farmhouse on the site. Booth came in mid-August, along with Richard Watson Gilder and President and Mrs. Cleveland. Jefferson and Cleveland had met in October 1887, when Jefferson set aside three boxes for the president and his party at McVicker's Theatre in Chicago. The following year, Cleveland was defeated by Benjamin Harrison in his bid for reelection. In July 1888 Mrs. Cleveland spent a few days at the Gilder cottage located on Sippican Harbor in Marion, Massachusetts. She was favorably impressed and suggested locating a summer house in the region to the former president. Cleveland asked Gilder: "Are there any fish up around Marion?" and Gilder brought him to see Jefferson. Jefferson held forth on the bluefish and sea bass in Buzzards Bay, and the two men struck up an acquaintance that became a friendship revolving around fishing. Cleveland eventually rented a summer house near the Gilders in Marion in the early summer of 1889, returned the following year, and in 1891 bought a house he called Gray Gables near Jefferson's home in Cape Cod. There the two men wiled away their summer vacations, along with Gilder; Jefferson's eldest son, Charles Burke; the newspaper editor L. Clarke Davis; the actor Lawrence Barrett; Mrs. Drew; her granddaughter Ethel Barrymore; William Warren; and Edwin Booth.[491]

Like Jefferson, Cleveland needed a solitary place to fish. Together they would retreat to a private pond and keep fishing, even during hail storms, fortified with "a generous supply of Mumms Extra Dry." Away from the public eye, Jefferson could take a drink. During the summer, Cleveland's skin would turn brown and harden from constant exposure to the sun and wind; Jefferson burned as badly on the last day of the season as on the first. Summer visitors described him as having a face that looked "very like raw meat," protected by a cap with a hood covering his head, neck, and cheeks and a peak protecting his exposed eyes, nose, and mouth. He wore dull-colored trousers and three or four different fish jackets buttoned up tight. He told visitors that he thought that bright clothes scared the fish, but Jefferson also enjoyed the relaxation of sloppy clothes. When Crow's Nest was photographed, he was shown outside, on the verandah, in the yard, or in his painting studio over the stable. The clothes he wore, albeit formal from a modern viewpoint, would have looked bizarre against the antiques and dutch tiles and cherry woodwork of the home's lush interior. When the opulent interiors of the home were photographed, Jefferson was never in the picture. Jefferson did not want audiences to see "Rip" living in the midst of luxury.[492]

The summer of 1888 would be the last time Jefferson saw his cousin William Warren. In late September, Warren died at his home in Boston after an illness of several weeks, diagnosed as a brain disease. He was almost seventy-six years old. The funeral took place on September 24 in Boston's Trinity Church. Jefferson attended with his wife and sons Charles and Joseph. Also present were his cousin Mrs. John Blake Rice of Chicago, who was Warren's sister; Oliver Wendell Holmes; C. W. Couldock; and Mayor O'Brien of Boston. Warren had never married. He left his niece (Joe's wife, Sarah Jefferson) $5,000, and Joe himself received a silver loving cup he had presented to his cousin. Jefferson had no time to mourn. In the tradition of his family, he began his 1888–89 fall tour that evening in Baltimore. The summer was over, and he was back on the road.

Jefferson closed that season in Holyoke, Massachusetts, on January 5, 1889. By March 5 he was in New Iberia, where he wrote a revealing letter to William Winter. He was replying to Winter's birthday greetings.

My dear Willie

"By sudden floods and fall of Water" we were cut off from the savage world for several days so that your telegram of congratulation had to be floated out to me in a dug out. . . . It is a pleasure to grow old, if we are kindly thought of by our friends and respected by our enemies.

Of course you know my age; you must have it recorded in that obituary notice . . . that is filed away in the dead head list . . . in your office—Sixty—but I do not realize it—possibly because I am so strong and well. I am truly grateful for this good fortune and still more that I am as nearly content as it is possible for mortal to be. This is the best of all. I don't think I am so bitter as I used to be for I [have] learned to scan my own faults more closely and to look with forbearance upon the shortcomings of others.

I shall act in New York for six or eight weeks next season so I hope to see more of you. I wish you were here now—the roses are all in bloom and the woods alive with song birds.[493]

It is the only Jefferson letter extant that reveals his personal feelings, and its rarity makes it assume an importance that is probably
unmerited. Jefferson was sixty when he wrote it. After Edwin Booth,
he was the most famous actor in America. His health was good, and
he was very wealthy. He had three homes and a wife half his age. His
youngest child was four years old, and he was probably still a sexually
vital man. But he was sixty. William Warren was dead; Couldock and
Booth were failing. Jefferson was aware that there was an obituary
notice waiting for him. He is having an intimation of mortality—a
blue day on the bayou.

Still the reference to past bitterness is startling. What did someone
this wealthy, this successful, this beloved, have to be bitter about?
Jefferson implies that the bitterness he has experienced stemmed not
from some dissatisfaction with his own life as much as from a dissatisfaction with those around him. He implies that he has felt himself
better than other people, has seen their faults (but not his own), and
has finally learned humility in what he is experiencing as old age. But
it may have been a ploy. Jefferson was playing humble to a man he
must have known was writing his biography, and Jefferson loved to
play humble. The typical Jefferson joke about himself has at its heart
the thought: "Here is this very famous man who is forgetting something or someone or has been forgotten." The stories in which
people do not recognize Jefferson parallel the third act of Rip too
closely to be convincing. So Jefferson, playing the humbled man,
may be performing for Winter's benefit.

Yet he is alone for a moment, isolated physically by the weather,
recalling past bitterness. People are not bitter just because they think
they are superior. They are bitter because they believe their superiority is not recognized by others or because, despite their superiority,
they are entrapped in a life that is, in their estimation, beneath them.
Certainly the former could not have been true of Jefferson. Although
he may have suffered some eclipse in the shadow of Edwin Booth,
Jefferson was one of the most recognized public figures in America.
But he was certainly trapped—trapped in a role that he could never
outgrow, trapped in an economic system that drove him relentlessly
from city to city, night after night, and trapped possibly in the role of
being a celebrity—a role he craved and simultaneously despised.
Jefferson wanted to fish and paint, to slop around in casual clothes,
but the luxurious homes, the opulent lifestyle, the clambakes with

their prodigious amounts of food, the letters to and from critics, the fact that he was fishing with Grover Cleveland—all reminded him that he was not Rip. He was and would forever be a star, surrounded by press agents and managers who made their living off him, people who were dependent on him and on whom he was dependent, but people from whom he was essentially aloof. The letter from Louisiana implies an acceptance of his situation in life.

It took approximately two years to build Crow's Nest. By May 16, 1890, Jefferson and Sarah were staying with his son Charley in the latter's home at Buzzards Bay, awaiting the completion of their new house, which Jefferson intended to open with "a strictly private housewarming" at which the guest list would be approved by the Clevelands. The two families entertained each other, and the house was filled with family and friends. Sarah Jefferson, described as "slender blue-eyed and looking ten years younger than she really is," presided over a constant round of visitors while still mothering Willy, "a tall manly boy, who knows a lot for a youth of 14, but who is none the less a boy for all that." C. W. Couldock and Edwin Booth came in 1890. Both men were approaching the end of their lives. Booth looked "like a ghost" and moved through the house so quietly that "they hardly know that he is in the house." After breakfast at nine, he would take out a cigar and spend his time smoking and reading and going for a walk once a day. On August 11 the Jeffersons gathered in back of Charles Burke's home for a New England clambake replete with four bushels of clams, one dozen chickens, half-a-dozen large bluefish, and a bushel of sweet and Irish potatoes. Charles did the cooking, and Jefferson's sister Connie acted as hostess. After dinner the guests lay down in the grass to watch the younger family members boat-race across the bay.[494]

The summer of 1892 saw Grover Cleveland's battle for a second nomination as the Democratic presidential candidate. On June 22 the Jefferson family joined the Clevelands at Gray Gables to listen to the returns of the New York Democratic convention "by a special wire in the gun-room," with Charles Burke keeping tally, as the delegations cast the votes that would again make Cleveland the Democratic nominee. According to American newspapers, Jefferson sat up all night with Cleveland reading telegrams and was the first to congratulate the candidate on his nomination. One Western newspaper noted that "by sacrificing a night's rest, the actor's name appeared in thousands of daily papers throughout the country." The *New York Dramatic Mirror* found the remark "contemptible, and discreditable to the journal in which it appears." Publicity may not have been Jefferson's intent, but the result was the same. Thomas' wife, Eugenie Jefferson, recounts a different version.

> Towards daylight, when there remained no doubt as to his nomination for a second term, and he had received the congratulations of all present save one, Mr. Cleveland turned to look for Mr. Jefferson. He was standing before the great landscape window . . . his hands folded behind his back, gazing . . . upon the reflection of the rising sun . . . in the waters of Buzzards Bay; forgetful of all save that beautiful picture. Mr. Cleveland crossed the room to where he stood.
>
> . . . "Joe aren't you going to congratulate me?" Mr. Jefferson started, turned to him, and grasping his hand warmly said, "Oh, I do—believe me, I do! but—good God!" turning again to the beautiful scene . . .—"if I could paint like *that*"—his hand sweeping the horizon—"you could be Emperor of the world and I wouldn't exchange places with you!"[495]

By March 16, 1893, Jefferson, having finished his fall and winter 1892–93 tour, was up in Buzzards Bay, enjoying the scenery "in its winter dress" and "luxuriating in a soft hat and a checkshirt." A group of Massachusetts state senators visited, and Joe provided and apparently partook of "a large decanter of Kentucky whiskey." In a letter to Cleveland, by then beginning his second term as president, he wrote:

> I set a large decanter of Kentucky whiskey on the table to which I am bound to say they did full justice—no blue grass senators would have been more loyal to their state.
>
> After the second round I came up smiling and held forth on the bridge question [the issue of whether or not to build a bridge between the mainland and Cape Cod]. I informed them that while our common community could & will do without Hawaii, we would fall into unestimable [sic] harm, if we failed to annex Gray Gables [Cleveland's home] to Buzzards Bay.
>
> I trust that you will place this matter before the cabinet and urge immediate action.

The tone of Jefferson's letter implies that the relationship between the two men was growing closer. Rumors spread that Jefferson was to be appointed to "a position of honor" in Cleveland's second administration, but he was not interested. Jefferson was always careful to avoid exploiting his relationship with the president. When asking if he might drop by the Cleveland's home in New York after dinner to introduce an acquaintance, he wrote:

If you say "no" both he and I will understand why—If "yes," we promise not to stay more than five minutes.

Pray do not trouble yourself to write a reply. The bearer of this will advise me your "yes" or "no."

Jefferson even added a postscript saying: "Don't bother your self to write."[496] His relationship with the president always preserved some sense of reserve, even after Cleveland had left the White House. Jefferson referred to William Winter as Willie and Edwin Booth as Ned, but it was always "Mr. and Mrs. Cleveland."[497] On July 10, 1895, Grover Cleveland, then at Gray Gables, wrote to Jefferson in a tone that illustrates the charming banter in which they liked to engage.

. . . am told that you . . . find recreation in the rod and reel. I think it not amiss . . . to suggest a . . . spot where you might be able to find some sport. . . . On the Sandwich road, a mile or two from Bourne, is a sort of abandoned farm, now owned by . . . Joseph Jefferson. This farm was originally purchased . . . by Mr. Jefferson on account of a trout stream running through it; but . . . he . . . now pretty thoroughly neglects it. I am told he is a little capricious that way. . . . Almost anybody about Bourne can tell you where the Jefferson farm is; and I am sure the owner would not object to your fishing there.

A vision of the two men fishing was provided by Richard Watson Gilder on May 11, 1896, at a dinner in Buzzards Bay in honor of former President Cleveland. Gilder reminisced:

He will fish through hunger and heat, lightning and tempest. While the elder and wiser Jefferson and I will go off and dry our clothes, the young Jefferson—our Cape Cod Prince Charley— and the ex-President will keep on while light holds and bass bite. . . . [A] hail storm came up suddenly one day while we were in the middle of Peter's Pond. We put for shore and were soon . . . pelted with . . . hailstones, while the boats were . . . filling with ice-water. Joe Jefferson and I climbed a hill and dried our clothes in the kitchen of a . . . farm-house; but the President and Charley Jefferson . . . went back to work with the conviction that it was just the time that fish would bite. Pretty soon another storm came up and drove them to shore,—and up the hill for shelter, soaked, but laughing like boys. . . . Once when the surface of a Cape Cod lake reflected uncomfortably the noonday sun, Joe Jefferson and I pulled to shore and stretched ourselves restfully in the . . . shade of the trees. . . . Jefferson, looking off to where his son and the ex-President of the United States were at their . . . labors in the broiling heat, quietly remarked; "Well, it is lucky for us that you and I can do something besides fish!"

The ten-year-old Ethel Barrymore, upon seeing Grover Cleveland, is reported to have asked her grandmother, Mrs. John Drew: "Who was that fat man in the boat Mummum?"[498]

At noon on April 1, 1893, a gasoline tank in the basement of Crow's Nest began to leak. Nellie Symonds, the housekeeper; Miss Collins, the maid; and Helen McGrath, the family cook, were in the cellar, and Miss McGrath "discovered what she supposed was water covering the floor." She called the hired man, Wright, to take a look, and he, seeing that the "water" was oil from the gasoline tank, shouted for the women to flee for their lives. Instantly there was a huge explosion as the gasoline met the fire in the furnace. Wright grabbed Nellie Symonds and Miss Collins and fought his way to the open air above. He came back for Helen McGrath, but "was met by a blinding sheet of flame." Burned and bleeding, he was unable to get past the fire, and Helen McGrath, the Jefferson's cook for twenty-five years, perished in the flames that filled the basement.

Upstairs Sarah Jefferson was ill in bed, and her youngest sons were playing in the attic. Hearing screams below, the children dashed out of the house to safety. Sarah got up and, clutching a dressing case full of diamonds, rushed down the stairs without dressing. Blinded by smoke, she began to go in the wrong direction when her son Frank caught hold of her hand and led her outside, where the servants covered her with buffalo robes. "Her nervous system suffered a severe shock," and she was immediately removed from the premises and put under a physician's care. By then the local townspeople were gathering, making efforts to rescue the doomed cook. A southwest wind saved the adjoining Jefferson homes from destruction, but Crow's Nest burned to the ground.

Hundreds of local inhabitants rushed to the scene as flames blazed over Buzzards Bay, but virtually the entire contents of the house were lost, including Jefferson's personal and stage wardrobe, a portrait of Mrs. Siddons by Sir Joshua Reynolds, a self-portrait by Reynolds, a portrait of Jefferson by Sir David Wilkie, a portrait of a lady by Sir Thomas Lawrence, and pictures by Corot, Daubigny, Troyon, Van Marke, Michel, Rousseau, Diaz, A. Maure, Courtourier, and Montecelli, as well as a Corot palette. The paintings were worth $150,000, the furnishings $250,000, and the house itself $300,000.[499]

Charles Burke telegraphed from New York that he was setting out at once. Jefferson himself learned about the fire by letter four days later in Memphis; he immediately wired: "My house at Buzzards Bay burned to the ground. No lives lost, thank God." He apparently did not know of Helen McGrath. Afterwards he wrote to his eldest son:

> My dear Charlie:
>   Your letter was received, announcing what was saved from the fire—certainly there was much more than I expected. I thank you for your attention—I shall build again as soon as I get home and I will reward all those who lent their aid.
>   I will go over the valuation tomorrow and send it to you. . . . There doesn't seem to me any reason why I should not get all the insurance.[500]

Jefferson, the supposedly frivolous actor who joked his way through meetings with businessmen at The Players, had made sure he was insured, and it softened the blow. The insurance did not cover the estimated value of the house and its contents, but Jefferson was wealthy enough not to worry. When he later saw his daughter-in-law, Eugenie Paul Jefferson, she said: "Oh Father how unfortunate! All your beautiful paintings gone!" He replied: "Never mind, my dear, think what fun I am going to have buying more!" Sarah grabbed her diamonds; Joe would have saved the paintings. When he met Francis Wilson in Milwaukee on April 17, he laughed at the thought of the "natives" tugging away at heavy furniture, while Corots, Diazes, Troyons, Daubignys, and Mauves were threatened with destruction.

"I am glad we were away when it burned down, because curiosity would have taken some of us to the cellar where the explosion occurred, and like our poor cook, whom we had in our family for years, we should probably have perished."

"Did I understand you were insured?"

"Yes, for $67,000; but the paintings of my father and mother are gone."

The cook had died; his wife was prostrate; his house had burned to the ground. Still Jefferson did not return home. He could not: the spring 1893 season began on April 4, and he would not miss a performance. It was the family tradition in which he had been trained.[501]

Jefferson immediately wrote to a friend, the Boston architect Garrytt D. Mitchell, to begin work on a new home to occupy the site of the first Crow's Nest. Mitchell designed the house and presented plans to Jefferson and his wife when they reached Boston at the end of the spring 1893 tour. The next day Jefferson sent word to Mitchell that he was hired to superintend construction, which began in October 1893 as Jefferson was leaving for his 1893–94 tours. The rebuilt structure was scheduled to be finished by May 1, 1894. Joe returned by May 24, but the family was unable to move in until July. Even then work continued for at least two years. In the summer of 1896 Richard Watson Gilder wrote that the house had been delayed "because of the number of alterations in the plans."[502]

The result was a massive iron-framed composite of an American country house and an English manor, located on a cliff overlooking Buttermilk Bay. The extant foundations, made of enormous local boulders, sloped down the sides of the cliff, forming a sub-basement, and grey lichen-covered stone walls extended up to the second story. Above the second floor and on the gables were dark-red unburned bricks; a deep-brown gabled roof was made of hammered copper. On the third floor was an upper balcony with an "eyebrow" window. This led to Jefferson's painting studio and allowed him to paint *en plein air* when the weather was good. A cloisonné vase that had survived the destruction of the old house was fitted into an exterior corner of the new, and the chimneys were made of broken art tiles

and topped with brownish yellow seltzer-water bottles that produced a soft cooing sound when the wind blew.

The entrance to Crow's Nest was marked by two stone pillars set
in the middle of a wood, from which a macadamized road wound

Figure 22. Crow's Nest, the Jeffersons' second home in Buzzards Bay.
Courtesy of the Bourne Historical Society, Bourne, Massachusetts.

between pines and flowering bushes. The front door of the house
faced the water, so visitors, driving through the forest that surrounded
the mansion, came upon it from the rear. In the main hallway the walls
were a deep Indian red and the wainscoting and ceiling were carved
oak. Persian rugs covered the polished oak floor, and on the walls
hung paintings by Sir Joshua Reynolds, Daubigny, Greuze, and Van
Marcke. Nearby was an old carved English oak settle showing the
town of Chester.

The dining room, large enough to entertain the entire Jefferson
family, also had wainscoting, carved friezes, and a ceiling made of oak.
Old Dutch plaques decorated the walls, and the fireplace was framed
by Delft tiles. The mantle posts of carved oak had once been part of an
old French sideboard, and on the wall were Rembrandt's *The Burgo-
master's Wife* and Moreland's *Bell Inn*. By the time of Jefferson's

death, Crow's Nest, equipped with electric light, contained over $9,000 worth of furniture, carpets, rugs, bric-a-brac, paintings, and books.[503]

The drawing-room, where visitors waited while their visiting cards were brought up to Jefferson, was done in green and gold with a mantle of carved wood, showing Rip Van Winkle in the middle and Bob Acres and Doctor Pangloss on the sides. Here Jefferson hung Sully's *The May Queen*; Inman's portrait of the English actor William Charles Macready as William Tell; and Sir Thomas Lawrence's portrait of John Philip Kemble. On the same floor was a small library, near the rear entrance of the main hall, devoted entirely to the study of visual art. Visitors, after being told that "Mr. Jefferson begs you to step up to the library," crossed to the end of the hall, where a carved-oak staircase led to the second floor. There they entered a spacious library lined with bookshelves and boasting a semicircular bay window with a magnificent view of the bay.

In the fall of 1894, as he approached sixty-six, Jefferson began to search for yet another home, in a warmer climate. This is probably an indication of some setback in his respiratory condition as well as a reaction to the state of Sarah's health. On October 11, 1894, four days before the fall tour began, he appeared in a "testimonial performance" of *Lend Me Five Shillings* for the Twelfth Night Club, a New York women's club. Sarah was to perform the part of Mrs. Capt. Fobbs, which Jefferson described as a "walking lady" role, but on October 5, 1894, he wrote to a member of the club that she is "quite ill" and unable to undertake the part. By October 29 he was in Cincinnati, but Sarah was still "not quite strong enough to travel." She remained at the Fifth Avenue Hotel in New York.[504] When the fall tour ended, they decided to go south.

The Jeffersons spent the winter of 1895 in Punta Gorda, Florida. Travel to Florida entailed a three-day train trip. Travelers, approximately thirty to a train, were serviced by black porters who ran a buffet at one end of the cars, handed out pillows to passengers in their seats, made up each bed out of two or three mahogany boards and a concealed mattress, and blacked the boots of passengers. In northern climates, travelers were warmed with car heaters. As the train went south, they could open the doors to let in the warming air. Jefferson remained in Punta Gorda until March 3, 1895. He was probably there because of Henry Flagler, John D. Rockefeller's associate, who was

developing Florida as a site for vacation homes. It is clear from a letter
to Flagler that Joe, despite the fact that he had just rebuilt his Cape
Cod home, was considering moving south again. He visited both
Lake Worth and St. Augustine, did some hunting and fishing, and
apparently planned to explore more of the region—but, as he wrote
to Flagler: "On our arrival here Mrs. Jefferson was taken ill and has
been confined to her room nearly ever since. She seems now a little
stronger and it is our present intention to start for St. Augustine on
Friday next—arriving at the Ponce De Leon that evening."[505]

Sarah's health did not improve. The Jeffersons returned to Buzzards Bay when the spring 1895 tour ended, and on July 2, 1895,
Jefferson wrote: "I regret to say that my wife is ill and in bed—but we
hope to see her up in a few days.—The dreadful 4th is at hand and my
baker's dozen of Boys are busy in hopes of making everybody here
uncomfortable with patriotic confusion."[506] Apparently Jefferson's
health was also poor during the summer of 1895, because Grover
Cleveland wrote on August 13: "I am glad you are home again with
improved health." The deterioration in both his and Sarah's physical
condition led Jefferson to focus on Florida as a retirement home.
Despite health problems, however, Jefferson was already at work on
what would become one of the most famous moments of his career—
the 1896–97 all-star production of *The Rivals*.

18

THE ALL-STAR *RIVALS*
1896–1897

By the fall of 1893 Jefferson's productions were literally falling apart. The *New York Mirror* wrote:

> In his individual work Mr. Jefferson is a great artist, but he is far from artistic in . . . his surroundings. Even so . . . composed an actor . . . must have viewed with dismay the . . . characteristics of the performance of *Rip Van Winkle* at the Garden last Thursday night.
>
> The scenery was of the shabbiest . . . description. It might have been bought at a sheriff's sale of the contents of a jaytown "opera house."
>
> [S]cenes were handled in the clumsiest manner. Drops got entangled with wings in the hoisting process. . . . The village of Falling Water—represented by a long set-piece on which there was grass . . . the color of billiard table cloth and two or three up-to-date houses which had done service in Act One, in Act Three, rebelled. . . . In the middle of one of Rip's best scenes, it began to wobble and with strange noises, it . . . fell forward, where it lay until it was placed again in a horizontal position.
>
> Mr. Jefferson, who saw this scenic earthquake, was not . . . disturbed by it. Indeed, his serenity in the face of the bad acting . . . of his company and the bungling manipulation of the third rate scenery was . . . sublime.

> It was a . . . tribute to Mr. Jefferson's art that he was able to exert his spell . . . in spite of these drawbacks—many of which . . . were traceable directly to his own *laisser aller*.[507]

While in Cleveland, in the fall of 1895, Jefferson emphatically denied that he was thinking of retiring from the stage at the end of the season. He announced his intention of acting as long as audiences were there to see him and he felt strong enough to do so. During the interview he praised Henry Irving, then touring America: "There's a wonderful man who lives only for his art. There's not a mean bone in him. He spends money lavishly on his productions, and America owes him a debt . . . for what he has taught us about beautiful and appropriate stage settings." The *New York Dramatic Mirror* countered: "Would we might say that Jefferson lives only for his art and that he had lavished money on his productions. Were this so we should not read in the same issue of the Cleveland paper . . . : 'Mr. Jefferson's company is not a first class one, and his entire performance is not up to a $2 standard.'"[508]

By 1895, Jefferson, at the age of sixty-six, was facing failing health and critical disdain. He needed to reassert his preeminence in the American theatre. On May 31, 1895, he produced an all-star performance of *The Rivals* to celebrate the occasion of C. W. Couldock's retirement from the stage. During the curtain calls, Joseph Brooks, one of the afternoon's producers, publicly offered Jefferson and associates $100,000 for a twenty-week tour of the production. Jefferson whispered his answer so that no one heard. Brooks, who had managed Jefferson, knew that this was not what he would accept, but he may have planted the seed, because both Francis Wilson and Nat Goodwin credited this performance with inspiring Jefferson to produce an all-star revival of *The Rivals* the following year.[509]

By February 21, 1896, he was in New Orleans, having already partially cast the production and freely advising on the costumes. Jefferson had his own costumes (now owned by the Museum of the City of New York), designed by Herman, but the rest of the cast were responsible for their wardrobe. Joe, however, did not hesitate with his opinion. He told Wilson, who was to perform the minor role of David, to wear "pumps, white stockings, red plush breeches, long yellow vest, white necktie with huge bow, and a long old-fashioned square-cut livery. . . . I would say a red or black close crop [wig]."[510]

On February 27, 1896, he wrote to Charles Burke from Pass
Christian, Mississippi:

> I don't like the lady you mention for our company. Her
> reputation is nationally bad—and she drinks.
>
> Of course it will be better to have a star for Lucy, if we could
> get one, but our forces are so strong that any neat pretty little
> actress will do.
>
> The reputation of our company in the eyes of first-class
> audiences who will pay high for their entertainments is of great
> consequence.[511]

Jefferson wanted the actress Olga Nethersole to play Lydia Languish and wrote to Charles Burke, who was suggesting and hiring
actors:

> Parker House
> Boston.
>
> Dear Charly:
>
> The cast, if it can be had, would, of course, be strong.
>
> I will see Miss Nethersole, but I understand that she goes to
> England in about 7 weeks.
>
> I don't think Nat Goodwin will like to play Sir Lucius.
>
> You do not say anything about Mrs. Drew, but I take it for
> granted that she will play.[512]

The itinerary was already set by late April, and Jefferson wrote,
from Boston, to Francis Wilson, who had written to ask for help: "I
find it . . . out of the question to rehearse in Springfield until Monday. If you . . . get here Saturday . . . , I can give you an hour or two
at my hotel, the Parker House."[513]

C. B. Jefferson and Joseph Brooks produced the show with Julia
Marlowe as Lydia Languish, her husband Robert Taber as Captain
Absolute, W. H. Crane as Sir Anthony, Joseph Holland as Falkland,
Nat C. Goodwin as Lucius O'Trigger, Edward M. Holland as Fag,
Francis Wilson as David, Mrs. John Drew as Mrs. Malaprop, Fanny
Rice as Lucy, and, of course, Jefferson as Bob Acres.[514]

Francis Wilson came up to Springfield, Massachusetts, on the train
from New York with Mrs. Drew, Nat C. Goodwin, Edward and
Joseph Holland, Fanny Rice, and Joseph Brooks. Fanny brought her
family along complete with baby. They drove in carriages to Pullman
cars that were sidetracked by the Connecticut River. In addition to

sleeping quarters, the cars provided a drawing room, a dining room, and a morning room. William H. Crane and his wife stayed in Springfield at the Massasoit House, because he had a cold and was avoiding speaking, lest he contract laryngitis the day before opening.

Figure 23. Joseph Jefferson in *The Rivals*. Courtesy of the Museum of the City of New York Theatre Collection.

At Sunday dinners in the dining car, the cast sat hierarchically, like a family. Jefferson and Mrs. Drew were at opposite ends of the main table, playing father and mother. Goodwin, Julia Marlowe, and Robert Taber were down one side, and eventually Crane, Mrs. Crane, and Wilson down another, like the older children of the family. Four smaller tables held the "youngsters," as it were. At one sat the Rice family—Baby Rice, Grandma Rice, Fanny Rice, and her husband, Dr. Purdy. At another the three Jefferson "boys," Charley, Tom, and Joe. The Holland brothers occupied a third table by themselves, and at the fourth sat Jefferson's youngest son, Willie, along with two female understudies—Miss Ratcliffe and Mrs. H. M. Pitt.[515]

After dinner the cast went to the Massasoit House; got W. H. Crane out of bed; experimented with the ether, iodoform, and cocaine that he was using to improve his throat; and began to rehearse under Jefferson's supervision. The actors were nervous about performing in front of one another for the first time, and when Francis Wilson's scene came, he actually locked the door so that none of the cast could watch. The other actors had to pound on it for admittance when their cues came. Jefferson was too deaf to notice anything. Julia Marlowe later remembered that throughout the tour "rehearsals were casual; the call would be . . . that those could come who wished. There was much . . . good fellowship and little . . . discipline. . . . My habit of precision . . . made me . . . prey to . . . anxiety."[516]

Jefferson's all-star *Rivals* opened with virtually no rehearsal on the day after its star reached Springfield. Backstage, Joe met Carl Kettler, who was working as Nat Goodwin's valet. Goodwin shared Jefferson's dressing room, and Kettler was asked to help comb Bob Acres' wig. When Jefferson began to get into costume, he discovered that he had forgotten to shave; Kettler came to his rescue. During the tour that followed, Kettler helped Jefferson clean the palette and brushes he used for painting, and finally Charles Burke offered him a job if he ever had occasion to leave Goodwin. Kettler would become the mainstay of Jefferson's old age.

On stage, Goodwin, Joseph Holland, Taber, and Wilson discovered that the version of *The Rivals* they had been reading or rehearsing was not the version Jefferson performed. Jefferson would improvise, for instance, frequently interrupting the speeches of fellow actors without warning. On opening night other members of the cast were so confused they required prompting, which Jefferson provided in front of the audience. Francis Wilson, in a newspaper interview the following fall, remembered that "Mr. Jefferson has introduced many lines . . . into *The Rivals* and has so altered . . . business and condensed . . . the scenes [that Sheridan wouldn't recognize the play]."[517]

Audiences could not have cared less; the reaction to the production was phenomenal. The Chicago correspondent for the *New York Dramatic Mirror* referred to the final curtain call as the disclosure of the "royal ten." Ticket prices at the American Theatre in New York and the Lafayette Square Theatre in Washington ranged from $5.00 to $1.00 and could be purchased a week before the performance. Every seat was filled, and as soon as the doors opened, people jammed into the theatre to fill the $1.50 standing room places. There were ten women there for every man, and even in the top gallery, spectators were well dressed. In Washington, President and Mrs. Cleveland turned out, along with members of the cabinet and their wives. Mark Hanna, William McKinley, and their wives came to see the show. Thirty-eight hundred people saw the play in Louisville, and in Buffalo messenger boys stood in line for five days in order to procure a ticket for their employers.[518] In St. Louis tickets went on sale a week in advance at 9 A.M., and

> The street in front of the theater was so jammed with . . . pur-chasers that passers-by were forced to take to the gutter. Two extra policemen were necessary to handle the crowd. The pur-chasers were whipped into a line which extended from the box office clear past the St. James Hotel on Broadway up Walnut Street halfway to Sixth, and as the morning progressed, the line became longer.
>
> All the doors save one were closed and locked. Through this, the line was admitted, and as each one bought his ticket, he was let out through the lobby door into the drugstore. Two stalwart attaches stood guard here and would allow no one to enter. . . .
>
> Several smooth individuals turned a pretty penny by salting places in the line and selling them . . . to individuals who were willing to pay any price for a good seat. Two and three dollars were paid in several instances for these positions. Other men who had positions were paid to buy tickets for . . . latecomers. Some of them had commissions of from fifteen to twenty seats, but owing to the fear that speculators would secure the tickets, no one was allowed to buy more than ten. Several speculators were, however, in evidence, and they will probably be able to double the price of the tickets.
>
> By nine A.M. every seat in the parquette was taken, and the indications were that before the day was over, standing room would be at a premium. Many . . . swells . . . resigned them-selves and their dress suits . . . to seats in the gallery.[519]

The production made a fortune. The New York matinee on May 7 took in $8,000; the receipts in Philadelphia were $8,200; and the Chicago matinee netted $7,250, exactly the amount taken in at the New York opening. The total Chicago engagement of three performances took in over $20,000; receipts were over $5,000 in Cincinnati and nearly $3,000 in Indianapolis. The Boston matinee took in $6,996.50. Jefferson and Crane each made $40,000 on the tour; Francis Wilson and Nat Goodwin made $10,000; but Mrs. Drew earned only $2,500.[520]

Artistically the show was less successful. According to the critic for the *New York Dramatic Mirror*, Jefferson's Acres was "the . . . finest exemplification of the comedian's art that the stage of this country has produced for a score of years," but the results of the production as a whole were artistically unsatisfying.

> Every actor in *The Rivals'* cast . . . worked . . . to get the most out of his part. The result . . . was incongruous. . . . The ripe method of Mrs. John Drew contrasted glaringly with Mr. Crane's modern sense of art. The finesse . . . of Joseph Jefferson [was] offset by the grotesquery of Francis Wilson. . . . Nat Goodwin was not at his happiest as Sir Lucius O'Trigger. His brogue was hard and forced and of the will-o'-the-wisp variety —now you heard it and now you didn't. Mr. Crane's Sir Anthony Absolute had the merit of . . . sincerity. Robert Taber balanced the cynicism and hypocrisy of Jack Absolute with . . . earnestness. . . . It was one of the satisfying performances of the day. Mrs. Taber's Lydia Languish was charmingly natural.
>
> In the thankless parts of Falkland and Fag, the Holland brothers "fed" their comrades so unobtrusively that they deserve . . . warm praise. They kept the parts where they belonged —in the background.
>
> As much cannot be said for Francis Wilson's David. . . . In his one "bit of fat" he elaborated . . . extravagantly. . . . His self-assertiveness nevertheless pleased the audience, and he was rewarded with two . . . scene calls. His dialect . . . would have puzzled a philologist.[521]

The itinerary was brutal. The company traveled by train, eating, sleeping, and performing together. In twenty-seven days they played thirty-two performances in twenty-eight cities, sometimes changing venues between matinee and evening performances, living in the deluxe set of Pullman railway cars that Jefferson hired for the occasion and going by carriage every day to and from the theatre. The tour was unusual, because it took place during the summer theatrical doldrums. This allowed Jefferson to obtain the quality of cast he wanted and to be assured of little competition. To compensate for the heat, the cast was provided with electric fans in both the railroad cars and their dressing rooms, as well as ice cream, cake, and punch backstage during performances. Nevertheless Francis Wilson reported that Jefferson was exhausted by the hot weather.[522] Goodwin remembered:

> We visited . . . principal cities, never playing over two nights in one place. Business was enormous, the management clearing . . . thousands of dollars during the four weeks tour. We were the recipients of many attentions, our time being spent driving, dining and visiting various public institutions and colleges. We held impromptu receptions nightly behind the scenes. A large table was always spread on the stage laden with viands, and many distinguished people partook of our hospitalities. Our happiest times were spent in the private car where we would congregate after the play and spend a few hours in anecdote and song.[523]

The production's scenery, created by Walter Burridge, traveled with the company from theatre to theatre and could be set up quickly, because Jefferson was still using wings and drops rather than box sets. Joe controlled the scenic design, but the other actors decided what they would wear, and he was not always pleased with their desire for historical authenticity. Julia Marlowe recalled that

> I had bought a new and correct dress for my character of Lydia Languish, with the sides built out, bustle wise, as was the fashion of that day.
>
> Mr. Jefferson accosted me on the first night behind the scenes. "Miss Marlowe, Miss Marlowe, what made you get a dress like that?"
>
> "Why, this is the correct costume, Mr. Jefferson."
>
> "Yes, yes yes—but those—those things at the sides; they make you look enormous. I wouldn't have them. No-no—I would do away with them."
>
> "But that would ruin the dress. It's absolutely the proper style."
>
> "Nonsense," said Mr. Jefferson, and snapped his fingers in the direction of the audience. "They don't know anything about all

that—not a bit of it—nothing, nothing at all. An ounce of effect is worth a pound of correctness," said he.

I wore my dress all the same. . . .

A moment later, Mr. Jefferson addressed himself to Mr. Taber, playing Captain Absolute. "What's that metal thing you have about your neck, my boy?"

"Why, that's part of my uniform, sir."

"And that stiff collar which seems to choke you and that white wig. Why you've ruined . . . your good looks. What do you do that for?"

"But this is the uniform of the time, Mr. Jefferson I took a lot of trouble to get the exact thing."

"Nonsense," said Mr. Jefferson. "Waste of time and money, too." He closed one eye and tapped Mr. Taber on his chest several times. "They"—a glance toward the audience—"don't know anything about that. Nothing at all. Effect, effect my boy. That's what you want. Hang the wig. And this thing and the high collar. Off with them."[524]

Neither Marlowe nor her biographer, Charles Edward Russell, who saw the production and who was writing in 1926, when Marlowe was still alive, was satisfied with the results.

> *The Rivals*, performed by the All-Star cast, was a thing . . . to see for the sake of future boasting. . . . From any point of view of art it was negligible. . . . *Lydia Languish* was a part that Julia Marlowe could have played in her sleep and wherein she could contribute little but her name on the playbills.

Among members of the cast, viewpoints about Jefferson's performance varied. Russell at one point noted: "Mr. Jefferson played *Bob Acres* as he had always played it and was the main show. . . . In like manner, according to Nat Goodwin, Jefferson's performance was unvarying—"always the same, never a change, standing in the same position, no altering of intonation or gesture, everything given by rote, but always with fine effect." Yet at another point, Russell wrote:

> Mr. Jefferson had a way of varying his business and introducing unexpected . . . stunts that drove . . . other actors frantic. On one occasion, a scene with *Sir Lucius*, he reached the cue word, but instead of stopping for Goodwin's rejoinder, he kept

on saying: "Don't it, *Sir Lucius?* Eh, *Sir Lucius?* Ain't it so, Sir Lucius?" until Goodwin . . . was thrown . . . off the cue and could do nothing but follow Mr. Jefferson about the stage mumbling and stuttering. I think it an odd revelation of the actor's psychology that when Mr. Goodwin . . . called attention to this lapse, Mr. Jefferson was unaware that he had gone off and was . . . honestly sorry. He had been so . . . accustomed to playing with a support trained to his peculiarities that he had forgotten they were his.

Marlowe's version of the story is even less flattering to Jefferson.

Nat Goodwin, although not lacking in assurance, found himself disconcerted while acting with Mr. Jefferson, who would not stick to the text but provoked audiences to laughter by grimaces, gestures, drawn-out exclamations and repetitions. . . . Goodwin . . . would beg for a rehearsal at which Mr. Jefferson would correctly give the cue saying "There you are Nat. That's your cue."
"Yes," Mr. Goodwin would say. "I recognize it, but at night you talk all around that cue and keep the people in an uproar so that I can't fit my lines in anywhere."
Mr. Jefferson would promise amendment, but the unhappy Mr. Goodwin suffered still.

The problems that Goodwin faced with Jefferson may have accounted for the poor reviews he received. The *St. Louis Post Dispatch* wrote that his Sir Lucius paled in comparison with memory of Florence.[525] On the other hand, Jefferson may have realized that he had a weak Sir Lucius and made up for it by improvisation. His ad-libbing was part of his acting technique, a verbalized subtext kept going through the play and often overheard by other actors onstage and sometimes by the audience.

For instance . . . at the closing of the second act in *The Rivals*, where Bob throws himself upon the lounge, overcome by the thought of being . . . in a duel, Jefferson, with back to audience and with head rolling from side to side in pitiful comic despair, [ad-libbed]:
"Oh my God! my God! What a damned fool I am!"[526]

Jefferson knew exactly what worked for him both as Bob Acres and as Joseph Jefferson, the beloved American actor audiences had come to see. Goodwin describes his shameless milking of a curtain speech at the end of Act II. After the entire company was called out, Jefferson stepped forward and began with a homage to Sheridan, followed by a

> reference to the artistic rendering that they were giving his work, the . . . pleasure it afforded him and his comrades to have the privilege of acting such a comedy. . . . Then with a . . . trembling voice, he would bewail the fact that Sheridan was not permitted to view this . . . interpretation of his work. Choking with sobs . . . , he would refer to past performances by lamented actors and thank the audience for its attention. Concluding with a semi-congratulatory reference to its being permitted to view this . . . artistic performance, the . . . old gentleman would make his bow, . . . wiping away a tear, amid the plaudits of the throng.[527]

Goodwin resented Jefferson not only for his manipulation of the audience, but also for his financial success. He claimed that Jefferson contributed nothing to the American theatre—built no theatres, produced no original plays, and created no new characters other than Rip. The latter, although untrue, was the common image of Jefferson in 1896. Goodwin's description of the Jefferson family after each performance is devastating. "The sprint from the theatre to the private car, participated in by Joseph Brooks, the Jefferson boys, and the . . . old gentleman (with Charles Jefferson in the lead, with the nightly receipts). . . . They would arrive at the car—panting—and, falling into their seats, . . . divide the artistic spoils, 'the Dean' taking fifty per-cent."

This scene described a financial arrangement that Goodwin came to resent. The cast were paid fixed salaries by Jefferson, but the company got not only its guaranteed fee but also a percentage of the house—a percentage that went directly to the Jeffersons. It is the percentage of the box office that the Jeffersons counted each night while the salaried actors looked on.

In spite of artistic and financial subordination, touring with Jefferson could be a pleasant experience offstage. Marlowe remembered that on train trips, Mr. Jefferson was . . . amusing, a . . . storyteller and an amiable host. He made etchings, printed them on a . . . wringer and presented them to us. He also painted in oils using a feather. . . . One day Mr. Jefferson, who had been laughing with rest of us at Nat Goodwin's imitations, said, "Now, Nat, imitate me."

"Oh, no!" Mr. Goodwin protested. "Oh, no, governor, I couldn't imitate you." But while he spoke he was giving the most marvelous imitation of Mr. Jefferson, our chief being . . . unaware of the fact. The rest of the table was convulsed with laughter as Mr. Jefferson continued to beg for an imitation, and Goodwin in Mr. Jefferson's . . . voice avowed he . . . could not do it.[528]

Even when he was making fun of Jefferson, Goodwin referred to him as "governor." Everyone knew who was the boss, and the boss was, with age, becoming increasingly self-absorbed. By 1889 even Jefferson had begun to joke about it. Francis Wilson writes that at their first meeting

Mr. Jefferson explained that he was absent-minded . . . , and told of having written a letter to his wife the other night, and not wishing to forget to post it he carried it in his hand, got into a car, paid his fare on entering, and sat down. Later, the conductor, forgetting Mr. Jefferson had paid, touched him on the shoulder and held out his hand. Mr. Jefferson . . . put the letter into the conductor's hand, saying:

"Mail this for me, will you please?"

"I haven't time to mail your letters!" yelled the fare-taker.[529]

In like manner Nat Goodwin tells a story about a fellow actor, Sol Smith Russell, which indicates either an incredible naïveté on Jefferson's part or an alarming inattention to the world around him. Russell found his way to a dressing room shared by the two men in Chicago. He was so drunk he kept falling asleep on his feet as he complimented them and finally had to be led out of the room by Goodwin.

Jefferson appeared much gratified. "Sol is awfully pleased apparently and was most gracious," he said. I answered, "Yes for a tired man, Sol spoke remarkably well." Jefferson, who was very literal asked, "Is Sol tired?" I replied, "He ought to be with the load he is carrying."

Said Jefferson, "What load is he carrying?"

Figure 24. Joseph Jefferson as Bob Acres in *The Rivals*.
Courtesy of the Performing Arts Research Center,
New York Public Library.

"A basket of lovely peaches," quoth I.

"I didn't notice he had a parcel with him," replied Jefferson.

"He is tanked up to the collar button," I said. "Oh what a lovely skate he has!"

"Tanked up to the collar button and skate? What the devil are you talking about? You have a vernacular, my dear Nat, that requires translation. What are you talking about?"

"Didn't you notice his condition?" I asked. "He's loaded to the eyebrows."

"Tight?" asked Jefferson.

"As a new drum," I replied.

"I can't realize it," said Jefferson. "My eyesight prevented my scanning his face as accurately as I could wish. I noticed his conversation was a bit measured, but very well expressed. I can't believe he was under the influence of liquor. Are you sure?"

I replied . . . "You can't deceive an artist."

Jefferson simply screamed at this remark and during the afternoon repeated the incident several times to each and every member of the company.[530]

The Rivals' cast gave a farewell performance at the Fifth Avenue Theatre in New York during the summer of 1896. Afterwards they met on stage, and Nat Goodwin presented Jefferson with the sword he had used as Acres' second in the dueling scene. Later Jefferson took him to his dressing room, removed his wig, and said: "My boy, I want you to play Bob Acres. I now crown you Bob Acres. This wig I have worn for years, and I now bequeath it to you." Another version of the story has Jefferson saying "Take it, Nat. And may it bring you success."[531] There were rumors of an all-star production of *The School for Scandal* the following season, with Jefferson as Sir Peter Teazle, but Jefferson squelched them fast. He had not enjoyed this recent experience.

> The all star cast was a sensational affair but proved one thing very thoroughly—that when a good actor makes a failure, it is greater than that of an unknown person in the part. . . .There were three failures in the all-star cast, one of which was that estimable actress, Julia Marlowe. She did not . . . enter into the part at all. The company was a . . . charming one. . . . We all lived in the four cars which were provided for us and during the

whole four weeks of the trip, I never heard a cross word . . .
from any one. . . . Once in a while Mrs. Drew would say something sarcastic to Mr. Goodwin and he would answer in kind,
but it was . . . good natured . . . banter.

At first sight Jefferson's admission about a "good actor" failing
seems humble and unguarded until one reads on and finds that he is
not necessarily talking about himself. He may have been aware of the
production's problems, but there is little evidence that he was aware
of his own. If Jefferson never heard a cross word among ten star
actors living togther for four weeks in a railway train, it is probably
because he was going deaf.[532]

19

"A BACK NUMBER"— RETIREMENT AND DEATH

1896–1905

Until a year before his death, Jefferson continued to tour. His fall engagements gradually declined from ten weeks in 1896–97 to seven in 1903–04, but until the end, he was able to push out a month to five weeks of performances every spring.[533] The length of the tours varied according to his health; the winters spent in Florida and the warmth of the spring invigorated him, but even in the years of increasing ill-health, when he was forced to cancel performances, Jefferson still played three to five weeks every season.

His summers were spent at Buzzards Bay, fishing with Richard Watson Gilder and Grover Cleveland and surrounded by his seven children, nine grandchildren, and two great-grandchildren. His winter vacations took place first in New Iberia and later in Palm Beach. He fished; and of course he painted, writing from Louisiana in 1897:

> Think of it; I have been twelve weeks without painting, . . . but I shall be at it . . . early to-morrow. . . . The weather . . . is delightful. The roses are climbing over our veranda, and my grandson is climbing over my chair.
>
> I am working away at my painting, and hope . . . to do some work that will be creditable in the way of American landscape.

He also gardened, writing to Francis Wilson in August 1901: "How the summer has flown! I dig in the garden in the morning and paint all of the afternoon. Time slips away, and I haven't got half done that I want to have behind me—I am going on for seventy-three. God will soon make a sweet little angel of me; so I must hurry up."[534]

He saw his children and his grandchildren married, some of them in elaborate garden ceremonies, with orchestras imported from Boston and, in Willy's case, a bride sporting a heart-shaped sapphire pendant surrounded by diamonds, and a best man, described in newspapers as a "golfer and society man."[535]

But in the midst of his leisure, Jefferson was always planning to work. On tour, he was indefatigable. In one week in Baltimore he "played seven performances, made seven speeches, delivered a lecture, formed the centre of a street procession, ate five special dinners, sat up several evenings with the boys as late as two and three o'clock in the morning and attended to various other duties"—"without," in his own words, "fatigue or ennui."

That he was without *ennui* is doubtful. Jefferson had become very cynical about *Rip*. While in Philadelphia in the fall of 1900, he journeyed to Princeton by train to give a lecture and wrote to Lawrence Barrett: "I must leave Princeton Junction at 2:23 in order to get back to Philadelphia in time for the 'Dramatic Swindle.'"[536] His daughter-in-law, Eugenie, remembered him playing charades, performing as the child Meenie wearing a Dutch hat made from a tea-table cover. Another story of the period, told to E. L. Sothern, whose father had appeared with Jefferson in *Our American Cousin*, illustrates the same point.

> This morning . . . I found Henry Watterson and Joe in close confidence, regaling themselves with reflections on the laxity of the present generation and politics. Something brought to Watterson's mind a line in *Rip Van Winkle*, but he could not recall the words. He squinted his game eye at Joe, and Joe covered his own game ear and said "eh?" to the three-cornered Wattersonian glance. He tried to remember the line, did Jefferson, stumbled hopelessly and then said:
>
> "Oh I don't know what it is."
>
> "What do you mean by 'don't know it'? Haven't you been playing it eighty years?" shouted Watterson.
>
> "Oh, well I *play* the piece; I don't *know* it!" said Jefferson, in his soft musical voice, with its odd little snarl at the periods.[537]

Figure 25. Jefferson in old age, *ca.* 1890's

That Jefferson was without fatigue is impossible, but he could not stop. He pushed on, by now plagued with rumors of his retirement. He told Francis Wilson: "The newspaper criticisms . . . of late are very mournful in tone. They write, 'this may be the last time you will ever see him! He must soon pass away!' They sound more like obituary notices than critiques. I expect to see shortly, 'None but the family are invited—no flowers, etc.'"

Sounding more and more like C. W. Couldock, insisting at his retirement benefits that he would still accept an engagement, Jefferson began denying, in town after town, "the rumor, locally current, that he would retire from the stage and not be seen again in that city. 'When I do retire,' he told a St. Louis audience, 'it shall be after it has been announced to the public, and I shall not make the announcement as long as I have health'." He could even get nasty on the subject. During a dinner party a drawling guest asked: "Aw—Mr. Jefferson—aw—when are you—aw—going—aw—to retire from the stage?" Jefferson replied: "I am only waiting for you to say the word!"[538]

Of course part of this problem was that Jefferson's press agents, presumably with his permission, used the threat of his retirement as an inducement for audiences. By mid-July 1898 he had signed contracts to appear at the Fifth Avenue Theatre during the 1898–99 season. According to his press releases, this was "to signalize his farewell to the stage," but Jefferson was still performing in 1904. In May 1903 a satirical article appeared about his farewell tours:

> "Jerome," demanded Joseph Jefferson yesterday afternoon of Eddy his faithful press agent, "has everything been carefully arranged for my opening to-morrow night?"
>
> "Yes sir. . . . Cords and cords of your press matter now block the city editor's path to his desk; the public has been carefully apprised of the fact that this is the last of your series of farewell tours."[539]

Eventually the fatigue became undeniable. On Saturday, October 6, 1901, Jefferson performed in Dayton, Ohio, got up at 6 A.M. on Sunday, and took a train to Chicago. By the time he got there, he could not remember where he had been. He admitted to reporters:

> I am absolutely tired out. We have been traveling nearly all day, and I arose at six o'clock this morning. I have finished only the first week of my tour, and . . . I have enjoyed every minute. . . . Where did I play last night? Why, I played *Rip Van Winkle* at—. Let me see. Where did I play last night? Really I grow ashamed of myself. I really must be getting forgetful.

"Dayton, Dayton, Ohio". . . that's the name of the town. Very pretty place too. I really do not know why the name escaped me, but it did. We played there last night to a splendid house, and with the end of my performance came the completion of my first week's tour.

There is no truth whatever in the report that this is my last year. . . . I have set no time for withdrawing from the stage, and I don't propose to set any time. If the American people are kind enough to accord me the honor of their patronage, I shall endeavor to please them, as, I hope, I have done in the past. No indeed, this is not my last year, by any means. At least, I sincerely hope not.

But I really haven't anything to say to you today. I'm not an important personage who can tell you very much that you would like to know. Besides that, I'm tired—very tired—and if you will excuse me I think I will go to my rooms.[540]

This was the real version of Billy Florence's inability to distinguish Hartford from New Haven. Jefferson could not remember where he had been. Word of the Dayton gaffe spread, and the Chicago correspondent for the *New York Dramatic Mirror* immediately took up the cause in his hero's interest.

Mr. Jefferson . . . took occasion . . . Monday night to stop before the curtain in the rags of Rip, after the first act, and rebuke a reporter who had interviewed him . . . and had intimated that the veteran could not remember Dayton, Ohio, his last one-night stand, and was consequently failing mentally and would soon retire from the stage. After the performance that evening, I saw him trot briskly into Rector's at the head of a party consisting of Mrs. Jefferson [and] their son William, . . . and the way the old gentleman did justice to a midnight luncheon and seemed to be the life of the party did not indicate . . . any mental or physical collapse. Every actor likes to forget one-night stands. In response to an invitation to spend a morning in police court with me, Mr. Jefferson wrote a note. He did not dictate but wrote it himself in a dashing hand not guilty of a tremor. His alleged collapse is all rot. I expect to take my grandchildren to see him. Any man who could do Rip, Caleb Plummer and Mr. Golightly all inside of nine hours, as he did last Saturday, is far from a wreck.[541]

Despite his continued ability to perform, there could be no doubt that Jefferson was beginning to fail physically. On September 14, 1897, he and Sarah went from Buzzards Bay to Portland, Maine, to inaugurate a theatre named for him. Francis Wilson was present and noted that Jefferson's hearing was deteriorating, or, as Joe put it, "his deafness was improving." He also noted that Jefferson took a "slight stimulant" before going on "to calm his nervousness." That Jefferson needed to calm himself before an audience at the age of sixty-eight is doubtful. The stimulant may well have served to pick him up and keep him going. In Washington, during the fall 1897 tour, Wilson noted that Jefferson "sleeps   about ten hours a day, goes to bed at twelve, falling to sleep immediately and rises about eight A.M. In the afternoon, his custom is to lie down about five P.M. and sleep until six-thirty or seven P.M." This is hardly the schedule of a convalescent, but more and more, Jefferson needed to rest.

Eventually his well-being both at home and on the road was supported by the presence of Carl Kettler, who had so impressed him as a valet the previous year. While in New Orleans in March 1897, Jefferson had met Kettler again and immediately offered him a job. Kettler finally began work as Jefferson's "private secretary and valet" in Boston in the fall of 1897. Devoted to the man he referred to as the "Governor" or the "Master," he moved his family to Buzzards Bay and renovated one of the local houses. He was with Jefferson at home and on the road. Backstage he rubbed Joe's legs to combat the rheumatism setting in and tickled the soles of his feet with a feather while Jefferson, clad in a brown padded Chinese smoking jacket, slept between matinees and evening performances. Joe believed that the tickling helped his circulation.[542]

Like any elderly person, Jefferson was surrounded by death, and he now had the leisure to mourn. On September 5, 1897, he traveled to Philadelphia for the funeral of Louisa Lane Drew, who had played Mrs. Malaprop with him for seventeen years. Joe sent a huge heart of autumn leaves and attended the brief church service at St. Stephen's with Francis Wilson. As the coffin was borne up the aisle, Wilson noted Jefferson's "bowed head and trembling lip." Finally, at the interment in Glenwood Cemetery, he stood bareheaded with Sol Smith Russell; the actor and playwright Denman Thompson; Mrs. Drew's son, John; and her grandson, Lionel Barrymore, and joined in the Lord's Prayer.[543]

By the winter of 1897–98, Jefferson was ill enough to retire to Palm Beach, Florida. He took the luxurious new Florida Limited, which left Pennsylvania Station in New York. The train was equipped with a Pullman drawing-room, sleeping cars, dining cars, and a library car furnished with easy chairs, sofas, and writing desks where passengers were provided with stationery. The observation car had large plate-glass windows on the sides and ends.[544] This was more than just a winter vacation, because on January 1, 1898, he wrote to his son Tom, who was now acting on his own:

> I congratulate you all on the success of your undertaking. If my illness has been the means of giving you all the opportunity to develop your talent, I have not suffered in vain—though I hope you will get on without my having to repeat the dose—for the present at least.
>
> I trust that you will go on earnestly and in harmony. These qualities are the key-note to success and happiness. The income derived from our own labour is always more gratifying than that gained from any other source.
>
> There is no reason to doubt that you may go on in the present course with great pleasure and profit. Toney is as much pleased as I am at the good news of your success and joins me in wishing you a happy New Year.[545]

As he wrote to Laurence Hutton, Jefferson considered himself a "back number," and from this point on Palm Beach became his winter home. Eventually he purchased real estate there, erecting summer homes or "villas" on lots facing Lake Worth and two large business buildings in downtown Palm Beach. Early in February 1898 he wrote to Charley: "It is the garden spot of the earth. . . . Without exception it is the most lovely place I have ever seen."[546]

But Jefferson was not done touring. He came north in March 1898 for a spring season. His health was improved, and he had decided to revive *The Rivals*. According to the *New York Dramatic Mirror:*

> The original purpose of the actor . . . was to have made it [the New York engagement] . . . his farewell to the New York public, but . . . he changed his plan, and if all goes well we shall have him with us again next year.
>
> To lend interest to the present performance of *The Rivals*,

Mr. Jefferson has surrounded himself with a . . . good company, and for this the public owes him a debt of gratitude, which . . . may obliterate recollections of inadequacies . . . that are associated with the dean of the American stage. . . .

The comedy was set with poor scenery, although it looked as if newly painted. The stage management was of the primitive order. Characters came on and off in front of the "tormentors," while Mr. Jefferson and members of his company interrupted the action by taking scene-calls. These were typical of many things not in the spirit of . . . dramatic art.[547]

According to Otis Skinner, who was a member of the company, Jefferson was very superstitious, and during the New York run he came backstage and said: "The play will go badly tonight. There is a woman dressed in mourning sitting in a box." The presentiment proved accurate. Jefferson was scheduled to switch from *The Rivals* to *Rip* on November 7, but on November 5 he failed to appear because of a severe cold. The cold turned serious, and the Fifth Avenue Theatre went dark. Joe was to appear in *Lend Me Five Shillings* for the Actors' Fund of America benefit at the Broadway Theatre on November 10. By November 8 over five hundred tickets had been sold, but that day the *New York Times* announced it was probable that his appearance would have to be canceled, as well as a lecture at Columbia University that Friday. Jefferson was unable to meet either obligation. He "spent a comfortable day" at the Holland House Hotel. On November 13 the *New York Times* announced that he had recovered and was to resume acting the next day, but on the fourteenth the rest of the New York engagement was canceled owing to Jefferson's "continued indisposition."

Charles Burke announced that his brothers would continue the tour of *Rip* and *The Rivals*, making their first appearance in Pittsburgh at a Thanksgiving matinee. His motives were financial. Jefferson's sons were his managers, and they were renting the theatre in New York directly, not just sharing in its profits or receiving a guarantee. Their overhead was $2,500 a week plus $1,500 for salaries. They were obligated to pay the rental and the company whether the actors performed or not. After two weeks of Jefferson's illness, they were out $8,000. In addition, the $11,000 advance ticket sale had to be refunded.[548] Charles Burke announced:

An expensive company has been engaged to support father during the short season booked for him, and . . . we ought to utilize the services of the actors engaged. Tom has only played one of father's parts, I believe, Golightly, in the farce *Lend Me Five Shillings*. We have found that local managers are willing to stand for him, and that ought to settle the matter. . . . Tom will do the best he can, and he's not a bad actor, by any means.[549]

Charles Burke seems to damn his brother with faint praise. And indeed Thomas had reasons for fear based on past experience.

Once the old gentleman did not feel equal to playing a one-night stand in Canton, Ohio; so he deputized his son [Tom] to play "Rip" in his place. The bill did not record the change, and therefore the young man received the full measure of applause that his father . . . gets. After the performance, he went to the . . . hotel and bought the finest cigar he could find, and as he smoked, he soliloquized . . . :

"Well, . . . I guess I am something of an actor. . . . I . . . flatter myself the old man couldn't have done better. . . . "

While he was . . . musing, a native stepped up to the cigar stand.

"See the show?" asked the clerk.

"Yep."

"What did you think of it?"

"First rate, all except 'Rip.' Seems to me the old man's failing."[550]

The "old man" was failing, and Tom had been elected to play Rip. He had actually been performing since 1884, but a family legend grew up around what was perceived as his debut. It was not a debut —Tom was simply taking over the family business—but his situation exemplifies the ambiguity of Jefferson's relationship with his sons. Their professional lives were dependent on him, and when he was not touring, he lived surrounded by them. With the exception, however, of Charles Burke, who had a career as a theatrical producer and manager outside of his father's tours, none of Jefferson's sons ever thrived professionally away from the family company. When Joseph, Jr., and Thomas and William Winter Jefferson toured on their own, they were seldom able to perform in the venues that had welcomed their father. Part of the reason is that Jefferson scheduled them that way. He would not brook competition; he would eventually cut down on his touring, but he did not give it up until 1904. Consequently, eventually Jefferson played the major cities, and his sons played the hinterlands. He knew he was the one the public came to see; he knew he was the one who would bring in the money; and his children knew it too. When Eugenie Paul Jefferson wrote a reminiscence of her father-in-law, she included a significant section about her husband, Thomas. It reads as a pathetic attempt to pretend that he was his father's artistic heir. According to Eugenie, Thomas was at home in Montclair, New Jersey, when his brother, Charles Burke, phoned to say that their father was ill.

> Charles Burke told Tom to come to New York at once to rehearse the part of Rip, which he would perform in a week. Tom's reaction was "I was so startled that I wanted to run—I don't know where—anywhere." He arrived at the hotel to find Joe very ill.
>
> "Well, my son," he said, "you will have to take my place; let me see how well you are going to do it."
>
> "But," he stammered, "how can I? I do not know the lines. I have never even tried to play Rip."
>
> "You *can* do it, my boy, I know you can," father said, and then and there, he insisted upon rehearsing [Tom] in the most important scene in the play. "I shall never forget it. There lay my dear father about to die (as we all feared)—and there was I lying upon the floor going through the waking-up scene from his play, *Rip Van Winkle!*"[551]

In 1898 Jefferson's sons planned to perform in Pittsburgh, Chicago, and St. Louis and then have Jefferson rejoin them in Washington, but their father remained at the Holland House in New York. Given the fact that he owned a home in New Jersey, the decisions to stay in the city and to drop out of the tour indicate the severity of his condition. On November 16, Charles Burke announced that his father would leave for Point Comfort to rest for a few weeks. Even facing what was a life-threatening illness, Jefferson got out of bed on November 18 and lectured on "The Drama" at Columbia College.[552]

Surely, if there were ever proof of his obsession with work and reputation, this was it. Jefferson's health was poor enough by November 1898 that he said to Laurence Hutton:

> "In the natural course of events, Laurence . . . you'll have something to say about me after I'm gone; and I know you will say it . . . kindly. . . . There are certain things about myself, as an actor, that I want said, which I can't say and which can't be said by anybody *yet*! Will you say them for me when the time comes? I'll write them down and send them to you." [Hutton later wrote] He did write them down . . . voluminously . . . , and he sent them; but alas! they never reached my hand. It was . . . discovered that a hotel bell boy had stolen and destroyed the document, had appropriated the stamps and had sold the signature to a collector of autographs.[553]

Although publicly they announced that they felt "no alarm about his condition," privately Jefferson's family was worried. He remained at the Holland House, but planned to go south on November 24. The day proved stormy, and he decided to stay. Finally, on November 26, his physicians "took him" to Point Comfort to "fully regain his health." By December 3, he was resting in Norfolk, Virginia.[554]

He spent the winter of 1898–99 in Florida, from which he shipped Grover Cleveland a gift of snappers and sheepsheads. Cleveland, now retired from public life, sent a letter thanking him and saying: "I am busy doing nothing or next to nothing." Jefferson must have understood only too well. On March 8, 1899, he wrote to Charles Burke from Palm Beach, orchestrating his son's trip to Florida the way he had orchestrated productions.

> The fishing here is not good, . . . as the fine weather has sent the fish into deep water. You ought to have a Tuxedo coat and black pants and vest for wear of an evening, also a bike suit for the wheeling. I need not suggest anything of this kind of Willie, as he is an authority—so you had best consult him. You need not bring any fishing tackle. I have everything. Can you leave Woonsocket on Sunday as to leave for here Sunday night? Try and do so if you can, as there is much you should see at Miami and Palm Beach. I will have all matters arranged here as to what

we shall do so as to save time. Of course I would like Tom to come also and will be only too glad to have him.[555]

But money and possibly the need to perform were too alluring to allow for full retirement. By 1898 Jefferson was the most financially successful actor in America. The *New York Dramatic Mirror* estimated that he had played *Rip Van Winkle* five thousand times and made five million dollars, figuring an average of a thousand dollars a performance in gross receipts. In mid-December, less than a month after his doctors had to take him south to recuperate, he was planning a return to the stage—a five-week spring tour in *Rip*, *The Cricket on the Hearth*, and *The Rivals* in the South, moving to the larger eastern cities, and ending in upstate New York. On March 3, 1899, one month before the tour began, his sister, Cornelia Jefferson Jackson, died in New York at the age of sixty-two. She had been suffering for five years from cancer of the stomach. Jefferson was in Palm Beach when it happened.[556] He replaced her, and the tour went on.

During the 1899–1900 season the family company continued to perform, opening on September 4 in New London, Connecticut, but Jefferson joined them only for performances between October 3 and November 25, and then later for a five-week tour starting April 1, which included three weeks at the Fifth Avenue Theatre in New York. Newspapers contended that the company made so much money when Jefferson appeared that he paid them twice as much for a ten-week season as other managers paid for twenty or thirty weeks. Given Jefferson's reputation for inexpensive productions, however, this may have been a publicist's attempt at positive press. The Jefferson company, headed by his sons, continued to tour all year.[557]

As always, they traveled by train. In the fall of 1902 Jefferson contended that he rehearsed the plays while going from city to city: "After luncheon on the train we clear out the tables from the dining car and all the company gives a rousing presentation as the train bowls from town to town." This contention, however, was probably designed to refute criticism about the sloppiness of his productions. Jefferson actors knew these plays backwards. A more appropriate image of the troupe's bowling "from town to town" has its younger members, Joe's sons and godson Jefferson Winter, wiling away the hours playing cards, especially poker. Jefferson hated cards, and this game in particular. If the boys spotted him approaching, the warning would go out: "Duck duck! Here comes father!" But Joe would often catch them, and when he did, he would stroll by silently with a contemptuous smile, or sometimes stop and harangue them:

> Oh don't stop! Please don't stop on my account. . . . I like to see young gentlemen enjoying themselves in such a . . . friendly way. All friends, aren't you? that's what you pretend to be. But it's all pretense! Who ever heard of friends sitting down . . . to take each other's money away? And at such a game—a game the essence of which is to . . . mislead your adversaries. Delightful, isn't it? I wonder you don't try waiting for each other up dark alleys and do it with clubs. But go on, go on! Don't let my prejudices interfere with your . . . enjoyment![558]

Jefferson was well aware of just whose money the "boys" were spending and that he needed to plug on as an actor to support them.

> You see it's this way. I divide with the boys . . . , and along toward the spring, they usually get . . . cramped for money. So I run out for five weeks, give the boys half the profits, and that carries them through the summer. . . .
>
> When September rolls around, the boys are once more wearing a worried look, whenever their tailor gets within hailing distance; so I take another . . . tour of five weeks—and there we are, a happy family again.

Willie was particularly needful of his father's financial help. Having slipped away to Europe, he cabled home: "Send five hundred dollars at once." Jefferson cabled back: "What for?" And the reply came: "For Willie."[559]

By December 20 Willie had arrived at what the *New York Dramatic Mirror* called Jeffersonville, Florida. The joke is a reference to Palm Beach, where Jefferson had settled in an oceanfront cottage called The Reef, just north of the Breakers, the city's premier hotel, with his wife, his son Joe Jr., and what a local newspaper described as "a retinue of servants."[560] He fished the waters of the St. Lucie and Indian rivers and continued his work as a developer in the area. On February 19, 1901, the day before his seventy-second birthday, he was visited by a writer for *Ladies' Home Journal* named James Metcalfe. The two men went fishing together, and Metcalfe told his magazine readers that Jefferson was slender, but not with the leanness of age. His hair, mostly black streaked . . . with gray, and . . . showing a . . . contempt for . . . the barber, blows . . . in the breeze. He has pulled on blue overalls over his ordinary attire as a precaution against the contingencies of fish and bait. His fingers are as quick and deft at knotting a line or adjusting a sinker as those of a boy. . . . "I catch more fish than I can eat—my appetite not being a large one. . . ." [He] talks of fishing, as we leave the hotel to take our boat, he pedaling slowly alongside on the tricycle which he uses for short journeys possible about Palm Beach. We come to a little pier, where we are met by Captain Jarvis, of Mr. Jefferson's boat. The boat "Marion" is named after Mr. Jefferson's granddaughter. . . . [The fish] go to the captain as a sort of perquisite. What he can't use, he sells, and eventually they are eaten by some one. . . . "And that reminds me," he continues, "that Helen Keller . . . asked me how I justified my killing so many fish. I explained to her that the fish is naturally a cannibal and is constantly killing other fish—hundreds of 'em—and so, by killing one fish, I save the lives of hundreds of others. 'I suppose it's for that humane reason, then, that you catch them,' she replied."[561]

Jefferson's contention that "my appetite [is] not a large one" was borne out by Metcalfe's observation that he had only milk and a sandwich for lunch and "did not join in the after-luncheon smoke, stating that if he had not given up tobacco . . . years ago he felt sure that he would not be with us." The loss of appetite and the reference to his longtime lung disability point to deteriorating health. Jefferson was losing strength. Within a year the tricycle had become a tricycle chair—a wicker four-wheeled sedan chair in which he was pedaled around by Carl Kettler. Edwin Booth's grandson, C. Edwin Booth Grossman, who visited him the following summer, reports that although Jefferson could no longer walk long distances, he could get in and out of the chair, "agile as a boy."[562]

Yet even though he had difficulty walking, Jefferson kept acting. A correspondent in Detroit wrote that "those who have reported Mr. Jefferson . . . in failing health have . . . not seen his acting this season, for some in the audience Monday night remarked that they had seen him in the same character over a third of a century ago, and he was as good as ever." One newspaper in 1902 estimated that

Figure 26. Jefferson in Palm Beach with his valet, Carl Kettler.
Courtesy of the Historical Society of Palm Beach County, Florida.

Jefferson was earning $40,000 a year, but by then he was focused on the symptoms of old age and impending death. During his sixth winter in Palm Beach, he told an interviewer: "Of course I like this country for it once restored my health. That is of vital importance to me. Good health is one's best possession. Isn't it?" And on May 23, 1903, he wrote to Laurence Hutton from Buzzards Bay:

My Dear Laurence:

When John L. Sullivan, the prize fighter, heard of the death of Edwin Booth he exclaimed, "It's a great loss—there's damned few of us left—" this is why I address you as "dear Laurence" and why I would have you address me as dear Joe—because there's "damned few of us left—". . . So many old friends have gone on the long journey that it is pleasant to hear myself called "Joe."[563]

Ironically it was not Jefferson but his son-in-law, B. L. Farjeon, that summer, who died of a ruptured blood vessel at his residence in Hampstead in London on the morning of July 23, 1903. Farjeon, at the age of sixty-five, was only nine years younger than Joe. He left behind three sons, Harry, Joseph Jefferson, and Bertie, and a daughter, Eleanor.[564] The mournful tone of the summer continued in a letter from Grover Cleveland, with whom Jefferson had spent the summer fishing for tautog, squeteacue, and trout. In mid-September, when the Clevelands were about to leave their summer home for Princeton, the former president wrote:

> I cannot leave without telling you, in this cold way, how much I have enjoyed your companionship during this vacation time and how large a figure you will be in the pleasant retrospection. I can hardly believe our summer's stay here is over; but I suppose these vacations will seem shorter and shorter until the end of the chapter. [I] hope that Fate will be kind to us all and permit us to meet when summer comes again.[565]

That same year Jefferson, by now knowing that the end was coming, wrote to a New York journalist identified only as The Spectator: "How times goes on so heedless of us all! What a short-lived creature is man myself excepted—by the by, seventy-five next birthday. In a few years we shall be sweet little angels, wings and all, and, as the old gambler said on his death-bed, 'If we meet, I'll fly you for $5.'"[566]

Jefferson's last stage appearance was on Saturday, May 2, 1904, in Patterson, New Jersey. He performed Rip at the matinee and Caleb Plummer and Mr. Golightly in the evening. After the second act of *The Cricket on the Hearth,* he was called before the curtain several times and finally made a speech. Eugenie Jefferson recalled: "Removing the torn and brimless hat worn in the part of Caleb Plummer, he shuffled in his tattered shoes, to the center of the stage, and in his quaint, old-fashioned way thanked the audience for the honour bestowed. It was the actor's last speech."

Joe had been invited to a supper that night, but he declined and headed for the 11:01 train back to New York. The intermissions had been abbreviated so he could make the train. He had removed his white tie as the curtain came down and was hurrying to his dressing room, taking off the curly blond wig he wore as Golightly. Jefferson brushed his hair, bringing it forward above his ears, and Carl Kettler replaced his stage evening coat with his traveling coat. Almost immediately, he was in a waiting carriage on his way to the railway station.[567] If his exit seems in hindsight like "going out with a whimper," it must be remembered that Joe did not regard it as an exit at all. It was just the end of another season. He did not know it was the end of his career.

Athough reelected president of The Players on May 9, 1904, Jefferson ceased to appear at its functions, and the club began to list its vice-president as its head in the New York directory. By May 29 he was back at Buzzards Bay and, recognizing that he was failing, asked his daughter Margaret to come to America and bring her children. In addition to Margaret's four children, Jefferson had four grandchildren by Charles Burke (Margaret Jefferson McDonough, Josephine Jefferson Rolfe, Sarah A. Jefferson, and Lauretta Jefferson Corlette), four grandchildren by Thomas L. (Eugenia Scott, Cornelia, Lauretta Raymond, and Joseph Jefferson), and two grandchildren by Joseph W. (Warren Jefferson and Marion Jefferson). He employed Charley, Tom, and Joe Jr. directly, and he had long supported Margaret's family with generous checks and gifts, including one of the first gramophones in England, which he sent along with a recording of his voice doing speeches from *Rip*.[568]

The Farjeon family traveled by boat to Boston, where Charles Burke met them, then by train to Buzzards Bay, and afterward by carriage to the house, where Joe was waiting for them on the veranda. They spent the summer in picnics and clambakes, swimming, canoe trips, table-games, and parlour theatricals and concerts. Margaret rubbed lambs-fat behind her father's ears "to soften hardenings that made him slightly deaf." Grover Cleveland came over to fish with Joe and play cribbage with him and Margaret in the evening. Joe's granddaughter, Eleanor Farjeon, remembered that "He spent much of the day in the garden tending his roses, wearing easy garments and large straw hat. 'All old people,' he said, 'should have a garden. It is so full of hope.'"[569]

That summer Jefferson went fishing with Grover Cleveland and

Cleveland's investment broker and friend, E. C. Benedict, on Benedict's yacht, the *Oneida*, in Buzzards Bay. The conversation "drifted to the subject of a future life." Benedict later wrote that "Mr. Jefferson expressed himself as very grateful for having had more than his share of the joys of this life, and as being prepared to meet, at any moment, the common fate of all. He said he had lately been 'scribbling some doggerel' on the subject, and he recited his lines to us." Jefferson had apparently memorized the poem, because when Benedict asked him for a copy, Joe did not have one with him. Although he may have considered the poem "doggerel," he was always ready to perform. In February 1905, shortly before Jefferson's death, Benedict, having once again reminded him of his promise, received the following poem, which would later be published as part of The Players' memorial service for Jefferson.

Immortality

Two caterpillars crawling on a leaf,
By some strange accident in contact came;
Their conversation, passing all belief,
Was that same argument, the very same,
That has been "proed and conned" from man to man,
Yes, ever since this wondrous world began
  The ugly creatures,
    Deaf and dumb and blind,
  Devoid of features
    That adorn mankind,
Were vain enough, in dull and wordy strife,
To speculate upon a future life.
The first was optimistic, full of hope;
The second, quite dyspeptic, seemed to mope.
Said number one, "I'm sure of our salvation."
Said number two, "I'm sure of our damnation;
. . . .
They argued through the summer; autumn nigh,
The ugly things composed themselves to die;
And so to make their funeral quite complete,
Each wrapped him in his little winding-sheet.
The tangled web encompassed them full soon,
Each for his coffin made him a cocoon,

All through the winter's chilling blast they lay
Dead to the world, aye, dead as human clay.
Lo, spring comes forth with all her warmth and love;
She brings sweet justice from the realms above;
She breaks the chrysalis, she resurrects the dead;
Two butterflies ascend encircling her head.
And so this emblem shall forever be
A sign of immortality.[570]

The Farjeon family planned to stay until Jefferson's fall tour began. He was hiring actors in early August 1904 (Jefferson Winter and his wife, Elsie Leslie) and had been planning to open the season in Boston on October 17. But in the late summer he went out in a fishing party of four friends to Big Sandy Pond and spent the day there. As the group was returning, a heavy mist settled over the landscape; Jefferson caught cold and sent for a doctor immediately upon his return. As late as September 10, 1904, he was still announcing an Allentown opening on September 14 in *Rip Van Winkle*, but by early fall he was very ill, and in September the tour was canceled. By the time Margaret and her children sailed for London, he was unable to say good-bye to Eleanor. But he rallied enough in late October to make the trip to Florida, with Sarah and two servants. He said to a reporter:

I'm going South, you know. I'll start for Washington next week, and then go down to St. Augustine. I'll have plenty to do. I'm feeling stronger every day. I go out and walk, and I take a drive. Oh I was very weak, but that's all over.

I'll do a lot of gardening in Florida. I know something about it, too, I can tell you; Do you know, I raise all our fruit and vegetables. And then . . . I am a fair fisherman. And I have a paint box—and brushes . . . now that I'm not going to act any more. . . . I am seventy-five, you know, and so no doubt am entitled to be old—and I have been a little weak of late, I'll admit that—but isn't it funny I feel as young as a boy? I was warned you know, not to tire myself talking to you and I would not do anything to displease the nurse or the dear ones about me but I enjoy all this—just a little bit excited or warmed up, but it's all right.

I'm leaving the limelight to go into the sunshine and I leave a blessing behind me and pray for a blessing before me. It has been dear to me—that life of illumined motion—and it has been so magnificently repaid. If I could send an eloquent message to the world I would, but somehow words fail me when I try to say it. I have been doubly repaid by the sympathetic presence of the people when I was playing and the affection that seems to follow me, like the sunshine streaming after a man going down the forest trail that leads over the hills to the lands of morning. No, I can't put it in words.

Perhaps it is a good thing to quit the stage before the people have a chance to change their minds about me.[571]

As Jefferson made his way south again in the winter of 1904, he asked his art dealer to purchase Theophile de Bock's *Landscape Evening*. The dealer later recollected:

When asked why he wished to buy additional works of art while he was so ill, he replied: "They give me so much pleasure now that I have given up my acting. Is it not fortunate that I have left to me my paintings and my love of nature? Please purchase these paintings for me and forward them to Palm Beach, Florida where I can have the enjoyment of them during the winter."[572]

By October 11, 1904, Thomas was touring in *Rip* and Joseph Jr. and William in *The Rivals*. Jefferson wrote to Tom:

I received your letter and am glad to hear that you are holding your own. There is no doubt that my retirement from the stage will be a benefit to you.

I told Charlie that if he can arrange it, I will give him and yourself my full production—scenery, properties, costumes, etc. so it will not cost you a cent.

I will come up from the South and be present on your opening night. I am improving slowly.[573]

By February 10, 1905, he was well enough to go fishing and sent a frozen sheepshead to Grover Cleveland's family in Princeton.[574] By March 6, 1905, however, Cleveland wrote to a mutual friend:

Speaking of Mr. Jefferson I cannot escape the feeling that he is not doing as well in point of health as his friends could wish. I am bound to confess, however, that this feeling is not based

Figure 27. Jefferson in Palm Beach, Florida, on his seventy-sixth birthday, February 20, 1905. This probably is the last photograph taken of Jefferson.

upon any unfavorable information, but very well may be only a 'vain imagining' on my part.[575]

As late as February 18, 1905, Jefferson planned to reappear on the stage in Boston starting Easter Monday, to make a speech between the acts while his son Thomas appeared in *Rip Van Winkle*.[576] He was then to come to New York and make his farewell appearance on the stage at Joseph Jefferson Holland's benefit at the Metropolitan Opera House on March 24. During the early part of 1905, he told his family:

> I shall never act again. It will seem strange to me at first to act no more, but I shall soon get used to it. I now begin, what I have looked forward to these many years—my long, long holiday, in which I shall uninterruptedly enjoy nature in outdoor life, my painting, my books, and pleasant companionship with wife, children and dear friends. I begin my holiday at last.

Francis Wilson wrote hoping that Jefferson would do Rip, Bob, and Caleb one more time, but Jefferson wrote back: "I am still a very sick man, but I am well enough to wish you success."[577]

There were those who did not lament Jefferson's retirement. One newspaper commented:

> Why, he's been retired for years, hasn't he? To the old-timers here to be off Broadway is to be off the earth. Jefferson has not played at a first class theater here for nearly ten years. The nearest he aproached Broadway in the last five seasons was on the occasion when he played the Harlem Opera House with his eternal "Rip" and "Bob Acres." The oldest inhabitant does not remember ever having seen him in anything else. . . . Jefferson kept . . . piling up money with his shabby productions of the old favorites. It is doubtful if he spent a . . . thousand on scenery in the last five years. . . . It puzzles the average up-to-date manager to understand how he maintained his grip on the public so long.[578]

On March 10, 1905, Jefferson made his last public appearance at an afternoon tea given by the Fortnightly Club at Palm Beach at a cottage called Ocean View. That same day he wrote a letter to the ill Joseph Jefferson Holland to be read at the latter's benefit on March 24. The letter is pure Jefferson. It is Jefferson at his most charming, mixing comedy and sadness; it is also Jefferson at his self-indulgent, self-promoting worst. It was read at the benefit of his godson, but it is all about himself. In paying tribute to another, he simply could not resist reminding everyone of who he was and what he had done—but then he was also giving them the story they wanted and doing it in a way that made them laugh and cry.

My Dear Joe:

As I have known you from . . . your birth . . . , it is natural that I should feel deeply interested on the occasion of this most auspicious testimonial.

Your father and I were friends for forty years. . . . I was requested by your parents to officiate as godfather to Joseph Jefferson Holland. Of course, I consented. I met them at the church, your mother in tears, your father wreathed in smiles; you rebelled at the ceremony, and no wonder for you were surrounded by enough . . . starched . . . ruffles to make any young one low spirited. I, of course, promised to bring you up on the way you should go and the way you did go was tremendous. . . .

Our next domestic relations were of a more solemn character. A telegram from your mother announced to me the death of your father. I hastened to town and taking your brother with me, repaired to the church your mother attended and asked the minister if the funeral could take place from his church. He consented, but when I mentioned that Mr. Holland was an actor, he withdrew his consent. "But," he remarked, "there is a little church around the corner where you might get the pastor to bury your friend." To which I replied, "If that is so, then God bless the little church around the corner." And I am glad to say that it has kept its baptismal appellation to this day, and I am glad to know that in the same year I was godfather to yourself and christened The Little Church Around the Corner.

And now, my dear Joe I feel it must be gratifying for you to know that though through your illness you have fallen by the wayside, it has been from no fault of your own and that thousands of eager hands have been stretched forth to raise you to happiness and comfort and believe me, no one rejoices in this more than your affectionate godfather JOSEPH JEFFERSON.[579]

On March 1 Jefferson made a trip to Charles Burke's home at Hobe Sound, a few miles above Palm Beach, to visit Grover Cleveland, who was vacationing there. He stayed for about a week, fishing with Cleveland, and participated in a Dutch supper at which he ate too much. By the time he returned, he was ill with what was initially diagnosed as indigestion due to a "slight indiscretion in eating." By March 18 he was said to be recovering, but by April 6, 1905, he was bedridden and dying. His old friend, Henry Flagler, entered the bedroom at The Reef and said: "Joe, I want to embrace you." The two old men kissed each other several times, and then Jefferson said: "I don't think that I will see you alive again."

The local newspaper began to keep an almost day-to-day death watch. On April 17 Dr. R. B. Potter, the local physician who cared for Jefferson, summoned a specialist from St. Augustine for a consultation, which lasted a full day. Early on April 19 Jefferson rallied and was able to eat grapefruit and a bowl of broth. He dictated letters to five of his personal friends, and his son Frank reported that Jefferson felt confident of his recovery. By Thursday, Potter was predicting recovery, but on Friday, Jefferson refused food and began growing weaker. By Saturday night, April 22, his condition had deteriorated, and he was having trouble sleeping. The family, who had gone to bed, were wakened. By noon on Sunday, April 23, Jefferson's doctor told the family that there was no hope for recovery, and Sarah; his sons, Charles Burke and Frank; his nurse, Mrs. Mabel Bingham; Doctor Potter; and Carl Kettler gathered around his bedside in the front room on the second floor, where Jefferson had requested to lie so that he could see the sea from the window. He was unconscious most of Sunday. At noon he asked for food, but could not keep it down. He died on Sunday, April 23, 1905, at 6:15 P.M. It was Easter Sunday, and the day traditionally designated as Shakespeare's birthday.[580]

Within thirty minutes of Jefferson's death, word was telegraphed around the nation. Thomas Jefferson was about to start an engagement as Rip in Boston when his father died. He had been visiting his sister, Josephine, who lived in a Boston suburb, and received a telegram from Charles Burke when he returned at 8 P.M. to the Hotel Touraine. Tom immediately canceled the engagement. William and Joseph Jefferson, Jr., had just closed *The Rivals* in Toledo. They were passing through Cleveland when the news reached them. William Winter immediately announced that he was canceling all engagements for his theatrical company and leaving the stage indefinitely.

Former President Cleveland issued a statement from his home in Princeton. Tributes appeared in national newspapers from Richard Mansfield, Marc Klaw, John Drew, and Daniel Frohman. Dozens of prominent actors sent a telegram to Charles Burke Jefferson requesting that the body lie in state at The Little Church Around the Corner in New York for one day so that the Reverend George C. Houghton could conduct a service, but Burke replied that Jefferson had requested a simple service at Crow's Nest. The flags of all public buildings in West Palm Beach were flown at half-mast, and the city's schools were suspended for the day. On Cape Cod, Jefferson's neighbors and their children gathered a great mound of arbutus as a tribute to him. In New York a photographer draped his picture in crepe and placed it in his window. Men removed their hats as they passed.

Jefferson's body was placed in the most expensive casket ever seen in Palm Beach. A formal procession, organized by the Masonic Harmonia Lodge No. 138, accompanied the casket, carried by six pallbearer Masons, from The Reef to the railroad station. They were followed by two rows of Masons, fourteen of whom bore elaborate floral offerings. Henry Flagler had sent a special train from St. Augustine to Palm Beach to carry Jefferson's body and family members north. The casket was placed in a case and lifted onto the baggage car, where it was hidden with flowers. Sarah was escorted to the train by Charles Burke followed by other members of the family. Accompanying her on the train ride were Charles Burke, Frank, Marion Jefferson (a daughter of Joseph Jefferson, Jr.), Aunt Nellie Symons, Carl Kettler, and several of the family's servants. The body left Palm Beach on Monday night at 9:05 P.M. As it pulled out, hundreds of spectators lifted their hats and bowed their heads in respect.[581]

The train arrived in Jacksonville, Florida, on April 25 and left immediately for the North. It stopped at Baltimore for a few moments, and the Concordia Lodge F. and A. M. placed a wreath of white roses on the casket. It arrived in Jersey City on April 26 at 5 P.M. A crowd had gathered at the station, and police reserves had to clear a way for the casket. In Jersey City other family members gathered as the casket was lifted from the baggage car and placed in a large transportation box, which was then concealed with masses of roses and other flowers. In New York it was lowered on an elevator to the baggage room, removed from the transportation box, and placed in a hearse. The coffin was taken for several hours to the Stephen Merritt funeral home. At 11 P.M. it was transferred to Grand Central station to leave for Boston on the midnight train. In New York, W. W. Smith, the undertaker, joined the cortege and accompanied the body to Boston, where Thomas Jefferson had remained to make arrangements for its reception and transfer to Buzzards Bay. The casket was held in a receiving vault until family members could gather.[582]

Car No. Ninety arrived at Buzzards Bay on Wednesday afternoon. Jefferson's body was transferred to the library at Crow's Nest and placed in a simple casket lined with black cloth and surrounded by floral tributes. The young funeral director in charge left a remembrance of the event now at the Bourne Historical Society:

> I took his body up in my arms out of the casket and carried it to my operating board in that enormous library, in order to give it better appearance for the funeral next day. As I stood looking down at him, I remembered so clearly, battling my way into the Providence Opera House not too many years before this time, to see him play *Rip Van Winkle*. I paid five dollars for a seat, and it was worth it. Here I was looking at his silent form stretched out in front of me. The words of Wolfe, on the Plains of Abraham, Quebec, came back to me: "The paths of glory, lead but to the grave."

Funeral services were held at Crow's Nest at 11 A.M. on Sunday, April 30, 1905. The house was filled with Jefferson's four sons, his two daughters, his grandchildren and great-grandchildren. The casket was placed in the east front room, which was filled with flowers. Immediate members of the family sat upstairs; friends and close neighbors sat in the hall and west front room. Only the male members of the family attended the service. Women stayed upstairs or in adjoining rooms where they could hear the service without being seen in their mourning. The Reverend Mr. Edward A. Horton of Boston, chaplain of the Massachusetts senate, began with a reading of Jefferson's favorite poem—Tennyson's "Crossing the Bar." Following the service, the body was then brought to Bay View Cemetery at Sandwich, eight miles away, about one-thirty or two in the afternoon. Cottages along the way were decked with flags at half-mast. As Jefferson's body arrived in Sandwich, the bell of the First Parish church tolled seventy-six times.[583]

Jefferson was buried in a lot selected in 1903 by his son Charles Burke in the Bay View Cemetery on the western end of Sandwich, Massachusetts. His five sons accompanied the casket along with scores of friends and about five hundred local people. In all, twenty-two carriages, scoured from all over the area, arrived at the cemetery. Three of them were filled exclusively with flowers. Services were brief. Dr. Horton read the Unitarian funeral service, and as the coffin was lowered into the grave, Jefferson's valet, Carl Kettler, standing at its head, said, "There's the last of the master," and walked hurriedly away. Then all withdrew except Charles Burke Jefferson, who remained for a moment alone.

Charles Burke left. The young funeral director removed the grave mats and was about to signal the sexton to come forward and fill in the grave when a carriage drove up. Two men stepped out and asked the undertaker to wait a minute. They took off their hats. One of the men dropped a bouquet of flowers into the open grave; they stood there silently for almost five minutes before leaving. The two were Mr. Blake, the governor of New York, and the most famous American artist of the period, John Singer Sargent. That night a policeman remained at the grave, which continued to be watched for several days.

The lot faces east on the northern end of the cemetery and is set back from the cemetery's stone wall about a hundred feet. The cemetery slopes toward the old turnpike road to Plymouth, from which Jefferson's gravestone is clearly visible. It is a ten-ton boulder covered with moss, fifteen feet across and originally twelve feet high. It came from the wood near Great Herring Pond. When its owner learned that the Jefferson family wanted to use the rock, he offered to present it to them. When they insisted on paying, he sold it for one cent.

Figure 28. The grave of Joseph Jefferson at Sandwich, Massachusetts. Bas-relief by Charles A. Walker.

APPENDIX

THE TOURS OF JOSEPH JEFFERSON

Fall 1866–Spring 1904

Prior to 1878 the identification of the venues of Jefferson's tours is incomplete. In 1878 the *New York Dramatic Mirror* began to publish weekly itineraries of all touring companies. For each year, the cities and dates are listed with the name of the theatre if available. Information about particular tours and venues is provided after each list. Endnotes follow the entire set of itineraries. Numbers in parentheses refer to the page number of the newspaper listed.

The 1866–67 venues were:

New York, New York	September 3–October 27, 1866. Olympic Theatre.
Philadelphia, Pennsylvania	October 30. One month. Chestnut Street Theatre.
Washington, D. C.	November 26. One week. National Theatre.
Baltimore, Maryland	December 3. One week. Holliday Street Theatre.
Washington, D. C.	December 10. One month. National Theatre.
Baltimore, Maryland	January 7, 1867. One month. Holliday Street Theatre.
Mobile, Alabama	February 18. One week. Mobile Theatre.
New Orleans, Louisiana	February 27. One month. Varieties Theatre.
Mobile, Alabama.	April 1. Two weeks. Mobile Theatre.
Cincinnati, Ohio	April 22. National Theatre.
Baltimore, Maryland	May 20. One week. Holliday Street Theatre.
Philadelphia, Pennsylvania	June 3. One month. Walnut Street Theatre.

For his benefit in Philadelphia, Jefferson appeared as Woodcock in *Woodcock's Little Game*, Sampson in *The Windmill*, and Tobias Shortcut in *The Spitfire*, and also performed a comic duet with Josie Orton, who played Gretchen in *Rip*. He continued that bill until November 13, when he appeared for one night in *The Quack Doctor, A Regular Fix,* and *Robert Macaire.* On November 15 he began to perform Asa Trenchard and Tobias Shortcut and remained with that bill throughout the week. From November 19, 1866, through November 22, 1866, he performed *Rip* alone, but on his last two nights he added *A Regular Fix* as an afterpiece.

Jefferson had planned to play Washington even before he opened in New York. His Washington performances were advertised two weeks in advance, and tickets went on sale a week before the opening. The National Theatre was a refurbished version of Grover's Theatre, serviced by horse-drawn streetcars that passed its front door every few minutes. Commuters to Alexandria, Virginia were assured that the last train waited until 11:30 P.M., after the close of performances, a move motivated by the tendency of some members of the audience to leave the theatre early while performances were still in process. Jefferson opened as Bob Acres in *The Rivals* and Hugh de Brass in *A Regular Fix.* The theatre was packed, and when he made his first entrance, "the whole house resounded—with the most enthusiastic and long continued demonstrations, it being some minutes before he was allowed to proceed, . . . and when the curtain fell, the enthusiasm was such that he was compelled to come out . . . and acknowledge the reception in words of gratitude . . . , tempered with the drollery becoming the character in which he had figured. . . ." At his third performance, Jefferson changed the bill to Caleb Plummer and Mr. Golightly. He performed this bill twice and on Friday switched to Dr. Pangloss and Tobias Shortcut in *The Spitfire.* These were repeated once before Jefferson left Washington. The Washington engagement ended on December 1, 1866.

He opened at the Holliday Street Theatre Baltimore on December 3, 1866, playing Rip for six performances with a benefit on Friday night.

He then reopened in Washington on Monday, December 10, as Doctor Ollapod in The *Poor Gentleman* and Diggory in *The Spectre Bridegroom.* On Tuesday he performed Dr. Pangloss and Hugh de Brass and on Wednesday opened as Asa Trenchard, using *A Regular Fix* as the afterpiece. This same bill was repeated on Thursday, and for his second benefit on Friday, December 14, he performed Newman Noggs, using *Lend Me Five Shillings* as an afterpiece. This bill was repeated on Saturday. Jefferson brought an actress to play Dame Van Winkle and two children from the Baltimore company to Washington.

Jefferson's second Baltimore performance was advertised as early as November 29. He reopened at the Holliday Street Theatre on January 7, 1869, playing a variety of pieces but at first avoiding *Rip,* which had already been seen there. He began with Caleb Plummer and Hugh de Brass, went on to Dr. Pangloss, Tobias Shortcut, Mr. Golightly, and even Jesse Rural in *Old Heads and Young Hearts.* He reopened *Rip* at the beginning of his second week, performed it for a week, and then went back to other characters for three performances, reviving *Rip* for two evenings and then switching to Asa Trenchard and Tobias Shortcut. He took a benefit every Friday night. At the beginning of the fourth week, Jefferson tried a brand new character, Hugh

Chalcote in T. W. Robertson and Artemus Ward's *Ours*. The play was currently playing at the Princess Theatre in London and Wallack's Theatre in New York. Jefferson played it for a week and went back to *The Ticket-of-Leave Man* and *Mazeppa*. By the time he closed in Baltimore on February 9, he had performed fifteen roles.

Jefferson opened at the Mobile Theatre with a three-night run of *Rip* on February 18. He went on to *Our American Cousin* on the fourth night and then, for his benefit, *Mazeppa* and *Lend Me Five Shillings*. Houses were described as "immense."

He opened *Rip* at the Varieties Theatre in New Orleans on February 27. The New Orleans reviewer had seen him perform it "repeatedly" at the Adelphi in London and was lavish in his praise of Jefferson's realism, his attention to detail and his ability to stay in character and not play to the audience: "He is a perfect master of detail, and will sometimes—very rarely—venture a 'hit,' but certainly not to the vicious degree common to so many of our so-called great American tragedians and comedians, whose reputations rest upon such depraved pandering to the 'groundlings.'"

Jefferson performed Rip in New Orleans until March 11, 1867, and then moved on to nine other roles. Business was good despite rainy weather, which turned the city's streets to mud. He did not return to *Rip* until his last week, when he gave three performances culminating on March 30. In New Orleans, Jefferson's other roles were Asa Trenchard in *Our American Cousin*, Bob Acres in *The Rivals,* Hugh de Brass in *A Regular Fix*, Cassimir in *Mazeppa*, Mr. Golightly in *Lend Me Five Shillings*, Dr. Pangloss in Coleman's *The Heir-at-Law*, Diggory in *The Spectre Bridegroom*, Caleb Plummer in *Dot*, and Dr. Ollapod in *The Poor Gentleman*.

In early April, Jefferson returned to Mobile for two weeks, opening on April 1 as Bob Acres in *The Rivals*. The children who had performed in *Rip Van Winkle* with him in New Orleans accompanied him to Mobile.

On May 20 Jefferson returned to Baltimore for the third time that season to play a week's engagement at Ford's Holliday Street Theatre. Here he performed with "the electric light" (probably an arc light) introduced "for the first time in America" and "by which coruscations in the clouds are produced so as to resemble real lighting." In Baltimore, Jefferson played five roles in six nights, and Rip was given only half the time. Jane Anderson Germon was a member of the company. Henrik Hudson's crew were clothed in new costumes from Paris. Jefferson performed Rip for three nights and then went on to Bob Brierly in *The Ticket-of-Leave Man*, which was advertised as having been performed "in Tasmania (Van Dieman's Land), the penal colony of Great Britain, where it was witnessed by about five hundred of the men who are known as hiring 'tickets of leave.' On his third Friday benefit, Jefferson switched to a bill of *Mazeppa* and *Lend Me Five Shillings*. He then performed in rapid succession Dr. Pangloss, Asa Trenchard, and Tobias Shortcut, and went back to Rip for his fourth and last benefit.

Venues for the 1867–68 season were:

New York, New York   September 9, 1867. Two months. Olympic
                            Theatre.
Chicago, Illinois   November 4. Three weeks. McVicker's Theatre.
St. Louis, Missouri   November 25. Olympic Theatre.
Cincinnati, Ohio   December 23. Two weeks. National Theatre.
New Orleans, Louisiana   January 28, 1868. One week. Varieties Theatre.
Mobile, Alabama   February 10. One week.
Memphis, Tennessee   March 9. One week. New Memphis Theatre.
                            Two-day extension through March 17.
Louisville, Kentucky   March 23. One week.
Washington, D. C.   April 13. Two weeks. National Theatre.
Baltimore, Maryland   May 11. Two weeks. Holliday Street Theatre.
Philadelphia, Pennsylvania June 1. Four weeks. Walnut Street Theatre.
Pittsburgh, Pennsylania   Date and place unknown.
Nashville, Tennessee   Date and place unknown.
Boston, Massachusetts   Date and place unknown.
Detroit, Michigan   Date and place unknown.
Toledo, Ohio   Date and place unknown.
Fort Wayne, Indiana   Date and place unknown.

On November 4, 1867, Jefferson opened in Chicago in *Rip* at McVicker's Theatre, playing six nights a week and a Saturday matinee. On the first Friday of his run, he was given a benefit night. The local reviewer wrote: "The house was in every respect a brilliant though not a very appreciative one." By the end of Jefferson's second week in Chicago, the local newspaper was suggesting that he might try some other roles, but *Rip* continued to pack audiences in through November 23, 1867. Each Friday he took a benefit. As was now his custom, he changed characters in his last week, appearing as Bob Acres in *The Rivals* and Hugh de Brass in *A Regular Fix*. Reviews of *Rip* in Chicago were favorable—and brief, as if there were nothing more to say other than "it is the finest piece of acting of the modern stage." The reviews for Bob Acres and Hugh de Brass were very favorable.

In Cincinnati, at the National Theatre, Jefferson performed Rip as well as other roles. He played Wednesday and Saturday matinees and gave Christmas and New Year's days' matinees. The house was "quite fair" for the Christmas matinee and "packed to suffocation" that evening. Jefferson got a benefit each Friday night. He performed *Rip* through the Thursday of his second week and then switched to other characters. Jefferson closed in Cincinnati on January 4, 1868.

On January 28, 1868, he opened at the Varieties in New Orleans, where he presented nine plays in a week and only one performance of *Rip*. Jefferson played *Mazeppa* and *Lend Me Five Shillings* on January 28 and 29; *The Poor Gentleman* and *The Spitfire* on January 30 and 31; *The Heir-at-Law* and *The Spectre Bridegroom* on February 1; a matinee of Boucicault's *Arrah-Na-Pogue* and an evening performance of *Rip Van Winkle* on February 2; *Mazeppa* and *The Spitfire* on February 3; and *Newman Noggs* and *Mazeppa* on February 4, his last night.

On February 10 Jefferson opened at the Mobile Theatre in Alabama for a six-night run. His final performance there was on February 18, 1868. Although he did Rip four times and no other play more than twice, Jefferson still performed a total of eight plays in Mobile to excellent houses despite inclement weather.

On March 9 Jefferson opened at the New Memphis Theatre with *Rip Van Winkle*. He took a benefit on March 14, the last night of his run. He stayed on for two extra days, performing Mr. Golightly and Tobias Shortcut on March 16 and Rip on March 17.

He played Rip in Louisville for a week beginning March 23. The management announced that it would not raise prices for Jefferson's performances.

He began performing Rip in Washington at the National Theatre on April 13. On April 20, he switched to *The Rivals* and *A Regular Fix*; on April 21, *The Heir-at-Law* and *The Spitfire*; on April 22, *Mazeppa* and *Lend Me Five Shillings*. From then on Jefferson performed *Rip*.

On May 11 Jefferson opened in *Rip* at the Holliday Street Theatre in Baltimore. Advertisements read: "The poem by WASHINGTON IRVING. The drama by BOUCICAULT. The impersonation by JOSEPH JEFFERSON. The scenery by GETZ." Half of the twelve performances were devoted to Rip and the rest to seven other roles. On May 22, 1868, Jefferson, about to close in Baltimore, wrote to Noah Ludlow, indicating that he had been performing there and in Washington, had plans to go to St. Louis, and would be in Chicago in September.

Dear Mr. Ludlow

    I am only just in receipt of your letter and I have been playing here and in Washington and there has been some delay in forwarding.

    . . . It may be some months before I come west. . . . My movements are . . . uncertain. Buckstone has made me an offer for the Haymarket next year, and if things don't improve commercially in this country, I shall again visit Europe.

    . . . Find time to write. . . . I shall be in Chicago in September and I might stop over.

On June 1 Jefferson opened *Rip* at the Walnut Street Theatre in Philadelphia. He played for four weeks, six nights a week, taking a benefit every Friday. The response, according to the theatre's advertisements, was so overwhelming that patrons were advised to purchase seats early, and tickets were placed on sale six days in advance. The first three weeks were devoted to Rip. On the fourth week, he performed Asa Trenchard, Hugh de Brass, Tobias Shortcut, and Bob Brierly, returning to Rip only for the final matinee. Jefferson's sister, Connie, was a member of the company, performing the role of Sam Willoughby in *The Ticket-of-Leave Man*. After a strong financial opening, attendance at *Rip* dropped off due to an epidemic of the "worms" and stormy weather. Jefferson performed Asa Trenchard and Hugh de Brass at his final Friday benefit and used Bob Brierly and Tobias Shortcut for his final evening performance on June 27, 1868.

The venues for the 1868–69 season were:

Chicago, Illinois	August 31, 1868. Two months. McVicker's Theatre.
Milwaukee, Wisconsin	October 26. Five days. Milwaukee Music Hall.
Detroit, Michigan	November 2, 1868. One week.
Buffalo, New York	November 9. One week. Buffalo Academy of Music.
Detroit, Michigan	November 15. One week.
Cleveland, Ohio	November 23. Two weeks. Academy of Music.
Cincinnati, Ohio	December 21. Two weeks. National Theatre.
Indianapolis, Indiana	January 4, 1869. Academy of Music.
St. Louis, Missouri	January 18. Olympic Theatre.
Lafayette, Indiana	Late January. Three performances.
Louisville, Kentucky	February 1. Two weeks. Opera House.
Cincinnati, Ohio	February 15. One week. National Theatre.
Columbus, Ohio	Late February.
Frankfort, Kentucky	February 24–25. Major Hall.
Lexington, Kentucky	February 26–27. Academy of Music.
Dayton, Ohio	March 1. Two nights.
Pittsburgh, Pennsylvania	Mid-March. Two weeks. Opera House.
Washington, D. C.	March 30, 1869. Two weeks. National Theatre.
Baltimore, Maryland	April 12. Two weeks. Holliday Street Theatre.
Boston, Massachusetts	May 3. Four weeks. Boston Theatre.
Philadelphia, Pennsylvania	May 31. Walnut Street Theatre.

Jefferson's opening at the Buffalo Academy of Music on November 9, 1868, was advertised as early as November 5. He played six evening performances and a matinee. The matinee took in $500–600.

Jefferson's opening in Cleveland on November 23 was advertised as early as November 20, by which time he was already in town. He played to "standing room only." The theatre was run by his former partner, John Ellsler, and Mrs. Ellsler played Gretchen. He was originally scheduled to play a week and three nights, but the engagement was extended for three "farewell" nights.

In Cincinnati, Jefferson's opening on December 21 was advertised as early as December 15. It was the second year in a row he had played Cincinnati on Christmas day. Jefferson played a matinee on Christmas day and performed five plays in addition to *Rip*. James O'Neill played Hendrick Vedder, the young sailor, and after Jefferson he received the most applause, partly because of his good looks. Women in the audience even threw bouquets.

In Louisville, houses were crowded during Jefferson's first week despite inclement weather and muddy streets. More boxes and seats were reserved than had ever been taken before. During the second week, the weather continued so poor that women were unable to attend. That and the fact that it was Lent prevented a complete financial success.

Seats in Washington went on sale four days in advance, and the management imposed an extra charge for reservations. Nightly the theatre was "crowded to its utmost capacity with most brilliant and delighted audiences." Jefferson performed nothing but Rip for his first week there. President Grant attended the play on April 2, 1869. On his last Saturday night, Jefferson took a benefit.

During his second season that year in Cincinnati, Jefferson performed *The Heir-at-Law* on Monday night, *Rip Van Winkle* on Tuesday night, *The Rivals* on Wednesday night, *A Regular Fix* on Thursday night, *Rip* on Friday night and for the Saturday matinee, and *The Spitfire* and *Lend Me Five Shillings* on Saturday night.

Jefferson was petitioned to appear in Frankfort, Kentucky, by the governor and both branches of the state legislature.

In Baltimore, Joe played six evenings and a Saturday matinee. On opening night "the doorways and corridors of the theatre were not only jammed and packed, but the throng extended from the sidewalk to the middle of the street." Even standing room was sold out. During a two-week engagement he played Rip for a week and for the Monday and Tuesday evenings following, then switched to Bob Brierly, Bob Acres (for his benefit), and Hugh de Brass. He played a Rip Saturday matinee and closed on April 24. His cousin, Jane Germon, was a member of the company.

Jefferson opened *Rip* at the Boston Theatre on May 3, 1869, playing Monday through Saturday, six nights a week and a Saturday matinee. It was Jefferson's first Boston appearance since his return from England, and he did nothing but Rip. During the second week, Jefferson substituted a Wednesday matinee for the Saturday evening performance, an unusual event in the period. This pattern continued during the third and fourth weeks of the run, which closed with the Saturday matinee of May 29, 1869. The production in Boston, done with the theatre's stock company, featured Mrs. Junius Brutus Booth (a.k.a Agnes Booth, a.k.a. Marian Agnes Land Rookes, a.k.a. Agnes Land Perry) and Edwin's sister-in-law, as Gretchen; and the theatre advertised "splendid new scenery and mechanism."

By May 31 Jefferson was at the Walnut Street Theatre performing Rip. By this time his performance and Boucicault's script were so famous that audiences were reminded of one of its most famous lines in their program—Rip's blessing of Little Hendrick and Meenie in the first act, which is echoed again at the end of the play:

> Here's your goot health,
> Unt your families—
> Unt may dey all live long
> Unt prosper.

By May 1869 Jefferson was already contracted to play under the Spalding, Bidwel and MacDonough management in St. Louis, New Orleans and Memphis for the 1869–70 season.

Venues during the 1869–70 season were:

New York, New York	August 2, 1869. Seven weeks. Booth's Theatre.
Brooklyn, New York	September 23. The Academy of Music.
Newark, New Jersey	September 27.
Buffalo, New York	October 10. One week.
Chicago, Illinois	November 1. One month. McVicker's Theatre.
Indianapolis, Indiana	November 30. One week. Academy of Music.
St. Louis, Missouri	December 12. One week. Olympic Theatre.
Memphis, Tennessee	December 20. Two weeks. Memphis Theatre.
New Orleans, Louisiana	January 10, 1870. Three weeks. Varieties Theatre.
Mobile, Alabama	January 31. One week. Mobile Theatre.
Cincinnati, Ohio	Late February. Engagement postponed, because Jefferson was ill.
Macon, Georgia	Date and place unknown.
Washington, D. C.	March 21. Two weeks. National Theatre.
Baltimore, Maryland	April 4. Two weeks. Holliday Street Theatre.
Boston, Massachusetts	April 18. Boston Theatre.
Cincinnati, Ohio	May 10. Two weeks. National Theatre.
Louisville, Kentucky	May 24. One week. Wiswell's Hall.
Philadelphia, Pennsylvania	May 30. Three weeks. Walnut Street Theatre.

Jefferson's New York engagement was to begin on June 14, 1869, an unusual procedure given the fact that the New York theatre tended to shut down in the summer. In the end he opened the seven-week run of *Rip* at Booth's Theatre in New York on August 2. It was his first appearance in the city in two years. Advertised as much as twelve days in advance in New York newspapers, the play was produced with new scenery, costumes, properties, and machinery. Booth's Theatre was also brand new, having just opened on February 3, 1869. Jefferson performed nothing but Rip seven times a week (six evenings and a matinee). With the exception of Master Willie Seymour, who had previously played the young Hendrick Vedder and who appeared with Joe in Philadelphia, the cast was brand new. Both the production and Jefferson initially received ecstatic reviews. A week after the opening, not even standing room tickets were available. The *New York Times* praised the scenery, in which it saw the style of the French landscape painter Gustave Doré, a man whose works Jefferson owned and admired. The same newspaper, however, in a "think-piece" criticized Jefferson for excessively subordinating the play's supporting roles to his own even more than called for in the script. This, apparently, was particularly true in the last scene of Act I, in Rip's cottage. While his wife, Gretchen, scolded him, Jefferson's Rip had by this time taken to playing elaborate pantomimed tricks on her. This lengthened the scene and actually made Gretchen seem more sympathetic in the reviewer's mind. In addition, Jefferson had begun to include jokes, which reminded the reviewer of the repartee between the interlocutor and Mr. Bones in a minstrel show. Jefferson's farcical intrusions into the scene may have been the result of the work of his Gretchen, in this case Fanny Morant, who, according to the reviewer, began to play her role in the style of Lady Macbeth. This is not surprising because Morant had been Booth's leading lady in heavy tragic roles.

When the run at Booth's Theatre was done, Jefferson toured to Brooklyn, where he gave four performances under the management of C. W. Tayleure at the Brooklyn Academy of Music, ending his New York stay on September 24, 1869. Jefferson had first met Tayleure at the Olympic Theatre in the fall of 1867, when Tayleure managed the theatre in which Jefferson performed Rip.

The reception in Newark "was very enthusiastic and the house was crowded." Jefferson was still supported by members of the company from New York.

On November 1 Jefferson opened *Rip* for a week at McVicker's Theatre in Chicago. He played six nights and a matinee each week, although the management also scheduled an unusual Wednesday matinee on November 18. After three weeks of *Rip*, Jefferson performed two nights of *The Heir-at-Law* and *The Spitfire*, followed by two nights of *The Rivals* and *A Regular Fix*. On November 26 he took a farewell benefit at which Charles Burke Jefferson, then eighteen, made his debut, playing Diggory in *The Spectre Bridegroom*, while his father performed Mr. Golightly in *Lend Me Five Shillings* and Tobias Shortcut, a bill they continued the following night. On Thanksgiving day, November 18, Jefferson gave performances at 3 P.M. and 8 P.M. On the occasion of Charles Burke Jefferson's debut, the *Chicago Tribune* reported: "For a 'first time,' young Jefferson did remarkably well. He has an excellent idea of comic situations and seems never to be at a loss to fill up occasional interstices with natural and laughable action. Of course his voice has not as yet a sufficient degree of culture and is not as completely under his control as the requirements of comic acting would demand."

On opening night in Memphis, despite terrible weather, the theatre was crowded "to suffocation." During Jefferson's first week, Memphians crowded the dress circle and parquette, some of them in the same seat every night for four nights. On his second Friday performance, Jefferson took a benefit. He performed nothing but *Rip* for six nights a week and a Saturday matinee.

When he opened *Rip* at the Varieties Theatre in New Orleans on January 10, 1870, there was not a vacant seat even in the upper tier, and a large number of New Orleans women sat in the second gallery, where they normally would never have been seen because the space had been traditionally associated with prostitutes. Just as he had in 1866, Jefferson ran *Rip* in New Orleans for a two-week run, and during the third week appeared in five other plays. He played *Rip* six days a week, with both matinee and evening performances on Saturday. On January 24 Jefferson performed *Our American Cousin*, switching to *Mazeppa* and *Lend Me Five Shillings* on January 26. He returned to Rip on January 27, and for his farewell benefit on January 28 he did *A Regular Fix*, *Mazeppa*, and *The Spectre Bridegroom*, in which his son, billed as Master Charles Jefferson, appeared as Diggory. The New Orleans run ended with a Saturday matinee of *Mazeppa* and *The Spectre Bridegroom*. That evening Jefferson gave an extra performance as Hugh de Brass in a benefit for the theatre's manager, W. R. Floyd. He appeared on the program with his boyhood idol John E. Owens. The *New York Clipper* reported:

> At the end of the farce he was called out and . . . thanked the citizens of New Orleans for their kindness . . . and asked the kind support of those present for his son, Charles Jefferson, who would appear as Diggory in *The Spectre Bridegroom*, which he did in a manner every way worthy the name he bears. He possesses a . . . share of his father's talent and it all rests . . . with himself to show that with . . . experience he possesses the hereditary ability of his family. The sensation of the week was the performance given on Saturday evening for the benefit of Mr. Floyd [manager of the Varieties Theatre] and at which both J. E. Owens and Mr. Jefferson appeared . . . as Hugh de Brass. . . . Such a bill attracted an immense audience, the house being packed from pit to dome. . . . Part of the company proceed, with Mr. Jefferson, to Mobile. . . .

On January 31, February 1, and February 2 Jefferson, supported by members of the Varieties Theatre company, played *Rip* at the Mobile Theatre. The local critic loved the performance, finding fault only with the incessant cracking of peanut shells, which prevented parts from being heard: "Those pea-nuts *must* be shelled. Why, there was one man, in the rear of the orchestra boxes, . . . who kept half a dozen from hearing Rip Van Winkle in those pathetic subdued passages; and by the perpetual crack, crack, of his d-d pea-nuts."

Initially billed for only three days, Jefferson stayed on in Mobile to perform *Lend Me Five Shillings* and *Mazeppa* on Thursday and Friday and to do a noon matinee and evening performance of Rip on Saturday. On Thursday, bad weather and the delay of the mail boat, presumably laden with potential customers, caused him to cancel the two new shows and play Rip again. For Jefferson's Friday night benefit, Charles Burke, still billed as Master Charles Jefferson, played Diggory in *The Spectre Bridegroom*. William Winter notes that at the end of February 1870 Jefferson was still in Mobile, where he became quite ill, but local papers provide no confirmation.

Beginning March 21, Jefferson played at the National Theatre in Washington, D.C., with the theatre's stock company, which featured a number of people who would later perform with him in his own touring company: Edwin Varrey, Thomas Hamilton, Charles Burke Jefferson, Joe's cousin Jane Germon, and Jane's granddaughter "little Bessie Germon." The performance was advertised six days in advance, and ticket prices were raised by twenty-five cents. The Washington correspondent for the *New York Clipper* wrote that

"The practice of making an extra charge for reserved seats . . . during Mr. Jefferson's engagements should be discontinued. A dollar and a quarter for an orchestra chair in any theatre outside of New York is a war price, especially when the company supporting a star is not of the best material. . . . Little Meenie and Hendrick are beautifully portrayed by the clever little children assuming the parts, but the remainder of the cast is not entitled to much praise." In Washington, Jefferson played a Saturday matinee. On Friday evening he had a benefit.

Jefferson played only Rip during his first eight performances in Washington (first week plus second Monday) and then switched from *Rip* to other pieces in his repertoire on the last week of a two-week run; "attendance was as large as when 'Rip' was on the boards." On Monday, March 29, 1870, he opened *The Heir-at-Law* and *Lend Me Five Shillings*; on Wednesday and Thursday he switched to *The Rivals* and *A Regular Fix*. On Friday, for his second benefit, he did Hugh de Brass and Diggory in *The Spectre Bridegroom*, and C. B. Jefferson appeared as Shortcut in *The Spitfire*. Reviews for Charles Burke were not positive: "The character that this young gentleman assumed, the merits of which consist more in . . . stage business than in any artistic personation, prevents too favorable criticism. Mr. C. B. Jefferson, however, made the most of his part, and added by the popular interest of 'the Jefferson,' was . . . well received." On Saturday afternoon and evening, Charles Burke and Joe shared the stage, with Jefferson as Mr. Golightly and Charley as Diggory.

The following week, Jefferson opened *Rip* at the Holliday Street Theatre in Baltimore, played it for six nights and a Saturday matinee, and then switched to Bob Brierly, Dr. Pangloss, and Mr. Golightly. He performed Bob Acres and Hugh de Brass for his farewell benefit on April 15, doing Brierly for the Saturday matinee and a triple bill of *The Spectre Bridegroom, A Regular Fix,* and *The Spitfire* for his final Saturday evening performance. A local correspondent for the *New York Clipper* complained about "tedious waits between the acts and a terrible long wait between the comedy and the farce" when *The Heir-at-Law* and *Lend Me Five Shillings* were performed.

Opening on April 18, Jefferson played Rip for fifteen nights and three matinees at the Boston Theatre. "Large and enthusiastic audiences" greeted him "at every performance, not withstanding the inclemency of the weather," in part because he had played *Rip* there only once before and then only for two weeks. The correspondent for the *New York Clipper* wrote: "The scenery displays the poor resources in that direction of the Boston Theatre and is really too shameful for a first class theatre." Jefferson ended the Boston engagement with the matinee of May 7, 1870. He played Saturday matinees in Boston beginning at 2:30, but did not perform on Saturday evenings.

After Boston, Jefferson played Cincinnati, opening on May 10 for two weeks and performing to "good houses," although the local correspondent for the *New York Clipper* thought that "the company supporting him is not good."

Arrangements for Jefferson to perform in Philadelphia had been made as early as July 10, 1869. Beginning May 30, 1870, at the Walnut Street Theatre in Philadelphia, he performed nothing but Rip for three weeks, playing six nights a week and a Saturday matinee "with the privilege" of extending his run. In Philadelphia, Jefferson had a Friday benefit each week. The 1869–70 tour closed on June 18, and Jefferson returned home to Hohokus.

Venues for the spring 1871 tour were:

Washington, D.C.	April 10, 1871. One week. National Theatre.
Baltimore, Maryland	April 17. Holliday Street Theatre.
Boston, Massachusetts	May 1. Three weeks. Boston Theatre.
Bridgeport, Connecticut	May 31. Two days.
Philadelphia, Pennsylvania	June 5. Two weeks. Walnut Street Theatre.

The Washington engagement was deemed "successful" by the local correspondent for the *New York Clipper*.

In Baltimore, matinees were announced for the benefit "of the ladies and the little ones, at cheap prices." On Friday, Jefferson got a farewell benefit.

Jefferson performed Rip at the Boston Theatre from May 1 through May 20; the correspondent for the *New York Clipper* recorded a "crowded house" on opening night despite bad weather and noted that Jefferson, for all of his success, was never called "before the curtain" in Boston.

Jefferson then went on to the Walnut Theatre in Philadelphia, June 5–17, playing Rip six nights a week and a Saturday matinee.

On June 29 he performed Mr. Golightly at a matinee benefit for the widow and family of the deceased James Symonds, stage manager of the Olympic Theatre in New York. The theatre's management donated the space, and Jefferson was supported by its stock company. Symonds, who had been Jefferson's manager in Australia, had been living with Jefferson, both in New Iberia and in Hohokus, where he died on April 22, 1871, at the age of forty-five, having been in poor health for a long time. He was buried at Cypress Hills Cemetery on April 24. Symonds and his mother, Nell, had become members of the Jefferson "family."

Jefferson was already booked for the succeeding season by late June. Venues for the 1871–72 tour were:

Brooklyn, New York	September 4, 1871. One week. Brooklyn Academy.
Buffalo, New York	September (date uncertain). One week. Academy of Music..
Cincinnati, Ohio	September 18. Two weeks. Originally scheduled for early September 1871, then later for October 1871. Pike's Opera House.
Indianapolis, Indiana	October 2. Two weeks. Academy of Music.
Detroit, Michigan	Circa November 3. Three nights and a matinee.
Cleveland, Ohio	November 6. One week. Academy of Music.
Rochester, New York	November 13. Three days. Opera House.

Syracuse, New York	November 16. Three days. Weiting Opera House.
Albany, New York	November 20. One week. Trimble Opera House.
Troy, New York	November 27. Three days. Griswold Opera House.
Columbus, Ohio	December 6. Two days.
St. Louis, Missouri	December 11. Two weeks. Olympic Theatre.
Nashville, Tennessee	January 1, 1872. Four nights and a matinee. Opera House.
New Orleans, Louisiana	January 8. Originally scheduled for the Academy of Music. Varieties Theatre.
Galveston, Texas	February 6. One week. Tremont Opera House.
Houston, Texas	February 12–13.
Harrisburg, Pennsylvania	February 20.
Louisville, Kentucky	April 1–4. Opera House.
Terre Haute, Indiana	April 8–9.
Springfield, Illinois	April 10.
Jacksonville, Illinois	April 11.
Quincy, Illinois	April 12–13.
Peoria, Illinois	April 15–16. Rouse's Opera House.
Bloomington, Illinois	April 17.
Logansport, Indiana	April 18.
Fort Wayne, Indiana	April 19.
Toledo, Ohio	April 20.
Akron, Ohio	April 22.
Meadville, Pennsylvania	April 23.
Oil City, Pennsylvania	April 24–25.
Titusville, Pennsylvania	April 26–27.
Williamsport, Pennsylvania	April 29–30. Elliot's Academy of Music.
Wilkes-Barre, Pennsylvania	May 1–2.
Scranton, Pennsylvania	May 3–4.
Trenton, New Jersey	May 6–7.
Wilmington, Delaware	May 8–9.
Newark, New Jersey	May 10.
Boston, Massachusetts	May 13. Three weeks.
Baltimore, Maryland	June 3. One week. Ford's Grand Opera House.

Jefferson appeared under the management of his son Charles Burke. William S. Lockyer was the advance agent. In Brooklyn, Jefferson played Rip for six performances a week including a Saturday matinee. Business was initially slow, but picked up for the Saturday matinee and evening performances.

Opening night in Indianapolis brought in between $1,700 and $1,800.

In late October, Jefferson and Charles Burke were in Chicago assisting theatre people who were the victims of the great fire.

In Detroit, Jefferson opened to the largest audience ever seen in the city, with every seat in the parquette sold before 5 P.M.

The Cleveland performances were advertised on November 3 for a November 6 opening. Tickets went on sale the following day. Jefferson again performed Rip to Mrs. Ellsler's Gretchen, and the Ellsler daughter Effie played Meenie. The auditorium was "crowded nightly" despite rainy weather. And for the first time in Cleveland, Jefferson played a *Rip* matinee, with Jefferson proceeds going to the destitute actors of Chicago.

In Rochester, "notwithstanding the inclemency of the weather, people were turned away nightly."

In Troy, "notwithstanding the increased price of admission, he succeeded in drawing good houses (but not crowded)."

In St. Louis, the theatre was "literally jammed" despite "an advancement over the standard rates of admission."

In Nashville, Jefferson drew the largest attendance of any actor since the Civil War.

For his benefit in New Orleans on January 19, Jefferson performed Doctor Pangloss and Mr. Golightly.

Jefferson was scheduled to perform at the Greenwall brothers' Tremont Opera House in Galveston, Texas. By this time he was accustomed to sending his valet and stage manager Sam Philips ahead to rehearse with the stock company. Philips rehearsed for three days and then was told that the company had gone on strike and that he would have to start over with a completely new group of actors. This was Saturday. Jefferson was to open on Monday. Jefferson arrived on Sunday from New Iberia and insisted that the actor who had been dismissed and whose dismissal had led to the strike be reinstated. While the act is recorded as one of benevolence by his daughter-in-law, Eugenie Paul Jefferson, it was clearly in Jefferson's financial interest for the show to go on. The correspondent for the *New York Mirror*, however, announced that because of inclement weather, the management had closed the Opera House in Galveston after the preceding Tuesday performance and spent the rest of the week rehearsing *Rip*. Eugenie Jefferson's version is the more likely one. To have spent almost a week rehearsing was unheard of in the nineteenth century, particularly in as remote a place as Galveston. The house was crowded on opening night despite "the severe 'norther' blowing and the weather extremely cold." On Friday night, Jefferson performed *Lend Me Five Shillings* and *A Regular Fix* for his benefit.

Jefferson performed in Harrisburg, Pennsylvania, on February 20. Although the performance was advertised only a day in advance, the local newspaper predicted that by the evening of the performance, all seats in the theatre would be sold out, despite the fact that two other actors had performed Rip there that year.

In Springfield, Illinois, Jefferson performed "to a very large audience."

In Peoria, Illinois, the theatre was filled with people from "Pekin, Canton, Washington, El Paso and other neighboring towns."

In Baltimore, Jefferson played *The Heir-at-Law* and *A Regular Fix* at his Friday benefit.

The brief fall 1872 tour was managed by Charles Burke Jefferson, and the advance agent was William S. Lockyer. The venues were:

Augusta, Maine	September 2, 1872.
Lewiston, Maine	September 3.
Portland, Maine	September 4.
Biddeford, Maine	September 5.
Portsmouth, New Hampshire	September 6.
Lawrence, Massachusetts	September 7.
Salem, Massachusetts	September 9
Lowell, Massachusetts	September 10.
Lynn, Massachusetts	September 11.
Chelsea, Massachusetts	September 12.
North Bridgewater, Massachusetts	September 13.
New Bedford, Massachusetts	September 14.

The venues of the Spring 1873 tour were:

Baltimore, Maryland	January 1–4, 1873. Ford's Grand Opera House.
Tour in Georgia.	Place and date unknown.
Charleston, South Carolina	January 27–29. Academy of Music.
Richmond, Virginia	Circa January 30.
Washington, D.C.	February 22. At least one week. Wall's New Opera House.
Brooklyn, New York	March 3. Four days. Brooklyn Academy.
Boston, Massachusetts	March 17.
Hartford, Connecticut	March 18.
Memphis, Tennessee	March 24. The New Memphis Theatre.
Pittsburgh, Pennsylvania	March 31. One week. Pittsburgh Opera House.
Reading, Pennsylvania	April 14.
Lancaster, Pennsylvania	April 15.
Easton, Pennsylvania	April 16.
New Haven, Connecticut	April 17.
Paterson, New Jersey	April 18.
Albany, New York	April 22–23.
Utica, New York	April 24.
Syracuse, New York	April 25–26.
Buffalo, New York	April 30–May 1. St. James Hall.
Lockport, Pennsylvania	May 2.
Erie, Pennsylvania	May 3.
Toledo, Ohio	May 5–6.

Adrian, Michigan	May 7.
Jackson, Michigan	May 8.
Lansing, Michigan	May 9.
East Saginaw, Michigan	May 10. Jackson Hall
Saginaw City, Michigan	May 12.
Bay City, Michigan	May 13. Opera House.
Detroit, Michigan	May 14–15.
Milwaukee, Wisconsin	May 16–17.
Bloomington, Illinois	May 19.
Galesburg, Illinois	May 20.
Rock Island, Illinois	May 21.
Davenport, Iowa	May 22.
Dubuque, Iowa	May 23.
Janesville, Wisconsin	May 24.
Madison, Wisconsin	May 26.
La Crosse, Wisconsin	May 27.
St. Paul, Minnesota	May 28, 30.
Minneapolis, Minnesota	May 29, 31.
St. Joseph, Missouri	June 11. Tootle Opera-house.

Jefferson reappeared in an evening performance of Rip on January 1, 1873, at Ford's Grand Opera House in Baltimore. The local newspaper commented that "it is very probable that the present will be the last engagement ever played by Mr. Jefferson in Baltimore." The announcement was possibly a ploy to bring in audiences; if so, it worked. Jefferson performed Rip for four nights and received $3,000. The *New York Clipper* reported that Jefferson intended to spend most of the winter in New Iberia.

Jefferson played Charleston under the management of his old boss John T. Ford. Seats for the performances on January 27–29 were advertised as early as January 21 and went on sale on January 24. The theatre even took orders "from the country" by mail or telegraph. As of the Saturday night before opening, half of the seats in the parquette and dress circle remained unsold, but by opening night on Monday, every seat was filled, and the aisles were crowded with standing spectators. John T. Ford arrived from Baltimore on either January 25 or 26, and Jefferson arrived from New York with his wife and daughter Margaret. They all stayed at the Charleston Hotel. Other members of the company, including Mrs. G. C. Germon, Miss Bessie Germon, Charles Burke Jefferson, and William S. Lockyer, arrived from Baltimore. They stayed at the Pavilion Hotel. What Ford had done was bring members of the Baltimore company south to support Jefferson. They presumably did not stay in as expensive a hotel as the Jeffersons could afford. On Wednesday, January 28, Charles Burke Jefferson performed a matinee (referred to as a morning performance) of *The Spitfire* and *The Spectre Bridegroom*. Charles's performances were labeled a debut and seen as particularly appropriate in Charleston, as it was the place his paternal grandmother had first appeared in America. In its review of his work, the local newspaper commented that "The young man was . . . nervous . . . , but the idea of the two characters was capital and warrants the belief that he will grow up to be a worthy rival of his father." It poured during Jefferson's last day in Charleston, but the house was packed, and omnibuses and hacks lined King Street from Market to Wentworth to take the spectators home. Jefferson's three performances took in more money than any Charleston attraction for a comparable period of time.

Attendance in Pittsburgh was "very large." Charles Burke Jefferson performed there at the matinee of April 5.

In Buffalo, Jefferson played to "large houses . . . but the support was not very good. The absence of proper scenery, appointments and mounting was painfully visible," according to the *New York Clipper* correspondent.

Jefferson's audience at the Opera House in Bay City, Michigan, was the largest ever assembled in that building.

In Detroit, however, his company did not draw the usual large houses. The correspondent for the *New York Clipper* attributed the poor attendance to the fact that the city had lately had a number of high-priced entertainments.

On February 22, 1873, approximately a week before the second inauguration of Ulysses S. Grant as president, Jefferson opened Wall's New Opera House in Washington, D.C., with *Rip Van Winkle*. Designed to replace the National, which had burned down, the theatre was managed by John T. Ford. The building was not quite finished on opening night, and "a portion of the paint on the chairs was carried off on the overcoats of gentlemen and dresses of ladies." The performance seemed a bit lackluster in the first act to the local critic, who felt "there was a little less of rollicking fun in 'Rip' in the first act, and a little more pathos in the last act, than in former representations" and that "the support was not above the average." Jefferson appeared in *Rip* every night for a week, but at the Saturday matinee his son Charles Burke Jefferson played his father's roles in *The Spitfire* and *The Spectre Bridegroom*.

Charles Burke Jefferson was the manager of the 1873–74 tour. Venues were:

New York, New York	September 1–October 4, 1873. Booth's Theatre.
Philadelphia, Pennsylvania	November 10–22. Two weeks. Walnut Street Theatre.
Washington, D.C.	December 8. One week. National Theatre, also known as Ford's Opera House.
Richmond, Virginia	December 15.
Norfolk, Virginia	December 17.
Charleston, South Carolina	December 19. Academy of Music.
Savannah, Georgia	December 20.
Augusta, Georgia	December 22.
Atlanta, Georgia	December 24.

Macon, Georgia	December 25.
Columbus, Georgia	December 26.
Montgomery, Alabama	December 27.
New Orleans, Louisiana	January 12, 1874. One week. Varieties Theatre.

November 10–22, 1873, Jefferson appeared as Rip for twelve nights and one matinee at the Walnut Theatre in Philadelphia. Even standing room was at a premium during his first week. For the second Saturday matinee he performed Shortcut in *The Spitfire*. On the last day of the engagement, November 22, Charles Burke appeared as Shortcut in *The Spitfire* during the matinee performance.

There was standing room only every night during the Washington run. Jefferson performed Rip for the first three nights, then switched to Bob Acres and Hugh de Brass. For his benefit on December 11, he did Dr. Pangloss and Mr. Golightly. Again Charles Jefferson appeared as Shortcut for the Saturday matinee. On Saturday evening, Jefferson did Rip again, and by then, hundreds of people were turned away.

Jefferson's performance in Charleston was advertised four days in advance. Tickets went on sale two days in advance, and the free list (comps reserved for shareholders in the theatre) was suspended. Private boxes were $10 and $15. Jefferson and Charles Burke arrived the day of the performance and stayed at the Charleston Hotel. With them came nine members of the Jefferson troupe, who stayed at the Pavillion Hotel.

In New Orleans, Jefferson opened as Rip on January 12, 1874, played Rip on January 13, switched to Dr. Pangloss and Mr. Golightly on January 14, did Bob Acres and Hugh de Brass on January 15 and 16, then played Rip again for the Saturday matinee. That evening saw *Our American Cousin* performed with another actor playing Asa Trenchard, along with *The Spitfire* with Charles Burke Jefferson as Tobias Shortcut.

Verifiable venues during the spring 1874 were:

Lexington, Kentucky	No date.
Louisville, Kentucky	No date.
Cincinnati, Ohio	Circa April 26, 1874
Akron, Ohio	No date.
Titusville, Pennsylvania	April 30, 1874.
Brooklyn, New York	May 18. One week. Brooklyn Academy.

Jefferson traveled from Lexington to Louisville, Kentucky, in the company of his then valet, Sam Philips. When he discovered a poor man on the train taking his two daughters to see their sick mother, Jefferson helped pay the man's fare and gave him $40. The story, published by Jefferson's daughter-in-law, Eugenie, may have been designed to counteract Jefferson's reputation for being tight with money.

On April 26, 1874, he was in Cincinnati, where he met Edwin Booth (who referred to him in a letter as J. J. Rip Esqre) for "a most delightful chat (of several hours duration)," and then went on to Akron. While in Cincinnati, Booth wrote to William Winter: "Joe & I have been acting . . . here & in Louisville, both drawing tremendous houses, & we've had two or three charming 'seances'—the one just ended was full of genial 'spirits,' who seemed to revel in our society—they led us from 'grave to gay' & back again, 'till the 'brazeen tongue,' or rather the tiny ticker warned that 'Time & Trains wait for no 'uns'— he'll soon be at 'Ho-hokus-pokus' beneath his roof-tree." Booth's word choice here is tantalizing. Jefferson was certainly to develop an interest in spiritualism later in life, but the "seances" and the spirits referred to are probably alcoholic.

Venues for the 1874–75 tour were:

Chicago, Illinois	September 7–October 3. One month. McVicker's Theatre.
Grand Rapids, Michigan	October 14.
Toledo, Ohio	October 16.
Dayton, Ohio	October 19.
Springfield, Ohio	October 20.
Columbus, Ohio	October 21.
Canton, Ohio	October 22.
Youngstown, Ohio	October 23.
Jamestown, New York	October 24.
Wheeling, West Virginia	October 26. Hamilton Opera House.
Johnstown, Pennsylvania	October 27. Main-street Opera House.
Altoona, Pennsylvania	October 28.
Danville, Pennsylvania	October 29.
Pittston, Pennsylvania	October 30.
New York, New York	November 9–28. Three weeks. Booth's Theatre.
Philadelphia, Pennsylvania	November 30. Walnut Street Theatre.
St. Louis, Missouri	Early January 1875. Olympic Theatre.
Memphis, Tennessee	January 11.
Boston, Massachusetts	May 3. Two weeks. Boston Theatre.

In Chicago, houses were crowded every evening, although prices were raised. On his last night, Jefferson played Bob Acres and Hugh de Brass. During his last week in Chicago, Jefferson played a matinee aimed at children.

In Wheeling, West Virginia, Jefferson's performance of *Rip* was advertised five days in advance; reserved tickets for the orchestra and dress circle were $1.50; unreserved seats in the orchestra and dress circle were $1.00, and family circle seats were fifteen cents. The local newspaper, however, noted that "all the seats, domes, stairs and about all in the gallery have been reserved, and 'standing room' will be the only 'seat' to be had by the less fortunate ones." Although the local reviewer loved Jefferson, the rest of the production was uninspired: "Leaving Jefferson out, the remainder of the acting was flat, stale and unprofitable. Gretchen was . . . fairly done, and the little folks in the first act did better than their elders in the third."

On November 9 he performed what was billed as a farewell engagement at Booth's Theatre in New York. Jefferson appeared for three weeks every night of the week except Saturday, substituting a Saturday matinee for the evening performance and adding a special Thanksgiving matinee. The *New York Tribune*, reviewing the performance on November 11, reported:

> Mr. Jefferson appeared at Booth's Theater last night—returning to this stage after a considerable absence—and acted Rip Van Winkle. Two thousand persons . . . were in the house, and their . . . applause, upon the comedian's first entrance and at familiar points in the course of the representation, testified . . . to the affectionate admiration in which Mr. Jefferson is held.

In an illuminating article published at about the time of Jefferson's performance, the *New York Times* pointed out that audiences of the period were harassed by excessive use of music to underscore the action, long waits in the interval while scenery was being changed, ticket scalpers operating in the lobbies of theatres (Booth's is not named), and ladies' bonnets, which seriously blocked the view of the stage. Jefferson closed in New York with a November 28 matinee.

In Memphis, Jefferson performed with the company from the Olympic Theatre in St. Louis.

Jefferson opened *Rip* at the Boston Theatre for ten nights and two matinees on May 3, 1875, but did not perform on Saturdays. He played opposite the standard stock company in the theatre, which advertised that "for this production Mr. GETZ has been busily employed for some weeks and he will show Entirely New and MAGNIFICENT SCENERY." During the second week, the run was extended by one performance, when Jefferson performed both a Saturday matinee and an evening show. The run closed on May 15, 1875.

Between the end of the spring 1875 season and the beginning of the fall 1877 season, Jefferson was in England. The venues for the fall 1877 tour were:

Harrisburg, Pennsylvania	December 3, 1877.
Elmira, New York	December 4.
Syracuse, New York	December 5.
Utica, New York	December 6.
Rochester, New York	December 7.
Troy, New York	December 8. Matinee and evening.
Hartford, Connecticut	December 9.
Bridgeport, Connecticut	December 10.
New Haven, Connecticut	December 11.
Providence, Rhode Island	December 12. Providence Opera House.
Brooklyn, New York	December 14–15. Matinee.
Washington, D.C.	December 17. One week. National Theatre.
Baltimore, Maryland	December 24. Two weeks. Ford's Opera House.

The performance in Troy, New York, was a disaster. There were hardly a hundred people at the matinee, and the house was only two-thirds filled in the evening. A woman who had bought a gallery ticket, thinking it was in the first tier, was refused a refund, and her husband issued a lawsuit for $100. At 8 P.M., as Jefferson was about to go on, two deputy sheriffs appeared in his dressing room and confiscated his costume. At that moment Augustin Daly, who had refused the refund, appeared with a lawyer, and the curtain finally went up at 8:30.

Jefferson's performance in *Rip Van Winkle* at the Providence Opera House was advertised as early as December 7, 1877. He was touring with the Augustin Daly stock company. Reserved seats were $1.50, general admission was $1.00, and the family circle was fifty cents.

In Washington, Jefferson played Rip for four nights and then switched to Bob Acres and Hugh de Brass.

Rip, advertised as "dramatized by . . . Boucicault and realized by . . . Jefferson," opened at Ford's Opera house in Baltimore on December 24, 1877. Joe performed on Christmas eve, twice on Christmas day, and through the Tuesday following Christmas week with the local stock company as support. He also used Rip on New Year's eve and for the matinee and evening performances on New Year's day. Midway through his second week in Baltimore, however, he switched to Hugh de Brass, Bob Acres, and Mr. Golightly, returning to Rip for his closing Saturday matinee and evening shows. During his second week in Baltimore, Jefferson's cousin, Jane Anderson Germon, appeared as Mrs. Malaprop. *The Rivals* was accompanied by an afterpiece, first *A Regular Fix* and then *Lend Me Five Shillings*. Jefferson was still able to command a benefit night (the second Friday of the run), but was now expected to play matinees. Prices were increased by only twenty-five cents during the engagement.

Samuel Philips served as Jefferson's business manager for the spring 1878 tour. Known venues were:

Philadelphia, Pennsylvania	April 1, 1878. Two weeks. Walnut Street Theatre.
Boston, Massachusetts	April 22. Two weeks. Boston Theatre.
Rochester, New York	May 13–14. Lyceum Theatre.
Buffalo, New York	May 15. The Academy of Music.
San Francisco, California	June 3. Four weeks. California Theatre.
Salt Lake City, Utah	July 15. Salt Lake Theatre.
Denver, Colorado	July 22–24. Forrester Opera House.

On April 1 Jefferson began two weeks at the Walnut Street Theatre in Philadelphia. It was his first appearance there in four years. He played seven performances a week, including a Saturday matinee. By the end of his run, he had already made arrangements to appear at the Broad Street Theatre next season.

On April 22 Jefferson began a two-week engagement at the Boston Theatre, where he continued through May 4, when he did a benefit for the theatre's doorkeepers and ushers.

Attendance at Buffalo was only "fair."

Every seat was sold for opening night in San Francisco. Jefferson performed for six nights a week and a matinee. On June 14, for his benefit, he did Bob Acres and Hugh de Brass. Jefferson opened in *Baby* on June 17 and performed it for a week. He did *The Rivals* and *A Regular Fix* on June 24 and June 25, *The Heir-at-Law* and *Lend Me Five Shillings* on June 26 and 27, took a farewell benefit on June 28 as Rip, and did a Rip matinee and evening performance the following day. The local reviewer thought his Dr. Pangloss too light and insufficiently pedantic. Business was not as good during the last week as it had been during the rest of the run. His cousin Elizabeth Anderson Thoman, now Elizabeth Saunders, was a member of the San Francisco stock company. While in San Francisco, Jefferson telegraphed his acceptance of an engagement at the Fifth Avenue Theatre the following season.

Jefferson's performances in Salt Lake City, beginning July 15 were advertised as early as July 10. He played *Rip* for one night only. The next day, the local critic noted "it was an artistic effort but somewhat lacking in vim and intenseness. . . . Such acting as was seen last night is a treat to lovers of the drama, but $500 is a very costly price for it." The reference was to the fact that Jefferson was paid $500 a night to perform.

The two performances of *Rip* in Denver were advertised as early as July 12 and went on sale July 15. Patrons from nearby towns were informed that "upon receipt of letter or telegram" they could "have a person placed in line who will secure the number of seats desired." Only a certain number of tickets could be bought by each person, thus insuring that ticket brokers would not be able to purchase large blocks. Special rates were given on all railroads leading into Denver, good for July 22 through 25. "Twelve young ladies" were hired as auxiliaries ("Those who can sing preferred"). Jefferson arrived in Denver on the Colorado Central with his wife and sons, Joseph, Jr., and Tom. They stayed at the American Hotel. Jefferson went off to hunt and fish for trout at Sisty's ranch near Morrison for several days. The local reviewer, after the second night, noted: "The play ran smoother as the support became more familiar with their 'business' and more at home with the stellar attraction." After his Denver engagement, Jefferson remained in Colorado, fishing in Middle Park for several months.

Known venues for the fall 1878 tour were:

Chicago, Illinois	September 9, 1878. Three weeks. McVicker's Theatre.
St. Louis, Missouri	September 30. Two weeks. Olympic Theatre.
Cincinnati, Ohio	October 14. Grand Opera House.
New York, New York	December 15. Fifth Avenue Theatre.

Jefferson opened the fall 1878 season in Chicago, performing six nights a week and a Saturday matinee. He did not play a Wednesday matinee.

Rip opened at the Olympic Theatre in St. Louis on September 30 "until further notice." Jefferson played six nights a week and a Saturday matinee, supported by the company's stock actors. Nearby towns got up theatre parties to see *Rip Van Winkle* despite a $5 charge for tickets.

In Cincinnati, Jefferson performed with the St. Louis company. He played to fair houses for the first two nights and large houses thereafter.

Jefferson returned to New York on December 16 for a three-week engagement at the Fifth Avenue Theatre. He played every night of the week and Saturday matinees, but not a Christmas or a New Year's day matinee. Business continued to increase during the first week of the new year. The *New York Clipper* pointed out that Jefferson had made numerous small changes in the play's details and that his own performance had become "more colloquial." Samuel Philips and his wife played with Jefferson in New York as did Jefferson's son, Thomas, who performed Seth under the stage name of Henry Thomas.

Venues for the spring 1879 tour were:

Washington, D.C.	March 24, 1879. One week. National Theatre.
Brooklyn, New York	March 31. One week. Park Theatre.
Williamsport, Pennsylvania	April 10. Lyceum Theatre.
Harrisburg, Pennsylvania	April 11. Grand Opera House.
Philadelphia, Pennsylvania	April 14. Three weeks. Broad Street Theatre.

In Brooklyn, houses were crowded all week and packed at the Saturday matinee and evening performance. On Saturday evening the theatre's assistant manager, George R. Edesen, appeared in front of the curtain and thanked the audience on Jefferson's behalf, promising that the star would return in October.

In Philadelphia, as the Broad Street's Easter attraction, Jefferson played Rip in evening performances, while a group of children performed *H.M.S. Pinafore* in the afternoon (except Saturdays, when Jefferson performed Rip). The engagement lasted three weeks until April 26. Jefferson initially announced that *The Rivals* was in rehearsal; however, *Rip* was apparently profitable enough for the entire run of twelve nights and two Saturday matinees. Patrons outside the Philadelphia area could even wire in orders for tickets.

Venues during the fall 1879 tour, which consisted of performances of *Rip Van Winkle*, *Lend Me Five Shillings*, and *The Rivals*, were:

Cumberland, Maryland	August 30, 1879.
Akron, Ohio	September 3. Canceled.
Chillicothe, Ohio	September 3 or 4.
Columbus, Ohio	September 5. Grand Opera House.
Springfield, Ohio	September 6. Black's Opera House.
Cincinnati, Ohio	September 8. One week. Pike's Opera House.
Richmond, Indiana	September 15. Grand Opera House.
Indianapolis, Indiana	September 18–20. Park Theatre.
Detroit, Michigan	End of September. Two nights and a matinee. Opera House.
Cleveland, Ohio	September 29–30. Euclid Avenue Opera House.
Erie, Pennsylvania	October 1.
Syracuse, New York	October 2. Wieting Opera House.

Waterbury, Connecticut	October 27. City Hall.
Hartford, Connecticut	November 4. Roberts' Opera House.
Manchester, New Hampshire	November 5. Smyth's Opera House.
Portsmouth, New Hampshire	November 6.
Lewiston, Maine	November 7.
Portland, Maine	November 8. City Hall.
Lawrence, Massachusetts	November 10.
Haverhill, Massachusetts	November 11.
Salem, Massachusetts	November 12. Mechanic Hall.
Lynn, Massachusetts	November 13.
Providence, Rhode Island	November 14–15. Providence Opera House.
Lowell, Massachusetts	November 20. Huntington Hall.
New Haven, Connecticut	November 21–22. Coe's Opera House.
Philadelphia, Pennsylvania	November 24. One week. Broad St. Theatre.
Baltimore, Maryland	December 1. One week. Ford's Opera House.
Washington, D.C.	December 8. One week. Ford's Opera House
Savannah, Georgia	January 21–22, 1880. Savannah Theatre.
Atlanta, Georgia	January 26. DeGive's Opera House.
Columbus, Georgia	January 27. Springer Opera House.
Selma, Alabama	January 28.
Montgomery, Alabama	January 29.
Nashville, Tennessee	January 30–31. Two nights and a matinee. The Vendome.

On September 12, 1879, while in Cincinnati, Jefferson wrote to William Winter: "William Jefferson [Winter] who has just joined me gave me your letter. I regret to hear of your illness and am grieved to find you writing in such low spirits. For God's sake don't let anything between us give you the slightest trouble. I shall be in New York in four weeks and hope to see you." With the exception of Cincinnati, *Rip*'s popularity held.

Jefferson had not been in Detroit for four years, and his appearance brought out large crowds.

In Cleveland, advanced sales were excellent, and Jefferson played to packed houses there on September 29 and 30, 1879. The performance was advertised as early as September 20. Tickets went on sale on September 25; seats sold rapidly, but Jefferson's *Rip* no longer commanded advanced prices.

In Manchester, New Hampshire, there was an advance sale of nine hundred tickets.

Jefferson gave a performance of *Rip* to a "crowded house" at the Mechanic Hall in Salem, Massachusetts, on November 12, 1879.

Jefferson's performances of *Rip Van Winkle* (for two nights and a matinee) at the Providence Opera House on November 14 and 15 were advertised as early as November 6, 1879. Tickets went on sale November 11 at 9 A.M. He performed to "immense houses" at "regular prices" with his own dramatic company under the management of Charles H. Thayer.

In Philadelphia Jefferson opened on November 24, performing only Bob Acres and Mr. Golightly, probably because he had appeared in the city the preceding spring and felt that Rip's popularity had been sufficiently exploited there. Jefferson performed every night, Thanksgiving day, and a Saturday matinee.

On December 1 Joe opened *The Rivals* and *Lend Me Five Shillings* at Ford's Opera House in Baltimore. The production had been advertised the preceding Friday. On Thursday he switched to Rip and played it for the rest of the week, including a Saturday matinee. The newspaper noted that there would be no Wednesday matinee.

On December 8 he opened for a week at Ford's Opera House in Washington, playing *The Rivals, Rip Van Winkle,* and *Lend Me Five Shillings* to crowded houses. Ford had actually advertised the Washington performances in Baltimore the preceding week.

In Savannah on January 21 and 22, 1880, Jefferson played "to good business."

In Atlanta on January 26 he performed "to the largest audience this season."

Jefferson's performance in Nashville on January 30 drew "the largest audience of the season standing room being at a premium." After Nashville the company disbanded.

Venues for the spring 1880 tour were:

Boston, Massachusetts	April 14, 1880.
Lancaster, Pennsylvania	May 1. Fulton Opera House.
Trenton, New Jersey	May 3. Taylor Opera House.
New Brunswick, New Jersey	May 4.
Newark, New Jersey	May 5.
Paterson, New Jersey	May 6.
Jersey City, New Jersey	May 7–8.
Burlington, Vermont	May 10.
Montreal, Canada	May 11–12.
Ottawa, Canada	May 13.

On April 24, Jefferson wrote to William Winter that he considered changing the bill to comedy, but "the theatre is too large and Rip is still playing to great houses."

In Montreal, Jefferson played "to overflowing houses."

The venues for the fall 1880–winter 1881 tour were:

Philadelphia, Pennsylvania	September 13, 1880. Three weeks. Arch Street Theatre.
Wilmington, Delaware	October 4.
Lancaster, Pennsylvania	October 5. Fulton Opera House.
Harrisburg, Pennsylvania	October 6. Grand Opera House.

Reading, Pennsylvania	October 7. Academy of Music.
Pottsville, Pennsylvania	October 8. Academy of Music.
Easton, Pennsylvania	October 9.
Newark, New Jersey	October 11–12.
Paterson, New Jersey	October 13.
Albany, New York	October 14.
Troy, New York	October 15–16.
Boston, Massachusetts	October 18. Two weeks.
Worcester, Massachusetts	November 1–2.
Fall River, Massachusetts	November 3.
New Bedford, Massachusetts	November 4.
Providence, Rhode Island	November 5–6. Providence Opera House.
Springfield, Massachusetts	November 8.
Holyoke, Massachusetts	November 9.
Hartford, Connecticut	November 10–11.
New Haven, Connecticut	November 12.
New York, New York	November 15. Two weeks. Grand Opera House.
Poughkeepsie, New York	November 29.
Utica, New York	November 30. Opera House.
Syracuse, New York	December 1.
Rochester, New York	December 2.
Detroit, Michigan	December 3–4.
Chicago, Illinois	December 6. Two weeks.
Evansville, Indiana	December 20.
Terre Haute, Indiana	December 21. Opera House.
Fort Wayne, Indiana	December 22.
Indianapolis, Indiana	December 23–25. Dickson's Grand Opera.
Louisville, Kentucky	December 27. One week.
Cincinnati, Ohio	January 3, 1881. One week. Pike's Opera House.
Lexington, Kentucky	January 10–11.
Dayton, Ohio	January 12. The Grand Theatre.
Springfield, Illinois	January 13.
Columbus, Ohio	January 14.
Wheeling, West Virginia	January 15. Matinee and evening. Opera House.
Akron, Ohio	January 17.
Youngstown, Ohio	January 18. Opera House.
Meadville, Ohio	January 19.
Buffalo, New York	January 20–22. The Academy of Music.
Brooklyn, New York	January 24. One week.
Baltimore, Maryland	January 31. One week. Albaugh's Holliday Street Theatre.

Pittsburgh, Pennsylvania   February 7. One week (originally scheduled
                                for Washington). Opera House.
Cleveland, Ohio   February 14. One week. Opera House.
Pittsburgh, Pennsylvania   February 21. One week.
Nashville, Tennessee   February 28–March 2. Performance on Feb-
                                ruary 28 missed.
Memphis, Tennessee   March 3–5. (Originally scheduled March
                                3–5, but changed to February 24–26 be-
                                fore being changed back to the original
                                dates.)
St. Louis, Missouri   March 7. One week (originally scheduled for
                                March 7, but changed to February 28 be-
                                fore being changed back to the original
                                date). Olympic Theatre.

In Philadelphia Jefferson performed *The Rivals* for three weeks, six nights a week, plus a Wednesday and Saturday matinee.

On October 6 Jefferson was in Harrisburg, Pennsylvania, where, accompanied by Mrs. John Drew and by his son, Joseph Jefferson, Jr., he visited his grandfather's grave. A reporter accompanied them and told his readership: "Mr. Jefferson is enjoying excellent health and avers he is fully as vigorous and buoyant in spirit as he was twenty years ago." What Jefferson was implying was that *Rip* was as good as ever. The audience that evening was "large appreciative and select."

Jefferson performed in Reading to "a very large audience."

Jefferson performed Bob Acres at the Providence Opera House on Friday, November 5, and the Saturday two o'clock matinee on November 6. On Saturday evening he did *Rip Van Winkle*. The performance was advertised as early as November 3, when tickets went on sale for $1, seventy-five cents, fifty cents, and twenty-five cents.

On November 15 he opened in New York at the Grand Opera House for a two-week engagement as Rip. He played a matinee every Wednesday and Saturday, but his appearance merited only two lines in the *New York Times* theatrical page. His performance was unreviewed and swamped by the publicity attending Sarah Bernhardt's *Camille* and the arrival of Tommaso Salvini, the great Italian realistic actor. Jefferson remained at the Grand Opera House through Thanksgiving, when *Rip* was given a Grand Holiday Matinee and closed on November 27, 1880.

By December 6 the Jefferson company, under the management of Charles Burke Jefferson, was in Chicago. Although the season was primarily devoted to *The Rivals*, Jefferson slipped in performances of *Rip Van Winkle*.

Rip was performed "to immense business" in Terre Haute.

On December 27, Jefferson opened in Louisville for a week. He began with three performances of *The Rivals* and ended the week with *Rip*, a pattern typical of the tour. He had not appeared in Louisville in six years; consequently he attracted a "large and fashionable audience."

On January 3, 1881, he performed *The Rivals* at Pike's Opera House in Cincinnati, playing Bob Acres every night except January 8, when *Rip Van Winkle* was given.

On January 10 and 11, he played Lexington, taking in $1,119 on *The Rivals* and $1,301 on *Rip*.

In Wheeling, West Virginia, the parquet and dress circle were seventy-five cents for unreserved seats and $1.00 for reserved seats; the family circle was fifty cents for unreserved seats and seventy-five cents for reserved seats; matinee prices were twenty-five and fifty cents for unreserved seats and seventy-five cents for reserved seats. Tickets went on sale two days in advance. Speculators grabbed them up and sold them at advanced prices. The local newspaper speculated that "this will be the last opportunity to see Mr. Jefferson in our city." The Wheeling and Elm Grove Railroad Company ran trains after the performance to take spectators home.

On January 31, 1881, Jefferson opened for a week at Albaugh's Holliday Street Theatre in Baltimore, playing *The Rivals* on Monday, Tuesday, Wednesday, and Thursday evenings and a Wednesday matinee, and *Rip van Winkle* on Friday evening and two performances on Saturday. The run was advertised first on the Thursday preceding opening night.

On February 14, Jefferson opened for a week at the Opera House in Cleveland. The house was crowded, and those who did not obtain seats early had to settle for standing room.

Jefferson's company "missed two railroad connections between Pittsburgh and Louisville," and consequently Joe was unable to open his engagement at the Masonic Theatre in Nashville on February 28. Rather than disappoint the audience and lose income, he played a matinee and evening performance of *The Rivals* on March 1 and a matinee and evening performance of *Rip* on March 2.

Jefferson opened at the Olympic Theatre in St. Louis for one week on March 7, 1881. He performed *The Rivals* on Monday, Tuesday, and Wednesday evenings plus a Wednesday matinee, and then switched to *Rip* for Thursday, Friday, and Saturday evenings and the Saturday matinee. There was no extra charge to see him. The weather was poor, and the opening night of *The Rivals* was sparsely attended; but after that, people were turned away every night, and only half the people who came to the Saturday matinee could be accommodated. The *Missouri Republican* noted that "it has been long since a comedy 'star' was seen in St. Louis surrounded by actors."

The spring 1881 tour venues were:

Bloomington, Illinois	April 14, 1881.
Decatur, Illinois	April 15.
Springfield, Illinois	April 16.
Topeka, Kansas	April 18.
St. Joseph, Missouri	April 19.
Leavenworth, Kansas	April 20. New Opera House.

Atchison, Kansas	April 21.
Lincoln, Nebraska	April 22.
Omaha, Nebraska	April 23.
Des Moines, Iowa	April 25. Moore's Opera House.
Ottumwa, Iowa	April 26.
Keokuk, Iowa	April 27.
Burlington, Iowa	April 28.
Iowa City, Iowa	April 29.
Rock Island, Illinois	April 30. Matinee.
Davenport, Iowa	April 30.
Cedar Rapids, Iowa	May 1–2.
Dubuque, Iowa	May 3.
La Crosse, Wisconsin	May 4.
Minneapolis, Minnesota	May 5. Grand Opera House.
St. Paul, Minnesota	May 6–7. Metropolitan Opera House.

The theatre in Decatur was crowded on April 15.

Jefferson's performances of Caleb Plummer and Mr. Golightly in St. Joseph, Missouri were described as "fine, evenly balanced and . . . enthusiastically received by the largest and most fashionable audience of the season to date."

At the New Opera House in Leavenworth, Kansas, Jefferson played to a "light house. Support only fair. In some other piece he would have drawn well, but 'Rip' is overdone"—meaning that too many people had seen it.

In Omaha, Nebraska, May Woolcott, who played Dot in *The Cricket on the Hearth,* caught her skirts on a step getting off the train and fell onto the platform, breaking her nose and bruising herself. Jefferson was forced to cancel *Cricket* and substitute *Rip.*

On April 25 in Des Moines, Iowa, April 26 in Ottumwa, Iowa, and April 28 in Burlington, Iowa, Jefferson played to "large and fashionable audiences."

In Iowa City, on April 29, he played to "immense business."

Following the close of the spring 1881 season, the *New York Mirror*, the country's leading dramatic newspaper, announced that Mrs. John Drew, Frederick Robinson, and Maurice Barrymore had retired from the company. Mrs. Drew's intention to return was announced within a month.

Venues for the fall 1881 tour were:

Albany, New York	September 5–6, 1881. Tweedle Opera House.
Poughkeepsie, New York	September 9.
Newark, New Jersey	September 10. Matinee.
Trenton, New Jersey	September 10. Evening.
New York, New York	September 12. Two weeks. Union Square Theatre.
Oswego, New York	September 28 (originally September 26, but that date was canceled out of respect for the funeral of the assassinated president, James Garfield).
Syracuse, New York	September 27.

Auburn, New York	September 28.
Rochester, New York	September 29.
Cincinnati, Ohio	October 7. Pike's Opera House.
St. Louis, Missouri	October 9. One week. Olympic Theatre.
St. Louis, Missouri	October 16. Grand Opera House. Extra performance.
Columbus, Missouri	October 18–19.
Chicago, Illinois	October 31. One week.
Erie, Pennsylvania	November 3.
New York, New York	November 14. Two weeks. Grand Opera House.
Boston, Massachusetts	December 3. One week. Globe Theatre.
Brooklyn, New York	December 5. One week.
Philadelphia, Pennsylvania	December 12. One week. Arch Street Theatre.
Buffalo, New York	December 19. One week. The Academy of Music.
Pittsburgh, Pennsylvania	December 26. One week. Opera House

The company opened at the Union Square Theatre in New York on September 12, 1881, in *The Rivals* and performed through September 26, 1881. (The *New York Times* praised Jefferson's decision to present something other than *Rip*.) Both his characterization and his cutting of the text were reviewed favorably. The opening was advertised a week in advance in large ads featuring the names of supporting company members headed by Mrs. John Drew.

Jefferson's performances in St. Louis the week of October 9 were packed. His popularity in the city was attested to by the fact that he opened on a Sunday evening, an event virtually unprecedented in the nineteenth-century American theatre. He then played *The Rivals* Monday through Friday evening, including a Wednesday matinee, and switched back to *Rip* for the Saturday matinee and evening performances. On opening night, every foot of the house, including standing room, was occupied. The demand was so great that at the end of his engagement at the Olympic, Jefferson gave yet another extra Sunday evening performance at the Grand Opera House.

The Chicago performances played to standing room only.

Jefferson was originally slated to play Bob Acres at the Globe Theatre in Boston but changed to Rip. He opened there on December 3 and played a double bill of *The Cricket on the Hearth* and *Lend Me Five Shillings* on Monday, Tuesday, and Wednesday evenings as well as the Wednesday matinee. He switched to *Rip van Winkle* for the Thursday, Friday, Saturday evening, and Saturday matinee performances. Matinees were at two o'clock, and evening performances were at 7:45. The theatre was illuminated by "Edison Incandescent Light." According to the local reviewer, "The house was crowded [on opening night], and on the following nights standing room only. *Rip Van Winkle* is as fresh and delightful as of yore. . . . Rose Wood's Gretchen is . . . unsatisfactory in its . . . hardness. . . . She makes the character a . . . termagant, and one almost detests her, whereas Gretchen was surely deserving of pity for the suffering she endured from Rip's dissipation and profligacy."

Venues for the spring 1882 tour were:

Washington, D.C.	April 10. One week. National Theatre.
Philadelphia, Pennsylvania	April 17. One week. Arch Street Theatre.
Cleveland, Ohio	April 24. One week. Euclid Opera House.
Chicago, Illinois	May 1. Two weeks. McVicker's Theatre.
Indianapolis, Indiana	May 11. Grand Opera House.
Dayton, Ohio	May 12.
Toledo, Ohio	May 13–14. Wheeler's Opera House.
Taunton, Massachusetts	May 15. Music Hall.
Chelsea, Massachusetts	May 16. Academy of Music.
Salem, Massachusetts	May 17.
Lowell, Massachusetts	May 18. Huntington Hall.
Lawrence, Massachusetts	May 19.
Haverhill, Massachusetts	May 20.
Lynn, Massachusetts	May 22. Music Hall.
Portland, Maine	May 25. New Portland Theatre.
Lewiston, Maine	May 26. Music Hall.
Bangor, Maine	May 27. Matinee and evening. Bangor Opera House.

The fall 1882 tour, under the management of Charles Burke and H. S. Taylor, featured *The Rivals, The Poor Gentleman,* and *Rip Van Winkle.* Venues were:

Bradford, Pennsylvania	September 4, 1882.
Jamestown, New York	September 5.
Akron, Ohio	September 6.
Xenia, Ohio	September 7.
Zanesville, Ohio	September 8.
Columbus, Ohio	September 9. Matinee and evening. Comstock's Opera House.
Chillicothe, Ohio	September 11.
Dayton, Ohio	September 12.
Xenia, Ohio	September 13.
Bellefontaine, Ohio	September 14.
Sandusky, Ohio	September 15.
Youngstown, Ohio	September 16. Opera House.
New York, New York	September 18. Six weeks. Union Square Theatre.
Worcester, Massachusetts	November 3. Worcester Theatre.
Springfield, Massachusetts	November 4.
Boston, Massachusetts	November 6. One week. Globe Theatre.
Brooklyn, New York	November 13. One week.
New York, New York	November 20. Two weeks.
Philadelphia, Pennsylvania	December 4. One week. Arch Street Theatre.
Washington, D.C.	December 11. One week. National Theatre.
Louisville, Kentucky	December 18–20.

Indianapolis, Indiana	December 21–23. Grand Opera House.
St. Louis, Missouri	December 25. One week. Olympic Theatre.
Nashville, Tennessee	January 1, 1883.
Atlanta, Georgia	January 2–3.
Rome, Georgia	January 4.
Selma, Alabama	January 5.
Montgomery, Alabama	January 6. Montgomery Theatre.
New Orleans, Louisiana	January 8. One week. Grand Opera House.

(The tour paused briefly after its New Orleans engagement, and Jefferson had a rest in New Iberia, where Mrs. John Drew was a guest at his plantation.)

Galveston, Texas	January 15–17.
Houston, Texas	January 18–20.

Jefferson toured with the same company he had worked with the previous year. Only the actor playing Captain Absolute, the most difficult role for Jefferson to cast, had changed.

The company opened with *The Rivals* at the Union Square Theatre in New York on September 18, 1882. Jefferson played six performances a week plus a Saturday matinee for the next six weeks. The *New York Times* found his acting "even more finished and delicate than that of last season." The *New York Mirror* reported: "Splendid audiences of representative New Yorkers have attended every one of Mr. Jefferson's performances. . . . The . . . excellent cast assists him . . . in his delicious Bob Acres, and no doubt *The Rivals* would . . . fill out the . . . term of his sojourn . . . , but yielding to . . . demand, Mr. Jefferson will . . . appear as Dr. Ollapod in *The Poor Gentleman*. Rip and Mr. Golightly in *Lend Me Five Shillings* are said to be contemplated." Jefferson closed in New York on October 28.

November 6–11 he performed *Rip* at the Globe Theatre in Boston. At the matinee, hundreds of people were turned away.

The same production, however, was received with mixed reviews when Jefferson played the Grand Opera House in New York beginning November 20. The *New York Mirror* praised his performance but damned the supporting cast. Despite the review, however, Jefferson's box office receipts were "large," and he attracted a younger audience, who had not yet seen what was by now a traditional American production.

December 4–9 he was playing in repertory at the Arch Street Theatre in Philadelphia, opening on Monday, December 4, with *The Rivals*, playing *The Poor Gentleman* on Tuesday, Wednesday, and Thursday, and ending up with *Rip* on Friday and Saturday matinee and evening.

In Indianapolis in late December, "attendance was good at all the performances and especially on Friday night, when *The Poor Gentleman* was the play." The supporting company was described as "excellent beyond praise."

On December 25, starting with a Christmas day matinee crowded to the vestibule, Jefferson opened at the Olympic Theatre in St. Louis, Missouri. *Rip Van Winkle* was performed at the Monday (Christmas day) matinee and the

Wednesday matinee; *The Rivals* was performed on Monday and Tuesday evenings; *The Poor Gentleman* was performed on Wednesday, Thursday, and Friday evenings. The *St. Louis Post Dispatch* called Jefferson's Rip "as finished a piece of work as ever," but the *Missouri Republican* admitted that "Christmas audiences are not Jefferson audiences," as they preferred variety shows. The newspaper went on to point out that Jefferson was reviving old English comedies, instead of doing Rip incessantly, "at some expense to himself." It also noted that Jefferson had condensed the five-act *Poor Gentleman* into three acts.

On January 8, 1883, Jefferson opened at the Grand Opera House in New Orleans. The company played *The Rivals* on Monday, Tuesday, and Wednesday and then moved to *Rip Van Winkle* on Thursday, Friday, and Saturday (both matinee and evening). Charles Burke Jefferson appeared as Hendrick Vedder, the young sailor in the third act of Rip.

By April 13 members of Jefferson's company for the spring 1883 season were being announced in the *New York Mirror*. The company toured with two double bills, *The Heir-at-Law* and *The Poor Gentleman*; and *The Cricket on the Hearth* and *Lend Me Five Shillings*. The venues that can be identified were:

Pittsburgh, Pennsylvania	April 23, 1883. Opera House.
Sandusky, Ohio	May 2.
Chicago, Illinois	May 7. Three weeks.

In Pittsburgh, Jefferson appeared at the Opera House, which was managed by his old partner John Ellsler.

The fall 1883 tour, consisting of *Rip Van Winkle*, *The Cricket on the Hearth*, *The Rivals*, and *Lend Me Five Shillings*, toured to the following venues:

New York, New York	September 3, 1883. One week. Third Avenue Theatre.
Cleveland, Ohio	September 16. One week. Euclid Avenue Theatre.
Adrian, Michigan	September 24.
Philadelphia, Pennsylvania	October 1 (originally scheduled for September 24). One week (originally scheduled as two weeks). Arch Street Theatre.
New York, New York	October 8. Six weeks. Union Square Theatre.
Chicago, Illinois	November 19. One week. McVicker's Theatre.
Rockford, Illinois	November 26.
Peoria, Illinois	November 27. Canceled on account of Jefferson's loss of voice.
Bloomington, Illinois	November 28. Canceled on account of Jefferson's loss of voice.
Indianapolis, Indiana	November 29–December 1. Grand Opera House. Canceled on account of Jefferson's loss of voice.

Cincinnati, Ohio	December 3. One week. Robinson's House, a.k.a. Grand Opera House. Canceled on account of Jefferson's loss of voice.
Pittsburgh, Pennsylvania	December 10. One week. Grand OperaHouse.
Louisville, Kentucky	December 17. One week.
St. Louis, Missouri	December 24. One week. Olympic Theatre.
Baltimore, Maryland	December 31. One week. Holliday Street Theatre.
Washington, D.C.	January 7, 1884. One week.
Wilmington, North Carolina	January 14. Opera House.
Charleston, South Carolina	January 15–17.
Savannah, Georgia	January 18–19. Savannah Theatre.
Augusta, Georgia	January 21–22. Masonic Theatre.
Macon, Georgia	January 25. Ralston Hall.
Columbus, Georgia	January 26. Springer Opera House.
Montgomery, Alabama	January 27. Montgomery Theatre.
Birmingham, Alabama	January 30.
Nashville, Tennessee	January 31–February 2. Grand Opera House.

Jefferson opened in *Rip Van Winkle* on September 3, 1883, for six nights and a matinee at Mr. and Mrs. McKee Rankin's Third Avenue Theatre at Third Avenue and 31st Street in New York. The Rankins were retired actors, and the Third Avenue was a new venture, complete with electric lights, in a working-class neighborhood far from the fashionable theatres of New York. It catered to lower-class people through cheap seats and popular entertainments. "The theatre was crowded, and Mr. Jefferson was greeted with spontaneous enthusiasm. His performance of Rip had its usual lightness, grace and humor. This performance has been seen on many occasions; yet it retains its . . . freshness."

Upon Jefferson's second appearance in New York, at the Union Square, the *New York Times* wrote: "The house was crowded to the utmost, and the applause was unstinted. . . . At the fall of the curtain, the audience, which had frequently applauded before, cheered and shouted and applauded . . . , and all the artists were forced to appear and reappear . . . before the noisy congratulations would be stilled." Jefferson remained in New York for six weeks. By October 21 the *New York Times* was reporting that his engagement was "entirely successful." As *The Cricket on the Hearth* and *Lend Me Five Shillings* entered their fourth week on October 29, the theatre remained crowded. The New York engagement closed on November 17.

In Peoria on November 27 Jefferson lost his voice and was forced to cancel his engagements. He also canceled in Bloomington, Illinois, Indianapolis, and in Cincinnati, where he rested under a doctor's care.

On December 24 Jefferson began a run at the Olympic Theatre in St. Louis, consisting of *The Rivals* (Monday evening), *Rip Van Winkle* (Tuesday, Christmas matinee, and Saturday evening), *The Cricket on the Hearth* (Tuesday,

Wednesday, and Thursday evenings, and Saturday matinee) and *Lend Me Five Shillings* (four performances in a double bill with *Cricket*). According to the local paper, opening on Christmas eve to a good audience was an exceptional triumph, because it was one of the two evenings of the year in which audiences were notoriously sparse (the other was Good Friday). The performance began an hour late because Jefferson did not arrive in St. Louis until after 8 P.M. The audience was informed that he would be late and offered their money back.

> Jefferson's company had arrived during the day, but the comedian . . . had stayed over in Louisville, owing to an aversion to night travel. In consequence, it was nearly nine P.M. before Maestro Vogel tapped his desk with his baton, and the *Semiramis* overture began. This finished, Mr. Downing, in the costume of Captain Absolute, stepped before the curtain and made a . . . speech, in which he stated that Mr. Jefferson had been delayed and might be there in a few minutes, but [that] those who wished to have their money refunded could do so or get tickets for any other night during the engagement. Mr. Downing laid too much emphasis on the latter part of his speech, and there was a . . . general exodus. . . . Before a . . . considerable portion of the sinews of war had been sold out, and before Mr. Vogel's harmonizers had worn out the portfolio of old-time waltzes and mazurkas, word came that Jefferson had arrived, and the play went on.

When the season ended, the company returned to New York by special railway car. This is the earliest indication that Jefferson was using such a car in his tours.

Venues for the spring 1884 tour were:

Boston, Massachusetts	April 14, 1884. Two weeks. Globe Theatre.
Pittsfield, Massachusetts	April 28.
Worcester, Massachusetts	April 29. Worcester Theatre.
Hartford, Connecticut	April 30–May 1.
New Haven, Connecticut	May 2–3. Opera House.
Newport, Rhode Island	May 5. Bull's Opera House.
Fall River, Massachusetts	May 6. Academy of Music.
New Bedford, Massachusetts	May 7. Opera House.
Lowell, Massachusetts	May 8.
Providence, Rhode Island	May 9–10. Providence Opera House.
Manchester, New Hampshire	May 12–13.
Portland, Maine	May 14–15. Portland Theatre.
Bangor, Maine	May 16–17. Opera House.
Waltham, Massachusetts	May 19 (originally scheduled for May 26). Music Hall.
Pittston, Massachusetts	May 20.
Greenfield, Massachusetts	May 21.

Rutland, Vermont   May 22.
Burlington, Vermont   May 23.
Saratoga, New York   May 24.

In Boston, Jefferson performed Caleb Plummer, Mr. Golightly, and Rip. The company included his standard repertory actors (Frederic Robinson, Rosa Rand, et al.) as well as his sister Cornelia and his son Thomas. Houses were "full" the first week and "packed" the second.

On May 2 and 3, Jefferson played New Haven, Connecticut, where the local correspondent for the *New York Mirror* wrote that

> there have been few more brilliant assemblages at this . . . house than that to which Joseph Jefferson bowed his acknowledgments. . . . *The Cricket on the Hearth* is a readable . . . story . . . but certainly not for the footlights. The interest with which the comedian imbued the subordinate part of Caleb Plummer and the excellence with which he played the theatrically opposite role in *Lend Me Five Shillings* shows the versatility of his genius. As the hero in the play founded on Irving's famous legend of the Catskills, he drew the largest house.

On Friday evening, May 9, at the Providence Opera House, Jefferson performed *The Cricket on the Hearth* and *Lend Me Five Shllings*. He did *Rip* for the Saturday matinee and evening, May 10 performances. His appearance was advertised as early as Wednesday, May 7, the day on which tickets went on sale.

The fall 1884 tour, featuring *The Cricket on the Hearth*, *Rip Van Winkle*, and *Lend Me Five Shillings*, played the following venues:

Detroit, Michigan	September 15, 1884. Whitney's Grand Opera House.
Kansas City, Missouri	September 22–23. Gillis Opera House.
Des Moines, Iowa	September 27. Grand Opera House.
St. Paul, Minnesota	September 29–October 1. Evening and matinee. Grand Opera House.
Minneapolis, Minnesota	October 2–4. Evening and matinee. Grand Opera House.
Eau Claire, Wisconsin	October 6.
Madison, Wisconsin	October 7.
Oshkosh, Wisconsin	October 8 (originally October 6). Grand Opera House.
Racine, Wisconsin	October 9.
Milwaukee, Wisconsin	October 10–11. Grand Opera House.
Ottawa, Illinois	October 13. Sherwood Opera House.
Davenport, Iowa	October 14.
Peoria, Illinois	October 15.
Keokuk, Iowa	October 16.
Springfield, Illinois	October 17. Chatterton's Opera House.
Bloomington, Illinois	October 18. Burley Theatre.

Indianapolis, Indiana	October 20. Dickson's Grand Opera House.
Dayton, Ohio	October 21.
Columbus, Ohio	October 22. Comstock's Opera House.
Louisville, Kentucky	October 23–25. MacAuley's Theatre.
Chicago, Illinois	October 27. One week. McVicker's Theatre.
Cleveland, Ohio	November 3–5.
Buffalo, New York	November 6–8. Academy of Music.
Rochester, New York	November 10.
Ithaca, New York	November 11.
Gloversville, New York	November 12.
Syracuse, New York	November 13. Wieting Opera House.
Paterson, New Jersey	November 15.
Scranton, Pennsylvania	November 17.
Easton, Pennsylvania	November 18.
Trenton, New Jersey	November 19.
Bethlehem, Pennsylvania	November 20.
Wilmington, Delaware	November 21.
York, Pennsylvania	November 22. York Opera House.
Baltimore, Maryland	November 24. One week. Holliday Street Theatre.
Philadelphia, Pennsylvania	December 1. One week. Arch Street Theatre.
Washington, D.C.	December 8. One week. National Theatre.

Performances in Des Moines were given to "one of the finest audiences of the season."

The house in Minneapolis was "packed at every performance."

In Milwaukee, the company performed "before the largest and most fashionable audience that has attended any performance since the opening of the season."

During the week of December 1, 1884, Jefferson performed at Mrs. John Drew's Arch Street Theatre every evening and on Wednesday and Saturday matinees.

The city set for the opening of the spring 1885 tour was originally Richmond, but by early April this had changed to Lynchburg, and the date was set for April 20. Late in January Jefferson began to have problems with his leading man, R. L. Downing. During the winter break, Downing had produced and starred in a play that was surprisingly successful, but he was contracted to a four-week spring tour with Jefferson and began to negotiate a release from his agreement.

During the spring of 1885, the Jefferson company performed at the following venues:

Lynchburg, Virginia	April 20, 1885.
Norfolk, Virginia	April 21.
Richmond, Virginia	April 22–24. Richmond Theatre.
Wilmington, Delaware	April 25.

Brooklyn, New York	April 27. One week. Brooklyn Theatre.
Boston, Massachusetts	May 4. One week. Globe Theatre.
Williamsburg, Virginia	May 18. One week.

Jefferson's performance in Richmond was called "one of the most brilliant of the season."

The *New York Mirror* wrote of his Brooklyn appearance: "Long before the rising of the curtain, nearly all the seats were occupied, the few that were not were being sold at a high rate by . . . speculators. . . . Mr. Jefferson was tended a warm reception. His *The Cricket on the Hearth* is an admirable piece of work, and the company were well up in their parts. The receipts from Monday to Saturday have every appearance of being . . . brisk."

Venues for the fall 1885 tour were:

Columbus, Ohio	September 30, 1885.
Fort Wayne, Indiana	October 1. Masonic Temple.
Elkhart, Indiana	October 2. Buckley's Opera House.
Chicago, Illinois	October 3. One week. McVicker's Theatre.
St. Louis, Missouri	October 12. One week. Olympic Theatre.
Cincinnati, Ohio	October 19. One week.
Indianapolis, Indiana	October 26–27.
Terre Haute, Indiana	October 28.
Louisville, Kentucky	October 29–31.
Baltimore, Maryland	November 2. One week.
Brooklyn, New York	November 9. One week. Brooklyn Theatre.
Boston, Massachusetts	November 16. One week. Globe Theatre.
Philadelphia, Pennsylvania	November 30. One week. Arch Street Theatre.
Washington, D.C.	December 7. One week. New National Theatre.

In St. Louis, Jefferson played three performances of a double bill of *The Cricket on the Hearth* and *Lend Me Five Shillings* (Monday, Tuesday, and Wednesday evenings) and four performances of *Rip* (Thursday, Friday, and Saturday evenings, and Saturday matinee). Jefferson was praised, but the local newspaper criticized the supporting cast as more effective in *Cricket* than in *Rip*.

Jefferson performed at the Arch Street Theatre in Philadelphia from November 30 through December 5, opening on November 30 with *The Cricket on the Hearth* and *Lend Me Five Shillings* for three evenings, followed by three evenings and a matinee of *Rip*. It was the same pattern he had followed in St. Louis.

In the spring of 1886, the Jefferson company played the following venues:

Washington, D.C.	April 19, 1886. One week. National Theatre.
Philadelphia, Pennsylvania	April 26. One week. Chestnut Street Opera House.
Trenton, New Jersey	May 4. Taylor's Opera House.
Newark, New Jersey	May 6–8.
Bridgeport, Connecticut	May 13. Hawes' Opera House.
Springfield, Massachusetts	May 14.

| Burlington, Vermont | May 15. |
| Montreal, Canada | May 17. One week. Academy of Music. |

Only three members of the company had performed with Jefferson before, one of them his sister, Cornelia Jackson, who appeared as Tilly Slowboy.

In Philadelphia he was reported as "delighting large audiences as only he can."

In Trenton the audience was "fine."

In Bridgeport *Rip* played to "a big house."

The Cricket on the Hearth, *Lend Me Five Shillings*, and *Rip* did "a splendid week's business" in Montreal, where Jefferson had not played in a number of years.

In the fall of 1886, the Jefferson company played at the following venues:

Denver, Colorado	August 23, 1886. One week.
Kansas City, Missouri	September 6.
St. Joseph, Missouri	September 10. Tootle's Opera House.
Sioux City, Iowa	September 11. Academy of Music.
Minneapolis, Minnesota	September 13–14 (performance on September 15 canceled). Grand Opera House.
St. Paul, Minnesota	September 17–18 (performance on September 16 canceled).
Duluth, Minnesota	September 20.
Chippewa Falls, Wisconsin	September 21.
Milwaukee, Wisconsin	September 22. Grand Opera House.
Detroit, Michigan	September 23–25. White's Theatre.
St. Louis, Missouri	September 27. One week. Olympic Theatre.
Chicago, Illinois	October 4. Two weeks. McVicker's Theatre.
Nashville, Tennessee	October 18–20.
Henderson, Kentucky	October 21. Opera House.
Evansville, Indiana	October 22.
Vincennes, Indiana	October 23.
Cincinnati, Ohio	October 25. One week. McCaull Opera House.
Cleveland, Ohio	November 1–3.
Buffalo, New York	November 46. Academy of Music.
Pittsburgh, Pennsylvania	November 8. One week. Opera House.
Philadelphia, Pennsylvania	November 15. One week. Arch Street Theatre.
Boston, Massachusetts	November 22. One week.
New York, New York	November 29. Three weeks. Star Theatre.

On September 27, 1886, Jefferson opened for a week at the Olympic Theatre in St. Louis, playing three performances of a double bill of *The Cricket on the Hearth* and *Lend Me Five Shillings* and four performances of *Rip*. Business was better in St. Louis than it had been the previous year, and *Rip* drew the largest crowds.

Jefferson opened for a week at Philadelphia's Arch Street Theatre on November 13. Again he played *The Cricket on the Hearth* and *Lend Me Five Shillings* on Monday, Tuesday, and Wednesday evening as well as the Wednesday matinee, and *Rip* on Thursday, Friday, and Saturday evenings and the Saturday matinee.

He opened in New York on November 29, where "Mr. Jefferson was greeted at the Star Theatre by a large audience that bestowed upon the performance . . . attention and applause rarely to be observed in a theatre. . . . After every act, he was called before the curtain."

In the spring of 1887, the Jefferson company played the following venues:

Fall River, Massachusetts	April 4, 1887. Academy of Music.
Haverhill, Massachusetts	April 9. Academy of Music.
Fitchburg, Massachusetts	April 11. Whitney's Opera House.
Newburyport, Massachusetts	April 12.
Newark, New Jersey	April 18.
Asbury Park, New Jersey	April 25.
Harrisburg, Pennsylvania	April 26. Opera House.
Reading, Pennsylvania	April 27. Academy of Music.
Pottsville, Pennsylvania	April 28. Academy of Music.
Wilkes-Barre, Pennsylvania	April 29. Music Hall.
New York, New York	May 2. One week. Grand Opera House.
New York, New York	May 10. Star Theatre. Couldock benefit.

On May 2, 1887, Jefferson opened as Rip at New York's Grand Opera House. He played six nights and a Wednesday and Saturday matinee. Tickets were fifty cents everywhere in the theatre. Although his performance received excellent reviews, the *New York Mirror* felt that "with the exception of the mountain scene, which had some points of excellence, the scenery was poor." The *New York Times*, however, had nothing but praise:

> Mr. Joseph Jefferson would be troubled to remember when he appeared as Rip Van Winkle to a more delighted audience. . . . He has not often played to a more numerous one . . . , for there were . . . few vacant seats in the Grand Opera House. . . . Mr. Jefferson and his audience were . . . fortunate last night in the character of his support. He . . . obtained the largest share of attention and moved many of his audience to tears or smiles . . ., but several minor characters were well represented. . . . At the close of the third act, Mr. Jefferson was compelled to take cognizance of repeated salvos of applause by appearing before the curtain, but in every scene, he was the same . . . Rip that has given pleasure to . . . thousands.

In the fall of 1887, the Jefferson company played at the following venues:

Albany, New York	September 19. Leland Opera House.
Utica, New York	September 20. Opera House.
Watertown, New York	September 21. City Opera House.
Ogdensburg, New York	September 22.
Oswego, New York	September 23. Academy of Music.
Seneca Falls, New York	September 24.

Bradford, Pennsylvania	September 26. Wagner Opera House.
Warren, Pennsylvania	September 27. New Warren Opera House.
Oil City, Pennsylvania	September 28. Opera House.
Youngstown, Ohio	September 29. Opera House.
Warren, Ohio	September 30.
South Bend, Indiana	October 1.
Chicago, Illinois	October 3. Two weeks. McVicker's Theatre.
New York, New York	October 17. Three weeks. Star Theatre.
Boston, Massachusetts	November 7. One week. Globe Theatre.
Philadelphia, Pennsylvania	November 14. One week. Arch Street Theatre.
New York, New York	November 21. One week. Niblo's.
Brooklyn, New York	November 28. One week. Park Theatre.
New York, New York	December 1. Actors' Fund benefit. Grand Opera House.
New York, New York	December 3. One week. Grand Opera House.

Jefferson played to a "large audience" in Utica.

He took in $1,200 at Watertown.

He performed to capacity crowds in Chicago.

By the middle of the second week of his first New York run, Jefferson had decided to switch from *Rip* to *The Cricket on the Hearth* and *Lend Me Five Shillings* for the Monday, Tuesday, and Wednesday night performances of the third week. On November 3 he gave a professional matinee of *The Rivals* for other theatre professionals, then continued to perform as Acres for the rest of the week.

From November 7 through November 12, 1887, Jefferson played at the Globe Theatre in Boston. He opened on Monday, November 7, with a double bill of *The Cricket on the Hearth* and *Lend Me Five Shillings* and continued to play this combination on Tuesday night and the Wednesday matinee. The rest of the week, including the Saturday matinee, was set aside for *Rip*. He was managed by his sons C. B. and Thomas, and his business manager was H. C. Husted. Only four members of the company were new. The local reviewer had only praise for Jefferson's Caleb Plummer, lamenting the fact that "in a few more years, . . . he shall have past off the stage," but expressed mixed feelings about the rest of the company.

> Mr. Jefferson's supporting company, as seen last night, was almost perfection. The leaders were Miss Emma Vaders as Dot and Mr. Varrey as John Perrybingle. Miss Vaders presented [a] picture of the bluff and honest truckman's . . . wife, a picture which was . . . marred . . . by her tendency . . . to make ultra-tragic the . . . situations. She could not have "looked the character" better. Mr. Denham, the gentleman who was intrusted with the part of Tackleton, was . . . marvelous in make-up and in power of grimacing, but his performance left it not altogether clear whether the villain . . . was a . . . tormentor of . . . Caleb or a . . . good-natured man who chose to

. . . mimick . . . the burlesque stage villain . . . to make the women think him a very bad man. . . . The latter theory had . . . the better of it. Miss Rachel Noan added . . . to the cast by a . . . performance . . . of Bertha, the blind daughter. Her simulation of blindness, with wide open eyes, was effective and not overdone. . . . She gave a good deal of effectiveness to the scene . . . wherein the daughter discovers the deception that her father has led her through and realizes the extent of his sacrifices for her. Miss Connie Jackson's Tillie Slowboy . . . appears to be accepted as the ideal of this . . . young female.

On November 21, Jefferson reopened in New York to perform *Rip* for a week at Niblo's. "All the well known points were applauded, and the actor was, several times, called before the curtain." The brief review in the *New York Times* was positive. Jefferson played six evenings and matinees on Wednesday and Saturday. There was a special Thanksgiving matinee on November 24, and the final matinee was filled to overflowing with children. On December 1, 1887, Jefferson and Mrs. Drew performed an act of *The Rivals* at the Actors' Fund benefit at the Grand Opera House in New York. The *New York Times* reviewer wrote:

> The Grand Opera House was crowded yesterday afternoon from one o'clock until five, and the Actors' Fund is richer by a large sum of money. The entertainment offered . . . did not differ much in character from those usually provided for similar purposes. The quality was . . . good. The audience . . . got its money's worth. Mr. Jefferson's Bob Acres was seen, writing the challenge to Beverly, learning about . . . fighting gentlemen from Sir Lucius, remonstrating with . . . David and arranging with Jack for the manufacture of reputation of prowess. Mrs. Drew's . . . portrayal of Mrs. Malaprop was also seen in the . . . interview with Captain Absolute concerning Beverly's "interceded" letter. These two . . . pieces of . . . acting were appropriately supplemented by the Sir Lucius O'Trigger of Mr. Charles Walcott. . . . The receipts were $3,156.75, the largest amount ever obtained for the fund by a single performance. The expenses were also small. All the performers cheerfully contributed their services without price. . . . None of the ladies who took part in the entertainment charged the fund for carriage hire. . . . Boxes were occupied by Miss Ellen Terry, Mrs. F. W. Vanderbilt and Mr. Tony Pastor.

In the spring of 1888, the Jefferson company played the following venues:

Lexington, Kentucky	March 19, 1888. New Opera House.
Knoxville, Tennessee	March 20. Staub's Theatre.
Atlanta, Georgia	March 21. DeGive's Opera House.
Chattanooga, Tennessee	March 22. New Opera House.
Savannah, Georgia	March 23. Savannah Theatre.
Charleston, South Carolina	March 24. Academy of Music.
Jacksonville, Florida	March 26.

Macon, Georgia	March 27. Academy of Music.
Columbus, Georgia	March 28. Springer Opera House.
Birmingham, Alabama	March 29.
Selma, Alabama	March 30.
Mobile, Alabama	March 31. Mobile Theatre.
New Orleans, Louisiana	April 2. One week. Grand Opera House.
Galveston, Texas	April 9–10. Tremont Opera House.
Houston, Texas	April 11.
Austin, Texas	April 12.
San Antonio, Texas	April 13–14. Grand Opera House.
Waco, Texas	April 16. Garland Opera House.
Memphis, Tennessee	April 27–28. New Memphis Theatre.
Cairo, Illinois	April 30. Opera House.
Nashville, Tennessee	May 1. The Vendome.
Louisville, Kentucky	May 2.
Indianapolis, Indiana	May 3.
Columbus, Ohio	May 4.
Cleveland, Ohio	May 5. Opera House.
Detroit, Michigan	May 7. Matinee and evening. White's Grand.
Flint, Michigan	May 9. Music Hall.
Grand Rapids, Michigan	May 12. Redwood's Grand.
Muskegon, Michigan	No date. Opera House.

In the fall of 1888, the Jefferson company played the following venues:

Baltimore, Maryland	September 24, 1888. One week.
Pittsburgh, Pennsylvania	October 1. One week. Grand Opera House.
Chicago, Illinois	October 8. Three weeks. McVicker's Theatre.
New York, New York	October 28. Two weeks. Fifth Avenue Theatre.
Brooklyn, New York	November 10. One week. Colonel Sinn's Park Theatre.
Newburg, New York	November 12. Academy of Music.
Plainfield, New Jersey	November 13.
Scranton, Pennsylvania	November 14. Academy of Music.
Williamsport, Pennsylvania	November 15. Lyceum Theatre.
Rochester, New York	November 16–17. Lyceum Theatre.
Brooklyn, New York	November 19. One week.
Bridgeport, Connecticut	November 26. Proctor's Grand Opera House.
Waterbury, Connecticut	November 27. Jacques Opera House.
Hartford, Connecticut	November 29. Opera House.
Worcester, Massachusetts	November 30. Worcester Theatre.
Pittsfield, Massachusetts	December 1.
Boston, Massachusetts	December 3. Two weeks. Park Theatre.
Washington, D.C.	December 17. One week. Albaugh's Theatre.
Jersey City, New Jersey	December 24. One week.

Providence, Rhode Island	December 31, 1888–January 2, 1889. Providence Opera House.
Wobasocket, Rhode Island	January 3.
Brockton, Massachusetts	January 4. City Theatre.
Holyoke, Massachusetts	January 5.

In Newburg Jefferson played to a "packed house."

In Scranton, "every part of the house was full, except a few seats in the top gallery." The local reviewer, however, suggested that as the company was better suited to *The Cricket on the Hearth* than to *Lend Me Five Shillings*, it would improve the evening if the farce appeared before the sentimental drama.

In Williamsport he played to "large, refined and elated audiences" and "received encore after encore."

In Rochester he performed to "large audiences."

In Hartford and Pittsfield he was greeted by "crowded houses."

Jefferson's performances at the Providence Opera House on December 31, 1888, through January 2, 1889, were advertised as early as December 23, an unusual amount of time, possibly because they were over the New Year's holiday. He performed *The Cricket on the Hearth* and *Lend Me Five Shillings* on the evening of December 31 and the matinee of January 1, and *Rip Van Winkle* on the evenings of January 1 and 2. Ticket prices for the evening were $1.75, fifty cents, and 25 cents; tickets for the matinee were $1, seventy-five cents, fifty cents, and twenty-five cents.

During the spring 1889 season, the Jefferson company played the following venues:

Cincinnati, Ohio	April 15, 1889. Heuck's Theatre.
Louisville, Kentucky	April 17. MacAuley's Theatre.
Nashville, Tennessee	April 19. The Vendome.
Memphis, Tennessee	April 24. Memphis Theatre.
Springfield, Missouri	April 27.
Kansas City, Missouri	April 29–30. Gillis Theatre.
Omaha, Nebraska	May 1. Opera House.
Denver, Colorado	May 2.
Marshall, Colorado	May 3.
Sioux City, Iowa	May 4. Peavey Grand Opera House.
Des Moines, Iowa	May 5. Foster's Opera House.
Minneapolis, Minnesota	May 6–8. Grand Opera House.
St. Paul, Minnesota	May 9–11. Metropolitan Opera House.
Milwaukee, Wisconsin	May 13.
South Bend, Indiana	May 14.
Indianapolis, Indiana	May 15. Grand Opera House.
Terre Haute, Indiana	May 16. Naylor's Opera House.
Dayton, Ohio	May 17. The Grand Theatre.
Youngstown, Ohio	May 18. Opera House.

Detroit, Michigan	May 20.
Buffalo, New York	May 21–22.
Watertown, New York	May 23. City Opera.
Utica, New York	May 24. Opera House.
Yonkers, New York	May 25.

The opening day of the advance sale in Cincinnati brought in over $1,000.

In Louisville Jefferson played to "one of the largest audiences that ever gathered in the house."

In Nashville "the theatre was packed from orchestra rail to gallery, and a prettier audience, it would be hard to imagine."

Ticket prices were raised in Kansas City, and still "the largest audiences of the season were in attendance."

In Sioux City he played to "standing room only."

In Des Moines Jefferson drew "packed houses."

In Utica he played to "one of the largest houses of the year."

During the fall 1889 tour, the Jefferson-Florence company played the following venues.

New York, New York	October 14, 1889. Three weeks. Star Theatre.
Boston, Massachusetts	November 11. Two weeks. Park Theatre.
New Haven, Connecticut	November 27.
Albany, New York	November 28. Matinee and evening. Lyceum Theatre.
Utica, New York	November 29.
Rochester, New York	November 30. Lyceum Theatre.
Haverhill, Massachusetts	No date.
Philadelphia, Pennsylvania	December 2. Two weeks. Arch Street Theatre.
Baltimore, Maryland	December 16. One week. Ford's Opera House.
Brooklyn, New York	December 23–25. Matinee on Christmas day. Brooklyn Academy of Music.
Harlem, New York	December 26–28. Opera House.
Detroit, Michigan	January 2, 1890. Opera House.
Cleveland, Ohio	January 3–4.
Dayton, Ohio	January 8. The Grand Theatre.
St. Louis, Missouri	January 13. One week. Olympic Theatre.
Chicago, Illinois	January 20. Two weeks. McVicker's Theatre.
Denver, Colorado	February 3. One week. The Tabor Theatre.
Memphis, Tennessee	February 14–15. Memphis Theatre.
New Orleans, Louisiana	February 17. One week. St. Charles Theatre.
Nashville, Tennessee	February 24–25. The Vendome Theatre.
Chattanooga, Tennessee	February 26. New Opera House.
Atlanta, Georgia	February 27. Opera House.
Knoxville, Tennessee	February 28. Staub's Theatre.
Lexington, Kentucky	March 1. Opera House.

Cincinnati, Ohio	March 3–5. Heuck's Theatre.
Pittsburgh, Pennsylvania	March 6–8. Grand Opera House.
New York, New York	March 10. Three weeks. Fifth Avenue Theatre.
Philadelphia, Pennsylvania	March 31. One week. Arch Street Theatre.
Boston, Massachusetts	April 7. One week.
Manchester,	
New Hampshire	April 16.
Brockton, Massachusetts	April 18. City Theatre.
Worcester, Massachusetts	April 19. The Musee Theatre.
New Bedford, Massachusetts	April 23.
Fall River, Massachusetts	April 24. Academy of Music.
Hartford, Connecticut	April 26. Opera House.
Wilmington, Delaware	April 28.
Wilkes-Barre, Pennsylvania	April 29. Music Hall.
Scranton, Pennsylvania	April 30. Academy of Music.
Trenton, New Jersey	May 1. Taylor Opera House.
Brooklyn, New York	May 2–3.

Featured in the fall 1889 tour was Joe's son, Joseph, Jr. (calling himself Joseph Warren), whom the *New York Times* proclaimed "an acceptable Fag." C. B. and Thomas Jefferson served as managers, and Harry A. Lee was the advance agent.

The New York *Star* reported about the opening night in New York: "The house was crowded. Even the pouring rain did not deter fashionable people from coming early . . . to see the play from beginning to end."

For the two performances in Albany on Thanksgiving day prices were doubled, but the "sale was big." The audience for the matinee on Thanksgiving day was small, but the evening house was "very large."

Jefferson drew a "large house" in Rochester.

The Philadelphia correspondent for the *New York Dramatic Mirror* reported that "No event of the season has awakened so great an interest or drawn audiences as large and refined."

On January 13, 1890, the Jefferson company, with W. J. Florence, Mrs. John Drew, and Viola Allen, opened in *The Rivals* at the Olympic Theatre in St. Louis, Missouri, and played for a week. The management considered the company enough of a star attraction to increase prices. On January 16 Jefferson wrote to William H. Thomson of The St. Louis Club: "I sent a note to you this morning to the club thanking you for your card of invitation. I regret that it will be quite impossible for me to come to you on Sunday as I understand that we leave St. Louis early on that morning."

In Detroit they were greeted by "the largest and finest audience ever assembled at any one time in any theatre in this city. . . . They were all received with applause and cheers. At the end of the second act, Jefferson and Florence were called out. The applause continuing, Mrs. Drew was added; then Mr. Varey; then Mr. Paulding; then Miss Allen and finally the entire company. Cries of bravo and cheering were heard all over the house which was filled from pit to dome, and hundreds were turned away."

The Vendome Theatre in Nashville was "crowded."

The sale of tickets in Lexington "was the largest for years, every seat having been sold at advanced prices." The company, however, failed to appear because of a railroad wreck.

In Wilkes-Barre the performance was a great success despite problems in the audience.

> The house was a large one. All the boxes were occupied, and the galleries were called into requisition by the most cultured people of town. . . . When Mrs. Drew, Florence and Jefferson came in front of the curtain together, in response to an encore, the applause was deafening. . . . The very pretty epilogue, in which each by turns participated, was nearly spoiled by the hoodlums on the back seats of the gallery, who always make a stampede for the doors about three minutes too soon. . . . At its close, Market Street was blocked to an unusual degree with street cars, coaches, cabs and private conveyances. The company travels in its private cars, furnished in the highest style, with a full complement of waiters and maids.

Tickets in Scranton went on sale two days before the performance, and "all of the choice seats were soon taken," although it was still possible to obtain a seat on the day of the performance. The local reviewer had some doubts about Florence's performance as O'Trigger, but the "house was in raptures continually, and the recalls were numerous."

In 1890–91 the Jefferson-Florence company played the following venues:

New York, New York	October 13–November 8. Palmer's Theatre.
Boston, Massachusetts	November 17–29. Park Theatre.
Philadelphia, Pennsylvania	December 1–14. Arch Street Theatre.
Washington, D.C.	December 16–20. New National Theatre.
Albany, New York	December 22.
Utica, New York	December 23. Opera House.
Syracuse, New York	December 24. Wieting Opera House.
Watertown, New York	December 25.
Buffalo, New York	December 26–27.
Cleveland, Ohio	December 29–30.
Youngstown, Ohio	December 31.
Fort Wayne, Indiana	January 1, 1891.
Decatur, Illinois	January 2.
Peoria, Illinois	January 3.
St. Louis, Missouri	January 5–10. Olympic Theatre.
Chicago, Illinois	January 12–20.
Galesburg, Illinois	January 21. New Auditorium.
Davenport, Iowa	January 22.

Cedar Rapids, Iowa	January 23. Green's Opera House.
La Crosse, Wisconsin	January 24.
St. Paul, Minnesota	January 26–8. Metropolitan Opera House.
Minneapolis, Minnesota	January 29–31. Grand Opera House.
Dubuque, Iowa	February 4.
Des Moines, Iowa	February 5.
Sioux City, Iowa	February 6.
Omaha, Nebraska	February 7. Grand Opera House.
Kansas City, Missouri	February 9–11. Gillis Theatre.
Wichita, Kansas	February 13.
St. Joseph, Missouri	February 14.
Memphis, Tennessee	February 16–17. The Grand Theatre.
Nashville, Tennessee	February 18. The Vendome.
Chattanooga, Tennessee	February 19. New Opera House.
Atlanta, Georgia	February 20–21.
Louisville, Kentucky	February 23–24. MacAuley's Opera House.
Columbus, Ohio	February 25. Grand Opera House.
Toledo, Ohio	February 26. Wheeler Opera House.
Detroit, Michigan	February 27–28.
Indianapolis, Indiana	March 2. Grand Opera House.
Dayton, Ohio	March 3. The Grand Theatre.
Lexington, Kentucky	March 4. New Opera House.
Cincinnati, Ohio	March 5–7.
Pittsburgh, Pennsylvania	March 9–14. The Dusquesne Theater.
Baltimore, Maryland	March 16–21. Ford's Opera House.
Wilmington, Delaware	March 25.
Scranton, Pennsylvania	March 26.
Wilkes-Barre, Pennsylvania	March 27. Music Hall.
Trenton, New Jersey	March 28. Taylor Opera House.
Chicago, Illinois	March 31–April 18. McVicker's Theatre.
New York, New York	May 19. Benefit performance. Madison Square Garden.

Harry A. Lee served as Jefferson's advance man. The New York opening of the Jefferson-Florence company was advertised as early as October 2 for an October 13 opening, and tickets went on sale on October 7. When the New York engagement closed, Jefferson remained in New York City for an extra week, staying at 27 Madison Avenue and planning to play at the Academy of Music in Brooklyn during Christmas week. The plans did not materialize.

Between November 17–29 the company performed *The Heir-at-Law* and *The Rivals* at the Park Theatre in Boston. Each show played for a week, with a Saturday matinee at two o'clock.

On December 12, when the company was in Philadelphia, W. J. Florence invited a group of twelve New York friends for a supper party. Mr. and Mrs. A. M. Palmer, the manager of New York's Madison Square Theatre and president of the Actors' Fund Association (of which Florence was a trustee), and Colonel and Mrs. John A. Cockerill took the three o'clock express from New York. Jefferson and Florence met them at the Broad Street station in Philadelphia and took them to their hotel. They saw the performance that evening and then had dinner with Florence and Mr. and Mrs. Kendal at midnight.

By December 15, 1890, Jefferson was performing *The Heir-at-Law* and *The Rivals* at the New National Theatre in Washington in what was being billed as his "Annual Engagement." Sheridan's comedy was played on Monday, Tuesday, Wednesday evenings, and Saturday matinee, whereas Colman's was performed on Thursday, Friday, and Saturday evenings.

In Utica they played to a "fair-sized audience."

In Syracuse the company played "to a big house at advanced prices."

In Peoria "every seat in the house was sold a week ahead at $2 a seat for the whole of the parquette."

On January 5, 1891, Jefferson and Florence opened *The Rivals* in the Olympic Theatre in St. Louis. They played *The Rivals* on Monday, Tuesday, Wednesday nights and Saturday matinee and performed *The Heir-at-Law* on Thursday, Friday, and Saturday nights. "The attendance during the first week's engagement was large and fashionable as well as enthusiastic at each performance." The *St. Louis Post Dispatch* commented that Jefferson was continuing to make changes in the script, almost nightly.

In Cedar Rapids they played to a "packed house at advanced prices."

In St. Paul "the house was packed by brilliant and appreciative audiences."

The company ran into trouble in Louisville when the local newspaper, the *Commercial*, demanded fourteen complimentary seats at the theatre, which was controlled by the syndicate of Jefferson, Klaw, and Erlanger. The theatre's owner, John T. Macauley, and Jefferson's manager limited the newspaper to twelve, particularly because Jefferson would be in town for only one day and the fourteen seats amounted to $28.00. The newspaper subsequently engaged in a journalistic attack on any shows that Charles Burke and his partners Klaw and Erlanger brought to town. When, a year later, the newspaper ran a story saying that the mortgage on the theatre was to be foreclosed, Jefferson, Klaw, and Erlanger sued for $40,000.

The season ended in Chicago, but Jefferson and Florence accepted an invitation to give a matinee, on May 19, of the third act of *The Rivals* at the Madison Square Garden Theatre in New York to benefit the erection of the memorial arch at Washington Square. Tickets went for twice their usual price, and the house was full. In the box were former President Cleveland and Mr. and Mrs. Richard Watson Gilder. Mrs. Cleveland, who was four months pregnant with the child who would be known as Baby Ruth, did not attend. At the Washington Square benefit, the Jefferson-Florence company came on next to last. At the end of the tour, Florence went to Europe, and Jefferson went to Buzzards Bay.

The Jefferson-Florence company's venues during the 1891–92 season were:

Richmond, Virginia	October 5, 1891.
New York, New York	October 12–23.
Brooklyn, New York	October 30. Brooklyn Academy of Music.
Boston, Massachusetts	November 2. One Week. Hollis Theatre.
Philadelphia, Pennsylvania	November 9. One Week. Arch Street Theatre.
Buffalo, New York	November 16.
Grand Rapids, Michigan	November 18.
Detroit, Michigan	November 20–21. Matinee and evening. Detroit Opera House.
Minneapolis, Minnesota	November 2–6. Matinee and evening. Grand Opera House.
Washington, D.C.	December 14. One week. New National Theatre.
Pittsburgh, Pennsylvania	December 21–23. Alvin Theatre.
Baltimore, Maryland	December 24–26.
Cincinnati, Ohio	December 28–30.
Paris, Kentucky	December 31.
Terre Haute, Indiana	January 1, 1892. Naylor's Opera House.
Indianapolis, Indiana	January 2. Grand Opera House.
Chicago, Illinois	January 4–16. McVicker's Theatre.
St. Louis, Missouri	January 18–23. Olympic Theatre.
Little Rock, Arkansas	January 25.
Memphis, Tennessee	January 26. Lyceum Theatre.
Nashville, Tennessee	January 27. The Vendome.
Atlanta, Georgia	January 28. DeGive's Opera House.
Augusta, Georgia	January 29. Grand Opera House.
Charleston, South Carolina	January 30. Owens' Academy of Music.
New Orleans, Louisiana	February 1–6. St. Charles Theatre.
Galveston, Texas	February 8. Tremont Opera House.
Houston, Texas	February 9. Sweeney and Coomb's Opera House.
Dallas, Texas	February 10. Opera House.
Fort Worth, Texas	February 11. Greenwall's Opera House.
Austin, Texas	February 12. Millett's Opera House.
San Antonio, Texas	February 13. Grand Opera House.
Los Angeles, California	February 17–20. Grand Opera House.
Oakland, California	February 23.
San Jose, California	February 24. California Theatre.
Stockton, California	February 25. Avon Theatre.
Seattle, Washington	February 27.
Portland, Oregon	February 29–March 5. Marquam Grand Opera House.
San Francisco, California	March 7–19. Baldwin Theatre.
Ogden, Utah	March 21. Grand Opera House.

Salt Lake City, Utah	March 22.
Denver, Colorado	March 24–26. People's Theatre.

In an unusual move, in New York, nine members of the company were listed in the advertisement below the two stars. The list was, of course, headed by Mrs. John Drew. Jefferson and Florence performed *The Rivals* for a week and then switched to *The Heir-at-Law* for the first three nights of the second week. The New York engagement lasted until October 24.

Audiences in Minneapolis were "pretty slim, because tickets had been raised from $1 to $3."

The Jefferson Comedy Company, as the twelve-person troupe was called after Florence's death, performed *The Rivals* in Charleston, South Carolina, on January 30, 1892. The performance was advertised as early as January 14. Ticket sales began on the evening of January 27. By 7 P.M. on the evening of the performance there was standing room only, and the City Railway Company announced that cars would be available at the corners of Market and Meeting streets and Wentworth and King streets to take spectators home at the close of the performance.

Jefferson's gross receipts for three nights and a matinee in Los Angeles alone were $5,890.

In Stockton, California, tickets of $1.00 and $1.50 produced poor business.

The fall 1892 tour played the following venues:

New York, New York	October 10–22, 1892. Star Theatre.
Brooklyn, New York	October 24–November 5.
Rochester, New York	November 10. Lyceum Theatre.
Buffalo, New York	November 11–12. Star Theatre.
Philadelphia, Pennsylvania	November 14–20. Walnut Street Theatre.
Washington, D.C.	November 21–26. New National Theatre.
Chicago, Illinois	November 28. Two weeks. McVicker's Theatre.
St. Louis, Missouri	December 12. One week. Olympic Theatre.
New York, New York	January 16, 1893. Hammerstein's Harlem Opera House.

The tour started on October 10 at the Star Theatre in New York City, where Jefferson, having concentrated on *The Rivals* for three years, was welcomed back as Rip. "The house was crowded," and the production described as having "the best setting that it has had since the notable revival at Booth's Theatre years ago." Of the fourteen members of the company, five were new to the Jefferson enterprise. C. B. Jefferson served as the manager. On October 18, 1892, Francis Wilson visited Jefferson at the theatre in New York.

> The line of ticket-buyers was so long that I decided to appeal personally to the manager. . . . I . . . found . . . Jefferson in the room adjoining the box-office. . . . On my mentioning California, he spoke of the delight of his recent experience there and said that he was going again next season and that he had, in fact, made arrangements to do so, and those

arrangements included a week's idleness to be devoted to revisiting the Yosemite Valley. . . . I was recommending him to leave his climbing of the Glacier Point Trail until the last day of his visit (a trail built since Jefferson's visit twenty years before).

Former President and Mrs. Grover Cleveland attended the performance on October 20 and were cheered by the audience.

The houses in Rochester and Buffalo were "crowded."

The Philadelphia performances played to standing room only.

The advance sale in Chicago indicated that Jefferson would be playing to "some of the biggest houses on record" despite the increase in prices.

On December 12, 1892, Jefferson opened for a week in *Rip* at the Olympic Theatre in St. Louis, Missouri. The *St. Louis Post Dispatch* noted that although he might not have been as light on his feet during the first two acts as he had been in the past, the performance was essentially unchanged.

The spring 1893 tour was under the management of Charles Burke Jefferson and featured only *Rip Van Winkle*. It included the following venues:

Louisville, Kentucky	Date unknown. MacAuley's Opera House.
Nashville, Tennessee	April 4, 1893. The Vendome.
Memphis, Tennessee	April 5.
Springfield, Missouri	April 6. Baldwin Theatre.
Kansas City, Missouri	April 7–8. The Coates Theatre.
St. Joseph, Missouri	April 10. Crawford Theatre.
Lincoln, Nebraska	April 12. The New Lansing Theatre.
Omaha, Nebraska	April 13. Boyd's Theatre.
Des Moines, Iowa	April 14. Grand Opera House.
Dubuque, Iowa	April 15. The Grand.
Milwaukee, Wisconsin	April 17. The Academy Theatre.
Detroit, Michigan	April 18–19.
Columbus, Ohio	April 21. Henrietta Theatre.
Indianapolis, Indiana	April 22. Grand Opera House.
Baltimore, Maryland	April 24–29. Ford's Grand Opera House.
Cincinnati, Ohio	May 1–6. The Walnut Theatre.

Jefferson completely filled MacAuley's Opera House for a matinee and evening performance of *Rip* in Louisville.

In Nashville he played to standing room only, with prices marked $1, $1.50, and $2.

In Memphis he played to a large house at advanced prices.

In Springfield, Missouri, Jefferson played to "a large and fashionable audience."

His performance at Boyd's Theatre in Omaha, Nebraska, with $2 being charged for "choice seats," proved to be the most profitable in the history of the house, taking in $2,312. Four or five hundred people were turned away.

Advance sales in Milwaukee indicated that Jefferson would play to a full house, and indeed the theatre was "packed with the best people" in town.

In Indianapolis the house was sold out a short time after the box office opened, grossing $2,000.

Audiences in Cincinnati, however, were disappointed. Jefferson suffered "a slight attack of dyspepsia," which his physician, Giles Mitchell, felt might develop into "acute gastritis." He barely finished the Friday evening performance and canceled the Saturday evening show, although it was sold out. All signs of illness, however, had disappeared by the time he took the train, and he was in good health when he arrived in New York on Sunday evening.

By April 7, 1894, Klaw and Erlanger had booked Jefferson for the fall 1894 tour, which began in Chicago. The repertoire included *Rip*, *The Cricket on the Hearth*, and *Lend Me Five Shillings*. The company numbered twenty, of whom five were new to Jefferson's troupe. One of them, playing a minor role, was William Winter, who was Joe's youngest son, William Winter Jefferson.

During the fall 1894 season the Jefferson company performed at the following venues:

Chicago, Illinois	October 15–27, 1894. McVicker's Theatre.
Cincinnati, Ohio	October 29–November 3.
Pittsburgh, Pennsylvania	November 5–10. The Duquesne Theatre.
Philadelphia, Pennsylvania	November 12–17. Walnut Street Theatre.
Washington, D.C.	November 19–24. National Theatre.
Norfolk, Virginia	November 27. Academy of Music.
Wilmington, Delaware	November 29. Grand Opera House.
Trenton, New Jersey	November 30. Taylor Opera House.
Utica, New York	December 1. Opera House.
Syracuse, New York	December 3. Wieting Opera House.
Rochester, New York	December 4. Lyceum Theatre.
Buffalo, New York	December 5. Star Theatre.
Detroit, Michigan	December 6. Detroit Opera House.
Columbus, Ohio	December 7. Grand Opera House.
Indianapolis, Indiana	December 8. English's Opera House.
Nashville, Tennessee	December 10–11. The Vendome Theatre.
Louisville, Kentucky	December 12–13. MacAuley's Opera House.
Memphis, Tennessee	December 14–15. Grand Opera House.
New Orleans, Louisiana	December 17–22. St. Charles Theatre.

Jefferson did "remarkably well" at McVicker's in Chicago.

He opened in Philadelphia to a "tremendous house."

On November 19 Jefferson began performing *Rip Van Winkle*, *The Cricket on the Hearth*, and *Lend Me Five Shillings* at the National Theatre in Washington, D.C. *Rip* was performed on Monday, Tuesday, Wednesday, and Thursday evenings as well as the Saturday matinee. The other two plays were done Friday and Saturday evenings.

In Trenton he received two curtain calls.

After his performance in Utica, Jefferson "was presented to the young women of Houghton Seminary, who gave him beautiful bouquets; he then spent Sunday evening at Mrs. Piatt's Seminary where he received more flowers."

In Rochester, he appeared before "a crowded house at advanced prices." From Rochester, Jefferson, sitting in his private car, wrote to Charles Burke:

> You will see by reading the enclosed slips that I exposed to the audience the trick of the manager in———who took the liberty of announcing my farewell engagement (the cars are in motion, so that you will find it hard to read my writing).
>
> See that Mr. McKee and Miss Bijou Fernandez get the enclosed letters; one contains a check for $50 for the Russell Fund, the other one for $5 for the children's Christmas Festival.
>
> Our house last night $1,670. Telegrams to Tom [of] advance [sales]:
> 1st day's sale in Detroit . . . . $ 1,100.
> 1st day's sale in Columbus . . . . 1,250.
> Our reception along the road is quite an ovation.

In Buffalo he played to a "crowded house."
In Detroit every seat was sold in advance.
In Columbus Jefferson played to "standing room only."
In Nashville he played to "crowded and delighted houses."
In Memphis, however, audiences were only "fairly large and satisfactory" at advanced prices.

Venues for the spring 1895 tour were:

Boston, Massachusetts	March 25–30, 1895. Boston Theatre.
Providence, Rhode Island	April 1–2. Providence Opera House.
Hartford, Connecticut	April 5. Proctor's Opera House.
Harlem, New York	April 8–13.
Brooklyn, New York	April 15–20.
Baltimore, Maryland	April 22–27. Ford's Grand Opera House.

Of the sixteen members in the company only two were new. On opening night in Boston "the great house was crowded out the doors, and all the week there had been an almost unprecedented demand for seats at the box-office." In a curtain speech on closing night, Jefferson denied the rumor that this was his farewell engagement.

Jefferson's performances in Providence, Rhode Island, on April 1 and 2 were advertised as early as March 23. He played *Rip* on the 1st and *The Cricket on the Hearth* and *Lend Me Five Shillings* on the 2nd. Seats went on sale on March 29 at 9 A.M. The *Providence Daily Journal* reported: "Every nook and cranny of the auditorium was occupied, and hundreds were turned away, unable to obtain even standing room. The orchestra was placed behind the scenes, and the space usually occupied by the musicians filled by closely seated auditors, while behind the rows and around the sides of the balconies and pit stood a dense crowd, which included many ladies."

In Baltimore, Jefferson was repeatedly called before the curtain and finally gave what was now his customary speech about having before him the "children and grandchildren of those whom he had tried to entertain in Baltimore just sixty years ago." Jefferson was quite accurate in his Baltimore statement. His family was playing there in 1835.

Venues for the fall 1895 tour of *The Cricket on the Hearth, Lend Me Five Shillings,* and *Rip Van Winkle* included:

New York, New York	October 14–November 9, 1895. Garden Theatre.
Albany, New York	November 13. Harmanus Bleeker Hall.
Utica, New York	November 14. Opera House.
Rochester, New York	November 15. Lyceum Theatre.
Buffalo, New York	November 16. Star Theatre.
Cleveland, Ohio	November 18–20. Euclid Theatre.
Grand Rapids, Michigan	November 23. Powers' Theatre.
Minneapolis, Minnesota	November 25–27. Grand Opera House.
St. Paul, Minnesota	November 28–30. Metropolitan Opera House.
Chicago, Illinois	December 2–14. McVicker's Theatre.
Toledo, Ohio	December 25–26. Wheeler Opera House.

Miss Mary Shaw, who later wrote about Jefferson, played Gretchen on this tour. She was one of three new faces in the company, which included Jefferson's sister, Connie Jackson. Jefferson, by this time, described Connie as "deaf as a post—no, not exactly that but she can't hear her cues."

Advertisements for the New York performances began as early as October 1, 1895, and tickets went on sale a week before opening. Jefferson was in New York as early as October 4, when he saw a matinee performance of *A Social Highwayman,* a play being performed by E. H. and Joseph Holland. Jefferson attended along with his wife, Nat C. Goodwin, Francis Wilson, and E. H. Sothern.

The *New York Dramatic Mirror* sent two critics. The first was favorable toward the production. The second had reservations.

> On Thursday evening Mr. Jefferson, in deference to the never ending public desire for *Rip Van Winkle,* revived that piece at the Garden Theatre. Although the rain pelted down just at the hour when people prepare for theatregoing, and although damp coats and wraps and dripping umbrellas gave a tinge of humidity to the auditorium, a large audience enjoyed the performance as hugely as it ever was enjoyed. Among the spectators we noticed a large number of elderly people . . . and many boys and girls. . . .
>
> Rip wears well. The old play, though a trifle archaic in construction, is perennially interesting, aside from its great value as a medium for one of the most remarkable of stage creations. . . .
>
> Mr. Jefferson's impersonation loses nothing of its many admirable

qualities with the progress of time. . . . The heart reaching tenderness of Rip's farewell; the curiously whimsical drollery of the scene with the spirits of Hudson's crew; the picture of the awakened sleeper on the brow of the mountain straining his eyes toward the village in the valley beneath; the scene of Meenie's recognition—all these and countless other elements of this marvelously fine characterization are mingled with the same effectiveness that all American playgoers know so well. . . .

Mary Shaw did not strike the true note as Gretchen. Her acting is saturated with spirit of modernity, and her methods scarcely suit the old-fashioned role of Rip's long-suffering spouse. John Jack was a capital Derrick Van Beekman. The rest of the cast was not altogether satisfying.

The prompter's voice was heard frequently during the evening. The stage management was atrocious and the scenery was handled so clumsily as to mar seriously the pleasure of the audience.

The *New York Times* pointed out that when Jefferson returned to *The Cricket on the Hearth*, he was no longer using Boucicault's version but one put together by Albert Smith.

> This was performed in such a manner last night that its deficiencies seemed greatly magnified. The Tilly Slowboy was still Jefferson's sister Cornelia Jackson. The supporting cast was generally woefully incompetent.
>
> Mr. Jefferson played with all his old moderation, and with some of his old humor and pathos. There were beautiful moments—as when Caleb on Christmas Eve, recalled the departure of his long-lost son. His diction was fine as ever. As usual, each word he uttered seemed to be the expression of that moment's thought. . . .
>
> Much of the failure last night was due to the amateurish Bertha and the preposterous Dot with the baby voice. How much was due to Jefferson's acting it is hard to say in the circumstances. But this Caleb was surely not the one we used to cry over and then laugh with before our tears were dry.
>
> In the farce Mr. Jefferson was assisted by Mary Shaw, who tried hard to make the slender part of Mrs. Phobbs seem rational. The charm of his Golightly was always the hint his acting gave of the mild, gentle, honest nature of the man beneath his superficial absurdities. That charm was not absent last night. . . .
>
> We should be sorry if Mr. Jefferson's engagement proved unprofitable but we fear his present programme and his present company will not suit New York.

The *Times'* prediction was apparently true. By the following Sunday, tickets could be secured for any performance. A notice on October 23 stated that Jefferson was drawing "crowded houses" but was switching to *Rip* in response to an onslaught of requests in the mail. If the houses were really crowded, it is unlikely that the switch would have been made. On October 31, Jefferson opened *Rip Van Winkle* for the last week of his New York run. *The Cricket on the Hearth* and *Lend Me Five Shillings* were given at the matinee on Wednesday, November 6, 1895.

The advance sale in Albany was "very large." The box office came to $2,400 for one night of *Cricket on the Hearth* and *Lend Me Five Shillings*, and Jefferson was called before the curtain to give a brief speech.

In Utica the Opera House was filled at advanced prices; all available standing room was occupied, and people were turned away from the doors. Jefferson was given a curtain call, and Mary Shaw received "great applause" as Gretchen.

The advanced sale in Cleveland, where prices were increased, was heavy.

In Grand Rapids the local critic even thought "the scenic features of the best."

Business was "excellent" in Minneapolis.

While in Chicago, Jefferson did a performance of *Lend Me Five Shillings* for a Thursday matinee at McVicker's Theatre in benefit of the Actors' Fund. It brought in $2,271. Business in Chicago was "enormous." Jefferson announced plans to go to California and then to have the company join him there for a tour that would take them back east.

The spring 1896 tour of *Rip, The Cricket on the Hearth,* and *Lend Me Five Shillings* played the following known venues:

Brooklyn, New York   April 6, 1896. One week. Columbia Theatre.
Philadelphia, Pennsylvania April 20. One week. Broad Street Theatre.
Boston, Massachusetts   April 27. One week.

On April 6, 1896, Jefferson began to perform again, a week-long engagement at the Columbia Theatre in Brooklyn playing Rip, Caleb Plummer, and Mr. Golightly. He opened with *Rip* on Monday, continued with it on Tuesday, Wednesday, and Thursday, and then switched to *The Cricket on the Hearth* and *Lend Me Five Shillings* on Friday and Saturday nights. *Rip* was always used for Saturday matinees. Of the fourteen other members of the cast, five were newcomers to the Jefferson camp, an unusually high number, which may indicate a pick-up cast.

Venues for the summer 1896 all-star production of *The Rivals* were:

Springfield, Massachusetts May 4, 1896. Court Square Theatre.
Hartford, Connecticut   May 5. Proctor's Opera House.
New Haven, Connecticut   May 6. The Hyperion Theatre.
New York, New York   May 7. Matinee.The New York Academy of
                              Music.
Brooklyn, New York   May 7. Evening.
Baltimore, Maryland   May 9. Matinee. Harris' Academy of Music.

Washington, D.C.	May 9. Evening. Albaugh's Lafayette Square Opera House.
Pittsburgh, Pennsylvania	May 11. The Alvin.
Louisville, Kentucky	May 12. The Auditorium.
Cincinnati, Ohio	May 13. The Walnut
St. Louis, Missouri	May 14. Matinee and evening. Olympic Theatre.
Chicago, Illinois	May 15–16. Two evening performances and a matinee. McVicker's Theatre.
Milwaukee, Wisconsin	May 18. The Academy Theatre.
Indianapolis, Indiana	May 19. The English Theatre.
Grand Rapids, Indiana	May 20. Powers' Theatre.
Toledo, Ohio	May 21. Matinee. Wheeler Opera House.
Detroit, Michigan	May 21. Evening. Detroit Opera House.
Columbus, Ohio	May 22.
Cleveland, Ohio	May 23. Matinee and evening. Euclid Opera House.
Buffalo, New York	May 25. Music Hall.
Rochester, New York	May 26. Cook Opera House.
Syracuse, New York	May 27. Matinee. Bastable Theatre.
Utica, New York	May 27. Evening. Opera House.
Albany, New York	May 28. Harmanus Bleeker Hall.
Boston, Massachusetts	May 29. Matinee.
Worcester, Massachusetts	May 29. Evening.
New York, New York	May 30. Fifth Avenue Theatre.

By late August 1896, Jefferson was forming his company for what was first announced as a ten-week and then changed to a fourteen-week season beginning in mid-October. He also consented to appear at a benefit of the Actors' Order of Friendship in New York that fall. The benefit took place on October 8 at the Academy of Music, and Jefferson and his company performed *Lend Me Five Shillings*. He also contributed sketches to be photogravured for the souvenir program. Venues for the fall 1896 season were:

Kansas City, Missouri	October 12–13, 1896. Coates Opera House.
Des Moines, Iowa	October 14. Foster's Opera House.
Sioux City, Iowa	October 15. Grand Opera House.
Grand Rapids, Michigan	October 19. Powers' Theatre.
Saginaw, Michigan	October 20. Academy of Music.
Bay City, Michigan	October 21. Wood's Opera House.
Detroit, Michigan	October 23–24. Hoyt's Theatre.
Cleveland, Ohio	Date unknown. Euclid Avenue Opera House.
Indianapolis, Indiana	October 27. The English Opera House.
Buffalo, New York	November 2. The Star Theatre.
Rochester, New York	November 3. Lyceum Theatre.
Utica, New York	November 4. Opera House.

Albany, New York	November 5. Harmanus Bleecker Hall.
Northampton, Massachusetts	November 6.
Poughkeepsie, New York	November 7. Collingwood Opera House.
Pittsburgh, Pennsylvania	November 9–14. The Alvin Theatre.
Baltimore, Maryland	November 16–21. Ford's Grand Opera House.
Cincinnati, Ohio (originally scheduled as St. Louis, Missouri)	November 23–28. The Walnut Theatre.
St. Louis, Missouri	November 30–December 5. Olympic Theatre.
Chicago, Illinois	December 7–19. McVicker's Theatre.

In Des Moines, the receipts were $1,800.

Jefferson played to an excellent house in Sioux City and was called before the curtain after each act.

Business was not good in Grand Rapids, because this was Jefferson's third appearance there in a year.

In Poughkeepsie Jefferson packed the house; almost all of Vassar's four hundred students attended. The "attachés" of the Collingwood Opera House wore yellow chrysanthemums in honor of the occasion, and the students presented Jefferson with a large bouquet of white chrysanthemums with a yellow V in the center.

The Chicago engagement was preceded by "an enormous advance sale." Jefferson played Rip for a week and was planning to switch to *The Cricket on the Hearth* and *Lend Me Five Shillings* the second week, but the demand for *Rip* was so great that he rescheduled it that second week for a Wednesday matinee and evening, a Thursday matinee and evening, as well as Friday and Saturday nights. Jefferson again laughed at rumors of retirement and announced that he was "good for many seasons yet."

The spring 1897 tour, consisting of *Rip, The Cricket on the Hearth*, and *Lend Me Five Shillings*, took less than a month as it wound its way through ten Southern cities. Jefferson's advance man was E. D. Schultz. The company of sixteen had four new members. Venues included:

New Orleans, Louisiana	March 22–26, 1897. St. Charles Theatre.
Selma, Alabama	March 30. Academy of Music.
Atlanta, Georgia	April 3.
Birmingham, Alabama	April 4. O'Brien's Opera House.
Jacksonville, Florida	April 6. Park Opera House.
Savannah, Georgia	April 7. The Savannah Theatre.
Charleston, South Carolina	April 9. Academy of Music.
Wilmington, North Carolina	April 10. The Opera House.
Roanoke, Virginia	April 12. Academy of Music.
Richmond, Virginia	April 24.

In Selma, Jefferson played to a $1,000 house.

In Birmingham he played to standing room only at advanced prices.

In Jacksonville the house took in $1,450.

The company's performance of *Rip Van Winkle* on April 9 in Charleston was announced as early as April 4. Tickets went on sale on April 6. People were lined up when the box office opened, and three hundred seats were sold immediately. The subsequent performance had standing room only.

In Wilmington the receipts were "the largest for any performance in many years."

Rip played to a $1,700 house in Roanoke.

On April 24 Jefferson gave an interview in Richmond, Virginia, in which he said: "I never expect to retire from the stage. As long as the American people want to see me, they can have me."

The fall 1897 tour of *Rip, The Cricket on the Hearth*, and *Lend Me Five Shillings* lasted two months. A typical pattern was established for these three plays during a one-week stand: Jefferson opened on a Monday, played Rip through Wednesday evening, switched to Caleb Plummer and Mr. Golightly on Thursday and Friday evenings, and then finished with a Saturday matinee and evening performance as Rip. This tour was performed by a company that included Jefferson's sons, William Winter Jefferson and Joseph Warren Jefferson, as well as his daughter-in-law, Blanche Bender. Six of the fourteen company members were new. Venues were:

Portland, Maine	October 7, 1897. The Jefferson.
Lawrence, Massachusetts	October 8. Opera House.
Boston, Massachusetts	October 11–16. Boston Theatre.
Providence, Rhode Island	October 18–19. Providence Opera House.
Hartford, Connecticut	October 21. Parsons' Theatre.
New Haven, Connecticut	October 22. Hyperion Theatre.
Bridgeport, Connecticut	October 23. Park City Theatre.
Brooklyn, New York	October 25–31. The Columbia Theatre.
Baltimore, Maryland	November 1–6. Ford's Theatre.
Washington, D.C.	November 8–14. New National Theatre.
Chicago, Illinois	November 22–28. McVicker's Theatre.
Minneapolis, Minnesota	November 29–December 1. Metropolitan Theatre.
St. Paul, Minnesota	December 2–4. Metropolitan Opera House.
Milwaukee, Wisconsin	December 6–7. Davidson Theatre.
Indianapolis, Indiana	December 11. English's Theatre.
Detroit, Michigan	December 13–14. Empire Theatre.

In Portland the theatre sold out three hours after the box office opened. Jefferson had to make curtain speeches after the first and second act.

Jefferson "packed the Boston at advanced prices. They had to keep two box-offices running . . . to accommodate the crowds buying tickets." He did "the biggest six consecutive nights' business ever known in the city's history. In all, more than 25,000 people saw him."

Jefferson's performances in Providence on October 18 and 19 were advertised as early as October 10. Tickets went on sale October 15. "The theatre was packed to the doors. The orchestra was forced from its accustomed place and the space filled with chairs."

The house was sold out in New Haven, and Jefferson consented to address the Yale boys with the stipulation that three questions on the drama, "written and sealed[,] be sent to him upon the platform."

In Brooklyn "it was thought best to advance the desirable seats to $2, an injudicious move as it resulted in no inconsiderable number of discernible vacancies during the engagement."

The spring 1898 season, consisting of *The Cricket on the Hearth* and *Lend Me Five Shillings*, lasted less than a month and was confined to New York, Pennsylvania, Delaware, and New Jersey. Venues for the tour included:

Buffalo, New York	April 4, 1898.
Rochester, New York	April 5. Lyceum Theatre.
Watertown, New York	April 6. City Opera House.
Utica, New York	April 7. Opera House.
Schenectady, New York	April 8. Van Curler Opera House.
Poughkeepsie, New York	April 9. Collingwood Opera House.
Philadelphia, Pennsylvania	April 11–23. Broad Street Theatre.
Harrisburg, Pennsylvania	April 25. Grand Opera House.
Wilmington, Delaware	April 26. Grand Opera House.
Easton, Pennsylvania	April 27.
Trenton, New Jersey	April 28. Taylor Opera House.
Orange, New Jersey	April 29. Columbus Theatre. Music Hall.
Elizabeth, New Jersey	April 30. Star Theatre.

In Rochester, Jefferson was enthusiastically called before the curtain.
In Watertown the house was "fair."
In Schenectady he "packed the house."
In Wilmington the house was "overflowing."

Venues for the fall 1898 tour were:

Albany, New York	October 4, 1898. Empire Theatre.
Schenectady, New York	October 5. Van Curler Opera House.
Bridgeport, Connecticut	October 6. Matinee. Park City Theatre.
New Haven, Connecticut	October 6. Evening. Hyperion Theatre.
Burlington, Vermont	October 7.
Springfield, Massachusetts	October 8. Gilmore's Court Square Theatre.
New York, New York	October 10–15. Extended to November 6. Extended again to November 19. Fifth Avenue Theatre. (Week of November 13–19 canceled due to Jefferson's ill health.)

The tour continued without Jefferson.

Advertisements for the New York engagement began as early as October 1, and tickets went on sale on October 3. In New York, Jefferson played *The Rivals* for six nights a week and a Saturday matinee at the Fifth Avenue Theatre. On the day after opening, the *New York Times* commented:

> Both in size and character, the audience that greeted the . . . actor . . . must have been as gratifying as . . . the applause that welcomed each of the best-known actors of the company and punctuated the performance throughout. There was no stint in that applause, and there were no vacant seats in the house. At the close of the scene in Bob Acre's chambers, where the challenge to Beverly is composed, Mr. Jefferson was called before the curtain and made the speech. . . . He gratefully returned thanks on behalf of himself and his company for the cordiality of the reception. . . .

Ffoliott Paget played Mrs. Malaprop in gowns obtained the previous summer in Europe. The material had taken first prize in the Brussels Exhibition.

The spring 1899 tour included the following venues:

Jacksonville, Florida	April 3, 1899.
Savannah, Georgia	April 4. Savannah Theatre.
Charleston, South Carolina	April 5. Academy of Music.
Macon, Georgia	April 7. Academy of Music.
Atlanta, Georgia	April 8.
Washington, D.C.	April 10–15. New National Theatre.
New York, New York	April 17–23. Harlem Opera House.
Philadelphia, Pennsylvania	April 24–29. Broad Street Theatre.
Brooklyn, New York	May 1–6.
Orange, New Jersey	May 8. Music Hall.
Wilkes-Barre, Pennsylvania	May 10.
Binghamton, New York	May 11. Stone Opera House.
Elmira, New York	May 12. Lyceum Theatre.
Rochester, New York	May 13. Baker Theatre.

In Macon *The Rivals* played "to a large and appreciative audience."

Jefferson's performance of *The Rivals* in Charleston, South Carolina, on April 5 was advertised as early as March 30, and tickets went on sale on March 31.

In Washington, Jefferson performed Rip on Monday, Tuesday, Thursday, and Saturday. On Wednesday and Friday he did Bob Acres. Business was "good."

Jefferson's return to the stage in New York was announced as early as April 7 and advertised as early as April 9. He opened with *Rip* on a Monday, played it on Tuesday and Thursday nights and Saturday matinee and evening, and switched to *The Rivals* on Wednesday and Friday evenings.

During the fall 1899 season, Jefferson played *Rip Van Winkle*, *The Cricket on the Hearth*, *The Rivals*, and *Lend Me Five Shillings*. The fall 1899 tour performed at the following venues:

Oswego, New York	October 2. Richardson Theatre.
Albany, New York	October 5. Empire Theatre.
Worcester, Massachusetts	October 6. Originally scheduled for October 12. Worcester Theatre.
Hartford, Connecticut	October 7.
Waterbury, Connecticut	October 10. Poli's Theatre.
Middletown, Connecticut	October 11. The Middlesex Theatre.
Springfield, Massachusetts	October 12. Gilmore's Court Square Theatre.
New London, Connecticut	October 13. Lyceum Theatre.
Holyoke, Massachusetts	October 14. Opera House.
Boston, Massachusetts	October 16–21. The Boston Theatre.
Baltimore, Maryland	October 23–28. The Academy of Music.
Pittsburgh, Pennsylvania	October 30–November 4.
Indianapolis, Indiana	November 14. English's Theatre.
Columbus, Ohio	November 15. The Southern Theatre.
Dayton, Ohio	November 16.
Decatur, Illinois	November 17. Powers' Grand Opera House.
Springfield, Illinois	November 18.
St. Louis, Missouri	November 20–25. The Olympic.

In fall 1899 at least five members of the company were new.

In Hartford the house was "crowded."

In Waterbury Jefferson played to a "large" audience.

In Middletown he performed to "the largest audience of the season."

In Holyoke business was only "fair."

In Boston Jefferson played *Rip Van Winkle* all week, switching to *The Rivals* for closing night. The receipts for the week were $18,233.50.

In Indianapolis Jefferson was "welcomed by an immense audience."

In Columbus "*The Rivals* packed the house, the entire house being sold three days in advance."

In St. Louis Jefferson played to a "large audience."

The spring 1900 company employed his sons, William Winter Jefferson and Joseph Jefferson, Jr.; his daughter-in-law, Blanche Bender; and six new company members. The troupe performed *Rip Van Winkle, The Rivals, The Cricket on the Hearth*, and *Lend Me Five Shillings*. The venues were:

Atlanta, Georgia	April 2, 1900. Matinee and evening. Grand Theatre.
Birmingham, Alabama	April 3. Jefferson Theatre.
Memphis, Tennessee	April 4. Lyceum Theatre.
Nashville, Tennessee	April 5. The Vendome.
Lexington, Kentucky	April 6. Opera House.
Louisville, Kentucky	April 7. MacAuley's Theatre.
Springfield, Ohio	April 9. Grand Opera House.
Canton, Ohio	April 10. The Grand Theatre.
Youngstown, Ohio	April 11. Opera House.

Buffalo, New York   April 12–14.
New York, New York   April 16–May 5. Fifth Avenue Theatre.

Jefferson began in Atlanta with a matinee of *Rip* that played to standing room only. Evening performances of *The Cricket on the Hearth* and *Lend Me Five Shillings* performed to a "big audience."

In Birmingham he played to standing room only in a theatre named for him.

Jefferson performed *The Rivals* in Nashville to "a packed house."

There was also standing room only in Lexington.

He packed the theatre in Louisville to capacity.

The Buffalo correspondent for the *New York Dramatic Mirror* noted that "one would not have thought from the size of the houses that welcomed [Jefferson] that Holy Week was in the calendar of the Buffalonians."

His New York opening was advertised as early as April 1, 1900. Jefferson arrived in New York on Sunday, April 15, and stayed at the Fifth Avenue Hotel. He opened in New York in *Rip Van Winkle*, playing opening night, April 16, to a well-filled house. Jefferson performed *Rip* all week, changing to *The Rivals* on his first Saturday night. The production in New York was criticized because the same furniture was used in no fewer than three different indoor scenes. Between the second and third acts of *The Rivals*, Jefferson made a curtain speech. He performed *the Rivals* for the first four nights of his second week, switching to *The Cricket on the Hearth* and *Lend Me Five Shillings* on his second Friday and Saturday nights. The *Times* wrote:

> While it would be folly to say that in these roles the veteran comedian's genius is as potent as ever, for especially as Plummer has his manner lately seemed to harden and his humour to wither; yet both are masterworks in their comparatively small way. The novelty in *The Cricket on the Hearth* is the performance of Tilly Slowboy by a little girl. Jefferson's Tilly Slowboy, in all his revivals of the crude Caleb Plummer play for many years, was his funny little sister Cornelia Jefferson Jackson. The character of Tilly, the nursemaid from the Work'us, is a bald caricature in Dickens' Christmas story, and a caricature Tilly has always been on the stage. It has not been unusual, in fact, for the first low comedian of the company to take that part and "gag" it to his heart's content. . . . Mr. Jefferson has changed all this now, and in the performances of *The Cricket on the Hearth* at the Fifth Avenue Theatre last week, the part was played . . . by a little girl.

During his third week in New York, Jefferson performed *Rip* on Monday, Tuesday, and Thursday nights as well as the Wednesday and Saturday matinees, *Cricket* and *Shillings* on Saturday night, and *The Rivals* on Wednesday and Friday nights. At the end of the New York run Jefferson made another speech in which he assured his audience "that this would not mark his last appearance in this city, and if his health permitted he would positively be seen here next season." The *New York Times* commented that one who remembers his acting of Rip in the late sixties would find it difficult to point out any passage in which the present performance differs in . . . a syllable or the turn of a finger from the Rip of his youth.

At the conclusion of the performance Mr. Jefferson was repeatedly called before the curtain, and in response to the demands for a speech said:

"I thank you cordially for the reception and applause which you have given me tonight, and if I did not address you when I appeared before the curtain at the end of the first act, it was because I did not wish to break the thread of the story.

"But if I had only thought, I needn't have feared that I would break the thread of the story, because I have played Rip before you so many times. It is now forty years since I first played the part you see me in to-night in this city, and it is a reasonable supposition that I played it before the fathers and mothers and grandfathers and grandmothers of you who are present before me this evening.

"It is sixty years since I first appeared as an actor. I was then but a child, and it is pleasant indeed for me to know that there are so many young people here to-night. It is not pleasant to know, however, that we are so soon forgotten. I do not want to become melancholy at this time, but when I discuss these things it is difficult to avoid becoming sad, for the actor can only live in the memory of those who have seen him. To them he is a revelation, to others a tradition.

"I can only say that if I have tarried here too long, you who come to see me are . . . as much to blame as I am, but when I am encouraged by such applause and by an assemblage so brilliant, I must say I have no intention of leaving the stage, and I must say that I thoroughly appreciate this welcome to-night. I felt there must be some friends as well as the 'general public' in this audience; so let me conclude by saying that I appreciate from my heart this more than kindly greeting."

Following Jefferson's final performance there in 1900, the Fifth Avenue Theatre was turned from a legitimate playhouse into a variety house in forty-eight hours, a sign of changes occurring in the American theatre.

During the fall 1900 tour, Jefferson played Rip, Caleb Plummer, Bob Acres, and Mr. Golightly. The venues were:

Northampton, Massachusetts	October 1. Academy of Music.
Albany, New York	October 3. Matinee and evening. Empire Theatre.
Utica, New York	October 5. Majestic Theatre.
Rochester, New York	October 6. Matinee and evening.
Chicago, Illinois	October 8–20. Powers' Theatre.
Cleveland, Ohio	November 1–3. Euclid Avenue Opera House.
Philadelphia, Pennsylvania	November 5–17. Broad Street Theatre.

St. Paul, Minnesota	November 22–24. Metropolitan Opera House.
Minneapolis, Minnesota	November 25–27. Metropolitan Theatre.
Bloomington, Illinois	November 29. Grand Opera House.
Indianapolis, Indiana	November 30. English's Theatre.
Columbus, Ohio	November 31. The Southern Theatre.
Philadelphia, Pennsylvania	December 5–17.
Brooklyn, New York	December 19–24. Columbia Theatre.

Business was excellent in Minneapolis, but the correspondent for the *New York Dramatic Mirror* thought the supporting company was only "fair."

The spring 1901 tour performed at the following venues:

Jacksonville, Florida	April 6. Park Opera House.
Birmingham, Alabama	April 10. Jefferson Theatre.
Louisville, Kentucky	April 13. Matinee and evening. MacAuley's Theatre.
Richmond, Kentucky	April 15. Matinee. White-Bush Opera House.
Lexington, Kentucky	April 15. Evening. Opera House.
Chattanooga, Tennessee	April 16.
Knoxville, Tennessee	April 17.
Roanoke, Virginia	April 18.
Norfolk, Virginia	April 19.
Richmond, Virginia	April 20.
New York, New York	April 22–27. Harlem Opera House.
Bridgeport, Connecticut	April 29. Park City Theatre.
New Haven, Connecticut	April 30. Hyperion Theatre.
Hartford, Connecticut	May 1. Parson's Theatre.
Springfield, Massachusetts	May 2. Court Square Theatre.
Salem, Massachusetts	May 3.
Portland, Maine	May 4. Jefferson Theatre.
Boston, Massachusetts	May 6–11. Boston Theatre.

In Birmingham there was standing room only.

In Lexington a line formed at 4 A.M. on April 10 to purchase tickets for Jefferson's performance; tickets went on sale thirty hours later.

Business in Bridgeport was light.

Jefferson played to packed houses in New Haven and Hartford.

He opened in New York on April 22, 1901, playing Rip on Monday, Tuesday, and Wednesday nights as well as the Saturday matinee, *The Rivals* on Thursday and Friday nights, and *The Cricket on the Hearth* and *Lend Me Five Shillings* on Saturday night. The show was advertised as early as the preceding Wednesday with seats going on sale the next day.

In Boston, Jefferson played Rip for six performances, including the Saturday matinee, *The Rivals* on Wednesday evening, and *The Cricket on the Hearth* and *Lend Me Five Shillings* on Saturday night. The week's box office was

$16,680. It was in Boston that he met Helen Keller and performed a scene from *The Rivals* for her, while she followed him with her finger on his lips.

The fall 1901 tour performed at the following venues:

Troy, New York	September 30. Griswold Opera House.
Utica, New York	October 1. Majestic Theatre.
Syracuse, New York	October 2. Wieting Opera House.
Rochester, New York	October 3. Lyceum Theatre.
Youngstown, Ohio	October 4. Opera House.
Dayton, Ohio	October 5. Victoria Theatre.
Chicago, Illinois	October 7–14, extended to October 19. Two weeks. Powers' Theatre.
Detroit, Michigan	October 21–23.
Toledo, Ohio	October 24. Valentine Theatre.
Columbus, Ohio	October 25. Southern Theatre.
Indianapolis, Indiana	October 26.
St. Louis, Missouri	October 28–November 2. One week. Olympic Theatre.
Pittsburgh, Pennsylvania	November 4–9. One week.
Washington, D.C.	November 11–16. One week. National Theatre.
Baltimore, Maryland	November 18–23. One week. Academy of Music.

In Dayton the sale of orchestra seats was only "fair," but the balcony was crowded. The local correspondent for the *New York Dramatic Mirror* felt that the supporting company was below Jefferson's usual standard.

The seat sale in Chicago was enormous.

A correspondent in Detroit wrote:

> The public was out in force on Monday evening, October 21, to greet Joseph Jefferson, . . . who opened for a half week stay in *Rip Van Winkle*, followed by *The Rivals* for Tuesday evening and *The Cricket on the Hearth* and *Lend Me Five Shillings* for the closing performance Wednesday night, in addition to which a matinee of *Rip Van Winkle* was given on Wednesday. Those who have reported Mr. Jefferson as in failing health have . . . not seen his acting this season, for some in the audience Monday night remarked that they had seen him in the same character over a third of a century ago, and he was as good as ever. Mr. Jefferson must have been . . . gratified to see . . . such a . . . number of admirers, the attendance being . . . the largest of the season, every seat being occupied and a goodly number standing. He was recalled at the close of the first act and made one of his timely speeches, recalling the fact that it was about thirty-three years ago since he made his first appearance in Detroit. . . .
>
> The audience for *The Rivals* was equally as large as on the first night, and a splendid presentation of the comedy was given by the whole co. The entire cast was recalled many times, and the audience would not be satisfied until Mr. Jefferson had made another speech.

In St. Louis, Jefferson opened on a Monday in *Rip*. "He was enthusiastically received by a packed house. *Rip* [was] also on the bill for Tuesday and Thursday evenings and Saturday matinee. Wednesday and Friday evenings, he performed in *The Rivals* and on Saturday evening in *The Cricket on the Hearth* and *Lend Me Five Shillings*." A horse show drew most of the "society" patrons away.

In Washington, Jefferson opened with *Rip*, gave *The Rivals* on Wednesday and Friday nights, *The Cricket on the Hearth* and *Lend Me Five Shillings* on Saturday nights, and *Rip* on Tuesday night and the Saturday matinee.

The spring 1902 tour began on March 28 and was under the management of Charles Burke Jefferson; the repertoire was *Rip Van Winkle, The Rivals, The Cricket on the Hearth*, and *Lend Me Five Shillings*. Venues for the tour were:

Mobile, Alabama	March 28, 1902. Mobile Theatre.
Atlanta, Georgia	April 2. Grand Theatre.
Memphis, Tennessee	Date unknown. Auditorium.
Chattanooga, Tennessee	April 8. New Opera House.
Knoxville, Tennessee	April 9. Staub's Theatre.
Roanoke, Virginia	April 10. Academy of Music.
Norfolk, Virginia	April 11. Academy of Music.
Richmond, Virginia	April 12. Academy of Music.
Philadelphia, Pennsylvania	April 14–26. Broad Street Theatre.
New York, New York	April 28–May 3. Harlem Opera House.

In Mobile Jefferson, "in response to continuous applause . . . came before the curtain and in a few well chosen words spoke of his early reminiscences of this place."

In Atlanta he played to immense houses.

In Richmond he had to leave the theatre by the darkened main entrance in order to avoid a group of women gathered at the stage door to meet him.

Jefferson's New York performance was advertised a week in advance. Tickets went on sale the Thursday before opening. He performed Rip on Monday, Tuesday, and Thursday nights as well as the Saturday matinee, *The Rivals* on Wednesday and Friday nights, and *The Cricket on the Hearth* and *Lend Me Five Shillings* on Saturday night. The *New York Times* reported him to be in excellent health.

The fall 1902 tour performed at the following venues:

Boston, Massachusetts	September 29–October 4, 1902. Colonial Theatre.
Chicago, Illinois	October 6–18. Powers' Theatre.
Cincinnati, Ohio	October 20–25. The Grand.
Columbus, Ohio	October 28. The Southern.
Toledo, Ohio	October 29. The Valentine.
Cleveland, Ohio	October 30–November 1. Euclid Avenue Opera House.
Pittsburgh, Pennsylvania	November 3–8. The Alvin.
Buffalo, New York	November 10–12. The Star.

Brooklyn, New York   November 17–22. Montauk Theatre.

On September 29, 1902, Jefferson opened at the Colonial Theatre in Boston with a company of seventeen, including four new members. He played Rip to an appreciative standing-room-only audience, which called him out for a curtain speech after the first act. He said that certain spectators among them were the grandchildren of audience members who had first seen him do the role thirty-five years before. The local newspaper praised not only Jefferson but the entire company. The troupe performed *Rip* on Monday and Tuesday nights and the Wednesday and Saturday matinees. On Wednesday and Friday nights they did *The Rivals*, and Saturday evening saw a double bill of *The Cricket on the Hearth* and *Lend Me Five Shillings*. *The Rivals* was similarly well received. Every scene was applauded; every actor given an ovation. At the end of the second act Jefferson was called out before the curtain and said: "I am glad that you enjoy it, for that makes us enjoy it. A dull audience makes a weary actor and a dull actor makes a weary audience." It was one of the most lucrative engagements ever played at the Colonial. After the first performance of *Rip*, every seat was sold, and even standing room was completely taken. One of the performances had to be halted when Jefferson's leading lady in *The Rivals* was taken ill with stage fright and was unable to go on for the third act.

During his second week in Chicago, Jefferson played *Rip* on Monday, Tuesday, and Thursday evenings as well as at the Wednesday and Saturday matinees; on Wednesday and Friday evenings he did *The Rivals*, and on Saturday night he performed *The Cricket on the Hearth* and *Lend Me Five Shillings*.

In Cincinnatti, the advanced sale was the heaviest of the season.

In Cleveland, Jefferson appeared for three nights and a matinee. He opened on a Thursday with Rip, played Bob Acres on Friday, did Rip for the Saturday matinee, and Caleb Plummer and Mr. Golightly at the Saturday evening performance.

Venues for the spring 1903 season were:

Jackson, Mississippi	Date unknown.
Nashville, Tennessee	April 13, 1903. The Vendome.
Memphis, Tennessee	April 14. Lyceum Theatre.
Jacksonville, Florida	April 15.
New Orleans, Louisiana	April 16–18. Tulane Theatre.
Mobile, Alabama	April 20. Mobile Theatre.
Birmingham, Alabama	April 21.
Atlanta, Georgia	April 22. Grand Opera House.
Macon, Georgia	April 23. Academy of Music.
Augusta, Georgia	April 24. Grand Opera House.
Savannah, Georgia	April 25. Matinee. Savannah Theatre.
Charleston, South Carolina	April 27. Academy of Music.
Columbia, South Carolina	April 28. Columbia Theatre.
Charlotte, Virginia	April 29.

Roanoke, Virginia	April 30. Academy of Music.
Richmond, Virginia	May 1. Academy of Music.
Norfolk, Virginia	May 2. Academy of Music.
New York, New York	May 4–16. Harlem Opera House.

Jefferson performed with a nineteen-person company of his old standbys (only one new member). Jerome Eddy served as his press agent.

In Nashville he went before the curtain and thanked his auditors for their enthusiastic reception, remarking that it was sixty years since he had first appeared in that city and thirty years since he had first played *Rip* there. Large floral offerings were presented to him.

Jefferson appeared for three nights and a matinee in New Orleans at the Tulane Theatre beginning Thursday, April 16. On closing night, after *The Cricket on the Hearth* and *Lend Me Five Shillings*, the curtain calls were so numerous as to require a speech. "In the course of his remarks, Mr. Jefferson stated that he desired to refute certain press rumors regarding his retirement, his health and age, and assured his audience that his health had never been better nor his retirement more remote and that as long as his health maintained its present standard, he would continue to act and that this was by no means his last tour."

In Savannah the lights failed at the end of the first act, and Jefferson did the end of the act in darkness. In a curtain speech after the first act, he apologized to the audience for the accident. At the end of the play, Joe was presented with a bouquet of red carnations and remembered that he had managed a theatre in Savannah fifty-two years before and that he had first played Rip there thirty years ago.

Jefferson's performance of *The Rivals* on April 27 in Charleston was advertised as early as April 25. The house was packed, and Jefferson made a short speech after the second act while the audience threw flowers at him.

Jefferson opened at the Harlem Opera House on May 4. He performed Rip on Monday, Tuesday, and Thursday nights and the Saturday matinee, *The Rivals* on Wednesday and Friday nights, and *The Cricket on the Hearth* and *Lend Me Five Shillings* on Saturday night. The same plays were presented on the second week of the run, except that the double bill was performed on Friday and Jefferson did *The Rivals* on Saturday night. On opening night, Jefferson repeated his determimation not to retire as long as health permitted it.

In the fall of 1903 the Jefferson company's venues were:

Chicago, Illinois	September 28–October 10, 1903. Powers' Theatre.
St. Paul, Minnesota	October 12–14. Metropolitan Opera House.
Minneapolis, Minnesota	October 15–17. Metropolitan Opera House.
Sioux City, Iowa	October 19. Grand Opera House.
Des Moines, Iowa	October 20. Foster's Opera House.
Omaha, Nebraska	October 21. Boyd's Theatre.
Kansas City, Missouri	October 23–24. Willis Wood Theatre.

St. Louis, Missouri	October 26–31. Olympic Theatre.
Louisville, Kentucky	November 3. MacAuley's Theatre.
Indianapolis, Indiana	November 4. English's Theatre.
Detroit, Michigan	November 5–7. Detroit Opera House.
Battle Creek, Michigan	November 9. Post Theatre.
Grand Rapids, Michigan	November 10. Powers' Theatre.
Fort Wayne, Indiana	November 11. Masonic Temple Theatre.
Akron, Ohio	November 12. New Colonial Theatre.
Canton, Ohio	November 13. The Grand Theatre.
Wheeling, West Virginia	November 14. Matinee and evening. Court Theatre.
Washington, D.C.	November 16. One week. New National Theatre

The company had two new members in the fall of 1903.

On closing night in Chicago, even standing room in the theatre was packed.

In Detroit, Jefferson performed *Rip Van Winkle, The Rivals, The Cricket on the Hearth*, and *Lend Me Five Shillings*.

In Battle Creek, Jefferson played to the largest house since the Post Theatre had opened, and took in $1,354.

In Wheeling, Jefferson played *Rip* in the afternoon and *The Rivals* in the evening. Prices were $2 for the orchestra, $1.50 for the dress circle, $1 for the balcony, seventy-five cents for the family circle, and fifty cents for the gallery. The performance was advertised six days in advance.

Jefferson opened with *Rip* in Washington and played it on Tuesday and Thursday evenings and the Saturday matinee. *The Rivals* was given on Wednesday and Friday nights and *The Cricket on the Hearth* and *Lend Me Five Shillings* on Saturday night.

In the spring of 1904 the Jefferson company played the following venues:

Macon, Georgia	April 4, 1904. Academy of Music.
Augusta, Georgia	April 5. Grand Opera House.
Charleston, South Carolina	April 6.
Columbus, South Carolina	April 7.
Charlotte, North Carolina	April 8. Academy of Music.
Atlanta, Georgia	April 9. Grand Opera House.
Montgomery, Alabama	April 12. McDonald's Theatre.
Mobile, Alabama	April 13. Mobile Theatre.
New Orleans, Louisiana	April 14–16. Tulane Theatre.
Natchez, Mississippi	April 18. Baker-Grand Theatre.
Jackson, Mississippi	April 19. The Century Theatre.
Memphis, Tennessee	April 20. Lyceum Theatre.
Nashville, Tennessee	April 21. The Vendome.
Lexington, Kentucky	April 22. Opera House.
Hamilton, Ohio	April 23. The Jefferson Theatre.
Philadelphia, Pennsylvania	April 25. One week. Broad Street Theatre.

Providence, Rhode Island   May 2. Providence Theatre.
Trenton, New Jersey   May 6. Taylor Opera House.
Paterson, New Jersey   May 7. Opera House.

By April 30, 1904, virtually all the seats in the parquet of the Providence Opera House had been sold for Jefferson's performance of *The Rivals* on May 2. Prices were $2.00, $1.50, $1.00, seventy-five cents, and fifty cents. "A large audience . . . filled every seat in the . . . Opera House. . . . Curtain calls were frequent, and to those at the end of the second act, . . . Jefferson responded with his customary happy speech and his assurance that the company were enjoying the performance quite as thoroughly as was the audience." In the company were Jefferson's godson, Jefferson Winter; Joseph Jefferson, Jr.; William Jefferson; and Joseph Jefferson, Jr.'s wife, Blanche Bender.

For information on the 1866–1867 season, see Celebrity Index, Chestnut Street Theatre Free Library of Philadelphia; Weldon B. Durham, ed., *American Theatre Companies, 1749–1887* (New York: Greenwood Press, 1986), 213; *Philadelphia Inquirer,* August 6 (3), October 29 (8), November 5 (2), November 8 (8), November 9 (2. 8), November 13 (5), November 15 (8), November 19 (2), November 23 (8) 1866; *New York Clipper,* November 17 (255), November 24 (262), December 1 (270), December 15 (286), December 29 (302) 1866; February 9 (351), March 9 (383), March 30 (406), April 6 (414, 415), April 20 (14), April 27 (22), June 29 (94), July 6 (102) 1867; *Daily National Intelligencer* (Washington), September 12 (2), September 28 (1), October 15 (2), October 25 (2), October 26 (2), December 3 (1), December 6 (1), December 11 (1), December 31 (1)1866; *American and Commercial Advertiser* (Baltimore), November 29 (1), December 1 (1, 2), December 3 (2), December 7 (2) 1866; January 8 (1), January 10 (1), January 11 (1), January 25 (1), January 28 (1, 2), May 20 (1), May 23 (1) 1867; Winter, *Life and Art,* 185; Broadside dated January 1867, Glase Scrapbook, Free Library of Philadelphia; *Daily Picayune* (New Orleans), February 27 (5), March 3 (3), March 12 (5, 9), March 17 (7), March 21 (5), March 23 (5), March 27 (5), March 28 (5), March 29 (5) 1867; Kendall, 331; *Mobile Daily Advertiser and Register,* February 15 (2), February 19 (2) 1867; and *Public Ledger* (Philadelphia), June 3 (1), June 7 (1), June 21 (3), June 26 (1) 1867.

For information on the 1867–68 season, see ALS Mast. Willie Seymour, August 17, 1867, The William Seymour Family Papers, Theatre Collection, Princeton University; *New York Dramatic Mirror,* January 29, 1905: 8; Winter, *Life and Art,* 185; *Chicago Tribune,* November 3 (2), November 4 (4), November 9 (4), November 16 (4), November 23 (4), December 21 (4) 1867; *Chicago Times,* November 5, 1867: 3; *New York Clipper,* August 10 (142), September 14 (182), October 5 (206), October 21 (222), October 26 (230), November 2 (238), November 9 (246), December 14 (286), December 28 (299) 1867; January 4 (311), January 11 (318), January 18 (326), February 15 (358), March 14 (390), April 4 (414), April 11 (6), April 18 (14), April 25

(22), June 20 (86) 1868; *Cincinnati Commercial,* December 22 (8), December 26 (8), December 27 (8), December 29 (8), December 31 (8) 1867; *Louisville Daily Democrat,* March 22, 1868: 2; Joseph Jefferson, "To My dear Mr. Ludlow," May 22, 1868(?), Missouri Historical Society Archives, St. Louis; *American and Commercial Daily Advertiser* (Baltimore), May 11 (1), May 14 (1) 1868; Daniel J. Watermeier, *Between Actor and Critic* (Princeton: Princeton University Press, 1971), 31; and *Daily Memphis Avalanche,* March 8 (2), March 13 (2), March 15 (2) 1868.

For information on the 1868–69 season, see *Chicago Tribune,* September 5 (4), September 14 (4), September 19 (4), October 4 (2), October 7 (4) 1868; *Milwaukee Sentinel,* October 26, 1868: 4; Clapp, 1: 49; Gladys Malvern, *Good Troupers All: The Story of Joseph Jefferson* (Philadelphia, Macrae Smith Co., 1945), 64; *New York Dramatic Mirror,* January 29, 1905: 8; July 4, 1908: 6; *Mobile Daily Register,* November 15 (1), December 28 (1) 1868; "Joseph Jefferson in the Capital City," Clipping Scrapbook, Jonathan Bourne Historical Center, Bourne, Massachusetts; James B. Runnion, "Joseph Jefferson," *Lippincott's Magazine* 4 (1869): 170; *Daily National Intelligencer* (Washington D.C.), March 25 (1), April 1 (2), April 3 (1), June 5 (1) 1869; *Daily National Intelligencer and Washington Express,* October 5 (1), October 21 (1), 1869; *American and Commercial Advertiser* (Baltimore), April 8 (1), April 12 (2), April 21 (2) 1869; *New York Clipper,* September 5 (174), October 3 (206), October 10 (214), October 17 (222), October 31 (288), December 5 (278), December 12 (286), December 26 (302) 1868; January 9 (348), January 23 (334), January 30 (342), February 13 (358), February 20 (366), March 6 (382), March 27 (408), May 1 (30), May 8 (38), May 15 (46) 1869; Broadsides dated May 3, 12, 29, 1869, Boston Theatre, Boston Public Library; *New York Times,* November 8, 1883: 4; Broadside dated May 27, 1869, UCLA Archive; Broadside dated May 28, 1869, Glase Scrapbook, Theatre Collection, Free Library of Philadelphia; *Cincinnati Commercial,* December 15 (8), December 22 (8), 1868; Broadside dated June 7, 1869, Paradise Valley Historical Society Collection, Paradise Valley, Pennsylvania; Broadside dated August 2, 1869, Mrs. Patricia Flynn, Kennebunkport, Maine; Bradford, *Atlantic Monthly,* 86; *Buffalo Commercial Advertiser,* November 5 (2), November 9 (2), November 16 (3), 1868; *Cleveland Daily Plain Dealer,* November 20 (3), November 24 (3), November 27 (3), December 3 (3) 1868; Winter, *Life and Art,* 186, 193; Davis, 67; and Broadside, Manuscripts, Rare Books, and University Archives, Tulane University Library, New Orleans.

For information on the 1869–1870 season, see *Mobile Daily Register,* January 29 (2), February 2 (2, 3), February 3 (8), February 4 (3), February 5 (3) 1870; *Daily Picayune* (New Orleans), January 10 (5), January 11 (2), January 16 (5), January 23 (5), January 27 (5), January 28 (5) 1870; *Memphis Daily Appeal,* December 18 (1), December 21 (4), December 24 (4), December 28 (4), December 30 (3), December 31 (1) 1869; *Chicago Tribune,* November 1 (4), November 14 (2), November 17 (4), November 18 (4),

November 26 (4), November 27 (4) 1869; *Boston Daily Advertiser,* April 18 (1), April 23 (1), 1870; *Public Ledger* (Philadelphia), May 30, 1870: 1; *Daily Morning Chronicle* (Washington, D.C.), March 16 (2), March 21 (2), March 24 (2), March 28 (2), March 30 (2), March 31 (2), April 2 (1, 2) 1870; *New York Times,* August 1 (7), August 3 (4), August 4 (7), August 6 (4), September 16 (4, 7), September 23 (7) 1869; *New York Clipper,* June 5 (70), June 19 (86), July 10 (110), August 14 (150), September 11 (182), September 18 (190), October 2 (206), October 9 (215), November 13 (254), November 27 (270), December 11 (286), December 18 (295) 1869; January 8 (318), January 15 (326), January 29 (339), February 5 (350), February 12 (358), February 19 (367), March 5 (383), April 2 (414), April 9 (7), April 23 (23), April 30 (31), May 7 (88), May 21 (54), May 28 (62), June 4 (70), June 18 (87) 1870; and Broadsides dated April 18, May 6, 1870, Boston Theatre, Boston Public Library.

For information on the fall 1870 season in New York, see Chapter 11. Jefferson performed only at Booth's Theatre in New York.

For information about the spring 1871 tour, see Winter, *Life and Art,* 173, 187; "Joseph Jefferson in the Capital City," n.p.; Copeland, 92; Celebrity Index, Free Library of Philadelphia; *Public Ledger* (Philadelphia), June 5 (1), June 17 (1) 1871; *New York Times,* April 9 (5), April 19 (5), June 27 (4), June 29 (7)1871; *Baltimore American and Commercial Advertiser,* April 17 (2), April 18 (2), April 20 (4) 1871; *Boston Theatre,* 173; *New York Clipper,* April 1 (414), April 15 (14), April 22 (22), April 29 (30, 31), May 13 (46), May 27 (62), June 10 (78), July 8 (110) 1871; and Watermeier, 31.

For information about the 1871–72 season, see *New York Clipper,* June 24 (94), July 1 (102), July 8 (110), July 22 (128), August 5 (142), August 12 (150), August 19 (158), August 26 (166), September 2 (174), September 16 (191), November 11 (204), November 18 (263), November 25 (271), December 2 (278), December 9 (286), December 16 (294), 1871; January 13 (327), January 20 (334), February 17 (366), February 24 (375), March 23 (406), April 6 (6), April 20 (22), April 27 (30), May 11(47), May 18 (55), June 15 (86) 1872; Eugenie Jefferson, 175–176; *Cleveland Daily Plain Dealer,* November 3 (3) November 7 (3), November 10 (3), November 11 (3) 1871; *State Journal* (Harrisburg, Pa.), February 19 (4), February 20 (4), June 15 (86), June 22 (94) 1872; and *Boston Theatre* 185.

For information on the spring 1873 season, see *Baltimore American and Commercial Advertiser,* January 1 (2, 4), January 3 (4), January 4 (4), January 6 (4) 1873; *New York Clipper,* August 3 (142), August 17 (158), September 14 (190), September 21 (198) 1872; January 11 (326), March 15 (398), March 23 (406), April 5 (6), April 12 (14), April 26 (30), May 10 (46), May 17 (55), May 24 (62), June 14 (86) 1873; and *Charleston News,* January 20 (4), January 24 (4), January 27 (2, 4), January 28 (4), January 29 (4), January 30 (4) 1873.

For information about the fall 1873, spring 1874, and 1874–75 seasons, see Celebrity Index, Free Library of Philadelphia; *Public Ledger* (Philadelphia),

November 30, 1874: 3; *Daily Picayune* (New Orleans), January 15 (1), January 17 (1) 1874; *New York Clipper,* November 8 (254), November 15 (262), November 22 (271), November 29 (278), December 13 (294), December 20 (302), December 27 (310) 1873; January 10 (326, 327), January 24 (342), January 31 (350), March 27 (444), May 2 (38), May 22 (60), September 12 (190), September 19 (199), September 26 (206), October 10 (222), October 24 (238), November 7 (251), November 14 (259), November 21 (267), November 28 (278), December 5 (286) 1874; January 16 (335), February 20 (375), April 17 (22), May 8 (46) 1875; *Wheeling Daily Register,* October 21 (2), October 26 (2, 3), October 27 (3) 1874; Eugenie Jefferson, 172–173; Winter, *Life and Art,* 188; *New York Times,* August 16 (3), August 27 (4), September 10 (5), November 9 (7), November 23 (7) 1874; May 24, 1875: 4; *News and Courier* (Charleston), December 16 (2), December 18 (2), December 20 (4) 1873; *Public Ledger* (Philadelphia), November 10 (1), November 22 (1) 1873; Broadsides dated May 3, Saturday, 1875, Boston Theatre, Boston Public Library; and Farjeon, *Portrait of a Family,* 103.

For information on the fall 1877 season, see *Sun* (Baltimore), December 18 (1), December 21 (1), December 24 (1), December 26 (1, 2), December 27 (1), December 28 (1), December 31 (1) 1877; January 2 (1), January 4 (1), January 5 (1) 1878; *New York Clipper,* November 10 (262), November 24 (279), December 8 (294), December 15 (303), December 29 (318) 1877; January 5 (327), January 12 (335) 1878; and *Providence Journal,* December 7 (3) 1877.

For information about the spring 1878 season, see *New York Clipper,* April 13 (22), April 20 (30), April 27 (38), May 4 (46), May 11 (54), May 18 (63), May 25 (70), June 15 (78), June 29 (110), July 6 (118), July 13 (126), July 22 (142) 1878; Clapp, 1: 104; Winter, *Life and Art,* 189; *New York Dramatic Mirror,* July 4, 1908: 6; Davis, 71; Celebrity Index, Free Library of Philadelphia; Program, Glase Scrapbook, Free Library of Philadelphia; Brown, 3, 22; Letter 100, Box 64, UCLA Special Collections; Lee, 61; *Public Ledger* (Philadelphia), April 1 (1), April 13 (1) 1878; *Daily Alta California* (San Francisco), June 2 (4), June 11 (4), June 12 (4), June 13 (1), June 23 (2, 4), June 27 (1), June 28 (1, 4), June 30 (2) 1878; *Deseret Evening News* (Salt Lake City), July 10 (2), July 16 (3) 1878; and *Rocky Mountain News* (Denver), July 12 (4), July 14 (1, 4), July 18 (4), July 21 (4), July 24 (4) 1878.

For information about the fall 1878 season, see *New York Clipper,* September 7 (190), September 14 (198), September 21 (207), October 12 (280), October 19 (258), October 26 (246), December 15 (299), December 21 (310), December 28 (318) 1878; *New York Times,* November 15 (11), December 17 (5), December 25 (4), December 30 (7) 1878; January 1, 1879: 7; Olympic Theatre program, September 30, 1878, Missouri Historical Society Library, St. Louis; and *New York Mirror,* January 4, 1879: 1, 2.

For information on the spring 1879 tour, see *New York Mirror,* February 8 (4), March 29 (7), April 5 (2), April 12 (7), April 19 (2, 7), April 26 (2), May

24 (4) 1879; *Public Ledger* (Philadelphia), April 14 (1), April 15 (1), April 26 (1) 1879.

For information on the fall 1879 season, see *New York Mirror,* June 5 (6), 1886, June 28 (5), August 2 (3), August 16 (3), September 13 (2, 3, 4), September 20 (2), October 4 (2, 3), October 11 (2, 3), October 25 (3, 4), November 1 (3, 6), November 8 (3, 6), November 15 (3), November 22 (3, 6), November 29 (3), December 13 (2, 6), December 20 (6) 1879; January 10 (2), January 31 (2, 6), February 7 (2, 6) 1880; Hunter, 77; Celebrity Index, Free Library of Philadelphia; Winter, *Life and Art,* 189, 193; *Sun* (Baltimore), November 28 (1), December 3 (1), December 4 (1) 1879; Joseph Jefferson, "To My Dear Willie," September 12, 1879, MS Collection 1427, Historic Hudson Valley, Tarrytown, New York; *Cleveland Plain Dealer,* September 20 (4), September 25 (4), September 26 (1, 4), September 30 (4), October 1 (1) 1879; *Providence Journal,* November 6 (3), November 10 (3), November 11 (3) 1879; and *Public Ledger* (Philadelphia), November 24 (1), November 27 (1), November 29 (1) 1879.

For information on the spring 1880 season, see *New York Mirror,* April 17 (9), May 1 (2, 5), May 8 (3), May 15 (9), May 22 (9) 1880.

For information on the fall 1880 and winter 1881 tours, see *New York Mirror,* August 21 (3), December 18 (3), December 25 (6), 1880; January 1 (3, 4), January 8 (3, 4), January 15 (2, 3), January 29 (4), February 19 (3), February 26 (9), March 5 (8) 1881; *Sun* (Baltimore), January 26 (1), January 28 (1) 1881; *New York Times,* November 14, 1880: 11; *Harrisburg Daily Patriot,* October 6 (4), October 7 (1) 1880; *Daily New Era* (Lancaster, Pa.), October 5, 1880: 3; *Reading Daily Eagle,* October 7 (4), October 8 (1) 1880; *Providence Daily Journal,* November 3, 1880: 3; The Robinson Locke Scrapbooks, 78: New York Public Library for the Performing Arts; Malvern, 80; Program dated January 14, 1881, Glase Scrapbook, Free Library of Philadelphia; *Missouri Republican* (St. Louis), March 6 (3), March 7 (3), March 8 (4), March 9 (4), March 13 (3) 1881; *Wheeling Register,* January 15, 1881: 2, 4; and Joseph Jefferson, "To My dear Willie," October 7, 1880, MS. Collection 1427, Historic Hudson Valley, Tarrytown, New York.

For information on the spring 1881 tour, see *New York Mirror,* February 12 (6), March 19 (6), April 23 (5, 9), April 30 (5), May 7 (5), May 14 (4) 1881; and *Missouri Republican* (St. Louis), March 13, 1881: 3.

For information on the fall 1881 and spring 1882 tours, see *New York Mirror,* July 16 (9), August 20 (10), September 3 (8), September 17 (3), October 1 (8), October 8 (8), October 15 (4), October 22 (5), October 29 (4), November 5 (4), November 19 (4), December 10 (4) 1881; April 15 (10, 11), May 6 (7, 10), May 13 (5, 8), May 27 (8) 1882; June 7 (10), June 14 (2) 1884; Celebrity Index, Free Library of Philadelphia; *Globe Theatre Programme,* December 3–December 8, 1888, Boston Public Library; *Pittsburgh Commercial Gazette,* December 26, 1881: 4; *Missouri Republican* (St. Louis), October 9 (3), October 11 (4), October 16 (3) 1881; *New York Times,*

September 4 (11), September 13 (5) 1881; Winter, *Life and Art,* 193, 215; Joseph Jefferson, "To My dear Willie," August 19, 1881, MS Collection 1427, Historic Hudson Valley, Tarrytown, New York; Clapp, 3: 311; Joseph Jefferson, "To Mr. Cist," October 7, 1881, the Historical Society of Pennsylvania; and *Public Ledger* (Philadelphia), April 17 (1), April 21 (4) 1882.

For information on the fall 1882 tour, see *New York Times,* September 15 (7), September 17 (9), September 19 (5), October 15 (9) 1882; *New York Mirror,* September 30 (2), November 5 (2), November 18 (4), December 2 (2), December 9 (4), December 30 (5) 1882; January 21, 1883: 7; Hunter, 83; Celebrity Index, Free Library of Philadelphia; Winter, *Vagrant Memories,* 18; Program 6: 93, MS 4467, Box 11, the Historical Society, Washington, D.C.; *Public Ledger* (Philadelphia), December 4, 1882: 1; Clipping File, John Callahan, Kutztown, Pennsylvania; *St. Louis Post Dispatch,* December 23 (7), December 26 (8) 1882; and *Missouri Republican* (St. Louis), December 24 (3), December 26 (5), December 31 (3) 1882.

For information on the spring 1883 tour, see *New York Mirror,* April 14 (8), April 21 (8), April 28 (18), May 12 (8), May 19 (4), June 2 (4) 1883.

For information on the fall 1883 tour, see Joseph Jefferson, "To My dear Willie," Envelopes, July 20, August 21, September 29, October 13, 1883, Ms. Collection 1427, Historic Hudson Valley, Tarrytown, New York; *New York Mirror,* July 7, 1882: 6; July 21 (7), August 4 (8), September 8 (3) 1883; September 1 (9), September 22 (4, 8), September 29 (3), November 17 (4, 9), December 1 (9), December 8 (4, 6, 9), December 15 (8, 9), December 29 (4, 6) 1883; January 3 (6), January 12 (2), January 19 (5, 8), January 26 (4, 5, 9), February 2 (8) 1884; January 3, 1885: 10; *New York Times,* September 3 (3), September 4 (4), October 7 (4, 5, 15), October 9 (7), October 21 (9) 1883; *Missouri Republican* (St. Louis), December 23 (3), December 25 (5) 1883; Autograph dated Chicago May 8, 1833, Archives, Sandwich Glass Museum, Sandwich Historical Society; Brown, 3: 225; Celebrity Index, Free Library of Philadelphia; and Program dated October 11, 1883, Glase Scrapbook, Free Library of Philadelphia; Clipping File, Historical Society of Pennsylvania, Philadelphia.

For information on the spring 1884 tour, see *New York Mirror,* February 2 (3), April 12 (6, 9), April 19 (8), April 26 (4, 5, 8, 9), May 3 (5, 8), May 10 (5, 9), May 17 (5) 1884; Hunter, 86.

For information on the fall 1884 season, see Broadside, Theatre Collection, Free Library of Philadelphia; Glase Scrapbook, Free Library of Philadelphia; Hunter, 86; *New York Mirror,* October 4 (5, 6), November 22 (6), December 8 (6), December 15 (7) 1884; *New York Times,* November 30, 1884: 15; and *Providence Daily Journal,* May 7, 1884: 3.

For information on the spring 1885 season, see *New York Mirror,* January 17 (6), January 24 (3), January 31 (4), February 14 (6), April 11 (7), May 2 (4, 8), 1885.

For information on the fall 1885 season, see Winter, *Life and Art,* 194;

Glase Scrapbook, Free Library of Philadelphia; Celebrity Index, Free Library of Philadelphia; *Public Ledger* (Philadelphia), November 30, 1885: 1; *New York Mirror,* September 10 (5), September 14 (10), November 28 (4), December 19 (6, 9) 1885; Clipping Book, John Callahan, Kutztown, Pennsylvania; *St. Louis Post Dispatch,* October 16, 1885: 5; and *Missouri Republican* (St. Louis), October 11 (3), October 13 (8), October 14 (10) 1885.

For information on the spring 1886 season, see *New York Mirror,* May 8 (4), May 15 (8) 1886.

For information on the fall 1886 season, see *New York Mirror,* July 6 (3), August 21 (9), August 28 (8), September 4 (5, 8), September 11 (5, 8), September 25 (2, 4, 5), October 2 (3), October 16 (4), October 23 (5), October 30 (4, 8), November 6 (8), November 13 (4, 5, 7), December 4 (2) 1886; Celebrity Index, Free Library of Philadelphia; Ruth Chiles, "The Birmingham Theatres 1886–1900," Master's thesis, Birmingham-Southern College, 1936, 31; Clipping File, John Callahan, Kutztown, Pennsylvania; *St. Louis Post Dispatch,* October 2, 1886: 12; and *Public Ledger* (Philadelphia), November 15, 1886: 1.

For information on the spring 1887 season, see *New York Mirror,* March 26 (5, 9), April 2 (5, 8), April 9 (9), April 23 (5, 8, 9) 1887.

For information on the fall 1887 season, see *New York Mirror,* August 6 (6), August 20 (8), September 17 (9), September 24 (5, 8), October 1 (4, 5), October 15 (4, 9), October 29 (9), November 5 (2, 3), November 12 (4, 9), November 22 (4), November 26 (2), December 10 (2) 1887; *New York Times,* October 27 (2, 8), October 28 (5), October 30 (2), November 22 (4), December 20 (2) 1887; Joseph Jefferson, "To George Knight," November 2, 1887, The Players, New York City; *Rip Van Winkle* folder, Free Library of Philadelphia; Joseph Jefferson, "To Col. Lamont," September 27, 1887, *Grover Cleveland Papers,* 2nd ser., Library of Congress, Washington, D.C.; Celebrity Index, Free Library of Philadelphia; Glase Scrapbook, Free Library of Philadelphia; *San Antonio Express,* February 13, 1937: 11; Joseph Jefferson, "To My Dear Wallack," MS 1428, Historic Hudson Valley, Tarrytown, New York; *Globe Theatre Programme,* Week of November 7–November 12, 1887, Boston Public Library; and Clipping File, Edwin A. Barron, New York Public Library for the Performing Arts.

For information on the spring 1888 season, see *New York Mirror,* March 10 (5, 7, 9), March 31 (5, 8), April 7 (8), April 28 (4, 8), May 5 (4), May 12 (8), May 19 (5), May 26 (5) 1888.

For information on the fall 1888 season, see *New York Mirror,* September 1 (8), September 22 (8), October 6 (4), October 13 (4), November 17 (5, 8), November 24 (8, 9), December 2 (4), December 9 (4, 5, 9), December 16 (11, 13), December 22 (8) 1888; January 5, 1889: 5; Glase Scrapbook, Free Library of Philadelphia; *New York Times,* November 11, 1888: 2; *Scranton Republican,* November 15, 1888: 3; and *Providence Daily Journal,* December 23 (8), December 29 (5) 1888.

For information on the spring 1889 season, see *New York Mirror,* April 20 (10, 13), April 27 (10, 17), May 4 (11, 12), May 11 (11, 12) 1889.

For information on the 1889–90 Jefferson-Florence Company tour, see Newspaper clipping, Sarah B. Hull Scrapbook, 63, Missouri Historical Society, St. Louis; *New York Dramatic Mirror,* September 14 (13), October 19 (8), November 16 (9, 13), November 30 (11, 13), December 7 (5, 9, 11, 13), December 14 (13), December 21 (9), December 28 (9, 12) 1889; January 11 (10), January 18 (9, 11), January 25 (9), February 1 (10), February 8 (4, 10), February 15 (12), February 22 (10, 12), March 8 (11, 12), March 15 (10, 12), April 5 (8, 13), April 12 (10), April 19 (13), April 26 (13) 1890; *Scranton Republican,* April 29 (3), May 1 (5) 1890; Program, Olympic Theatre, January 13, 1890, Missouri Historical Society Archives, St. Louis; Clipping File, John Callahan, Kutztown, Pennsylvania; *St. Louis Post Dispatch,* January 14 (3), January 19 (19) 1890; Program, February 17, 1890, Manuscripts, Rare Books and University Archives, Tulane University Library; Celebrity Index, Free Library of Philadelphia; "Joseph Jefferson Talks of his Art at the University of Pennsylvania," article dated November 1900, 301: 44, Robinson Locke Collection, New York Public Library for the Performing Arts; and Viola Allen Clipping File, New York Public Library for the Performing Arts.

For information about the 1890–91 tour of the Jefferson-Florence company, see *New York Dramatic Mirror,* October 18 (4, 11), November 8 (13), November 22 (12), November 20 (3), December 6 (12), December 13 (12), December 20 (4, 12), December 27 (10, 12) 1890; January 3 (11, 12), January 10 (10), January 17 (4, 5, 9, 10, 12), February 7 (10), February 21 (5), February 28 (11), March 7 (10, 11), March 14 (9, 10, 12), March 21 (10, 12), March 28 (9, 13), April 11 (5), April 8 (9), May 16 (5), May 23 (6), May 30 (3) 1891; January 27, 1892: 8; *New York Times,* October 2 (6), October 5 (12), October 10 (7), October 17 (8), October 26 (13) 1890; November 24, 1891: 9; Joseph Jefferson, "Letter to Mr. Henry S. Russell, Jr.," Autumn 1889, Miscellaneous Manuscripts Collection, Mrs. Copley Amory, AMI–AND Box 7, Library of Congress, Washington D.C.; *Sandwich Independent,* May 7, 1919, Bourne Archives, Sandwich, Massachusetts; Joseph Jefferson, "Letter to 'Dear Sir,'" November 10, [1889?], Ferdinand J. Dreer Autograph Collection, Historical Society of Pennsylvania, Philadelphia; Photograph, 1889, Miscellaneous Manuscripts Collection, Box 133, Library of Congress; Brown, *A History of the New York Stage,* 3: 340–341; Winter, *Life and Art,* 130; Clipping Book, John Callahan, Kutztown, Pennsylvania; *St. Louis Post Dispatch,* January 6, 1891: 10; Program dated November 14–November 29, 1890, Glase Scrapbook, Free Library of Philadelphia; Celebrity Index, Free Library of Philadelphia; Program dated December 15, 1890, MSD 420, Theater & Concert Collection, Historical Society of Washington, D.C.; Playbill, Olympic Theatre, January 5, 1891, Missouri Historical Society, St. Louis; and *Pittsburgh Post,* November 20, 1891: 1.

For information about the 1891–92 tour of the Jefferson-Florence company, later the Jefferson Comedy Company, see *New York Dramatic Mirror*, August 12 (8), October 10 (4), October 17 (15), October 31 (3), November 7 (13), November 28 (4, 10), December 26 (10, 13) 1891; January 2 (10), January 9 (9), January 16 (9), January 23 (10, 13), January 30 (10), February 6 (9, 12), February 13 (12, 18), February 20 (12), February 27 (10, 13), March 12 (10, 13), March 19 (10) 1892; January 29, 1905: 8; Brown, 3: 520; Celebrity Index, Free Library of Philadelphia; Joseph Jefferson, "To Mr. and Mrs. Clees," November 11, 1891, Autograph Collection of Simon Gratz, Historical Society of Pennsylvania, Philadelphia; Playbill dated December 14, 1891, National Theatre programs 1877–1903, Martin Luther King Library, Washington, D.C.; Barnes, 188; *New York Times*, September 29 (8), October 13 (4), October 18 (7), October 24 (2), November 7 (13), November 28 (4, 10), December 26 (10, 13) 1891; January 2 (10), January 9 (9), January 16 (9), January 23 (10, 13), January 30 (10), February 6 (9, 12), February 13 (12, 18), February 20 (12), February 27 (10, 13), March 12 (10, 13), March 19 (10), April 30 (4) 1892; *Trow's Directory*, 677; *Pittsburgh Post*, November 17 (1), November 20 (1), December 12 (3) 1891; *Evening News* (Detroit), November 19 (3), November 22 (2) 1891; *Minneapolis Tribune*, November 19 (4), November 20 (5) 1891; *Sunday News* (Charleston), January 14, 1892: 3; and *News and Courier* (Charleston), January 27 (8), January 30 (8) 1892.

For information on the fall 1892 tour, see *New York Dramatic Mirror*, October 8 (8), October 15 (2, 14), October 29 (13), October 29 (4), November 12 (13), November 19 (10, 11, 12), November 26 (13), December 3 (9), December 3 (9) 1892; January 3, 1893: 3; Rip Van Winkle File, Free Library of Philadelphia; Wilson, 287–288; Program dated October 18, 1892, UCLA Archives; Edmond M. Gagey, *San Francisco Stage* (New York: Columbia University Press, 1950), 180; Program dated October 11, 1892, Special Collection, University of California, Davis; Program dated November 21, 1892, National Theatre Programs 1877–1903, Martin Luther King Library, Washington, D.C.; Program dated November 28, 1892, Free Library of Philadelphia; Clipping Collection, John Callahan, Kutztown, Pennsylvania; and *St. Louis Post Dispatch*, December 13, 1892: 2.

For information on the spring 1893 tour, see *New York Dramatic Mirror*, April 5 (5, 7), April 8 (5, 7, 14), April 15 (5, 6, 13), April 22 (5, 6, 7, 10), April 29 (5, 6, 7, 10, 11), May 6 (5, 11), May 13 (8, 11), May 20 (4), June 10 (14), July 15 (8) 1893; Wilson, 281–283; and Clipping Collection, John Callahan, Kutztown, Pennsylvania.

For information on the fall 1894 tour, see *New York Dramatic Mirror*, August 18 (13), October 20 (10, 13), October 27 (14), November 10 (10), November 17 (10), November 24 (14), December 1 (6, 13), December 8 (8, 16), December 15 (4, 8, 9, 10), December 22 (9, 10), December 29 (4, 13) 1894; Program dated November 19, 1894, National Theatre Programs, 1877–1903, Martin Luther King Library, Washington, D.C.; and Eugenie Jefferson, 147–148.

For information on the spring 1895 tour, see *New York Dramatic Mirror,* March 23 (13, 17), March 30 (7), April 6 (4, 10, 14), April 27 (5, 8), May 4 (4), May 11 (11) 1895; and Broadside, March 31, 1895, Glase Scrapbook, Rip Van Winkle Folder, Free Library of Philadelphia.

For information on the fall 1895 season, see Nevins, *Letters,* 404, 406; Joseph Jefferson, "To Laurence Hutton," October 19, 1895, Laurence Hutton Correspondence Collection, Princeton University Library; Glase Scrapbook, Rip Van Winkle Production File, Free Library of Philadelphia; Brown, 3: 525; *New York Dramatic Mirror,* October 26 (18), November 2 (18), November 16 (7, 8, 11), November 23 (4, 7, 10, 12, 13), November 30 (4, 7), December 7 (4, 7, 10, 12), December 14 (3, 12), December 28 (10) 1895; Box marked Joseph Jefferson, Theatre Collection, Museum of the City of New York; Eugenie Jefferson, 236; *New York Times,* October 1 (7), October 15 (5), October 31 (7) 1895; and *Providence Daily Journal,* March 23 (7), March 26 (7), April 2 (5) 1895.

For information on the spring 1896 season, see *New York Dramatic Mirror,* April 25 (12, 22), May 2 (9, 14) 1896; and *Philadelphia Inquirer,* April 19, 1896: 22.

For information on the all-star tour of *The Rivals,* see Program, *The Rivals,* May 7, 1896, Collection of Mrs. Patricia Flynn, Kennebunkport, Maine; Clipping Collection, John Callahan, Kutztown Pennsylvania; *New York Dramatic Mirror,* May 9 (5, 14), May 16 (4, 14,15, 16), May 23 (13), May 30 (4, 6), June 6 (4) 1896; and Wilson, 220, 223.

For information about the fall 1896 season, see *New York Dramatic Mirror,* August 29 (13), October 3 (13), October 17 (4), October 24 (4), October 31 (7, 12), November 7 (5, 16), November 14 (3, 6, 7, 10), November 21 (3, 4), November 28 (13), December 5 (10), December 12 (11, 12, 14), December 19 (10) 1896; January 2 (12), January 23 (12) 1897; and Wilson, 289–290, 301.

For information about the spring 1897 season, see *New York Dramatic Mirror,* March 13 (10), March 27 (3), April 3 (4), April 10 (4), April 17 (5), April 24 (4, 7, 8) 1897; Eugenie Jefferson, 178–179; *Sunday News* (Charleston), April 4, 1897: 3; *News and Courier* (Charleston), April 5 (8), April 6 (8) 1897; and Francis Wilson, *Life of Himself* (Boston: Houghton Mifflin, 1924), 197.

For information about the fall 1897 season, see *New York Dramatic Mirror,* October 16 (6, 9), October 23 (4, 5, 9), October 30 (22), November 6 (3, 6, 19), November 27 (12), December 4 (3), December 11 (3, 10), December 18 (3, 4) 1897; Program, November 1, 1897, Box marked Joseph Jefferson, Museum of the City of New York; Program, November 8, 1897, MS 447, Box 2, Historical Society of Washington, D.C.; Rip Van Winkle File, Free Library of Philadelphia; Ruth Chiles, "The Birmingham Theatres 1886–1900," Master's thesis, Birmingham-Southern College, 1936, 159; Envelope, November 28, 1898, MS 1427, Historic Hudson Valley, Tarrytown, New York; Wilson, 131, 133–134; Tompkins, 454; and *Providence Daily Journal,* October 10 (10), October 15 (7) 1897.

For information about the spring 1898 season, see *New York Dramatic Mirror,* April 9 (6, 10), April 16 (6), April 23 (6, 10), April 30 (4, 6, 7, 8), May 7 (5) 1898.

For information on the fall 1898–winter 1899 season, see *New York Dramatic Mirror,* October 1(4, 6, 9, 14), October 8 (4, 5, 10, 14), October 15 (6, 10), October 29 (10), November 26 (10), December 3 (4), December 10 (12), December 24 (6, 7, 10, 12) 1898; January 7 (5, 7), January 28 (8, 10), February 4 (7, 10, 11), February 11 (7, 10), February 25 (7, 10), March 4 (6, 7, 10, 23), March 18 (6), March 25 (6)1899; *New York Times,* October 1 (12), October 2 (14), October 11 (7) 1898; and Joseph Jefferson, "To Edwina Booth Grossman," October 28, 1898, Winslow Purchase file, The Players.

For information about the spring 1899 tour, see *The Players* (New York: n.p., 1899), 36; Nevins, 509; Glase Scrapbook, Free Library of Philadelphia; Clapp 2: 174; Program dated April 10, 1899, National Theatre Archives, Washington, D.C.; *New York Dramatic Mirror,* December 17 (14), December 31 (14) 1898; January 7 (14), February 12 (14), April 1 (4, 5, 10, 23), April 8 (10, 12), April 15 (10, 12), April 22 (4, 10, 16), April 29 (6, 10) 1899; *New York Times,* April 9 (17), April 16 (17), April 17 (2) 1899; Robinson Locke Collection, 33, New York Public Library for the Performing Arts; and *News and Courier* (Charleston), March 30, 1899: 8.

For information on the fall 1899–spring 1900 season, see *New York Dramatic Mirror,* August 26 (12), September 30 (10, 14), October 7 (10), October 14 (4, 5, 6, 10, 12), October 21 (5, 10, 13), October 28 (6, 13), November 4 (4), November 12 (12), November 18 (4, 6, 10), November 25 (3), December 2 (5, 10), December 9 (10), December 16 (4, 5, 10), December 30 (8) 1899; January 6 (4, 5, 10), January 13 (10), January 27 (3, 10), March 10 (5, 10), March 31 (4, 10) 1900; Tompkins, 471; Joseph Jefferson, "To Mr. and Mrs. Thomas Shirley Clarke," September 17, 1899, The Players; New York City; and "Joseph Jefferson: Actor, Painter, & Fisherman," *Post Scripts . . .* (Summer 1988), 3.

For information about the spring 1900 season, see *New York Dramatic Mirror,* November 25 (14), December 9 (14) 1899; March 31 (3, 4, 5, 7, 10), April 7 (7, 15), April 14 (3, 4, 5, 6, 15, 23), April 21 (3, 7, 15, 16, 17), April 28 (3, 16, 17), May 5 (16), 1900; *The Players* (New York: n.p., 1900), 36; Joseph Jefferson, "To Edwina Booth Grossman," April 16 and April 18, 1900, The Players; Eugenie Jefferson, 225; *New York Times,* April 1 (11), April 16 (8), April 17 (9), April 22 (11), April 24 (8), May 6 (11) 1900; "JJPs Search for Mementoes and Open Membership Drive," Newspaper clipping, Sandwich Historical Society, Sandwich, Massachusetts; *Palm Beach News,* March 30, 1900: 3; Rip Van Winkle File, Free Library of Philadelphia; T. Allston Brown, 3: 80; "Joe Jefferson is a Real Diplomat," "The Jefferson Family," 307: 37, 39, Robinson Locke Collection, New York Public Library for the Performing Arts; Nevins, 520; and Wilson, 88–89.

For information on the fall 1900–winter 1901 season, see Joseph Jefferson,

"To Treasurer of the Philistine," August 15, 1900, Miscellaneous Manuscript Collection, Box 127, Hubbard, Elbert & Family, Library of Congress, Washington, D.C.; Joseph Jefferson, "To Laurence Hutton," August 23, 1900, Laurence Hutton Correspondence Collection, Princeton University Library; *New York Dramatic Mirror,* September 22 (6), October 6 (5, 10), October 13 (4, 7, 10, 12), October 27 (4, 10, 12), November 3 (3, 10), November 10 (3), November 17 (3, 10, 24), November 24 (16), December 1 (15), December 22 (60) 1900; January 12, 1901: 15; "Joseph Jefferson Talks of His Art at the University of Pennsylvania," article dated November 1900, 301, Robinson Locke Collection, New York Public Library for the Performing Arts; Clapp and Edgett, *Players of the Present,* 183; Joseph Jefferson, Rip Van Winkle Files, Glase Scrapbook, Free Library of Philadelphia; Joseph Jefferson, "To Meyers & Hediace," December 24, 1900, Manuscript Collection, New York Public Library at 42nd Street; Wilson, 86, n. 1.

For information about the spring 1901 and fall 1901 seasons, see *New York Dramatic Mirror,* February 16 (15), March 23 (15), April 6 (15), April 13 (4, 5), April 20 (4, 5, 10, 15, 23), April 27 (4), May 4 (4), May 11 (4), May 18 (12), June 12 (13), September 21 (6, 10), September 26 (23), October 5 (5, 6, 10), October 12 (8, 9, 10, 12, 24), October 19 (6, 7, 10, 24), October 26 (6, 10, 24), November 2 (3, 4, 6, 7, 10, 12), November 9 (3, 10, 12), November 16 (10), November 23 (3, 4, 10, 12, 13, 24), November 30 (4, 10, 13) 1901; January 12 (8), January 25 (5, 10), 1902; Joseph Jefferson, "To William Clarke," April 23, 1901, The Players; Rip Van Winkle Folder, Free Library of Philadelphia; *The Players* (1901) 35, 37; Wilson, 93, 135–136; Tompkins, 482; *New York Times,* April 17 (10), April 19 (16) 1901; Joseph Jefferson, "To Mr. Thomas," September 22, 1901, Heartman Collection, New York State Historical Society, New York City; Program dated November 11, 1901, National Theatre Archive, Washington, D.C.; "Observations," article dated October 13, 1901, Robinson Locke Collection, 301: 50; "Greatness of Greek Drama Defended," article dated October 21, 1900, 301: 51; and "Jefferson Talks of Stage Realism," article dated November 1, 1901, 301: 53, New York Public Library for the Performing Arts.

For information on the spring 1902 tour, see *New York Dramatic Mirror,* January 25 (8), February 15 (15), February 22 (15), April 5 (10, 24), April 12 (4, 6, 7, 10, 13, 15, 23), April 19 (4, 7, 5, 12, 15, 24), April 26 (6, 10, 15, 17, 24), May 3 (10, 15), May 10 (2), May 17 (15), May 24 (5), May 31 (5)1902; *New York Times,* April 20 (15), April 27 (9), May 1 (6), May 9 (7) 1902; Joseph Jefferson, "To Edwina (Booth) Grossman," March 29, 1902, The Players; *The Players* (New York: n.p., 1902), 36; "Joseph Jefferson Answers Last Call," Clipping Archives, The Jonathan Bourne Historical Society, Bourne, Massachusetts; Joseph Jefferson, "To My Dear Mr. Rogers," July 25, 1902, Philip H. Ward Collection, Box 14, Van Pelt Library, University of Pennsylvania, Philadelphia; "Jefferson Preaches a Sunday Sermon," article dated April 21, 1902, 302: 28; "An Offer Joseph Jefferson Could Not Accept," article dated April 27, 1902,

302 :30; "Hurl Questions at Mr. Jefferson," article dated April 30, 1902, 302: 31, Clipping, May 4, 1902, 302:37, Robinson Locke Collection, New York Public Library for the Performing Arts; and Probate Inventory, July 29, 1905.

For information about the fall 1902 season, see Rip Van Winkle Collection, Free Library of Philadelphia; *New York Dramatic Mirror,* July 5 (14), July 12 (13), September 20 (7, 12), September 27 (7), October 4 (5, 6, 10), October 11 (12, 24), October 18 (10, 12, 25), October 25 (12, 14, 15, 27), November 1 (4, 5,7, 9), November 8 (3, 4, 8, 10, 15, 24), November 15 (3, 10), November 22 (8, 12) 1902; "Failed Through Stage Fright," article dated October 5, 1902, Robinson Locke Collection, 302: 41; "Rip Van Winkle is a Busy Man. Jefferson at Work," *Inter Ocean*, October 12, 1902, Robinson Locke Collection, 302: 42, New York Public Library for the Performing Arts.

For information on the spring 1903 season, see Joseph Jefferson, "To Mrs. Edwina Booth Grossman," January 4, 1903, The Players; Joseph Jefferson, "To My Dear Mr. Currly," February 1, 1903, Autograph Collection of Simon Gratz, Historical Society of Pennsylvania, Philadelphia; Eugenie Jefferson, 225; "Joseph Jefferson is 75," Robinson Locke Collection, 302: 67, The New York Public Library for the Performing Arts; *New York Dramatic Mirror,* April 18 (5, 10, 23, 24), April 25 (2, 5, 7, 10, 24), May 2 (7, 15, 24), May 9 (6, 7, 10, 23), May 16 (5) 1903; *The Players* (New York: n.p., 1903), 51; *New York Times,* May 3 (4, 13), May 6 (3), May 9 (9), May 10 (11), May 12 (5), May 14 (9), May 15 (10), May 16 (7), May 18 (7)1903; *News and Courier* (Charleston), April 25 (8), April 28 (8) 1897.

For information on the fall 1903 and spring 1904 seasons, see Rip Van Winkle Collection, Free Library of Philadelphia; Lee, 54; *New York Dramatic Mirror,* September 26 (10), October 17 (10), October 24 (3, 4, 5, 12), October 31 (2 ,3, 5, 10, 15), November 7 (2, 6, 10), November 14 (3, 4, 7, 8, 12, 15, 17, 26, 29) 1903; April 9 (7), April 16 (4, 5, 6, 8), April 30 (6, 7), May 7 (3, 7, 9) 1904; *Wheeling Register,* November 3 (12), November 14 (3), November 15 (12) 1903; Program, April 16, 1904, Manuscript Collection, Tulane University Library, New Orleans; and *Providence Daily Journal*, May 1 (14), May 3 (8) 1904.

ENDNOTES

Introduction   *pages xv–xviii*
1. Daniel Frohman, *Daniel Frohman Presents* (New York: Scribner, 1935), 127; Francis Wilson, *Joseph Jefferson* (New York: C. Kendall & W. Sharp, 1906), 31.

1. A Property Child, 1829–1837   *pages 1–19*
2. William Winter, *Life and Art of Joseph Jefferson* (New York, 1894), 158; Russell F. Weigley, ed., *Philadelphia: A 300–Year History* (New York: W. W. North & Co., 1982), 218, 281; Gordon E. Kershaw, "600 Spruce Street: Case Study of a House," unpublished paper, University of Pennsylvania, December 18, 1963, 3, 8, 28.
3. Charles Burke was born March 27, 1822. William Winter, *The Jeffersons* (Boston, 1881), 94, 122; *Lancaster Journal,* October 21, 1831: 2; Francis Wemyss, *Chronology of the American Stage from 1752 to 1852* (1852; reprint. New York: Benjamin Blom, 1968), 26–27; Winter, *Life and Art,* 133, 156; *United States Gazette* (Philadelphia), November 14, 1818: 3; April 11, 1829: 3; Broadside dated January 28, 1829, Chestnut Street Theatre, January 1, 1829–March 12, 1849 file, Free Library of Philadelphia; *Notices of Marriages and Deaths in Paulsons's American Daily Advertiser, 1831–1833,* vol. 79 of *Collections of the Genealogical Society of Pennsylvania* (Philadelphia: n.p., 1903), 13; *New York Dramatic Mirror,* March 30, 1901: 14; Nathan Haskell Dole, *Joseph Jefferson at Home* (Boston, 1898), 21.
4. Philadelphia's *United States Gazette* lamented that "the current that has set against his profession these last few years, has not been without its effects upon his interests." The *New York Clipper* contended that the elder Jefferson had been financially ruined in an attempt to save his brother-in-law, William Warren, from bankruptcy. Michael Baker, *The Rise of the Victorian Actor* (Totawa, N.J.: Rowan & Littlefield, 1978), 65; *United States Gazette* (Philadelphia),

December 23, 1829: 2; *New York Clipper,* February 1, 1862: 332; Charles Durang, *History of the Philadelphia Stage Between the Years 1749 and 1855,* 2nd Series 148. This is a series of newspaper articles published in the *Philadelphia Sunday Dispatch* between 1854 and 1861 and then bound in folio by the Pennsylvania Historical Society. A microfilm of the volume is in the New York Public Library at Lincoln Center.

5. *American and Commercial Daily Advertiser* (Baltimore), January 8 (3), January 14 (3), February 2 (3), February 19 (3), February 26 (32), April 26 (3), May 6 (3), May 8 (3) 1830; *United States Gazette* (Philadelphia), September 1, 1829: 3; *Daily National Intelligencer* (Washington), September 9, 1829: 3; March 4 (3), April 22 (3), May 3 (3), May 19 (2), May 31 (2), June 7 (2) 1830.

6. Euphemia Anderson left the company to join a troupe in Annapolis, Maryland; she died there of a "long and lingering disease." Elizabeth Chapman was known in the family as "Aunt Bess." She had recently been widowed by the death of her husband, actor-manager Samuel Chapman. *Maryland Gazette* (Annapolis), July 15, 1830: 3; "Chat with Mrs. Germon," Germon: Mrs. Jane, Clipping Collection, New York Public Library at Lincoln Center; *Paulson's,* 79, 511.

7. The Washington Theatre was completed in 1821 and located on 6,617 square feet of land on Louisiana Street between Four-and-one-half and Sixth streets. It had been used by Philadelphia's Chestnut Street company as "a sort of summer retreat." The Jeffersons, who had been part of that company, knew it well. *Daily National Intelligencer* (Washington), August 6, 1829: 2; December 1, 1830: 2; Joseph Cowell, *Thirty Years Passed Among the Players in England and America* (New York, 1844), 82; I. Mudd, "Early Theatres in Washington City," *Records of the Columbia Historical Society, Washington, D.C.,* 5 (1902): 77; *New York Dramatic Mirror,* May 22, 1897: 9; Frances Anne Kemble, *Journal, 1832–33,* 2 (London, 1835): 119.

8. Joseph Jefferson III, "Letter to Mr. Cist," October 7, 1881, The Historical Society of Pennsylvania, Philadelphia.

9. Only five of the plays done had three performances, and only one, *The Flying Dutchman,* was performed more often.

10. *Daily National Intelligencer* (Washington), January 12, 1831: 3; Joseph Jefferson I, letter, April 5, 1830, The Historical Society of Pennsylvania, Philadelphia. William Winter refers to Jefferson's wife as Euphemia, although the *Daily National Intelligencer* calls her Jane. Since their eldest daughter was named Euphemia, the former name is more likely.

11. John Jefferson (1804–1831), the younger brother of Joe's father, had apprenticed as a theatre manager of touring companies for Philadelphia's Chestnut Street Theatre. He was described by Joe's biographer, William Winter, as the most brilliant, well educated, and versatile member of the family, an opinion presumably based on Winter's conversations with Jefferson family members. The *American and Commercial Daily Advertiser* (Baltimore), May 20, 1825: 3, notes that the "dresses" for the spectacular musical *Cherry*

and Fairstar were "designed by Mr. John Jefferson." In addition to expanding the range of John Jefferson's talents, this citation is interesting, because it is rare to find anyone in the period referred to as a designer. Fifty-six years later, one of Harrisburg's older citizens, Wien Forney, Jr., remembered the governor, his cabinet, judges of the state Supreme Court, and leading lawyers attending the theatre and financially underwriting Jefferson's season. Winter, *Jeffersons*, 94, 122; Wemyss, *Chronology*, 78; *Lancaster Journal*, April 29 (2), November 4 (2) 1831; *Harrisburg Chronicle*, August 22, 1831: 2; Paul E. Glase, "Annals of the Reading Stage: Early Theatre and Playbills," *Historical Review of Berks County* 12 (1946): 6; *Miner's Journal* (Pottsville, Pa.), August 21 (3), August 28 (3) 1830; July 2 (2), July 23 (3) 1831; *Berks and Schuykill Journal* (Reading, Pa.), June 4, 1831: 2; J. Monroe Kreiter, Jr., "The Tomb of Jefferson," *New York Clipper*, Clipping Collection, The Museum of the City of New York.

12. The Red Lion Tavern was located on West King Street in Lancaster; Mr. Boyer's Ball Room was in a tavern at the corner of Prince and Market Square in Reading. Felix Freichmann, "Amusements in Lancaster 1750–1940," *Papers Read Before the Lancaster County Historical Society* 45 (1941): 42; William Frederick Worner, "Theatre on West Chestnut Street, Lancaster," *ibid.* 37(1933): 161–162; *Lancaster Journal*, August 20, 1830: 3; May 13 (3), September 2 (2), September 9 (2) 1831; *York Dispatch*, September 18, 1942: 19; *Harrisburg Chronicle*, August 22, 1831: 2; *Pennsylvania Intelligencer* (Harrisburg), August 13, 1831: 3.

13. John's accident followed a benefit performance of *The School for Scandal*. Reports of his death differ; his fall was caused either by an apoplectic fit or by a slip on an orange peel. He died a few hours after his fall and was buried in the Episcopal burying ground. The *New York Clipper* reports the date of his death as September 4, 1831. Durang, 52; *Republican Banner* (Nashville), July 13, 1872: 4; *Miner's Journal* (Pottsville, Pa.), July 2, 1831: 2; *United States Gazette* (Philadelphia), August 25, 1828: 2; Broadside dated January 7, 1829, Chestnut Street File, January 1, 1829–March 12, 1849, Free Library of Philadelphia; *Marriages and Deaths from the Newspapers of Lancaster County Pennsylvania 1831–40* (Westminster, Md.: Family Line Publications, 1988), 72; *New York Clipper*, February 1, 1862: 332.

14. One of Joe's earliest biographers, James B. Runnion, wrote of Jefferson II in 1869:

> Jefferson loved his art too well to be successful in this most practical branch of it. His application was not equal to his fondness, and his work, like his character, was sketchy. It showed talent, but it lacked finish. The man and the artist were too much merged together to achieve great things. The family connection with the stage, and Jefferson's own familiarity with life behind the scenes, attracted him from the art which he should have made the study and practice of his life [scene painting].

> Yet his excessive modesty, in spite of serious application, kept him from making his appearance for several years, although he became a theatrical manager in the mean time.

James B. Runnion, "Joseph Jefferson," *Lippincott's Magazine* 4 (1869): 170.

15. The first Washington season lasted from December 5, 1831, to May 30, 1832. As Joe's grandmother died on January 11, 1831, at the age of fifty-six, she must have discovered him imitating Frimbley when he was not quite two years old. That the performance took place is verified by Jefferson's *Autobiography* and by the recollections of the veteran stock tragedian, Edmon S. Connor, who remembered "little Joe" dressed in white tights with a white wig and chalked face, posed on top of a small round table, imitating Frimbley's portrayal of "Ajax Defying the Lighting" and "The Discobulous." Winter, *The Jeffersons,* 123; *Paulson's,* 79, 122; *New York Times,* June 5, 1881: 10.

16. Jefferson's grandfather, father, and one of his Anderson cousins were also in the production. *New York Clipper,* October 17, 1877: 269.

17. The story does not appear in Elizabeth Jefferson Chapman's reminiscences as published by William Winter in *The Jeffersons.* Jefferson recollects that the production starred J. R. Scott, who performed *Pizarro* with the Jefferson company, but not until January 21, 1834. Joe would have been almost five years old at the time and a far more seasoned performer than the anecdote suggests. It is more likely that the Rolla in question was Harry Isherwood and that the performance took place on January 21, 1831, when Joe was not quite two years old. Elizabeth Chapman had played the child in an 1817 production and was to play Cora in an 1832 production. *New York Clipper,* October 17, 1877: 269; *Daily National Intelligencer* (Washington), January 21 1831: 3l; Richard Brinsley Sheridan, *Pizarro* (London, 1887), 179, 181, 189, 219; Howard Carroll, *Twelve Americans: Their Lives and Times* (1883, Freeport, New York, 1971), 356; *Autobiography,* 5–6; Francis Wilson.

18. Jefferson was feeling "the rude approach of age" and appeared only twenty-six times in a long season. After February 1832 he performed primarily at benefits, playing Sir Peter Teazle, Dogberry, and Polonius, parts he had done for years. The most utilized member of the company was Elizabeth Chapman (1810–1890), Jefferson I's third daughter, who within the next three years was to become one of the leading actresses of the Park Street Theatre in New York. *Daily National Intelligencer* (Washington), April 25, 1832: 2.

19. The *Pennsylvania Intelligencer* and the *Pennsylvania Telegraph* listed Jefferson's age as sixty-two. The old actor's grave was finally marked by a marble slab erected by Judge John Bannister Gibson of the Supreme Court of Pennsylvania. In 1867, when Joe was a star, it became necessary to move his grandfather's gravestone from the Episcopal cemetery. A resident of Harrisburg described the situation.

> The Episcopalians found it necessary to enlarge their Sunday school building, an extension which encroached upon the ground . . . for burial.

... Arrangements were ... made to remove all the dead ... to the Harrisburg [Mt. Kalmia] Cemetery. ... A gentleman in the city wrote to Joseph Jefferson in New York. ... Mr. Jefferson requested this gentleman to purchase a lot in the cemetery and have his grandfather's remains placed therein. This was done, ... the lot being surrounded by an ... iron fence. The slab which Judge Gibson ... placed ... over the remains has been raised ... to form a tomb, the expense for ... which was borne by the living Joseph Jefferson. The younger Joseph Jefferson never passes this shrine; he visits it Summer and Winter when in this city, and ... in cold winter, had to remove the snow and ice from the slab before the inscription could be read.

The above reminiscence, written in 1880, reflects the image that Jefferson conveyed to his public. Newspaper accounts in 1867 note that Attorney General Brewster and state senators Cameron and Coleman bore the expense of the reburial and that Cameron actually offered to deposit the remains in his own family lot in the new cemetery. While in Harrisburg on April 26, 1887, Jefferson visited his grandfather's grave. He found "a marble box about eighteen inches high, tightly cemented together and surmounted by a marble slab six feet long and three feet wide." A wire fence surrounded the plot, and Jefferson decided to erect a marble coping or low fence to dignify the site. The gravestone has recently been restored by the state of Pennsylvania. Jefferson I died intestate, and approximately one year after his death his children contacted a Philadelphia lawyer about inheriting their father's tenement and lot on Powell Street. *New York Mirror,* July 17, 1880: 7; *Daily National Intelligencer* (Washington), April 25 (3), May 28 (3), August 8 (3), 1832; *Lancaster Journal,* June 29, 1832: 3; Durang, 148; *Nashville Union,* August 4, 1843: 2; R. Pennsette, letter to Joseph Jefferson, August 7, 1833, The Historical Society of Philadelphia; Letter from Wien Forney, Jr., Harrisburg, Pa., dated July 12, 1880; *Harrisburg Daily Patriot,* October 7, 1880: 1; *New York Clipper,* June 29, 1867: 24; Glase Scrapbook, Free Library of Philadelphia; J. Monroe Kreiter, Jr., "The Tomb of Jefferson," *New York Clipper,* clipping file, The Museum of the City of New York; *Pennsylvania Intelligencer* (Harrisburg), August 9, 1832: 3; *Pennsylvania Telegraph* (Harrisburg), August 8, 1832: 3; *Pennsylvania Reporter* (Harrisburg), August 10, 1832: 3.

20. While on tour during the summer of 1832, the MacKenzie-Jefferson company supported the touring English star Thomas Abthorpe Cooper. *Lancaster Journal,* July 6, 1832: 2; Wemyss, *Chronology,* 76; Durang, 2; Lawrence Barrett, *Edwin Forrest* (Boston, 1882), 46.

21. James B. Runnion noted:

Perhaps [Jefferson II] never would have made an appearance in character, had it not been for a circumstance which involved his keeping faith with the public—a matter in which he was strictly conscientious. This circumstance occurred in 1832, when he was managing a theatre in

Washington. An unusually large audience assembled . . . when a play was to be given in which the comedian of the company was cast for the leading part. While the orchestra played the . . . overture, . . . there was great commotion behind the scenes. The comedian was nowhere to be found, and manager Jefferson was in despair. Waiting until the last, unwilling to make an apology or dismiss the audience, and urged . . . by . . . the company, Mr Jefferson resolved to play the part. . . . The part was one which Jefferson had studied . . . , but in which . . . he could never make up his mind to appear. Yet, with no preparation . . . he made his *debut*, and attained a marked success.

Daily National Intelligencer (Washington), October 3, 1832: 3; Runnion, 170; William Dimond, *The Hunter of the Alps* (New York, 1804), 18.

22. To "jump Jim Crow" was to perform the song and steps that went along with the musical number for which Rice was famous. Francis Wilson, who performed in Jefferson's version of *The Rivals,* contends that in 1895 Mrs. John Drew told him "that she was present at Rice's benefit performance and remembered well Mr. Jefferson's appearance and mimicry of Rice, which was received with uproarious laughter." Mrs. Drew, then Louisa Lane, born January 10, 1818, would have been fifteen at the time. There is, however, no evidence that she was a member of the Jefferson company in 1833. Brander Matthews and Laurence Hutton, *Actors and Actresses: Joseph Jefferson* 2 (Harvard, *ca.* 1889), n.p; Amy Leslie, *Some Players' Personal Sketches* (Chicago, 1899), 289. Wilson, 22; *New York Dramatic Mirror,* January 5, 1895: 2; January 12, 1901: 14.

23. MacKenzie also led a tour to Lancaster, Pennsylvania, in late November 1832. The Baltimore-Washington division of the Jefferson company hurt the theatre in both cities. With its financial resources split, the group had little money for newspaper advertising. Advertisements became smaller and less frequent in Washington and seldom appeared in Baltimore—which in any case had a poor reputation for theatre. The Anglo-American managers, Francis Wemyss and Joseph Cowell, thought Baltimore "the worst theatrical town in America." Cowell blamed the Chestnut Street company of Philadelphia: "Baltimore had for years been visited by Warren and Wood with the same jog-trotting company and the same old pieces, till they had actually taught the audience to stay away."

The problem, however, may have been the city's size and lack of culture. In 1837 the French traveler Count Francesco Arese reported: "Taking everything into consideration, Baltimore is, in its atmosphere, much more the small town than Philadelphia and very much more than New York." *American and Commercial Daily Advertiser* (Baltimore), January 2, 1833: 3; Wemyss, *Theatrical Biography,* 148; Cowell, 82; Count Francesco Arese, *A Trip to the Prairies and in the Interior of North America (1837–1838)* (New York: Harbor Press, 1934), 13.

24. Fanny toured with her father, Charles Kemble. Her journal was, in the opinion of her scandalized contemporary, New York businessman Philip Hone, totally uncensored: "I cannot believe that she . . . intended it should see the light. . . . It was evidently written on the evening of the very day [the events occurred]." Kemble, 1: viii; Bayard Tuckerman, ed., *The Diary of Philip Hone, 1828–1851* 1 (New York, 1889), 126.

25. Fanny's opinion of the company and the quality of its performances was shared by Philip Hone. In Washington, on business, he visited the theatre to see the young actress he had admired in *Hamlet* and had entertained socially. Hone remarked that "Fanny Kemble in the Washington theatre is like a canary bird in a mousetrap." Kemble, 2, 112–114.

26. Allan Nevins, ed., *The Diary of Philip Hone, 1828–1851* (New York: Dodd Mead & Co., 1936), 116; Kemble, 2: 136.

27. Jefferson recollected having performed with the elder Booth "when I was but five years of age" and shortly after Booth's son Edwin was born (November 13, 1833). Jefferson's chronology was not absolutely accurate, but then he was speaking in 1893 about an event that had occurred sixty years before. It is also possible that the performance with Booth could have taken place in Baltimore on January 21, 1833, when Jefferson was not quite four. *Daily National Intelligencer* (Washington), January 8, 1834: 3; Joseph Jefferson, "In Memory of Edwin Booth," Thomas B. Reed, ed., *Modern Eloquence* (Philadelphia: John D. Morris and Co., 1901), 691; Wilson, 144; *American and Commercial Daily Advertiser* (Baltimore), January 21, 1833: 3.

28. Box seats went from seventy-five cents to one dollar. Pit seats went from thirty-seven and a half cents to fifty cents. *New York Clipper,* November 24, 1877: 277.

29. *Daily National Intelligencer* (Washington), November 26, 1833: 3; January 15 (3), April 12 (6), April 18 (3), May 19 (3) 1834; Runnion, 170.

30. Fanny Kemble complained: "I cannot act tragedy within half a yard of the people in the boxes." Kemble, 2, 123; *Daily National Intelligencer* (Washington), January 9 (3), September 11 (2), September 25 (2) 1835; Tyrone Power, *Impressions of America during the Years 1833, 1834 and 1835* 1 (London, 1836): 210.

31. John S. Buckingham, the English temperance lecturer and traveler, noted in 1838 that "gas is as yet nowhere in Washington, and oil is very scantily supplied." *Daily National Intelligencer* (Washington), August 6, 1829: 2; James Silk Buckingham, *America: Historical and Descriptive,* 1 (London, 1841): 321.

32. Francis J. Grund, *The Americans in their Moral, Social and Political Relations,* 2 (London, 1841): 119.

33. The Northern Exchange was located on Third Street below Green. Jefferson closed the theatre when the Third Street portion of the building was scheduled to be demolished to provide space for an extension of Spring Garden Street. After Jefferson's managerial stint ended, he and Cornelia

continued to perform at the Northern and Walnut Street theatres. Alexander MacKenzie returned to the bookstore business in Washington, and three of the Jeffersons went to New York. David Ingersoll began to appear at the Bowery Theatre, and his wife, Mary-Anne, made her New York debut as Mrs. Ingersoll on August 14, 1834. That fall, Elizabeth Chapman also opened in New York as Ophelia. According to the American historian George C. D. Odell, "Mrs. Chapman was the best leading lady the Park had for years, her personal charm, her intellect (common to the Jeffersons), her instinct for acting and her ability as a songstress, ranking her . . . as one of the most versatile actresses of Park history." Successful in both high comedy and tragedy, Mrs. Chapman performed at the Park through July 2, 1835. *Evening Post* (New York), May 27 (3), August 13 (3), September 1 (3), 1834; July 2, 1835: 3; George C. D. Odell, *Annals of the New York Stage*, 4 (New York: Columbia University Press, 1938): 2; Arthur Herman Wilson, *A History of the Philadelphia Theatre, 1835 to 1855* (Philadelphia: University of Pennsylvania Press, 1935), 130–34; Glazer 177; *United States Gazette* (Philadelphia), January 8 (3), January 9 (3), January 31 (3), February 9 (3), March 18 (3), March 24 (3), April 1 (3), April 2 (3), April 9 (3) 1835; *Daily National Intelligencer* (Washington), May 22, 1835: 1.

34. Joseph and Cornelia appeared in Wilmington in January 1835, and were joined in April by Mary-Anne Ingersoll and Jane Anderson. They played a short engagement in Wilmington from April 21 until May 2, 1835, after which the Jeffersons rejoined the parent troupe in Philadelphia. By July 4 they were back in Wilmington, with Jefferson sharing the managerial responsibilities. They played Wilmington from July 4 to August 21. *Delaware Gazette and American Watchman* (Wilmington, Del.), April 21 (3), April 28 (2), July 21 (3) 1835; *American and Commercial Daily Advertiser* (Baltimore), May 16 (3), May 25 (3), November 10 (3) 1835; Broadside, Walnut Street Theatre, September 27, 1812–November 27, 1849, Theatre Collection, Free Library of Philadelphia; *United States Gazette* (Philadelphia), April 27, 1835: 3.

35. Following this pantomimic episode, Alexis calls to the entering Lowina: "Mother, dear mother, I perish with the cold," one of two lines allotted to the part. William Barrymore, *The Snow Storm; or Lowina of Tobolskow* (Baltimore, 1833), 21.

36. In 1835 Joe's half-brother, Charles Burke, then thirteen years old, left the family in Philadelphia for a brief period and went to New York, where he played at the Franklin Theatre on September 7. The Jeffersons played in Baltimore until December 2. While there, they were reunited with Elizabeth Chapman, Joe's aunt. In June 1835 she became engaged to a Baltimore businessman, Augustus Richardson, and according to Charles Durang, was forced to give up a $3,500-a-year salary and retire from the stage "in conformity with the usual respectable position in society." She was married in Baltimore on July 7, 1835, but her retirement was brief. When her husband ran into financial problems, she returned to the stage as Mrs. Richardson, first in Washington and later in Baltimore and New York.

In December 1835 Joseph and Cornelia Burke Jefferson moved back to Washington to appear at the new National Theatre. Ironically, they found themselves in competition with a company run by their brother-in-law, Alexander MacKenzie, at their old Washington theatre. MacKenzie's company featured Hester Jefferson MacKenzie, Mary-Anne Jefferson Ingersoll, Jane Anderson, and, in a starring engagement, Elizabeth Jefferson Richardson. By Thanksgiving, however, MacKenzie's troupe had folded, beset by competition and poor reviews, and the MacKenzies joined the National Theatre, where their three-year-old daughter was described by a reviewer as "the interesting infant . . . who enacted her part very prettily." *United States Gazette* (Philadelphia), July 13 (2), August 24 (3), August 28 (3) 1835; *Evening Post* (New York), September 7 (3), December 12 (3) 1835; *American and Commercial Daily Advertiser* (Baltimore), July 9 (2), September 29 (3), September 30 (3), October 6 (3), November 14 (3) 1835; T. Allston Brown, *History of the American Stage* (1870; rpt. New York: Benjamin Blom, 1969), 193; Mary Shaw, "The Human Side of Joseph Jefferson," *Century Magazine* 85 (1913): 380; Durang, 36; Wemyss, *Chronology*, 80; *Evening Star, for the Country* (New York), September 18 (1), November 17 (3) 1835; *Daily National Intelligencer* (Washington), October 15, 1835: 3; March 16, 1836: 3; *New York Clipper,* February 1, 1862: 332.

37. In 1824 Joe and Cornelia had performed at the Chatham Garden Theatre. The Franklin, "far out of the fashionable districts," was located at 175 Chatham Street between James and Oliver Streets. It was twenty-five feet wide and seated six hundred to a thousand people in its pit and three tiers of boxes. *Evening Post* (New York), September 29, 1835: 3; Odell, 4: 89, 91; Joseph N. Ireland, *Records of the New York Stage from 1750 to 1860,* 2 (New York, 1867): 165; Mary C. Henderson, *The City and the Theatre: New York Playhouses from Bowling Green to Times Square* (Clifton, New Jersey: J. T. White, 1973), 66; *Evening Star, for the Country* (New York), July 28 (3), September 11 (2), September 22 (2) November 20 (3), 1835; Dole, 21.

38. Jefferson's recollection of the building's number and of Sefton's tenancy is borne out by the city directory of the period. Sefton was an English actor born in Liverpool, with whom the Jeffersons had worked at the Walnut Street Theatre in Philadelphia in January 1835. His line of business at the Franklin was that of first low comedian. A plate by C. A. Vanderoof published in the *Autobiography*'s original edition identifies the cemetery. The site, the oldest Jewish cemetery in Manhattan, had been purchased in 1682 by a band of Sephardic Spanish and Portuguese Jews fleeing to New Amsterdam from the Spanish inquisition. Federal Writers' Project, *New York City Guide* (New York: Pantheon Books, 1982), 117; *Autobiography,* 15; Broadside dated January 17, 1835, Walnut St. Theatre, September 27, 1842–November 24, 1849 file, Free Library of Philadelphia; *New York Dramatic Mirror,* January 19, 1901: 14; *New York Clipper,* September 26, 1868: 198; *Longworth's American Almanac New-York Register and City Directory* (New York, 1836), 357, 593.

39. Ludlow set Jefferson's salary at $30 a week during a season of at least

twenty-four weeks and $22 a week during a summer season of at least eighteen weeks. Cornelia was offered work at $25 a week in the winter and $18 a week in the summer. Charles Burke was offered $10 a week, winter and summer. Jefferson and his wife were each to get two benefits a season, receiving a third of the receipts on each benefit night. "Master Burke" was also to get two benefit nights. Letter Book of Ludlow & Smith (1835–1844), 75, Missouri Historical Society, St. Louis.

40. Jane Anderson, who specialized in chambermaids and old women, married Greenbury C. Germon, and Elizabeth Anderson married Jacob A. Thoman, a character actor from Philadelphia. Mary-Anne Ingersoll appeared at her brother's benefits at the Chatham. Charles Burke, then fourteen, found work performing boys' parts and comic songs at the National Theatre on the northwest corner of Church and Leonard streets along with Cornelia Jefferson and Mary-Anne Ingersoll. Elizabeth Richardson performed star engagements at the Franklin and appeared, along with David Ingersoll, in her brother's benefits. Elizabeth later divorced Jacob Thoman, who by 1878 was an inmate at the Forrest Home for indigent elderly actors in Philadelphia. She remarried and appeared in San Francisco theatres as Mrs. Saunders. Greenbury C. Germon died in Chicago on April 14, 1854. *Evening Post* (New York), May 9 (3), June 1 (3), June 6 (3), June 13 (3), August 23 (3), October 20 (3) 1836; March 1 (3), May 6 (3) 1837; Ireland, 2: 93, 158, 170, 171, 194, 201; Jack H. Neeson, "The Devil in Delaware. A Study of Theatre in New Castle County," diss., Case Western Reserve U., 1959, 1:106; *Quincy (Ill.) Whig,* May 2, 1840: 2; *Autobiography,* 14; *New York Times,* March 30, 1898: 7; *New York Clipper,* January 26 (349), February 2 (357), March 16 (405), March 29 (413) 1878.

41. Odell, 4: 180–3, 246; *Evening Post* (New York), July 18 (3), September 21 (3), September 23 (3), September 30 (3) 1837; "Mrs. Jane Germon," Clipping Collection, New York Public Library for the Performing Arts; Broadsides dated January 17, 1835 and March 13, 1835, Walnut Street Theatre, September 27, 1812–November 27, 1849 file, Free Library of Philadelphia.

42. Count Francesco Arese wrote: "Balls, suppers . . . dinners, and other gayeties are . . . suspended, because of the . . . bad state of business. . . . This last month there have been a hundred bankruptcies for more than a hundred million francs." The anonymous author of *The Actor* remembered that "the Commercial revulsion of 1837, which spread like a hurricane through the land, affected every branch of the arts." Arese, 206; *The Actor; or a Peep Behind the Curtain* (New York, 1846), 175.

2. The Jeffersons in the West, 1836–1847 *pages 20–32*

43. By June 1836 MacKenzie was in Buffalo, where his and Hester's infant son, Jefferson, died on June 6, 1836. By the time he came west, David Ingersoll's career was not going well. Joseph Ireland wrote of him: "His personal appearance was fine, and his natural abilities were . . . of a superior order; and had discretion guided his career, he might have lived to become the first of American actors."

"Discretion" is Ireland's euphemism for sobriety. Charles Durang wrote that Ingersoll "fell victim to dissipation which finished his career at an early age, which career with common prudence would have been . . . brilliant." *Daily National Intelligencer* (Washington), June 6, 1836: 3; Alexander MacKenzie, *A Letter to the Rev. Samuel C. Aikin* (Cleveland, 1836), 1; Gerhard Walter Gaiser, "The History of the Cleveland Theatre from the Beginning to 1854," diss., State U. of Iowa, 1953, 333; Marion Cole, "Theatrical and Musical Entertainment in Early Cleveland 1796–1856," thesis, Case Western Reserve U., 1958, 71–72; Ireland, II: 88; Neeson, I: 107.

44. Isherwood and the MacKenzies performed at the City Theatre in Detroit between June 6 and September 2, 1837, and later at the Detroit Museum until September 9. In later life Isherwood became the scenic artist at Lester Wallack's Theatre in New York.

According to Charles Durang, Ingersoll's "irregular and wild disposition combined with a heart given to ill-considered generosity which knew no bounds in its offerings" led him to drink and poverty. Ingersoll initially left MacKenzie and Isherwood to play Lexington, Kentucky. A fellow actor found him "in the last stage of distress and gave him a hundred dollars." Ingersoll drifted south to Nashville, where a disease described as "inflammation of the brain" set in, and he died at the Exchange Hotel on August 6, 1838. Gaiser, 43; *New-York Daily Times*, September 1, 1853: 5; Douglas Charles McKenzie, "The Acting of Joseph Jefferson III," diss., U. of Oregon, 1973, 64; *Observer and Reporter* (Lexington, Kentucky), April 14 (3), April 28 (3), May 9 (3), May 16 (3), May 26 (3), May 30 (3), June 2 (3) 1838; Durang, 203; *Daily Republican Banner* (Nashville), May 5 (2), July 3 (2), July 12 (2), August 7 (3) 1838; *Nashville Whig*, August 8, 1838: 3.

45. The MacKenzie-Isherwood company performed in Cleveland until September 26, 1837, and opened in Chicago shortly after October 7, 1837. *Chicago American*, November 4, 1837: 2; *Sangamo Journal* (Springfield, Ill.), March 10 (3), March 24 (2) 1838; *Chicago Democrat*, December 27 1837: 3.

46. The Jeffersons toured to Syracuse, Utica, Auburn, Waterloo. and Rochester. *New York Mirror*, September 29, 1888: 2.

47. In Buffalo the Jeffersons performed with a company that included Warren's sister, Anna, who was married to the celebrated Yankee comedian Danforth Marble. *New York Mirror*, September 29, 1888: 2; *Philadelphia Record*, August 11, 1909: 13.

48. Isherwood appears to have intended to remain with the Jeffersons. He built the Rialto theatre and petitioned the Common Council of Chicago for a license. But Joe's father was not impressed with the painted drop curtain, and a company this size certainly did not need two scenic artists. By mid-August 1838, Isherwood was back in Detroit, and Jefferson had taken his place as MacKenzie's partner. Common Council Records, Chicago, Illinois, Petition of Isherwood and MacKenzie for Theatre License, Document 635; Remonstrance against Theatre in Rialto, Filed May 1, 1838, Document 629; Minority Report of

Committee on Theatres, Document 505, The Illinois State Historical Library, Springfield; *Chicago Times,* May 7, 1876: 2; April 1, 1891: 6; Joseph Jefferson, "To J. H. McVicker," Christmas 1882, Chicago Historical Society; *Chicago American,* September 5, 1839: 2; *Autobiography,* 22–24; Otis & Eddy Account Book, Chicago Historical Society 121; *Detroit Free Press,* August 13, 1838: 3.

49. *Autobiography,* 24; *Philadelphia Record,* August 11, 1909: 13; Otis & Eddy Account Book, 121; Day Book, *Chicago American,* Chicago Historical Society, 30, 52.

50. Jane Germon remembered the trip to Galena:

> We reached the stage-coach station early in the morning, nearly starved. The only restaurant . . . was a . . . shanty made of rough boards. It was the most uninviting looking place, for the wind was whistling through the cracks. . . . We were to take breakfast there, but when I saw the place I groaned: "Nothing good to come out of that place."
>
> But I was . . . surprised. What do you think they gave us for breakfast? Wild turkey, pork chops . . . and buckwheat cakes and honey. The people in the neighborhood of Chicago didn't have such luxuries as tea and coffee; so we had to get along without them, but they gave us a substitute for tea that was made of herbs. . . . I didn't care much for the tea, but I never forgot the taste of that wild turkey!

Mrs. Jane Germon Clipping Collection, New York Public Library for the Performing Arts; *Autobiography,* 25; *North Western Gazette and Galena Advertiser,* October 27, 1838: 2; Don B. Wilmeth, "The MacKenzie-Jefferson Theatrical Company in Galena, 1838–1839," *Journal of the Illinois State Historical Society* 60 (1967): 26; Robert Dale Farrell, "The Illinois Theatrical Company 1837–1840," thesis, U. of Illinois, 1964, 26; August L. Chetlain, *Recollections of Seventy Years* (Galena, 1899), 176.

51. The Jeffersons performed a benefit for the Galena fire department on February 4, 1839. By February 22 they were on their way to Mineral Point, Wisconsin, stopping for two performances in Galena, where they returned in early April 1839. The *Autobiography*'s story about the company's wardrobe, scenery, and properties falling through the ice is probably apocryphal. Jefferson failed to mention the incident in a conversation "in the latter part of the 80's" with August Chetlain, who was a resident of the region. Moreover, William Warren, who was twenty-seven in 1839, did not mention it in a letter to J. H. McVicker about his early days in Illinois. *Northwestern Gazette and Galena Advertiser,* February 7, (2), February 21 (3), 1839; Chetlain, 176; Bruce E. Mahan, "The Iowa Thespians," *Palimpsest* 4 (1923): 22; Charles L. Geroux, "The History of Theatres and Related Theatrical Activity in Dubuque, Iowa 1837–1877," diss., Wayne State U., 1973, 1: 41, 73 n., 83.

52. Between Burlington, Iowa, and Springfield, the Jeffersons played Peoria, Quincy, Alton, and Pekin, Illinois. In Quincy they opened in the Court House on May 13, 1839. They ran into "bad weather" and played to houses that were

"thin" to "tolerably well-filled" until June 5, 1839, when they took the steamer *Ben Franklin* to Alton. They performed in Alton through June 8, 1839, and then in a pork house in Pekin, Illinois. That spring they also toured to Palmyra, Missouri. Chetlain, 178, 187; *Autobiography*, 27; *Daily Picayune* (New Orleans), May 28 (2), June 3 (2) 1839; Farrell, 42, 44, 47; *Quincy Whig*, May 11 (3), June 1 (2), June 8 (2) 1839; *Daily American* (Chicago), June 6, 1839: 2; *The Alton Telegraph*, June 8, 1839: 2; *Palmyra Missouri Whig and General Advertiser Weekly*, May 23, 1840: 2; *Sangamo Journal* (Springfield), June 21, 1839: 2; Ruth Hardin, "Lincoln and the Jefferson Players," *Journal of the Illinois State Historical Society* 40 (1947): 445.

53. Religious revivals posed problems for theatrical companies in the period. The *Daily Picayune* (New Orleans), June 3, 1839: 2, reports: "According to the *Chicago Democrat* the theatrical company of that city . . . is . . . timid about visiting Chicago since the revival, but as steamboats are bringing on . . . many . . . sinners, . . . a theatre can soon be well supported." *Autobiography*, 28–30; *Sangamo Journal* (Springfield, Ill.), June 21, 1839: 2; John Carroll Power, *History of the Early Settlers of Sangamo County, Illinois* (Chicago, 1881), 273; Hardin, 334.

54. Between Springfield and Chicago, the Jeffersons played Jacksonville, Peru, and Ottawa. By the third week of August, when the company was in Juliet (now Joliet), Joe's father was in Chicago, preparing the Rialto (which had suffered a fire during the summer) for their third season. Day Book, *Chicago American*, Chicago Historical Society, 106; *Daily Chicago American*, June 2, 1839: 2; *Chicago American*, August 19, 1839: 2.

55. A number of the company's members, including William Warren and Mary-Anne Ingersoll, had become ill on tour. *Oliver Twist* had premiered the preceding February at New York's Park theatre with Joe's aunt, Elizabeth Jefferson Richardson, in the title role. Odell, IV: 283; *Chicago Daily American*, September 16 (2), September 23 (3), September 30 (2) 1839; *Daily Chicago American*, September 3, 1839: 2.

56. By November 4, the Jeffersons were in Aurora. In Springfield the Jeffersons performed in the dining room of W. W. Watson's saloon on the south side of the square. It was Watson, not Abraham Lincoln, who arranged for a reduction in the licensing tax levied against the company. *Chicago Daily American*, October 30 (2), November 2 (3), November 4 (2) 1839; *Daily Georgian* (Savannah), November 6 (3), December 11 (3), December 18 (3) 1839; *Daily Chronicle & Sentinel* (Augusta, Ga.), January 21, 1840: 3; *Sangamo Journal* (Springfield), November 29, 1839: 2; Phillips, 632; Hardin, 45.

57. *Sangamo Journal* (Springfield), December 6, 1839: 2.

58. Between Springfield and St. Louis, the Jeffersons played Jacksonville, Carrollton, and Alton. Sol Smith wrote to Ludlow on March 17, 1840:

I hear from St. Louis that McKenzie was to open on the 10th—his reign will be short—but I fear he will annoy you for a time.

William G. B. Carson, *Managers in Distress* (St. Louis: St. Louis Historical Documents Foundation, 1949), 19; *The New York Dramatic Mirror*, February 16, 1901: 14; *Daily Missouri Republican* (St. Louis), March 9 (2), March 20 (2), March 24 (2), March 28 (2), March 30 (2) 1840; "A Walk in the Streets of St. Louis in 1845," *Missouri Historical Society Collections* 6 (1928): 33–40; *Sangamo Journal* (Springfield), February 7, 1840: 2; Hardin, 446; *Alton (Ill.) Telegraph,* February 22, 1840: 2; *Daily Missouri Republican* (St. Louis), February 17 (2), March 9 (2) 1840.

59. Addams, then twenty-nine, had worked with the troupe during their first and second Washington seasons there, had toured with them to Lancaster, Pennsylvania, in the fall of 1832, and had been Fanny Kemble's unfortunate Romeo in the disastrous 1833 Baltimore production. Although once compared in talent to the great nineteenth-century tragedian Edwin Forrest, Addams "was addicted to putting that enemy in his mouth that steals away the brains." By 1841, according to the Anglo-American actor-manager F. C. Wemyss, "*drink had done its work*—the mind of the actor is gone; he is incapable of committing a new part to memory; there was not even an attempt to produce an effect."

By April 4, 1840, the Jeffersons were in Alton, Illinois, filling out the supporting roles in *Richard III*. Thereafter Joseph and Cornelia Jefferson led a troupe to Quincy, Illinois, while Alexander and Hester MacKenzie organized another company to tour rural Missouri. In May 1840 they were in Jefferson City; two weeks later, they played Palmyra; by June 12, 1840, the reunited company was in Fulton, where the widowed Mary-Anne Ingersoll married James Wright; by July 1840 they were in Boonville; by July 31, 1840, they were again playing Galena; and on October 10, 1840, they played Fayette and announced their intention of playing Huntsville on the way back to Galena. By fall, the Wrights had left, and the rest of the troupe moved to Springfield in the second week of December 1840. *Daily National Intelligencer* (Washington), January 7 (3), January 9 (3), January 16 (3), November 6 (3), November 10 (3) 1832; January 24 (3), January 25 (3) 1833; Ireland, II: 110; *American and Commercial Daily Advertiser* (Baltimore), January 7, 1833: 3; *United States Gazette* (Philadelphia), January 5, 1835: 3; *Alton Telegraph,* April 4, 1840: 3; *Quincy Whig,* May 2, 1840: 2; *Jefferson (Mo.) Republican,* May 2, 1840: 2; May 23, 1840: 2; *Daily Chicago American,* June 19, 1840: 2; *North Western Gazette and Galena Advertiser,* July 31, 1840: 3; Elwood Bowen, *Theatrical Entertainments in Rural Missouri Before the Civil War, University of Missouri Studies* 32, (Columbia, Mo.: University of Missouri Press, 1956), 50–51.

60. The week before they appeared in Vincennes, the company played a short run in Terre Haute, Indiana. According to the Vincennes settler, who claimed to have been a relative of the Jeffersons, the company intended to reach Florida when they departed and left behind a trunk of costumes, music, plays, etc., as security against a loan for the journey. It is doubtful that the Jeffersons ever intended to travel to Florida; they lacked the financial means for so long a journey. In fact they considered spending the winter of 1841–42 in Springfield

again and petitioned the city council for a license. The council, however, decided that a $75 license would be granted only if the company paid the $30 they already owed, and the Jeffersons did not return. They opened in Nashville on September 23 for a fifty-two-night season. When the Jeffersons moved to Nashville, Greenbury C. Germon (who had rejoined the company) and Jane Anderson Germon left to join Ludlow and Smith in St. Louis. Potter's Nashville season ran until November 30, 1841. Carson, *Managers*, 22, 93, 102, 116; *Daily Missouri Republican* (St. Louis), August 22 (2), September 5 (2), October 3 (2), October 28 (2) 1840; *Sangamo Journal* (Springfield), December 15 (3), December 18 (3) 1840; John Hanners, "Early Entertainments in Terre Haute, Indiana, 1810–1865," thesis, Indiana State U., 1973, 72–3; *Chicago Tribune*, December 12, 1880: 19; *Vincennes Saturday Gazette*, May 29 1841: 2; Minutes of the City Council of Springfield, Ill., 1840–50, City Clerk's Office, Springfield, Ill., 35; *Daily Republican Banner* (Nashville, Tenn.), September 23, 1841: 3; Claude Ahmed Arnold, "The Development of the Stage in Nashville, Tennessee 1807–1870," thesis, U. of Iowa, 1933, 33, 65.

61. Article by Frank C. Bangs, Scrapbook on Joseph Jefferson, Townsend Walsh Collection, New York Public Library for the Performing Arts; Guy Herbert Keeton, "The Theatre in Mississippi from 1840 to 1870," diss., U. of Tennessee, 1979, 125; *The Mississippian* (Jackson), December 16, 1841: 2; Davidson County, Tennessee, County Court Clerk, Marriages 1837–1863, 2: 69.

62. Prior to Vicksburg, the Jeffersons performed in Natchez. *Mississippi Free Trader and Natchez Daily Gazette*, February 28 (2), May 13 (1) 1842; William Bryan Gates, "The Theatre in Natchez," *Journal of Mississippi History* 3 (1941): 119.

63. The Jeffersons played nearby Fort Pickering. Hill, 52; Wanda Melvina Luttrell, "The Theatre in Memphis, Tennessee, from 1829–1860." Master's thesis, Louisiana State University, 1951, 10, 11; *American Eagle* (Memphis), June 17, 1842: 2; *Autobiography*, 31; Scrapbook on Joseph Jefferson, Townsend Walsh Collection, New York Public Library for the Performing Arts.

64. After Memphis, the Jeffersons drifted to New Orleans. In Mobile, Fisher's employer, E. DeVendel, president of the gas company, became involved in a scheme to lease and run the Royal Street Theatre for the 1842–43 season in partnership with a local restauranteur and tavernkeeper, Jules Dumas. DeVendel withdrew from the partnership before the season began. Charles J. B. Fisher eventually made his stage appearance in Dion Boucicault's *London Assurance* on March 25, 1843. Mary Morgan Duggar, "The Theatre in Mobile 1822–1860." Master's thesis, University of Alabama, 1941, 99; Cowell, 97; Sol Smith, *Theatrical Management in the West and South for Thirty Years* (1858; rpt. Bronx, N.Y.: Benjamin Blom, 1968), 166; *New York Dramatic Mirror*, January 26, 1901: 14; *The Mobile Register and Journal*, March 25, 1843: 3.

65. The Steamboat *Creole* arrived in New Orleans from Mobile on October 3, 1842. The full company first gathered at the theatre in Mobile on November 12.

Mobile Register and Journal, October 11, 1842: 2, 3; *Courier de la Louisiana* (New Orleans), October 3, 1842: 2.

66. *New York Clipper,* February 1, 1862: 332.

67. *Autobiography,* 36; Winter, *The Jeffersons,* 147; John McClure, Magnolia Cemetery, Mobile; Caldwell Delaney, City of Mobile Museum Department, personal interviews, June 19, 1981; *North Western Gazette and Galena Advertiser,* December 23, 1842: 3; *Daily Picayune* (New Orleans), November 30, 1842: 2; *Mobile Daily Register,* February 8, 1870: 2.

68. The theatre was closed on November 25, 26, and 28. A limited performance was presented on November 26, but most of the company did not participate. *Autobiography,* 60.

69. On January 24, 1843, Jefferson did a comic song between the acts of James Hackett's *Rip Van Winkle.* Jefferson places Macready and Booth in Mobile at this period in his *Autobiography,* but there is no evidence for this. On May 23 a leading socialite named Madame Le Vert sponsored a benefit for young Joe and his sister. As a star in the late nineteenth century, Joe reminisced about this period in a conversation with his coactor and biographer Francis Wilson.

> "After my father died, his partner, MacKenzie, took full charge of the company, and when minstrels became so popular, the craze having been inaugurated by Dumbleton, we all blacked up and did songs and dances."
>
> "'We all'—who were 'we all'?"
>
> "My half-brother, Charley Burke, James Wright, who was afterwards prompter at Wallack's Theatre, and myself," he answered.
>
> "Did the ladies cork their faces?"
>
> "Oh no."
>
> "What songs did you sing?"
>
> "'Lucy Long,' 'Good-night Ladies,' and all the old melodies."

Wilson, 77–8; *Mobile Register and Journal,* January 9 (3), January 24 (3), April 21 (3), May 23 (3) 1843.

70. In 1897 Jefferson employed Julia Dean's niece and namesake to play a village girl in *Rip Van Winkle* and May Fielding in *The Cricket on the Hearth.* When Jefferson questioned her right to use the name, the young woman produced family Bibles, birth records, newspaper clippings, autographed photographs, and letters attesting to her claim. Learning that her aunt, who had died in childbirth on May 19, 1869, lay in an unmarked grave in Laurel Grove Cemetery in Port Jervis, New York, Jefferson said: "What a pity that so sweet a woman and so great an actress should be so soon forgotten. The profession ought to erect a tombstone in her memory." He proposed "getting up a benefit" for the purpose. The young niece declined, indicating her intention of saving her money for a monument. Forty-one years after Dean's death, the niece finally put up a tombstone. Nathan Dole contends that this Julia Dean performed with Jefferson in Mobile, but there is no trace of her in

advertisements. Clipping dated November 4, 1905; Paul Howard, "The Julia Deans—Yesterday and Today," *New York Mirror,* October 30, 1909, Robinson Locke Collection, 148, New York Public Library for the Performing Arts; Wilson, 270–271; Dole, 59.

71. Both Jefferson and Joseph Cowell, who was an actor in the troupe, attest to the Mobile company's lack of success, and Sol Smith reported: "Mr. Dumas . . . cooked up the drama in various styles—boiled, fried, roasted, broiled or on the half shell—involving a loss of whatever ready money he may have been possessed of."

In Jackson, Mississippi, in 1903, Jefferson recalled passing through Mississippi when only fourteen years old with "his brother's theatrical company which traveled in an ox wagon." The Jeffersons played Memphis again in late June 1843. Sol Smith, 166; *New York Dramatic Mirror,* May 7, 1903: 15; *Mobile Register and Journal,* April 3 (3), May 23 (3), May 27 (2), June 13 (2) 1843; Cowell, 101; *Autobiography,* 38–40; *Nashville Union,* June 16, 1843: 2; *Daily Republican Banner* (Nashville), August 28, 1843: 2.

72. Jefferson's role in the company was, however, minor enough that Noah Ludlow had completely forgotten him when Ludlow came to write his own autobiography in 1880. *Autobiography,* 45.

73. The Jeffersons opened with the Ludlow and Smith company in Mobile in the fall of 1844. Newspaper issues are missing, but they certainly performed there from December 5, 1844, through April 21, 1845. The two children got the last benefit on April 21. They performed in Saint Louis from May 13 through November 1, 1845. In an article entitled "What becomes of actors during vacations," the *St. Louis Reveille* of July 30, 1845, reported that "the little Jeffersons are practicing some new steps." Young Cornelia, whose name appeared far more often than Joe's in newspaper advertisements, danced "the Grand Pas Hongrois" taught to her by the company's dancing master. Kendall, 151; *Mobile Register and Journal,* December 5, 1844: 3; January 11 (3), January 17 (3), April 4 (3), April 11 (3), April 14 (3), April 18 (3), April 19 (3), April 21 (3) 1845; Duggar, 137; *Daily Missouri Republican* (St. Louis), May 13 (2), June 20 (2), August 16 (2), September 27 (2), October 1 (2), October 4 (2), November 1 (2) 1845; *Spirit of the Times* (New York), August 3, 1845: 308.

74. *Autobiography,* 49; *St. Louis Reveille,* July 4 (3), July 6 (2) 1845.

75. *Daily Picayune* (New Orleans), November 21, 1845: 3, March 24, 1846: 3.

76. "A portion of the Mobile and St. Charles theatre company left with Sol Smith in the Missouri for St. Louis. . . . Another portion left for Texas on the Galveston with Smyth Clark, the manager, and others for Cincinnati, Pittsburgh and New York." Since the safety of the theatre building in Houston was apparently suspect, the company manager requested that a committee of seven Houstonians inspect the theatre and published a report that they had found "the foundation and framework of the building . . . perfectly safe and secure." *Autobiography,* 57; *Daily Picayune* (New Orleans), April 14 (2), April 16 (2),

August 7 (2) 1846; Jack Harlan Yocum, "A History of the Theatre in Houston, 1836-1954." Diss., University of Wisconsin, 1955, 126-127.

77. *Autobiography*, 66-67.

78. *Memoirs of a Maryland Volunteer. War with Mexico* (Philadelphia, 1873), 43.

79. The American officer, George Gordon Meade, described Matamoras.

> The volunteers continue to pour in, and . . . I do not see it with much satisfaction. They are . . . ignorant of discipline and . . . restive under restraint . . . a . . . disorderly mass, who will give us . . . more trouble than the enemy. Already are our guard houses filled . . . with drunken officers and men who go to the town, get drunk and commit outrages on the citizens.

Kenly writes:

> After supper we went to the theatre and recognized our . . . friends whom we had met at the mouth of the river. Such an audience! The Texas Rangers were there, pistols and knives in their belts, many with swords at their sides, others with long rifles, while drunken volunteers from . . . every southern State of the Union were mingled with regulars of the horse, foot, and artillery arms of the service, in a medley of . . . riotous dissipation.

George Gordon Meade, *Life and Letters*, 1 (New York: Charles Scribner's Sons, 1913): 91; Kenly, 51; James Longstreet, *From Manassas to Appomattox* (1908, Bloomington: Indiana University Press, 1960), 20.

80. *Daily Picayune* (New Orleans), August 16, 1846: 2.

81. A correspondent for *Spirit of the Times* described the site of Jefferson's business as "a large square surrounded by chine trees. The houses surrounding the square are of brick or stone, the lower parts used as stores or offices and the second story as dwellings. . . . Streets diverge from the plaza. . . . The cathedral occupies a large space on one side of the square and is an unfinished mass of masonry. Directly opposite to the cathedral is the prison. There are a great many stores and quite a large market place." *Spirit of the Times* (New York), May 13 (187), September 5 (329) 1846; *Autobiography*, 68; K. Jack Bauer, *Zachary Taylor: Soldier, Planter, Statesman of the Old Southwest* (Baton Rouge: Louisiana State University Press, 1985), 175; "Bronze Will Mark Adobe," Joseph Jefferson III file, Theatre Collection, Museum of the City of New York. The author is indebted to Professor Ben McArthur for the information about Jefferson's Matamoras tobacco shop. It comes from an ad in *The American Flag*, quoted in Leroy Graf's "Soldier Entertainment a Hundred Years Ago," in *Theatre Annual 1946*, page 57.

82. An army officer serving as correspondent for a New York newspaper described Matamoras as "the meanest looking and filthiest city I have ever seen. The greater part of the genteel population have left, and in about one house in three, among the more humble class, one of the family was . . . searching the heads of the others . . . for lice, and the very sight set my head

itching to such a degree that I was not satisfied until I reached camp." In Brazos Santiago, the Jeffersons performed with Mrs. Hart, a former member of the Houston company, before returning to New Orleans. *Spirit of the Times* (New York), June 13, 1846: 187; *Autobiography,* 78; *Daily Picayune* (New Orleans), November 4, 1846: 2.

83. Owens died on December 7, 1866, at his country home near Towson, Maryland. Although English born, he was identified with the Yankee character of Solon Shingle, a part that Jefferson would play until he began to do the Boucicault version of Rip. At one point Owens was said to be the richest actor in America, but imprudent investments in California mining stocks reduced his savings. *New York Mirror,* December 11, 1886: 6.

84. Jefferson's mother and sister remained in New Orleans through early February of 1847. *United States Gazette* (Philadelphia), March 19 (3), June 4 (3), June 27 (3), July 27 (3), July 29 (3), July 30 (3), August 1 (3), August 3 (3), August 7 (3), August 10 (3), September 29 (3), October 17(3), October 30 (3), October 31 (3), December 7 (3), December 11 (3), December 24 (3), December 31(3) 1846; *The Evening Mirror* (New York), December 14, 1846: 2; *Autobiography,* 83–88; *Daily Picayune* (New Orleans), February 5, 1847: 1; *Cumberland* (Md.) *Alleganian,* April 17, 1847: 4.

3. Apprenticeship in the East, 1847–1850   *pages 33–43*

85. Bangs was paid $6 a week for general utility work at the Old National Theatre in Washington in 1851. By the end of the first season, he had advanced to the position of second walking gentleman, and his salary had been increaed to $18 a week. As a leading juvenile at Ford's Theatre in Baltimore, playing roles such as Romeo, Bangs made $25 a week his first season and $30 a week during his second season. At the Greene Street Theatre in Albany, as a leading man, he received $40 a week. *New York Mirror,* March 8, 1884: 10; *New York Dramatic Mirror,* November 27, 1897: 17.

86. *New York Dramatic Mirror,* August 27, 1901: 3.

87. *Ibid.,* July 19, 1902: 15.

88. *Daily Journal* (Wilmington, North Carolina), November 3, 1851: 2.

89. By watching Charles Burke, Jefferson gained exposure to versions of Dickens' *The Cricket on the Hearth* and *Nicholas Nickleby,* works in which he would find his characterizations of Caleb Plummer and Newman Noggs. One of Jefferson's earliest biographers, L. Clarke Davis, remembered Charley as "tall and slender, almost emaciated in form, with a countenance that he could render . . . grotesque or . . . sad. So great was his control of it that, in the long line of characters which he played, it seemed like the faces of many men." *New York Mirror,* March 8, 1884: 10; *New York Dramatic Mirror,* November 27, 1897: 17; *Autobiography,* 88; *Public Ledger* (Philadelphia), January 2, 1847: 3; L. Clarke Davis, "At and After the Play," *Lippincott's Magazine* 24 (July 1879): 60.

90. Peale's Museum was located in the former Masonic Hall. There Jefferson was able to watch his half-brother play Bob Acres in Sheridan's *The Rivals,*

another role that Jefferson would later make his own. *Public Ledger* (Philadelphia), February 15 (3), February 18 (3), February 26 (3), March 10 (3) 1847.

91. One of the few references to Jefferson, in the fall of 1847, was as one of a group of actors to appear in a benefit for the Washington Independent Rifle Company on December 17, 1847. Charles Burke opened at the Bowery Theatre in New York on Monday, July 19, 1847. He scored a reasonable success and was described in reviews as "a very clever low comedian." *Public Ledger* (Philadelphia), May 15 (3), June 22 (3), July 13 (3), July 17 (3) 1847; *Autobiography,* 88; *Evening Mirror* (New York), 19 July, 1847: 3; *Spirit of the Times* (New York), August 21, 1847: 308.

92. One of the plays done in Baltimore was J. S. Dalrymple's *The Naiad Queen; or The Revolt of the Naiads,* and the cast list that precedes the published text indicates that Jefferson played the role of Manfredo. It is essentially a lineless chorus role in "a grand romantic operatic spectacle," in which a band of robbers encounter a chorus of nymphs. Jefferson, at the age of nineteen, was still functioning as a utility actor, an extra in spectacles. The company lasted until July 10, 1847. Included in the company were Mrs. John Drew, then Mrs. Mossop, who was to appear with Jefferson in the 1880's, as well as Mrs. McLean, who had worked with the Jefferson company in Chicago. While in Baltimore, Jefferson may have lived in an actors' boarding house. Another of its residents, Dr. G. A. Kane, then a journalist, later remembered:

> The hostess was a good-natured, gray-eyed old lady. The house did not have all the modern improvements, but it was a comfortable, if not a luxurious, home. The old lady had two boys, Mike and Matt. Matt was a "basket boy," that is, he carried a champagne basket, with the actors' dresses in it, to and from the theatre.
>
> In the cozy rooms of the "Hotel O'Brien," we would sit and listen to the elder [Junius Brutus] Booth. . . . Glass in hand, he would read for us our parts as only he could read them. His son Ted [Edwin Booth] would come with the old man and wait to see him home, for fear he would drink potations pottle deep. Never shall I forget Booth's recital of the Lord's Prayer; it was one of the most intense pieces of elocution I ever heard. The young actors would look and listen, watch every movement, gesture and tone of his voice. After a fine bit of pathos, the old man would take a pull at the beer—for we could not afford anything better.
>
> Joe Jefferson was one of our party. He was a very careful actor, always making the most of a point. Joe, in those days, was our second low comedy man and was helping his father to paint scenes, in both of which labors he did not get more than eighteen dollars a week.
>
> Charley Burke was one of us. He was a fine mime; had a merry eye, a sweet voice and was a superb dancer.

Dr. Kane's reminiscences have to be taken with a grain of salt. Joe's father was dead by the time Jefferson returned to Baltimore, and Charley Burke was in New York, but Kane is certainly placing Edwin Booth correctly in time. J. S. Dalrymple, *The Naiad Queen* (Boston: William V. Spencer, n.d.), 2; *American and Commercial Daily Advertiser* (Baltimore), June 30, 1847: 3; July 5, 1847: 3; *New York Mirror,* June 14, 1884: 8.

93. On the same night that Jefferson had his benefit, Mrs. Burke had hers at Burton's Arch Street Theatre. It was an unusual circumstance for two family members. Jefferson disappeared from view during the summer and fall of 1848, although cast lists at Burton's indicate performances by both Mrs. Burke and by Jefferson's sister, Cornelia. *Public Ledger* (Philadelphia), July 28, 1848: 3. Mention of Jefferson in Philadelphia newspapers ceases between July 1847 and July 1848. He did appear at the Arch Street Theatre on February 23 and 24, 1848. *Public Ledger* (Philadelphia), February 23 (3), February 24 (3) 1848.

94. *Public Ledger* (Philadelphia), October 23, 1848: 2.

95. Eleanor Farjeon, *Portrait of a Family* (New York: Frederick A. Stokes Company, 1936), 59.

96. Burke left for Richmond, Virginia. *Public Ledger* (Philadelphia), December 23, 1848: 3, January 12 (3), January 16 (3) 1849; *Pennsylvanian* (Philadelphia), December 23, 1848: 3; January 16 (3), February 20 (3) 1849.

97. The following day Jefferson played Tilly Slowbury, the dim-witted female servant in *The Cricket on the Hearth*. It was the role his sister Connie would later perform in the Jefferson company and one of Joe's few forays into what the modern period would see as a cross-dressing role. In 1849, however, Jefferson's acting a female role would have had none of the sexual or political implications that such a performance would carry today. Tilly is a nonsexual eccentric comic servant role. *Public Ledger* (Philadelphia), January 16, 1849: 3; John M. Morton, *The Midnight Watch* (London: n.d.), 2.

98. James was the father of the playwright Eugene O'Neill. Arthur and Barbara Gelb, *O'Neill* (New York: Harper's, 1964), 23–24.

99. On March 23 a benefit for Jefferson was announced at the Circus and National Theatre. *Pennsylvanian* (Philadelphia), January 15 (3), January 16 (3), January 17 (3), March 23 (3) 1849; *Autobiography,* 118, 120-121.

100. Ellsler was six years Jefferson's senior and had begun his theatrical career as an office assistant in Peale's Museum. He progressed to an assistant property man and finally became an actor in the company. *Pennsylvanian* (Philadelphia), April 18, 1849: 3; *New York Mirror,* July 31, 1886: 6; *New York Dramatic Mirror,* August 29, 1903: 14.

101. Burke had opened at the Bowery Theatre on July 19, 1847, as Ebenezer Calf in *Ole Bull*. It was, however, his work as Diggory in *The Spectre Bridegroom* that made him a Bowery favorite. Both parts were to become part of Jefferson's repertoire. On April 30, 1849, Burke opened at Burton's Theatre in Chambers Street in New York, an engagement that lasted until May 2. By July 1848, Burke's wife had joined him there. Ireland, 474; *Spirit of the Times* (New York), July 8, 1848: 240; *Cumberland (Md.) Alleganian,* August 5, 1848: 2; *New York Herald,* April 30 (2), May 2 (3), May 23 (1) 1849.

102. Chanfrau's father was a fruit seller near Chatham Square. G. C. Foster wrote of the National:

> On the steps we encounter . . . police officers, as we enter the vestibule, and attempt to pass on. [The] ladies before us . . . appear to be on intimate terms with the doorkeeper, who gives them a chuck under the chin as they pass through, leaving a strong flavor of bad gin behind them. These are women of the town.

The atmosphere inside the theatre, particularly as the house lights were up for the entire performance, had little to do with dramatic art.

> The dress-circle is filled with diaphanously-robed ladies, who raise enormous instruments to their eyes—something between a telescope and a pair of goggles . . . while the men in the pit are, by the help of similar contrivances, scanning the gazers themselves. . . . We are at the entrance of the "Saloon"—a large, bare, dreary looking groggery with a fattish young woman in a gilt-watch chain and half mourning at either end, behind a little counter . . . with rank smelling bottles and collapsed doughnuts. Between the acts, the room . . . fills with gentlemen who can't wait for their next drink 'til the play is out and have left their ladies in the boxes by themselves, to be stared out of countenance by the loafers and libertines in the pit.

In 1902 Jefferson reminisced:

> Well can I remember the times in New York City when the infamous "Third Tier," for the use of the "half world" was one of the acknowledged sections of every theatre. Imagine such a condition existing at present!"

New York Mirror, October 11, 1884: 11; G. C. Foster, *New York by Gas-Light* (New York, 1850), 87 88; *New York in Slices* (New York, 1849), 102; "Rip Van Winkle is a Happy Man," Robinson Locke Collection, 302: 38, New York Public Library at Lincoln Center.

103. Frank C. Bangs described Charles Burke as "Singularly made up, physically, from "top to toe," he was over six feet in height, very thin, of angular build and yet not ungraceful. . . . A small round head, set low on square broad shoulders, and arms of unusual length."

Burke opened at Chanfrau's on June 4, 1849, as Paul Pry and later appeared as a character familiar to audiences from the local scandals—the pickpocket Capt. Tobin in *Three Years After or Sequel to the Mysteries and Miseries of New York,* a piece written specifically for Frank S. Chanfrau. (The latter appeared in his noted character of Mose, the New York fireman.) Burke also played in *The Heir-at-Law,* which his half-brother would later use as a touring vehicle for almost fifty years. But Burke, unlike Jefferson, did not play the eruditely preposterous Dr. Pangloss, but rather the country bumpkin Ezekiel Homespun. Burke took his benefit on the 29th, and the *New York Herald* wrote:

Last evening Mr. Burke took a benefit, and had a . . . crowded house.
. . . The performances commenced with a new burlesque entitled *Josey the Spartan*, and a . . . funny affair it was. It is a burlesque on *Douglass*, and of all the young Norvals, . . . Burke's version . . . is the funniest. His long thin figure, encased in tartan tights, his version of the famous speech . . . tickled the fancies of the audience . . . . The applause at the conclusion was vociferous, and Mr. Burke was called before the curtain.

By June 25, Chanfrau's National was the only theatre in town operating at full capacity during the sweltering summer, its boxes and pit continually filled in part because the theatre was well ventilated. Burke left the company in early July 1849, but came back for one performance in the middle of the month, after which his name disappeared from its advertisements. By August 7, Chanfrau's had been in continual operation for a year, a record hailed as "the longest season ever accomplished by any theatre in the Union." It finally closed on August 25, 1849, to be redecorated and refurbished for its opening on September 10. *New York Herald*, June 3 (3), June 6 (4), June 8 (4), June 25 (1), June 28 (1), June 30 (2), July 1 (1), July 3 (1) 1849; Frank C. Bangs, *Recollections of Players II*, Clipping Collection, New York Public Library at Lincoln Center.

104. On August 6, 1849, Margaret danced the Fox Hunters Jig at Chanfrau's. *New York Herald,* August 5 (3), August 7 (3), August 12 (3) 1849; Winter, *Life and Art*, 192; John Bouve Clapp and Edwin Francis Edgett, *Players of the Present* (New York: The Dunlap Society, 1901), 183; Manhattan Deaths 1861 F-Z, The City of New York Department of Records and Information Services, Municipal Archives; Eleanor Farjeon, 58; *New York Dramatic Mirror,* September 12, 1901: 12; June 12, 1902: 3; *Baltimore American and Commercial Advertiser*, February 20, 1861: 1; *New York Clipper,* February 1, 1862: 332.

105. The actress Fanny Herring provides a view of Burke as a stage manager.

Chanfrau [was] managing the . . . Chatham Street Theatre and advertised for . . . ballet girls. I determined to apply and was engaged. Charles Burke . . . was the stage-manager. Each girl's name was called from a list, and when I answered to mine, Burke said, "Are you the daughter of Mrs. Herring of the Bowery?" I replied "Yes." "I thought so," said he, "for you bear a great resemblance to your . . . mother, and if you make as good actress . . . , you will do well." . . . I asked Mr. Burke if I could not have one of the small speaking parts, but it was given to my room-mate. She made a poor showing, and the manager came around and said, "Give those lines to that little dark haired girl. I bet she can do it better." The other girl was a fair-haired, frail little thing. I said to Mr. Burke, "She will be all right tomorrow night," but she was worse; so the part was given to me. I felt . . . badly for her sake, but I spoke the lines and the manager said, "I told you so. She is a good one." Later the lady who played the Fairy Queen was taken ill and I was given her part. I wore her costume. I was required to come up a trap. I had never done such a thing, and as I went up the trap, my lines went up too; my costume became caught and was pulled off my shoulders. This gave me real "stage fright," for I could not either move or speak. The audience laughed. The prompter gave me the words, but I could not take them, and the audience laughed again. That made me angry, and off I walked. Mr. Burke said, "Go on again, little one; you are all right." I did and spoke every line.

New York Herald, August 25 (1), August 26, (4), September 4 (3), September 9 (4), September 10 (3) 1849; *New York Dramatic Mirror,* June 12, 1902: 3.

106. By September 14, five days after he had opened, Jefferson had the lead role of Hans Meritz, "the honest blacksmith who so unexpectedly loses his lady-love only to gain as the play's title suggests, *Somebody Else."* Margaret Lockyer played Louise opposite him. The review next morning contained a brief but favorable mention of his work. Just as Jefferson was appearing opposite his future wife, Charles Burke began appearing opposite twenty-eight-year-old Mrs. Mary Sutherland, whom he would marry after his first wife's death.

Margaret Burke died in Philadelphia on November 16, 1849, at the age of thirty-two. She was buried on November 18 after a service at the home of her stepfather, Lewis Bond, in Rose Alley above Tamang Street in back of Commissioners' Hall. Mary Sutherland survived Charles Burke and died in Paris on November 15, 1877, of rheumatism of the heart at the age of sixty. Her remains were placed upon a steamer sailing from Le Havre on November 23, 1877, and arrived in New York on December 4. After a funeral in The Little Church Around the Corner, she was buried in Cypress Hill cemetery on December 10, 1877, in a plot owned by the American Dramatic Fund, of which she was annuitant. *New York Herald,* September 11 (2), September 14 (3), September 15 (1) 1849; *Public Ledger* (Philadelphia), November 17, 1849: 2; *New York Clipper,* December 8 (294), December 15 (302) 1877.

107. Charles Burke was also active as a playwright, and Jefferson appeared in his brother's "national drama" entitled *Revolution* on October 1, 1849. Burke, who had, according to the *New York Herald,* "in so many dramatic compositions, given satisfactory proofs of his talents as an author," appeared in the play as Mesopotamia Jenkins, "a true-grit Yankee lad." *New York Herald,* October 1, 1849: 2.

108. I. Pocock, *Rob Roy or Auld Lang Syne* (New York, n.d.), 3–60.

109. On January 9, 1850, Jefferson was taken suddenly ill, and his part had to be taken by another member of the company, but he was listed again in the casts for the following night. The "bread and butter" play of the company was an Arabian burlesque entitled *The Female Guard or A Lad in a Lamp.* By mid-January 1850 it had been performed thirty-eight times supposedly to between one hundred thousand and one hundred fifty thousand people. The printed edition of Burke's version of *Rip Van Winkle* has Jefferson playing Seth to Burke's Rip at the Arch Street Theatre in Philadelphia in 1850. Rip's famous

toast, "Here's your good health and your families', may they all live long and prosper," occurs in several variants in the Burke text. *New York Herald,* January 6 (1), January 7 (4), January 10 (1), January 11 (3), January 20 (1) 1850; Charles Burke, *Rip Van Winkle: A Legend of the Catskills* (New York: Samuel French, n.d.), 2, 8–9, 22, 27.

110. In 1879 L. Clarke Davis wrote that Jefferson's friend and fellow actor, John Sleeper Clarke (later to marry Edwin Booth's sister Asia) told him

> that in the delivery of these lines no other actor has ever disturbed the impression that the profound pathos of Burke's voice, face and gesture created. . . . Mr. Clarke played Seth with Mr. Burke for many consecutive nights, and he relates that . . . each . . . night, though he was . . . aware of what was coming, . . . when those lines were spoken, his heart seemed to rise in his throat, . . . and his cheeks were wet with tears; for Burke's manner of pronouncing them was so tender and pathetic that not only the audience, but even the actors on the stage, were affected.

L. Clarke Davis, 75.

111. *New York Herald,* March 1(1, 3), March 2 (3), April 11 (3), May 15 (4) 1850.

112. Jefferson and Williams appeared in *In and Out of Place. New York Herald,* April 30, 1850: 1; *New York Dramatic Mirror,* April 27, 1901: 14.

113. By the time he returned to the Chatham, Burke had re-married, and Mrs. Sutherland appeared with him as Mrs. Burke. *New York Herald,* May 10 (1), May 12 (2), May 14 (1, 3) 1850.

114. Eleanor Farjeon, 59.

115. *Idem,* 61; *Autobiography,* 127.

116. L. Clarke Davis, 75.

117. *New York Herald,* February 22 (1), March 27 (2) 1850.

118. Edward Wagenknecht, *Merely Players* (Norman: University of Oklahoma Press, 1966), 190.

119. The occasion of Connie's appearance was Joe's first benefit in New York. According to *The New York Herald,* Connie "delivered her role with considerable ability and was greatly applauded." On July 5, Jefferson played Iago in a minstrel Shakespearean parody called *Otello* opposite T. D. Rice, with whom he had performed as a small child. On June 29, 1850, Burke took a farewell benefit with Jefferson in the cast. *New York Herald,* May 17 (3), May 18 (2), May 22 (3), June 9 (3), July 5 (3), July 8 (4) 1850.

120. By July 8, Jefferson's name appeared in the cast lists in Brooklyn. By July 9, his wife was playing opposite him. Fanny Herring, who was a member of the company felt that they were not financially successful. Back at the Chatham, Margaret did not appear in cast lists until August 22, but Connie Jefferson was a member of the company by August 15. *New York Herald,* July 4 (3), July 9 (5), Aug 5 (3), August 15 (3), August 22 (3) 1850; *New York Dramatic Mirror,* July 12, 1902: 3.

121. It is probable that Jefferson played the First Witch when Booth did *Macbeth* and played a minor role when Booth appeared in *The Mountaineers*. Although Jefferson's name is not mentioned in the abbreviated cast list published in the paper for *The Mountaineers*, he had performed the play earlier that year. On November 18 Charles Burke rejoined the company as a touring star, but Jefferson had left to go south. *New York Herald*, September 19 (3), September 20 (3), October 3 (3), October 4 (3), October 5 (3), November 18 (3) 1850; Joseph Jefferson, "In Memory of Edwin Booth," 691.

4. A Provincial Manager: A Provincial Actor, 1850–1857
pages 44–63
122. Mason had appeared with the Jefferson family in Chicago in 1839. Of Jefferson's Dr. Ollapod, a critic for Melbourne's daily newspaper *The Argus* later wrote:

> Nothing could be better than his treatment of the . . . *tete-a-tete* with . . . Lucretia Mactab, when in . . . ignorance of her acquaintance, she abuses "the Goths and Vandals of the country, where every sheepish squire has the air of an apothecary." His feelings of . . . astonishment, of chagrin, and of awkwardness culminating in the sheepish admission, "I deal a little in Galenicals myself," are so . . . managed that he would be ranked as a comedian of rare taste and expression were he beheld in this scene alone. Mr. Jefferson makes up for the part . . . as effectively as he plays it. His appearance in the "tasteful uniform of the Galen's Head Volunteeer troop—a small scarlet jacket turned up with a rhubarb-colored lapel," . . . adds much to the merriment of the scene.

Daily Morning News (Savannah, Georgia), January 6 (3), January 14 (2)1851; *Argus* (Melbourne), November 3, 1864: 5.

123. When the troupe left, Mason stayed on in Savannah until at least January 18, playing Jefferson's roles. Jefferson's first appearance in Charleston was on January 22. *Daily Morning News* (Savannah), January 18, 1851: 3; *Charleston Courier*, January 17 (3), January 21 (2), January 22 (3), February 25 (3)1851.

124. *Charleston Courier*, March 5, 1851: 3.

125. L. Clarke Davis was the editor of the Philadelphia *Public Ledger*, the husband of the novelist Rebecca Harding Davis, and the father of the novelist Richard Harding Davis. His listing of 1849 as the date Jefferson began work as a manager is off by at least two years. The impoverishment of the company is illustrated by a notice in the Savannah *Daily News:* "We . . . suggest to Mr. F. CROCKER, that it would be well to pay a little more regard to the dressing of his characters. His modern frock coat and black pants were sadly out of place last night. He should remember that such garments were not worn two centuries ago." L. Clarke Davis, "At and After the Play," *Lippincott's Magazine of Popular Literature and Science*, 24 (July 1879): 60; Allan Nevins, *Grover Cleveland* (New York: Dodd, Mead & Co., 1932), 459; *New York*

Times, October 23, 1860: 4; *New York Dramatic Mirror,* June 12, 1897: 2; *Daily News* (Savannah, Georgia), April 26, 1851: 2.

126. *Public Ledger* (Philadelphia), April 6, 1850: 3; *Georgia Journal and Messenger* (Macon), March 19 (3), March 26 (2, 3) 1851; W. Stanley Hoole, *The Ante-Bellum Charleston Theatre* (Tuscaloosa: University of Alabama Press, 1946), 130; Gravestone, Charles B. Jefferson, Sandwich, Massachusetts; "The American on the Stage," *Scribner's Monthly* 18 (July, 1879): 331.

127. Charles Burke's retelling of the family legend is borne out by a newspaper advertisement announcing the appearance of "Master Jefferson" along with his parents at a benefit for his father and two other actors on the last night of the Savannah engagement, April 30, 1851. "Charles Jefferson Talks of His Famous Father," newspaper clipping, 1906, Bourne Historical Center, Bourne, Massachusetts; Eugenie Jefferson, 240; *Daily News* (Savannah, Georgia), April 30, 1851: 2.

128. Jefferson, John Ellsler, and Deering were listed as the lessees of the Savannah theatre, meaning they were the heads of the company. Jefferson, however, was also advertised as stage manager for the troupe of ten men and five women, a position equivalent to artistic director today. The performance of *The Rivals* took place on April 16, 1851. The Jefferson-Ellsler-Deering Company also played Wilmington, North Carolina, in 1851, performing nightly for a month to good business, and Jefferson was a great hit as Diggory. *Daily News* (Savannah, Georgia), April 8 (3), April 16 (3) 1851; L. Clarke Davis, 67; *New York Mirror,* January 19, 1884: 8.

129. Burke hired Joe, Connie, and his wife, Iona, for the Arch Street Theatre. The company of thirty-four actors and an orchestra began performing on August 27 after two days of rehearsal. At first, Jefferson was assigned to roles that his brother would normally have performed, again an example of generosity on Burke's part. By October 2, 1851, however, Joe's roles had reverted to Charley, presumably because Joe had left the company to resume his managerial career. *Public Ledger* (Philadelphia), August 25 (3), August 27 (3), September 13 (3), October 2 (3) 1851; Broadside Collection, Arch Street Theatre, September 18, 1851–December 31, 1852, Free Library of Philadelphia.

130. *Daily Journal* (Wilmington, North Carolina), October 18 (3), October 22 (3), October 29 (2) 1851.

131. Jefferson opened in Wilmington with the intention of playing only until October 31. He then planned to proceed to Savannah, opening there on November 4. But business in Wilmington must have been good, because the company stayed there though November 15.

Booth arrived in Charleston the weekend prior to opening on the steamship *Commodore Vanderbilt* from Wilmington, but there is no evidence that Edwin was with him. In 1893, however, Jefferson recalled: "Over forty years ago his father one of the great tragedians of the world, came to act in the city of Charleston, South Carolina. I was the boy stage-manager of the theatre there. His father was ill. I called on him to see if I could do anything. I found the elder Booth lying upon a sofa, attended by his son. They were not at a hotel; they were living at the house of an old friend."

Jefferson and Ellsler took a benefit in Charleston on March 4, 1852. Advertisements for the theatre disappeared after February 14, but the theatre reopened on February 23. *Daily Journal* (Wilmington, North Carolina), October 31 (2), November 7 (2), November 15 (3) 1851; *Charleston Courier,* December 30, 1851: 2, February 2 (3), February 23 (3), March 4 (2, 3), March 8 (3), March 10 (3), March 22 (2) 1852; "Revealing All Julia Dean's Secrets," *Chicago Record Herald,* February 1, 1914, Robinson Locke Collection 48, The New York Public Library at Lincoln Center; *Memorial Celebration of the Sixtieth Anniversary of the Birth of Edwin Booth,* n.p.

132. *Charleston Courier*, March 30, 1852: 3; *Daily Chronicle and Sentinel* (Augusta, Georgia), March 31 (3), April 7 (2), April 22 (2), April 24 (2), April 27 (1) 1852.

133. On April 26 the company left by train for Columbia, South Carolina. Returning to Wilmington on May 11 on a mail steamer, they opened that night and stayed until May 29. They had been scheduled to begin on May 10, but accidentally got stranded at Charleston when they "got down to the wharf just as the board pushed out into the stream." They arrived on May 11 in the U. S. mail steamer *Commodore Vanderbilt.* Jefferson took a benefit on May 28. *Daily Journal* (Wilmington, North Carolina), May 10 (2), May 11 (3), May 28 (3) 1852; *Daily Chronicle & Sentinel* (Augusta, Georgia), April 24, 1852: 3.

134. *New York Daily Times,* July 8, 1852: 3.

135. *New York Dramatic Mirror,* March 29, 1890: 4; *New York Times,* March 23 (13), March 25 (5), October 20 (6) 1891.

136. At Niblo's, Jefferson performed eight roles. Twenty years later *New York Clipper* remembered that he "attracted considerable attention" during this engagement. In New York, Jefferson performed again with John Sefton. While he was playing at the Albany Theatre, Mr. and Mrs. John Drew as well as Jefferson's cousin Jane Anderson Germon were performing at the Albany Museum. At the Albany Theatre, his roles included Dogberry in *Much Ado About Nothing. New York Clipper,* May 25, 1879: 57; *New York Daily Times,* December 4 (5), December 17 (5), December 31 (5) 1852; Jefferson Winter, "As I Remember," *Saturday Evening Post* 193 (August 7, 1920): 42; *Daily Albany Argus,* December 18, 1852: 3, January 20 (3), January 31 (3) 1853; *Spirit of the Times,* January 22, 1853: 583.

137. In the course of the season at the Athenaeum, Jefferson played Francis in *King Henry IV, Part I* and Slender in *The Merry Wives of Windsor*, both to James K. Hackett's Falstaff. When the company appeared at a matinee, Jefferson performed three roles. *Daily Evening Transcript* (Boston), February 12, 1853: 3; *Daily Picayune* (New Orleans), October 16, 1846: 2; Playbills dated March 17, March 19, March 21, March 26, March 29, April 8, 1853, Howard Athenaeum, Boston Public Library.

138. The part was Timothy Quaint in *Soldier's Daughter*. *Spirit of the Times* (New York), April 2, 1853: 74.

139. At the Eagle Theatre, Jefferson was regularly featured playing Diggory in *The Spectre Bridegroom* and Dr. Ollapod in *The Poor Gentleman*. *Daily Evening Transcript* (Boston), April 13 (3), April 19 (3), April 22 (3), April 25 (3) 1853.

140. Winter, *Life and Art* 193; Eleanor Farjeon, 60.

141. For his own benefit on March 7, 1854, Jefferson performed Mark Meddle in *London Assurance* and Jerry Hawthorn in *Tom and Jerry*. Charles Burke performed as a touring star at the Chestnut while Jefferson was a member of the company, and this would have been an opportunity for Jefferson to see his brother play Dr. Ollapod in *The Poor Gentleman*—a role Joe was already making his own. Burke's wife was also in the company. John Jack, a member of the troupe who later toured with Jefferson, remembered Burke's influence on Jefferson's Rip.

> Burke was possessed of remarkable comic talent, combined with abilities for pathetic portrayal which, in many impersonations, permitted him to draw forth an intermingling of laughter and tears, . . . and if pecuniary success was not his . . . , he was certainly the bringer of . . . good fortune to others. . . . Burke's characterization of Rip Van Winkle . . . must have been no small factor in the . . . achievement of his . . . half-brother, Joseph Jefferson.

New York Dramatic Mirror, April 3, 1897: 2; Broadside dated December 16, 1853, Tulane University Library, New Orleans, Louisiana; *Spirit of the Times* (New York), April 22 (120), April 29 (12) 1854; *Public Ledger* (Philadelphia), August 30 (3), September 1 (3), 1853; January 10 (3), February 3 (3), February 7 (3), March 7 (3), May 5 (3) 1854; *Cummings' Evening Bulletin* (Philadelphia), August 23 (3), September 26 (5), October 10 (5) 1853; February 3 (3), February 7 (3), February 11 (3), March 7 (1, 3), March 11 (3) 1854.

142. The Baltimore Museum opened with Colman's *The Heir-at-Law*, and the opening-night audience was so large that it was impossible to obtain standing room after the play began. *The Heir-at-Law* featured Jefferson as Dr. Pangloss. Margaret, "of the Chestnut Street Theatre, Philadelphia," played opposite him in the one-act farce that followed. The following evening, Jefferson performed Bob Acres. *New York Dramatic Mirror*, February 16, 1901: 14.

143. Under Jefferson's management, the museum mounted a variety of main pieces while repeating a repertoire of comic afterpieces. Julia Dean performed her standard repertoire of plays such as *Romeo and Juliet*, Sheridan Knowles' *The Hunchback*, August von Kotzebue's *The Stranger*, and Bulwer-Lytton's *The Lady of Lyons*. On October 6, Jefferson, finding himself without a star for the main piece, performed three comic roles in three one-act farces on the same bill. On November 4, 1854, he took a benefit, performing in three one-act farces that had not been previously seen that season in Baltimore. Although

Margaret was initially given star billing right below her husband, her name disappeared quickly from the abbreviated newspaper cast lists. When he appeared in farces, Jefferson worked opposite other female members of the company. That October, Margaret became pregnant again. She was still performing in late November. *American and Commercial Advertiser* (Baltimore), August 28 (2), August 29 (2, 3), September 4 (3), October 6 (3), October 25 (3), November 3 (3), November 4 (3), November 29 (3) 1854.

144. On November 13, 1854, *New York Times* published a list of City Mortalities, November 4–11, 1854. Of the 404 deaths reported, 61 were from consumption, by far the largest killer. Burke's obituary read:

We regret that we are called upon to chronicle the death of Mr. CHAS. S. T. BURKE, the distinguished Comedian, who departed this life on Friday evening last, at the Florence Hotel, corner of Broadway and Walker-street, aged thirty-two years. The disease which has cut off Mr. BURKE, . . . before he had reached his prime, was consumption, which was an hereditary compliant with him, his mother . . . having died of the same disease. . . . Mr. BURKE had been for many years laboring under a serious pulmonary difficulty.

Mr. BURKE was born in Philadelphia, in 1822. . . . At an early age, he commenced his career on the stage. He gradually arose in his profession till he obtained a rank among the first comedians of this country. In New-York and Philadelphia, Mr. BURKE was eminently successful, and in our Western theatres, where he often played star engagements, he was always a . . . favorite and was greeted by crowded houses. Mr. BURKE was stage manager for Mr. CHANFRAU, when that gentleman directed the Chatham Theatre. Many will remember him at that time and also at BURTON's Theatre, where he played a short engagement to commence the season of 1850–51. Since that time, as frequently as his health would allow, he has played star engagements in various cities and towns throughout the United States. He was, for a time, stage manager of the Chestnut-street Theatre, Philadelphia. His last engagement in New-York was in August, 1853, when he filled the Bowery Theatre during two weeks. He then went to Baltimore, as manager of the new Vaudeville Theatre. This post he resigned in November following and soon after resolved to try a trip to California, hoping that . . . his health might be restored. He was warmly received at San Francisco, but his illness grew worse, and he returned to New York about six weeks since. On Saturday, his remains were conveyed to Philadelphia, accompanied by Mr. JEFFERSON. . . . A number of Mr. BURKE's . . . professional associates accompanied the remains to Jersey City. Mr. BURKE leaves a widow but . . . no children.

In all walks of life, Mr. BURKE enjoyed a popularity unexcelled. . . . He was . . . at home in all low and eccentric comedy parts, and during a brief engagement, we have seen him appear successively as Yorkshire man,

Yankee, Frenchman and Cockney, and in whatever *role* he undertook, he was certain to keep his audience in . . . constant laughter by his quiet humor. In his private life, Mr. BURKE's character was unexceptionable, and among those who were his friends the fondest memories of past associations will exist.

A different picture of Charley is provided by Dr. G. A. Kane, who claimed to have known him in Baltimore and later in California in the 1840's.

Burke came out to California in the early days and made a great deal of money and a fine reputation, but dissipated habits soon ended his career. He died in New York. Upon his death-bed, he gave Joe his play [*Rip Van Winkle*] and begged him not to drink or gamble and told him to play Rip and some good would come out of it. . . . Poor Charley! He was born too soon. What money and reputation would he not have made if he had lived in these days [1884], when actors wear the best of clothes, board in first-class hotels, drink champagne, smoke 25 cent cigars, wear mustaches, sport kid gloves, twirl gold-headed canes, have their pictures hung up in store windows and are interviewed by report-ers? Yes, Charley was born too soon.

Winter, *Life and Art,* 115; Deaths, 21, The City of New York Department of Records and Information Service, Municipal Archives, n.p; *New York Daily Times,* November 13, 1854: 4; *American and Commercial Advertiser* (Balti-more), November 9 (4), November 15 (3) 1854; *New York Mirror,* June 14, 1884: 8.

145. At first, *The Naiad Queen* was popular enough not to require any comic afterpiece, but on December 25, 1854, afterpieces were added, and from then on, Joe often performed two roles in an evening. In addition to acting, Jefferson performed at least one "doleful song," specifically "Villikins and his Dinah." Margaret Jefferson was singled out for praise by the local critic as the lieutenant of the army of female warriors. On Christmas day the Baltimore Museum company gave a matinee of *The Naiad Queen,* and Joe and Margaret performed *The Alarming Sacrifice* as an afterpiece. On April 27, Jefferson received a benefit and played Jacques Strop in *Robert Macaire* as an afterpiece to the "Oriental spectacle." On January 6, 1855, Joe and Margaret appeared in the museum's "Saturday Afternoon Festival" when *The Naiad Queen* was presented in a rare matinee. When Jefferson produced another scenic spectacle, *Aladdin or The Wonderful Lamp,* Margaret played one of the roles. As he did with *The Naiad Queen,* Jefferson added both an afterpiece and a Saturday matinee to *Aladdin* after the show's first eighteen performances. He also buoyed up attendance by advertising the number of performances *Aladdin* had played, numbers he tended to inflate, claiming that the show had reached its sixtieth performance when it had barely reached its fortieth. Margaret continued to perform into her seventh month of pregnancy. *American and Commercial Advertiser,* December 6 (2), December 15 (2), December 25 (2) 1854; January 6 (3), January 30 (3),

February 5 (3), March 17 (2), April 11 (3), April 27 (2, 3), April 30 (3), May 12 (3), May 23 (2) 1855.

146. *Lend Me Five Shillings* was first produced at the Haymarket Theatre in London on February 19, 1846. By the time Jefferson performed it, it was already established within the repertoire of American afterpieces. It opens in a room adjoining a public ballroom at a hotel. When the curtain rises, Mr. Golightly is flirting with Mrs. Major Phobbs. She rejects him, and in revenge Golightly exits to gamble and loses every shilling in his pocket. When Mrs. Major Phobbs suddenly indicates that she desires him to call a carriage and escort her home, however, Golightly instantly accepts, forgetting that he has no money. He frantically goes from person to person, trying to borrow five shillings. When he tries to pawn his coat, he discovers that the coat has been stolen. Because of a series of mishaps, the more money he tries to borrow, the more he winds up owing. Meanwhile Golightly mistakes the identity of the woman with whom he has been flirting, and a duel almost ensues. But the error is cleared up, and at the end of the play, Golightly, still broke, appeals to the audience directly to "lend me five shillings." John Maddison Morton, *Lend Me Five Shillings* (New York: M. Couglas, n.d.), 531; Jefferson Winter, 42.

147. On February 7, 1855, Jefferson performed for the first time yet another role for which he would later become famous—Newman Noggs in *Nicholas Nickleby*. He was not, however, performing the Boucicault version in which he later made his reputation. *American and Commercial Advertiser* (Baltimore), February 7, 1855: 3.

148. On July 1, 1855, Jefferson and John Sleeper Clarke rented the Howard Athenaeum and Gallery of Arts on the upper floors of a large building on the northeast corner of Baltimore and Charles streets in Baltimore. They renamed it the Charles Street Theatre and began to perform. There is no sign of the theatre after two days of advertisement in the local newspaper, and this may have been a temporaray way of making money. Winter, *Life and Art,* 193; J. Thomas Scharf, *Chronicles of Baltimore* (Baltimore, 1874), 443, 526; *American and Commercial Advertiser* (Baltimore), May 29, 1855: 2, 3.

149. *New York Dramatic Mirror,* February 23 (14), March 26 (14), April 20 (14) 1901.

150. Mary Devlin delivered the opening address in Jarrett's theatre in Washington. Joseph Jefferson, "In Memory of Edwin Booth," *Modern Eloquence,* 692.

151. Jefferson's personal financial situation apparently allowed him to make a contribution to the American Dramatic Washington Monument Association, an attempt to raise money from theatre professionals for the building of the monument.

An alarming notice indicated that the profits of the Washington venture were gained at the cost of potential danger.

Last Wednesday night, there was . . . a *house* as ought to satisfy any Manager . . . but the thought would intrude itself, as I looked . . . upon the densely-packed throng, that, should a panic be raised, a cry of fire, or the . . . actual danger from fire amidst the combustible material about the stage, what a horrible catastrophe would . . . be recorded! [A]mid the confusion . . . of such an event, out of the estimated number of 2,500 spectators, at least 1,000 would meet with *certain* death. It could not be otherwise, for in going out in an orderly manner from the boxes through the *one narrow* doorway, and at the foot of the stairs meeting the crowd from the parquet, and there jammed, it requires some twenty or thirty minutes to clear the house.

While Jefferson opened the Washington theatre, the Baltimore Museum turned into a concert hall for two days. In Washington, the local critic wrote:

Rain and muddy streets could not keep . . . people from the Theatre on Saturday night. There was not merely a full, but a crowded house. . . . The drama is . . . a novelty in Washington, . . . and when the manager presents an entertainment . . . on but one or two evenings of each week, they [the audience] go thither in throngs, without scanning . . . the character of the entertainment.

American and Commercial Advertiser (Baltimore), October 3 (3), October 6 (3) 1855; Wilson, 298; *New York Mirror,* April 18, 1885: 9.

152. On November 14, 1855, Jefferson played Dromio of Ephesus in Washington. *American and Commercial Advertiser* (Baltimore), October 18 (3), October 29 (3), October 31 (2), November 7 (3), November 8 (3) 1855; "Joseph Jefferson in the Capital City," Clipping, Bourne Historical Center; *Daily National Intelligencer* (Washington, D.C.), October 2 (1), October 9 (2), October 22 (3), October 23 (3), November 5 (3), November 14 (3), November 17 (1), November 19 (3), November 26 (3), November 28 (3), November 30 (3) 1855.

153. Winter, *Life and Art,* 193; *American and Commercial Advertiser* (Baltimore), December 12 (3), December 14 (3), December 31 (3) 1855; *Daily National Intelligencer* (Washington), December 17, 1855: 1.

154. Fifty years later, after he had been involved in several all-star tours, Jefferson pronounced the 1853 *School for Scandal* "an artistic failure," because the actors were not accustomed to playing together and considered themselves of equal importance. Jefferson also performed two roles on one evening in two different theatres on January 3, 1856, when he played Mr. Bobtail at the Holliday Street Theatre and Jack Cabbage at the Museum. *Daily National Intelligencer* (Washington), December 28 (1), December 31 (1) 1855; *American and Commercial Advertiser* (Baltimore), December 27, 1855: 2, January 1 (3), January 3 (3) 1856; "Why 'All Star' Casts Fail," Robinson Locke Theatre Collection, 302: 40, New York Public Library at Lincoln Center.

155. Margaret Jefferson performed only comic roles opposite her husband,

whereas Mary Devlin performed both serious and comic plays. Jefferson appeared for a second time as Newman Noggs at the Holliday Street Theatre on January 21, 1856, as part of a benefit for the Holliday's leading lady, Mrs. I. B. Phillips. *American and Commercial Advertiser* (Baltimore), January 7 (3), January 8 (2), January 9 (3), January 15 (3), January 21 (2, 3), February 20 (2) 1856.

156. A week later, the Baltimore company gave its last performance, and on March 13 Jefferson opened with members of the Museum Company at the Charles Street Theatre. The Charles Street venture lasted only a few days, but the Baltimore Museum reopened, and Jefferson worked in both cities until March 17, 1856. From then on, he concentrated on Washington. Mary Devlin also appeared both in Baltimore and in Washington. *American and Commercial Daily Advertiser* (Baltimore), March 13, 1856: 2.

157. In early April, Washington's National Theatre was taken over for a week by an opera troupe; consequently on April 7 its regular company opened a brief engagement at the Richmond Theatre with Jefferson serving as both stage manager and "well known star." They performed there through April 15, 1856, with Jefferson appearing again opposite Agnes Robertson, who had begun work with him in Washington and followed the company to Virginia. *Daily National Intelligencer* (Washington D.C.), March 1 (1), March 3 (1), March 18 (1), April 4 (1), April 9 (1), May 31 (1) 1856; *Spirit of the Times* (New York), March 29, 1856: 84; *New York Dramatic Mirror,* September 30, 1899: 3; *Richmond Enquirer,* April 4, 1856: 3.

158. Davis, 67.

159. "Joseph Jefferson in the Capital City," Clipping Collection, Jonathan Bourne Historical Center, Bourne, Massachusetts.

160. Wilson, 80; William Winter, "Joseph Jefferson," *Harper's New Monthly Magazine* (August 1886): 395.

161. John Jack, who was a member of Jefferson's company in the late nineteenth century, remembered that Jefferson was playing Touchstone in *As You Like It* when word came that the child was dying, but there is no other evidence that Jefferson ever performed the role. Winter, *Life and Art,* 193; *Autobiography,* 157; *New York Times,* October 23, 1860: 4; Eugenie Jefferson, 229–30; *New York Dramatic Mirror,* March 26, 1901: 14.

162. In Richmond, Jefferson performed at least ten roles, including Dr. Pangloss, Mr. Golightly, Shortcut in *The Spitfire,* and Diggory in *The Spectre Bridegroom. Richmond Enquirer,* November 14, 1856: 3; *Daily National Intelligencer* (Washington), November 22 (1), November 26 (1) 1856.

163. The Richmond theatre had a parquette, a dress circle, a second tier of boxes, and two tiers of galleries. Patrons paid between twenty and fifty cents. Jefferson played Golightly in *Lend Me Five Shillings,* Bob Acres in *The Rivals,* and Dromio of Syracuse to John Drew's Dromio of Ephesus in *A Comedy of Errors.* In an afterpiece called *The Waterman,* Jefferson sang "so well that he was loudly encored." *Porter's Spirit of the Times* noted that he "is no less appreciated

[in Richmond] for his talents as a comedian than for his estimable qualities as a gentleman." *Richmond Enquirer,* December 5, 1856: 3; February 20 (3), February 27 (1) 1857; *Porter's Spirit of the Times,* December 20, 1856: 264.

164. Joseph Jefferson, "In Memory of Edwin Booth," *Modern Eloquence,* 691.

165. Margaret Jefferson also performed in Richmond, sometimes opposite Joe, and played Lady Teazle at her benefit in March 1857. *The Players* (n.p.: The Gilliss Press, 1894), 38. *Richmond Enquirer,* March 10, 1857: 3.

166. After a two-week run as Schnapps in *The Fairy Queen,* Jefferson went on to his other traditional comic roles. For his benefit on June 26 he played Dr. Ollapod in *The Poor Gentleman.* Business, however, was not good. Jefferson's name never appears in newspaper advertisements after his benefit, and after August 10 the theatre passed to new management. *New York Dramatic Mirror,* January 5, 1895: 2; *Public Ledger* (Philadelphia), May 16 (4), June 1 (3), June 26 (3) 1857.

167. *New York Daily Times,* August 18, 1857: 5.

5. The Years With Laura Keene, 1857–1859   *pages 64–78*

168. The *New York Daily Times* estimated that there were "about *twenty* theatres, concerts rooms, &c., open nightly, holding upon an average probably fifteen hundred persons. If the admission fee averages half a dollar, here are nearly $15,000 expended every night, or nearly $100,000 every week for amusements."

The Metropolitan was located in the LaFarge Building, on Broadway opposite Bond street. Keene's management was, from the first, fraught with difficulties. Scenery for the opening night production was vandalized, and Keene had to postpone the theatre's premiere and substitute another play.

The New York Daily Times located Keene's second theatre at 624 Broadway, on the east side of the street, below Bleecker and a few doors above Houston Street, half a block north of Niblo's Garden. The *Spirit of the Times* located the building two doors above Houston between Bleecker and Houston. Its appearance, the work of the theatrical architect John M. Trimble, merited almost a full column in the *Spirit of the Times.* Although its description of the theatre's interior makes a modern reader feel that it must have overpowered any play presented there, particularly in a period when house lights remained on during performances, the space was considered intimate for its time, and described as a "little jewel of a place." *New York Daily Times,* December 24, 1855: 6; November 19, 1856: 4; February 1, 1858: 4; Ben Graf Heneke, *Laura Keene—A Biography* (Tulsa, Oklahoma: Council Oak Books, 1990), 59–66; *Porter's Spirit of the Times,* October 25, 1856: 136.

169. Jefferson's sister Connie had been a minor member of Keene's company in 1856, and may have made her aware of his work. Connie played one

of the ensemble roles in *Camille*, but appeared primarily in the one-act farces that ended each evening. She continued her work in the company through the 1857 season. The *Spirit of the Times* goes on to note that

> the . . . struggle among . . . places of public amusement . . . appears to be, which shall excel . . . in bringing out something *new*. . . . New York has been "put to its purgation" with . . . theatrical novelties. . . . Miss Keene, on Monday evening, brought out a new piece. . . . The plot is . . . old . . . take it all in all, it is one of those *very* correct pieces—very *good* but . . . a *bore*. Like every thing . . . which Miss Keene supervises, the piece is well put on the stage, and her own part well sustained.

New York Daily Times, December 12, 1856: 6; September 28, 1857: 3; *Spirit of the Times,* (New York) May 23 (180), May 30 (192) 1857.

170. On September 1, 1857, Jefferson appeared opposite Laura Keene in a comedy entitled *A Conjugal Lesson*, a play he had performed with his wife in Richmond. The *New York Daily Times* critic wrote:

> In it there are but two characters sustained by MISS LAURA KEENE and MR. JEFFERSON; the former a neglected wife, the latter a husband who affects the club and the small hours of the morning. The piece exhibits . . . the drunken *nonchalance* of the spouse and the vexation of the wife, ending in suspicion and jealousy on both parts. The latter passion is aroused by the *contretemps of Mr. Lullaby,* returning from the club with a coat which does not belong to him. His wife examines the pockets. . . . She finds a pocket-book, a handkerchief and a pair of . . . gloves, without exciting her suspicion; but presently she fishes out a . . . *billet* from a . . . ballet dancer, at which discovery she rushes from the room in an agony. *Mr. Lullaby* is aroused from his slumbers somewhat sobered and . . . comes upon the pocket-book which he . . . supposes . . . abandoned by some destroyer of his domestic happiness. The scene between the two which ensues is . . . amusing, of course, with a satisfactory explanation.
>
> *A Conjugal Lesson* is . . . a screaming comicality. It affords the widest scope for MR. JEFFERSON's comic powers. . . . The house was in a constant roar. He is . . . the best low comedian in this City; . . . painstaking, yet completely abandoned, and at his ease.

New York Daily Times, September 1 (3), September 3 (4) 1857.

171. *New York Daily Times,* September 1, 1857: 4.

172. The afterpiece performed with *The Heir-at-Law* was *The Castle Spectre or A Ghost in Spite of Himself*, in which Jefferson played Diggory with "such droll contortions of face and body" that he "convulsed the house with laughter by his extravagant . . . playing." *Spirit of the Times* (New York), September 5, 1857: 360.

173. Tolles, 161; *New York Daily Times,* September 7, 1857: 6.

174. *The Sea of Ice* opened on November 5. It was the third time it had run

in New York, but the first time it had ever been successful. The *New York Times* wrote: "In Baltimore . . . the piece had a long run, and as MR. JEFFERSON played the principal comic character there, it is reasonable to believe that he had something to do with it and that his talent will continue to a similar result in New York." The *New York Times,* October 30 (6), November 4 (6), November 6 (4), November 9 (6) 1857.

175. *The Sea of Ice* featured a scenic spectacle that Keene emphasized in her advertisements, which also reprinted the entire review from the *Spirit of the Times*—surely one of the first times this occurred in the history of the American theatre. The play ran until December 19, 1857, giving forty-three consecutive performances, and was later revived for nine additional performances in the winter and spring of 1858. *Spirit of the Times* (New York), October 25, 1864: 434; *The New York Times,* November 12 (6), November 16 (6), November 20 (6), November 23 (6), December 12 (6), December 19 (6) 1857; January 5, 1858: 4.

176. *Spirit of the Times* (New York), December 26, 1857: 552; Winter, *Life and Art,* 193.

177. For his benefit, Jefferson performed Toby Twinkles in *All That Glitters Is Not Gold,* Mr. Brown in *My Neighbor's Wife,* and Diggory in *The Spectre Bridegroom,* soon to be billed as "his great character." The *Spirit of the Times* told its public that "this same modest and unassuming Mr. Jefferson stands . . . high in the estimation of our play-going public, as well as in that of the critics." *Spirit of the Times* (New York), February 13 (12), February 20 (24), February 27 (36) 1858; *New York Times,* February 13 (6), February 25 (3) 1858.

178. Eleanor Farjeon, 28.

179. Edwin Booth, "To Joseph Jefferson," April 26, 1858, The Hampden-Booth Theatre Library at The Players, New York City. The letter is transcribed in Asia Booth Clarke, *The UnLocked Door* (New York: Faber and Faber, 1938), 17, 194–6.

180. On April 15, 1858, Keene advertised that *Blanche of Brandywine* had been in preparation for many weeks "with new and BEAUTIFUL SCENERY, APPROPRIATE MUSIC, COSTUMES AND PROPERTIES." *The New York Times,* April 15 (3), April 19 (4), April 21 (2), April 22 (3), May 6 (1) 1858.

181. A New York reviewer wrote:

A patriot drama . . . with a comic negro as the principal character, was produced here last night with complete success. It is called *Blanche of Brandywine*—and the misfortunes of the lady, who is beloved by an unprincipled English nobleman and beleaguered by a . . . revengeful Tory, form the connecting thread of the story, if indeed the story be connected at all. The heroine is played by MISS KEENE, and the very little she has to do is done effectively. The dramatist should have provided more liberally for such an accomplished artist. . . . Some excellent pictures are presented by MISS KEENE; the costumes are . . . accurate; and most of the scenery is

admirable. For the rest, *Blanche of Brandywine* owes her success to the drollery of MR. JEFFERSON and the chattering of the negro *Sampson.*
Spirit of the Times (New York), May 1, 1858: 144.

182. *Blanche of Brandywine* (New York, 1858), 3f.

183. The New York season closed the week of Jefferson's benefit, and Keene arranged for the thirty-three-member acting company's transfer to Mrs. D. P. Bowers's Walnut Street Theatre in Philadelphia, where they opened on May 17 for a month. Mrs. Bowers and her company (including Jefferson's sister Connie) came to New York and performed at Keene's theatre. *Spirit of the Times* (New York), May 15 (168), May 22 (180), May 29 (192) 1858; *Public Ledger* (Philadelphia), May 17 (3), June 3 (3) 1858; *New York Times,* May 12, 1858: 3.

184. Paradise Valley was hospitable to actors and became a nineteenth-century theatrical summer resort. James B. Runnion, Jefferson's first biographer, reported in 1869:

> Some time ago . . . Jefferson saw [John Sefton, the actor who shared a New York tenement with Joe's family in 1836] near his house in Paradise Valley. He found Sefton . . . standing in the middle of a . . . stream. . . . Sefton stood . . . watching . . . a little pig which the stream was carting down its current. . . . Jefferson . . . dropped his fishing—tackle and took his sketch-book to transfer the ludicrous scene to paper. Sefton appreciated the humor of the situation and only objected when Jefferson began to fill in the background with a dilapidated old barn, at which the old gentleman demurred on account of its wretched appearance. The artist insisted that it was picturesque, however, and proceeded to put it down. Sefton had to submit, but he had his revenge by writing back to New York that "Jefferson is here, drawing the worst 'houses' I ever saw."

"To draw a house," of course, refers to the ability of an actor to fill the seats of a theatre. Runnion, 171; "Leisure Hours" Archives, Theatre Museum of the City of New York; Eleanor Farjeon, 67; Eugenie Jefferson, 162; *Porter's Spirit of the Times,* July 31, 1858: 352.

185. Eleanor Farjeon, 45, 61.

186. The season opened on August 25. Keene attempted to cash in on the excitement generated by the laying of the Atlantic cable with a one act "fairy extravaganza" entitled *Love and Lightning* in which Jefferson had the lead, but the *New York Times* blasted the piece as "unworthy of the occasion and the theatre in which it is played." The cable failed and so did the play. In *The Rivals* Keene appeared as Lydia Languish and E. A. Sothern as Captain Absolute. In *The School for Scandal* Jefferson performed opposite Keene's Lady Teazle and Sothern's Charles Surface. Jefferson also got the chance to dance a breakdown in *Jenny Lind* and to sing in *Fra Diavolo,* a "nonsensical burlesque" that featured his niece Effie Germon, the daughter of Jane Anderson Germon. *Spirit of the Times* (New York), August 21 (336), August 28 (348), September 11 (372),

September 18 (384) 1858; Oggel, xii; *New York Times,* September 4 (4), September 8 (3), September 9 (4) 1858; *New York Dramatic Mirror,* January 26 (14), April 6 (14), 15 June 15 (12) 1901; Daniel Walker Howe, "Victorian Culture in America," *Victorian America* (Philadelphia: University of Pennsylvania Press, 1976), 3.

187. In 1880 the *New York Mirror* wrote that the play was "a mere sketch [presumably by Tom Taylor] . . . that was found among the effects of Josh Silisbee [the Yankee actor] after his death and purchased for a mere song." Jefferson then took it "in hand" and "rearranged" it so that his became the leading role. In another version of its history, the play had originally been brought to the theatrical impresario and actor Lester Wallack by Bancroft Davis, a friend of his father's. Wallack decided he could not use it and said that it needed a great Yankee character actor. He recommended Jefferson. In 1865 Jefferson testified in a court trial: "first saw the manuscript of this play at Miss Keene's; a professed agent of Mr. Taylor's was here then."

Jefferson's costar, E. A. Sothern, initially had no interest in the role of Lord Dundreary. Sothern's son, E. L. Sothern, credited Jefferson with his father's decision to take the role of Dundreary, a role that became as identified with Sothern as Rip Van Winkle was with Jefferson. E. L. Sothern's anecdote below reinforces the perception, which came to be widely held, that Joe was tight with money.

> My father and Jefferson used to ride horseback . . . every morning . . . in the park at New York, and they shared the expenses. Joe says that his sole object in persuading the governor to play Dundreary was to keep both the horses, because if his friend lost his engagement, he couldn't afford to ride, and Joe couldn't stand the expense alone. . . . In his heart he felt my father's judgement was correct. It was . . . a beast of a part. When father made the immense hit in *Our American Cousin,* nobody was more dumbfounded than Jefferson.

Nils Erk Enkvist, *Caricatures of Americans on the English Stage Prior to 1870* (Port Washington, N.Y.: Helsingford, 1951), 124–27; Lester Wallack, *Memories of Fifty Years* (New York, 1889), 159; *New York Mirror,* May 8, 1880: 9; Leslie, 33.

188. "The traditional Down-Easter wore long hair and short trousers and talked through his nose. Mr. Jefferson's Yankee wore long trousers and short hair and talked from his mouth. The innovation was so successful that it forever banished the old-time stage Yankee from the boards." Sara Stevens, who played the milkmaid with whom Asa falls in love, recalled the play's rehearsal process:

> On the first reading . . . , I sat beside [Jefferson] and looking up into his face said: "How I should like the part of *Mary Meredith!*" And he replied "I think you should have it." . . . After he had received his part of *Asa Trenchard,* I said to him: "Won't you please play it in your own hair? I think your style of wearing it is just suited to the character, and it

would seem so much more appropriate." He paid me the compliment of accepting my suggestion so far as to have a wig made with the hair arranged exactly as he was in the habit of wearing it. And he said afterward that my remark gave him the first idea of dressing *Asa Trenchard* like the gentleman he is. I remember that he wore a beautiful suit of light gray cloth of fine texture. . . . His hat was of the same color.

Davis 68; Clapp and Edgett, 346.

189. The *New York Times* commented that "to [Jefferson's] exertions we ascribe the success of the piece for we do not think that MR. TOM TAYLOR's . . . merits in this case would have insured that result." Keene advertised that by December 27, 1858, 100,000 people had seen the play; by January 3, 1859—115,000; by January 10—130,000; by January 17—140,000; by January 24—150,000; by January 31,—160,000; by February 14—180,000; by February 21—190,000; by February 28—200,000; by March 7—211,000. Extra matinee performances were scheduled for Thanksgiving and Christmas as well as New Year's day, 1859. When the company gave a benefit for the Mount Vernon Fund Association on December 29, Keene donated "the entire gross receipts without deducting even the printing and advertising expenses toward the purchase of the Washington estate." On the occasion of its one hundredth consecutive performance, Keene gave out copies of "Our American Cousin Polka arranged for the Piano-forte with a beautiful illuminated title page, the publisher's price of which is thirty-five cents or almost equal to one ticket of admission" free of charge to each woman in the audience. *Spirit of the Times,* December 11 1858 (528), December 18 (548) 1858; January 1 1859: 564; *New York Times,* October 19 (4), November 15 (3), November 16 (4), December 20 (3), December 27 (4), December 29 (3) 1858; January 3 (6), January 10 (6) 1859; January 24 (3), January 31 (3), February 4 (3), February 10 (3), February 14 (3), February 21 (3), March 7 (3) 1859; *New York Mirror,* May 8, 1880: 9; *New York Clipper,* October 20, 1866: 220.

190. In late January 1859 the *Spirit of the Times* reported:

Determined to . . . spend two hours . . . with *Our American Cousin,* we wended our way to this pretty little house the early part of the week, reaching it a quarter of an hour before the time in order to procure a good seat. We were somewhat startled to find at the ticket office a note *"Standing Room Only!"* but were not thereby deterred from making an effort. 'Twas in vain, however, and no alternative remained but to back out (with much difficulty) and leave room for some unfortunate . . . whose perseverance . . . deserved a square foot of standing room. We have not the least doubt that this piece might be kept upon the stage until the end of the season with profit, but Mr. Jefferson has made engagements to play it elsewhere, and it must therefore be withdrawn before that time arrives.

Jefferson's position as a star meant that he no longer had to perform nightly in both the main piece and the comic one-act afterpiece. The one exception was his benefit night on February 12, 1859, when he appeared as Diggory in *The Spectre Bridegroom* and Asa Trenchard. At a second benefit on February 19, Jefferson and Keene revived one of their hits from the 1857–58 season, *A Conjugal Lesson,* and performed it as an afterpiece with *Our American Cousin.* *Spirit of the Times* (New York), January 22, 1859: 600; *New York Times,* February 11 (3), February 12 (3), February 19 (3) 1859; Gamaliel Bradford, *Portraits and Personalities* (Boston: Houghton Mifflin Company, 1933), 100.

191. *New York Daily Times,* September 28, 1857: 3.

192. *Autobiography,* 198.

193. *Ibid.,* 198–200.

194. *Ibid.,* 204.

195. John Creahan, *The Life of Laura Keene* (Philadelphia, 1897), 75–76.

196. Winter, *The Jeffersons,* 180–181; Veranne Bryan, *Laura Keene* (Jefferson, North Carolina: McFarland & Company, 1993), 167.

197. When *A Midsummer Night's Dream* finally opened on April 18, 1859, Blake, not Jefferson, played Nick Bottom, the weaver. The fact that they could play the same role may have contributed to the quarrel.

6. Boucicault and Stardom, 1859–1861   *pages 79–98*

198. On April 18, 1859, the *Spirit of the Times* announced that "Mr. Jefferson ... will probably rest a short time and then show some of our principal cities the kind of 'Cousin' we have been listening to for the past ever-so-many months." In late April, Jefferson began a tour to Buffalo, New York; Halifax, Nova Scotia; and Portland, Maine. His performances in Portland were not "enthusiastically received," although his benefit on May 1 was "well attended." By June 4 the same paper was announcing Jefferson's determination to "sail for Liverpool within a month" to perform *Our American Cousin* in "London, probably at the Haymarket early in the season."

Mary Devlin's letter notes: "I was quite ill, and but for Mr. Jefferson's entreaties, would have given up all thoughts of pleasure. . . . Mrs. Jefferson and myself play for Joe's benefit on Saturday, then leave for P Valley, stay one week and return to the city. . . ." *New York Clipper,* April 23 (6), April 30 (14), May 21(39), June 11 (62, 63) 1859; *Porter's Spirit of the Times* (New York), March 12 (30), July 23 (336) 1859; Terry L. Oggel, ed., *The Letters of Mary Devlin* (New York: Greenwood Press, 1987), 4.

199. In late April and early May, Jefferson performed in Buffalo, New York. In late May 1859 he and Sothern performed *Our American Cousin* in Halifax, Nova Scotia. In Boston, after Asa Trenchard, Jefferson switched to Solon Shingle in *The People's Lawyer,* Clod Meddlenot in *The Lady of the Lions* (a spoof of Bulwer-Lytton's romantic drama, *The Lady of Lyons*), and other comic pieces. A planned production of *The Courier of Lyons or the Attack on the Mail,* in which Jefferson was scheduled to appear, never materialized. On the last night of his engagement, the company produced *Blanche of Brandywine,* which it held over for a performance on the Fourth of July. A rumor spread in New York that *Our*

American Cousin had been performed five to seven times on the Fourth of July, but there is no evidence of this in the Boston newspapers. Jefferson closed in Boston with a farewell benefit on July 7. At Niblo's Gardens, Jefferson appeared in four characters in a complimentary benefit tendered him by William E. Burton, his old boss and now the Gardens' manager. Among the pieces was *A Conjugal Lesson*, the farce he had performed with Laura Keene during the 1858–59 season. *Boston Evening Transcript,* January 15 (3), June 27 (3), July 1 (3), July 7 (3) 1859; *Porter's Spirit of the Times* (New York), April 16 (120), April 30 (144), May 7 (160), May 21 (192), May 28 (208), June 4 (204), June 18 (228), July 9 (304) 1859; Playbills dated June 22, July 2, July 5, July 6. 1859, Howard Athenaeum, Boston Public Library; *New York Times,* July 20 (7), May 22 (7) 1859; *New York Clipper,* July 9 (94), July 16 (102), July 30 (118), August 6 (126) 1859.

200. Boucicault and Jefferson both worked for William Stuart, the lessee and proprietor of the theatre. Stuart had taken a five-year lease on the theatre and hired Boucicault as his stage director and Boucicault's wife, Agnes Robertson, as his leading lady. Jefferson was their lead comic actor. But Stuart also had to borrow money from several investors in order to open, among them his friend Thomas Fields, who was appointed "trustee" to protect these investments. The situation would prove problematic.

The theatre, newly rebuilt on the site of the "Metropolitan," had just been completed. The *New York Times* noted that Jefferson had delayed his departure for England to participate in its opening. Effie Germon, Jefferson's first cousin once-removed, was also a member of the company. Although Jefferson made his reputation in Boucicault's adaptation of *The Cricket on the Hearth*, he later used a version by Albert Smith, a monologue entertainer and well-known wit. *New York Times,* August 29 (4), September 1 (7), September 9 (4), December 26 (2) 1859; *New York Dramatic Mirror,* November 9, 1895: 13.

201. Jefferson had played Caleb Plummer in Charleston in 1852, probably in a version witten by W. T. Townsend. W. T. Townsend, *The Cricket on the Hearth* (London: Thomas Hailes Lacy, n.d.), 1–24.

202. Laurence Hutton, *Plays and Players,* 197–199.

203. *The Argus* (Melbourne), July 14, 1862: 5, 8; November 14, 1864: 5.

204. By the time Jefferson Winter performed with his godfather, Joe was no longer doing the Boucicault version. The lines in the original read:

Caleb: Oh dear, o mum, No it can't be.
Edward: Ain't it.
Caleb. If my Ned, my boy, from the golden South Americas were alive.
Dot. He is, he is, and there he is.
Caleb. My Son.
Edward: Father!
Caleb. It is, it is oh mum, oh lord, here, look here, Ned, ho! ho! ho! my boy, my son.

Missouri Republican (St. Louis), December 30, 1885: 3; Winter, "As I Remember," 42; Ms. Dion Boucicault, *Dot*, J. L. Toole promptbook, New York Public Library at Lincoln Center.

205. Towse went on to discuss an important distinction between Jefferson's characterization and Dickens' original:

> There is not a trace in Mr. Jefferson's *Caleb* of the dull, vacant, hopeless depression which the novelist paints with so pathetic a touch. He has not the dull eye and vacuous manner . . . of a spirit crushed by perpetual . . . misery, because there is not in the comedian himself any sympathy with this . . . phase of human nature. His own temperament is buoyant, hopeful, placid and sunny, and he naturally—it might be said necessarily—invests *Caleb* with some of his own . . . humor . . . without robbing the part of any of its exquisite pathos. He . . . heightens . . . the picture by . . . contrast. . . . There is nothing . . . more touching than those scenes where *Caleb* listens while *Dot* reveals to *Bertha* the story of his . . . deceit and where he recognizes the son whom he deemed lost in "the golden South Americas." The play of emotion on Mr. Jefferson's face at the moment of recognition, as wonderment, doubt and hope are succeeded by certainty and . . . joy,—his deprecatory, spasmodic action as he turns away from what he evidently fears is a delusion of the senses and his fired rush into the arms of his son,— are triumphs. . . . The minutest "business" is transacted with a . . . precision which could not . . . be surpassed. Nowhere is there a sign of premeditation . . . ; all is done simply, naturally and without strain.

J. Rankin Towse, "Joseph Jefferson as 'Caleb Plummer,'" *Century* 27, 476–477.

206. *Spirit of the Times* (New York), September 29, 1859: 396; *New York Times,* September 27 (7), September 29 (4) 1859.

207. *New York Times,* October 17, 1859: 4.

208. By the third week of the season, Boucicault had gone to Thomas Fields and asked that Stuart be removed as head of the theatre and that Fields take over. The request was repeated on October 6, 1859. Fields and Stuart agreed, and Fields went from being a backer to being a theatre proprietor. Stuart became his assistant. Stuart then asked Boucicault and Robertson to become shareholders in the theatre instead of salaried actors. Boucicault countered with an offer in which he agreed to write two plays for the theatre, one of which was a "Mississippi piece" that he had been thinking about "for the last three or four years." This was to be ready on approximately December 1. In return for his services as a playwright and director and for Robertson's work as an actress, Boucicault asked for twelve percent of the net weekly profits or $100 per week until at least January 15, 1860, or until *The Octoroon*, as the "Mississippi piece" was called, closed. Stuart, Fields, and Boucicault struck a bargain during the week of October 10, 1859, and on October 19 the first of the two promised plays, Boucicault's burlesque *Chamouni,* opened. It failed. *The Octoroon* was

five weeks from completion, and Boucicault needed a new play quickly. *Smike* was the result. *New York Times*, November 1, 1859: 7; *New York Clipper*, September 24, 1859: 182.

209. Winter, *Life and Art,* 193; Eleanor Farjeon, 48, 79; Eleanor Farjeon, "Joe in Paradise," *"Rip Van Winkle": The Autobiography of Joseph Jefferson* (New York: Appleton-Century-Crofts, 1950), xvi.

210. *The Times*' reviewer wrote:

> Mr JEFFERSON's *Newman Noggs* is . . . a surprise, such as each new *role* becomes in the hands of this admirable actor. Mr JEFFERSON always puts off his individuality with his great-coat in the Green-room, . . . absorbing himself so absolutely in the character . . . that you are . . . tempted to believe he can never emerge . . . to fill any other part. When he was *Caleb Plummer*, who believed that he ever played *Asa Trenchard*? Now that he is *Newman Noggs*, who will believe that he was ever *Caleb Plummer*?

New York Times, November 2, 1859: 4.

211. *Daily National Intelligencer* (Washington), December 17, 1866: 2.

212. It was not until *Smike*'s success was assured that Boucicault was willing to admit he had actually adapted it from Dickens' novel. Toward the end of its run, the play was paired with *Dot* in an evening of Dickens. Jefferson used *Smike* for his benefit on November 21, along with a one-act Yankee character farce entitled *Solon Shingle*. *New York Times,* November 4 (7), November 21 (6) 1859.

213. Wilson, 268.

214. *New York Times,* December 5 (7), December 20 (2) 1859; November 20, 1860: 4.

215. The controversy may have been engineered by Boucicault to stir up business. *Spirit of the Times* (New York), December 17, 1859: 213; *New York Times,* December 26, 1859: 4.

216. Two days before *The Octoroon* opened, Boucicault and Robertson demanded that the theatre's profits be divided nightly, not weekly. Fields refused. After the opening Robertson claimed that as a result of the play's controversial nature, she had received "letters threatening me with violence, and when I go on the stage, I do so in fear of some outrage to myself or to my husband." She publicly implored the theatre's manager, William Stuart, and his partner, Thomas C. Fields, to withdraw the play. Relations between the Boucicaults and Stuart and Fields deteriorated. Stuart, on December 12, had a surreptitious copy of the prompt script made. His suspicions were well founded. That evening, Boucicault took the original script home, supposedly for alterations, and also tried to make off with the orchestral arrangements. The next day, December 13, Robertson quit the company, and Boucicault attempted to withdraw *The Octoroon* from production. Stuart then fired Boucicault as stage manager, hired two actors from the company to replace him and Robertson on less than a day's notice, turned Boucicault and Robertson away from the stage door, and removed Boucicault's name, as author, from advertisements for *The*

Octoroon. When Stuart continued to run *The Octoroon* after the Boucicaults left, Boucicault sued him on the basis of violation of copyright and claimed that Stuart was using a surreptitious copy and that the negative political feeling against the play was injurious to his and Robertson's career. In court, Jefferson contended that "no sign of disapprobation of the piece or of any of the sentiments therein has ever escaped the audience on any occasion of the representation of said play, but, on the contrary, every evidence of satisfaction and good will." Field and Stuart countered Boucicault's claim of copyright violation by contending that the play had opened before Boucicault had applied for a copyright. By January 14, 1860, the *Spirit of the Times*, which hated the play, was proclaiming: "*The Octoroon* is gradually losing its interest; the play has become tiresome, and its sectional tendency is . . . being comprehended, and people . . . refuse to witness its performance. We predict that all engaged in this vile misrepresentation of Southern life will . . . regret it; at all events, all engaged in it will be proscribed from the Southern stage." *Spirit of the Times* (New York), December 14, 1859: 552, January 14, 1860: 588; Richard Fawkes, *Dion Boucicault* (London; Quartet Books, 1979), 111; *New York Times,* December 16 (6), December 22 (4), December 26 (2) 1859.

217. On January 23, 1860, Jefferson opened *Lesbia*, Matilda Heron's adaptation of a French drama set in Renaissance Italy, to excellent reviews. Despite his claims to being a director, Jefferson was called a stage manager when he testified on behalf of a fellow actor named George Jordan, who was suing Laura Keene. Keene had cast Jordan in a role he refused to play because he had been engaged as a leading man. Keene had subsequently docked his salary to recover losses. Jefferson testified "that a man employed to do leading business was not always entitled to the choice of parts. He did not think there was a leading part at all in the play . . . that the part . . . was not such a part as he should cast the leading man for . . . that the leading man was entitled to the best part in a play, if it was in his line of business."

Jefferson's testimony, supposedly for Jordan the plaintiff, may indicate that animosity still existed between him and Keene, although the specifics of what he said could be taken as supporting either side. Meanwhile he hired Jordan to perform in his next production at the Winter Garden. *New York Times,* January 6 (2), January 7 (3), January 24 (7), January 25 (3), January 31 (3) 1860.

218. On February 6, while *Oliver Twist* was playing in New York, Jefferson, Mrs. John Wood, and a company drawn from the Winter Garden troupe opened at the Boston Academy of Music. Jefferson stayed for only a week, performing four plays. He returned to acting in New York on February 20, 1860, much to the delight of the *New York Times*: "MR. JEFFERSON is, as heretofore, irreproachable, . . . never exceeding the bounds of good taste."

On March 5 Jefferson opened as Sir Brian de Bore Guilbert, the villain in a burlesque version of *Ivanhoe* opposite a female Ivanhoe, played by Jefferson's comic partner, Mrs. John Wood. The part required him to "execute the most daring acts of horsemanship," and the "great tournament scene was given here as a grand circus act, with a ring, and all the well-known appurtenances of riding-master, clown &c." Jefferson used the play for his benefit on March 12, 1860, an event that attracted the largest crowd ever seen at the Winter Garden. Again the *New York Times* was lavish in its praise. "MR. JEFFERSON . . . as *Sir Brian*, keeps the house in a . . . roar, and . . . shows how easy it is for an . . . . artist to provoke . . . merriment without the slightest descent to vulgarity. We doubt . . . if there has ever been a popular comedian in this country who abstained more absolutely from stage clap traps—who ignored more utterly the easy laughter of coarse suggestions—than MR. JEFFERSON."

On March 10, Joe, along with most of the other notables playing in New York, participated in a grand Benefit Festival in aid of the widow and family of the late actor George Wilkins. The benefit took place at the Academy of Music at 1 P.M.

On March 19 Jefferson opened as Baptiste LaBlanc in a version of Longfellow's *Evangeline*, written by Mrs. Sydney Frances Cowell Bateman and starring her daughter, the former child actress Kate Bateman. In the course of the production, the author's husband, dissatisfied with Jefferson's performance, protested, "It is the best comic part my wife ever wrote," to which Jefferson replied, "It is the worst comic part I ever played." The *New York Times*, which was very kind to the production, agreed with Jefferson's assessment of the role: "The part is of course written up for . . . MR. J. JEFFERSON, who . . . makes the most of it. What little that 'most' may be is due to the actor rather than the authoress, for *Baptiste* is decidely a 'stagey' conception." Eugene Tompkins, *The History of the Boston Theatre* (Boston: The Riverside Press, 1908), 80; *Boston Daily Advertiser,* February 4, 1860: 3; *New York Times,* February 21 (5), March 5 (5), March 6 (8), March 10 (5), March 12 (7), March 14 (1), March 20 (4) 1860; Winter, *Life and Art,* 170; *Spirit of the Times* (New York), February 11 (12), February 25 (36) 1860; Winter, *The Jeffersons,* 183.

219. Jefferson opened for two nights at the Holliday Street Theatre in Baltimore on April 16 and for four nights in Washington on April 18 with a company from the Baltimore theatre. In Baltimore he played four roles in two days; in Washington he played seven roles in four days, performing as many as three roles a performance. *Baltimore American and Commercial Daily Advertiser,* April 16 (2), April 17 (2) 1860; *Daily National Intelligencer* (Washington), April 19, 1860: 1; *New York Times,* April 7, 1860: 5.

220. By mid-June 1860 Jefferson was famous enough to have a local amateur dramatic association named for him. His benefit, however, was panned by the *New York Clipper*. Jefferson appeared as Paul Pry and the newspaper's critic wrote that "instead of the intrusive busybody . . . , we had something too like Asa Trenchard and in fact, too like Mr. Joseph Jefferson himself." By mid-July 1860 the *Spirit of the Times* noted that "we are growing *ratherish* tired of burlesques, and as now Mr. Jefferson has a company fully *up* to first rate standard pieces, we hope that he will give us something that we can give a full column to, and with not a word save of highest praise."

Since Jefferson was present in New York through the month of July, he probably attended the wedding of his best friend, Edwin Booth, to Mary Devlin at Booth's house (154, now 113, West 11th Street). Jefferson had introduced the two. Mary had lived with his family and spent two summer vacations with the Jeffersons in Paradise Valley.

When Tom Taylor, who had written *Our American Cousin*, sent Jefferson a script entitled *The Fool's Revenge* in 1860, based on Hugo's *Le Roi S'Amuse*, Jefferson took it to Mary, "telling her to insist on Edwin's looking at it, the character being tragic and not suited to a comedian." Booth would later make this play one of his great successes. *New York Mirror,* May 8, 1880: 9; *New York Clipper,* May 19 (38), June 16 (71), June 30 (86), July 28 (118) 1860; *Spirit of the Times* (New York), July 14 (280), August 23 (336) 1860; *New York Times,* May 17 (7), June 4 (7) 1860; Oggel, 47; Charles Townsend Copeland, *Edwin Booth* (Boston: Small, Maynard & Company, 1901), 51; Asia Booth Clarke, *The Elder and the Younger Booth* (Boston: 1882), 152.

221. The *New York Times,* however, sent a reviewer to see *Our American Cousin* shortly before the season closed on Friday, August 31, and recorded a far more favorable impression:

> When will *Asa Trenchard* cease to light his cigar with that fabulous amount of money represented by a piece of paper, which he carries in his vest pocket? When will *Lord Dundreary* accomplish that sneeze? Not while . . . [the] theatre can be crowded as it was last night . . . . We dropped in . . . before the curtain fell on the first act, and then there was scarcely standing room, although the play has been performed this season and last near two hundred nights.

Spirit of the Times (New York), April 14 (120), May 21(180), June 23 (240), July 14 (280), July 28 (304), August 18 (344) 1860; "Joseph Jefferson in the Capital City," Washington Clipping Scrapbook, Jonathan Bourne Historical Center, Bourne, Massachusetts; Winter, *The Jeffersons,* 183–184; *New York Times,* July 23 (7), August 29 (4) 1860.

222. "In the evening went to Laura Keene's theatre to see young Jefferson as Goldfinch in Holcroft's comedy of *The Road to Ruin.* Thought Jefferson, the father, one of the best actors he had ever seen; and the son reminded him, in look, gesture, size and make of the father. Had never seen the father in Goldfinch but was delighted with the son." Irving was probably referring to Jefferson's grandfather rather than his father. Winter, *Life and Art,* 184; Pierre M. Irving, *The Life and Letters of Washington Irving,* 4 (New York:1864): 253; *New York Clipper,* September 1, 1860: 158.

223. Irving's *Sketch Book* had been published in 1819, and *Rip Van Winkle,* one of the short stories in it, had been dramatized as early as 1828. The American comedian, James H. Hackett, was using it as a starring piece as early as 1830. Hackett's son, ninety years later, wrote: "My mother used to tell me that Joe Jefferson played the part like a German, where *Rip* was a North River

Dutchman, and in those days, dialects were very marked in our country. But my father soon became identified with the part of *Falstaff*, and he used to say, 'Jefferson is a younger man than I; so I'll let him have *Rip*. I don't care to play against him.'"

During the summer of 1859, Jefferson also visited Washington Irving's home, Sunnyside, and did a silhouette of Irving. Two other silhouettes in the collection are attributed to Jefferson but are unsigned. Silhouette of Washington Irving signed by Joseph Jefferson and dated August 1859, MS Collection, Historic Hudson Valley, Tarrytown, New York; Montrose J. Moses, ed., *Representative Plays by American Dramatists* (Boston: Little Brown and Company, 1921), 17–22.

224. *Philadelphia Inquirer,* June 6, 1871: 7.

225. While railways were often dirty and dangerous, some lines had begun to cater to the demands of their customers for comfort:

> The carpets, the cushions, the chairs with backs, that can be put either way, the room for moving about, the lights, and the warm-airpipes put all, except our first-class [horse-drawn] carriages, to shame. The ingenious contrivance, on the New York and Erie Railway, of a funnel which conveys air down into a chamber, where it is purified by spray forced up from jets below and then makes its way through the car is a specimen of American railway indulgence to Summer travelers. The slanting windows and the screens of tarred canvass for throwing off the dust show the same consideration, while the use of a bell instead of a whistle on leaving stations proves a regard for the human ear.

New York Daily Times, April 6, 1857: 2.

226. Jefferson's Washington opening was advertised two months in advance, an unprecedented amount of time in the period. He opened in *The Heir-at-Law* and as Jacques Strop in *Robert Macaire*. In the course of the run, he also performed Bob Acres, Asa Trenchard, Diggory in *The Spectre Bridegroom*, Mr. Golightly, and Rip. Jefferson later claimed that he had first performed Rip at Washington's Carusi's Hall in 1859. Both A. I. Mudd and I have confirmed that this was inaccurate. On November 16, Jefferson did Newman Noggs and Paul Pry at a farewell benefit, and on Saturday afternoon he gave a rare matinee of *Our American Cousin*. His engagement ended on November 17 with performances of both Newman Noggs and Rip on one bill.

On November 19 Jefferson began playing a twelve-day engagement at the Holliday Street Theatre in Baltimore with a repertoire of eleven plays. His roles included Rip, Bob Acres, Doctor Pangloss, Caleb Plummer, Newman Noggs, Diggory, Golightly, and Asa Trenchard. The *New York Clipper* told its readers that "his Rip Van Winkle has been pronounced by the press to be a great piece of acting." The admiration he now inspired is attested to by the *Baltimore American and Commercial Advertiser:* "Mr. Jefferson was always a good actor, but he has so . . . improved that those who remember him at the Museum some years back will scarcely recognize him in his finished impersonations."

On December 3 Jefferson opened in Richmond at the New Richmond Theatre, where he played for two weeks as Dr. Pangloss, Diggory, Asa Trench-ard (for his first benefit), Jacques Strop in *Robert Macaire*, Newman Noggs, Tobias Shortcut in *The Spitfire*, Caleb Plummer (for his second benefit), and Scout in *The Village Lawyer*. In Richmond, *Dot* was called *Caleb Plummer. Daily National Intelligencer* (Washington), September 4 (3), November 5 (3), September 16 (3) 1860; *Spirit of the Times* (New York), August 18, 1860: 344; *Baltimore American and Commercial Advertiser,* November 17 (3), November 19 (3), November 20 (3), November 21 (3), November 22 (2), November 23 (3) 1860; *New York Clipper,* November 24 (252), December 1 (263), December 8 (271), December 29 (294) 1860; *New York Times,* December 24, 1860: 4; *Richmond Enquirer,* December 4 (2), December 7 (3), December 11 (2), December 14 (3) 1860; *Evening Star* (Washington), April 6, 1859: 2; A. I. Mudd, article, Robinson Locke Collection, 302, 65, The New York Public Library at Lincoln Center.

227. *New York Clipper* agreed, noting that "our friend J. J. was amusing but nothing to the extent we have found him to be in parts better suited to his specialty"—by which the writer meant Yankee roles. *New York Times,* December 25, 1860: 5; *New York Clipper,* January 5, 1861: 302.

228. The *New York Times* commented:

> The good judgement of the management in giving us a taste of comedy, after the surfeit of tragedy which we have had for some months, has not been productive the last week of as golden results [money] as might . . . have been anticipated. This arose mainly . . . from the character of the piece and from the circumstance that MR. JEFFERSON is not acknowledged in his new character of star, not from any shortcomings of the engagement, the change having been . . . politic and the piece of *Rip Van Winkle* . . . admirably placed on the stage.

The *Spirit of the Times* reported that Jefferson was "reaping a golden harvest," but the diary of Emille Marguerite Cowell, told a different story:

> Not a hundred dollars in the Winter Garden last night. Jefferson opened there on Monday last in a new piece called *Rip Van Winkle*. His week's engagement being over, Stewart [*sic*] the manager wanted him to go, but he prefers to stay for the next fortnight *without salary* to leaving New York after one week's engagement.

Mrs. Cowell's viewpoint on Jefferson's success may have been tempered by the fact that she generally disliked his acting. She later went to see him in a burlesque of the equestrian drama *Mazeppa*, a play that required Jefferson to undertake what advertisements described as a "daring feat of horsemanship." She was not impressed.

> Sam kindly took Sidney [their daughter] and me to the Winter Garden (only next door) to see *A Conjugal Lesson* and *Mazeppa* and stayed with us during the first piece. Mr. Jefferson was very funny in that, but Sid and I were disgusted with his "rendition" of Mazeppa. Perhaps our having seen Mr. Robson in the part increased our fastidiousness, but the result of our opinions was far from flattering to Mr. J.
>
> Robson's Mazeppa was interesting in spite of occasional bathos, but Jefferson's was such a vile, pompous "Jeames"-like villain that we could not care for him in any portion of the piece, except the imitation of the circus riders.

New York Times, December 31, 1860: 3; *Spirit of the Times* (New York), December 29, 1860: 228; M. Wilson Disher, *The Cowells in America Being the Diary of Mrs. Sam Cowell During her Husband's Concert Tour in the Years 1860–1861* (London: Oxford University Press, 1934), 228, 237.

229. *New York Times,* January 21, 1861: 5.

230. Joe opened for a week's run at the Holliday Street Theatre in Baltimore on January 28, 1861, playing Asa Trenchard and Mr. Lullaby in *A Conjugal Lesson*. The opening night audience was appreciative but not numerous, according to the local newspaper, because *Our American Cousin's* popularity had been used up. Jefferson immediately switched to Newman Noggs, Cassimir in *Mazeppa,* and what was advertised as "Charles Dickens' great Rip Van Winkle." The audiences increased throughout the week. On February 1, Joe took a benefit, playing Caleb Plummer, and the run ended the following evening. *Baltimore American and Commercial Advertiser,* January 26 (4), January 28 (4), January 29 (1, 4), January 30 (4), January 31 (1, 4), February 1 (1, 4), February 2 (4) 1861.

231. The *New York Times* described her final illness as "short." The *Baltimore American and Commercial Advertiser* described it as "sudden." The *New York Clipper* referred to "a brief illness." Manhattan Deaths 1861 F-Z, The City of New York Department of Records & Information Services, Municipal Archives; Eleanor Farjeon, *Portrait of a Family* (New York, Frederick A. Stokes and Company, 1936), 23; *New York Times,* February 20, 1861: 5; *Baltimore American and Commercial Advertiser*, February 20, 1861: 1; *New York Clipper*, March 2, 1861: 366.

232. *New York Clipper,* September 15, 1866: 182, May 25, 1872: 57; *New York Daily Times,* December 31, 1855: 2; *New York Mirror,* June 14, 1884: 8; "In His Easy Chair Joseph Jefferson Evokes Memories of the Past," *New York Herald*, October 16, 1904, Robinson Locke Collection, 302: 92–93, The New York Public Library at Lincoln Center; Sothern, 771.

233. Eugenie Jefferson, 241.

234. *Autobiography*, 229; Winter, *Life and Art*, 173, 193; *New York Dramatic Mirror*, January 29, 1905: 8; Clipping Scrapbook, Jonathan Bourne Historical Center, Buzzards Bay, Massachusetts; *Spirit of the Times* (New York), June 8, 1861: 288; Davis, 68.

235. "Charles Jefferson Talks of His Famous Father," n.p.

236. Eugenie Jefferson, 240.

237. On May 16 the *New York Times* also wrote:

> With the exception of the Winter Garden, where Mrs. JOHN WOOD and Mr. JEFFERSON keep large audiences in a . . . state of jubilation, the theatres have not been . . . cheerful during the past week. The usual business of the season has been brought to an abrupt end. People find more amusement in an "extra" than in the most popular place of amusement, and as that modest recreation, ever at war prices, is more economical than a seat in the parquet, people have taken to it with . . . kindliness. . . . At the Winter Garden, Mrs. JOHN WOOD, assisted by Mr. JEFFERSON, continues to attract the most brilliant houses of the season, and this, too, with the repetition of the oldest of old pieces. . . . An entire change of bill takes place to-morrow night, which has been set aside for the farewell benefit of Mr. JOSEPH JEFFERSON, prior to his departure for California. . . . Mr. JEFFERSON will perform once more his daring act of horsemanship. . . . In parting with Mr. JEFFERSON, we lose one of the most polished low comedians now on the stage.

On May 17 Mrs. Cowell reported "very good business at the Winter Garden," but she had not changed her mind about Jefferson's abilities:

> I forgot to mention going to the Winter Garden, last Wednesday and Saturday, to see Mr. Jefferson and Mrs. Wood. It was not much matter as they really were not very clever nor entertaining. Mrs. Wood seems to have greatly lost her voice but may account for a certain depression of spirits I observed, and Mr. Jefferson is getting so dreadfully "legitimate" as to ignore fun altogether.

New York Times, April 29 (7), May 12 (5) 1861; Disher, 322, 343, 386.

238. Farjeon, 23, 71.

239. *New York Times*, December 27, 1859: 3; April 4, 1861: 5; James R. Anderson, *An Actor's Life* (London: The Walter Scott Publishing Co., Ltd., 1902), 247.

240. *Daily Alta California* (San Francisco), July 3 (4), July 8 (4) 1861.

241. *Evening Bulletin* (San Francisco), July 6, 1860: 3.

242. *Daily Alta California* (San Francisco), July 10 (1), July 12 (1), July 20 (1) 1861.

243. *Evening Bulletin* (San Francisco), July 12 (3), July 26 (1) 1861; *Daily Alta California* (San Francisco), July 24 (1), August 3 (1) 1861

244. Jefferson opened as Simon Lullaby in *A Conjugal Lesson* and went on

to perform Cassimir in *Mazeppa,* Bob Acres, Dr. Pangloss, Diggory in *The Spectre Bridegroom,* Caleb Plummer (with his cousin Elizabeth Saunders as Tilly Slowboy), Asa Trenchard, Rip, and Salem Scudder. In late September 1861 he performed Schnapps in *The Naiad Queen.* Newspaper reviews, according to the *New York Clipper,* were favorable. When times got tough in San Francisco he performed in *Pocahontas, The Wind Mill, Sketches in India,* and *The Governor's Wife.* On October 25, Jefferson appeared as Meddle in *London Assurance. New York Clipper,* August 3 (124), August 10 (135), August 17 (142), August 24 (150), November 2 (231), November 9 (239), November 30 (263), December 7 (271) 1861.

245. According to Jefferson's *Autobiography:*

> Before my arrival I had been "overbilled." . . . If a circus had been coming, the placards could hardly have been more numerous. Those fatal documents known as the "opinions of the press" had been so freely circulated that every one was aware not only of what I could do but what I had done and must therefore take for granted what I was going to do. All power of judging for themselves had been denied both the public and the local press. I felt that I should fail, and I did fail.

New York Times, November 29, 1860: 2; *Autobiography,* 229–230.

246. "Charles Jefferson Talks of His Famous Father," n.p.

247. William Winter contends that Jefferson was in California until early November, but the *Autobiography* contends that he sailed from San Francisco on September 10, 1861. *Autobiography,* 229, 231; *Spirit of the Times* (New York), June 8, 1861: 288; Winter, *Life and Art,* 172–173; *New York Clipper,* November 16 (247), December 7 (268) 1861.

7. Years Abroad—Australia, New Zealand, 1861–1865
pages 99–110

248. Jefferson and his biographer, William Winter, contended that the party left on September 10, 1861, but sailing dates in newspapers show otherwise. In Jefferson's memory, as reported in his *Autobiography*, the voyage took fifty-seven days, and the *Nimrod* landed on November 4, 1861, at Sydney. Charles Burke Jefferson remembered being seventy-nine days at sea. All of this is incorrect.

The name "Symons" appears in Australian newspapers as "Simmonds," the name the manager had sometimes used in America. Charles Burke Jefferson, writing in 1906, remembered the agent's name as Jim Simmons. The *Nimrod* was also spelled Nimroud. *Sydney Morning Herald,* January 8, 1862: 4; Eugenie Jefferson, 242; Winter, *Life and Times,* 172; "Charles Jefferson Talks of His Famous Father," n.p; Farjeon, 23.

249. According to Charles Burke Jefferson, his father asked Symons for the $7,000 Jefferson had earned in San Francisco, but Symons had lost the money at cards the night before they left. Jefferson borrowed money from a fellow

passenger, pawned his and Symons' watches as well as a diamond ring, and raised the money. Charles Burke was ten when the incident supposedly occurred. Jefferson does not mention it in his autobiography, and given how careful he was with money, it seems unlikely he would have trusted anyone else with $7,000 or been willing to work with anyone who would lose it at a card game.

Jefferson incorrectly remembered the name of the manager, which was Tolano, as Rolamo. "Charles Jefferson Talks of His Famous Father," n.p.

250. *Sydney Morning Herald,* January 11 (1), February 3 (1), February 4 (1, 5) 1862.

251. "Charles Jefferson Talks of His Famous Father," n.p; Eugenie Jefferson, 242–243.

252. Jefferson performed most of his characters at least twice and only three of them (Rip, Cassimir, and Asa Trenchard) for more than a week. He started with Rip for three days and then turned to Dr. Pangloss and Newman Noggs. On February 15, 1862, he performed Rip and Cassimir for a farewell benefit in honor of the Eleven of all England, a visiting cricket team. The house was "crammed," and the Governor-in-Chief of Australia as well as the Mayor of Sydney attended. On February 1 he went on to Asa Trenchard, performed for the first time in Australia; on February 24 he played Caleb Plummer; on February 27, Bob Acres and Mr. Golightly; and on March 3 he opened as Salem Scudder, the latter advertised as having been performed for upwards of three hundred consecutive nights. The actual number of initial New York performances had been about fifty. On March 6, 1862, Jefferson performed a complimentary benefit for his manager "James Simmonds" in honor of the latter's return to Australia. For his benefit, Jefferson played Dr. Ollapod in *The Poor Gentleman. Sydney Morning Herald,* February 6 (1), February 10 (1), March 4 (4), March 13 (1) 1862.

253. After opening night, the *Argus* reported:

> His style is new to the Melbourne boards . . . through the whole of *Rip Van Winkle*—in which . . . considerable liberties have been taken with the . . . story—he succeeded in engaging the . . . attention of his audience, and he twice received the honour of an *encore*. . . . In *Mazeppa*, Mr. Jefferson gave the audience [a] different specimen of his ability, and, by his . . . acting, singing and dancing, continued to add . . . to the . . . favorable opinion . . . formed regarding him.

Sydney Morning Herald, March 20 (4), April 11 (5) 1862; *Argus* (Melbourne), March 22 (4), March 27 (8), April 1 (5) 1862.

254. *A Regular Fix,* written by James Maddison Morton, the author of *Lend Me Five Shillings,* was first presented in London in 1860 and in New York in 1863, which makes it likely that Jefferson had received a copy by mail. Discovered in a drawing room the night after a ball, Hugh de Brass, having fallen asleep there the night before, awakes to find himself in "a regular fix." He has no idea where he is; he knows no one in the house, and he ought to leave but is forced to

stay (and to justify his presence) because a bailiff is waiting outside to arrest him for debt. His troubles increase when he discovers that the house's owner, Mr. Surplus, is one of his creditors. Consequently de Brass must invent a completely new identity, which he does with an elaborate story that always begins "amidst the gathering thunder clouds." Constantly forgetting his fictitious name, de Brass becomes more entangled in his fabrication until everyone he has duped confronts him. Just then he discovers that a distant uncle has died, making him a baronet with seven thousand pounds a year. When asked why he has been behaving so strangely, de Brass begins "Amidst the gathering thunderstorm" as the curtain descends. "Charles Jefferson Talks of His Famous Father," n.p; *Argus* (Melbourne), April 4 (8), April 7 (8) 1862; John Maddison Morton, *A Regular Fix* (New York, n.d.), 3–20.

255. For information on Jefferson's Melbourne performances of Bob Acres, Simon Lullaby, and Dr. Pangloss, see *Argus* (Melbourne), April 10 (5), April 17 (8), April 19 (5), May 23 (5) 1862.

256. *Argus* (Melbourne), May 24 (4), May 27 (5), June 25 (6), June 16 (8), June 26 (8), June 30 (8), July 3 (5, 12), July 14 (5, 8), July 21 (8), July 24 (5), July 30 (5), August 4 (8), August 9 (8), August 18 (8) 1862.

257. The *Argus* critic wrote: "Mr. Jefferson's Bottom was an essay rather than an achievement. It was like the first sketch for a . . . picture by a good artist. . . . Such a . . . sketch suggested the possibility of its being painted out at some future time and a . . . new picture put upon the canvas. Nevertheless, it was humorous, for it is impossible for Mr. Jefferson to be otherwise." Almost immediately Jefferson accompanied *Midsummer Night's Dream* with a one-act, the plan he had previously considered at Laura Keene's. Performances ran through September 5, at which point Jefferson left the Royal Princess's Theatre. *Argus* (Melbourne), August 9 (8), August 18 (8), August 23 (5) 1862.

258. The Haymarket was the sixth theatre to be erected in Melbourne or its suburbs in seven years. The *Argus* critic noted that

> attendance was not . . . "overflowing." . . . People expected a crowded house and a . . . rush for seats and so abstained from attending. Possibly it was conjectured that an accident might result. . . . The pit was the only portion of the Haymarket Theatre that was incommodiously full last night, while the dress and upper circles and the stalls were well filled but nothing more. Some speculative individual . . . bought up three-fourths of the dress-circle tickets, in the hope of re-selling them at a premium, but as the playgoers of Melbourne were indisposed to pay 7s. or 8s to witness a performance on Monday evening which they could see for 5s. on the night following, numbers of these tickets . . . remained unsold.

A rare broadside advertising the production in Ballarat exists in the New York Public Library for the Performing Arts. *Argus* (Melbourne), September 8, 1862: 8.

259. He returned to Melbourne from the mining towns, reopening on

December 26 in *Rip* to a crowded house paying unusually high prices, and stayed until the end of January 1863. By April 1, 1863, Symons was advertising Jefferson's reappearance "for a limited number of nights" at the Royal Haymarket, beginning Easter Monday. *Argus* (Melbourne), December 22 (8), December 24 (8), December 27 (5) 1862; January 5 (8), January 12 (8), January 15 (8), January 16 (5), January 20 (3), January 21 (12), January 22 (12), January 26 (12), January 27 (5), January 29 (5), January 30 (12), April 1 (8), April 6 (8), April 7 (5), April 11 (5), April 13 (8), April 14 (5), April 18 (8), April 20 (5, 12), April 21 (5), April 25 (8), April 27 (5), April 28 (5), May 2 (12), May 4 (12), May 5 (5), May 9 (12), May 11 (5, 12), May 14 (12), May 15 (5), May 16 (5), May 23 (12), May 26 (4), May 30 (12), June 8 (5), June 13 (12), June 15 (12), June 20 (12), June 25 (12), June 26 (5) 1863; Robinson Locke Collection, 301: n.p., New York Public Library for the Performing Arts; John West, *Theatre in Australia* (Stanmore, New South Wales: Cassell Australia, 1978), 42–44; Alex Bagot, *Coppin the Great: Father of the Australian Theatre* (London: Cambridge University Press, 1965), 237; *Sydney Morning Herald,* June 23, 1864: 6.

260. *Argus* (Melbourne), April 11, 1862: 4; *South Australian Register* (Adelaide), June 30 (1), July 7 (1), July 8 (1), July 10 (1), July 21 (2), August 11 (1) 1863; *Sydney Morning Herald,* September 26 (1), October 3 (1), October 10 (1), October 23 (1) 1863.

261. Jefferson traveled to Melbourne on the City of Melbourne. It is at this point in his *Autobiography* that he describes meeting Mr. and Mrs. Charles Kean, who were playing at the Royal Haymarket Theatre, under James Symons' management. *Sydney Morning Herald,* October 29, 1863: 4; *Argus* (Melbourne), November 2, 1863: 4; *Autobiography,* 241–255.

262. *Bendigo Advertiser,* November 11 (1), November 12 (1), November 13 (1), November 14 (1), November 16 (1), November 18 (1), November 19 (1), November 21 (1) 1863; *Argus* (Melbourne), November 23 (12), November 26 (12), December 5 (12)1863; *Otago Daily News* (Dunedin, New Zealand), November 14, 1863: 5.

263. Eleanor Farjeon, 72.

264. Jefferson began his New Zealand stay with a two-week vacation in a Maori village called Wikawite. Annabel Farjeon, *Morning Has Broken* (London: J. MacRae, 1986), 1, 3, 8; Eleanor Farjeon, 18; *Otago Witness,* January 23, 1864: 5; *Who Was Who, 1897–1916* (London: A. C. Black Limited, 1920), 236.

265. Jefferson gave at least four performances of *Rip* and *Our American Cousin* in Launceston. *Argus* (Melbourne), February 6, 1864: 4; *Mercury* (Hobart Town, Tasmania), February 15 (2), February 20 (1) 1864; *Advertiser* (Hobart Town, Tasmania), March 23, 1864: 3; *Launceston Examiner* (Launceston, Tasmania), February 18, 1864: 6, 7.

266. *The Ticket-of-Leave Man* had first been done in London on May 27, 1863; consequently Jefferson must have been mailed a copy of the text. "Charles Jefferson Talks of His Famous Father,"n.p; Tolles, 278.

267. Upon closing in Hobart Town, most of the company, along with Charles Burke Jefferson, sailed back to Melbourne, while Jefferson and a fellow actor went on to Launceston. *Mercury* (Hobart Town, Tasmania), March 1 (2), March 3 (1), March 3 (2), March 4 (2), March 5 (2), March 8 (2), March 9 (2), March 23 (1), March 26 (1), April 4 (2), April 5 (2), April 6 (2), April 7 (2) 1864.

268. *South Australian Register* (Adelaide), July 7 (1), July 11 (1), July 16 (2), August 8 (2), August 10 (1) 1864; *The Sydney Morning Herald,* September 2 (1), September 12 (4), September 14 (1), September 17 (5), October 10 (1), October 11 (1), October 13 (1), October 15 (4) 1864; *Argus* (Melbourne), September 7 (4), November 25 (5), November 26 (8), November 28 (5) 1864.

269. "Charles Jefferson Talks of His Famous Father," n.p.

270. *Autobiography,* 277–279.

271. It was not until 1938 that the manuscript was finally published with a preface by Eleanor Farjeon, Margaret's daughter. Eugenie Jefferson, 246–247; Asia Booth Clarke, 11, 22, 23, 25; *New York Mirror,* May 26, 1888: 6; Oggel, 45.

272. "Charles Jefferson Talks of His Famous Father," n.p.

8. Jefferson as Rip, 1865–1867   *pages 111–129*

273. Jefferson spent ten days in Lima, waiting for a boat to Panama, visiting the theatre there, where a French comic-opera troupe was performing, and in Callao, where he saw a religious tableau. The steamer from Colon to Southampton stopped at St. Thomas and Jamaica. *New York Mirror,* June 14, 1884: 8.

274. Townsend Walsh, *The Career of Dion Boucicault* (1915; reprint, New York: Benjamin Blom, 1967), 109–110.

275. In his *Autobiography,* Jefferson notes, somewhat archly that "Boucicault did not seem to fancy the selection, thinking the subject stale, but we talked the matter over and soon came to terms. He undertook to rewrite the drama for a consideration agreed upon between us. He never seemed to think much of his own labor in this play; but I did, and do still, with good reason." Charles Burke Jefferson, who was fourteen at the time, later remembered: "It is amusing to recall that Boucicault did not like the play and would . . . stop working . . . on it to tell father that it would be a failure. But father kept saying: 'Go on with the play. I'm willing to risk it.'" Davis, 68; *Daily Picayune* (New Orleans), January 23, 1870: 11; *Autobiography,* 302; "Charles Jefferson Talks of His Famous Father," n.p; Eugenie Jefferson, 249.

276. Wilson, 266–268.

277. He told Francis Wilson: "The actors [at the Adelphi] . . . were inclined to be skeptical as to [*Rip's*] chances for success, . . . but I was so much in earnest and had my subject so well in hand that I . . . won their respect, . . . and I was patronizingly called by the older members of the company their 'transatlantic kid.'" Wilson, 39.

278. Performances began at 7 P.M. with a one-act farce. *Rip* was performed

at 8, and at 10:30 another one-act farce ended the evening. Charles Burke Jefferson remembered: "When Rip was . . . put on, my father's name did not appear in big letters. There was no star part for him in the programme. The play was handed out as the work of Boucicault. That name was enough to draw the crowd. Rip had been created by Boucicault just as father wanted it."

Even after the play was an enormous success, Boucicault continued to have his doubts. William Winter later wrote:

> After a while Boucicault . . . could attend Jefferson's performance. "I looked down," said Jefferson, "and I saw his old shiny bald head, and I acted *Rip* as well as I could. When it was over, he came round to see me, and he said: 'Joe, I think you are making a mistake: you are shooting over their heads.' I replied: 'I am not even shooting *at* their heads—I'm shooting at their *hearts*.'"

Times (London), September 4, 1865: 6; Wilson, 40; William Winter, *Other Days* (New York, George H. Doran, 1908), 75; Eugenie Jefferson, 139.

279. *Adelphi Calendar*, 38; Howard Carroll, *Twelve Americans: Their Lives and Times* (New York, 1883), 387–8; Program dated September 4, 1865, Collection of Mrs. Patricia Flynn, Kennebunkport, Maine; *Times* (London), September 6, 1865: 12; Henry Morley, *The Journal of a London Playgoer* (London, 1866), 310–313

280. *Rip Meeting the Dwarf,* American Mutoscope and Biograph Co., 1902, photographed from the Library of Congress Paper Film Collection by Primrose Productions, Los Angeles, California, 1955, for the Film Archives of the Academy of Motion Picture Arts and Sciences, Library of Congress Film Archives; *The Chicago Times,* November 5, 1867: 3.

281. Pierce, 697.

282. *Idem,* 700.

283. Clara Morris, "Joseph Jefferson Who Is Passing," April 16, 1905, Robinson Locke Collection, 302: 114, The New York Public Library for the Performing Arts.

284. Pierce, 698.

285. The validity of the film as a replication of Jefferson's stage work is discussed in Stephen Johnson, "Evaluating Film as a Document of Theatre History: The 1896 Footage of Joseph Jefferson's Rip Van Winkle." Johnson identified the film as having been shot by W. K. L. Dickson on Jefferson's New Jersey farm. The Biograph Company advertisement contends that it was shot in Buzzards Bay. Both are possible, but the rockiness of the ground and the date makes the New England setting more probable. The film seems to have been photographed in summer, and by 1896 Jefferson would normally have been in Buzzards Bay by that time. Stephen Johnson, "Evaluating Film as a Document of Theatre History," *Nineteenth Century Theatre* 20 (Winter 1992), 101–122; "Rip," Library of Congress, Washington, D.C.; Kemp R. Niver, *Motion Pictures from the Library of Congress Paper Print Collection*

1894–1912 (Berkeley: University of California Press, 1967), alphabetical listing under Rip; Kemp Niver, comp., *Biograph Bulletins 1896–1908* (Los Angeles: Locare Research Group, 1971), 82.

286. *Chicago Tribune,* September 6, 1868: 2.

287. *Rip Van Winkle,* performed by Joseph Jefferson, *Traditions of Acting* 2, Crest Cassettes, audiocasette.

288. L. Clarke Davis describes the same moment.

> His utterance of the . . . words, "Would you drive me out like a dog?" is . . . unsurpassed. . . . His sitting with his face turned from the audience during his dame's tirade, his . . . dazed look as he rises, his . . . groping from his chair to the table, are . . . actions conceived in the . . . spirit of art. . . . The theatre does not "rise at him": it does more. . . . it is deadly silent for minutes after . . . but for some sobbing women. . . . In a moment the . . . drunkard, stung . . . by the taunts of his vixenish wife, throws off the shell which has encased his better self, and rises to the full stature of his manhood,—a man . . . stricken, but every inch a man. All tokens of debauchery are gone; . . . all traces of the . . . indolence and humor. His tones . . . are clear and low and sweet—full of doubt that he has heard aright the words of banishment—full of . . . pain and pity and dismay. And so, with one parting farewell to his child, he goes out into the storm and darkness.

Chicago Tribune, September 6, 1868: 2; L. Clarke Davis, "Among the Comedians," *Atlantic Monthly* 19 (1867): 751–752.

289. Jefferson encouraged O'Neill to "read Shakespeare first, for breadth and depth and height of thought and fancy, and for insight into human nature read all the standard old comedies." Gelb, 23–24.

290. Eugenie Jefferson,165; Mary Shaw, "The Stage Wisdom of Joseph Jefferson," *Century Illustrated Monthly Magazine* 83 (1912): 733.

291. Shaw, "Stage Wisdom," 731–737.

292. In February 1887 the editor of *Harper's New Monthly Magazine,* aware of the criticisms that groups like the Women's Christian Temperance Union might have about *Rip Van Winkle,* wrote: "A man would hardly be bettered by a sermon who would not go out from seeing this play more kindly and thoughtful and patient. . . . It fills us with pity and sympathy and . . . forbearance. Surely there is no spectacle more humanizing, . . . none which dissolves harsh judgments . . . more certainly than this poem, this picture." "Jefferson in 'Rip Van Winkle,'" "Editor's Easy Chair," *The Nation* 9 (1869): 248.

293. *Wheeling Daily Register,* October 27, 1874: 3.

294. *New York Times,* December 17, 1878: 5.

295. Jefferson's insistence on the fairy-tale quality of the play also led him to reject Boucicault's suggestion that the reawakened Rip sit at a table and eat. Richard Watson Gilder wrote: "Jefferson will not allow him to eat, because he

has become . . . a myth, no longer a mortal. Neither will he let Rip yawn on waking from his twenty years' sleep. A man yawns, says Jefferson, after sleeping one hour or twenty hours, not after sleeping twenty years." *Autobiography*, 454; Gilder, 411.

296. On September 9, 1865, the English actor James R. Anderson wrote in his diary: ". . . went to the Adelphi Theatre to witness Joseph Jefferson's . . . Rip van Winkle. . . . After the performance, I saw him in his dressing-room and congratulated him . . . on his success. It is [a] pleasure . . . to shake a deserving brother actor by the hand, . . . especially when he hails from the United States, where I myself have ever been received with . . . liberality."

The Times claimed 172 performances in London. In Manchester, Jefferson tried a new part in Boucicault's *The Parish Clerk* but was not successful. Anderson, 276–277; Eugenie Jefferson, 141, 143; *Times* (London), September 13 (9), October 25 (8), December 27 (10) 1865; February 24 (8), March 2 (7), March 24 (8) 1866; *Adelphi Calendar*, 39; *Autobiography*, 303, 310, 321; Winter, *Life and Art*, 183; *New York Dramatic Mirror*, September 27, 1890: 3; "In His Easy Chair Joseph Jefferson Evokes Memories of Past," *New York Herald*, October 16, 1904, Robinson Locke Collection, 302: 92–93, The New York Public Library for the Performing Arts.

297. The Olympic was under the directorship of Leonard Grover. The performance was advertised as early as August 26 in *New York Times*. On September 23, 1865, Mary Farren wrote to the American theatrical entrepreneur Sol Smith: "Joe Jefferson has made a great hit in London." Although it was Jefferson's first appearance in New York in five years, the *New York Daily Tribune*, looking forward to the opening, remembered his past performances: "Mr. Jefferson was . . . distinguished for . . . pathos and . . . humor in the character of Rip Van Winkle, and, to judge by . . . the London press, time has . . . deepened the emotional effect . . . of this personation."

The *New York Daily Tribune*'s review, first printed on October 5, 1866, was very positive.

> Those who were present at the Olympic Theater . . .—and the house was . . . crowded in every part—will not . . . forget . . . the applause . . . which hailed Mr. Jefferson's appearance. . . . Time has dealt kindly with Mr. Jefferson. He seems to be more robust than . . . he was. . . . He was several times called before the curtain, and at the end of the play, he made a graceful speech, expressive of his gratification at the welcome accorded him.

Only the *New York Clipper* voiced any doubts.

> As an actor . . . [Jefferson] has improved . . . little. Before he left this country, he was . . . one of the best eccentric actors on the American stage; although . . . his engagement in London added to his reputation, . . . we find him . . . as he was. . . . This London reputation is all humbug.

> If an actor does not possess some histrionic ability, all the reputation of London . . . cannot make him a good actor.

The *Clipper* was not really lambasting Jefferson; it was denigrating the idea that to prove himself, an American actor had to be successful in London. The newspaper actually admired Jefferson's Rip, declaring it "one of the finest pieces of acting the modern stage has witnessed." Mary Farren, To "My dear Uncle Sol," September 23, 1865, Missouri Historical Society Archives, St. Louis; *New York Clipper*, September 1 (166), September 8 (174), September 15 (182, 183) 1866; November 2, 1867: 234.

298. Robert C. Toll, *On With the Show* (New York: Oxford University Press, 1976), 159.

299. Milton Rugoff, *America's Gilded Age* (New York: Holt, 1989): 1.

300. Toll, 159.

301. The *New York Daily Tribune* described *Our American Cousin* as "a play which we . . . detest," and the replacement was delayed until October 4, 1866, because business improved. *New York Clipper*, September 29, 1866: 198.

302. Although the *New York Daily Tribune* had some doubts about the scenery and the acting of subordinate roles in *The Cricket on the Hearth*, it lavished praise on Jefferson's performance: "His . . . art enables him to embody [the character of Caleb] with . . . detail. There is no evidence of elaboration in his acting. Your attention is not drawn to any . . . peculiarity. You see . . . *Caleb* before you, and your . . . heart goes out to him."

The *New York Clipper* criticized Jefferson's supporting cast while praising his acting. Attendance on opening night was good but not crowded, and the *Clipper* described the house as "a cold . . . audience; . . . it required Mr. Jefferson's . . . pathetic scenes to arouse them. . . ." Caleb is actually a subordinate role in the play, but audiences now came to see Jefferson. His name was placed in larger type and separately from other cast members in the company's advertisements. During the season he also performed Mr. Woodcock in Maddison Morton's *Woodcock's Little Game* and Tobias Shortcut in *The Spitfire*. *New York Clipper*, October 13 (214), October 20 (220, 222), October 27 (280) 1866; *New York Tribune*, September 1 (7), September 3 (7), September 5 (3), September 7 (2), September 10 (2), September 17 (7, 10), September 26 (7, 8), October 1 (4), October 4 (7), October 15 (7), October 25 (7) 1866; Winter, *Life and Art*, 183–184.

9. "My Latest Novelty," 1867–1870   *pages 130–141*

303. *New York Clipper*, November 3, 1866: 238; January 19, 1867: 326.

304. *Times* (London), September 11 (8), September 15 (7) 1865; *Porter's Spirit of the Times* (New York), January 31, 1857: 353.

305. *New York Times*, January 5, 1881: 10.

306. For a full discussion of the staging of the play, see Stephen Johnson, "Joseph Jefferson's Rip Van Winkle," *Drama Review* 26 (Spring 1982), 4–20.

307. For information about the Jefferson's tours, see Appendix.

308. Wilson, 18, 19, 67, 69; *Sun* (Baltimore), December 8, 1879: 1.

309. Cornelia Jefferson and Jefferson's cousin Effie Germon opened on August 6 in Baltimore in *The Woodcutter of Baghdad*. Among his duties, Jefferson served as the production's design consultant, importing scenery, properties, and costumes from Paris. The Olympic had as its business manager Clifton W. Tayleure, who eventually became one of Jefferson's managers. Tayleure was born in Charleston, South Carolina, on June 30, 1832, and thus was three years younger than Jefferson. He made his stage debut in 1850 in Richmond and but gave up acting in 1855 to become the business manager and treasurer for John T. Ford's Holliday Street Theatre in Baltimore, where he presumably met Jefferson.

The Olympic had just been repainted, recarpeted, and reupholstered. The dirty laces that had formerly hung over the boxes had been replaced by new draperies, and *Rip* was presented with new scenery. The *New York Times* reported that

> Mr. JEFFERSON appears to speak without . . . study or . . . hesitation, as if upon the inspiration of the moment. The rest of the acting after Mr. JEFFERSON's was rather conventional . . . , with the exception of the little girl and boy, who in the first act play the tiny lovers. . . . The lady who played the part of Rip's wife was bad enough to justify a divorce. Her rage in the first act was spasmodic and stagey, and her grievings in the last act were funereal at times and at times funny.

New York Clipper, July 13 (110), August 10 (142), August 17 (150), September 14 (182), September 21 (190) 1867; August 29, 1868: 162.

310. In 1903 Jefferson was quoted as saying: "Fifty years ago no theater was allowed to open its doors on Saturday night, it being considered too near Sunday to admit of stage performances. This, I am quite satisfied gave rise to the Saturday matinee." There is, however, no indication in nineteenth-century newspapers that this was true. "Joseph Jefferson's Optimism," November 24, 1903, Robinson Locke Collection, 302: 56, New York Public Library at Lincoln Center.

311. *New York Dramatic Mirror*, March 22, 1890: 2; *New York Times*, October 1, 1860: 4.

312. Philadelphia audiences had not appreciated the panorama, in part because the Philadelphia production had been sloppy, and its scenery was not coordinated well with the actors. *New York Clipper*, August 24 (154), September 28 (198), November 2 (234) 1867.

313. When *A Midsummer Night's Dream* was eventually performed at the Olympic, Cornelia Jefferson played Titania and the noted clown, George L. Fox, played Bottom. In the next two months after Jefferson left the Olympic, *A Midsummer Night's Dream* took in almost $70,000. *New York Times*,

September 9 (1), September 10 (4), September 19 (7), September 23 (4), September 28 (4) 1867.

314. *Daily National Intelligencer* (Washington), September 4, 1867: 2.

315. Both Rice and Marble had married Henry Warren's sisters. Four days before the wedding, Julia Dean, Jefferson's first sweetheart, opened at McVicker's Theatre. Mr. and Mrs. Barney Williams were also performing at McVicker's, and as Williams had been Jefferson's best man at his first wedding, it is likely they attended his second. Jefferson and Sarah Warren were married by the Reverend W. H. Ryder. *Chicago Tribune*, December 20 (4), December 21 (4) 1876; *New York Clipper*, December 21 (294), December 28 (299) 1867.

316. *New York Dramatic Mirror*, March 3, 1894: 22; January 29, 1905: 8; Winter, *Life and Art*, 194; Olive Logan, *Before the Footlights and Behind the Scenes* (n.p., 1869), 458; Tombstone, Sarah Jefferson, Buzzard's Bay Massachusetts, James B. Runnion, "Joseph Jefferson," *Lippincott's Magazine* 4 (1869): 170; *Daily National Intelligencer* (Washington, D.C.), December 24, 1867: 2.

317. According to the Washington *Daily National Intelligencer*, Owens was "probably the wealthiest actor on the American stage" with "property . . . said to be considerably in excess of half a million dollars." *New York Clipper*, March 14 (390), April 4 (414), April 11 (6), April 18 (14), April 25 (22) 1868; Eugene Tompkins, *The History of the Boston Theatre* (Boston: The Riverside Press, 1908), 155; *Memphis Sunday Appeal*, December 19, 1869: 2; *Daily National Intelligencer*, (Washington, D.C.), June 15, 1869:1; *Mobile Daily Register*, February 10 (2), December 11 (3, 4) 1868.

318. Above all, the high prices may have affected business adversely in Denver. The original three performances were cut to two, and seats were still available on the night of the second performance. *New York Clipper*, July 27, 1872: 142; *Deseret Evening News* (Salt Lake City), July 10 (2), July 11 (2), July 16 (13) 1878; *Rocky Mountain News* (Denver), July 14 (4), July 23 (4) 1878.

319. *Sunday Morning Appeal* (Memphis), December 19, 1869: 4.

320. The following week the *Tribune* reported that "The management will . . . get tired out before the public. Meyers is seriously talking of enlarging the box office and chartering a bank, . . . and McVicker has not made such a success since the days when he played Richard III on Dearborn street and threw an audience into convulsions by sneezing in a tragic role." *Chicago Tribune*, October 25, 1868: 2.

321. The *Tribune* contended that the plot of *A Midsummer Night's Dream* was difficult to understand and advised its audiences to read the text before attending the production.

> It has been running three weeks, but the receipts . . . have not yet been equal to the expenses. It is not because the scenic effects are not grand . . . or that the costumes are not rich . . . or that there is an absence of lovely women or that the acting and singing are not good or that the house is not comfortable. We only wish that we could account for the slim houses

upon some hypotheses that would not reflect on the culture and intelligence of Chicago play-goers. The truth stands out . . . that the students of Shakespeare are not numerous in our midst.

James B. Runnion praised Jefferson for supporting what he considered an artistic triumph but a financial failure:

> The Philadelphia public have not forgotten the tribute which Jefferson paid to art in the production of *A Midsummer Night's Dream*. The piece was afterward produced in the West, newly appointed and in every way as complete, but it did not meet with a patronage equal to the money that had been expended upon it.

The panorama in *A Midsummer Night's Dream* is probably the piece of scenery referred to by Runnion as follows:

> Not many months since [Jefferson] bought a panorama, because he admired it and put it in charge of an agent who had been with him a long time. The panorama failed to attract in spite of its merits, and the agent wrote back that he despaired of ever doing anything with it besides losing money. "Never mind," was Jefferson's answer: "it will be a gratification for those who do go to see it, and you may draw on me for what money you need." But the result was, that the panoramic beauties now blush unseen in the garret of a Philadelphia theatre.

The production of *A Midsummer Night's Dream* toured after Chicago, playing Cincinnati in February 1869. *New York Clipper,* December 5, 1868: 278; February 6, 1869: 350; James B. Runnion, 170–171, 176; *Chicago Tribune,* October 29, 1868: 4.

322. The Milwaukee newspaper, however, notes that audiences were "large and fashionable." *Chicago Tribune,* August 29 (4), September 6 (2), September 13 (2), September 28 (4), October 4 (2), October 18 (2), November 1 (2) 1868; *Milwaukee Sentinel,* October 29, 1868: 1.

323. Hunter, 58; "Joseph Jefferson in the Capital City," Clipping Scrapbook, Jonathan Bourne Historical Center; Winter, *Life and Art,* 187; Celebrity Index, Free Library of Philadelphia; Wilson, 1; Watermeier, 25–28; *New York Clipper,* December 31, 1870: 310.

10. Home, 1868–1870   *pages 142–155*

324. Farjeon, *Portrait of a Family,* 78.

325. The *New York Clipper* gives Joseph Jefferson Jr.'s birthdate as July 7, 1869. He was brought up as a rich man's son, educated at Columbia Grammar School, the Challier Institute in New York, the English Grammar School in London, and Upson Seminary in Connecticut. He made his professional acting debut in Denver at the age of sixteen. In his early professional career he attempted to disassociate himself from his father by using his middle name

Warren as a stage name (Joseph Warren); by 1899, however, he had reverted to Joseph Jefferson, Jr. He spent much of his adult life touring in vehicles made famous by his father. On August 13, 1908, Joe Jr. wrote to the American theatres impresario Charles Frohman:

> Dear Sir:
> As you doubtless know, my brother and I have been playing in *The Rivals* for the past several seasons and take that comedy out again this season. My object in writing you is this. I am very tired of playing from thirty to thirty-five weeks of one night stands & would like to get an engagement in some good company. Do you think you would have an opening for me the season following this? While I am a young man, I have been on the stage since 1885, when I first joined my father's company.

Joseph Jefferson, Jr., wound up in vaudeville and died on May 1, 1919.

The site of Jefferson's Hohokus home was originally called Ranlett Place, because the property had been "formerly owned and improved by the late William H. Ranlett architect and subsequently by Mr. Forrester, who sold it to 'Old Rip.'" The Hohokus house, although much altered, is still standing, and the trout streams are part of an exclusive men's fishing club approximately three-quarters of a mile away on the Saddle River. *Who Was Who in America,* 1 (Chicago: Marquis Who's Who, 1968), 631; Winter, *Life and Art,* 194; Article dated May 7, 1919, from the *Sandwich Independent,* Archives, Sandwich, Massachusetts; Joseph Jefferson, "To Charles Frohman," August 13, 1908, The William Seymour Family Papers, Princeton University Theatre Collection; *New York Clipper,* July 17 (118), July 24 (126) 1869; Bergen City Courthouse, Book IJ7: 42.

326. Bergen County Courthouse, Land Record dated November 10, 1874. Book 9M, 150; Arnold Gingrich, *The Joys of Trout* (New York: Knopf, 1971), 13, 36, 64.

327. Eugenie Jefferson, 79.

328. "Among Mr. Jefferson's pictures are a portrait of Garrick as Abel Drugger, by Zoffany; Macready as William Tell, by Inman; Edmund Kean as Richard III, by Hardy; a miniature of Madame Vestris [the nineteenth-century English actress and theatrical impresario]; a portrait of Mr. Jefferson's grandfather as Solus; another of his mother as Jessica, by Nagle; and another by the same artist, of his father. Among the other modern painters represented are Doré, Diaz, Boldoni, Simonetti, Marny, Herring, Corot and—Jefferson." Francis Wilson notes that Jefferson was interested in modern Dutch painting—works by Maris, Israel, Mauve, and Neuhuys. L. Clarke Davis, "At and After the Play," 70, 73–4; Wilson, 79.

329. The quotation comes from a catalog of a show of Jefferson's own paintings in Washington. The exhibition was presumably very successful, because the Fischer Galleries scheduled another show of fifty-five of Jefferson's oil paintings the following year, most of them canvases 26-by-36 inches, from

December 10 to 29, 1900. Souvenir Catalogue, New York Historical Society; *Exhibition of 55 Oil Paintings by Joseph Jefferson at the Fischer Galleries* (Washington, D.C., 1900), title page, 33, Historic New Orleans Collection.

330. Apparently Jefferson did not like Sargent's work, having told a journalist named Homer Fort that "Sargent has painted me. . . . His brush-work is all right, but he doesn't touch me." The American artist whom Jefferson admired was N. R. Brewer, who painted him as Rip. Jefferson's valet would come with him to Brewer's studio in New York to help make him up. "Joseph Jefferson and his Favorite Artist," *Leslie's Weekly*, May 1, 1902, Robinson Locke Collection 302: 33, The New York Public Library for the Performing Arts.

331. *New York Times*, March 11, 1890: 4; *Sunday Mirror* (St. Louis), April 1, 1894: 13, Clipping Collection, John Callahan, Kutztown, Pennsylvania.

332. Wilson, 226. *Time*, March 25, 1996: 73.

333. Malcolm Daniel, *Eugene Cuvalier, Photographer in the Circle of Corot* (New York: The Metropolitan Museum of Art, 1996), 10.

334. Joseph Jefferson, "My Farm in Jersey," 689–690; *New York Dramatic Mirror*, June 19, 1897: 3.

335. Otis Skinner, *Footlights and Spotlights* (Indianapolis: The Bobbs-Merrill Co., 1923), 255.

336. Farjeon, *Portrait of a Family*, 81; Dole, 63.

337. Gamaliel Bradford, "Joseph Jefferson," *Atlantic Monthly* 129 (1922): 92.

338. Jefferson appeared before a notary public in New Orleans and purchased Orange Island from Faustin Dupuy for $28,000. He paid $17,000 in cash and agreed to pay the rest off in two years at eight percent interest. Jefferson deposited $5,000—what would now be called earnest money—with the bank of Pike, Brother & Company in New Orleans and agreed to forfeit this money if he did not come up with the rest of the $17,000 in ninety days. The final sale occurred on May 21, 1870. Winter, *Life and Art*, 187; Agreement and Promise of Sale dated March 4, 1840, Archives, Joseph Jefferson House, Jefferson Island, New Iberia, Louisiana.; Glenn R. Conrad, "Wilderness Paradise," *Attakapas Gazette* 53, Archives, Joseph Jefferson House, Jefferson Island, New Iberia, Louisiana.

339. At the time of the purchase it was called Orange Island after the fruit (also known as Louisiana Sweets) that grew in its large orchard. The lake's name is derived from the French word for wool-comber, because its shape resembled that of eighteenth-century wool combs. A visitor in 1890 described it as follows: "The word 'island' seems . . . a misnomer in the light of its lack of . . . encompassing water, for it is only . . . sea marsh. The grand marais extends on two or three sides whilst . . . Lake Simonette bounds the place on the northeast ward."

By April 6, 1895, Jefferson received word that a bed of rock salt had been found on his Louisiana property. He had suspected as much, had initiated the sinking of a shaft in search of it, and salt had been hit at the depth of 180 feet. The Jefferson house is still standing and its external appearance is fundamentally the same. When Jefferson lived in the house, its grounds were rustic. The dignified English gardens that now surround the residence, as well as its interior decor, were contributed by the family of J. L. Bayless, to whom Jefferson's heirs sold the property in 1917. *Daily Picayune* (New Orleans), June 8, 1890: 13; *New York Dramatic Mirror,* April 6, 1895: 2.

340. Grace B. Agate, "Joseph Jefferson, Painter of the Teche," *National Historic Magazine* 24, Archives, Joseph Jefferson Home; *Transit Readers' Digest* (December 12, 1966), n.p., Archives, Joseph Jefferson Home, Jefferson Island, New Iberia, Louisiana; Writers' Program of the Work Projects Administration in the State of Louisiana, comp., *Louisiana: A Guide to the State* (New York: Hastings House, 1945), 438; *Times-Picayune* (New Orleans), August 30, 1925: 7; Charles Dudley Warner, "The Arcadian Land," *Harper's New Monthly Magazine* (1887): 350; Farjeon, *Portrait of a Family,* 81; Eugenie Jefferson, 64–65, 74; *Daily Picayune* (New Orleans), November 12, 1885: 4; William Hosea Ballou, "Joseph Jefferson at Home," *Cosmopolitan* (1889): 121–127; *New York Mirror,* June 14 1884: 8; July 31 1886: 7; Wilson, 54; Francis Wilson, *Life of Himself* (Boston: Houghton Mifflin, 1924), 199.

341. Eugenie Jefferson, 13–14.

11. The Little Church Around the Corner— Blindness, 1870–1875 *pages 156–165*

342. Booth continues: "For my part—my only (or rather my chief) object is to get away that I may let my ground lie fallow & gather *i'the West* the harvest waiting there for me. If he don't come here (Of course I know, he won't go to any other theatre in the city) I must pitch in myself." Watermeier, 25–26.

343. Jefferson was originally announced as appearing at Booth's Theatre in October. By the end of June 1870 the date had been fixed as mid-August. Originally booked for four months, Jefferson later agreed to an engagement that would cease "when the nightly gross receipts should fall below a given sum." Initially he had insisted on having Saturday evenings free, but almost as soon as the play opened he relented. When the Manhattan run closed, Booth moved Jefferson and the entire company to the Brooklyn Academy of Music for five performances from January 10, 1871, through January 14, just as C. W. Tayleure had done the preceding year. He did not, however, bring the scenery, and the sets used were far below the quality seen in Manhattan. *Baltimore American and Commercial Advertiser,* April 4 (2), April 11 (2), April 16 (2) 1870; *Chicago Tribune,* April 17, 1870: 2; *New York Times,* January 4 (7), January 9 (4, 7) 1871; *New York Clipper,* February 28 (374), April 9 (6), April 23 (22), June 5 (70), June 25 (94), July 18 (118), August 13 (150), August 27 (166), October 29 (288) 1870; January 21, 1871: 334.

344. *New York Times,* January 1, 1871: 3.

345. "Editor's Easy Chair," *Harper's New Monthly Magazine* 42 (March 1871): 615.

246. In the winter of 1870 William Winter had attempted to organize a

benefit performance for George Holland. He enlisted the aid of Edwin Booth. Plans for the benefit dragged on. On April 25, 1870, Booth again wrote to Winter: "I would suggest that you fix on June the 30th (Thursday) for the Holland benefit. At that time Jefferson & the others will . . . be idle. To do it earlier will . . . interfere . . . with several of their projects."

The benefit was actually held on May 18, 1870, while Jefferson was touring and unable to participate. Hunter, 58; "Joseph Jefferson in the Capital City," Clipping Scrapbook, Jonathan Bourne Historical Center; Winter, *Life and Art*, 187; Celebrity Index, Free Library of Philadelphia; Wilson, 1; Water-meier, 25–28; *New York Clipper*, December 31, 1870: 310.

347. The funeral took place on December 22, 1870, at 1 P.M. Jefferson and his daughter Margaret, then seventeen years old, who was best friends with Holland's daughter, Katie, accompanied the black-walnut casket from Holland's home at 509 Third Avenue to the church, where it was "placed in the recess immediately inside the main entrance, and the cover being removed, the friends of Mr. HOLLAND passed around it, single file." Among the mourners were the distinguished American producers Augustin Daly and Lester Wallack. The Reverend Dr. Houghton read the burial service; the casket was then closed and borne by six men to the hearse. After the funeral, the cortege made its way to Cypress Hill Cemetery, where Holland's body was buried in a lot belonging to the American Dramatic Fund. *New York Times*, December 22 (9), December 23 (2) 1870; *New York Dramatic Mirror*, May 2, 1896: 22; Farjeon, *Portrait of a Family*, 86; *New York Mirror*, August 13, 1887: 8; *Frank Leslie's Illustrated Newspaper* (New York), January 3 (283), January 21 (306) 1871.

348. The following ballad, sung by the San Francisco minstrels, had words by George Cooper and music by D. S. Wambold:

> God bless the little church around the corner.
>   The shrine of holy charity and love
> Its doors are ever open unto sorrow,
>   A blessing fall upon it from above.

In Quincy, Illinois, in the spring of 1871, a member of the "blonde burles-quers . . . sang 'The Little Church Around the Corner,' and the persistent audience compelled her to repeat it as many as four times." *Frank Leslie's Illustrated Newspaper* (New York), January 21 (306), February 11 (367) 1871; *New York Clipper*, January 7 (818), January 21 (329), March 4 (882), April 8 (7) 1871.

349. At the Holland benefit, Jefferson appeared along with Effie Germon, the daughter of his cousin Jane Anderson Germon. At the close of the performance, he was called before the curtain "and compelled to say a few words of gratitude." The afternoon's receipts were $1,270 and the evening performance's $3,731.50, for a total of $5,001.50. Jefferson made a personal contribution of $75 to the fund. It was one of the largest personal contributions made. The results of these benefits, however, did not benefit the George Holland family as much as anticipated. The proceeds, instead of going to the Holland's widow directly,

were invested in disappointing stocks, and she and her two younger children wound up living on $600 a year or $12 a week plus whatever her two eldest sons, George and Edmund, both actors, were able to provide. They did not even have the money to erect a tombstone over Holland's grave. *York Clipper,* January 28 (349), June 17 (86) 1871; September 21, 1872: 198.

350. By 1872 Jefferson's fame as Rip was nationwide. In as small a town as Harrisburg, Pennsylvania, a young actor named Joseph H. Keane performed Rip and was billed as "the only successful rival of the eminent Joseph Jefferson." *Daily Picayune* (New Orleans), January 7 (1, 16), January 14 (1, 3), January 17 (1) 1872; *State Journal* (Harrisburg), November 28, 1872: 4; *New York Clipper,* September 30 (206), October 28 (289) 1871; January 27, 1872: 342.

351. *Daily Picayune* (New Orleans), January 21, 1872: 11.

352. Winter, *Life and Art,* 188.

353. The threat of blindness does not seem to have limited Jefferson financially. The day he was operated on, he arranged to have a three-acre parcel of land bought for Charles Burke in Hohokus for $11,300, and while recuperating, he purchased another eleven acres, filled with maple and sugar maple trees, for $5,000. Bergen County Courthouse, Book 08, 17, 614; Wilson, 6; *New York Clipper,* June 22 (94), August 24 (166) 1872; January 11, 1873: 326.

354. The Jeffersons sailed to England on the steamship *Cuba.* Their eleven-day return journey began in Liverpool on August 16, on the steamship *Russia. New York Dramatic Mirror,* January 29, 1905, 8; Winter, *Life and Art,* 188; "Joseph Jefferson in the Capital City," Bourne Historical Center; *New York Times,* August 27 (8), August 31 (7), September 2 (5), September 7 (4), September 28 (7) 1873; *New York Clipper,* April 5 (6), June 21 (94), July 19 (126), August 23 (166), September 6 (182) 1873; Celebrity Index, Free Library of Philadelphia.

355. Winter, *Life and Art,* 194; *Chicago Tribune,* February 21, 1875: 7.

356. Davis, "In and After the Play," 70.

12. England and America, 1875–1877   *pages 166–174*

357. Charley and Lauretta were married in his father's home in Hohokus by the Reverend R. L. Dickinson of Christ Church, Ridgewood. When Lauretta died in their cottage in New Iberia, Charley left her room—"beds, pillows, coverings, undisturbed." Farjeon, *Portrait of a Family,* 104, 105; *Daily Picayune,* January 8, 1890: 13; *New York Clipper,* July 10, 1875: 118; "When Jefferson Came to Chicago," *Sunday Record Herald* (Chicago), April 30, 1905, Robinson Locke Collection, 302: 135, The New York Public Library for the Performing Arts.

358. *Times* (London), February 12, 1876: 8.

359. In England, Jefferson continued to paint and to send paintings to America. On April 18, 1876, Edwin Booth wrote to William Winter:

Joe has a picture for the Academy but fears it will be crowded out— there are so many more offered than can be accommodated; Joe was urged by some high up party to send his picture (I forget who); it is said to be excellent & McD. [Thomas B. McDonough, American theatrical agent] says we'll some day find J. J. ranked among our great painters, I hope so—that is, if he sends us those pictures.

Before his London run began, Jefferson painted a picture for Edwin Booth and sent it to Booth via William Winter. *Autobiography,* 345, 346; Farjeon, *Portrait of a Family,* 109; Ballou, 125; Watermeier, 54, 66.

360. *Times* (London), November 1 (8), November 3 (8) 1875.

361. The London run was an enormous success. *Rip* stood by itself until December 1, when the management of the Princess Theatre added a one-act farce to precede it and a one-act farce to follow. The farces, like *Rip*, proved to be long-running hits. The first piece was not changed until January 24, 1876, and the second continued to run until March 13. The opening play, *The Irish Tutor*, was later switched with the closing play, *Mr. and Mrs. Peter White.* On April 28, both farces were changed, and *A Quiet Family* opened the evening with *Sylvester Dangerwood* closing it. On February 26, at 2 P.M., Jefferson did a performance of *Rip* to benefit the Royal General Theatrical Fund.

Beginning March 13, 1876, the *Times* advertisement began to list the number of times Jefferson had performed *Rip* during this run and the number of weeks remaining. It was announced that the production would be withdrawn to allow Jefferson to fulfill provincial engagements. Later Jefferson played at the Theater Royal in Glasgow, Scotland. While Jefferson performed in Edinburgh, his son Tom made his professional debut as Cockles in *Rip Van Winkle. Times* (London), November 5 (7), December 1(8), 1875; January 24 (8), February 12 (8), February 26 (8), March 2 (8), March 13 (10), April 21 (8) 1876; Watermeier, 54; Eugenie Jefferson, 230.

362. Ballou, 123.

363. The mansion in Scotland—twenty rooms filled with antique furniture, —rented for five pounds. While there, Sarah Jefferson became ill. Eugenie Jefferson, 173; *New York Mirror,* June 14, 1884: 8; *New York Dramatic Mirror,* January 29, 1905: 8; Winter, *Life and Art,* 189, 193–194; *Autobiography,* 345, 364, 372; Farjeon, *Portrait of a Family,* 8, 93–123; Clarke, 18; Watermeier, 56.

364. The benefit in March was for a comic actor named Compton, who had been forced to retire by a lengthy painful illness. Advertisements asked the "renters" of Drury Lane, who were entitled to seats in the last row of the dress circle and the last row of the first balcony, not to exercise their rights so that these seats could be sold. *Times* (London), March 1 (8), March 2 (8), March 22 (8), March 28 (8), March 30 (6), April 2 (6), April 12 (8), April 28 (10), May 22 (8) 1877.

365. Winter had been in London all summer. *Times* (London), July 16 (8), August 11 (8) 1877; Watermeier, 84; *New York Dramatic Mirror,* June 19, 1897: 3; William Winter, *The Poet and the Actor,* New York Public Library; William Winter, *The Trip to England* (Boston, 1881), 57–74.

366. The evening at the Haymarket consisted of three plays, opening with J. R. Planche's *Charles XII,* in which Jefferson did not perform. The review continues: "Mr. Jefferson received far more assistance from his colleagues in [*Lend Me Five Shillings*] than he did in [*A Regular Fix*]. The acting in the second farce . . . was mostly very poor." Winter, *Life and Art,* 217; Winter, "Joseph Jefferson," *Harper's New Monthly Magazine* 73 (1886): 396; *Times* (London), June 5 (8), June 11 (1), June 13 (8) 1877.

367. In Edinburgh, performances were advertised as early as August 8. They began at 7:45 P.M. and ended at 10:30. Edinburgh audiences requested a "morning performance" (matinee), but Jefferson refused. He took a benefit on August 24, 1877. *Scotsman* (Edinburgh), August 8 (1), August 23 (1), August 27 (5) 1877.

368. "The Old Cabinet," *Scribner's Monthly* 15 (1877–1878): 130.

369. Included in the party on the trip home from England were Jefferson's now-married sister, Mrs.[Cornelia] Jackson, her young son, Joe, Sarah, infant Willie, Josephine Jefferson, Thomas Jefferson, Master Joseph Jefferson, Jr., and Aunt Nell Symons. *New York Times,* October 17, 1877: 8; Farjeon, *Portrait of a Family,* 119, 130, 134; Winter, "Joseph Jefferson," 396.

370. Daly had originally intended to present Jefferson at the Fifth Avenue Theatre, but his lease on that space ran out before Jefferson could open. The *New York Times* review continued: "The support which Mr. Jefferson had last evening was derived . . . from Mr. Daly's old 'Fifth Avenue Company.' Mr. Hardenberg, Mr. Davidge, Mr. Maurice Barrymore and others were in the cast, and Mr. Jefferson introduced to the public of New York Miss Constance Hamblin in the role of *Gretchen.* The lady is a good actress."

Maurice Barrymore was to tour with Jefferson in *The Rivals* in 1880. In 1877 he played the young sailor Hendrick in the third act of *Rip.* His future father-in-law, John Drew, played Seth, the role that Jefferson had done opposite Charley Burke.

Jefferson's future daughter-in-law, Eugenie Paul, played Katchen, one of the village maids. Eugenie Paul was the daughter of Sarah E. and W. H. Paul, manager of the Walnut Street Theatre in Philadelphia, where Jefferson often performed. All of her brothers and sisters were actors as well. Eugenie had already been on the stage for several years under the name of Lottie Francis. *New York Times,* October 21 (11), October 30 (5) 1877; Eugenie Jefferson, 89; *New York Clipper,* October 21 (246), November 3 (254), November 10 (262), November 17 (270) 1877; December 7, 1878: 295.

371. Jefferson performed for eight weeks until December 1, 1877. He did not appear on Saturday evenings, which were devoted to Daly's hit *Under The Gaslight.* Jefferson's performances included Thanksgiving night (although not Thanksgiving matinee) and a special Saturday evening performance on December 1 to end his New York run. After the last performance, Jefferson was called before the curtain and said: "Ladies and gentlemen: I have not come prepared with a speech; I can only say I thank you. Were I to speak all night I

could not say more. Farewell." *New York Times,* November 4 (7, 11), November 10 (7), November 18 (11), November 25 (7, 11), December 2 (7) 1877; *New York Clipper,* October 21 (246), December 1 (286) 1877.

372. Charlie also told Margaret that Tom was performing in New Orleans. *New York Dramatic Mirror,* January 29, 1905: 8; Winter, *Life and Art,* 189; National Theater Programs 1877–1903, Martin Luther King Library, Washington D.C.; *New York Clipper,* January 12, 1878: 335.

373. Margaret gave birth in London on February 13, 1881, to her first daughter, named Eleanor after her Aunt Nell Symons. She was called Nellie, Nelly, or Nell during her childhood and would become Jefferson's most famous grandchild, a much-honored writer of more than eighty children's books as well as volumes of poetry, plays, and a biography of her family. She also wrote the lyrics for the popular modern song "Morning has Broken."

Margaret had two more sons—Joseph Jefferson Farjeon, born in 1883, and Herbert Farjeon, born in 1887. Farjeon, *Portrait of a Family,* 136, 137, 144; Wilson, 74; *The New York Clipper,* December 8 (294), December 15 (302), December 22 (310) 1877; September 7, 1878: 190.

13. The Jefferson Company   *pages 175–188*

374. *New York Times,* December 17, 1878: 5.

375. Jefferson performed *Lend Me Five Shillings* at a matinee benefit for Southern cholera victims at the Fifth Avenue Theatre on September 5, 1878, with Joseph Jefferson, Jr., as Sam.

376. *New York Mirror,* January 18, 1879: 342.

377. Alfred L. Bernheim, *The Business of the Theatre* (New York: n.p., 1932), 30; *New York Mirror,* March 22, 1879: 4.

378. Jefferson certainly had the money to spend. When J. H. McVicker, the Chicago theatrical manager, declared bankruptcy on July 29, 1878, it was revealed that he owed Jefferson $5,000, which the actor had put up to enable McVicker to rebuild his theatre after the Chicago fire. *New York Clipper,* August 10, 1878: 158.

379. Mary Shaw, "The Stage Wisdom of Joseph Jefferson," 731–737.

380. *New York Mirror,* September 29, 1883: 4; Eugenie Jefferson, 310.

381. *New York Mirror,* December 2, 1882: 2.

382. The review goes on to say that "*Rip* 'was not . . . carefully mounted . . . , and the cast was not a . . . strong one, but everything went off smoothly; the 'waits' between the acts were commendably short, and Mr. Jefferson was honored with several calls before the curtain.'" *News and Courier* (Charleston, South Carolina), January 9 (2), January 15 (2), January 16 (4), 17 January 17 (4), January 18 (4) 1884.

383. *New York Mirror,* May 13, 1882: 4.

384. *New York Dramatic Mirror,* May 11, 1889: 3.

385. Elsie also remembered Jefferson taking her and Aunt Connie to visit an old artist named Weber in Cincinnati. There they had a lunch of home-made

pumpkin pie and claret. Elsie Leslie Lyde, "My Stage Life," *Some Stage Favorites of To-Day* (New York, 1893), n.p.

386. When Waverly died, Jefferson was rehearsing *Rip* in New York City, leaving Hohokus early in the morning and commuting back at night. The letter continues: "I wish you could have been here this week but I am in the train at nine A.M. this morning and don't get out till seven." Skinner, 255; Joseph Jefferson, "To My dear Willie," August 30, 1883, MS. Collection 1427, Historic Hudson Valley, Tarrytown, New York.

387. Robinson Locke Collection 78, New York Public Library at Lincoln Center.

388. Donald Dale Jackson, "John Barrymore: A Profile Is Just About Everything," *Smithsonian* 28 (1997): 88, 90.

389. In early 1880 the *New York Mirror* wrote: "Neither Jefferson nor Booth have a New York agent. . . . He [Jefferson] is very wealthy and does not care to act the entire season. He accepts only the plums and is well managed by his son Charles Jefferson."

At first, Taylor handled only two other stars, nowhere as important as Jefferson, and was the special New York representative for twenty of the leading theatres in America. He claimed that regional theatre managers were becoming increasingly demanding and would book nothing but the best attractions. *New York Mirror,* February 14, 1880: 5; Bernheim, 35.

390. Jefferson went back briefly to Hohokus, New Jersey, at the end of January 1883. Envelope, January 26, 1883, MS 1427, Historic Hudson Valley, Tarrytown, New York; *New York Mirror,* January 27, 1883: 6.

391. Joseph Jefferson, "To Mr. Dan Palmer," February 14, 1883, The Hampden-Booth Theatre Library at The Players.

392. Robert Grau, *The Business Man in the Amusement World* (New York: Broadway Publishing Co., 1910), 290–291.

393. *New York Times* noted that during the 1879–80 season that Jefferson gathered a small company for the purposes of presenting *The Rivals. New York Times,* November 14, 1880: 11.

394. Joseph Jefferson, "My dear Willie [Winter]," April 1, April 10, April 24, July 24, 1880, MS Collection, Historic Hudson Valley, Tarrytown, New York.

395. The fact that Jefferson refers to her as Mrs. J. is a Victorian custom. Most Victorians avoided the use of first names, even when married. In fact the reference to Sarah as "Mrs. J." really indicates the informality of the Jefferson home and Jefferson's closeness to William Winter. Joseph Jefferson, "To My dear Willie," n.d., MS Collection 1427, Historic Hudson Valley, Tarrytown, New York; Pool, 56.

14. Jefferson: The Public Man   *pages 189–210*

396. On July 25 1882, Jefferson was elected a Trustee of the Actors' Fund of America. *New York Mirror,* July 29, 1882: 3; *The New York Dramatic Mirror,* December 23, 1899: 83; August 29, 1903: 14.

397. The pictures had been borrowed from George Browne's chop house.

398. On October 4, 1882, Jefferson was one of five actors who presented a loving cup to his cousin William Warren at a tribute upon the occasion of Warren's fiftieth anniversary on the stage. On June 6, 1892, he was part of a tribute at the Academy in Philadelphia in honor of Mrs. John Drew, who had just relinquished the lesseeship and management of the Arch Street Theatre, which she had managed since the death of her husband in 1862. Along with Edwin Booth, he signed a testimonial to Mrs. Drew and appeared on the program in her honor. *New York Times*, June 5 (4), June 14 (5) 1880, October 7 (12), October 28 (6) 1882; Pool, 77; *New York Dramatic Mirror* June 4, 1892: 4, 6.

399. Joseph Jefferson, "To Laurence Hutton," March 10, 1896, Laurence Hutton Correspondence Collection, Princeton University Library; Menu, Lotos Club Dinner for Joseph Jefferson, April 4, 1896, Joe Jefferson Club, Saddle River, New Jersey; *New York Dramatic Mirror,* March 14 (14), April 4 (14), April 11 (15) 1896.

400. *New York Times,* March 16 (13), March 23 (13) 1890.

401. Hunter, 86; *New York Mirror,* October 4 (5, 6), November 22 (6), December 8 (6), December 15 (7) 1884; *New York Dramatic Mirror,* June 1, 1889: 2; *New York Times,* November 30, 1884: 15.

402. The Couldock tribute, which took place at the Star Theatre in New York, cleared nearly $5,000. *New York Mirror,* April 16 (6), May 7 (2), May 14 (6), June 11 (2) 1887; *New York Times,* May 1 (15), May 3 (5), May 8 (2), May 11 (4) 1887.

403. Couldock had turned eighty on April 26, 1895. Jefferson's son, Thomas, bought a seat for $10. The total sale netted $5,869. Remaining seats after the auction were sold at $5, $3, and $2 in the orchestra, $5, $3, and $1.50 in the first balcony, and $1 for the second balcony and general admission. By May 26 not a seat was left, and a plan was underway to place extra seats on the orchestra floor. Jefferson began to rehearse the actors for *The Rivals* daily on May 21, 1895, ten days before the performance, a move necessitated by the fact that only two of the company members had ever performed before with him. The critic for *New York Times* reported:

> The "front" scene between Jack and Sir Lucius . . . employed while the late Mr. Florence was associated with Mr. Jefferson, was . . . omitted, so that Mr. Goodwin, making his first appearance as the Irish duelist, did not remark that "the quarrel is very pretty as it stands" and "we should only spoil it by trying to explain it." . . . A false note was struck by Miss McHenry, whose red satin skirt, lace apron and ostrich feathers were as foreign to the affected "simplicity" of a Lucy as her over-exuberance of spirits.

The *Illustrated American* of June 15, 1885, reported that

> a few days since Joseph Jefferson, the *doyen* of the American stage, when speaking of a report that the venerable actor Couldock, was about to enter the Forrest Home, repelled the suggestion with . . . resentment.

Jefferson . . . generously hinted that his own . . . hand was ready to descend into his capacious pocket to prevent such a close for Mr. Couldock's long and honorable career, provided the benefit arranged for the aged player did not result satisfactorily.

In addition to tickets, souvenirs for the benefit brought the profits to $6,500. The benefit's profits were invested and earned Couldock an annual income of $1,200 a year. *New York Dramatic Mirror* April 6 (5), April 13 (2, 8), May 4 (2, 25), May 11 (2), May 18 (11) 1895; December 3, 1898: 17; *The Players,* 39; Joseph Jefferson, "To William Bispham Jr.," May 1, 1895, The Hampden-Booth Theatre Library at The Players; *New York Times,* May 12 (21), May 17 (15), May 19 (12), May 26 (12), June 1 (5) 1895; F. F. L., "The Forrest Home not a Poorhouse," *Illustrated American* 17 (June 15, 1895): 744.

404. Jefferson's Gravedigger was called "deliciously humorous—a gem of artistic low comedy." Wallack was very ill and died in September 1888. He was buried on September 10. Jefferson was a pallbearer at his funeral, held at the Church of the Transfiguration in New York—by then known, of course, as "The Little Church Around the Corner." Lester Wallack, 27–28; Brown, 3: 444–445; *New York Mirror,* May 26 (2), September 15 (7) 1888; January 8, 1889: 9.

405. Richard Watson Gilder, "A Few Words about Joseph Jefferson and His Art," *Christian Union* 5 (1893): 410; John D. Barry, "A Talk with Richard Watson Gilder," *Illustrated American* 17 (January 12, 1893): 39–41.

406. Rosamond Gilder, ed., *Letters of Richard Watson Gilder* (New York: Houghton Mifflin Company, 1916), 67.

407. *Ibid.,* 68.

408. On September 28, Cable revisited the Gilders and found Jefferson there with the great Polish actress Modjeska. They were talking about Shakespeare.

409. Cable writes of Jefferson: "When he closes his mouth, it comes together with a firmness up and down and a sweetness across that is pretty to see. His eyes and brows do the same thing at the same time. Wish you could see it." George W. Cable, "To L. S. C.," September 25, 1882, Lucy Leffingwell Cable Bikle, *George W. Cable: His Life and Letters* (New York: Russell & Russell, 1967), 81, 82, 102, 106; Nevins, 37; Philip Butcher, *George W. Cable* (New York: Twayne Publishers, 1962), 67.

410. During the summer of 1884, he wrote to a would-be author: "I am so much engaged in my studio that I have not time to give your play the attention I am sure it deserves. When I come to Boston, if you will leave it with me, I will read it and give you my opinion. . . . I congratulate you on your success as a stage manager and hope to do the like for you as an author." Ms. 1427, Historic Hudson Valley, Tarrytown, New York.

411. Rosamond Gilder, 68; Skinner, 255.

412. Francis Wilson saw Jefferson in "costume" in Buffalo on May 25, 1896, giving a lecture to the Women's Union at Union Hall. When the

chairperson, Mrs. Frank Wade, introduced Jefferson in Buffalo, she said; "Mr. Jefferson, here are five hundred of your friends." *New York Mirror*, September 29, 1883: 3; *New York Times*, October 7, 1883: 4, 15; Wilson, 98.

413. Wilson, 105.

414. *New York Dramatic Mirror*, June 4, 1892: 4, 6.

415. Francis Wilson reports that in 1896, while taking questions from the audience, Jefferson would occasionally put an open hand in back of his ear and ask his questioner to raise his voice. Wilson, 105.

416. Rosamond Gilder, 295–296.

417. Apparently Jefferson had lowered his prices during the 1898 tour, and his opinion about the Theatrical Trust counted. Harrison Grey Fiske, editor of the *New York Dramatic Mirror* printed it in every edition. "When the Trust was formed I gave my opinion as against it, considering it inimical to the theatrical profession. I think so still." *New York Dramatic Mirror*, October 16 (2, 6), October 23 (12), October 30 (4, 5), November 6 (3), December 11 (14), December 18 (2) 1897; January 22 (14), February 5 (2) 1898; Wilson, 310, 316, 319; Eugenie Jefferson, 179.

418. *New York Dramatic Mirror Theatrical "Trust" Supplement No. 11*, January 22, 1898: 3.

419. *New York Times*, October 26, 1895: 13.

420. The dinner was held in the Constable building, 111 Fifth Avenue. Two hundred members were present, including Richard Watson Gilder, William Bispham, Laurence Hutton, E. C. Benedict, and Daniel Frohman. Former President Grover Cleveland, Augustin Daly, and Bronson Howard sent letters of regret. The printed menu was elaborate, with a large bust portrait of Jefferson and pictures of him as Bob Acres and Rip. Jefferson was introduced by Hamilton W. Mable, the toastmaster. Joe responded: "It is . . . embarrassing to be presented as such a virtuous man as Mr. Mable makes me out to be, . . . and if I don't get mixed up in some scandals . . . soon my friends will begin to suspect me." He then complimented the guests on their singing of "The Star-spangled Banner" and "Marching through Georgia," although he said that in the latter song the voices of the guests were pitched in keys enough to have unlocked the prison bars of the Spanish Inquisition.

On March 31, 1898, yet another testimonial dinner was given in Jefferson's honor, this time at the Colonial Club. Grover Cleveland, unable to attend, sent a charming letter that was read aloud, and the main speech of the evening was given by William Winter, who by then had known Jefferson for almost forty years. Winter ended with a nine-stanza poem of exquisite nineteenth-century doggerel:

> Like the rainbow that pierces the clouds where they darken,
> He came ev'ry sorrow and care to beguile:
> He spoke—and the busy throng halted to harken;
> He smiled—and the world answered back with a smile.

Wilson 321; William Winter, *The Poet and the Actor*, New York Public Library.
421. *Autobiography*, 439.
422. Wilson, 153, 236.
423. *New York Dramatic Mirror*, January 10, 1891: 2.
424. On October 9, 1886, Booth wrote to his daughter Edwina:

> Jefferson called and left me with the MS of his reminiscences. . . . So far as he has written it, it is intensely interesting and amusing and well written in a . . . chatty style; it will be the best autobiography of any actor yet published.

On October 15 Booth again wrote to Edwina: "Jefferson came with more of his MS yesterday, which was even more interesting than the first chapters." Joseph Jefferson III, Letter to Edwin Booth, October 7, 1886, The Hampden-Booth Theatre Library at The Players; Grossman, 74–75.
425. Jefferson had already had word of the *Autobiography* leaked to the press, and notice of his writing appeared in the *New York Mirror* of October 16, 1886. He continued to work on his reminiscences in Boston and New York, and when the fall 1886 tour was over, in New Iberia. A reporter visiting him in Louisiana recalled that the days

> were given over to reading aloud from the autobiography upon which Mr. Jefferson was . . . at work and to long walks through the woods. . . . In the morning, Mr. Jefferson would sit on the piazza on a big wicker chair and read bits of the autobiography. Occasionally he would lay down the manuscript and tell a story, and the Spectator would say, "Now you must put that in."
> "And do you . . . think that would interest the public?"
> And after some argument, in it would go.

Jefferson initially conceived of his autobiography as a "subscription book" with a gilt top, a half-morocco book selling at the coffee table price of $3.00, but he was eventually persuaded, probably by Richard Watson Gilder, to let it come out in serialized form in a magazine. Gilder's publishing house, Century Press, initially wanted to publish only excerpts, but Jefferson refused. He eventually sold the publication rights for $6,000 plus a ten percent royalty, and Century got the right to serialize portions.
The *Autobiography* "had the best holiday sale of all the books of the year." According to the bookseller Brentano: "It is unlike any previous dramatic work I ever handled inasmuch as its sale has been limited to no particular class. The average theatrical work is sought only by a small coterie of collectors who buy every book of the kind in order to augment their libraries. But the Jefferson memoirs are asked for by everybody." Joseph Jefferson III, "To Edwin Booth," October 7, 1886, The Hampden-Booth Theatre Library at The Players; Grossman, 74, 75; "Joseph Jefferson as the Spectator Knew Him,"

Outlook 80 (May 6, 1905): 18; Wilson, 237; *New York Dramatic Mirror,* January 10, 1891: 2.

426. On January 6, 1888, sixteen men met at Delmonico's restaurant in New York to incorporate The Players. They included Edwin Booth, the club's founder and the eventual donor of its building, Samuel L. Clemens, Augustin Daly, Laurence Hutton, Brander Matthews, and General William Tecumseh Sherman. Jefferson, who was not present at the initial meeting, became a member of the board but not an officer. Articles of incorporation were drawn up the next day, marking the official founding of the club, and those present announced their intention to "to buy a building, establish a library and provide a place of the deposit of relics and pictures." The club's official purposes were:

> To provide for social intercourse among the members of the dramatic profession, artists, and the patrons of art.
> For the formation of a dramatic library and a house for dramatic records.
> To collect historical data of the stage in general and of the American stage in particular.

Jefferson was not present in New York on December 31, 1888, when The Players opened its doors at 16 Gramercy Park. Edwin Booth, however, toasted the opening of the club, using the "loving cup" that William Warren had bequeathed to Jefferson and that Joe, in turn, had given to The Players. Laurence Hutton, who served as secretary at The Players' meetings, worshiped Jefferson. He remembered an early meeting of the board at which

> Some unimportant motion was made, seconded—seconded, I think, by Jefferson himself—and was about to be put to vote without discussion, when I interrupted. I explained that I had been occupied . . . with the recording of the previous motion . . . and that I would like to say a word or two upon the subject, giving my . . . reasons . . . why the matter . . . should not . . . be . . . settled. Jefferson . . . said, "I think Laurence is right!" Booth saw the expression of my face, and cried: "Look at the boy! . . . he is blushing like a girl!" And I *was* blushing like a girl with pleasure, at the epithet. Jefferson, without thinking of it, had called me by my first name, and for the first time! It was a small matter to him. It was not a small matter to me.

New York Mirror, January 14, 1888: 8; *Constitution of The Players* (New York, 1888), 5; *New York Times,* January 1, 1889: 5; Laurence Hutton, "Recollections of Joseph Jefferson," *Harper's Weekly* 49 (May 6, 1905), 657.

427. The text of the speech was as follows:

> I cannot attribute this . . . reception . . . either to Mr. Booth or to myself but rather to the office we are called upon to fulfill.
> If you will glance at the . . . audience assembled . . . you will perceive . . . that this is neither the time nor place . . . for a lengthened address.
> I will not mention the word "charity." The . . . donations and . . .

merchandise which you have showered upon this institution show that you . . . appreciate . . . the value of that word.

In this vast place it is quite natural that not more than one-half of the audience can see or hear what I say, which perhaps, is one of the advantages you will derive from my address.

I find that I am shut out from one-half of the audience by the house of the immortal Shakespeare. This is not the first time that I have been obscured . . . by him. I can say, however, that there is one actor under this roof whom he has never obscured. . . . Your applause shows that you know to whom I refer, and if he ever has to open a fair, and make a speech, I hope he will say a good word for me.

As the name of Shakespeare comes up before me, . . . I will venture a short poem:

> May I say that all the varied gifts of his possession
> The wondering world asks, What was his profession?
> "Of course he was a lawyer," says the lawyer.
> "He must have been a sawyer," says the sawyer.
> The corner druggist says he was a chemist.
> The skilled mechanic dubs him a machinist.
> The thoughtful sage declares him a great thinker,
> And every tinman swears he was a tinker.
> And so he is claimed by every trade and factor.
> Your pardon, gentlemen, he was an actor.
> Pray take my hand and come with me
> To where once stood the famous mulberry tree
> Then on to Stratford church. Here take a peep
> At where the fathers of the hamlets sleep
> They hold a place of honor for the dead,
> The family of Shakespeare at the head.
> Before the altar of this sacred place
> They have been given burial and grace.
> And oh, my comrades, brothers in art,
> Permit me just one moment to depart
> From this my subject, urging you some day
> To seek this sacred spot and humbly pray
> That Shakespeare's rage toward us will kindly soften,
> Because, you know, we've murdered him so often.
> I ask this for myself, a poor comedian,
> What should I do had I been a tragedian!

Now then let me conclude my brief address. I have been requested to thank the . . . workers in this cause—the general public and the theatrical profession—for their . . . liberality and loyal support, and so I announce this fair to be formally opened.

The fair netted $8,628.71. *New York Times,* May 3 (5), June 3 (9) 1892.

428. *New York Dramatic Mirror*, July 2 (2), July 9 (4), July 23 (4) 1892; *New York Times,* January 2, 1894: 4.

429. Joseph Jefferson, "In Memory of Edwin Booth," *Modern Eloquence,* 693.

430. *New York Dramatic Mirror,* April 29 (3), May 6 (11), May 13 (8) 1893; *New York Times,* June 6 (1), June 8 (5), June 10 (12) 1893; William E. Bryant, "Joseph Jefferson at Home," *New England Magazine* 12 (1895): 203–4.

431. The doors opened at 2:45 P.M., and audience members were forced to line up early because there were no reserved seats. Thirteen hundred invitations were sent out. Below is a newspaper account of Jefferson's opening remarks:

And now it would seem that my duty's done; but can I quit this scene without telling you how closely allied I was in friendship with Edwin Booth? We were boys together. We have acted on the same stage. He was but sixteen years of age when I . . . met him—the sweetest nature and the most noble face I ever looked upon. His splendid social and dramatic career was marked by me from its beginning to its close. Pardon me if I press too closely upon his early domestic life, but I was the confidant between him and the sweet lady to whom he gave his first love—was cognizant of his youthful courtship, his early marriage, and the bereavement that followed. . . . I have acted with him upon the stage and rambled with him through the woods. We shared our youthful joys . . . , and in after years, he leaned upon my arm when broken down by illness and overwork.

It was but little more than a year ago that we strolled together upon the seashore, and if I remember his . . . words aright, he considered no man happy until he could enjoy the success of his enemies. Surely this was an elevated condition for one who was about to step . . . from this world to the next.

We all know Edwin Booth's public benevolence, but his private charities were only revealed to his friends, and even these he would have concealed . . . had it been possible. May I mention one? When he returned to San Francisco, after twenty years' absence, he discovered the abode of an old lady who had acted with him in . . . years gone by. He found her in poverty, and his charitable hand surrounded her with comfort for the rest of her life. [The actress was Elizabeth Saunders, Jefferson's first cousin.]

Another: Over forty years ago, his father . . . came to act in the city of Charleston. He was attended by his son Edwin. They were living at the house of an old friend. I saw them under this hospitable roof. Thirty years afterwards, . . . Charleston was shaken . . . by a terrible earthquake, and that same house . . . was crushed to earth and its inmates injured and ruined. Before the fallen telegraph wires had been lifted an hour, a message of comfort to that afflicted family was flashed over the wires by Edwin Booth, with a splendid gift that placed them beyond the reach of want.

The article goes on to say that

> Mr. Jefferson then related an incident . . . that had just been brought to his attention by Laurence Hutton. An elderly colored woman had asked the doorkeeper politely for admission. She had explained that her name was Betty Carter, that she had been an old servant of Edwin Booth. She said she had lived with him up to the death of his first wife and had been the slave of the elder Booth on his plantation. She had come all the way from Baltimore and was now sitting in the front row. Mr. Jefferson then asked those present to listen with rapt attention to the words of those who would follow him.

Jefferson and Irving later dined with Irving's stage manager, Bram Stoker, now most famous as the author of *Dracula*, and with the future president of the United States, William McKinley. *New York Times*, October 12, 1893: 4; Rip Van Winkle file, Free Library of Philadelphia; *Memorial Celebration of the Sixtieth Anniversary of the Birth of Edwin Booth held in the Madison Square Garden Concert Hall November The Thirteenth MDCCCXCIII [1893] by the Players*, 17; Bram Stoker, *Personal Reminiscences of Henry Irving* 2 (1906); Reprint, Hamden, Connecticut: Greenwood Press, 1970), 230; *New York Dramatic Mirror*, September 2, 1893: 4.

432. Walter Oettel reports: "Soon after his installation as president, he hung one of his canvasses, a water-mill scene, on the west wall of the Billiard Room and had a special light fixed over it. . . . [No other member] would have been permitted to hang one of his pictures in the Clubhouse."

Another version of this story has Jefferson hanging a landscape entitled *Summer* in the lobby and Maurice Barrymore commenting: "You know summer is not half so bad as it's painted."

On November 1, Jefferson presented The Players with a painting of Sir Henry Irving as Beckett, which he had commissioned a young German American named Eugene to produce. The portrait hung at Knoedler and Company galleries at Fifth Avenue at 34th Street. Walter Oettel, *Walter's Sketch Book of The Players* (New York: The Gotham Press, 1943), 30; James Kotsilibas-Davis, *Great Times Good Times: The Odyssey of Maurice Barrymore* (Garden City, New York: Doubleday & Co., Inc., 1977), 165; Winter, *Life and Art*, 309; *New York Dramatic Mirror*, May 7, 1892: 4; Wilson, 113, 128; *The New York Times*, May 1, 1892: 10.

433. The loving cup, designed by W. Clark Noble and manufactured by the Gorham Company, had three handles representing Jefferson's most popular characters—Rip, Dr. Pangloss, and Bob Acres. Between the handles were panels in bas relief, one representing a scene from Rip, another the dueling scene from *The Rivals*, and a third with Rip's famous toast inscribed on it. The top ornamentation consisted of three masks—Tragedy, Comedy, and Art—and three figures of Fame entwined with a garland of laurels. The cup was financed by subscription, using funds donated by other members of the

theatrical profession. At the time of the testimonial, only a silvered-over plaster cast was ready. It was placed on a revolving pedestal on the stage.

Frohman opened the proceedings and then introduced John Drew, who delivered some remarks. Then Agnes Booth, Edwin's niece, read a poem that William Winter had written. Frank Mayo made a speech acknowledging Jefferson as "the head and front of the American stage." *New York Times,* November 9, 1859: 9.

434. The stage children were Percita West, Baby Parker, Little Lola, Roy Richardson, Violet Moore, and Johnnie McKeever. Jefferson thanked the group, noting: "I see it seems that I have won the cup." He quoted one of his sons as saying that the inscription should read "For a Good Boy" on one side and "For an Old Boy" on the other. He paid tribute to Billy Florence and Edwin Booth and then cited a performance of *Julius Caesar*—with Edwin Forrest as Caesar, Booth as Cassius, and E. L. Davenport as Brutus—as particularly unforgettable. Jefferson ended with a anecdote about Edwin Forrest and a tribute to J. H. Stoddart and Charles Couldock, the only other surviving members of the Laura Keene company, in which he had first become a star. Frohman then presented him a scroll with the subscribers' names as well as a laurel wreath on behalf of the actor Richard Mansfield, who was aspiring to the mantle of the late Edwin Booth. Mansfield was the closest anyone could come to being America's greatest tragic actor in 1895; it must have seemed appropriate for him to present the wreath to America's greatest comic actor.

On March 28 the loving cup was finally completed and presented to Jefferson at the Fifth Avenue Hotel by a presentation committee including Daniel Frohman, William H. Crane, and John Drew. *New York Dramatic Mirror,* November 16 (3), November 23 (2) 1895; *New York Times,* November 1 (13), November 9 (9) 1895; January 26, 1896: 10; Wagenknecht, 191; Wilson, 113; Clipping Scrapbook, Jonathan Bourne Historical Center, Bourne, Massachusetts.

435. Joseph Jefferson, "To Mother of Mrs. Roy R. Denslow," April 12, 1895, The Hampden-Booth Theatre Library at The Players, New York City.

15. "For Heaven's Sake, Get a New Play," 1880–1889
pages 211–222

436. Joseph Jefferson, "To Laurence Hutton," Summer 1903, Laurence Hutton Correspondence Collection, Princeton University Library.

437. L. J. C., "Joe Jefferson, My Joe," Clipping File, The Historical Society of Pennsylvania, Philadelphia, Pennsylvania.

438. *New York Mirror,* July 31, 1886: 7.

439. William Winter, *Other Days,* 66–67.

440. In Jefferson's version of *The Rivals*, the first act ended after the comic scene between Captain Absolute and Sir Anthony; the second ended after scenes between Acres, Sir Lucius, and Captain Absolute, in which it is arranged that the former shall fight the mysterious Beverly; and the third act consisted of

scenes from the two final acts of the original play, so rearranged that the scenes in which Acres takes part followed one another. *New York Times,* September 13, 1881: 5; *New York Dramatic Mirror,* December 28, 1895: 14; Wilson, 218; Kotsilibas-Davis, 151–152.

441. In the fall of 1891 the *New York Times* wrote:

> We are curious to know why Mr. Jefferson has substituted the word "churchyard" for "abbey" in Sir Lucius's famous suggestion to Bob about the disposal of the squire's body if "anything happens." Is it because his . . . experience as actor and manager has taught him to trust nothing to the intelligence of his audiences. . . . It seems to be a pity to alter a phrase that has become classical.

Not everyone agreed with Jefferson's revisions of the play. In the fall of 1881 the *Missouri Republican* critic, although basically positive about Jefferson's version, noted that "the cutting of Faulkland, . . . was made necessary by the limitations of a traveling company, and this may be credited to business policy." The Boston correspondent for the *New York Mirror* wrote:

> I do not like the liberty that has been taken with Sheridan's work. There is . . . no harm done, nor is the sense of the play lost, but *The Rivals* has held the stage for . . . years, . . . and the character of Julia (although not a strong one) was always cast to the leading lady. . . . Some of Acres' scenes have been compressed and made stronger by the alteration. . . . The liberties do not extend much out of Acres' domain. . . . The stage was beautifully set, and the decorations, costumes etc., of a superior order. Business has been large.

New York Times, October 18, 1891: 13; *Missouri Republican* (St. Louis), October 11, 1881: 3; *New York Mirror,* October 30, 1880: 3.

442. Wilson, 110–111.

443. Jefferson told Francis Wilson that he had spent a long time training his hair for the role. Wilson, 276; Eugenie Jefferson, 27.

444. In 1887 the *New York Mirror's* critic wrote: "We have no desire to lecture Mr. Jefferson for his version of Sheridan's masterpiece. We simply object to the piece being billed as *The Rivals* without any mention of the elisions and alterations on the programme. . . . It has been urged . . . that he lacks histrionic versatility. His methods and personality bear a decided similarity, whether he appears as Golightly, Caleb Plummer, Bob Acres or Rip Van Winkle." *New York Mirror,* October 22, 1887: 1–2.

445. *New York Mirror,* November 3 (1), December 8 (4) 1888.

446. *New York Times,* October 18, 1887: 5.

447. *Ibid.,* October 16, 1898: 18.

448. *New York Mirror,* September 25, 1880: 3; *Public Ledger* (Philadelphia), September 14, 1880: 4.

449. *New York Times,* November 14 (7), November 24 (9) 1881; September

15 (7), September 17 (9), September 19 (5, 15) 1882; *New York Mirror,* November 18, 1882: 4; *Public Ledger* (Philadelphia), December 12, 1881: 1; *Pittsburgh Commercial Gazette,* December 27, 1881: 4.

450. In the fall of 1899 Joe toured with his godson, Jefferson Winter, as a member of the company. The two did not always get along. Winter remembered Jefferson as "old and sometimes a trifle testy if not immediately deferred to." He also saw himself as "young and foolish," but he admired Jefferson's work as an actor. During a particular scene in *The Rivals,* Jefferson came close to making his young godson laugh on stage. When Joe realized what was happening, he was incensed and admonished him: "[F]or heaven's sake, my boy, don't you laugh! If you laugh the audience won't." It was the moment . . . when Acres reveals to Captain Absolute his hair done up in curl papers . . . the expression in his eyes, as after glancing furtively about, he suddenly removed his hat and displayed his sandy-red hair in pickle, was ludicrous." Joseph Jefferson III, "To John Rogers, Jr.," December 29, 1888, April 15, 1889, Rogers Collection, New York Historical Society; Jefferson Winter, 22.

451. By 1885, Jefferson's tours were planned at least nine months in advance. The fall 1884 tour ended in early December, and by mid-January 1885 he was negotiating to open his fall tour in Cincinnati on October 15. Negotiations for touring, however, were complex, and by mid-February Jefferson was scheduled to open at McVicker's Theatre in Chicago. In actuality, he opened in Columbus, Ohio, on September 30. Jefferson was caught in the machine of the touring system.

16. The Jefferson-Florence Company, 1889–1892
pages 223–235

452. *New York Dramatic Mirror,* February 2 (3), March 9 (5) 1889; November 28, 1891: 3.

453. *New York Mirror,* June 2, 1888: 6.

454. *Ibid.,* June 9, 1888: 9.

455. *New York Dramatic Mirror,* March 30, 1889: 1.

456. Wilson, 9.

457. Skinner, 255.

458. *New York Dramatic Mirror,* August 31 (2), September 14 (1) 1889.

459. *New York Herald,* October 15, 1889: 5.

460. "A few years ago one hardly ever saw a dress coat at the theatre. Now nearly the entire male audience is in evening clothes [and] women [go] to the play [in] cumbersome hats and wraps." *New York Herald,* October 27, 1889: 11.

461. Couldock was a replacement. On June 18, 1889, John Gilbert, who was to play Sir Anthony Absolute in the fall, died in Boston at the age of seventy-nine. He had Bright's disease of the kidneys and an attack of pneumonia in the right lung. Gilbert had acted Polonius in the famous all-star production of

Hamlet in honor of Lester Wallack, in which Jefferson had played the First Gravedigger, and he had worked with Jefferson since 1888. *New York Dramatic Mirror*, March 30 (2), June 2 (4) 1889.

462. *New York Herald*, October 15, 1889: 5; *The New York Dramatic Mirror*, March 15, 1890: 4.

463. *New York Dramatic Mirror*, October 19, 1889: 4; *New York Herald*, October 15, 1889: 5.

464. When Francis Wilson first met Jefferson during the tour's Boston engagement, he noted that the actor was thin, his face wrinkled, and his brown hair mixed with gray. A photograph of the period shows Jefferson as Bob Acres and Florence as Sir Lucius O'Trigger. Jefferson, although clearly aged, has strong legs, could still wear tights, and appears booted as he stands in a strong, athletic pose. The strength of his legs is also apparent in the motion picture clips of *Rip*. Wilson, 4.

465. *Wilkes-Barre Record*, April 30, 1890: 8.

466. The review begins: "Jefferson, like Booth, draws largely from the floating populations during his metropolitan engagements. This, together with the element that only patronizes the theatre on special occasions or when old favorites come . . . makes larger and more cordial audiences than those of merely fashionable composition. A house of this sort was present at the Fifth Avenue on Monday evening when the stellar triumvirate presented *The Rivals* again." *New York Dramatic Mirror*, March 15, 1890: 4.

467. *New York Times*, March 11, 1890: 4.

468. *Ibid.*, March 9 (13), March 16 (13) 1890.

469. *New York Dramatic Mirror*, April 5, 1890: 8; *Times-Democrat* (New Orleans), March 27, 1890: 4.

470. The validity of this accusation may be testified to not only by Mrs. Drew's retirement but by the poor health experienced by the young male lead Frederick Paulding in the summer after the tour's conclusion. *New York Dramatic Mirror*, June 21, (3), July 12, (3) 1890.

471. *New York Dramatic Mirror*, July 19, 1890: 3.

472. Florence returned on the *Etruria*, and on September 8 a reporter found him "walking up Broadway, looking as stout and jolly as ever."

> Did I bring Mrs. Florence home with me? No. She will remain in England for another year. She has a . . . suite of rooms overlooking Trafalgar Square and seems to enjoy herself. . . . She likes to act, but . . . there isn't . . . much pleasure in one-night stands. . . . We may . . . resume our joint starring tours . . . , but it will be . . . later on.

New York Dramatic Mirror, September 13, 1890: 6.

473. *New York Dramatic Mirror*, October 4, 1890: 6.

474. Florence was very generous. He forwarded $800 a week to his wife in England and spent the rest on friends. Upon his death, a relative said: "Billy

Florence made, since his connection with Joseph Jefferson, $50,000 a year; he spent $49,000."

475. *New York Times,* October 14, 1890: 4.

476. One day, while getting into makeup and costume, Jefferson and Florence decided to make a phonographic record of their work, now unfortunately lost.

> The first phonographic record ever made by Mr. Florence was made in the dressing room of Mr. Jefferson at Palmer's Theatre. . . . Mr. Florence came into the dressing room dressed and "made up" for Sir Lucius O'Trigger and found Mr. Jefferson . . . interested in a phonograph which a gentleman of this city, who has become known to his friends as a "phonograph crank," had taken there, and on the invitation of the "crank," Mr. Jefferson and Mr. Florence joined in placing in the waxen cylinder the scene from *The Rivals* in which Sir Lucius and Bob Acres are arranging the preliminaries for the duel, beginning with a snatch of a song by Florence and ending with Jefferson's funny plaint: "You oughtn't to talk to a man like that, at a time like this, to a man like that."

Another recording, also lost, was made a year later.

> Only a little over a month ago [September 1891], when the Jefferson-Florence company was rehearsing at the Star theatre . . . Charles Burnham, acting manager of the Star for Mr. Moss, and who is also the possessor of a phonograph, induced the two actors to make a record for him. They gave the same scene from *The Rivals,* but Mr. Jefferson momentarily stumbled in his part, and Mr. Florence prompted him in his every-day tone of voice. This "prompt" went on the record, and is repeated every time the scene is reproduced, making the cylinder more curious as a souvenir than if it contained only the words of the scene.

Wilson, 281, 282, 283; *New York Times,* September 22, 1891: 13.

477. *New York Dramatic Mirror,* March 7, 1891: 11.

478. *Ibid.,* November 28, 1891: 3; *New York Times,* November 17 (1), November 18 (1), November 20 (5), November 21 (2), November 23 (5) 1891; *Pittsburgh Post,* November 20, 1891: 1; Barnes, 190.

479. *Evening News* (Detroit), November 20, 1891: 1; *Minneapolis Tribune,* November 20, 1891: 2.

480. James, who was forty-nine, had worked under Mrs. Drew's management at the Arch Street Theatre in Philadelphia.

The evening performance was filled with hundreds of students from Michigan University and cadets from the Michigan Military Academy. Jefferson was called out at the end of the first act, and when the final curtain went down, the "college boys present let loose . . . with their usual cries, and the 'Rah, Rahs' of Cornell, Michigan University, Michigan Military Academy and Detroit high school were repeated over and over. The company left immediately for Minneapolis." Mrs. Drew did not appear in Detroit.

On April 6, 1892, eleven days after he closed in Denver, Jefferson arrived back in New York, traveling in his private railway car. Upon arrival, he announced that

> he will act no more in the old comedies. He took them up . . . to show the critics that he was . . . able to play . . . other roles beside Rip Van Winkle, and having accomplished that design and doubled his large fortune . . . , he will return to Rip and play nothing else during the rest of his career. Mr. Jefferson will probably play an extended engagement in Chicago during the World's Fair.

The statement was untrue; Jefferson continued to perform plays other than *Rip* through his final performance in 1904. *New York Dramatic Mirror,* December 5, 1891: 10; April 9 (2, 4), April 16 (3) 1892; October 5, 1895: 2; *New York Times,* April 3, 1892: 13; *Pittsburgh Post,* November 20, 1891: 1; *Evening News* (Detroit), November 20, 1891. 1, Joseph Jefferson, "To Sol Smith Russell," February 2, 1892, The Hampden-Booth Theatre Library at The Players.

17. Private Life at Buzzards Bay   *pages 236–251*

481. On August 25, 1884, Edwin Booth wrote to his daughter from Newport, Rhode Island: "I expected Jefferson to-day, but he can't come until Wednesday and his stay will be curtailed, and my anticipated pleasure of fishing and picnicking with him and his folk is dashed." On July 15, 1885, having just returned from Canada, Jefferson wrote to Booth:

> My Dear Ned:
>   I send you today a noble salmon killed by myself and cured and smoked in our camp last week on the Mirramicki River in Canada.
>   It will make a fine relish for breakfast cooked just about two minutes.
>   I would have called when in Boston to acknowledge the receipt of [your daughter's] wedding cards but Thayer, your agent, told me you were away. If I had not been barnstorming at the time, I would have honored my family with a sight of the bride and groom. We all send our congratulations. I expect you are a little lonely.
>   Can't you put in some time with us here? I wish you would. I have some new things you would like to see—don't fail to keep open dates for the Plantation next winter if you get as far as New Orleans.
>   Ever yours
>   Joe

Grossman, 253; Joseph Jefferson, "To Edwin Booth," July 15, 1885, The Hampden-Booth Theatre Library at The Players.

482. "Joseph Jefferson as the Spectator Knew Him," *Outlook* 80 (May 6, 1905): 18.

483. Wilson, 54.

484. Eugenie Jefferson, 64–65; Bradford, 91.

485. William Hosea Ballou reported that Jefferson had a salmon reserve in Skiff Lake, Nova Scotia. Booth wrote to his daughter, Edwina: "Jefferson has sent me a huge salmon from Canada, killed and smoked by himself." Ballou, 126; Grossman, 64; *New York Mirror*, August 22 (4), September 19 (6), October 24 (6) 1885.

486. *New York Mirror*, June 11, 1887: 9.

487. *Ibid.*, May 27 (5), June 3 (5) 1882; William E. Bryant, 195; "When Joe Jefferson Lived at Crow's Nest," *Cape Cod News*, September 21, 1938, Sandwich Massachusetts Archives.

488. This rumor is reinforced by an article in the *Independent* of October 13, 1895:

> Until the town of Bourne was set off a few years ago, Buzzards Bay was a part of Sandwich. Mr. Jefferson had . . . fallen in love with the town and, after a view of it from an elevation. . . , declared that in natural beauty, it could not be surpassed by any town in New England. . . . President Cleveland and Mr. Jefferson both desired to build in Sandwich before Buzzards Bay knew them for its own. President Cleveland looked at one or two estates. One in particular seemed to strike his fancy. It had been on the market for some time, but there was no purchaser. When it became known that the distinguished gentleman thought favorably of it, the price . . . took a quick upward turn, but it rose too high; the evidence of cupidity was too apparent and no sale was effected. The sudden desire for quick wealth robbed Sandwich of the honor of having among its summer residents, the first citizen of the land and America's foremost actor.

In 1898 Josephine Robb, writing in the *Ladies' Home Journal*, contended: "When Mr. Jefferson first made his home there, it was suggested that the name of the nearest station be changed from Buzzards Bay to Jeffersonville, but with his characteristic modesty, . . . Mr. Jefferson did not agree with the railroad directors who wished this alteration. Josephine Robb, "Rip Van Winkle as He is at Home," *The Ladies' Home Journal* 15 (May 1898): 2.

489. *Chicago Record Herald*, April 24, 1905: 1.

490. Newspaper clipping, Sarah B. Hull Scrapbook, 47, Missouri Historical Society, St. Louis.

491. Gilder was probably involved in more than a social occasion. As an editor at Century Press, he spent his time getting the rights to Jefferson's *Autobiography* on "good terms," which were subsequently ratified by telegram from his publisher, Roswell Smith. In October 1889, Jefferson's *Autobiography* began publication in installments by *Century Magazine*. *Sandwich Observer*, March 27, 1888: n.p., Bourne Archives, Sandwich, Massachusetts; Cullity, n.p; Grossman, 87; Gilder, 162, 169, 181; Winter, *Life and Art,* 191, n. 1; Probate Inventory dated July 29, 1905, Municipal records, Barnstable, Massachusetts, Collection of Michael Burgess, Buzzards Bay, Massachusetts; Eugenie Jefferson, 81; *New*

York Dramatic Mirror, March 23 (2), April 27 (2) 1889; Allan Nevins, *Grover Cleveland,* 451; Richard Watson Gilder, *Grover Cleveland* (New York: The Century Co., 1910), 7, 53, 57.

492. Joseph Jefferson, "Letter to John Rogers, Jr.," July 8, 1889, Rogers Collection, New York Historical Society; Joseph Jefferson, "To Grover Cleveland," July 9, July 12, 1889, Grover Cleveland Papers Series 2, January 12, 1889–September 18, 1889, Library of Congress, Washington D.C.; *New York Dramatic Mirror,* May 18, 1889: 6; *Sandwich Observer,* July 23, 1889, Bourne Archives, Bourne Massachusetts; Gilder, *Grover Cleveland,* 58.

493. Joseph Jefferson, "Letter to Willie," March 5, 1889, Miscellaneous Manuscripts Collection, Library of Congress.

494. Joseph Jefferson, "To Grover Cleveland," May 16, 1890, Grover Cleveland Papers, Series 2, 1889, Library of Congress; *New York Dramatic Mirror,* August 25, 1888: 8, May 10, 1890: 3; Notes on "Crows Nest," Bourne Historical Society; Newspaper clipping Sarah B. Hull Scrapbook, 47, Missouri Historical Society, St. Louis.

495. Eugenie Jefferson, 202.

496. Hugh Coyle, "To Grover Cleveland," April 1, 1893, Grover Cleveland Papers, Series 2, March 20–April 14, 1893, Library of Congress, Washington, D.C.

497. Bradford, 93.

498. Nevins, *Letters,* 401; Gilder, *Grover Cleveland,* 60, 62; *New York Dramatic Mirror,* June 13, 1896: 9; Kotsilibas-Davis, 292.

499. Fortunately a number of works by Mauve, Israëls, Daubigny, and Corot had been on loan to a New York exhibit and had arrived back in Buzzards Bay only the day before. They were still in packing boxes and easily removed. Mauve's *Return of the Flock,* which Jefferson had bought for $2,500, was on loan to the Chicago World's Fair. Another of the paintings saved was Israëls' *The Madonna of the Cottage.* The figures on the valuation of the house may be greatly exaggerated. Because Jefferson was on tour when the fire occurred, some of his theatrical wardrobe was obviously saved. I am deeply indebted to Michael Burgess for his invaluable and indefatigable researching of the Jefferson family homes. *Register* (Sandwich, Massachusetts), April 7, 1893: 1; Michael Burgess, "Tragic Fire Struck 'Crow's Nest' 100 Years Ago Today," *Bourne Courier,* April 1, 1993: 7; *New York Times,* November 24, 1880: 2; Winter, *Life and Art,* 191; Eugenie Jefferson, 25–26, 40, 44.

500. Eugenie Jefferson, 25, 27–28.

501. The family stayed in the Buzzards Bay area. By April 18, 1893, while Jefferson was on tour, and less than three weeks after the fire, Sarah Jefferson and Nell Symons, the old family nurse, returned to occupy the Whittier cottage, now called The Inn on Buttermilk Bay. *New York Dramatic Mirror,* April 5 (5, 7), April 8 (5, 7, 14), April 15 (5, 6, 13), April 22 (5, 6, 7, 10), April 29 (5, 6, 7, 10, 11), May 6 (5, 11), May 13 (8, 11), May 20 (4), June 10 (14), July 15 (8) 1893; Wilson, 281–283.

502. Josephine Robb, writing in 1894, reviewed the homes of the rest of the Jefferson clan.

> In the houses around Crow's Nest live Mr. Jefferson's sons. Charles Jefferson, the eldest son, is . . . farther away from the manor than the others, but in his . . . cottage live . . . his sister, Miss Josephine Jefferson [who acted as Charles Burke's housekeeper after his wife's death], and his four daughters. The two elder girls are married—Margaret to Glen McDonough, the playwright; Josephine to Charles Rolfe of Boston. There is a little cottage close at the left of Crow's Nest where Joseph Warren Jefferson, with his wife, Blanche, and their two . . . babies, make their home. . . . On the right of Crow's Nest is the home of Thomas Jefferson, the second son. Mr. and Mrs. Thomas Jefferson have four children. . . . In another . . . cottage lives "Auntie Con," known . . . as Mrs. Jackson. . . . At the manor house at Crow's Nest the family consists of the master and mistress, their son Will, who is twenty-one years old and unmarried, and Frank, a charming boy of thirteen, the youngest of Joseph Jefferson's children.

Daily Picayune (New Orleans), March 27, 1894: 8; Joseph Jefferson, "To Edwina Booth Grossman," April 18, May 24, 1894, The Hampden-Booth Theatre Library at The Players; Joseph Jefferson, "To L. J. Cist, April 24, 1894, Autograph Collection of Simon Gratz, Historical Society of Pennsylvania, Philadelphia; *The Players* (New York, 1894), 43; Josephine Robb, 1–2; Clipping Collection, John Callahan, Kutztown, Pennsylvania; *New York Dramatic Mirror*, March 10 (2), April 7 (4), April 28 (7) 1894; Henry Harrison, "An Afternoon with Joseph Jefferson," *Woman's Home Companion*, 31 (January 1904), Robinson Locke Collection, 302: 57; "When Jefferson Came to Chicago," *Sunday Record-Herald* (Chicago), April 30, 1905, Robinson Locke Collection, 302: 136, New York Public Library for the Performing Arts; Rosamond Gilder, 295–6.

503. On January 15, 1894, Jefferson was in Florida, where he bought a Rembrandt called *The Burgomeister's Wife*, or *Portrait of Petronella Buys, Wife of Burgomeister of Curdon*, from Knoedler & Company. He wrote to Charles Burke:

> Mr. Roos of Knoedler & Co., was here spending a few days with me. By his advice and, I may add, by my own inclination, I have bought the "Burgomeister's Wife," by Rembrandt. This . . . rare work only costs me $25,000. He asked me not to mention the price except in my own family, so don't touch on that to anyone. With love,
>
> J. JEFFERSON.

Jefferson's art was a good investment. He paid $30,000 for Mauve's *The Departure of the Flock*, for which he was later offered $150,000. He paid $25,000 for the Rembrandt, and its value soared; he bought a piece by Mayer von Breman in a Montreal store for five pounds and later sold it for $1,500. His total collection was estimated upon his death at $300,000, and his total worth in personal property at $500,000. Michael Thomas Burgess, "Post Scripts," Bourne Historical Society; Horace S. Crowell, "To Mrs. Grover Cleveland," February 18, March 11, 1894, Grover Cleveland Papers, Series 3, November 21, 1893–May 16,1894, Library of Congress; Probate Inventory dated July 29, 1905; Wilson, 142; Eugenie Jefferson, 36, 45; *Pioneer* (Bourne, Massachusetts), October 31, 1893: n.p.; Robb, 2; Deluxe Catalogue, No. 56, 69; *New York Dramatic Mirror,* July 14, 1894: 4.

504. William E. Bryant, 203–204; Joseph Jefferson, "To Mrs. Harcourt," October 5, 1894, Museum of the City of New York; Joseph Jefferson, "To Mrs. Emmons," October 29, 1894, Maxcy-Markoe-Hughes Collection, Historical Society of Pennsylvania, Philadelphia; *New York Dramatic Mirror*, September 29 (7), October 13 (4), October 20 (10), November 24 (14), December 1 (10) 1894.

505. Joseph Jefferson, "To Mr. Cable," February 19, 1895, Manuscripts, Rare Books and University Archives, Tulane University Library, New Orleans, Louisiana; Joseph Jefferson, "To Henry C. Flagler," March 3, 1895, Flagler Museum Archives, Palm Beach, Florida; *New York Dramatic Mirror*, February 16, 1895: 12; Eugenie Jefferson, 45.

506. Joseph Jefferson, "To Sophie Markoe Emmens," July 2, 1895, Maxcy-Markoe-Hughes Collection, Historical Society of Pennsylvania, Philadelphia.

18. The All-Star *Rivals,* 1896–1897   *pages 252–266*

507. *New York Dramatic Mirror,* November 9, 1893: 13,14.

508. *Ibid.,* November 30, 1895: 15.

509. The tour is one of the most extensively documented periods of Jefferson's career. Francis Wilson, who played what he described as "the booby David," wrote a book about it, and Nat Goodwin and Julia Marlowe both describe it in their autobiographies. *New York Dramatic Mirror,* June 8, 1895: 10; Wilson, 189; *New York Times,* June 2, 1895: 20.

510. Wilson, 194–195.

511. Eugenie Jefferson, 255.

512. *Idem,* 253–254.

513. Wilson, 195.

514. Brown 3: 582; *New York Dramatic Mirror,* April 18 (17), May 9 (6) 1896; *New York Times,* December 7, 1899: 1.

515. Wilson, 199.

516. Nat Goodwin, who played Sir Lucius in the production, believed that the primary source of the company's problems were Jefferson's three sons, Willie, Tom, and Joe. Goodwin writes: "Some one had told [Jefferson] that I associated with his sons . . . ; consequently I was not a desirable person to have in any first class organization! He had given up . . . hope regarding his sons; so he thought that he would have a try at my redemption. My conduct was so

exemplary, however, that the third week, he apologized to me and . . . begged that, during the rest of the tour, I kindly look after him." Nat C. Goodwin, *Nat Goodwin's Book* (Boston: Richard G. Badger, 1914), 45–48; Wilson, 211.

517. Eugenie Jefferson, 177–178; Wilson, 199.

518. Program, *The Rivals*, May 9, 1896, MS 447, Box 5, The Historical Society of Washington D.C.; Wilson 214; *New York Dramatic Mirror*, May 16 (10, 14), May 23 (4, 12, 13), May 30 (4, 11) 1896.

519. By the next day, the Olympic Theatre in St. Louis had extended the number of performances and decided on a new ticket policy.

> A matinee performance of *The Rivals* . . . has been decided upon. The sale for the evening performance is the biggest on record for a dramatic presentation and left no more seats on the first floor or in the balcony after the box office had been open three or four hours. Admission to the gallery will be sold only on the night and afternoon of the performance. The sale for the matinee, to be given Thursday afternoon, May 14, at two o'clock, will begin at the theater Monday morning at nine o'clock.

As it turned out, the matinee in St. Louis was not a sellout, possibly because Americans were not accustomed to Thursday matinees. The balcony and gallery were crowded, but there were empty spaces in the orchestra. The evening performance, however, was jammed; even the standing room along the back and side walls was full. *St. Louis Post Dispatch*, May 7 (4), May 8 (3), May 15 (4) 1896; *Globe Democrat* (St. Louis), May 15, 1896: 4; Clipping Collection, John Callahan, Kutztown, Pennsylvania.

520. Knapp, 35; *New York Dramatic Mirror*, May 16 (10, 14), 1896; *St. Louis Post Dispatch*, May 8 (3), May 23 (12 13), May 30 (4) 1896.

521. *New York Dramatic Mirror*, May 16, 1896: 10.

522. Wilson, 238.

523. The company slept on the train except for the three-performance run in Chicago. The Chicago correspondent of the *New York Dramatic Mirror* wrote: "The company arrived on its . . . special train from St. Louis Friday morning and all registered at the Auditorium. . . . They report a glorious time on the rail. Nothing but money and fun. At the hotel, I met Mr. Crane, suffering from a bad throat, and I took him down to young Dr. Thomas. . . . I left him squirting all sorts of things down the comedian's throat, and at night his voice was a wonder. *New York Dramatic Mirror*, May 23, 1896: 12; Nat Goodwin, 182–183.

524. Jefferson had an instinctive eye for what would distract an audience. When Julia Marlowe accidentally dropped a rose on stage one night, just before one of his scenes, he rushed to snatch it up as he entered, later telling Francis Wilson: "I couldn't have acted with it there. . . . The eye is such a tyrant that it would have constantly sought the unusual on the scene. My attention would have been distracted and my scene ruined." E. H. Sothern, *Julia Marlowe's Story*

(New York: Rinehart & Company, Inc., 1954), 115–119; Wilson, 239–240.

525. *St. Louis Post Dispatch,* May 15, 1896: 4.

526. Wilson, 253.

527. Marlowe felt that both Jefferson, who was sixty-seven, and Mrs. Drew, who was seventy-eight, represented an older, less enlightened generation of actors:

> There was an ancient custom of taking calls on the scene while the actors who had not gone off were compelled to stand on . . . stage like . . . waxworks. That practice was adhered to by Mr. Jefferson. He and Mrs. Drew . . . would come on again and again at the door which had just closed on them and bow and bow and bow. I was one of the victims of that . . . breach of realism and had to wait to go on. . . .

> Another custom . . . with its origin in the old-time dimness of the stage lighted with candles was the following: Actors would pick up chairs, take them down to the footlights, seat themselves with their faces to the audience and there conduct their conversation so that the full countenance might be observed. That was continued by Mr. Jefferson and Mrs. Drew in spite of modern electric lights.

Marlowe's viewpoint is borne out by the St. Louis *Globe Democrat.*

> Each of the actors was given a splendid reception, and there were repeated recalls, not only at the end of every act, but there were individual calls, and each of the actors, after every exit, was forced to return to the stage and bow his or her acknowledgements. This . . . made the situation . . . awkward. . . . When [Jefferson] came [on], the demonstration was . . . tumultuous and lasted nearly five minutes.

528. Russell writes that "On the tour the All-Star cast . . . [was] friendly and comradely. . . . Mr. Jefferson was . . . paternally . . . sweet. . . . Four weeks in private cars hurtling about the country, playing in the afternoon at one place and in the evening at another, are tiresome and have nothing to do with art." Charles Edward Russell, *Julia Marlowe" Her Life and Art* (New York: D. Appleton and Company, 1926), 246–247.

529. Jefferson's lack of attention to the world around him may have been a sign of old age, although there is some indication that he was like this as a young man. He told Frances Wilson that in 1859 he was introduced to Senator Stephen A. Douglas, Lincoln's great opponent,

> and was invited to drink. On leaving the place one of the party who accompanied Mr. Jefferson asked if he knew what he had done.

> "I can't imagine—something dreadful, I'll be bound! What was it?"

> "Why Douglas paid for those drinks with a five-dollar piece and you pocketed the change!"

Wilson, 7–9.

530. Goodwin, 64–65.

531. At the end of the tour on May 29, Jefferson received a gift from Sir Henry Irving: the walking-stick used in the first performance of *The School for Scandal* in London in 1777. Irving had had the stick mounted and inscribed. *Post* (New York), February 11, 1897, Scrapbook, National Theatre Archive, Washington D.C.; Clipping Collection, John Callahan, Kutztown, Pennsylvania; Wilson, 279.

532. *New York Dramatic Mirror,* June 6, 1896: 12; Wilson, 274; Article dated November 18, 1899, Robinson Locke Collection, New York Public Library for the Performing Arts.

19. "A Back Number"—Retirement and Death, 1896–1905
pages 267–294

533. In 1897–98 the fall tour was eight weeks; the spring tour was a month. The fall 1898–99 tour lasted only five weeks, and for the first time in more than twenty years there was no spring tour at all. The fall 1899–1900 tour lasted only three weeks, although Jefferson still did five weeks in the spring. He bounced back the following year, doing a fall 1900–01 tour of almost three months and a five-week spring tour. In 1901–02 he did a nine-week fall tour and a five-week spring tour. The 1902–03 tour lasted nine weeks in the fall and a month in the spring. The 1903–04 tour lasted seven weeks in the fall and a month in the spring, culminating in Jefferson's last performance.

534. Wilson, 16.

535. On June 29 his grandchild Josephine, daughter of Charles and Edna Cary Jefferson, was married to Charles J. Rolfe, the son of a Harvard Shakespeare scholar, under a marquee on the lawn of her home near Crow's Nest. She walked down the aisle on her father's arm to the strains of an orchestra imported from Boston. The wedding breakfast was followed by a dance in the decorated boathouse. That fall, on September 28, her sister Margaret married Glen McDonough of New York at Buzzards Bay. In May 1901 William Winter Jefferson married the actress Christie MacDonald. The wedding, initially planned for New York, was eventually held at Crow's Nest.

> Miss MacDonald and her mother and sister went down . . . last week, after having visited the Jefferson family at the Touraine [Hotel in Boston]. The wedding ceremony was performed in the parlor of the Jefferson mansion at high noon by Rev. E. A. Horton of [Boston]. There were no bridesmaids, no ushers. The bride's sister, Belle, accompanied her and the best man was H. V. Dodd, the golfer and society man, from New York, who is a great friend of the groom. After the ceremony, a wedding breakfast was served and the special train brought the party back to [Boston]. The bride and groom left Boston for New York. When the party left Crow's Nest for the station, the bride and groom were forced into an open phaeton in which they were drawn to the station by the wedding guests, a distance of a mile and a half. As they rode, they were pelted with flowers and showered with rice. At the station, they were the

center of interest. The trunks were tied with white ribbon, and the special car was marked with chalk: "A bride is in this car." The bride's dress was of white *mousseline de soie*, with rare old lace. She had her long bridal veil fastened with a large diamond star. At her throat was a great heart shaped sapphire surrounded with diamonds, the gift of the groom. She carried bride's roses. The bride and groom will sail for Bremen [aboard the steamship Maria Theresa] on Tuesday and will spend the early summer in Germany, France and England, returning to America early in August and coming directly to Buzzards Bay to remain until it is necessary to resume professional work. . . .

Many handsome and costly gifts were received by the young couple. Joseph Jefferson gave her a complete chest of silver filled with all kinds of knives, forks, spoons . . . ; Mrs. Jefferson's present was a jeweled watch; Joseph Jefferson Jr. gave a silver tea service; Thomas Jefferson an antique finger ring of great value; Frank Jefferson a belt pin; Charles Jefferson a chafing dish; Mrs. Josephine Rolfe, nee Jefferson, a silver tea pot and Ffolliot Paget a pair of bon bon dishers.

Michael Burgess, "Stormy Marriage after Quiet Buzzards Bay wedding," *Upper Cape Cod Codder*, May 6, 1999: 27. *Boston Sunday Post*, May 12, 1901, Collection of Michael Burgess, Buzzards Bay, Massachusetts.

536. Joseph Jefferson, "To Laurence Hutton," November 2, 1900, November 13, 1900, Laurence Hutton Correspondence Collection, Princeton University Library.

537. Eugenie Jefferson, 36; Leslie, 228–229.

538. Wilson, 15.

539. The quotation continues: "Do you mean to say you have forgotten the frankfurters? . . . And the sauerkraut." After each performance at 11 P.M., before he took off his makeup, Jefferson had a "lunch" of frankfurters and sauerkraut in his dressing room. Article, May 4, 1903, Robinson Locke Collection, 302: 50, New York Public Library for the Performing Arts.

540. "Age Puts Mark on Actor," October 7, 1901, 301: 49, Robinson Locke Collection, New York Public Library for the Performing Arts.

541. *New York Dramatic Mirror*, October 19, 1901: 12.

542. Eugenie Jefferson, 178–179; Francis Wilson, *Life of Himself*, 197.

543. Mrs. Drew died on August 31, 1897, at Bevan House in Larchmont, New York.

544. Eugenie Jefferson, 179; *New York Dramatic Mirror*, January 29, 1898: 24.

545. Eugenie Jefferson, 318.

546. Upon first arriving, Jefferson stayed at the Royal Poinciana Hotel and wore his Rip Van Winkle costume to a Washington Birthday ball there. Joseph Jefferson, "To Laurence Hutton," May 18, 1898, Laurence Hutton Correspondence Collection, Princeton University Library; Eugenie Jefferson, 22.

547. *New York Dramatic Mirror,* October 15, 1898: 11, 18.

548. "Jefferson's Illness Expensive," November 15, 1898, 301: n.p., Robinson Locke Collection, New York Public Library for the Performing Arts.

549. "Tom Jefferson will Play Rip," November 15, 1898, Robinson Locke Collection, 148: n.p., Lincoln Center Public Library, New York.

550. "Joe Jefferson's Family of Actors," November 20, 1899, Robinson Locke Collection, 301: n.p., New York Public Library for the Performing Arts.

551. Eugenie Jefferson, 282.

552. Skinner, 253–256; *New York Times,* October 31 (10), November 3 (7), November 8 (5), November 9 (12), November 11 (7), November 13 (8, 17), November 14 (10), November 15 (6), November 17 (2), November 22 (7) 1898; Envelope, November 28, 1898, MS 1427, Historic Hudson Valley, Tarrytown, New York; *New York Dramatic Mirror,* November 12 (14), November 19 (15) 1898.

553. Laurence Hutton, "Recollections of Joseph Jefferson," *Harper's Weekly* 49 (May 6, 1905): 657.

554. *New York Dramatic Mirror,* December 3 (4), December 10 (2, 10, 12) 1898; Scrapbook, National Theatre Archives, Washington D. C., Envelope, MS 1427, Historic Hudson Valley, Tarrytown, New York; Clipping Collection, John Callahan, Kutztown, Pennsylvania; Wilson, 49, 52, 53; Tompkins, 464; *The New York Times,* November 22 (7), November 23 (7), November 25 (5), November 26 (7), November 28 (7), November 30 (7) 1898.

555. Eugenie Jefferson, 257.

556. Connie left one son, Charles J. Jackson. She was replaced in the cast of *The Cricket on the Hearth* by Virgie Glyndon, a ten-year-old who also played the child Meenie in the first and second acts of *Rip.* "Actress Connie Jackson Dies," March 4, 1899, Robinson Locke Collection, 301: n.p., New York Public Library for the Performing Arts.

557. Article dated November 18, 1899, Robinson Locke Collection, 301: n.p., New York Public Library for the Performing Arts.

558. Jefferson Winter, "As I Remember," 22.

559. Article dated December 6, 1904, Robinson Locke Collection, 302: 100, New York Public Library for the Performing Arts.

560. The *New York World* reported that Jefferson had retired from the stage, but on January 16 he wrote to the editor from Florida denying this and announcing his intention to "begin . . . engagements next season." He reiterated this assertion to the *New York Dramatic Mirror.*

Almost immediately upon arriving in Palm Beach in 1901, he began buying land from its ex-mayor, who had appeared on the stage with Joe in Memphis in 1868. Jefferson referred to him as "one of my boys." On a lot on the southeast corner of Clematis Avenue, Olive Street and 29th, Jefferson tore down the residence that had been standing and put up two commercial buildings, one known as the Jefferson block and the other the Jefferson Hotel. Its popularity with winter guests grew until Jefferson finally erected an annex on the opposite side of the street. On twenty acres south of town he laid out building lots for a development of winter villas, which became known as Jefferson's Lake View Extension. And on the northwest corner of Narcissus and Datura streets he built a winter home for himself and eventually owned six houses across the street. At the time of his death, he was still holding mortgages on five pieces of property in the area.

Thomas Jefferson took the Jefferson company out, playing *Rip Van Winkle*, beginning mid-January 1901. He toured simultaneously with his father, but of course to far smaller towns. "Rip Van Winkle Sleeps His Everlasting Sleep," April 28, 1905, Clipping, Scrapbook, Jonathan Bourne Historical Center, Bourne, Massachusetts; *Tropical Sun* (West Palm Beach), January 18 (6), February 15 (6) 1901; J. Wadsworth Travers, *History of Beautiful Palm Beach* (Palm Beach: no publisher, 1928), 31; Joseph Jefferson, "To Editor of *The New York World*," January 16, 1901, Museum of the City of New York; *The Players* (New York: n.p., 1901), 35; Probate Inventory, July 29, 1905.

561. James S. Metcalfe, "Goin' Fishin' with Joseph Jefferson," *Ladies' Home Journal* 18 (July 1901): 2.

562. C. Edwin Booth Grossman, "A Morning Fishing with Joseph Jefferson," *Theatre* 5 (July 1905): 53, Robinson Locke Collection, 302: 72, The New York Public Library for the Performing Arts.

563. Joseph Jefferson, "To Laurence Hutton," May 23, 1903, Laurence Hutton Correspondence Collection, Princeton University Library.

564. *Dictionary of National Biography,* Supplement, January 1901–December 1911 (Oxford: Oxford University Press, 1912), 2: 6; *New York Times,* July 24, 1903: 7; Affadavit signed by Joseph W. Jefferson, March 24, 1914, Municipal Records, Barnstable, Massachusetts; Collection of Michael Burgess, Buzzards Bay, Massachusetts.

565. Nevins, *Letters,* 570; Nevins, *Grover Cleveland. A Study in Courage,* 739.

566. "Joseph Jefferson as the Spectator Knew Him," 18.

567. Eugenie Jefferson, 205, 249; *New York Dramatic Mirror,* October 17 (13), October 27 (14), November 14 (4) 1903.

568. Nevins, *Letters,* 572; Rip Van Winkle File, Free Library of Philadelphia; *The Players* (New York: The Knickerbocker Press, 1905) 5; *The Players* (New York: no publisher, 1904) 39; Trow's Directory, 632; Eugenie Paul Jefferson, 48; Joseph Jefferson, "To Cashier of the Nassau Bank," September 8, 1902, Philip H. Ward Collection, Box 14, Van Pelt Library, University of Pennsylvania; Affadavit signed by Joseph W. Jefferson, March 24, 1914, Clipping Collection, Michael Burgess, Buzzards Bay, Massachusetts.

569. Eleanor Farjeon, "Joe in Paradise," xiii.

570. The section omitted reads:

> Our ugly forms alone would seal our fates
> And bar our entrance through the golden gates.

Suppose that death should take us unawares,
How could we climb the golden stairs?
If maidens shun us as they pass us by,
Would angels bid us welcome in the sky?
I wonder what great crimes we have committed,
That leave us so forlorn and so unpitied.
Perhaps we've been ungrateful, unforgiving;
"Tis plain to me that life's not worth the living."
"Come, come, cheer up," the jovial worm replied,
"Let's take a look upon the other side;
Suppose we cannot fly like moths or millers,
Are we to blame for being caterpillars?
Will that same God that doomed us crawl the earth,
A prey to every bird that's given birth.
Forgive our captor as he eats and sings,
And damn poor us because we have not wings?
If we can't skim the air like owl or bat,
A worm will turn 'for a' that."

Nevins, 459.

571. Eugenie Jefferson, 154; *New York Dramatic Mirror,* August 13 (13,), August 27 (11), September 10 (11), October 29 (13) 1904; "In His Easy Chair Joseph Jefferson Evokes Memories of Past," *New York Herald,* October 16, 1904, Robinson Locke Collection, 302: 92–93, Article dated October 1, 1904, Robinson Locke Collection, 302: 95, The New York Public Library for the Performing Arts.

572. *Deluxe Catalogue,* No 65.

573. Eugenie Jefferson, 288.

574. In early February Jefferson offered to tender a benefit to Joseph Holland, who was ill. The benefit was planned for March, and Jefferson's name was placed on the honorary committee. Nevins, *Letters,* 594; Wilson, 342; Eugenie Jefferson, 49; *New York Dramatic Mirror,* February 4, 1905: 15.

575. Nevins, *Letters,* 598.

576. *New York Dramatic Mirror,* February 18 (16), February 25 (13), April 1 (7)1905.

577. Wilson, 344.

578. "Broadway Won't Miss 'Rip'," Robinson Locke Collection, 302: 86, The New York Public Library for the Performing Arts.

579. There is little reason to believe that Jefferson would have received a telegram informing him of Holland's death, and he was definitely not out of town. He was performing *Rip* at Booth's Theatre. His version of the story makes it seem more dramatic. *New York Dramatic Mirror,* April 1, 1905: 7.

580. "Rip Van Winkle Sleeps His Everlasting Sleep," Clipping Scrapbook, Jonathan Bourne Historical Center, Bourne, Massachusetts; *New York Dra-*

matic Mirror, March 18 (13), April 1 (11) 1905; *Tropical Sun* (Palm Beach, Florida), April 19 (1), April 22 (1) 1905; *Chicago Record-Herald*, April 24, 1905: 1; *Daily Picayune* (New Orleans), April 24, 1905: 1; "Jefferson Is Reported to be Sinking Fast," April 19, 1905, Robinson Locke Collection, 302: 114, The New York Public Library for the Performing Arts.

581. Although the procession to the train suggests that Jefferson was a mason, there is no other evidence for this.

The train consisted of Flagler's and Vice-President J. R. Parrot's (general manager of the Florida East Coast Railroad) private cars, Nos. Ninety and Ninety-one, and a baggage car (No. Seven). *Tropical Sun* (West Palm Beach, Florida), April 26, 1905: 1; *Chicago Record-Herald,* April 25, 1905: 3; *New York Dramatic Mirror,* May 6, 1905: 11.

582. In Jersey City the family was joined by Joseph Jefferson, Jr., and his wife, Blanche Bender Jefferson; William W. Jefferson and his wife; Mr. and Mrs. Glen MacDonough (C. B. Jefferson's daughter and son-in-law); Jefferson's agent, Al Harris; Joe Junior's manager, Harry C. Smart; William Jefferson; Maury Phillips; C. B. Jefferson's manager, Leon Mayer; a former financial manager for Joseph Jefferson; and Jefferson's coactor, John Jack.

583. The pallbearers were Glen MacDonough and Charles J. Rolfe, both of whom were married to Jefferson's granddaughters; his former stage manager, Samuel Phillips; Carl Kettler; Richard Watson Gilder; Edward Black; Dr. George Barry; and J. A. Walker. That same Sunday the Reverend G. C. Houghton, rector of the Church of the Transfiguration, Jefferson's "Little Church Around the Corner," conducted a memorial service upon the request of The Players. *The Players* (New York: The Knickerbocker Press, 1905), 35.

BIBLIOGRAPHY

Books

Acklen, Jeanette Tillotson. *Tennessee Records: Tombstone Inscriptions and Manuscripts*. Nashville: Cullom & Ghertner, 1933.

The Actor; or A Peep behind the Curtain. New York: W. H. Graham, 1846.

Adams, Henry W. *The Montgomery Theatre, 1822–1835*. University of Alabama Studies, no. 9. Montgomery: University of Alabama Press, 1955.

Anderson, James R. *An Actor's Life*. London: The Walter Scott Publishing Co., Ltd., 1902.

Arese, Francesco. *A Trip to the Prairies and in the Interior of North America*. New York: The Harbor Press, 1934.

Bagot, Alex. *Coppin the Great: Father of the Australian Theatre*. London: Cambridge University Press, 1965.

Baker, Michael. *The Rise of the Victorian Actor*. Totowa, N.J.: Rowman and Littlefield, 1978.

Baker, Russell Pierce. *Obituaries and Marriage Notices from the Tennessee Baptist, 1844–1862*. Easley (S.C.): Southern Historical Press, 1979.

Barrett, Lawrence. *Edwin Forrest*. Boston, 1882.

Barrymore, William. *The Snow Storm: or Lowina of Tobolskow*. Baltimore, 1833.

Bauer, K. Jack. *Zachary Taylor: Soldier, Planter, Statesman of the Old Southwest*. Baton Rouge: Louisiana State University, 1985.

Bernheim, Alfred L. *The Business of the Theatre*. New York, 1932.

Bikle, Lucy Leffingwell Cable. *George W. Cable: His Life and Letters*. New York: Russell & Russell, 1967.

Birch's Views of Philadelphia: A Reduced Facsimile of the City of Philadelphia . . . as it appeared in the Year 1800 with photographs of the Sites in 1960 & 1982 by S. Robert Teitelman. Philadelphia: University of Pennsylvania Press, 1982.

Blake, Charles. *An Historical Account of the Providence Stage*. Providence: George H. Whitney, 1868.

Bowen, Elwood. "Theatrical Entertainments in Rural Missouri before the Civil War." *University of Missouri Studies* 32. Columbia, Mo.: University of Missouri Press, 1959.

Bradford, Gamaliel. *Portraits and Personalities*. Boston: Houghton Mifflin Company, 1933.

Brown, T. Allston. *History of the American Stage*. 1870. Reprint. New York: Benjamin Blom, 1969.

Bryan, Veranne. *Laura Keene*. Jefferson, N.C.: McFarland & Company, 1993.

Buckingham, James Silk. *America: Historical and Descriptive*. Vol. 2. London: Fisher, Son, & Co., 1841.

Burke, Charles. *Rip Van Winkle: A Legend of the Catskills*. New York: Samuel French, n.d.

Burnett, J. G., and Joseph Jefferson. *Blanche of Brandywine*. New York: Samuel French, 1858.

Butcher, Philip. *George W. Cable*. New York: Twayne Publishers, 1962.

Carroll, Howard. *Twelve Americans: Their Lives and Times*. New York, 1883.

Carson, William G. B. *Managers in Distress*. St. Louis, 1949.

Chetlain, Augustus L. *Recollections of Seventy Years*. Galena: The Gazette Pub. Co., 1899.

Clapp, John Bouve, and Edwin Edgett. *Players of the Present*. New York: The Dunlap Society, 1901.

Clarke, Asia Booth. *Edwin Booth*. Boston: Small, Maynard & Company, 1901.

————. *The Elder and the Younger Booth*. Boston, 1882.

————. *The Unlocked Door*. New York: G. P. Putnam's Sons, 1938.

Colman, George. *The Heir-at-Law*. London: Longman, Hurst Rees and Orme, 1808.

Constitution of the Players. New York, 1888.

Copeland, Charles Townsend. *Edwin Booth*. Boston: Small, Maynard & Company, 1901.

Cowell, Joseph. *Thirty Years Passed Among the Players in England and America*. New York: Harper & Brothers, 1844.

Creahan, John. *The Life of Laura Keene*. Philadelphia: The Rodgen Publishing Company, 1897.

Cullity, Rosanna, and John Cullity. *A Sandwich Album*. The Nye Family of America Association, Inc., 1987.

Dalrymple, J. S. *The Naiad Queen*. Boston: William V. Spencer, n.d.

Daniel, Malcolm. *Eugene Cuvalier: Photographer in the Circle of Corot*. New York: The Metropolitan Museum of Art, 1996.

Deluxe Catalogue of the Valuable Paintings Collected by the Late Joseph Jefferson. New York, 1906.

Dimond, William. *The Hunter of the Alps*. New York, 1804.

Disher, M. Wilson. *The Cowells in America: Being the Diary of Mrs. Sam Cowell during her Husband's Concert Tour in the Years 1860–1861*. London: Oxford University Press, 1934.

Dole, Nathan Haskell. *Joseph Jefferson at Home*. Boston, 1898.

Dorman, James H., Jr. *Theater in the Ante Belleum South 1815–1861*. Chapel Hill: The University of North Carolina Press, 1967.

Durham, Weldon B. *American Theatre Companies 1749–1887*. New York: Greenwood Press, 1986.

Elwood, George M. *Some Earlier Public Amusements of Rochester*. Rochester: *Democrat and Chronicle*, 1894.

Enkvist, Nils Erik. *Caricatures of Americans on the English Stage Prior to 1870*. Port Washington, N.Y.: Helsingford, 1951.

Farjeon, Annabel. *Morning Has Broken: A Biography of Eleanor Farjeon*. London: Julia MacRae Books, 1986.

Farjeon, Eleanor. *Portrait of a Family*. New York: Frederick A. Stokes Company, 1936.

———. "Joe in Paradise." Foreword to *Autobiography*. New York: Appleton-Century-Crofts, Inc., 1949.

———. *A Nursery in the Nineties*. 1935. Reprint. New York: Oxford University Press, 1980.

Fawkes, Richard. *Dion Boucicault*. London: Quartet Books, 1979.

Federal Writers' Project. *New York City Guide*. New York: Octagon Books, 1970.

Foster, G. C. *New York by Gas-Light*. New York, 1850.

Frohman, Daniel. *Daniel Frohman Presents*. New York: Claude Kendall & Willoughby Sharp, 1935.

Gelb, Arthur, and Barbara Gelb. *O'Neill*. New York: Harper's, 1964.

Gilder, Richard Watson. *Grover Cleveland*. New York: The Century Club, 1910.

Gilder, Rosamond, ed. *The Letters of Richard Gilder*. Boston: Houghton Mifflin, 1916.

Gingrich, Arnold. *The Joys of Trout*. New York: A. A. Knopf, 1971.

Goodwin, Nat C. *Nat Goodwin's Book*. Boston: Richard G. Badger, 1914.

Grau, Robert. *The Business Man in the Amusement World*. New York: Broadway Publishing Company, 1910.

Grossman, Edwina Booth. *Edwin Booth: Recollections by his Daughter*. 1894. Reprint. New York: Benjamin Blom, 1969.

Grund, Francis J. *The Americans in their Moral, Social and Political Relations*. 2 vols. Boston, 1837.

Henderson, Mary C. *The City and the Theatre: New York Playhouses from Bowling Green to Times Square*. Clifton, New Jersey: James T. White & Co., 1973.

Henneke, Ben Graf. *Laura Keene*. Tulsa: Council Oak Books, 1990.

Hoole, W. Stanley. *The Ante-Bellum Charleston Theatre*. Tuscaloosa: University of Alabama Press, 1946.

Howe, Daniel Walker. *Victorian America*. Philadelphia: University of Pennsylvania Press, 1976.

Hunter, Alexander. *New National Theatre: Washington D.C. A Record of Fifty Years.* Washington: R. B. Polkinhorn & Sons, 1885.

Ireland, Joseph N. *Records of the New York Stage from 1750 to 1860.* Vol. 2. New York, 1867.

Irving, Pierre M. *The Life and Letters of Washington Irving.* Vol. 4. New York, 1864.

James, Reese D. *Old Drury of Philadelphia. A History of the Philadelphia Stage, 1800–1835.* Philadelphia: University of Pennsylvania Press, 1932.

Jefferson, Joseph. *The Autobiography of Joseph Jefferson.* New York: The Century Co., 1889.

———."In Memory of Edwin Booth," "My Farm in Jersey," Thomas B. Reed, ed., *Modern Eloquence.* Philadelphia: John D. Morris and Co., 1901.

Kemble, Frances Anne. *Journal, 1832–33.* 2 vols. London: J. Murray, 1835.

Kendall, John S. *The Golden Age of New Orleans Theatre.* Baton Rouge: Louisiana State University Press, 1952.

Kenly, John R. *Memoirs of a Maryland Volunteer: War with Mexico.* Philadelphia: J. B. Lippincott & Co., 1873.

Kotsilibas-Davis, James. *Great Times Good Times: The Odyssey of Maurice Barrymore.* Garden City, New York: Doubleday & Co., Inc., 1977.

Larson, Carl F. W. *American Regional Theatre History to 1900: A Bibliography.* Metuchen, New Jersey: The Scarecrow Press, Inc., 1979.

Leslie, Amy. *Some Players' Personal Sketches.* Chicago, 1899.

Logan, Olive. *Before the Footlights and Behind the Scenes.* 1869.

Longstreet, James. *From Manassas to Appomattox.* 1908. Reprint. Bloomington, Indiana: Indiana University Press, 1960.

Longworth's American Almanac New-York Register and City Directory. New York, 1836.

MacKenzie, Alexander. *A Letter to the Rev. Samuel C. Aikin.* Cleveland, 1836.

McVicker, J. H. *The Theatre; Its Early Days in Chicago.* Chicago, 1884.

Malvern, Gladys. *Good Troupers All: The Story of Joseph Jefferson.* Philadelphia: Macrae Smith Company, 1945.

Marriages and Deaths from the Newspapers of Lancaster County Pennsylvania 1831–40. Westminster, Maryland: Family Line Publications, 1988.

Meade, George Gordon. *Life and Letters of George Gordon Meade.* 2 vols. New York: Charles Scribner's Sons, 1913.

Memorial Celebration of the Sixtieth Anniversary of the Birth of Edwin Booth held in the Madison Square Garden Concert Hall November the Thirteenth MDCCCXCIII. New York: The Players, 1893.

Morley, Henry. *The Journal of a London Playgoer.* London, 1866.

Morton, John Maddison. *Lend Me Five Shillings.* New York: M. Couglas, n.d.

———.*The Midnight Watch.* New York, n.d.

———. *A Regular Fix.* New York, n.d.

Moses, Montrose, ed. *Representative Plays by American Dramatists.* Boston: Little Brown and Company, 1921.

Nevins, Allan, ed. *The Diary of Philip Hone: 1828–1851.* New York: Dodd, Mead and Co., 1936.

———. *Grover Cleveland. A Study in Courage.* New York: Dodd, Mead & Company, 1934.

———, ed. *Letters of Grover Cleveland: 1850–1908.* Boston: Houghton Mifflin Company, 1933.

New York in Slices. New York, 1849.

Niver, Kemp R. *Motion Pictures from the Library of Congress Paper Print Collection 1894–1912.* Berkeley: University of California Press, 1967.

———, comp. *Biograph Bulletins 1896–1908.* Los Angeles: Locare Research Group, 1971.

Notices of Marriages and Deaths in Paulsons's American Daily Advertiser, 1831–1833. Collections of The Genealogical Society of Pennsylvania. Vol. 6. Philadelphia, 1903.

Odell, George C. D. *Annals of the New York Stage.* Vol. 2. New York: Columbia University Press, 1928.

Oettel, Walter. *Walter's Sketch Book of the Players.* New York: The Gotham Press, 1943.

Oggel, L. Terry, ed. *The Letters and Notebooks of Mary Devlin Booth.* New York: Greenwood Press, 1987.

Perry, E. G. *A Trip Around Buzzards Bay Shores.* Taunton, Mass.: Bourne Historic Commission, 1976.

Phelps. H. P. *Players of a Century: A Record of the Albany Stage.* 1880. Reprint. New York: Benjamin Blom, Inc., 1972.

The Players. N.p., The Gilliss Press, 1894.

Ibid. New York, 1904.

Ibid. New York: The Knickerbocker Press, 1905.

Pocock, I. *Rob Roy, or Auld Lang Syne.* New York, n.d.

Pool, Daniel. *What Jane Austen Ate and Charles Dickens Knew.* New York: Touchstone, 1993.

Power, John Carroll. *History of the Early Settlers of Sangamo County, Illinois.* Chicago, 1881.

Power, Tyrone. *Impressions of America during the Years 1833, 1834 and 1835.* 2 vols. London, 1836.

Rip Van Winkle as Played by Joseph Jefferson. New York: Dodd, Mead and Company, 1896.

Rugoff, Milton. *America's Gilded Age.* New York: Holt, 1989.

Russell, Charles Edward. *Julia Marlowe: Her Life and Art.* New York: D. Appleton and Co., 1922.

Scharf, J. Thomas. *Chronicles of Baltimore.* Baltimore, 1874.

Skinner, Otis. *Footlights and Spotlights.* Indianapolis: The Bobbs-Merrill Co., 1924.

Smith, Sol. *Theatrical Management in the West and South for Thirty Years.* 1858. Reprint. Bronx, New York: Benjamin Blom, 1968.

Sothern, Edward H. *The Melancholy Tale of Me.* New York: Charles Scribner's Sons, 1916.

———. *Julia Marlowe's Story.* New York: Rinehart & Company, Inc., 1954.

Stoker, Bram. *Personal Reminiscences of Henry Irving.* 2 vols. 1906. Reprint. Hamden, Connecticut: Greenwood Press, 1970.

Toll, Robert C. *On With the Show.* New York: Oxford University Press, 1976.

Tolles, Winton. *Tom Taylor and the Victorian Drama.* New York: Columbia University Press, 1940.

Tompkins, Eugene. *The History of the Boston Theatre.* Boston: The Riverside Press, 1908.

Townsend, W. T. *The Cricket on the Hearth.* London: Thomas Hailes Lacy, n.d.

Travers, J. Wadsworth. *History of Beautiful Palm Beach.* Palm Beach, 1928.

Tuckerman, Bayard, ed. *The Diary of Philip Hone: 1828–1851.* New York: Dodd, Mead and Company, 1889.

Wagenknecht, Edward. *Merely Players.* Norman: University of Oklahoma, 1966.

Wallack, Lester. *Memories of Fifty Years Ago.* New York, 1889.

Walsh, Townsend. *The Career of Dion Boucicault.* 1915; Reprint. New York: Benjamin Blom, 1967.

Watermeier, Daniel J. *Between Actor and Critic.* Princeton: Princeton University Press, 1971.

Weigley, Russell F., ed. *Philadelphia: A 300-Year History.* New York: W. W. Norton & Co., 1982

Wemyss, Francis. *Chronology of the American Stage from 1752 to 1852.* 1852. Reprint. New York: Benjamin Blom, 1968.

West, John. *Theatre in Australia.* Stanmore, New South Wales: Cassell Australia, 1978.

Weston, Effie Ellsler, ed. *The Stage Memories of John A. Ellsler.* Cleveland: The Rowfant Club, 1950.

Wilmeth, Don B., and Tice L. Miller, eds. *The Cambridge Guide to American Theatre.* New York: Cambridge University Press, 1993.

Wilson, Arthur Herman. *A History of the Philadelphia Theatre 1835–1855.* Philadelphia: University of Pensylvania Press, 1935.

Wilson, Francis. *Joseph Jefferson: Reminiscences of a Fellow Player.* New York: Charles Scribner's Sons, 1906.

———. *Life of Himself.* Boston: Houghton Mifflin, 1924.

Winter, William. *The Jeffersons.* Boston: James R. Osgood and Co., 1881.

———. *Life and Art of Joseph Jefferson.* New York: Macmillan and Co., 1894.

———. *Other Days.* New York: Yard and Company, 1908.

———. *The Poet and the Actor.* New York Public Library, n.d.

———. *Shadows of the Stage.* New York: The Macmillan Co., 1906.

———. *The Trip to England.* Boston, 1881.

Writers' Program of the Work Projects Administration in the State of Louisiana, comp. *Louisiana. A Guide to the State.* New York: Hastings House, 1945.

Articles

Ballou, William Hosea. "Joseph Jefferson at Home," *The Cosmopolitan* (1889): 121–127.

Barry, John D. "A Talk with Richard Watson Gilder," *The Illustrated American,* 17 (January 12, 1895): 39–41.

Bloom, Arthur W. "Tavern Theatre in Early Chicago," *Journal of the Illinois State Historical Society* 74 (Autumn 1981): 217–229.

———. "The Jefferson Company, 1830–1845," *Theatre Survey* 27 (1986): 89–153.

Bowen, Elbert R. "Amusements and Entertainments in Rural Missouri," *Missouri Historical Review* 47 (October 1952–July 1953): 307–317.

Bradford, Gamaliel. "Joseph Jefferson," *The Atlantic Monthly* 129 (January 1922): 85–92.

Bryant, William E. "Joseph Jefferson at Home," *New England Magazine* 12 (1895): 193–205.

Davis, L. Clarke. "Among the Comedians," *The Atlantic Monthly* 19 (June 1867): 750–761.

———. "At and After the Play," *Lippincott's Magazine* 24 (July 1879): 57–75.

"Editor's Easy Chair," *Harper's New Monthly Magazine* 42 (March 1871): 614–616.

Freichmann, Felix. "Amusements in Lancaster, 1750–1940," *Papers Read Before the Lancaster County Historical Society* 45 (1941): 42.

Gates, William Bryan. "The Theatre in Natchez," *The Journal of Mississippi History* 3 (April 1941): 71–129.

Gilder, Richard Watson. "A Few Words about Joseph Jefferson and his Art," *Christian Union* 47 (March 4, 1893): 410–411.

Glase, Paul E. "Annals of the Reading Stage: Early Theatre and Playbills," *The Historical Review of Berks County* 12 (1946–1947): 5–10.

Hardin, Ruth. "Lincoln and the Jefferson Players," *Journal of the Illinois State Historical Society* 40 (1947): 444–446.

Henshaw, Nevil G. "Joseph Jefferson: A Memory of Louisiana," *The Bohemian Magazine* 16 (1909): 737–747.

Hill, Raymond S. "Memphis Theatre, 1836–1846," *West Tennessee Historical Society Papers* 9 (1955): 48–58.

Huneker, James. "Joseph Jefferson. Our Most Beloved Actor—His Life and Art," *The World's Work* 10 (1905): 617–620.

Hutton, Lawrence. "Recollections of Joseph Jefferson," *Harper's Weekly* 49 (1905): 657.

"Jefferson in 'Rip Van Winkle'," "Editor's Easy Chair," *The Nation* 9 (1869): 248.

Johnson, Stephen. "Joseph Jefferson's Rip Van Winkle," *The Drama Review* 26 (Spring 1982): 4–20.

———. "Evaluating Film as a Document of Theatre History," *Nineteenth Century Theatre* 20 (Winter 1992), 101–122.

"Joseph Jefferson as the Spectator Knew Him," *The Outlook* 80 (May 6, 1905): 17–18d.

L., F. F. "The Forrest Home not a Poorhouse," *The Illustrated American* 17 (June 15, 1895): 744.

Lyde, Elsie Leslie. "My Stage Life," *Some Stage Favorites of To-Day.* New York, 1893.

Mahan, Bruce E. "The Iowa Thespians," *The Palimpsest* 4 (January 1923): 14–24.

Metcalfe, James S. "Goin' Fishin' with Joseph Jefferson," *Ladies' Home Journal* 18 (July 1901): 2–3.

Mudd, A. I. "Early Theatres in Washington City," *Records of the Columbia Historical Society* 5 (1902): 64–86.

"The Old Cabinet," *Scribner's Monthly* 15 (1877–78), 130.

Pierce, Gilbert A. "A Goodby to Rip Van Winkle," *Atlantic Monthly* 52 (1883): 695–703.

Reichmann, Felix. "Amusements in Lancaster, 1750–1940," *Papers Read Before the Lancaster County Historical Society* 45 (1941): 25–56.

Robb, A. Josephine. "'Rip Van Winkle' As He Is At Home," *Ladies' Home Journal* 15 (May 1898): 2.

Runnion, James B. "Joseph Jefferson," *Lippincott's Magazine* 4 (1869): 167–176.

Shaw, Mary. "The Stage Wisdom of Joseph Jefferson," *Century Magazine* 83 (1912): 731–737.

"A Walk in the Streets of St. Louis in 1845," *Missouri Historical Society Collections* 6 (1928): 33–40.

Warner, Charles Dudley. "The Acadian Land," *Harper's New Monthly Magazine* (1887): 335–354.

Wilmeth, Don B. "The MacKenzie-Jefferson Theatrical Company in Galena, 1838–1839," *Journal of the Illinois State Historical Society* 60 (Spring 1967): 23–36.

Winter, Jefferson. "As I Remember," *The Saturday Evening Post* 193 (August 7, 1920): 14–44.

Winter, William. "Joseph Jefferson," *Harper's New Monthly Magazine* 73 (August 1886): 395–396.

Worner, William Fredrick. "Theatre on West Chestnut Street, Lancaster," *Papers Read Before the Lancaster County Historical Society* 37 (1933): 161–162.

Newspapers

The Advertiser (Hobart Town, Tasmania), March 23, 1864.

Albany Argus, January 1–December 31, 1836.

Albany Evening Journal, January 2, 1836–June 30, 1838; January 2–December 31, 1847.

Alexandria Gazette, February 14, 1829–August 13, 1831.

The Alton (Ill.) Telegraph, March 7, 1840–May 29, 1841.

American and Commercial Daily Advertiser (Baltimore), January 1–June 31, 1825; January 2, 1833; January 1–June 30, 1831; January 1–December 31, 1835; January 8–May 8, 1840; January 2, 1837–December 31, 1841; January 1–December 29, 1847; *American and Commercial Advertiser,* August 28, 1854–March 13, 1856; *Baltimore American and Commercial Advertiser,* April 16–December 14, 1860; January 26– February 20, 1861; April 4–16, 1870.

American Eagle (Fort Pickering, Tenn.), January 25, 1842–April 26, 1844.

The Argus (Melbourne), March 22, 1862–November 28, 1864.

Baltimore Sunday Herald, January 11, 1903.

The Bendigo (Australia) Advertiser, November 11–21, 1863.

The Berks and Schuykill Journal, June 4–11, 1831.

Boston Daily Advertiser, February 4, 1860.

Bourne (Mass.) Courier, April 1, 1993.

Buffalo Patriot and Commercial Advertiser, January 4–November 15, 1837.

Buffalo Republican and Bulletin, September 22, 1837–December 31, 1840.

The Charleston Courier, January 4, 1837–December 31, 1839; January 17, 1851–March 30, 1852.

Chicago American, August 22, 1835–October 17, 1842; *Daily Chicago Amrican,* June 2–September 3, 1839; *Chicago Daily American,* September 16–November 4, 1839.

The Chicago Daily News, March 2, 1892.

Chicago Democrat, November 29, 1837–July 3, 1838.

The Chicago Record-Herald, April 24–25, 1905.

The Chicago Times, November 5, 1867; February 27–June 4, 1876; April 1, 1891.

Chicago Tribune, January 1–December 21, 1867; August 29–November 1, 1868; April 17, 1870; February 21, 1875; December 12, 1880; February 25–July 15, 1883.

Cincinnati Advertiser and Ohio Phoenix, January 4, 1837–November 5, 1838.

The Cincinnati Daily Gazette, January 29, 1838–April 10, 1839.

The Civilian and Galveston Gazette, June 1, 1844–November 20, 1847.

Cumberland (Md.) Alleganian, August 16, 1845–April 17, 1847.

Cummings' Evening Bulletin (Philadelphia), August 23, 1853–March 11, 1854.

Daily Albany Argus, December 18, 1852–January 31, 1853.

Daily Alta California (San Francisco), January 1–August 3, 1861.

The Daily Argus (Wheeling, W. V.), April 21–December 27, 1855.

Daily Buffalonian, May 26, 1838–April 16, 1840.

Daily Chronicle and Sentinel (Augusta, Ga.), January 6, 1840–June 30, 1845; March 31–April 27, 1852.

Daily Cincinnati Enquirer, April 10–September 30, 1841; *Daily Enquirer and Message,* January 4, 1842–August 8, 1845.

Daily Evening Transcript (Boston), September 1, 1837–March 31, 1838; January 1–December 31, 1853; *Boston Evening Transcript*, January 1–December 31, 1859; *Boston Daily Evening Transcript*, January 1, 1867–December 31, 1869.

Daily Georgian (Savannah), November 6–December 18, 1839.

The Daily Journal (Wilmington, N. C.), October 18, 1851–May 28, 1852.

The Daily Memphis Avalanche, March 8–March 15, 1868.

Daily Morning News (Savannah), January 6–18, 1851; *Daily News*, April 26, 1851.

Daily National Intelligencer (Washington, D.C.), August 6, 1829–June 7, 1830; February 27–September 9, 1831; January 8, 1834–May 15, 1837; February 7–March 31, 1845; July 24, 1855–February 3, 1857; September 4–September 16, 1860; August 4, 1866–March 16, 1868; June 15, 1869.

The Daily Picayune (New Orleans), May 25, 1838–January 14, 1840; August 6, 1840–December 11, 1842; July 2, 1844–July 16, 1845; October 17, 1845–April 10, 1847; December 17, 1866; January 23, 1870; January 7–21, 1872; November 12, 1885; June 8, 1890; March 27, 1894; April 24, 1905.

The Daily Pittsburgh Gazette, July 1, 1837–August 30, 1838; *Pittsburgh Commercial Gazette*, December 27, 1881.

Daily Republican Banner (Nashville), November 26, 1833–December 31, 1838; September 23, 1841; January 1, 1843–February 26, 1847; *Republican Banner and Nashville Whig*, September 16, 1853.

Delaware Gazette & American Watchman (Wilmington), March 8, 1833–March 4, 1836.

Deseret Evening News (Salt Lake City), July 10–July 16, 1878.

Detroit Daily Free Press, May 30–September 9, 1837.

Evening Bulletin (San Francisco), July 6–26, 1861.

The Evening Mirror (New York), October 16, 1846–December 31, 1847.

The Evening News (Detroit), November 20, 1891.

The Evening Post (New York), May 27, 1834–July 2 1835; May 9, 1836–September 30, 1837; October 16–January 31, 1839; May 1–June 11, 1839; January 2, 1847–December 31, 1847.

The Evening Star (Washington, D.C.), April 6, 1859; October 21, 1870–February 27, 1873.

The Evening Star for the Country (New York), April 3, 1835–March 16, 1836.

Frank Leslie's Illustrated Newspaper (New York), January 3–February 11, 1871.

Georgia Journal and Messenger (Macon), September 6, 1848–September 24, 1851.

Globe Democrat (St. Louis), May 15, 1896.

Harrisburg Chronicle, August 22, 1831.

The Harrisburg Daily Patriot, October 7, 1880.

The Herald (New York), January 1–June 30, 1836.

Lancaster Journal, August 20, 1830–November 30, 1832.

Launceston Examiner, February 18, 1864.

Louisville Daily Journal, January 2–June 27, 1837; January 30–June 30, 1840; January 1–December 31, 1841; February 2–March 10, 1845.

Maryland Gazette (Annapolis), April 17, 1828–December 29, 1831; January 5, 1832–October 22, 1835.

The Memphis Daily Register, February 10–December 11, 1868.

The Mercury (Hobart Town, Tasmania), February 15–April 7, 1864.

The Milwaukee Sentinel, October 29, 1868.

The Miner's Journal (Pottsville, Pa.), May 2, 1829–December 26, 1835.

The Minneapolis Tribune, November 20, 1891.

Mississippi Free Trader and Natchez Gazette, November 5, 1839–June 8, 1840; June 18–December 23, 1840; January 28–May 13, 1841; July 1–August 14, 1841; January 1–June 30, 1842; January 3–March 10, 1843; *Mississippi Free Trader*, January 4, 1843–December 30, 1846.

Mississippi Free Trader and Natchez Weekly Gazette, April 23–July 2, 1840; August 27–December 3, 1840; January 7–December 30, 1841; January 5–December 28, 1842.

The Mississippian (Jackson), March 8, 1839–January 1, 1841; January 15–December 16, 1841; January 6, 1843–March 5, 1845.

Missouri Republican (St. Louis), July 2, 1838–January 31, 1839; *Daily Missouri Republican*, January 2–June 31, 1840; January 1–December 31, 1841; June 9–November 11, 1842; November 22, 1843–December 31, 1844; January 4–November 8, 1845; *The Missouri Republican*, October 30, 1880; October 11–October 14, 1885.

Mobile Daily Advertiser and Register, September 1, 1866–February 29, 1868; *Mobile Daily Register*, February 10–December 11, 1868; February 8, 1870.

Mobile Daily Commercial Register and Patriot, October 20, 1840–December 31, 1842.

The Mobile Register and Journal, October 11, 1842; January 1, 1843–December 31, 1844; May 1, 1845–November 30, 1846.

Nashville Union, June 16, 1843–December 7, 1844; *Tri-Weekly Nashville Union*, January 9–February 4, 1845.

Nashville Whig, August 8, 1838; January 2–December 30, 1845; February 27, 1847.

New Orleans Commercial Bulletin, January 1–May 31, 1842.

The New York Clipper, January 5, 1861–May 25, 1879.

The New York Daily Times, September 18, 1851–September 28, 1857; *The New York Times*, October 30, 1857–December 31, 1860; August 24–November 2, 1867; December 17, 1878; June 5, 1881; March 30, 1898; July 24, 1903.

New York Daily Tribune, January 1, 1847–February 29, 1848; September 1–December 31, 1866.

The New York Herald, January 1, 1849–November 19, 1850; October 15, 1889.

The New York Mirror, January 4, 1879–January 18, 1889; *The New York Dramatic Mirror*, January 26, 1889–May 6, 1905.

The News and Courier (Charleston), January 9–18, 1884.

The Northwestern Gazette and Galena (*Ill.*) *Advertiser*, December 8, 1838–July 3, 1846.

Observer and Reporter (Lexington, Kentucky), April 14, 1838–May 30, 1838, March 28–May 1, 1839.

The Ohio State Journal and Columbus Gazette, December 22, 1835–October 27, 1837; *State Journal and Political Register*, October 27, 1837–December 31, 1838; *Ohio State Journal and Register*, December 28, 1838–April 10, 1839; *The Ohio State Journal*, April 17, 1839–August 18, 1841.

The Otago Daily News (Dunedin, New Zealand), January 23–November 14, 1863.

The Otago Witness (Dunedin, New Zealand), January 23, 1864.

Palmyra Missouri Whig and General Advertiser Weekly, May 23, 1840.

The Pennsylvania Intelligencer, August 13, 1831–August 9, 1832.

Pennsylvania Reporter (Harrisburg), August 10, 1832.

Pennsylvania Telegraph (Harrisburg), August 8, 1832.

The Pennsylvanian (Philadelphia), November 16, 1848–May 31, 1849.

Philadelphia Inquirer, August 1–November 26, 1866; June 6, 1871.

The Philadelphia Record, August 11, 1909.

The Pittsburgh Commercial Gazette, December 27, 1881.

The Pittsburgh Post, November 20, 1891.

Porter's Spirit of the Times (New York), March 1, 1845–July 23, 1859; *Spirit of the Times*, December 17, 1859–June 22, 1861.

The Post (New York), February 11, 1897.

Providence Daily Journal, January 1–December 31, 1836; *The Providence Journal*, December 7, 1877; November 6–November 11, 1879; November 3, 1880; May 7, 1884; December 23–December 29, 1888; March 23–April 2, 1895; October 10–October 15, 1897; May 1–3, 1904.

Public Ledger (Philadelphia), January 1, 1847–January 17, 1868; December 12, 1881.

Quincy (*Ill.*) *Whig*, June 6, 1840–August 28, 1844.

The Reading Daily Eagle, October 8, 1880.

The Register (Sandwich, Mass.), April 7, 1893.

Republican Banner (Nashville), July 13, 1872.

Richmond Enquirer, December 7, 1847–January 28, 1851; April 16, 1852–June 11, 1858; December 4–14, 1860.

Rocky Mountain News (Denver), July 14–July 23, 1878.

St. Louis Post Dispatch, October 16, 1885; May 7–May 30, 1896.

Sangamo Journal (Springfield, Illinois), February 17, 1838–December 18, 1840.

The Scotsman (Edinburgh), August 8–August 27, 1877.

The South Australian Register (Adelaide), June 30–August 11, 1863; July 7–August 10, 1864.

State Journal (Harrisburg), November 28, 1872.

The Sunday Morning Appeal (Memphis), December 19, 1869.

The Sunday Record Herald (Chicago), April 30, 1905.

The Sydney Morning Herald, January 8, 1862–October 15, 1864.

Telegraph and Texas Register (Houston), August 21, 1844–June 21, 1847.

The Times (London), September 4, 1865–March 24, 1866; November 1, 1875–August 11, 1877.

The Times-Democrat (New Orleans), March 27, 1890.

The Tropical Sun (Palm Beach, Florida), March 25, 1891–May 11, 1899; January 18–February 15, 1901; April 19–26, 1905.

The United States Gazette (Philadelphia), November 14, 1818; February 28, 1828–December 28, 1829; January 3, 1835–December 31, 1836; July 1–December 31, 1838; January 1, 1844–December 31, 1846.

Vicksburg Whig Register and Advocate, March 15, 1838–November 20, 1843.

Vincennes (Ind.) Gazette, January 3, 1835–December 19, 1841.

Weekly Buffalonian, June 2, 1838–January 19, 1839.

Wheeling Argus, January 8–December 23, 1847.

The Wheeling Daily Register, October 27, 1874.

Wheeling Times and Advertiser, July 14–November 28, 1840.

Wheeling Tri-Weekly, February 1, 1831–February 6, 1834.

The Wilkes-Barre Record, April 30, 1890.

The York Dispatch, September 18, 1942.

York Gazette, April 25, 1826–July 31, 1832.

Manuscripts

Agreement and Promise of Sale dated March 4, 1840, Archives, Joseph Jefferson House. Jefferson Island, New Iberia, Louisiana.

Alexander Autograph Collection. Princeton University.

Booth, Edwin. "To Joseph Jefferson," April 26, 1858. The Players, New York.

Boucicault, Dion. *Dot.* J. L. Toole promptbook. New York Public Library for the Performing Arts.

C., L. J. "Joe Jefferson, My Joe." Clipping File. The Historical Society of Pennsylvania, Philadelphia.

Cleveland, Grover. Collection. Princeton University.

Cleveland, Grover. *Papers,* September 12, 1887–October 24, 1887; January 12, 1889–September 18, 1889; September 20, 1889–March 10, 1891; December 14, 1889–October 5, 1891; August 27, 1892–September 19, 1892; September 20, 1892–January 20, 1893; January 21–March 19, 1893; November 12, 1892–November 21, 1894. Library of Congress.

Coyle, Hugh. "To Grover Cleveland," April 1, 1893. Grover Cleveland Papers, Series 2, March 20–April 14, 1893. Library of Congress.

Crowell, Horace S. "To Mrs. Grover Cleveland," February 18, March 11, 1894, Grover Cleveland Papers, Series 3, November 21, 1893–May 16, 1894. Library of Congress.

Davidson County, Tennessee, County Clerk, Marriages, 1837–1863. Nashville.

Day Book, *Chicago American*. Chicago Historical Society.

Dodge, Donald and Romber M., Collection. Princeton University.

Farren, Mary. To "My dear Uncle Sol," September 23, 1865. Missouri Historical Society Archives, St. Louis.

Hutton, Laurence. Correspondence Collection. Princeton University.

Jefferson, Joseph I. Letter, April 5, 1830. The Historical Society of Pennsylvania, Philadelphia.

Jefferson, Joseph, III. "To My dear Willie," April 1, April 10, April 24, July 24, October 7, 1880. MS. Collection 1427. Historic Hudson Valley, Tarrytown, New York.

———. "Letter to Mr. Cist," October 7, 1881. The Historical Society of Pennsylvania, Philadelphia.

———. "To J. H. McVicker," Christmas 1882. Chicago Historical Society.

———. Envelope dated January 26, 1883, MS 1427. Historic Hudson Valley, Tarrytown, New York.

———. "To Mr. Dan Palmer," February 14, 1883. The Hampden-Booth Theatre Library at The Players, New York City.

———. "To My dear Willie," August 30, 1883. MS. Collection 1427. Historic Hudson Valley, Tarrytown, New York.

———. "To Edwin Booth," July 15, 1885. The Hampden-Booth Theatre Library at The Players, New York City.

———. "To Edwin Booth," October 7, 1886. The Hampden-Booth Theatre Library at The Players, New York City.

———. "To Col. Lamont," September 27, 1887, Grover Cleveland Papers, Series 2, Library of Congress.

———. "To George Knight," November 2, 1887. The Hampden-Booth Theatre Library at The Players, New York City.

———. "To John Rogers, Jr.," December 29, 1888, April 15, 1889, July 8, 1889. Rogers Collection, New York Historical Society.

———. "To Willie," March 5, 1889. Miscellaneous Manuscripts Collection. Library of Congress.

———. "To Grover Cleveland," July 9, July 12, 1889. Grover Cleveland Papers, Series 2, January 12, 1889–May 18, 1889. Library of Congress.

———. "To Grover Cleveland," May 16, 1890. Grover Cleveland Papers, Series 2, 1889, Library of Congress.

———. "To Sol Smith Russell," February 2, 1892. The Hampden-Booth Theatre Library at The Players, New York City.

———. "To Edwin Booth Grossman," April 18, May 24, 1894. The Hampden-Booth Theatre Library at The Players, New York City.

———. "To L. J. Cist," April 24, 1894. Autograph Collection of Simon Gratz. Historical Society of Pennsylvania, Philadelphia.

———. "To Mrs. Harcourt," October 5, 1894. Museum of the City of New York.

———. "To Mrs. Emmons," October 29, 1894. Maxcy-Markoe-Hughes Collection. Historical Society of Pennsylvania, Philadelphia.

———. "To Mr. Cable," February 19, 1895. Manuscripts, Rare Books and University Archives, Tulane University Library, New Orleans.

———. "To Henry C. Flagler," March 3, 1895. Flagler Museum Archives, Palm Beach, Florida.

———. "To Mother of Mrs. Roy R. Denslow," April 12, 1895. The Hampden-Booth Theatre Library at The Players, New York City.

———. "To William Bispham, Jr.," May 1, 1895. The Hampden-Booth Theatre Library at The Players, New York City.

———. "To Sophie Markoe Emmens," July 2, 1895. Maxcy-Markoe-Hughes Collection. Historical Society of Pennsylvania, Philadelphia.

———. "To Laurence Hutton," March 10, 1896. Laurence Hutton Correspondence Collection. Princeton University Library.

———. "To Laurence Hutton," May 18, 1898. Laurence Hutton Correspondence Collection. Princeton University Library.

———. "To Edwin Booth Grossman," October 28, 1898. Winslow Purchase file. The Hampden-Booth Theatre Library at The Players, New York City.

———. "To Mr. and Mrs. Thomas Shirley Clarke," September 17, 1899. The Hampden-Booth Theatre Library at The Players, New York City.

———. "To Treasurer of the Philistine," August 15, 1900. Miscellaneous Manuscript Collection, Box 127, Hubbard, Elbert & Family. Library of Congress.

———. "To Laurence Hutton," August 23, 1900, November 2, 1900, November 13, 1900. Laurence Hutton Correspondence Collection. Princeton University Library.

———. "To Meyers & Hediace," December 24, 1900. Manuscript Collection, New York Public Library at 42nd Street.

———. "To Editor of *The New York World*," January 16, 1901. Museum of the City of New York.

———. "To William Clarke," April 23, 1901. The Hampden-Booth Theatre Library at The Players, New York City.

———. "To Mr. Thomas," September 22, 1901. Heartman Collection. New York Historical Society, New York City.

———. "To Edwina (Booth) Grossman," March 29, 1902. The Hampden-Booth Theatre Library at The Players, New York City.

———. "To My Dear Mr. Rogers," July 25, 1902. Philip H. Ward Collection, Box 14, Van Pelt Library. University of Pennsylvania, Philadelphia.

———. "To Cashier of the Nassau Bank," September 8, 1902. Philip H. Ward Collection, Box 14. Van Pelt Library. University of Pennsylvania, Philadelphia.

———. "To Mrs. Edwina Booth Grossman," January 4, 1903. The Hampden-Booth Theatre Library at The Players, New York City.

———. "To Laurence Hutton," May 23, 1903. Laurence Hutton Correspondence Collection. Princeton University Library.

————. "To Laurence Hutton," Summer 1903. Laurence Hutton Correspondence Collection. Princeton University Library.

————. "To My Dear Wallack," n.d. MS 1428, Historic Hudson Valley, Tarrytown, New York.

————. Miscellaneous Manuscript Collection, Box 133, Library of Congress.

Jefferson, Joseph, Jr. "To Charles Frohman," August 13, 1908. The William Seymour Family Papers. Princeton University Theatre Collection.

Kershaw, Gordon E. "600 Spruce Street: Case Study of a House." Unpublished paper, University of Pennsylvania, 1963.

Letter Book of Ludlow & Smith (1835–1844), 75. Missouri Historical Society, St. Louis.

Menu. Lotos Club Dinner for Joseph Jefferson. April 4, 1896. Joe Jefferson Club, Saddle River, New Jersey.

Minutes of the Board of Trustees of the Village of Springfield, Illinois of its Meetings from April 1832 to the Organizing of a City in 1839. Illinois State Historical Society.

Minutes of the City Council of Springfield, Illinois, 1840–50. City Clerk's Office. Springfield, Illinois.

Otis and Eddy Account Book. Chicago Historical Society.

Pennsette, R. "Letter to Joseph Jefferson," August 7, 1833. The Historical Society of Philadelphia.

The Players. Miscellaneous Manuscript Collection. Box 194, Library of Congress.

Probate Inventory of Estate of Joseph Jefferson, dated 29 July 1905. Barnstable, Massachusetts.

Dissertations and Theses

Arnold, Claude Ahmed. "The Development of the Stage in Nashville, Tennessee 1807–1870." Master's thesis, University of Iowa, 1933.

Bailey, Frances Margaret. "A History of the Stage in Mobile Alabama from 1824–1850." Master's thesis, State University of Iowa, 1934.

Bitz, Nellie. "A Half Century of Theater in Early Rochester." Master's thesis, University of Syracuse, 1941.

Callahan, John M. "A History of the Second Olympic Theatre of Saint Louis, Missouri, 1882–1916." Ph.D. diss., Kent State University, 1974.

Chiles, Ruth. "The Birmingham Theatres 1886–1900." Master's thesis, Birmingham-Southern College, 1936.

Crum, Mabel Tyree. "The History of the Lexington Theatre from the Beginning to 1860." Ph.D. diss., University of Kentucky, 1956.

Duggar, Mary Morgan. "The Theatre in Mobile 1822–1860." Master's thesis, University of Alabama, 1941.

Farrell, Robert Dale. "The Illinois Theatrical Company 1837–1840." Master's thesis, University of Illinois, 1964.

Free, Joseph Miller. "The Theatre of Southwestern Mississippi to 1840." Ph.D. diss., University of Iowa, 1941.

Gafford, Lucile. "A History of the St. Charles Theatre in New Orleans." Ph.D. diss., University of Chicago, 1930.

Gaiser, Gerhard Walter. "The History of the Cleveland Theatre from the Beginning to 1854." Ph.D. diss., State University of Iowa, 1953.

Geroux, Charles L. "The History of Theatres and Related Theatrical Activity in Dubuque, Iowa 1837–1877." Ph.D. diss., Wayne State University, 1973.

Hanners, John. "Early Entertainments in Terre Haute, Indiana, 1810–1865." Master's thesis, Indiana State University, 1973.

Keeton, Guy Herbert. "The Theatre in Mississippi from 1840 to 1870." Ph.D. diss., University of Tennessee, 1979.

Luttrell, Wanda Melvina. "The Theatre of Memphis, Tennessee, from 1829–1860." Master's thesis, Louisiana State University, 1951.

McDavitt, Elaine Elizabeth. "A History of the Theatre in Detroit, Michigan from its Beginnings to 1862." Ph.D. diss., University of Michigan, 1946.

McKenzie, Douglas Charles. "The Acting of Joseph Jefferson III." Ph.D. diss., University of Oregon, 1973.

Neeson, Jack H. "The Devil in Delaware. A Study of Theatre in New Castle County." Ph.D. diss., Western Reserve University, 1959.

Obee, Harold Brehm. "A Prompt Script Study of Nineteenth-Century Legitimate Stage Versions of *Rip Van Winkle*." Ph.D. diss., Ohio State University, 1961.

Ritter, Charles Clifford. "The Theatre in Memphis, Tennessee, from its Beginning to 1859." Ph.D. diss., University of Iowa, 1956.

Shockley, Martin Staples. "A History of the Theatre in Richmond, Virginia 1819–1838." Ph.D. diss., University of North Carolina, 1938.

Van Kirk, Gordon. "The Beginnings of Theatre in Chicago, 1837–1839." Master's thesis, Northwestern University, 1934.

Yocum, Jack H. "A History of Theatre in Houston, 1836–1954." 2 vols. Ph.D. diss., University of Wisconsin, 1954.

Miscellaneous

Archives. The Jonathan Bourne Historical Center, Bourne, Massachusetts.

Archives. Joseph Jefferson House. Jefferson Island, New Iberia, Louisiana.

Bangs, Frank C. Clippings. Townsend Walsh Collection. New York Public Library for the Performing Arts.

Barron, Edwin A. Clipping File. New York Public Library for the Performing Arts.

Broadsides dated January 7, 1829, January 28, 1829. Chestnut Street Theatre, January 1, 1829–March 12, 1849 file; Broadside, n.d., Walnut Street Theatre, September 27, 1812–November 27, 1849 file. Theatre Collection. Free Library of Philadelphia.

Broadside dated December 16, 1853. Tulane University Library, New Orleans.

Celebrity Index. Free Library of Philadelphia.

Clipping Collection. John Callahan. Kutztown, Pennsylvania.

Clipping Collection. Michael Burgess. Buzzards Bay, Massachusetts.

Common Council Records. Chicago, Illinois. The Illinois State Historical Library, Springfield.

Deaths, 21. The City of New York Department of Records and Information Service. Municipal Archives.

Delaney, Caldwell. City of Mobile Museum Department. Personal interview, June 19, 1981.

Drew, John, file. Robinson Locke Collection. New York Public Library for the Performing Arts.

Drew, Louisa Lane, file. Clipping Collection. New York Public Library for the Performing Arts.

Durang, Charles. *The Philadelphia Stage from 1749–1855.* 2 vols. Philadelphia: *Sunday Dispatch Newspaper,* 1858–1861. Bound in folio by Pennsylvania Historical Society.

Exhibition of 55 Oil Paintings by Joseph Jefferson at the Fischer Galleries. Washington, D.C., 1900.

Germon, Mrs. Jane. Clipping File. New York Public Library for the Performing Arts.

Heartman Collection. Rogers Collection. Reich Collection. New York Historical Society, New York City.

Hull, Sarah B., Scrapbook, 47. Missouri Historical Society, St. Louis.

Jefferson, Joseph, Collection. Mrs. Patricia Flynn. Kennebunkport, Maine.

Jefferson, Joseph, Clipping Collection. Henry B. Williams–E. Bradlee Watson Theatre Collection. Dartmouth College.

Jefferson, Joseph, Clipping Collection. Harvard Theatre Collection.

Jefferson, Joseph, III, File. Robinson Locke Collection. New York Public Library for the Performing Arts.

Jefferson, Joseph, File. Historical Society of Washington, D.C.

Jefferson, Joseph, III, File and Costume Collection. Theatre Collection. Museum of the City of New York.

Jefferson, Joseph, Files. The Historic New Orleans Collection.

Jefferson, Joseph, Collection. San Francisco Performing Arts Library and Museum.

Jefferson, Joseph, Scrapbook. Townsend Walsh Collection. New York Public Library for the Performing Arts.

Jefferson, Joseph. Silhouette of Washington Irving, dated August 1859. MS. Collection. Historic Hudson Valley, Tarrytown, New York.

Land Records. Bergen County Courthouse, New Jersey.

Manhattan Deaths 1861 F–Z. The City of New York Department of Records and Information Services. Municipal Archives, New York City.

Mathews, Brander, and Lawrence Hutton. *Actors and Actresses: Joseph Jefferson* 2. Harvard, *ca.* 1889.

McClure, John. Magnolia Cemetery, Mobile, Alabama. Personal interview, June 19, 1981.

Municipal Archives. Department of Records and Information Services. The City of New York.

National Theater Programs, 1877–1903. Martin Luther King Library, Washington, D.C.

Playbills dated March 17, March 19, March 21, March 26, March 29, April 8, 1853; June 22, July 2, July 5, July 6, 1859. Howard Athenaeum. Boston Public Library.

Program Collections, 1894–1959. National Theatre Archive, Washington, D.C.

Program Collections, 1877–1903. Martin Luther King Library, Washington, D.C.

Program Collections, Arch Street Theatre, October 9, 1828–April 6, 1849, September 1851–December 31, 1855; Chestnut Street Theatre, January 1, 1829–March 12, 1849; *Rip Van Winkle*, Walnut Street Theatre, September 27, 1812–November 27, 1849. Free Library of Philadelphia.

Program, *The Rivals*, dated May 9, 1896. MS 447, Box 5. The Historical Society of Washington, D.C.

"Rip." Film Archives. Library of Congress.

Rip Van Winkle. Performed by Joseph Jefferson. *Traditions of Acting* 2. Crest Cassettes. Audiocasette.

Tombstones. Jefferson Family. Sandwich, Massachusetts.

Warren, William. Clipping Collection. New York Public Library for the Performing Arts.

INDEX

*And yet, we are but tenants, let us assure ourselves
of this, and then it will not be so hard to make room for
the new administration, for shortly the great landlord
will give us notice that our lease has expired.*